MW00593253

Magazine Markets for
Children's Writers 2012

Writer's Institute
Publications

Copyright © Writer's Institute Publications™ 2011. All rights reserved.

Acknowledgments

The editors of this directory appreciate the generous contributions of our instructors and students, and the cooperation of the magazine editors who made clear their policies and practices.

SUSAN TIERNEY, Editor in Chief

SHERRI KEEFE, Associate Editor

MEREDITH DESOUSA, SUSAN TARRANT, Copyeditors

VICTORIA O'CONNOR, Editorial Assistant

CHERYL KAUER, Editorial Assistant

CLAIRE BROWN, Research Assistant

PAMELA KELLY, Editorial Director

Contributing Writers: KRISTEN BISHOP, SUSAN SULICH, SUSAN TARRANT

Cover Design and Production: JOANNA HORVATH
Cover illustrations supplied by Shutterstock Images LLC

The material contained herein is protected by copyright. No part of it may be republished, copied, reproduced, or adapted without the express written permission of the Institute of Children's Literature, 93 Long Ridge Road, West Redding, CT 06896-0811.

International Standard Book Number 978-1-889715-62-9

1-800-443-6078. www.writersbookstore.com
email: services@writersbookstore.com

Printed and bound in Canada.

Table of Contents

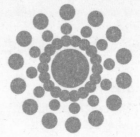

Listings

Submissions

Writing for Magazines: Explore, Diversify, Build

Hundreds of new magazines for readers young and old launched in 2011. Even in these difficult economic times, consumer magazines and trade magazines, for young readers and parents, religious or educational audiences, and in countless niches started up. Optimists believe the magazine industry may at last be on an upswing.

Arguably, the technology revolution is the biggest factor in publishing today, and it has affected magazine and book publishing somewhat differently. Magazines were "hit" first, and some might argue, hardest. The Internet suddenly allowed ezines to spring up overnight, many of them free. Readers began to ask why they would pay for a print publication when they could access one online for free. This was particularly true with children's and teen magazines. The Internet offers more immediacy, more inter-action, more visuals—everything contemporary teenagers and younger children want.

Yet now, the initial downside of the print/Internet competition appears to be turning into a upside for writers. Not only can you write for traditional print publications, but the markets in online magazines, websites directed for and about children, blogs, and even apps are daily growing in number. While this marketplace can change literally as fast as a few mouse clicks, it is an exciting and promising place for writers. Websites are breathing more life into many magazines, including those for children and teens.

The Markets Today

Magazine publishing can be a challenging industry in which to make a career. But you can build one, and grow as a writer. One way is to be sure you have a career with broad scope, and another is to specialize in a specific area. A career with scope means pursuing a combination of different kinds of markets and writing, even as you focus on the interests and subject of children. You can:

- Write purely for children's magazines, to enrich your own life and the lives of children, and earn some (though likely limited) income;
- Write for children, but expand into family and parenting magazines, or curriculum writing, religious publications, or magazines of a different scope that also interest children, such as some sports or hobby magazines; or
- Combine your writing for children's magazines with developing books for young readers, as well as related speaking engagements or editorial work.

To help you sell your writing and build a career, this 2012 edition of *Magazine Markets for Children's Writers* has been re-organized and redesigned. Now you can tailor your queries and submissions to any variety of markets you might choose. The 639 listings in the market directory are now divided into six sections:

● *For Children:* The first section of listings includes publications that are directed specifically to children and teens. These publish fiction, nonfiction, activities, poetry, and all the various genres kids and young adults read. Some are secular, and some religious. Some are general interest, and some address a specialized audience. These magazines are at the heart of being a children's writer.

A core group of high-quality children's magazines have long dominated here: *Boys' Life*, founded in 1911; *Highlights for Children*, founded in 1946; the Cricket and Cobblestone magazine groups from Carus Publishing; and *American Girl*. Smaller but well-established publishers include the Fun for Kidz magazines, and the health-oriented U.S. Kids magazines.

The biggest new publications for children and teens in the past year came from major players: Disney Publishing has announced a whole new group of magazines, some in conjunction with Pixar and Marvel. ESPN is now publishing *ESPNHS,* covering high school athletes in multiple regional editions.

We've also included start-up publications to keep an eye on in the coming year: JAKES *Country* is a relaunched version of two other magazines for kids and teens. *ChopChop* is a kids' food magazine. And we've also added companies that publish anthologies and are looking for short fiction or nonfiction, such as Dancing with Bear.

● *Classroom:* The second section of listings in *Magazine Markets for Children's Writers 2012* contains classroom magazines, which also target children and teen readers. The giants in school publications are Scholastic (*Scholastic Choices, Dynamath, Math, Scope*, and others) and Weekly Reader (*Current Health Kids* and *Current Health Teens*—which have new editors and direction this year).

Classroom magazines often use regular writers—a stable—familiar with their needs and contracted under work-for-hire arrangements. This is a market where you need to be familiar with curriculum, tightly tied to age needs in subject and depth of information or style and vocabulary of story. It's also a great boost to a career to become a regular member of a writing stable.

● *Educators:* The publications in this section are directed to teachers, children's and YA librarians, coaches, caregivers, and others whose lives involve the care and education of young people. This is an obvious market for teachers who are also writers, but these publications may also be open to gifted writers who know how to research, know the audience, and know children. Examples range from *Arts & Activities* to *Children's Advocate* to *Edutopia* to *HomeSchooling Today*.

Writers who want to earn income beyond writing exclusively *for* childen should consider the possiblities here. With these markets, writers can also earn credentials for other children's publishing: If you've published in a journal or magazine that indicates you know the needs of children, that's a plus on your résumé.

● *Parenting:* Always a growing market with many regional and national opportunities, parenting magazines can be the backbone of a career for writers who want to focus in some way on children. These publications constantly need material, and while many want local information, career-smart writers can take a "universal" idea with broad interest and redirect it locally—selling reprints or newly angled pieces to multiple markets, for multiple paydays.

Among the new parenting markets in *Magazine Markets for Children's Writers 2012* are *AKA Mom, Bamboo* (focuses on natural family health), *Little Bit* (covering kids' styles, parties, and more), and *Thriving Family* (Christian parenting).

• *Religious:* Sunday school and other religious publications abound, for children and families. The magazines read by children are included in the For Children section, while the magazines in this section target parents, religious educators, and others concerned with the spiritual and religious well-being of young people and families.

These can be divided generally into two groups, those specifically geared for a religious education curriculum (such as *Group*) and those targeted to a general family audience, such as *Birmingham Christian Family* or *Faith & Family.* Always be sure you thoroughly understand the doctrines and teachings of the religious denomination you are addressing.

• *Of Interest:* The listings in this directory include publications that may be of interest to children and teens. To provide our readers with as many potential markets as possible, we include magazines that cover such subjects as sports and hobbies, science fiction, fairy tales, and animals. Some are for older young adults—late teens (18–19) through early 20s.

What does this broad array and view of magazine publishing have to do with you, a writer who wants to focus on short fiction or articles for children? It offers you more choices, if you want to take advantage of them, to improve your writing skills and success selling your work. As a children's writer, you can take a few steps to the side to increase income: Write for children about healthy adventures, but then also write about health issues for parenting and other publications; health and medicine is a vital specialized market. Or consider multicultural fiction and nonfiction for many ages because it is a genre that continues to widen.

Keeping on top of the markets is both easier and more complicated than ever as digital versions of print magazines abound.

Magazine Markets for Children's Markets 2012 sifts through the chatter, with ongoing research and reporting, to find potential new markets and help you keep learning about the state of magazine publishing.

Love what you do and write for young people. But diversify, connect with markets, and build your career.

Idea Generation & Research

Some publishing truths are unchanging: If you want to be a published writer, you must identify and study your potential markets, you must tailor your ideas to the needs of those markets' readers and editors, and you must write well.

Ask yourself, what does a magazine do for kids? What place does it have in their lives? Why do they turn from the mailbox happily when a magazine just for them appears, or turn to an interactive ezine when they have a chance? And why do you want to contribute writing to magazines for children or others? How can you contribute?

Identify an Idea

As much as you learn about the magazine marketplace, you're reading up on it because you have individual writing interests and ideas, skills, and a love of children's literature. You may be full of ideas, or just the desire to have ideas. Either way, develop a regular idea generation process for yourself.

• Read periodicals and books targeted at children to spark your own ideas and stay on top of their interests.
• Create a folder, physical or electronic, with clippings when you come across ideas with potential.
• Use a journal to jot notes, thoughts, outlines, snatches of dialogue, quotes that inspire you, or even great words or turns of phrase.
• Look at magazine theme lists. Read

Resources about Children & Teens

- **Alloy.com:** www.alloy.com. From Alloy Media, a site that covers books, music, gossip, fashion, advice, and relatsionships for teen girls. Alloy is also the owner of gURL.com, a pop culture "online community and content site" for ages 13 and up.
- **American Library Association:** www.ala.org. The ALA lists some of the best websites for kids, from animals to literature, the arts, history, math and computers, science, and social sciences. Also check out the YALSA pages, which have resources for teens, including voting for teens' top ten favorite books of the year, and Teen Tech Week information. Do a search for the best websites for teens: www.ala.org/ala/mgrps/divs/yalsa/teenreading/trw/trw2005/profresources.cfm#teenweb_sites
- **Education.com:** www.education.com. A well-funded education initiative, Education.com has a panel of experts to help provide comprehensive information for parents about the education of their children, from birth through college and career.
- **Exploratorium:** http://apps.exploratorium.edu/10cool/index.php. Creates top ten lists on many subjects, including sites of interest to children, teens, and teachers.
- **Guys Read:** www.guysread.com. Guys Read is a literacy initiative started by author Jon Scieszka to encourage reading among boys all of ages. The site includes tips on promoting reading for parents, librarians, booksellers, and educators; reading lists for boys; and a forum area for site users to add recommendations.
- **IPL For Kids, IPL Teenspace:** http://ipl.org. Links to recommended reading for children and teens are among the pages on this research site.
- **KidsRead, TeenReads:** www.kidsreads.com, teenreads.com. Websites that focus on books and young readers. They include book reviews, interviews, and the opportunity for readers and authors to share their opinions.
- **Kidsites:** www.kidsites.com. Lists top websites for young people, ranging from Women@Nasa to Guitar Lesson World to ChessKIDS Academy and Chevron Cars. Some pages are under construction.
- **The Merchants of Cool:** www.pbs.org/wgbh/pages/frontline/shows/cool. The PBS program Frontline hosts this site about the relationship between marketing professionals (as purveyors of popular culture) and the hottest demographic in America, teenagers.
- **Parents Choice:** www.parents-choice.org. Parents Choice is an organization that reviews and lists the best products for children and teens, including magazines, books, DVDs, apps, software, television shows, toys, video games, and movies for young consumers. Its top website awards last year went, among others, to:
- **Teen Consumer Scrapbook:** www.atg.wa.gov/teenconsumer. Written by teens and sponsored by the Washington State Attorney General's Office, this consumer guide addresses topics especially of interest to young adults. Subjects have included modeling scams, CD clubs, piercing, sports drinks, tanning, driving laws, scholarship scams, and a host of other relevant concerns and issues.
- **Teenwire:** http://www.teenwire.com. This Planned Parenthood website provides information for teens on sexuality and relationships.
- **Youth Noise:** www.youthnoise.com. Information on volunteer work and teens taking action is provided by the Save the Chidlren Federation.
- **Youth at Work: Real World, Real Rights:** www.youth.eeoc.gov/cases.html. The U.S. Equal Employment Opportunity Commission is behind this informative site about teen workers and their rights.

Sample Curriculum Subjects by Grade

- **Kindergarten:** foundational reading skills, making sense of the alphabet and sounds; decoding words; story v. informational text or poetry, realistic v. make-believe; counting sequences; simple addition and subtraction; shapes; measuring; the states; school and neighborhood geography; the calendar; daily life in past times; being a citizen and following rules; traffic and map symbols; animals; Earth's resources; elements of art, music, dance, theater; healthy foods and play.
- **Grade 1:** follow a story line; recognize sentences; number sentences and place value; tell time; combine and divide shapes; the multicultural U.S.; U.S. symbols; weather; transportation of the past and today; time passage—past, present, future, generation, decade, century; animal and plant environments; solids, liquids, gases; simple musical forms.
- **Grade 2:** fables and folktales; language rhythms; point-of-view and story structure; measure lengths; work with time and money; addition and subtraction problems; graphs; measure motion of objects; life cycles; record scientific observations; sort common objects; map locations; government institutions in the U.S. and other countries; basic economic concepts.
- **Grade 3:** decipher a story's central message; literal and nonliteral language; multiply and divide; understand fractions; estimate measurements, time intervals, volume, mass; atoms and movement of light; diverse life forms and their environments; the planets and stars; physical and human geography (people in their environments); American Indian nations; history of local settlements and impact on the land.
- **Grade 4:** differences between poems, drama, and prose; recognize theme; describe characters in depth; perform multi-digit arithmetic; generate and analyze patterns; classify shapes by angle analysis; electricity and magnetism; processes behind the Earth's surface; state geography, history, culture, government, and economics.
- **Grade 5:** figurative language; differentiate chapters, scenes, stanzas; how characters face conflicts; visual and multimedia contributions to meaning; convert measurement units; decimals; physical elements and their properties; biological functions; weather maps; the making of the U.S. as a nation; early explorers; the colonial era; American Revolution; the Constitution; early to mid-1800s.
- **Grade 6:** pronouns; punctuation; vary sentence patterns; style consistency; ratios; compute multidigit numbers; real-world geometric problems; statistical variability; knowledge of energy and its forms; Earth's structure and geological components; ancient civilizations like Mesopotamia, Egypt, Hebrews, Greece, India, China, Rome.
- **Grade 7:** phrases and clauses; precise word choice; algebraic expressions and equations; proportional relationships; fractions and rational numbers; probability models; cell biology, genetics, and evolution; research techniques; fall of Rome; the Middle Ages in Europe, China, Islamic world, the Americas.
- **Grade 8:** recognize tenses, voice, mood; cite textual evidence; basic algebra; Pythagorean theory; statistical patterns and probability; knowledge of motion and velocity; understands atomic and molecular structure; basic understanding of chemical reactions; American constitutional democracy; the federal government; the American Northeast, South, West; slavery; the Civil War; the Industrial Revolution.
- **Grade 9:** use parallel structure; symbols; laws of energy and motion; periodic table of elements; gases, acids, and bases; Earth- and space-based astronomy; nuclear processes; cell biology; chronological and spatial thinking; historical interpretation.
- **Grade 10:** structure arguments; relationships among concepts; the author's motivation; Newton's laws; morality and philosophy in ancient Greece, Rome; Judaism, Christianity; Glorious, American, and French Revolutions; Industrial Revolution in U.S., Europe, Japan; imperialism; WWI and its aftermath; WWII; nation-building in the Middle East, Africa, Latin America, Asia; world economy and technological revolution.
- **Grade 11:** analyze primary sources; decipher and evaluate written arguments; chemistry; the Enlightenment and U.S. history; immigration; religion and America; U.S. as a world power; Great Depression; America in WWII and after; Civil Rights movement; contemporary social problems.
- **Grade 12:** organize complex ideas; physics; principles of American democracy, citizenship, and civil society; national, state, local governments; origins of political systems; economic principles.

trade publications like *Children's Writer* to find out topics of current interest and hear what editors have to say.

● Turn to newspapers and magazines for adults to spark ideas. Collect pictures if they are inspiring.

● Use your own educational background and knowledge base to begin to specialize in subjects and build your portfolio of clips.

● Use the Category Index on pages 351–386 to start the process of identifying topic areas and genres that might be of interest to you.

Reliable Research

Next, research your selected topic, and research it well. Topical, reader, and market research should all come together to create a perfect fit.

Children's and adult magazine editors want sources that are primary, expert, and thorough. Whether writing is popular, journalistic, or academic, the research bar has been set higher than ever today, paradoxically at the same time the possibilities for shoddy work have become greater. The explosion of websites full of information—with no definitive standards for their accuracy—has made it easier for writers to find and use inaccurate information.

The value of primary sources such as original documents, interviews (with an eyewitness, a scientist or historian, an athlete or coach for a sports article), professional studies, substantiated data, and so on, will continue to rise. Secondary sources—articles, books, and other information that analyze or explore a topic, but are not directly from an expert or original document—must be highly reliable.

Each primary and secondary source you use for your proposed work should be indicated in a query to underpin the solidity of your idea and make a promise of quality to the targeted editor. This is true whether you are researching for a nonfiction article or for a fictional short story. Here are several important research tips.

● *Learn how to optimize online searches.* Use proven search engines, and use key words wisely.

● *Select good sources.* Don't fall prey to the false sources of the virtual world. Try Google Scholar and university or organization websites. If you're interested in writing about optics in space for middle-graders, begin with the NASA site, for example, or *Scientific American* for article references, or SpringShare's LibGuides and ScholarGuides (www.springshare.com) for reputable sources.

● *Find experts to interview.* Research people—kids, interesting characters, local heroes, researchers—close to the source of your subject. Develop a strong interviewing technique.

● *Do field research.* Go to museums (art, science, local history), archives, or locations tied to your subject. *Do* whatever it is you're writing about, if appropriate. Writing a how-to about innovative summer games? Play them. Doing a seasonal piece on holiday meals in a foreign culture? Attend one. For a dinosaur or gardening article, go digging or hoeing. Visit a glass-blowing studio, or a sculptor, or a factory that makes pretzels or bats.

● *Visit potential settings for your fiction.* While some children's stories will not need much research, some do. Learn the geography, the climate, the atmosphere, or culture that will be the background for your fiction.

● *Read adult publications in the fields that interest you.* That is true whether the field is science, sports, education, history, or any other. Stay informed, and even begin to build a specialty.

● *Do photo research.* Photos can be particularly important to children's magazines, which often want graphics with articles.

Know the Reader

As you develop and refine a topic, you'll need to keep your young reader's age, skills, and interests in mind. Nothing will sink a submission faster than talking down to readers or aiming above their heads.

● Stay connected with the age through their culture: music, television and movies, books, social networking, sports, pop culture items, toys. Be sure to stay on top of trends; don't date yourself, for example, with references to Beanie Babies or Transformers.
● Explore what young children like, and are like today, on a daily basis. Volunteer in schools, scouting, or clubs. Visit the library, not just for your own research in books but to see what kids are doing and reading in their section.
● Read kids' websites, including the ones where they are the major contributors. Find out what they are talking about, what is new and what remains universal and timeless. Listen to their voices.

On pages 9 and 10 you'll find sidebars with resources about children and teens, and the subjects they study in school each year.

Know the Magazine

When you have a topic and an age range that appeals to you, use *Magazine Markets for Children's Writers 2012* to start your research into magazines. Use the Category Index to find publications interested in your topic. Compile a list of possibilities, as in the sidebar on angles below.

Be sure to study each listing on your target list looking for keys it gives you about editorial needs, readership, mission or editorial objective, style preferences, word counts, and themes, as well as submission formats.

Find copies of the top targeted magazines at the library, buy them at the newsstand, or order sample copies. Some magazines now have sample copies online. Read them from cover to cover, and analyze them for kinds of articles and departments, voice, depth of information, tone, length, and added material such as sidebars or graphics.

Look online for writers' guidelines, now widely available, or contact the magazine to request them. The listings in *Magazine Markets for Children's Writers 2012* indicate if and how they are available. Be sure to follow the guidelines to a T. Also check if the magazine has an editorial calendar or theme list.

Pay attention to the details, but know that some magazines are more vague than

Angling for Articles & Stories

When you do research to create article ideas, or in preparation for a specific piece, multiply your possibilities. Consider what other kinds of articles or stories you can generate from the same research. See the example below for several possibilities based on one topic.

Topic: Photograms

● *Ask:* ages 7–10, basic explanation of photograms with a simple experiment to illustrate and create one.
● *Art & Activities:* art educators, a look at the process of creating photograms, including photographic composition, and a look at artists who have worked in the form, including Man Ray.
● *Boys' Quest* or *Hopscotch:* Boys and girls, ages 6–14. Mystery where a photogram is at the heart of the solution.
● *ChemMatters:* grades 9–12, the chemistry behind photograms and their creation.
● *Scooter:* New York City parents, article on planning a family visit to MOMA and its photography exhibits, including photograms.

Magazine Review & Analysis

Reviewing magazines you may want to target with a query or submission is essential. Here is a sample of what you might look for if you were exploring magazines that publish history for children. Read and study your choices.

Magazine	Age	Freelance	Description	Submission	Payment
Appleseeds	8–10	80%	world cultures, history	query, source list	$50/page; all rights
Ask	7–10	50%	facts, nature, science, history	query, résumé	to 45¢/word; first rights
BabagaNewz	6–8	30%	Jewish history, tradition	query, résumé	varies; all rights
Bonbon	6–8	60%	Jewish history, tradition	query, author bio	none; one-time rights
ColumbiaKIDS	4–14	80%	Pacific Northwest history	complete manuscript	$200; first world rights
Dig	8–14	85%	archaeology, history	query, outline, bibliography	to 25¢/word; all rights
Highlights	6–12	99%	general interest, U.S. history	complete manuscript	$150+; all rights
National Geo. Kids	6–12	85%	surprising history, science	query, clips	varies; all rights
Scholastic News	Gr. 1–6	age	curriculum-tied	currently closed	varies
Sisterhood Agenda	13+	90%	African American heritage	complete manuscript	no payment; one-time

others in their guidelines, so studying sample issues becomes even more essential. You'll also want to consider what rights a publication purchases, its payment rates and policies, and its overall freelance potential. Use the Magazine Review & Analysis Form above to help you with this process. Here is some of what you should analyze:

● **Editorial objective or mission.** A magazine's goals may be stated in every issue, in its guidelines, and/or online. If not, try to discern it from a reading. The listings also provide these whenever possible. For instance, *Ask* "exists to give answers" to the questions children have about the world "in language they understand and in formats they enjoy." *Sporting Youth* "inspires kids to get active."

● **Audience.** Editors see meeting the needs of readers as central to their own missions. Know the abilities and interests of a given age of readers. Match characters and content to that age precisely. Reading sample issues can give you keys to doing this.

● **Content types.** Look at how many articles, stories, and departments make up an issue of a magazine. Note lengths. Note the editorial balance of the table of contents. It is advisable to look at the contents of a year's worth of issues, if possible, to see what topics have been covered and what might work but have not been covered in the last year.

● **Formats.** Some magazines use more photos than others, or are more or less interactive. Some like articles of limited length, but with one or more sidebars. Try to adapt your idea or story to a magazine's preferred layout.

● **Style.** Listen to the voice of a magazine. Determine if the tone is chatty, educational, upbeat, serious, or some other style. Analyze articles and stories for voice, sentence length, vocabulary choices, quantities of dialogue, how people or characters are presented. Writers' guidelines may give you an indication of the style and voice the editor seeks. *Justine* looks for a "young voice that doesn't patronize readers," while *YARN* wants "strong narrative voices and emotional honesty."

Determine which magazines match you as a writer, your idea, what you want to accomplish or earn. Then prepare to submit, following all the specifics of the writers' guidelines or information provided in the *Magazine Markets for Children's Writers 2012* listings.

Submissions

Magazines vary in what they require for submissions; the wise writer will be very careful to follow the requirements exactly. Possibilities include an email query, a mailed query, the complete manuscript by email or mail, clips or writing samples, an outline, a synopsis, a bibliography, a résumé, and some magazines even have online submission forms.

Queries, Cover Letters, Synopses

Every freelancer needs to master the art of the query. Queries can be brief and to the point, or they can be detailed (but should never be longer than a page or two) and include the many points an editor requests.

Try to write a strong, interesting lead paragraph, and make the body of the query support it. Overall, your query for a nonfiction article (and some fiction, although many editors prefer complete manuscripts for fiction) should do the following.

- *Lead* with an interesting statement of fact, a premise, an anecdote, or something else that will pull in the editor and arouse interest.

- *Provide* the title of the story or article and clarify the subject, audience age targeted, length, and availability or completion date.
- *Distinguish* your idea or story, revealing why it is new, compelling, or the right concept for this particular magazine at this particular time.
- *Set apart* your writing. Your query reveals your style, or your potential style and voice, and an editor will judge that. Reveal what makes your writing better or different, and right for the market. A too straightforward, business-like query could fade into the background. Yet, don't be chummy, too casual, or inappropriate.
- *Distinguish* you, your background, and/or your personal experience, and why you are the one to write the proposed work. Clarify that you are knowledgeable about the particular market and its needs.
- *Name* research resources briefly, for nonfiction particularly, including interview subjects or experts. Indicate the availability and sources of photographs.
- *Point* to any information attached: outline, synopsis, résumé, list of credits, clips, or other materials required by the publisher. (If kept within length limits, some of this information may be part of the body of the query itself rather than attached.)
- *Include* all the necessary contact information for an editor to respond.
- *Close* gracefully and professionally.

Don't overtalk or provide excess information. The art of creating a successful query is to know what information to include, how much, and to convey the heart of your proposed work. See a sample query on page 15.

If you're sending a complete manuscript, as required by the writers' guidelines, you'll use a cover letter instead of a query. This letter can merely indicate that the manuscript,

Sample Query

Dear Editor:

At the end of World War II, in the little village of Tangemunde, Germany, an ammunitions factory made enough baseball bats to supply the entire United States Army in Germany for games throughout the summer of the occupation.

My father-in-law, John Pfitsch, was instrumental in executing this modern-day version of the Biblical command to "beat their swords into plowshares." The U.S. Army was occupying the area and the commanding officer had given John the task of "doing something about" the ammunitions factory in the village. Being a coach, and seeing huge piles of hardwood stacked outside the factory, he naturally thought about baseball bats.

Would you be interested in a 1,000-word article based on this event? I believe it would be of interest to your readers, since the twofold theme, peace and baseball, is important to Americans of all ages.

Sincerely,

Patricia Curtis Pfitsch

and any other information requested in the writers' guidelines, is attached. Some editors also want a synopsis in the cover letter or query. See a sample cover letter on page 16.

Editors have individual preferences about how detailed writers should be in these synopses, especially for fiction. In the end, what counts is not how much or how long a letter is but how effectively it conveys the quality of your story and the market fit. Check writers' guidelines for requirements, and if there are no specifics on this point, be measured. Concisely describe your article or story and do it justice, but ultimately let the piece speak for itself.

You need to know what the market wants for its readership and editorial balance, interest, advertisers, and all the dimensions of magazine publishing. In writing your query, the question to ask is what is communicated and to what effect.

Outlines, Résumés, Clips, Bibliographies

Magazines may require attachments to the submitted query or manuscript, including outlines, résumés, clips, or bibliographies.

Outlines can be useful for writers and editors both. Some writers swear by them, and others never use them. But for freelance submissions, they may be a necessity. Learning to compose one to the right level of clarity and depth is a worthwhile skill. They can help you organize your thoughts, and present them well to a prospective magazine market.

Outlines summarize the contents of an article or story, in list form. As most of us remember from high school or college, an outline will include a thesis or general topic, and then include a number of concepts, with supporting ideas. The headings and subheadings usually include some descriptive details. See a sample on page 17.

Sample Cover Letter

Dear Editor:

The time: 1869. The place: A Nebraska sod house. John's father is delirious with fever. The nearest doctor? Fifteen miles away—unless John can stop the train at the two-thirty crossing . . . .

Enclosed please find my fiction story, "Two-thirty Crossing," which runs to 1,245 words. Although different from my story "Chicken Dream," which you published in August 20XX, or my historical article "One Winter Morning," which you have under consideration at this time, I hope you will find "Two-thirty Crossing" suitable for publication in *Cricket*.

I am a SCBWI member, write fiction and nonfiction for children and adults, and have been published in magazines such as *Nature Friend*, *Primary Treasure*, and *Joy-Full Noise*. In the event you are interested in "Two-thirty Crossing," but suggest changes, I will be happy to revise. Enclosed also find a SASE for notification. Thank you for your time.

Sincerely,

Leslie J. Wyatt

If you've already composed an article or story, you can work backwards and create an outline to reflect it. But much more common is to have a topic, know what you want to do with it before you've actually done your writing, and compose the outline to sell the piece to an editor. The editor may in fact have useful suggestions for changing the outline before agreeing to accept your submission.

Developing a good **résumé** to represent you and your writing is another important component of being a freelancer. It is best to have one specifically directed to your writing —not the same one you'd use if you were looking for a day job. A résumé helps an editor decide whether you're the person to write a given piece, based on your experience and credits.

Keep the résumé to one page, with your name and contact information at the top.

Don't go for fancy fonts or distracting designs, but try to make it look visually appealing, and for mailed submissions, use good paper.

If you're a beginner and your résumé is thin, don't despair. Highlight your writing-related skills and experience (Did you compose or edit the PTO or church newsletter? Write reports for your company?), and succinctly indicate your work experience and education. Also include relevant professional memberships. Even if you're unpublished, you can belong to the Society of Children's Book Writers and Illustrators (SCBWI), which also counts magazine writers in its members.

If you have writing credits, and they are reasonable in number, you might include them on the résumé. As they increase, an attachment specifically listing your article or story titles, the publications in which they appeared, and the date of publication, may be added. And again, if you're a novice, aim

Sample Outline

Cow Power: An Old Technology Made New

I. Pioneers traveling West used manure as fuel.
- A. Quote from Narcissa Whitman's Diary.
- B. No wood available to burn for cooking/heating, etc.
- C. Settlers welcomed cattle drives crossing their land.
  - 1. Cattle would add manure that the pioneers could collect for fuel.
- D. Sidebar: Author's experience collecting and burning cow chips.

II. In our search for inexpensive and environmentally responsible fuel, we're returning to the idea of burning manure.
- A. Carbon neutral—doesn't add to global warming.
- B. Renewable resource—always available.
- C. Inexpensive or free
  - 1. Farmers need environmentally responsible ways of disposing of animal waste.
  - 2. Urban sewage treatment plants.
- D. Sidebar: In Nepal, villagers are harvesting cow dung to produce biogas.
  - 1. New environmentally friendly 'household' digesters.
  - 2. Used in 140,000 kitchens in Nepal.
  - 3. Has saved 400,000 tons of firewood.
  - 4. Saved 800,000 liters of kerosene.
  - 5. Saved 600,000 tons of avoided greenhouse gases.
- E. Sidebar: Using manure to produce ethanol.
  - 1. Panda and e3 Biofuels.
    - a. Plan to use methane to heat corn and produce ethanol.
    - b. Not yet in operation.
- F. Sidebar: Is Ethanol really better for the environment than gas?
  - 1. Fuel needed to heat corn and produce ethanol.
    - a. Using manure helps here.
  - 2. Fuel needed to run tractors to produce corn.
  - 3. Fuel needed to ship ethanol away from plant.
    - a. Can't use pipelines because water in line will affect ethanol.

III. Does it work?
- A. Wild Rose Plant in Cashton, WI, has been supplying electricity to 650 homes since 2005.

IV. How does it work?
- A. Manure collected and heated in digester to produce methane gas.
- B. Methane—similar to natural gas—then used to power generators to generate electricity.
- C. Environmentally friendly by-products.
  - 1. Bedding material.
  - 2. Organic fertilizer to put on crops.
    - 1. Feed crops to cows.
    - 2. Produce more manure.

V. Circular processes are better for the earth.
- A. Putting resources back into the land.
- B. "Cow Power" creates a solution out of two problems.
  - 1) Waste storage.
    - a. Water pollution.
    - b. Odor problems.
  - 2) Fossil fuels.
    - a. air pollution/global warming.
    - b. diminishing resource.

Patricia Curtis Pfitsch

Sample Résumé

Leslie J. Wyatt

Address, Clinton, MO 64735 - username@iland.net -
www.lesliejwyatt.com - (660) 555-5555

Personal Statement
I am a focused, responsible, creative person who has a passion to impact the world through writing.

Work Experience
Freelance Writer   (1995-Present)
— Freelance writing for children and adults.
   o Fiction, nonfiction, and how-to articles for children and adults.
   o Speaking, conducting workshops, giving author visits.
   o Participating in literature festivals and book signings.
— Mentoring, critiquing, and editing other writers.
— Use of Microsoft Office Suite. Designing websites, newsletters, spreadsheets, and documents.

Publications
Nonfiction Articles
— *Highlights for Children:* "Horse Talk" (2009); "Sunflower House How-To" (2003); "Firepots and Gillam Weather" (2003).
— *Children's Writer:* "Kids and Hobbies" (2011); "Voila—Tension!" (2006); "Do Make a Scene" (2006); "Sending With Style" (2005); "Spice up Your Writing" (2005); "Friendship (Writing) Is Evergreen" (2004).
— *Homeschool Enrichment::* "Supermom Throws in the Towel" (2009); "The College Question" (2008); "Looking for the Bigger Picture" (2007); "Everybody All Together Now" (2005); "The Essence of High School" (2005); "Breathing Room" (2004); "Coffeecup Wisdom" (2004); "Hearing the Well Done" (2004); "No Magic Answers" (2003); "Lessons from the Quarter Mile" (2003).
— *Odyssey:* "Tornado!" (2003).

Short Fiction :
— *Cricket:* "Two-thirty Crossing" (2003); "The Hermit's Secret" (2003); "Chicken Dream" (1998).
— *Spider:* "Banana Moon" (2003).
— *Our Little Friend:* "Sorry, Snowball" (2010, 2005); "Love Grows and Grows" (2010, 2003).
— Harcourt/Brace curriculum: "Dad's Secret Weapon" (Reprint) (2006).
— *Primary Treasure:* "Secret Weapon" (2005); "Jump Rope Queen" (2011, 2003); "Rise and Shine" (2000); "Cousin Trouble" (1999).
— *Focus on the Family Clubhouse:* "Leading Man" (2003).
— *Club Connection:* "Spider and Fly" (2002).

Education
— Society of Children's Book Writers and Illustrators Writers' Retreat, April 2010, Potosi, MO.
— University of Montana, Missoula, MT, 1977-78. B.A. in music and French.

Sample Bibliography

Piano Man: A Profile of Ray Charles

– Ackerman, Paul et al. "A Touch of Genius: The Ray Charles Story." *Billboard*, 15 October (1966), RC1-RC16.
– Charles, Ray, and David Ritz. *Brother Ray: Ray Charles' Own Story*. New York: Da Capo, 1992.
– Feather, L. "Piano Giants of Jazz: Ray Charles." *Contemporary Keyboard*, vol. 7 (1980), 62.
– Fong-Torres, B. "Ray Charles." *Rolling Stone*, no. 126 (18 Jan. 1973), 28
– Marsh, Dave. "Ray Charles." *New Grove Dictionary of American Music*, 1st ed. Vol. 1. New York: Oxford UP, 1986, 405-07.
– Maher, Jack. "Ray Charles Carried the Ball—Then Everybody Else Began Scoring Big." *Billboard*, 10 Nov. 1962, 34.
– Palmer, Robert. "Soul Survivor Ray Charles." *Rolling Stone*, no. 258 (9 Feb. 1978), 11.
– Welding, P. "Ray Charles: Senior Diplomat of Soul." *Down Beat*, May (1977), 12.

Patricia Curtis Pfitsch

to prove yourself with your submission as a whole and your writing; when you do, your résumé will grow.

Clips, like résumés, grow with experience. Editors like to see these examples of published work (with a byline to show it is yours!) as proof of writers' ability to produce a high-quality finished product. Some editors prefer to see unedited writing samples: That way they are more sure they are seeing purely the writers' capabilities, and not the work of another editor as well. If that is what you are sending, of course you will want it to be your best, most polished work. If the sample is an article or story that has been accepted by another magazine but has not yet been published, indicate that.

When clips or samples are requested, the first rule is to select ones that are most closely matched to the magazine market you are pursuing. Don't sent a parenting article to a children's fiction market, for example. This is true of style as well. If you're submitting to a teen magazine that wants an upbeat and chatty style, send a sample or clip that shows you can write well in that way. Another consideration is that if the targeted magazine uses graphics or sidebars, try to send a clip that does the same.

If you are mailing your query or manuscript, photocopy the article or story to send. If you are emailing, and the clip is available online, include the URL. If not, check the writers' guidelines, and if you can scan the article and send an attachment, do so. If not, as a last resort, cut and paste the clip or sample into the body of the email.

Bibliographies for magazine articles and stories do not have to be scholarly affairs, but they should include the strongest possible sources, be thorough, accurate, and clearly formatted. Your bibliography illustrates to the editor that you are properly crediting your sources.

A good bibliography is well-rounded. It will have primary sources, including either original documents or interviews you have conducted, and respected secondary sources. If you are writing on an issue on which there are multiple perspectives, your bibliography

Sample Bibliography

"Horse Talk"

Books
- Budiansky, Stephen, The Nature of Horses, The Free Press, New York, 1997.
- Dines, Lisa, Why Horses Do That, Willow Creek Press, Minocqua, WI, 2003.
- Fisher, Sarah, Know Your Horse Inside Out, David and Charles, Cincinnati, OH, 2006.
- George, Jean Craighead, How to Talk to Your Animals, Harcourt Brace Jovanovich, New York, 1985.
- McBane, Susan, How Your Horse Works, David and Charles, UK, 1999.
- Morris, Desmond, Horse Watching, Crown Publishers, Inc., New York, 1988.

Websites
- Equusite, http://www.equusite.com/articles/behavior/behaviorSounds.shtml, June 25, 2008.
- Natural Horse Training, http://www.naturalhorsetraining.com, June 23-July 2, 2008.
- Monty Roberts: http://www.montyroberts.com/ju_ask_monty_0905.html#092805, July 5, 2008.

Interviews
- Scott, Sylvia, Founder of Whispering Way™ Natural Horsemanship Training, Virginia Natural Horsemanship Training Center LLC, 3850 Horse Farm Road, Blacksburg, VA 24060

Leslie J. Wyatt

should reflect that. Even if you are taking a definitive stand on a subject, you should show that you know what the "other" side argues.

Note that children's magazines have high standards for research today, and a bibliography that includes only two or three sources is likely to get you rejected post-haste.

Consider the research and bibliography requirements at *Highlights for Children,* which say in part: "We prefer research based on firsthand experience, consultation with experts, or primary sources. . . . Complete bibliographies as well as photocopies of key pages in references must be included." At *Cobblestone* (and other magazines of Carus Publishing Company), the guidelines request "an extensive bibliography of materials the author intends to use in preparing the article. . . . Authors are urged to use primary resources and up-to-date scholarly resources in their bibliography."

As for citation form for the entries in a bibliography, *The Chicago Manual of Style* (www.chicagomanualofstyle.org) or the *Associated Press Stylebook* (www.apstylebook.com) are both excellent references. See two sample bibliographies with slightly different formats, on pages 19 and 20.

Format, Mail, Email

"Form follows function" is an architectural adage, but is applied in other creative contexts as well. In submitting materials as a freelance writer, form may be said to come before the chance to function as a writer. If you send materials that are well-formatted and well-formulated, you will increase your chances of being accepted significantly.

Ask any editor: We've all received our share of handwritten and misdirected letters, stationery of strange color or scent, or just sloppy "stuffed" envelopes we want to toss. Editors are busy and professional people, and have little time for second-best. So send only your best.

Manuscript Format

The format for preparing manuscripts is fairly standard—an example is shown below. Double-space manuscript text, leaving 1- to 1 1/2-inch margins on the top, bottom, and sides. Indent 5 spaces for paragraphs. In the upper left corner of the first page (also known as the title page), single space your name, address, phone number, and email address. In the upper right corner of that page, place your word count. Center the title with your byline below it halfway down the page, approximately 5 inches. Then begin the manuscript text 4 lines below your byline. In the upper left corner of the following pages, type your last name, the page number, and a word or two of your title. Then, space down 4 lines and continue the text of the manuscript.

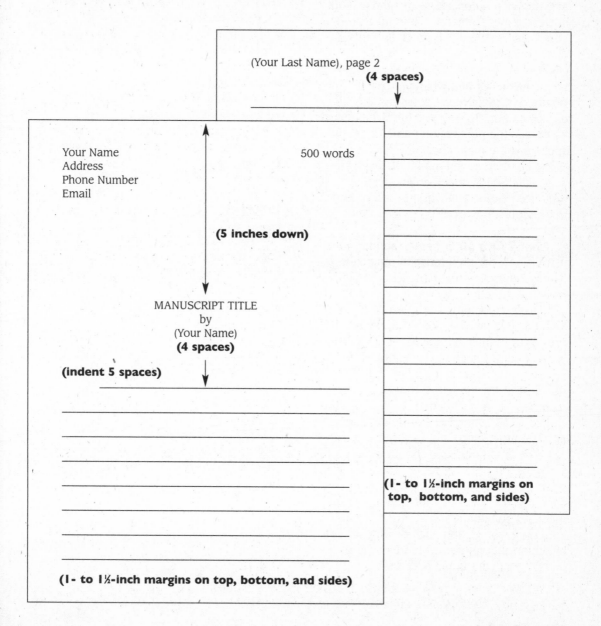

Mail format: For hard copy submissions sent by mail, the standard format for a manuscript is illustrated on page 21. Manuscripts should be double-spaced, with a margin of about one inch top, bottom, and sides. Indent paragraphs five spaces. The first page of a manuscript should include your name and contact information, the word count of the article or story, the title, and your byline. Following pages should include your name, and the page number. Use a standard font such as Times Roman in 12-point type. The paper quality should be good, and the ink dark and legible.

The manuscript should be accompanied by a cover letter and whatever else is required by the writers' guidelines, as discussed earlier. Be sure you have the editor's name and the publication name correctly spelled, and double-check the address. Remember when you mail it off to include a self-addressed stamped envelope, if requested. Some publications do not return manuscripts, however.

Email format: For email submissions—increasingly the preference in magazine publishing generally—the manuscript should be have the same format. You may be asked to send as an attachment in Word (DOC) or Rich text format (RTF), or cut and pasted from your manuscript into the body of the email. Check guidelines for editor preferences for the email subject line, but if that is not clear in the guideline, use "query" or "submission" and either your title or an indication of the genre. For example: "Query, YA article on the dangers of piercing."

Your email message should be as professional as if it were on paper. Email tends to be more casual, but sound professional, not chummy. Be sure that your spelling, grammar, and punctuation are correct. As in the hard copy submission, include all your contact information—name, address, phone—and not just your email address.

Fair Use & Quotations

Copyright protects your work from violation—from use or reuse that you have not permitted or sold. Under the *fair use* doctrine, however, your story or article may be used in limited ways without express permission. For example, a teacher could make a copy of an article under 1,000 words for class use without getting permission from you.

Fair use also means that you can quote the work of other writers in your own writing, but in a reasonable way. You don't want to abuse the copyrights of others.

If a piece of writing is in the public domain, you may quote from it at will, but you must still indicate your source. Any written work produced before 1923 is in the public domain. The author (and heirs) retains the copyright for anything written after 1978 for his or her lifetime, plus 70 years. If a work was written between 1923 and 1977, the copyright protection varies and should be checked.

However, if your use of an article, story, or book is limited, and your citation is clear, under fair use you may quote from it without express permission. There is no specific number for words that may be quoted attached to the fair use doctrine, which says material may not be a "substantial portion" of the work quoted. Thus, if you're quoting 200 words of a 1,000-word article you should seek permission; if it's 200 words from a 1,000-page book, you probably don't need to.

Finally, using quotes from a copyrighted work in a review, such as a book review, is considered an exception. It is fair use to quote without explicit permission in criticism and commentaries, news reports, scholarly works, for nonprofit use, and in parodies.

Getting Down to Business

With hard writing work, solid market research, and some good fortune, that query or manuscript you send off will elicit a *yes* from a pleased editor. It's time to consider the rights you're selling, and the payment.

Rights & Contracts

Many new writers are concerned about protecting their copyright before they have even sold one piece. Be assured: Even if you do not register and file any forms, you own the rights to your "original work of authorship," according to the U.S. Copyright Office of the Library of Congress. Moreover, copyright protection covers "both published and unpublished works."

Copyright is automatically secured when a work is created. You own your words, in the way you used them, in an original composition. Once you give a work a tangible shape, whether on paper or in a computer file, you own it; the critical copyright law term is "fixed in a tangible form of expression." What you cannot copyright or own is an idea or concept, or a title.

Should you want to register your work formally, you can find the information at www.copyright.gov/forms. Fees vary from $35 for online registration to $65 for paper registration. If you have a copyright, indicate that to an editor who accepts your article or story for publication.

The rights magazines purchase vary. You should consider which you are willing to sell as you develop your work and target markets. Also consider the fee offered.

The details should be indicated in a contract or letter of agreement with your editor or publisher. It is also not uncommon for the agreement to be informally conveyed in email or other written form; such an agreement is binding as long as both parties clearly consent. If you have an ongoing relationship with an editor, this arrangement may be more than satisfactory. If you are uncomfortable, however, you may formally write up your own understanding. For example, send a letter or email that says,

> I understand that *Kiddo Magazine* will purchase First North American serial rights to print my 1,000-word article for middle-graders titled 'The Myth of Math' for 10¢ a word. I will deliver the completed story to you on or before June 1, 2012."

Ask the editor to sign a copy of your letter or formally acknowledge acceptance in an email.

Remember that you do not have to agree to a publication's terms, and you can negotiate. Should you choose to do so, remain professional and reasonable. You will have more leverage if you have publishing credits and experience.

The rights you may sell or convey (to a nonpaying market) allowing a publisher to print and distribute your work include the following.

- *All rights:* The periodical purchases the right to use the work in any way it chooses, in the U.S. or abroad, in print or electronically, now and in the future. If you choose to sell all rights, be sure you understand you cannot again use or resell the work again yourself. You should consider whether the fee paid is adequate for handing over all rights, and whether you can negotiate for the return of certain rights, such as publishing the piece as part of a book. Writers' organizations such as the American Society of Journalists and Authors (ASJA) and the Authors Guild warn writers to be very careful of selling all rights, and generally advise against it.

- *All serial rights:* The publisher may publish your work in serials—newspapers, magazines, and so on. But you may keep rights to use it in other ways, such as in an anthology or as a book chapter.

Submission Tracking

Develop a means, such as this form, to track the status of the articles and stories you send out.

Magazine	Article/Story	Submitted	Status	Due	Publication	Payment
Highlights	John Trumbull & CT history	2/25/11	accepted	submitted	May 2012	5/30/11
Jack and Jill	retold myth, Aristaeus & bees	4/1/11	revising	5/15/11		
Natl. Geo. Explorer	Hurling, a Prehistoric Sport	4/6/11	rejected			
Dig	Hurling, a Prehistoric Sport	5/10/11	expanding bibliography	6/1/11		

● *First rights:* The publisher acquires the right to publish your work for the first time in any media specified, including print or electronic, without geographic limitations. But you retain reprint rights and all others.

● *First North American serial rights:* This may be the most common rights sold in the U.S. and Canada. The publisher may publish your work for the first time in North America. You retain reprint rights, and the right to sell the article outside North America.

First rights and first North American serial rights are "nonexclusive rights." The ASJA advises that even these can be a "rights-grab." The ASJA says,

These agreements often begin with a benign-sounding FNASR clause and then tack on extremely broad (though "non-exclusive") rights to use a writer's work in perpetuity in various media. The writer may still technically own the property, but the publisher may continue to re-use the work whenever it wishes—for no additional fee.

First rights are perfectly legitimate and appropriate, however, in most circumstances. Be sure that first rights mean one-time use, and if the publisher wants to use the piece in multiple media or in the future, you receive appropriate compensation.

● *Second or reprint rights:* A magazine or other publication acquires the right to publish the work, although it has already been published elsewhere. You may not grant these rights if the publisher who acquired first rights has not yet published the work. If you retain reprint rights, you may sell your work as many times as you wish.

● *One-time rights:* The periodical has the right to use your article, for the first time or as a reprint, once, and understands that it may be sold or published in another publication at the same time. One-time rights are most common in regional publications; the agreement is likely to include a geographical limitation. That is, you would be requested not to sell the article or story to another publication in the same area. If you sold an article to *Greenville Parent* in New York, you would be able to sell it at the same time to *Greenville Kids* in South Carolina, but not to *Greenville Family* in New York.

Another important consideration today is electronic rights, and the ongoing struggle to have writers paid fairly for the many changes in media now in existence and yet to come.

Electronic rights refer to online publication, ezines or electronic newsletters, CDs, audio, databases, apps, and any other digital form. Today, authors may be asked to sell first or other rights in both print and electronic form. Organizations such as the ASJA and Authors' Guild are waging an ongoing battle to make sure that electronic rights policies—which are still unfolding—are fair to authors. Many periodicals have arguably taken advantage of authors in regard to electronic rights over recent years.

The Authors Guild has led the charge for fair payment for electronic publication. It recommends that writers read contracts very carefully to see if they include electronic rights. Many publishers have added broad coverage of electronic rights in standard, or boilerplate contracts. The law—taken up to the U.S. Supreme Court—requires that publishers have your permission to publish your work in electronic databases.

If you are willing to sell simultaneous print and website rights—for the right fee—also check how long the article or story will be available electronically. Will it be archived or placed in a database and available long-term? Do you want it to be? Are there other considerations (like whether you can have a link to your blog or website attached to an archived article) that will mean making the article available is worth it to you for your own career purposes? Do not allow re-use unless you are compensated in some fashion.

Work-for-hire refers to an arrangement between publication and writer by which the writer produces an agreed-on work, but the publication owns all rights to it. The writer is given a one-time fee for the assignment. You are not an employee of the publisher, but you are an independent contractor who is commissioned to write articles and the work you produce is the work the property of the publisher. Work-for hire arrangements require a contract signed by both parties.

The ASJA, Authors Guild, and other writer advocacy groups are not admirers of work-for-hire arrangements because they make freelancers give up all control over the work they produce.

Famously, the Authors Guild and others took on the *New York Times* when, in the 1990s, the newspaper wanted writers to sign work-for-hire contracts that said that the *Times* would own all rights, in all nonprint media, all over the world, for anything published in print in the paper. But in 2001, the U.S. Supreme Court found in *Tasini v. New York Times et al.* that the newspaper and others were exceeding their rights and infringing on freelancers'.

The ASJA, in fact, recommends against all work-for-hire agreements, except for some books and corporate writing done for a specific purpose. When a publisher wants a work-for-hire agreement, the ASJA recommends that the writer try to get first serial rights instead, or put a time limitation on use of the work, or that the writer negotiate a higher fee.

Your goal as a writer is clear: Sell as few rights as you can, for the highest payment you can. Control your own work, and income. But also be practical: If you are a new writer, or new to a publication or writing arena, some compromise can help you secure more experience and more writing work for the future.

Payment

Payment policies at publishers vary. Some pay by word, some by column or page, and some have project-based fees or flat rates. Some publications pay on acceptance, and some on or after publication with a 30-, 60-, or 90-day window, or even longer. *On acceptance* means the editor needs time to read and evaluate the article. *On publication* means waiting for an editorial calendar to make room for the piece.

As the economy slowed, these policies often changed at publications that were looking to improve their cash flow. You need to work in the possiblities and timing of payment into your own financial situation. Track your submissions using a form such as the one on page 24. Know what you have sent out when, where the query or submission stands, your due dates, publication dates, and payment.

Building your writing career means attending to both creative and the business details. You can grow as a writer, widen your possiblities, and expand your publishing career.

Additional Writers' Resources

Writing & Style
- The Chicago Manual of Style: www.chicagomanualofstyle.org
- The Compulsive Copyeditor: www http://compulsivecopyeditor.wordpress.com
- Common Errors in English Usage: www.wsu.edu/~brians/errors/index.html
- Grammar Girl: http://grammar.quickanddirtytips.com

Writing Community
- Absolute Write: http://absolutewrite.com
- Education Writers Association: www.ew.org
- Goodreads: www.goodreads.com
- Mystery Writers of America: www.mysterywriters.org
- Science Fiction & Fantasy Writers of America: www.swfa.org

Career
- American Society of Journalists and Authors: www.asja.org
- The Authors Guild: www.authorsguild.org
- LinkedIn: www.linkedin.com
- Magazine Publishers of America: www.magazine.org
- National Writers Association: www.nationalwriters.com
- PEN Center: www.penusa.org
- Publishing Law Center: www.publaw.com

Children's Writing
- Children's Writer: www.childrenswriter.com
- Cynsations: http://cynthialeitichsmith.blogspot.com/
- Editorial Anonymous: http://editorialanonymous.blogspot.com
- Society of Children's Book Writers & Illustrators: www.scbwi.org

Listings

Listings Key

Cobblestone ———————————————————— Accepts fiction

Cobblestone Publishing, 30 Grove Street, Suite C, Peterborough, NH 03458
www.cobblestonepub.com

Editor: Meg Chorlian ————————————————————— Who to contact

Each theme-based issue of *Cobblestone* delves deep into a place, era, or event from American history. Its content is designed to meet curriculum standards while offering a lively and entertaining reading experience. Articles should be historically accurate and have a lively, original approach to the subject.
■ **Circulation** 27,000 ■ **Audience** 9–14 years ■ **Frequency** 9 times a year

> Profiles the publication, its interests, and readers

Freelance Potential Publishes 180 freelance submissions yearly: 85% written by nonstaff writers; 25% by authors new to the magazine; 20% by previously unpublished writers. Receives 50 queries monthly.

> Designates the amount and type of freelance submissions published each year; highlights the publication's receptivity to unpublished writers

Submissions Guidelines, theme list, and query due dates available at website. Query with cover letter, outline, bibliography, and clips or writing samples. All queries must relate to an upcoming theme. No unsolicited manuscripts. Accepts hard copy. SASE. Responds 5 months before theme issue publication.
■ *Articles:* 700–800 words. Sidebars, 300–600 words. Informational, profiles, interviews. Topics: American history, historical figures.
■ *Fiction:* To 800 words. Genres: historical, multicultural, biographical, adventure, retold legends.
■ *Depts/columns:* Word lengths vary. Interviews, short profiles, fun facts.
■ *Artwork:* Professional quality B/W or color prints and slides. Line art.
■ *Other:* Activities, to 700 words. Puzzles and games. Poetry, to 100 lines.

> Provides guidelines for submitting material; lists word lengths and types of material accepted from freelance writers

Sample Issue 52 pages. No advertising. Sample copy available at website.
■ "Walt Disney: Animation Pioneer," by John P. Brackin. A profile of Disney's accomplishments.
■ "Wrinkles, Scars, and Stitches," by Diana Kelly. How to achieve Hollywood-style make-up looks.

> Analyzes a recent sample copy of the publication; briefly describes selected articles, stories, departments, etc.

Rights and Payment All rights. Written material, 20¢–25¢ a word. Artwork, $15–$100. Pays on publication. Provides 2 contributor's copies.

> Lists types of rights acquired, payment rate, and number of copies provided to freelance writers

---

Icon Key

 New Listing   Epublisher   Not currently accepting submissions

 Overseas Publisher   Fiction makes up at least 10% of magazine editorial content

Magazines for Children and Teens

The magazines, ezines, and websites listed in this section of *Magazine Markets for Children's Writers 2012* represent the absolute core of the children's writer's market. These are the publications that kids, tweens, and teens turn to for a good story, engaging and informative nonfiction or fun activities. These are the publications of childhood—packed with age-specific content that's just for kids.

The titles represent the entire spectrum of children's magazines, and include the religious as well as secular. You'll find publications in all genres of fiction, general interest pieces, nonfiction on myriad topics, poetry, and activities—for audiences that range in age from infancy through the teen years

You'll also find new listings here that broaden the array of publishers that may be interested in what you have to offer their readers.

Alateen Talk

Al-Anon Family Group, 1600 Corporate Landing Parkway, Virginia Beach, VA 23454.
www.al-anon.alateen.org/alateen-talk

Editor: Mary Lou Mahlman

Filled with teenagers' own stories and thoughts, *Alateen Talk* is a newsletter written by and for members of Alateen and others who have been adversely affected by having an alcoholic or substance abuser in their lives. Members of Alateen are invited to share an experience from the heart with the focus on themselves—not the alcoholic, the non-drinking parent, or anyone else. ■ **Circulation** 4,000
■ **Audience** 6–18 years ■ **Frequency** Quarterly

Freelance Potential Publishes 85–120 freelance submissions yearly: 90% written by nonstaff writers; 75% by authors new to the publication; 80% by previously unpublished writers. Receives 8–12 unsolicited manuscripts monthly.

Submissions Alateen members only. Send complete manuscript. Accepts hard copy. SASE. Responds in 2 weeks. Guidelines available to Alateen members only.
■ *Articles:* Word lengths vary. Self-help, personal experience. Topics: social issues, family life, alcoholism and its effects on relationships.
■ *Depts/columns:* Staff-written.
■ *Artwork:* B/W line art.
■ *Other:* Poetry.

Sample Issue 8 pages. No advertising. Sample copy available.
■ "What I've Learned Being in the Program," by Stacey. A teen manages with the help of Al-Anon.
■ "One Day at a Time," by Ashley. Learning not to worry about yesterday or tomorrow.

Rights and Payment All rights. No payment.

American Careers

6701 West 64th Street, Suite 210, Overland Park, KS 66202. www.carcom.com

Editor in Chief: Mary Pitchford

Designed to promote career development and education for middle school and high school students, *American Careers* offers in-depth information on a variety of career choices. It also features how-to articles on career planning, life skills, and résumés. It is distributed through the school market. Articles should be written at a seventh- to tenth-grade reading level for a national audience. ■ **Circulation** 350,000 ■ **Audience** 12–18 years ■ **Frequency** Annually

Freelance Potential Publishes 5 freelance submissions yearly: 5% written by nonstaff writers; 1–2% by authors who are new to the magazine. Receives 8+ queries monthly.

Submissions Query with résumé and clips. Accepts hard copy. SASE. Responds in 1 month.
■ *Articles:* 300–750 words. Informational, how-to, profiles, personal experience. Topics: careers, career planning, education.
■ *Artwork:* Color prints, high-resolution digital images.
■ *Other:* Quizzes, self-assessments.

Sample Issue 64 pages. No advertising.
■ "The BIG Idea: Green." Ways to go green, and careers that support the environment.
■ "Speaking Up." Profiles a professional lobbyist.

Rights and Payment All rights. All material, payment rates vary. Pays on acceptance. Provides 2 contributor's copies.

American Cheerleader

333 7th Avenue, 11th Floor, New York, NY 10001. www.americancheerleader.com

Editor in Chief: Marisa Walker

American Cheerleader covers all things cheer-related—from profiles of teams and athletes to training tips and fitness advice. It also reports on cheerleading competitions and trends. Writers should have some sort of background in cheerleading and know the kind of determination and passion this sport takes. ■ **Circulation** 150,000 ■ **Audience** 13–18 years ■ **Frequency** 6 times a year

Freelance Potential Publishes 30 freelance submissions yearly: 40% written by nonstaff writers; 10% by authors who are new to the magazine; 20% by previously unpublished writers. Receives dozens of queries, a few unsolicited manuscripts monthly.

Submissions Editorial calendar available. Query with clips, or send complete manuscript. Prefers email to mwalker@americancheerleader.com; will accept hard copy. SASE. Responds in 3 months.
■ *Articles:* To 1,000 words. Informational, how-to, profiles, interviews, personal experience, photo-essays. Topics: cheerleading, cheerleaders and teams, workouts, competitions, scholarships, college, careers, popular culture.
■ *Depts/columns:* Word lengths vary. Safety, health, nutrition, beauty, fashion, fundraising, new products.
■ *Artwork:* High-resolution digital images, 35mm color slides.

Sample Issue 96 pages. Advertising.
■ "Eat Like a Champ," by Eve Pearson. How to make the right food choices before competitions.
■ "Double Life," by Brianne Carlon. Time management techniques.

Rights and Payment All rights. All material, payment rates vary. Pays on publication. Provides 1 contributor's copy.

American Girl

American Girl Publishing, 8400 Fairway Place, Middleton, WI 53562. www.americangirl.com

Editorial Director: Jodi Goldberg

Building the confidence, curiosity, and self-esteem of young girls is the goal of this magazine. Each issue includes inspiring profiles, entertaining articles, and craft and cooking ideas. It is always in search of new twists on familiar topics. Its Girls Express department—short profiles of girls who are into sports, the arts, or interesting hobbies; as well as true stories about girls who have had unusual experiences—offers the most opportunities for freelance writers. ■ **Circulation** 700,000 ■ **Audience** 8–12 years ■ **Frequency** 6 times a year

Freelance Potential Publishes 5 freelance submissions yearly: 4% written by nonstaff writers; 2% by authors new to the magazine; 2% by previously unpublished writers. Receives 65 queries monthly.

Submissions Guidelines available. Query. Accepts hard copy. Accepts simultaneous submissions if identified. Responds in 4 months.
■ *Articles:* 500–1,000 words. Informational articles, profiles, interviews. Topics: girls' interests.
■ *Depts/columns:* 175 words. Profiles, how-to pieces, craft ideas.

Sample Issue 72 pages. No advertising. Sample copy available at newsstands.
■ "Finding Her Voice." An autistic girl who learned to speak and interact through music therapy.
■ "Nature Nook." Eco-friendly craft projects for girls to make for their room decor.

Rights and Payment Rights vary. All material purchased under work-for-hire agreements. Written material, payment rates vary. Pays on acceptance. Provides 3 contributor's copies.

AppleSeeds

Cobblestone Publishing Company, 30 Grove Street, Peterborough, NH 03458. www.cobblestonepub.com

Editor: Susan Buckley

Written for kids in third and fourth grades, *AppleSeeds* explores world cultures and history. Each issue focuses on a particular place or country. The editors look for lively, age-appropriate articles that exhibit an original approach to the specified theme. Scientific and historical accuracy are a must. ■ **Circulation** 10,000 ■ **Audience** 8–10 years ■ **Frequency** 9 times a year

Freelance Potential Publishes 90–100 freelance submissions yearly: 80% written by nonstaff writers; 33% by authors new to the magazine. Receives 50+ queries monthly.

Submissions Guidelines, theme list, and query due dates available at website. Query with article description, source list, and proposed word count. Accepts email to susanbuckleynyc@gmail.com (attachments accepted; also include material in body of email). Responds in 2–3 months if interested.
■ *Articles:* 150–600 words. Informational, how-to, profiles, interviews. Topics: history, biography, biology, geology, technology, geography, literature, the environment.
■ *Depts/columns:* 150 words. Reading Corner (folktales and public domain literature), By the Numbers (theme-related math activities), Fun Stuff (hands-on activities), Your Turn, Experts in Action. From the Source (primary source material), 150–300 words.
■ *Artwork:* B/W and color prints.

Sample Issue 36 pages. No advertising. Sample copy available.
■ "Daily Lives of Egyptian Children," by Julie K. Cohen. The lifestyle of Egyptian children.
■ "Farmers: VIPs of Ancient Egypt," by Dorothy Phillips Mobilla. An explanation of why farmers were so important in Egypt.

Rights and Payment All rights. Written material, $50 per page. Artwork, payment rates vary. Pays after publication. Provides 2 contributor's copies.

Art Dawg ⭐

601 SW Otter Way, P.O. Box 2072, Bend, OR 97709. www.artdawgkids.com

Editor

Art Dawg exists to help children nurture their talent and curiosity. Subtitled "The Visual Arts Magazine for Kids," it is filled with articles on the visual arts and artists, and includes how-to's on everything from drawing to photography. Each issue also introduces readers to a classic art master, a contemporary artist, and possible career paths. Since learning about the arts increases children's abilities to learn across the spectrum, the mission of the magazine in an age when art budgets are being cut is to help parents, grandparents, and educators give children an alternative means to grow and come to love the arts. ■ **Circulation** Unavailable ■ **Audience** 5–12 years ■ **Frequency** Quarterly

Freelance Potential Unavailable.

Submissions Contact via the website only.
■ *Articles:* Word lengths vary. Informational, profiles, interviews, how-to. Topics: all types of visual arts and artists.
■ *Depts/columns:* Word lengths vary. Projects related to an artist's work.
■ *Other:* Puzzles, activities.

Sample Issue 28 pages. Sample articles available to view at website.
■ "Glass Guru." A profile of glass artist Dale Chihuly.
■ "When It Comes to Wildlife Photography, Steve Winters Is a Natural." Profile of the *Natural Geographic* photographer, and some of his biggest adventures.

Rights and Payment Unavailable.

Ask

Cricket Magazine Group, 70 East Lake Street, Suite 300, Chicago, IL 60601. www.cricketmag.com

Editor: Elizabeth Huyck

Young children have lots of questions about the world. *Ask* magazine exists to give them answers in language they understand and in formats they enjoy. Though most of its articles deal with facts about nature and science, all subjects are fair game. Writers must have experience in writing nonfiction articles for young children and demonstrate an ability to engage young readers with information that is presented in fun and entertaining ways. *Ask* is part of the Cricket family of children's magazines. ■ **Circulation** 36,000 ■ **Audience** 7–10 years ■ **Frequency** 9 times a year

Freelance Potential 50–75% written by nonstaff writers: 10–25% developed from freelance submissions; 10–25% assigned; 10–25% by authors new to the magazine; 1–10% by previously unpublished writers. Receives 25–50 queries monthly.

Submissions Guidelines and theme list available at website. Query with résumé, article overview, and writing samples that include at least 200 words of unedited copy on any nonfiction topic. Accepts hard copy and email to ask@caruspub.com. No simultaneous submissions. Responds in 2–8 weeks.
■ *Articles:* 1,200–1,600 words. Informational, interviews, profiles, biography, personal experience. Topics: science, animals, nature, technology, math, history, humor, geography, health, the arts.
■ *Depts/columns:* Word lengths vary. Science news and Q&As.

Sample Issue 34 pages. Advertising. Sample copy available at website.
■ "Why Animals Love to Play," by Ellen R. Braaf. How play prepares young animals for life in the wild.
■ "Do You Have a Musical Brain?" by Amy Tao. Understanding how and why the brain loves music.

Rights and Payment First North American serial rights. Written material, 25¢–45¢ a word. Pays on publication. Provides 2 contributor's copies.

BabagaNewz

Behrman House, 11 Edison Place, Springfield, NJ 07081. www.babaganewz.com

Editor: Aviva Werner

Designed for Jewish middle school students and their teachers, this ezine offers creative, innovative ways to explore Jewish traditions, holidays, values, and issues. Its perspective is hip, fun, and thought-provoking. ■ **Hits per month** 25,000 ■ **Audience** Grades 6–8 ■ **Frequency** Updated weekly

Freelance Potential Publishes 20 freelance submissions yearly: 30% written by nonstaff writers; 10% by authors new to the magazine. Receives 1–10 queries monthly.

Submissions Guidelines available by email request to aviva@babaganewz.com. Query with résumé. Accepts email to aviva@behrmanhouse.com. Response time varies.
■ *Articles:* Word lengths vary. Informational, profiles, personal experience. Topics: Israel; Jewish holidays, history, values.
■ *Other:* Games, crafts, puzzles, activities.

Sample Issue Sample issue available at website.
■ "The Myrtus Worm," by Howard Blas. An explanation of a computer virus aimed at Iran's nuclear weapon program, and why Israel is a suspect.
■ "Zachary Gordon: The Wimpy Kid," by Gerri Miller. Interview with the young movie star.

Rights and Payment All rights. Payment rates vary. Pays on acceptance.

Babybug

Cricket Magazine Group, 70 East Lake Street, Suite 300, Chicago, IL 60601. www.babybugmagkids.com

Submissions Editor

This magazine is designed in board book style for the littlest readers. Its brightly colored pages feature stories, poems, words, and concepts that help young children discover the world around them. It is part of the Cricket Magazine Group. ■ **Circulation** 50,000 ■ **Audience** 6 months–2 years ■ **Frequency** 9 times a year

Freelance Potential Publishes 30–40 freelance submissions yearly: 100% written by nonstaff writers; 50% by authors new to the magazine. Receives 200 unsolicited manuscripts monthly.

Submissions Guidelines available at website. Send complete manuscript. Accepts hard copy. Accepts simultaneous submissions if identified. SASE. Responds in 6 months.
■ *Articles:* 10 words. Informational. Topics: material that conveys simple concepts and ideas.
■ *Fiction:* 4–6 short sentences. Simple stories.
■ *Artwork:* By assignment only. Send sample tearsheets, photoprints, or photocopies to be kept on file.
■ *Other:* Parent-child activities, to 8 lines. Rhymes and poems, to 8 lines.

Sample Issue 24 pages. No advertising. Sample copy available at website.
■ "Little Mouse," by Eva Apelqvist. This energetic and rhythmic poem imaginatively describes the life of a mouse.
■ "Orchard Rain," by Louann Brown. This poem celebrates the wonders of the natural world, as a child enjoys petals *raining* from a tree.

Rights and Payment All or second North American serial rights. Written material, $25+. Artwork, $500 per spread, $250 per page. Pays on publication. Provides 6 contributor's copies.

Baseball Youth

Dugout Media, P.O. Box 983, Morehead, KY 40351. www.baseballyouth.com

Managing Editor: Nathan Clinkenbeard

This magazine allows kids to get lost in the world of baseball. Covering everything from youth leagues to the major leagues, *Baseball Youth* features profiles, interviews, advice, and training tips.
■ **Circulation** 100,000 ■ **Audience** 7–14 years ■ **Frequency** 6 times a year

Freelance Potential Publishes 10–20 freelance submissions yearly: 10% written by nonstaff writers. Receives 8 queries monthly.

Submissions Guidelines available. Query with word length and availability of artwork. Prefers email queries to nathanc@dugoutmedia.com (Word attachments); will accept hard copy. Availability of artwork improves chance of acceptance. SASE. Response time varies.
■ *Articles:* Word lengths vary. Informational, how-to, profiles, interviews, photo-essays, personal experience. Topics: youth baseball, major and minor league baseball, players, coaches, training, ballparks, baseball equipment, baseball cards.
■ *Depts/columns:* Word lengths vary. Baseball news, card collections, mascot interviews, fan club information, first-person essays, video game reviews.
■ *Artwork:* Color digital images or prints.
■ *Other:* Puzzles, quizzes, comics.

Sample Issue 46 pages. Sample copy available at website.
■ "Courage and Faith: Jaylon Fong." How a nine-year-old battled leukemia while playing on an all-star team, and ultimately achieved remission.

Rights and Payment All rights. Written material, payment rates vary. Payment policy varies.

Bayard Magazines

Bayard, 2 King Street, 1st Floor, Peterborough PE1 1LT, U.K. www.bayard-magazines.co.uk

Editor in Chief: Simona Sideri

An international magazine group that originated in France, Bayard publishes a line of English language magazines for children in the U.K. The beautiful publications have also won Parents' Choice Awards in the U.S. because of their high literary quality. They are *Adventure Box,* for ages 6–9; *Discovery Box,* for ages 9–12; and *Story Box,* for ages 3–6. *Story Box* is a read-aloud magazine meant to be shared by a parent or teacher with a child. Each issues features an engaging, age-appropriate story, illustrated nursery rhymes, animal facts, and fun puzzles. *Discovery Box* takes tweens into the worlds of nature, science, and history. It features lively articles that bring these topics alive, through photo-essays, science facts, and information about many countries. *Adventure Box* gets kids hooked on reading by giving them an exciting way to enjoy chapter books. Each issue features a story—chosen especially for newly independent and more advanced readers—divided into manageable chapters, with a summary and vocabulary list for each. It also includes word searches, puzzles, a comic strip, and fun facts about the natural world. Bayard Magazines also owns the Owl Magazines in Canada. ■ **Circulation** Unavailable ■ **Audience** 3–12 years ■ **Frequency** 10 times a year

Freelance Potential Freelance potential is at best limited. It is currently not open to submssions.

Submissions Not accepting submissions at this time.
■ *Articles:* Word lengths vary. Informational, photo-essays. Topics: history, geography, science, animals.
■ *Fiction:* Word lengths vary. Chapter stories. All genres.
■ *Depts/columns:* Vary with each magazine. They include Wonder with Whizkid (science topics), Animal World (animal facts), Time for a Rhyme, Do-It-Yourself activities. NatureBox (photos and facts about the natural world).
■ *Other:* Games, activities, rhymes, puzzles, fun facts.

Sample Issue 68 pages
- "Spy in a Muddle!" A class discovers a fun way to learn the capital cities of the European Union.
- "Learning To Be Wild." All about the experiment to set free the Mongolian wild horses.

Rights and Payment Unavailable.

Berry Blue Haiku

http://berrybluehaiku.blogspot.com

Editor: Gisele LeBlanc, Assistant Editor: Robyn Hood Black

Originally designed as a digital journal celebrating the Japanese poetic form, *Berry Blue Haiku* has evolved into a blog journal that publishes haiku and related resources for teens and adults. It also includes articles aimed at helping children of all ages learn to appreciate the genre and write poetry themselves. Haiku are two- or three-line poems conveying "a moment, thought, observation, or feeling through the use of concrete words and sensory images," according to the guidelines. ■ **Hits per month** Unavailable ■ **Audience** YA ■ **Frequency** Updated regularly

Freelance Potential Publishes several freelance submissions yearly.

Submissions Detailed guidelines available at website. Send complete manuscript. Accepts email to berrybluehaiku@gmail.com (no attachments; include "haiku submission" in subject line). Accepts simultaneous submissions if identified. Responds in 1 month.
- *Other:* Haiku and haiga, 2–3 lines; limit 5 per submission. Nature haiku with a seasonal word (kigo); modern, human haiku (senryu); and innovative haiku.

Sample Issue Available at website.
- Spring Haiku. A collection of seasonal haiku by multiple authors.
- "Spring Treasure Haiku," by Tina M. Cho. An activity article for ages 6+ to encourage the writing of haiku about the spring.

Rights and Payment First serial, nonexclusive worldwide electronic rights in perpetuity. No payment.

Beyond Centauri

P.O. Box 782, Cedar Rapids, IA 52406. www.samsdotpublishing.com

Managing Editor: Tyree Campbell

Beyond Centauri is a magazine of fantasy and science fiction designed specifically for tweens through young adults. It features short stories, informational articles, poetry, and reviews. It welcomes new authors, and often publishes the work of teenage writers. It will not accept work with foul, obscene, or otherwise "adult" language. ■ **Circulation** 150 ■ **Audience** 10–18 years ■ **Frequency** Quarterly

Freelance Potential Publishes 100 freelance submissions yearly: 95% written by nonstaff writers; 25% by authors new to the magazine; 20% by previously unpublished writers. Receives 40 unsolicited manuscripts monthly.

Submissions Guidelines available at website. Send complete manuscript. Accepts email to beyond-centauri@yahoo.com (manuscript in body of email or as RTF attachment). Responds in 2–3 months.
- *Articles:* To 1,500 words. Informational, opinion, media reviews. Topics: space exploration, science, technology, science fiction.
- *Fiction:* To 2,500 words. Flash fiction, to 1,000 words. Genres: science fiction, fantasy.
- *Artwork:* B/W or color illustrations.
- *Other:* Poetry, to 50 lines. Science fiction, fantasy themes.

Sample Issue 50 pages. No advertising. Sample copy available.
- "Gramma and the Giant Tomato Worm," by Rachel V. Olivier.
- "So You Wanna Write Poetry," by Brock Marie Moore. A poet explains her work.

Rights and Payment First North American serial rights. Articles, $7. Fiction, $6. Flash fiction, $2. Poetry, $2. Artwork, $6; $20 for cover art. Pays on publication. Provides 1 contributor's copy.

Blaze Magazine

P.O. Box 2660, Niagara Falls, NY 14302. www.blazekids.com

Editor: Brenda McCarthy

Blaze gives children a ride into the wonderful world of horses. It is filled with articles about horses and the natural world, and horse-based activities and games. Articles that employ a mix of entertainment and education will get the best reception here. It also accepts articles about other animals and the environment. ■ **Circulation** 4,000 ■ **Audience** 8–14 years ■ **Frequency** Quarterly

Freelance Potential Publishes 25–30 freelance submissions yearly: 50% written by nonstaff writers.

Submissions Query. Accepts email queries to brenda@blazekids.com. Availability of artwork improves chance of acceptance. Response time varies.
■ *Articles:* 200–500 words. Informational, how-to, profiles. Topics: horseback riding, training, breeds.
■ *Fiction:* Word lengths vary. Stories featuring horses.
■ *Depts/columns:* Word lengths vary. Short news items, arts and crafts.
■ *Artwork:* B/W and color prints and transparencies.
■ *Other:* Puzzles, games.

Sample Issue 40 pages. Advertising. Sample copy available at website.
■ "Palominos: The Golden Ones." Profile of the Palomino breed.
■ "Tooth Talk." Fun facts about horses' teeth, and how to keep them healthy.

Rights and Payment Rights vary. Written material, 25¢ a word. Payment policy varies.

Bonbon

2123 Preston Square Court, Suite 300, Falls Church, VA 22043. www.bonbonkids.com

Publisher: Sitki Kazanci

This bilingual magazine for Turkish children features articles and stories that reflect Turkey's culture, traditions, and values while conveying a message of tolerance and understanding. It is read by Turkish children living in America as well as by children living in Turkey. ■ **Circulation** 6,000 ■ **Audience** 6–14 years ■ **Frequency** 6 times a year

Freelance Potential Publishes 30 freelance submissions yearly: 60% written by nonstaff writers; 10% by authors new to the magazine; 25% by previously unpublished writers.

Submissions Query with brief author biography. Accepts email queries to info@bonbonkids.com (include "*Bonbon* query" in subject field). Responds in 2 weeks.
■ *Articles:* 250 words. Informational, profiles, interviews. Topics: Turkish language, culture, traditions, news, animals, nature, history.
■ *Fiction:* 500 words. Stories that feature Turkish traditions, culture, values.
■ *Other:* Comics, puzzles, games, jokes, activities. Poetry.

Sample Issue 26 pages.
■ "The Animal Rescuers." A story of a fun car trip told in both Turkish and English.
■ "Turkish Club," by Burçin Ögrenir. Playful illustrations assist in teaching vocabulary words.

Rights and Payment One-time rights. No payment.

Boys' Life

1325 West Walnut Hill Lane, P.O. Box 152079, Irving, TX 75015-2079. www.boyslife.org

Senior Writer: Aaron Derr

If it is of interest to boys, it is covered here. Published by the Boy Scouts of America since 1911, *Boys' Life* publishes articles that entertain and inform boys. Topics include outdoor adventure, scouting news, sports, video games, television, and films. All articles are commissioned and emphasize good character, kindness, adventure, and an appreciation of the world around us. ■ **Circulation** 1.1 million ■ **Audience** 6–18 years ■ **Frequency** Monthly

Freelance Potential Publishes 50 freelance submissions yearly: 80% written by nonstaff writers; 2% by authors new to the magazine; 1% by previously unpublished writers. Receives 160 queries monthly.

Submissions Guidelines available. Query. Accepts hard copy. SASE. Responds in 4–6 weeks.
■ *Articles:* 500–1,500 words. Informational, how-to, profiles, humor. Topics: sports, science, American history, geography, nature, the environment.
■ *Fiction:* By assignment only.
■ *Depts/columns:* To 600 words. Advice, humor, collecting, computers, pets.
■ *Other:* Puzzles, cartoons.

Sample Issue 52 pages. Advertising. Sample copy available.
■ "My Favorite Snakes," by Shawn Heflick. A biologist talks about the snakes he's met face to face.
■ "There and Back Again." An interactive map of a Illinois Boy Scout troop's Grand Canyon hike.

Rights and Payment First rights. Articles, $400–$1,500. Fiction, $750+. Depts/columns, $100–$400. Pays on acceptance. Provides 2 contributor's copies.

Boys' Quest

P.O. Box 227, Bluffton, OH 45817-0227. www.boysquest.com

Editor: Marilyn Edwards

A magazine for boys that can be used in the classroom or for pleasure reading at home, *Boys' Quest* is filled with articles offering information, adventure, fiction, and fun. Each issue is themed.
■ **Circulation** 12,000 ■ **Audience** 6–13 years ■ **Frequency** 6 times a year

Freelance Potential Publishes 100–150 freelance submissions yearly: 70% written by nonstaff writers; 40% by authors new to the magazine; 30% by previously unpublished writers. Receives 10 queries, 200 manuscripts yearly.

Submissions Guidelines and theme list available at website. Prefers complete manuscript; accepts queries. Accepts hard copy. Accepts simultaneous submissions if identified. Availability of artwork improves chance of acceptance. SASE. Responds to queries in 1–2 weeks, to manuscripts in 2–3 months.
■ *Articles:* 500 words. Informational, how-to, profiles, personal experience, humor. Topics: nature, pets, hobbies, sports, family, careers.
■ *Fiction:* 500 words. Genres: adventure, mystery, multicultural.
■ *Depts/columns:* 300–500 words. Science experiments, carpentry projects.
■ *Artwork:* B/W and color prints.
■ *Other:* Poetry. Puzzles, games.

Sample Issue 48 pages. No advertising. Sample copy available.
■ "Tips for Taking Great Photos," by Ann Lennsen. Tricks for capturing photos of fireworks, action shots, pets, and more.
■ "Do You See in Color?" Experiment to fool the brain to see colors when there is only black and white.

Rights and Payment First North American serial rights. Articles and fiction, 5¢ a word. Depts/columns, $35. Poetry and puzzles, $10+. Artwork, $5 a photo. Pays on publication. Provides 1 contributor's copy.

Brass

987 NW Circle Boulevard, P.O. Box 1220, Corvallis, OR 97339. www.brassmagazine.com

Editorial Director: Jennie Bartlemay

Brass magazine has a mission to make money matters interesting, simple, and relevant for young adults. It provides entertaining yet educational articles about financial issues, and profiles up-and-coming young adults who are making a difference. It prefers to work with freelancers between the ages of 16 and 29. Prospective writers should register at the website to receive the latest updates on current editorial needs, and to register areas of expertise. ■ **Circulation** 300,000 ■ **Audience** 16–25 years ■ **Frequency** Quarterly

Freelance Potential Publishes 15–20 freelance submissions yearly: 25–50% written by nonstaff writers; 10–25% by authors who are new to the magazine; 10–25% by previously unpublished writers. Receives 1–10 queries, 1–10 unsolicited manuscripts monthly.

Submissions Guidelines and editorial calendar available at website. Register at www.brassmagazine.com/contribute for full information. Prefers query. Accepts email to editor@brassmagazine.com (Word or PDF attachments). Responds in 1 week.
■ *Articles:* 500–1,000 words. Informational, self-help, how-to, profiles. Topics: personal improvement, professional advancement, education, fashion, sports, entertainment, health, travel, investments, saving strategies, banking, portfolio management.
■ *Depts/columns:* Word lengths vary. Starting a business, finance fundamentals, trends.
■ *Other:* Crossword puzzles.

Sample Issue 32 pages. Advertising. Sample copy available at website.
■ "Price PWNAGE: 10 Solutions to Cheaper Gaming." Affordable options for video game players.
■ "Nowhere To Ride: Andy Po Shakes Up a Skate Community," by Chris Thomas. A profile of a skateboarder who started a successful skateboard shop, then designed a community skate park.

Rights and Payment All rights. Written material, payment rates vary. Pays on publication. Provides contributor's copies.

Bread for God's Children

P.O. Box 1017, Arcadia, FL 34265-1017. www.breadministries.org

Editor: Judith M. Gibbs

This Christian publication offers children of all ages stories and articles designed to help them apply the Word of God to their everyday lives. Shorter stories for very young children (5 to 10 years old) are especially sought, as are stories about overcoming life's obstacles through faith in Jesus.
■ **Circulation** 12,000 ■ **Audience** Children–YA ■ **Frequency** Quarterly

Freelance Potential Of the articles published yearly, 25–50% are by freelancers; 25–50% are by authors new to the magazine; 25–50% are by previously unpublished writers. Receives 10–25 unsolicited manuscripts yearly.

Submissions Guidelines available at website. Send complete manuscript. Accepts hard copy. Accepts simultaneous submissions if identified. SASE. Responds in 2 months.
■ *Articles:* 500–800 words. Inspirational, informational, personal experience. Topics: religion, faith, nature, parenting.
■ *Fiction:* Children's, 500–800 words. YA, 900–1,200 words. Genres: inspirational, adventure.

Sample Issue 32 pages. Sample copy available.
■ "A Double Mother's Day." An adopted girl learns the circumstances of her adoption and begins to forgive the birth mother who gave her up.
■ "Pedro's Legos." Pedro is annoyed with his sister's help on his class project until a friend comments on the project's good design.

Rights and Payment First rights. Articles, $30. Fiction, $40 for children's; $50 for YA. Pays on publication. Provides 3 contributor's copies.

Brilliant Star

1233 Central Street, Evanston, IL 60201. www.brilliantstarmagazine.org

Associate Editor: Susan Engle

Designed for middle-school children, *Brilliant Star* presents the history and spirituality of the Bahá'í faith through stories, articles, and activities. All material must support the Bahá'í philosophy of humanity, love, and harmony. ■ **Circulation** 7,000 ■ **Audience** 8–12 years ■ **Frequency** 6 times a year

Freelance Potential Publishes 5 freelance submissions yearly: 80% written by nonstaff writers; 15% by authors new to the magazine; 5% by previously unpublished writers. Receives 2 queries, 10 unsolicited manuscripts monthly.

Submissions Guidelines and theme list available at website. Query with clips for articles. Send complete manuscript for fiction. Accepts hard copy and email queries to SEngle@usbnc.org. Accepts simultaneous submissions if identified (ARenshaw@usbnc.org for activities; AParelSewell@usbnc.org for artwork). SASE. Responds in 6–8 months.
■ *Articles:* To 350 words. Informational, how-to, personal experience, interviews, profiles, biography. Topics: historical Bahá'í figures, religion, history, ethnic and social issues, travel, music, nature.
■ *Fiction:* To 700 words. Early readers. Genres: ethnic, historical, contemporary, problem-solving.
■ *Depts/columns:* To 600 words. Religion, ethics, profiles of kids.
■ *Artwork:* Prints and illustrations.
■ *Other:* Poetry by children. Puzzles, activities, games.

Sample Issue 30 pages. Sample copy available via mail.
■ "The Route." A girl discovers her impact on those around her while delivering newspapers.

Rights and Payment All or one-time rights. No payment. Provides 3 contributor's copies.

Broomstix

P.O. Box 8139, Bridgewater, NJ 08807. www.broomstix.com

Editor: Natalie Zaman

Broomstix is an online magazine that embraces the pagan perspective. It features articles, creative writing, poetry, rituals, and activities that relate to the seasons, Mother Earth, and New Age topics, as well as feng shui, Reiki, and meditation. *Broomstix* also accepts writing and artwork from children. ■ **Circulation** 6,000 ■ **Audience** Children–YA ■ **Frequency** Quarterly

Freelance Potential Publishes 10 freelance submissions yearly: 30% written by nonstaff writers; 50% by authors new to the magazine; 75% by previously unpublished writers. Receives 5 unsolicited manuscripts monthly.

Submissions Guidelines and theme list available at website. Send complete manuscript. Accepts hard copy and email to broomstixforkids@yahoo.com. SASE for artwork only; manuscripts are not returned. Responds in 2 weeks.
■ *Articles:* To 750 words. Informational. Topics: nature-based spirituality, pagan rituals and Sabbats, the environment, social and multicultural issues, the arts.
■ *Fiction:* To 750 words. "Pagan Parables," including folktales and myths.
■ *Depts/columns:* 500 words. Hearth and Home, Pruitt the Druid, Wicc'ed Ways, craft projects.
■ *Artwork:* B/W and color prints. Line art.
■ *Other:* Theme-related and seasonal poetry.

Sample Issue Sample copy available at website.

- "Hag Schools the Inquisitive Witch!" by Gillian Greene. A mystical interview with a witch.
- "Treasure in the Cornfield," by Laura Beth Shope. A primer on hunting for arrowheads.

Rights and Payment One-time electronic rights. Written material, 1¢ a word, $5 maximum. Artwork, $1–$5. Pays 1 month after publication.

Bumples

www.bumples.com

Editor

This interactive ezine specializes in illustrated fiction for kindergarten and elementary students. Each issue features animal stories, mysteries, fantasies, sports stories, and poetry. Puzzles, question games, and activities accompany the stories, providing additional information in an entertaining way.
- **Hits per month** Unavailable ■ **Audience** 4–10 years ■ **Frequency** 10 times a year

Freelance Potential Publishes several freelance submissions yearly: 60% written by nonstaff writers.

Submissions Guidelines available at website. Send complete manuscript. Accepts email to editor@bumples.com (PDF attachments). Response time varies.
- *Fiction:* Ages 4-7, 800 words; ages 8-10, to 2,000 words. Genres: adventure, contemporary, mystery, fantasy, sports, animal stories.
- *Artwork:* Low-resolution digital images.
- *Other:* Poetry, line lengths vary.

Sample Issue 58 pages. Sample issue available at website.
- "Kimu & the Kelp Forrest " by Michelle Lee Brown. A future story about living under the sea.
- "My Tea Party at the Zoo" by Julie Mayer. A poem with narration.

Rights and Payment Rights vary. Fiction, 20¢ a word. Poetry, $3 a line. Artwork, payment rates vary. Payment policy varies.

Cadet Quest

Calvinist Cadet Corps, 1333 Alger Street SE, P.O. Box 7259, Grand Rapids, MI 49510.
www.calvinistcadets.org

Editor: G. Richard Broene

This Christian magazine for boys is filled with articles, fiction, projects, cartoons, and Bible lessons. Each issue of the magazine revolves around a theme, with a goal of showing readers how God is working in and around them every day. Only fiction submissions must fit a planned theme; nonfiction articles must simply be relevant or of interest to boys. ■ **Circulation** 8,000 ■ **Audience** Boys, 9–14 years ■ **Frequency** 7 times a year

Freelance Potential Publishes 25 freelance submissions yearly: 60% written by nonstaff writers; 10% by authors who are new to the magazine; 3% by previously unpublished writers. Receives 20–30 unsolicited manuscripts monthly.

Submissions Guidelines and theme list available at website. Send complete manuscript. Accepts hard copy and email to submissions@calvinistcadets.org (no attachments). Accepts simultaneous submissions if identified. SASE. Responds in 1–2 months.
- *Articles:* To 1,500 words. Informational, factual, profiles, interviews. Topics: religion, spirituality, stewardship, camping, nature, survival skills, crafts and hobbies, sports, the environment, serving God.
- *Fiction:* 1,000–1,300 words. Genres: inspirational, adventure, humor.
- *Depts/columns:* Word lengths vary. Cadet Corps news items, Bible lessons, craft projects.
- *Other:* Puzzles, cartoons.

Sample Issue 24 pages. Little advertising. Sample copy available.

Rights and Payment First and second serial rights. Written material, 4¢–5¢ a word. Other material, payment rates vary. Pays on acceptance. Provides 1 contributor's copy.

Calliope

Cobblestone Publishing, 30 Grove Street, Suite C, Peterborough, NH 03458
www.cobblestonepub.com/magazine/CAL

Editor: Rosalie F. Baker

Keeping its focus on helping readers explore world history, *Calliope* publishes articles and fiction on the history makers and cultures of the world. All material should relate to one of the upcoming themes. Query due dates for each issue are provided on the website. ■ **Circulation** 13,000 ■ **Audience** 8–14 years ■ **Frequency** 9 times a year

Freelance Potential Of the articles published yearly, 90% are written by nonstaff writers; 10–15% developed from unsolicited submissions; 25–75% by authors new to the magazine; 25–75% by previously unpublished writers. Receives 25–50 queries monthly.

Submissions Guidelines and editorial calendar available at website. Query with author biography, detailed outline, bibliography, and writing sample. Accepts hard copy. SASE. Responds in 3–6 months.

■ *Articles:* 700–800 words, plus sidebars. Informational, profiles. Topics: world history, geography, science.
■ *Fiction:* To 800 words. Genres: historical, multicultural, adventure, folktale, historical plays.
■ *Depts/columns:* Staff-written.
■ *Artwork:* B/W and color prints. Line art.
■ *Other:* To 700 words. Activities, word puzzles, games, crafts, recipes.

Sample Issue 48 pages. No advertising. Sample copy available at website.

■ "The Gates of Troy," by Rosalie F. Baker. An explanation of the Trojan War.
■ "Heracles and the Battle of Gerydon," by Charles F. Baker. The legend of Heracles is explored.

Rights and Payment All rights. Articles and fiction, 20¢–25¢ a word. Artwork, $15–$100. Other material, payment rates vary. Pays on publication. Provides 2 contributor's copies.

Careers and Colleges

2 LAN Drive, Suite 100, Westford, MA 01886. www.careersandcolleges.com

Editor: Anne Kandra

Careers and Colleges, produced as a print publication with an interactive companion website, serves as a guide for high school students as they start making decisions about their futures. Its articles cover career choices and everything teens will need to know about college—from financing it to making the best of dorm life. It seeks practical information that helps readers achieve their goals: to have a satisfying college experience and to lay the foundation for the career of their choice. ■ **Circulation** 752,000 ■ **Audience** 15–18 years ■ **Frequency** 3 times a year

Freelance Potential Publishes 6 freelance submissions yearly: 80% written by nonstaff writers; 10% by authors new to the magazine. Receives 4 queries monthly.

Submissions Guidelines available. Query with clips, or send complete manuscript. Accepts email to editor@careersandcolleges.com. Responds in 2 months.

- *Articles:* 800–2,400 words. Informational, how-to, profiles, interviews, personal experience. Topics: post-secondary education, independent living, campus life, career choices, social issues, personal growth.
- *Depts/columns:* Staff-written.

Sample Issue 32 pages. Advertising. Sample copy available at website.
- "Connecting with Colleges," by Katie McKoon. A primer for doing research on colleges.
- "A New Kind of Summer Camp," by Jessica Torner. An explanation of how involvement in summer programs can help students improve their chances during the admissions process.

Rights and Payment First North American serial and electronic rights. Written material, payment rates vary. Pays 2 months after acceptance. Provides 2 contributor's copies.

Celebrate

2923 Troost Avenue, Kansas City, MO 64109. www.wordaction.com

Senior Editor: Melissa K. Hammer

Celebrate is a take-home paper for use in religious education programs. It is filled with stories and Bible-based activities and games that help young children understand the glory of God and the role He can play in their lives. All material revolves around planned themes. The theme list is available by request. ■ **Circulation** 40,000 ■ **Audience** 3–6 years ■ **Frequency** Weekly

Freelance Potential Publishes 100 freelance submissions yearly: 90% written by nonstaff writers; 35% by authors new to the magazine; 30% by previously unpublished writers. Receives 16 queries monthly.

Submissions Guidelines and theme list available. Query. Accepts hard copy. SASE. Responds in 2–4 weeks.
- *Fiction:* Word lengths vary. Genres: inspirational, stories that show children dealing with issues related to a Bible story or lesson.
- *Other:* Bible stories, songs, finger plays, action rhymes, crafts, activities. Poetry, 4–8 lines.

Sample Issue 4 pages. No advertising. Sample copy available.
- "A Surprise Visit." The story of the angel coming to Mary.
- "Jesus Speaks to Saul." Saul's conversion on the road to Damascus.

Rights and Payment Rights vary. Written material, payment rates vary. Payment policy varies.

Chess Life for Kids

P.O. Box 3967, Crossville, TN 38557. www.uschess.org

Editor: Glenn Petersen

Chess Life for Kids is an official publication of the United States Chess Federation and is designed for scholastic members ages 12 and under. Each issue includes information on playing strategies for novices through experts, as well as reports on tournaments around the globe. ■ **Circulation** 22,700 ■ **Audience** To 12 years ■ **Frequency** 6 times a year

Freelance Potential Publishes 30 freelance submissions yearly: 75% written by nonstaff writers; 10% by previously unpublished writers. Receives 12–36 queries and manuscripts monthly.

Submissions Guidelines available at website. Prefers query with clips or writing samples; will accept complete manuscript. Prefers email to gpetersen@uschess.org (Word attachments); will accept hard copy. SASE. Responds to queries in 1 week, to manuscripts in 1 month.
- *Articles:* 800–3,000 words. Informational, how-to, historical, profiles, humor, personal experience, opinion. Topics: chess games and strategies, tournaments and events, personalities in the game.

- *Depts/columns:* To 1,000 words. Book and product reviews, short how-to's, brief player profiles.
- *Artwork:* High-resolution digital images.
- *Other:* Chess-oriented cartoons, puzzles, games.

Sample Issue 72 pages. Advertising. Sample copy available.
- "Tactical, Positional, and Opening Mistakes," by Daniel Gurevich. An exploration of the common mistakes players make.
- "How to Safely Checkmate a Bully," by Lisa Suhay. Explains the Bullyproof Chess program.

Rights and Payment All rights. Articles and depts/columns, $75 per page. Artwork, $35–$100. Other, $25. Kill fee, 30%. Pays on publication. Provides 2 contributor's copies.

ChickaDEE

Bayard Press Canada, 10 Lower Spadina Avenue, Suite 400, Toronto, Ontario M4V 2Z2 Canada. www.owlkids.com

Submissions Editor

Chickadee is a hands-on magazine for kids whose thirst for knowledge and appetite for humor are insatiable. Its interactive stories, puzzles, comics, animal features, and science experiments are designed to educate as well as entertain. Each issue is themed. Most of the material is assigned. Writers are welcome to submit their résumés in order to be considered. ■ **Circulation** 85,000 ■ **Audience** 5–9 years ■ **Frequency** 10 times a year

Freelance Potential Publishes 1 freelance submission yearly: 5% written by nonstaff writers.

Submissions Guidelines and theme list available. Most work is assigned. Send résumé. Accepts hard copy. No SASE. Responds if interested.
- *Articles:* Word lengths vary. Informational. Topics: animals, hobbies, science, history, sports.
- *Fiction:* 650–700 words. Genres: contemporary, historical.
- *Other:* Puzzles, games.

Sample Issue Sample copy available.
- "Outdoor Fun." Five crafts that kids can make and take outside.
- "Meet Cool Artists." The magazine's artists explain how they create the images for readers.

Rights and Payment All rights. Articles, payment rates vary. Fiction, $250. Pays on acceptance. Provides 2 contributor's copies.

Chirp

Bayard Press Canada, 10 Lower Spadina Avenue, Suite 400, Toronto, Ontario M5V 2Z2 Canada. www.owlkids.com

Submissions Editor

Designed for the very youngest readers, *Chirp* fills its pages with lively illustrations and colorful photographs, short articles, illustrated stories, and poems to entertain while preparing kids to read independently. Most work is assigned. ■ **Circulation** 60,000 ■ **Audience** 3–6 years ■ **Frequency** 9 times a year

Freelance Potential Publishes 1–3 freelance submissions yearly: 10% written by nonstaff writers; 1% by previously unpublished writers.

Submissions Guidelines available. Most work is assigned. Send résumé only. Accepts hard copy. No SASE. Responds if interested.
- *Articles:* Word lengths vary. Informational. Covers many topics of interest to young readers, including nature and the outdoors, art, dinosaurs.
- *Fiction:* 300–400 words. Genres: various, including nature stories, humor.

■ *Other:* Games, crafts, puzzles, rhymes.

Sample Issue Sample issue available.
■ "Learn How Crayons Are Made." Photos take the manufacturing process from beginning to end.
■ "Make Your Own Puppet Theater." How to put on a puppet show.

Rights and Payment All rights. Payment rates vary. Pays on acceptance. Provides 2 contributor's copies.

ChopChop

P.O. Box 43, Watertown, MA 02471. www.chopchopmag.org

Editor: Catherine Newman

Subtitled "The Fun Cooking Magazine for Families," this print magazine and website is published by ChopChop Kids, Inc., a Massachusetts-based nonprofit. It has a mission to educate children on how to cook, and to empower them to be active participants in pursuing healthy eating habits. In addition to fun and easy recipes, it publishes fun food facts, profiles of people who care about food, fitness information, and games. The magazine has an endorsement by the American Academy of Pediatrics.
■ **Circulation** 530,000 ■ **Audience** 5–12 years, families ■ **Frequency** Quarterly

Freelance Potential Unavailable.

Submissions Editor Catherine Newman can be reached at benandbirdy.blogspot.com. Executive Director Sally Sampson can be reached at sally@chopchopmag.com.
■ *Articles:* Word lengths vary. Informational, how-to, personal experience, profiles. Topics: food, nutrition, health and fitness, cooking.
■ *Depts/columns:* Word lengths vary. Gardening, recipes.

Sample Issue Sample articles are available for viewing at the website.
■ "Super Bold Tuna." Fresh ideas for this kitchen basic.
■ "Baked Potatoes with a Surprise Twist." Creative ideas for making baked potatoes that win over kids.

Rights and Payment Unavailable.

Cicada

Cricket Magazine Group, 70 East Lake Street, Suite 300, Chicago, IL 60601. www.cicadamag.com, www.cricketmag.com

Executive Editor: Deborah Vetter

Cicada publishes fiction, poetry, novellas, and creative nonfiction for young adults. It is open to submissions from adults and young writers ages 14 and up. Open to many genres, the magazine is especially interested in humor of all kinds, from satire to absurdist humor to lighthearted romance or screwball comedy. ■ **Circulation** 10,000 ■ **Audience** 14–23 years ■ **Frequency** 6 times a year

Freelance Potential Publishes 50 freelance submissions yearly: 90–100% written by nonstaff writers; 50–75% by authors new to the magazine; 25–50% by previously unpublished writers. Receives 150–250 unsolicited manuscripts monthly.

Submissions Guidelines available at www.cricketmag.com (for adults), and www.cicadamag.com (for ages 14–23).
■ *Articles:* To 5,000 words. Personal experience, creative nonfiction.
■ *Fiction:* 2,000–5,000 words. Genres: contemporary, coming-of-age, adventure, fantasy, historical, humor, realistic, science fiction. Novellas, to 9,000 words.
■ *Depts/columns:* Book reviews. Expressions (to 2,000 words), Creative Endeavors. Both are reserved for writers ages 14–23 only.
■ *Other:* Poetry, to 30 lines. Serious, humorous, rhymed, unrhymed.

Sample Issue 48 pages. No advertising. Sample issue available at website.
- ▪ "Prudent Paisley Gives Her Troubles Away," by Elizabeth A. Larsson. Story about a control freak who learns to loosen up a bit.
- ▪ "Bus 778," by Liz N. Clift. Personal experience piece about a memorable bus ride.

Rights and Payment Rights and payment rates vary. Pays on publication. Provides 2 contributor's copies.

Click

Cricket Magazine Group, 70 East Lake Street, Suite 300, Chicago, IL 60601. www.cricketmag, www.clickmagkids.com

Editor: Amy Tao

Click is a themed magazine of science and discovery. Led by Click the Mouse and his pals, children are brought on a journey through science, art, nature, and the environment. Because of its focused themes and presentations, all work is assigned; the editors choose the content and commission experienced writers to create it. ▪ **Circulation** 40,000 ▪ **Audience** 3–7 years ▪ **Frequency** 9 times a year

Freelance Potential 70% of its content is written by nonstaff writers; 10% by authors new to the magazine. Receives 1–10 queries monthly.

Submissions Theme list available at website. Experienced writers only. All work is assigned. Send résumé and clips. Accepts hard copy. SASE. Response time varies.
- ▪ *Articles:* To 1,000 words. Informational, interviews, photo-essays. Topics: the sciences, nature, the arts, technology, math, history.
- ▪ *Fiction:* Word lengths vary. Theme-related stories.
- ▪ *Other:* Poetry, cartoons, activities.

Sample Issue 40 pages. No advertising. Sample copy available at website.
- ▪ "Why Is Summer Hot?" by Kathleen Weidner Zoehfeld. How Earth's rotation and axis affect weather.
- ▪ "Sleepy, Sneezy, and Grumpy," by Charnan Simon. A story about a boy with a cold.

Rights and Payment Rights vary. Written material, payment rates vary. Payment policy varies.

Cobblestone

Cobblestone Publishing, 30 Grove Street, Suite C, Peterborough, NH 03458. www.cobblestonepub.com

Editor: Meg Chorlian

Each theme-based issue of *Cobblestone* delves deep into a place, era, or event from American history. Its content is designed to meet curriculum standards while offering a lively and entertaining reading experience. Articles should be historically accurate and have a lively, original approach to the subject. ▪ **Circulation** 27,000 ▪ **Audience** 9–14 years ▪ **Frequency** 9 times a year

Freelance Potential Publishes 180 freelance submissions yearly: 85% written by nonstaff writers; 25% by authors new to the magazine; 20% by previously unpublished writers. Receives 50 queries monthly.

Submissions Guidelines, theme list, and query due dates available at website. Query with cover letter, outline, bibliography, and clips or writing samples. All queries must relate to an upcoming theme. No unsolicited manuscripts. Accepts hard copy. SASE. Responds 5 months before theme issue publication.
- ▪ *Articles:* 700–800 words. Sidebars, 300–600 words. Informational, profiles, interviews. Topics: American history, historical figures.
- ▪ *Fiction:* To 800 words. Genres: historical, multicultural, biographical, adventure, retold legends.
- ▪ *Depts/columns:* Word lengths vary. Interviews, short profiles, fun facts.
- ▪ *Artwork:* Professional quality B/W or color prints and slides. Line art.
- ▪ *Other:* Activities, to 700 words. Puzzles and games. Poetry, to 100 lines.

Sample Issue 52 pages. No advertising. Sample copy available at website.
- "Walt Disney: Animation Pioneer," by John P. Brackin. A profile of Disney's accomplishments.
- "Wrinkles, Scars, and Stitches," by Diana Kelly. How to achieve Hollywood-style make-up looks.

Rights and Payment All rights. Written material, 20¢–25¢ a word. Artwork, $15–$100. Pays on publication. Provides 2 contributor's copies.

College Outlook

20 East Gregory Boulevard, Kansas City, MO 64114-1145. www.collegeoutlook.net

Editor: Kellie Houx

College Outlook publishes articles that speak to the concerns of high school seniors and their parents. Topics covered include choosing a college, financing an education, preparing for college life, and selecting a major. Student-centered articles that can be true resources for readers are valued here. Many authors are college administrators or counselors. ■ **Circulation** 440,000 (spring); 710,000 (fall) ■ **Audience** College-bound students ■ **Frequency** Twice a year

Freelance Potential Publishes 4 freelance submissions yearly: 10% written by nonstaff writers; 20% by authors new to the magazine; 10% by previously unpublished writers. Receives an average of 1 query every couple of months.

Submissions Guidelines available. Query with clips or writing samples. Accepts email to editor@collegeoutlook.net. Responds in 1 month.
- *Articles:* To 1,500 words. Informational, how-to, personal experience, humor. Topics: school selection, financial aid, scholarships, money management, college admissions procedures.
- *Artwork:* B/W and color transparencies.
- *Other:* Gazette items on campus subjects, including fads, politics, classroom news, current events, leisure activities, careers.

Sample Issue 40 pages. Advertising. Sample copy available at website.
- "Dress To Impress," by Brooke Pearl. Why personal appearance matters during interviews.
- "How To Work Effectively with a College Financial Aid Officer," by Howard Freedman. Navigating the financial aid maze.

Rights and Payment All rights. All material, payment rates vary. Payment policy varies. Provides author's copies.

ColumbiaKids

Washington State Historical Society, 1911 Pacific Avenue, Tacoma, WA 98402. http://columbia.washingtonhistory.org/kids

Manuscript Coordinator

This ezine features exciting and informative articles and stories based on Pacific Northwest history. It targets readers living in the region, but welcomes readers from around the country. Only well-researched pieces about Washington State or the Pacific Northwest will be considered. ■ **Hits per month** 5,000+ ■ **Audience** 4–14 years ■ **Frequency** Twice a year

Freelance Potential Publishes 20 freelance submissions yearly: 80% written by nonstaff writers; 80% by authors new to the magazine; 10% by previously unpublished writers. Receives 3–7 unsolicited manuscripts monthly.

Submissions Guidelines available at website. Send complete manuscript. Accepts hard copy and email to columbiakids@wshs.wa.gov (no attachments). SASE. Response time varies.
- *Articles:* 800–1,200 words. "Notorious Westerners" (biographies), "What Is THAT?" (investigation into something that was made, used, or invented in the Pacific Northwest).

- *Fiction:* 800–1,200 words. "One Day in History," fictional retellings of a historical event from a child's point of view.
- *Depts/columns:* 200–800 words. NW Legends, Making History (profiles of living people in the area), Pod Puzzle (audio mini-plays that give readers clues about a puzzle), NW HotSpot, WordPlay (poetry, work games, jokes), Amazing Places.

Sample Issue Sample issue available at website.
- "Crashing Concrete and Twisted Steel," by Lillian Thoren. Short story about the collapse of the Tacoma Narrows Bridge.
- "Dirty Dan Founds a Town," by Christine Myers. Biography of the founder of Fairhaven, WA.

Rights and Payment First world electronic and archival rights. Articles, $200. Depts/columns, $100 (NW HotSpot, $100–$500; WordPlay, $25–$100; Amazing Places, $50). Pays on publication.

Countdown for Kids

Juvenile Diabetes Research Foundation, 120 Wall Street, 19th Floor, New York, NY 10005. www.jdrf.org

Submissions Editor: Marieke Gartne

This magazine for children with diabetes provides information about the condition in age-appropriate language. Its articles explore ways to manage diabetes and still enjoy being a kid. Published writers and new authors are equally welcome—as long as they can share their knowledge of juvenile diabetes with readers without being boring or preachy. ■ **Circulation** Unavailable ■ **Audience** 10+ years ■ **Frequency** Twice a year

Freelance Potential Publishes 6–8 freelance submissions yearly: 50% written by nonstaff writers; 10% by previously unpublished writers. Receives 10 queries and unsolicited manuscripts monthly.

Submissions Query or send complete manuscript. Accepts hard copy. SASE. Response time varies.
- *Articles:* Word lengths vary. Informational, factual, self-help, profiles, interviews, personal experience. Topics: coping with Type 1 diabetes, health, fitness, careers, college, popular culture, social issues, diabetes research.
- *Depts/columns:* Word lengths vary. Diabetes news and information, career profiles, health advice.

Sample Issue 16 pages. Little advertising. Sample copy available.
- "Know Your Numbers," by Kalia Doner. How cholesterol, blood pressure, and body weight must are important in hitting target blood glucose levels.
- "Traveling with Diabetes," by John McIntosh. How being prepared means having more fun and less stress on vacations.

Rights and Payment First North American serial rights. Written material, payment rates vary. Pays on publication. Provides 1 contributor's copy.

Cricket

Cricket Magazine Group, 70 East Lake Street, Suite 300, Chicago, IL 60601. www.cricketmag.com

Submissions Editor

Entertaining the imaginations of tweens and early teens for decades, *Cricket* continues to be known for its high-quality fiction. It also features biographies, profiles, poetry, and activities. Submissions on all appropriate topics will be considered at any time during the year. *Cricket* is the flagship publication in Carus Publishing's Cricket Magazine Group. ■ **Circulation** 55,000 ■ **Audience** 9–14 years ■ **Frequency** 9 times a year

Freelance Potential Publishes 100 freelance submissions yearly: Articles and stories, 100% by non-staff writers; 50% by authors new to the magazine; 30% by previously unpublished writers. Receives 1,000 unsolicited manuscripts monthly.

Submissions Guidelines available at website. Send complete manuscript with word count; include bibliography for retold folktales and nonfiction. Accepts hard copy. Accepts simultaneous submissions if identified. SASE. Responds in 4–6 months.
- *Articles:* 200–1,500 words. Informational, how-to, biography, profiles. Topics: science, the arts, technology, history, natural history, architecture, geography, foreign culture, adventure, sports.
- *Fiction:* 200–2,000 words. Genres: realistic, contemporary, historical, humor, mystery, fantasy, science fiction, folktales, fairy tales, legends, myths.
- *Depts/columns:* Staff-written.
- *Other:* Poetry, to 50 lines. Puzzles, games, crafts, recipes, science experiments.

Sample Issue 48 pages. No advertising.
- "The Well Digger and the Princess," by Lloyd Alexander. Mideastern folktale about a young working man and a genie.
- "Beyond the Twilight Zone, Part 1," by Nikki McCormack. An cave exploration adventure.

Rights and Payment Rights vary. Articles and fiction, to 25¢ a word. Poetry, to $3 a line. Pays on publication. Provides 2 contributor's copies.

Dancing With Bear Publishing

www.dancingwithbearpublishing.com

Submissions: Rocky Renteria

Dancing With Bear is a new, royalty-paying book publisher that is interested in fiction and nonfiction that rejects the trends of sex and violence. It has put out the call for short stories to be collected into anthologies that are appropriate for everyone, including families and young adults. It also has a children's book line. Writers should check the website for upcoming "Special Submissions Calls" for anthologies. Many of its anthologies are seasonal or holiday-related. ■ **Circulation** Not applicable
■ **Audience** YA–Adults ■ **Frequency** Ongoing

Freelance Potential Welcomes first-time authors.

Submissions Guidelines available at website. Currently closed to all submissions except for special calls. Send complete manuscript, formatted to specifications in guidelines, author biography, and publishing history. Accepts email to submissions@dancingwithbearpublishing.com (Word and RTF attachments). Responds in 2 weeks.
- *Fiction:* 2,000–5,000 words. Short stories for a range of readers. Genres: family-oriented, contemporary, inspirational, religious, love stories.

Sample Issue
- *Valentine's Day 2012 Anthology*, by multiple contributors.
- *Easter 2012 Anthology*, by multiple contributors.

Rights and Payment Stories in anthologies, $50.

Davey and Goliath's Devotions

Augsburg Fortress Publishers, P.O. Box 1209, Minneapolis, MN 55440-1209.
www.augsburgfortress.org/dg/devotions

Lead Editor: Becky Weaver Carlson

Based on the characters of the popular 1960s television series, this magazine features a mix of Bible stories, activities, and games that help children experience faith lessons in a fun way. Freelance writers are commissioned to write a portion of each issue. To be considered, writers should send in a sample portion following the outline provided in the writers' guidelines. ■ **Circulation** 50,000
■ **Audience** 3–9 years ■ **Frequency** Quarterly

Freelance Potential Publishes 40 freelance submissions yearly: 100% written by nonstaff writers; 50% by authors new to the magazine; 25% by previously unpublished writers. Receives 4 queries monthly.

Submissions Guidelines available at www.augsburgfortress.org/media/company/downloads/ FamilyDevotionalSampleBriefing.doc. All work is assigned. Query with sample content per writers' guidelines. Accepts email to cllsub@augsburgfortress.org (with "Family Devotions" in subject line). Response time varies.
- *Articles:* 100–170 words. Informational, inspirational. Topics: Bible stories, Bible facts, prayers, Bible-related activities.
- *Depts/columns:* Questions and prayers, 15–20 words. Bible facts, memory verses, parenting tips, 30–50 words. Family discussion topics, 100–125 words.
- *Other:* Puzzles, mazes, activities, games.

Sample Issue 64 pages. No advertising. Sample copy available at website.
- "God's Chosen One." What will happen when God sends a new ruler?
- "Sharing 24-7." Suggestions on finding out more about how other families live.

Rights and Payment All rights. Written material, payment rates vary. Pays on acceptance. Provides 2 copies.

Devozine

1908 Grand Avenue, P.O. Box 340004, Nashville, TN 37203-0004. www.devozine.org

Editor: Sandy Miller

A devotional lifestyle magazine, *Devozine* helps Christian teens grow in their faith and discover how Christianity relates to the issues they face in their daily lives. Each of the bimonthly issues focuses on nine themes, one for each week. Each theme includes weekday meditations and a feature article for the weekend. ■ **Circulation** 90,000 ■ **Audience** 12–18 years ■ **Frequency** 6 times a year

Freelance Potential Publishes 400 freelance submissions yearly: 100% written by nonstaff writers; 50% by authors new to the magazine. Receives 12+ queries, 80+ unsolicited manuscripts monthly.

Submissions Guidelines and theme list available at website. Query for feature articles. Send complete manuscript for daily meditations. Accepts hard copy and email submissions to smiller@upperroom.org. SASE. Responds in 4 months.
- *Articles:* 500–600 words. Informational, profiles, personal experience, reviews. Topics: faith, mentoring, independence, courage, teen parenting, creativity, social issues, relationships.
- *Fiction:* 150–250 words. Genres: adventure, historical, multicultural fiction.
- *Depts/columns:* 75–100 words. Reviews, new product information.
- *Other:* Daily meditations, 150–250 words. Prayers and poetry, 10–20 lines. Submit seasonal material 6–8 months in advance.

Sample Issue 80 pages. No advertising. Sample copy available.
- "Elevating Entertainment," by Josh Moody. Profile of a young man who makes faith-based films.
- "More Than We Can Imagine," by Ciona D. Rouse. Article about a young woman who uses proceeds from her CDs to build ponds and other resources in Africa.

Rights and Payment First and second rights. Features, $100. Meditations, $25. Pays on acceptance.

Dig

Cobblestone Publishing, 30 Grove Street, Suite C, Peterborough, NH 03458. www.digonsite.com

Editor: Rosalie F. Baker

Dig publishes informative articles and fun activities designed to introduce children to the wonders of archaeology and history. Each issue is filled with photographs and articles about exciting discoveries and on-site reports from important digs. All submissions must relate to one of the upcoming themes. ■ **Circulation** 18,000 ■ **Audience** 8–14 years ■ **Frequency** 9 times a year

Freelance Potential Publishes 40–45 freelance submissions yearly: 85% written by nonstaff writers; 50% by authors new to the magazine; 10% by previously unpublished writers. Receives 20 queries monthly.

Submissions Guidelines and theme list available at website. Query with cover letter, outline, word count, and extensive bibliography. Accepts hard copy. SASE. Responds 5 months before theme publication date.
■ *Articles:* 700–800 words. Sidebars, 300–600 words. Informational, biography. Topics: archaeology, history, nature, science, technology.
■ *Fiction:* To 800 words. Genres: historical, biographical, adventure, folklore.
■ *Depts/columns:* To 700 words. Art, crafts, archaeology facts, discoveries, and projects.
■ *Artwork:* B/W and color prints. Line art.
■ *Other:* Activities, word puzzles, mazes, games.

Sample Issue 32 pages. No advertising. Sample copy available at website.
■ "The World's Oldest Mummies," by Paul G. Bahn. The mummies of Chile's Chinchorro people.
■ "What the Slices Reveal," by Robert B. Pickering. What CT scanning of mummies can reveal.

Rights and Payment All rights. Articles and fiction, 20¢–25¢ a word. Artwork, $15–$100. Other material, payment rates vary. Pays on publication. Provides 2 contributor's copies.

Disney Magazines

c/o Family Fun Magazine, 47 Pleasant Street, Northampton, MA 01060. www.familyfun.com

Submissions

In 2011, Disney Publishing Worldwide launched a new line of high-quality, kid-focused magazines based on its popular animated television shows and movies characters. This represents a change for Disney's U.S. magazine division, which had previously targeted moms exclusively with its monthly *Disney Family Fun* magazine. First up among the new kid magazines was *Phineas and Ferb*, based on the TV show popular among kids aged 9–14. That magazine was followed by *Thor*, *Cars*, and *Captain America*. Each of these magazines have content—articles, comics, adventure stories, and activities—inspired by Disney, Pixar, and Marvel titles and characters. ■ **Circulation** Unavailable ■ **Audience** Children, all ages ■ **Frequency** *Phineas and Ferb*, 6 times a year; *Cars*, monthly; *Captain America*, monthly.

Freelance Potential Not much is known about freelance opportunities at this time. Disney projects often use contract writers, and *FamilyFun* has been open to submissions.

Submissions Queries about freelance opportunities can be made via *FamilyFun*, queries.familyfun@disney.com.

Sample Issue 52 pages on average.
■ "Across the Second Dimension with Dan and Swampy." Interview with Phineas and Ferb characters, related to a new movie.
■ "The Firestorm Girls Handbook." Instructions on how to earn a "resisting-an-evil-dictator" patch.

Rights and Payment *FamilyFun* buys first serial rights. Written material, payment rates vary. Pays on acceptance.

Discovery Girls

P.O. Box 110760, Campbell, CA 95011. www.discoverygirls.com

Editorial Director: Sarah Verney

Discovery Girls features articles written by girls for girls—with some articles written by adults. Its content touches on topics that really matter to tween girls, in an effort to help girls grow and develop with confidence, a positive sense of self, and independence. Adult contributors must be able to channel their inner "tween" and write about issues that are important to young girls. ■ **Circulation** 220,000 ■ **Audience** 8–12 years ■ **Frequency** 6 times a year

Freelance Potential Publishes 10–18 freelance submissions yearly: 25% written by nonstaff writers; 50% by authors new to the magazine.

Submissions Query with sample paragraph, or send complete manuscript. Accepts hard copy and submissions through the website. SASE. Response time varies.
■ *Articles:* Word lengths vary. Informational, how-to, personal experience. Topics: friendship, family, self-esteem, peer pressure, fitness, health, beauty, entertainment, recreation, crafts, social issues.
■ *Depts/columns:* Word lengths vary. Celebrity news, relationship advice, embarrassing moments, opinions, health and beauty, book reviews.
■ *Other:* Quizzes, contests.

Sample Issue 58 pages. Advertising. Sample copy available at website.
■ "Three Sides of Jealousy," by Phoebe Kitanidis. The problematic triangle that forms when a third friend is added to a BFF duo.
■ "I Thought I Was Ugly," by Alexis. An appearance on *Oprah* helped change a girl's self-opinion.

Rights and Payment All rights. Written material, payment rates vary. Payment policy varies.

DNA Ya!

Diligent Media Corporation, First Floor, Oasis Building, Kamla Mills Compound, Lower Parel, Mumbia 400 013, India. http://epaper.dnaindia.com/

Editor

This English-language newspaper for older children and young adults is published by *DNA* (Daily News Analysis), a news publication distributed in India and also read in the U.S. The focus here is on current events, science, the environment, and Indian and world history, along with the pop culture, sports, and other topics that always appeal to kids. *Ya!* Tales is a section that runs fiction, or a serialized story. *DNA Ya!* is a Parents Choice Award winner in the magazine category in the U.S. ■ **Circulation** 270,000 ■ **Audience** 8–16 years ■ **Frequency** Weekly

Freelance Potential Unavailable.

Submissions For more information, contact youngadults@dnaindia.net.
■ *Articles:* Word lengths vary. Informational, profiles. Topics: current events, Indian history, India, personalities, the environment, science, language, nature.
■ *Fiction:* Individual short stories or serialized longer works. Genres vary.
■ *Depts/columns:* News, fun facts, reader opinion.
■ *Other:* Puzzles, crafts.

Sample Issue 12 pages. Little advertising. Sample copy available at website.
■ "Celebrating a Dahlicious Life." Article commemorates the worldwide popularity of Roald Dahl with a profile of the author and interesting facts about his life.
■ "A New New York." A look at New York City at the tenth anniversary of the 9/11 attacks.

Rights and Payment Unavailable.

Dramatics

Educational Theatre Association, 2343 Auburn Avenue, Cincinnati, OH 45219. www.edta.org

Editor: Donald Corathers

Written for theater students and teachers, *Dramatics* features informational articles on acting, directing, and set design. It also publishes profiles of theater professionals, reviews, and theater news. Articles on all areas of the performing arts, including film and television, are accepted. Submissions should engage an above-average high-school theater student and deepen his or her understanding and appreciation of the performing arts. ■ **Circulation** 37,000 ■ **Audience** YA theater students and teachers ■ **Frequency** 9 times a year

Freelance Potential Publishes 41 freelance submissions yearly: 80% written by nonstaff writers; 50% by authors new to the magazine; 25% by previously unpublished writers. Receives 40 unsolicited manuscripts monthly.

Submissions Guidelines available at website. Prefers complete manuscript; will accept query. Accepts hard copy. SASE. Responds in 2–4 months.
■ *Articles:* 750–4,000 words. Informational articles, interviews, book reviews. Topics: playwriting, musical theater, acting, auditions, stage makeup, set design, theater production.
■ *Fiction:* Word lengths vary. Full-length and one-act plays for high school audiences.
■ *Depts/columns:* Word lengths vary. Industry news, acting techniques.
■ *Artwork:* 5x7 or larger B/W prints; 35mm or larger color transparencies; high-resolution JPEGs or TIFFs. Line art.

Sample Issue 56 pages. Advertising. Sample copy available.
■ "Making Your First Short Film," by Joe Gold & Tammy Kaplan. Tips on everything from the right equipment to the right crew.
■ "The Toughest Crowd," by Harper Lee. An interview with playwright Mary Hall Surface on making theater for young audiences.

Rights and Payment First rights. Written material, $25–$400. Pays on publication. Provides 5 author's copies.

Eco-Kids Magazine

P.O. Box 3306, Hermit Park, Townsville, Queensland 4812 Australia. http://ecobites.com/articles/eco-kids-magazine

Editor

This magazine for kids and its companion website that targets adults form a green and eco-conscious community of readers worldwide. Seasonally themed articles on topics such as healthy lifestyles and environmental issues are offered in the magazine, as well as profiles of young people who are actively involved in environmental causes. ■ **Circulation** 30,000 ■ **Audience** Children ■ **Frequency** Monthly

Freelance Potential Publishes 15 freelance submissions yearly: 30% written by nonstaff writers; 50% by authors new to the magazine; 25% by previously unpublished writers.

Submissions Query or send complete manuscript. Accepts hard copy. SAE/IRC. Response time varies.
■ *Articles:* Word lengths vary. Informational. Topics: the environment, recycling, green living, healthy lifestyles.
■ *Other:* Word lengths vary. Healthy recipes, crafts.

Sample Issue Sample articles available at website.
■ "Happy Birthday." Earth Day is explained.
■ "41 Family Traditions." Ideas for getting the family to commemorate Earth Day in ways that benefit the yard, the community, or the Earth.

Rights and Payment Rights vary. Payment rates vary. Pays on publication. Provides 2 author's copies.

ESPNHS

ESPN Plaza, Bristol, CT 06010. www.rise.espn.go.com

Editor: Ryan Canner-O'Mealy

"Serving teen athletes and their fans," *ESPNHS* provides in-depth coverage of high scool sports, athletes, and coaches. Originally titled *ESPN Rise*, it changed its name in August 2011. It is produced in two different versions, one focusing on sports for boys, and another on girls' sports. Each version has various editions focusing on different regions of the country. It features team and athlete profiles, and season/tournament coverage, and training. A multimedia website complements the print version.
■ **Circulation** Unavailable ■ **Audience** High school athletes ■ **Frequency** Boy's sports, 7 times a year; Girls' sports, quarterly

Freelance Potential Regional editions may provide opportunities for local reporting

Submissions For more information contact rcomealy@risemag.com for the boy version, and laura.suchoski@espn.com for the girl version.
■ *Articles:* Word lengths vary. Informational, interviews, profiles. Topics: high school sports, teams, players, coaches, college recruitment.
■ *Depts/columns:* Word lengths vary. Training.

Sample Issue Individual sample articles are available at website.
■ "Rise Above." A successful Kentucky high school wide receiver born without a right hand.
■ "Signing Day Diary." An interview with a Top 20 Oklahoma State recruit about his signing experience.

Rights and Payment Unavailable.

Faces

Cobblestone Publishing, 30 Grove Street, Suite C, Peterborough, NH 03458 www.cobblestonepub.com

Editor: Elizabeth Carpentiere

This children's magazine takes its readers on a journey around the world, sharing engaging and fun stories about people, places, and cultures near and far. Topics include national and ethnic groups, global issues, biographies of international figures, and close-ups on various regions of the U.S. Upcoming themes and query due dates can be found at the website. ■ **Circulation** 15,000
■ **Audience** 9–14 years ■ **Frequency** 9 times a year

Freelance Potential 50–75% developed from unsolicited submissions: 50–75% written by nonstaff writers; 10–25% by authors new to the magazine; 1–10% by previously unpublished writers. Receives 50–75 queries monthly.

Submissions Guidelines and theme list available at website. Query with cover letter, synopsis, and résumé for fiction; cover letter, outline, and bibliography for nonfiction. Accepts hard copy and email to facesmag@yahoo.com (no attachments). Accepts simultaneous submissions. Responds in 6 months.
■ *Articles:* 800 words. Sidebars, 300–600 words. Informational, personal experience. Topics: culture, geography, the environment, cuisine, special events, travel, history, social issues.
■ *Fiction:* 500–800 words. Genres: retold legends, folktales.
■ *Depts/columns:* Staff-written.
■ *Artwork:* Color prints or transparencies, illustrations.
■ *Other:* To 700 words. Games, crafts, projects.

Sample Issue 52 pages. No advertising. Sample copy available at website.
■ "Connecting Sports with Peace," by Jodi Liss. Global sports that promote peace and civil rights.
■ "Oh, Canada," by Donna O'Meara & Karen Andric. The evolution of hockey.

Rights and Payment All rights. Articles and fiction, 20¢–25¢ a word. Other material, payment rates vary. Artwork, $15–$100. Pays on publication. Provides contributor's copies.

Face Up

Redemptorist Communications, 75 Orwell Road, Rathgar, Dublin 6, Ireland. www.faceup.ie

Editor: Father Gerard Moloney

This magazine offers teens lively and thoughtful articles and personal experience pieces on the social and spiritual issues most important to them. While it is part of the official ministry of the Irish Redemptorists, and a Catholic publication, its mission is not to preach religion but to tackle real issues facing today's Christian teens. ■ **Circulation** 12,000 ■ **Audience** 14–17 years ■ **Frequency** 8 times a year

Freelance Potential Publishes 60 freelance submissions yearly: 80% written by nonstaff writers; 25% by authors new to the magazine; 25% by previously unpublished writers. Receives 10+ unsolicited manuscripts monthly.

Submissions Guidelines and editorial calendar available at website. Send complete manuscript. Accepts email submissions to info@faceup.ie. Responds in 1 month.
- *Articles:* 900 words. Informational, how-to, profiles, personal experience. Topics: college, careers, current events, relationships, health, fitness, music, popular culture, celebrities, sports, multicultural and social issues.
- *Depts/columns:* 500 words. Opinions, essays, reviews, advice, self-help, profiles, interviews. Words of Wisdom.
- *Other:* Quizzes , crossword puzzles.

Sample Issue 48 pages. Little advertising. Sample copy available at website.
- "Dodging Bullets," by Meabh Smith. How one charity is raising funds to help the people of a violent Honduran slum.
- "A Degree of Madness." Unusual college courses, from acrobatics to Gaga-ology.

Rights and Payment Rights vary. Written material, payment rates vary. Pays on publication. Provides 2 contributor's copies.

Faze

4936 Yonge Street, Suite 2400, North York, Ontario M2N 6S3. Canada www.faze.ca

Editor in Chief: Dana Marie Krook

With the philosophy that every girl deserves the right to be young before becoming an adult, this magazine for Canadian girls offers insightful and inspiring looks at real life issues, youth culture, the arts, and lifestyle topics. ■ **Circulation** 120,000 ■ **Audience** Girls, 13–24 ■ **Frequency** 5 times a year

Freelance Potential Publishes 50–60 freelance submissions yearly: 35–40% written by nonstaff writers; 10% by authors new to the magazine; 10% by previously unpublished writers. Receives 10 queries monthly.

Submissions Guidelines available at website. Query with article idea, résumé, and writing samples. Accepts hard copy. Responds if interested.
- *Articles:* Word lengths vary. Informational, profiles, interviews, personal experience. Topics: current affairs, real-life and social issues, celebrities, entertainment, sports, science, travel, business, technology, health.
- *Depts/columns:* Word lengths vary. Short profiles, career descriptions, new products.

Sample Issue 66 pages. Advertising. Sample copy available.
- "Emily Osment: The Next Step," by Dana Marie Krook. Profile of the *Hannah Montana* actress.
- "Making a Difference, One Tummy at a Time," by Luisa Treble. A charity that raises money to feed children in Liberia, founded by a young Canadian woman.

Rights and Payment All rights. Written material, $50–$250. Payment policy varies. Provides 1 contributor's copy.

FLW Outdoors

30 Gamble Lane, Benton, KY 42054. www.flwoutdoors.com

Editor: Jason Sealock

This magazine for avid anglers covers all aspects of sport fishing, including techniques and tips, destinations, and tournaments. Each issue includes a pull-out section that is written specifically for children who are interested in fishing. It welcomes articles about fishing with children or other topics to get kids interested in the sport. ■ **Circulation** 100,000 ■ **Audience** 5–12 years; adults ■ **Frequency** 8 times a year

Freelance Potential 50% written by nonstaff writers: 10% by authors new to the magazine. Receives 25 queries monthly.

Submissions Guidelines available. Query with writing sample. Accepts email queries to info@ flwoutdoors.com. Responds in 1 week.
■ *Articles:* 200 words. Informational, how-to, profiles, humor. Topics: fish, fishing techniques, fishing gear, nature, the environment.
■ *Fiction:* To 500 words. Genres: adventure, nature stories.
■ *Depts/columns:* Word lengths vary. Tournaments, boat technology, fishing destinations, product reviews, environmental issues.
■ *Other:* Puzzles.

Sample Issue 88 pages. Advertising. Sample copy available at website.
■ "Gearing Up: Cold-Weather Comfort." Essential clothing for protecting the whole body from the cold.
■ "Your Rig: Rod Locker Storage," by Ross Robertson. Simple, inexpensive tips for storing fishing rods.

Rights and Payment First North American serial rights. Written material, $200–$500. Payment policy varies.

Focus on the Family Clubhouse

Focus on the Family, 8605 Explorer Drive, Colorado Springs, CO 80920. www.clubhousemagazine.com

Editor: Jesse Florea

Written for middle-grade readers, this Christian magazine features a mix of wholesome stories, faith-based articles, and activities that both educate and entertain. It looks for short fiction with strong takeaways, and stories based outside the U.S. that teach young readers something about the world. ■ **Circulation** 85,000 ■ **Audience** 8–12 years ■ **Frequency** Monthly

Freelance Potential Publishes 45 freelance submissions yearly: 25% written by nonstaff writers; 30% by authors new to the magazine; 10% by previously unpublished writers. Receives 80 unsolicited manuscripts monthly.

Submissions Guidelines available. Send complete manuscript. Accepts hard copy. SASE. Responds in 8 weeks.
■ *Articles:* 800–1,000 words. Informational, how-to, factual, interviews, personal experience, humor. Topics: sports, nature, travel, history, religion, current events, multicultural , noteworthy Christians.
■ *Fiction:* Humor, 500 words. Historical Christian fiction, 900–1,600 words. Adventure, mystery, contemporary, fantasy, science fiction, 1,600–1,800 words.
■ *Depts/columns:* 300 words. Short, humorous news articles emphasizing biblical lessons.
■ *Other:* Activities, quizzes, jokes, recipes. Submit seasonal material 8 months in advance.

Sample Issue 32 pages. Little advertising. Sample copy available.
■ "Silly Laws?" by Joanna Lutz. Explains how all laws have a purpose.
■ "Family Spree," by Bob Smiley. Funny story about families emphasizing love and the family bond.

Rights and Payment First rights. Articles, $150+. Fiction, $200+. Other material, 15¢–20¢ a word. Pays on acceptance. Provides 5 contributor's copies.

Focus on the Family Clubhouse Jr.

Focus on the Family, 8605 Explorer Drive, Colorado Springs, CO 80920. www.clubhousejr.com

Assistant Editor: Joanna Lutz

This sister magazine to *Clubhouse* targets young children with Christian-based fiction, nonfiction, and rebus stories. Stories can be written for beginning readers, or for parents to read aloud. Each issue also features crafts, activities, puzzles, and poetry. ■ **Circulation** 65,000 ■ **Audience** 4–8 years ■ **Frequency** Monthly

Freelance Potential Publishes 10–15 freelance submissions yearly: 45% written by nonstaff writers; 10% by authors new to the magazine; 5% by previously unpublished writers. Receives 60 unsolicited manuscripts monthly.

Submissions Guidelines available. Send complete manuscript. Accepts hard copy. No simultaneous submissions. SASE. Responds in 6–8 weeks.
■ *Articles:* To 600 words. Informational. Topics: science, nature, profiles, biographies of heroes of the faith.
■ *Fiction:* For beginning readers, 250–750 words. For read aloud, 700–1,000 words. Genres: contemporary, historical, inspirational. Bible stories, 800 words. Rebus stories, to 350 words.
■ *Depts/columns:* Word lengths vary. Personal anecdotes, recipes, crafts.
■ *Other:* Games, jokes, puzzles, comic strips.

Sample Issue 24 pages. No advertising. Sample copy available.
■ "The Silver Cup," by Jeanne Pallos. A story based on Genesis 44–45.
■ "A New Shepherd," by Joanna Lutz. Bible story of the good shepherd as told from the sheep's perspective.

Rights and Payment First rights. Articles and fiction, $100–$200. Poetry, $50–$100. Rebus, $75–$150. Puzzles, $30–$80. Pays on acceptance. Provides 3 contributor's copies.

The Friend

The Church of Jesus Christ of Latter-day Saints, 50 East North Temple, 24th Floor, Salt Lake City, UT 84150. www.lds.org/friend

Managing Editor: Jan Pinborough

The Friend features stories based on actual experiences that teach children about following the teachings of Jesus Christ—and the Mormon faith in particular. ■ **Circulation** 285,000 ■ **Audience** 3–12 years ■ **Frequency** Monthly

Freelance Potential 60% written by nonstaff writers.

Submissions Guidelines available at website. Send complete manuscript. Accepts hard copy and email submissions to friend@ldschurch.org. No simultaneous submissions. SASE. Responds in 2 months.
■ *True stories:* To 600 words. Young readers, preschool children, 250 words. Photo-essays, 200–300 words, 6–10 photos. Topics: Christian-themed, the Mormon church, faith, kindness, conflict resolution, service, family life.
■ *Depts/columns:* Word lengths vary. Children's submissions.
■ *Artwork:* B/W or color prints.
■ *Other:* Poetry, line lengths vary. Puzzles, activities, crafts.

Sample Issue 48 pages. No advertising. Sample copy available at website.
■ "Kindness To All Creatures," by Patricia R. Jones. True story about a Mormon president being kind to the animals on his farm.
■ "Jesus Begins His Ministry," by Diane L. Mangum. Story of how Jesus resisted Satan's temptations.

Rights and Payment First rights. Written material, payment rates vary. Pays only for queried and commissioned submissions. Pays on acceptance. Provides 2 contributor's copies.

Fun for Kidz

P.O. Box 227, Bluffton, OH 45817-0227. www.funforkidz.com

Editor: Marilyn Edwards

Filled with engaging articles and projects that make reading and learning fun, *Fun For Kidz* promotes family values with age-appropriate material. It was founded in 2002 by the same people that produce *Hopscotch* and *Boys' Quest* magazines, and looks for activities that deal with timeless topics, such as pets, nature, hobbies, science, and sports. ■ **Circulation** 7,000 ■ **Audience** 5–13 years ■ **Frequency** 6 times a year

Freelance Potential Publishes 100–150 freelance submissions yearly: 70% written by nonstaff writers; 40% by authors new to the magazine; 40% by previously unpublished writers. Receives 10 queries, 100 unsolicited manuscripts monthly.

Submissions Guidelines and theme list available at website. Send complete manuscript. Accepts email to submissions@funforkidz.com (reference the theme to which you are submitting in the subject field). Accepts simultaneous submissions if identified. Availability of artwork improves chance of acceptance. SASE. Responds in 4–6 months.
■ *Articles:* 500 words. Informational, how-to. Topics: nature, science, pets, hobbies, cooking, sports, careers.
■ *Fiction:* 500 words. Genres: adventure, mystery, humor.
■ *Depts/columns:* Word lengths vary. Activities, science experiments.
■ *Artwork:* B/W and color prints. Line art.
■ *Other:* Poetry. Puzzles, games, cartoons. Submit seasonal material 6–12 months in advance.

Sample Issue 48 pages. No advertising. Sample copy available at website.
■ "Busy Bees," by Shirley Anne Rama. A description of a bee's life.
■ "Bees in the Attic," by Theresa Martin. A house becomes a home for a swarm of bees.

Rights and Payment First North American serial rights. Articles and fiction, 5¢ a word. Poetry and puzzles, $10+. Artwork, $5–$35. Pays on publication. Provides 1 contributor's copy.

GirlMogul

309 Main Street, Lebanon, NJ 08833. www.girlmogul.com

Editor: Andrea Stein

This online community site was created to appeal to tween girls who are interested in becoming community leaders, activists, and entrepreneurs. It looks for age-appropriate, witty content that encourages girls to pursue their dreams. Games, quizzes, do-it-yourself projects, and book clubs are part of the mix. It is also in the process of launching a print magazine, which will soon open the door for even more submissions. ■ **Hits per month** Unavailable ■ **Audience** 7–13 years ■ **Frequency** Updated regularly

Freelance Potential Publishes several freelance submissions yearly: 15–20% written by nonstaff writers.

Submissions Query with author biography, or send complete manuscript. Accepts hard copy and email submissions to andrea@girlmogul.com. No simultaneous submissions. SASE. Response time varies.
■ *Articles:* Word lengths vary. Informational, how-to, profiles. Topics: relationships, careers, social issues, school, self-esteem, the environment.
■ *Depts/columns:* Word lengths vary. Crafts, quizzes, book reviews, DIY projects.

Sample Issue Sample articles available at website.
- "Awesome Slumber Party Ideas." Games to play at a sleepover.
- "Dealing with the Dreaded Friendship Triangle." How to best navigate this sticky social situation.

Rights and Payment First rights. No payment.

Girls' Life

4529 Harford Road, Baltimore, MD 21214. www.girlslife.com

Special Projects Editor: Lizzie Skurnick

This magazine is like a girl's best friend: It offers guidance and support on everyday issues such as relationships, self-esteem, school, fashion, and beauty. Profiles of girls who are making a difference are also featured, as is young adult fiction. ■ **Circulation** 400,000 ■ **Audience** 10–15 years ■ **Frequency** 6 times a year

Freelance Potential Publishes 40 freelance submissions yearly: 25% written by nonstaff writers; 20% by authors new to the magazine; 10% by previously unpublished writers. Receives 100 queries monthly.

Submissions Guidelines and editorial calendar available at website. Query with cover letter and detailed outline. Accepts hard copy and email queries to lizzie@girlslife.com. SASE. Responds in 3 months.
- *Articles:* 1,200–1,500 words. Informational, service-oriented. Topics: self-esteem, health, friendship, relationships, sibling rivalry, school issues, facing challenges, setting goals.
- *Fiction:* 3,000 words. Genres: girl-centered.
- *Depts/columns:* 300–800 words. Celebrity spotlights, profiles of real girls, advice, fashion, decorating tips, cooking, crafts, media reviews.
- *Other:* Quizzes; fashion spreads.

Sample Issue 80 pages. Advertising. Sample copy available.
- "Celebrate Your Sistahs." 20 reasons why BFFs rule.
- "Selena Spills It All." Interview with young actress Selena Gomez.

Rights and Payment All rights. Articles, $350+. Other material, payment rates vary. Pays on publication. Provides 1 contributor's copy.

Girlworks

47 Main Street South, P.O. Box 91559, Georgetown, Ontario L7G 5M9 Canada. www.girlworks.ca

Publisher: Janet Kim

This "magazine for smart girls" features articles about the complexity and diversity of girls and young women. Its articles tackle subjects ranging from style, beauty, and trends to issues such as self-esteem, body image, sexuality, loneliness, and depression. It looks for articles that are age-appropriate and written in a style that neither talks down nor preaches to readers. If a girl would be interested in it, the editors are likely to be interested in it, too. ■ **Circulation** 10,000 ■ **Audience** 11–16 years ■ **Frequency** 6 times a year

Freelance Potential Publishes 24 freelance submissions yearly: 20% written by nonstaff writers; 100% by authors new to the magazine; 5% by previously unpublished writers.

Submissions Guidelines available at website. Query with brief description, source list, intended word length, and unique angle or hook. Accepts email to publisher@girlworks.ca. Responds in 1–2 months.
- *Articles:* 400–800 words. Informational, how-to, profiles, interviews. Topics: money, careers, health, beauty, fashion, style, entertainment, art and design, sports, fitness, technology, girl-centered issues.
- *Depts/columns:* Word lengths vary. Beauty, crafts, media reviews.
- *Other:* Puzzles, quizzes, games.

Sample Issue 64 pages. Advertising. Sample copy available.
■ "Careergirl Interviews a Book Illustrator." Exploring the career of book illustration.

Rights and Payment First, second, or licensing rights. Written material, $50 a printed page. Pays on acceptance.

Go! Magazine

2711 South Loop Drive, Suite 4700, Ames, IA 50010. www.go-explore-trans.org

Program Coordinator: Rema Nilakanta

This is an online magazine for teens and young adults interested in a career in transportation, from Iowa State University's Institute for Transportation. It covers everything from the infrastructure of vehicles to the people behind the wheel. The site has changed to a cynamic site with continuously changing content. Throughout the year, *Go!* is in need of articles, bloggers, and transportation-related games, particularly those written by teens. A Spanish version, *Vamos!* is accessible through the *Go!* website. ■ **Circulation** 800 ■ **Audience** Teens, adults ■ **Frequency** Updated regularly

Freelance Potential Publishes 12–120 freelance submissions yearly. Receives 1–10 queries monthly.

Submissions Guidelines available. Query with short (to 200 words) description of article idea. Accepts electronic queries via the website. Response time varies.
■ *Articles:* 700–1,000 words. Informational, personal experience. Topics: transportation careers and issues, vehicles.
■ *Fiction:* Word lengths vary. Transportation-related.

Sample Issue Sample issue available at website.
■ "Truck/Semi-Truck Driver," by Bennett Stone. The qualifications and experience of a truck driver.
■ "Transportation Technology From the Future—Today!" by Bennett Stone. Highlights transportation innovations.

Rights and Payment First world electronic and archival rights. No payment. Holds writing contests with prizes.

Guardian Angel Kids

12430 Tesson Ferry Road, #186, St. Louis, MO 63128. www.guardian-angel-kids.com

Editor in Chief: Donna M. McDine

This interactive ezine, launched in 2010, offers original fiction, nonfiction, and poetry. Part of Guardian Angel Publishing, Inc., it also features games and activities based on characters from Guardian Angel Publishing books. Its editors seek distinct voices that do not preach or talk down to children. The themed issues promote health and safety, and feature some content aimed at parents and teachers. Guardian Angel Kids also accepts submissions from children to age 12. ■ **Hits per month** 300 ■ **Audience** 2–12 years, parents/teachers ■ **Frequency** Monthly

Freelance Potential Publishes 12–120 freelance submissions yearly: 75–100% written by nonstaff writers; 50–75% by authors new to the magazine; 75–100% by previously unpublished writers. Receives 50–75 unsolicited manuscripts monthly.

Submissions Guidelines, deadlines, and theme list available at website. Send complete manuscript. Accepts email to submissions@guardian-angel-kids.com (no attachments). Accepts simultaneous submissions if identified. Responds within 3 weeks of submission deadline.
■ *Articles:* To 500 words. Informational. Topics: health, safety, animals, sports, humor, activities, problem-solving.
■ *Fiction:* To 500 words. Genres: contemporary, multicultural, picture stories, adventure, humor, sports.

- *Other*: Poetry. Articles for parents and teachers on parenting, teaching, reading, writing, and related to the Guardian Angel mission, to 700 words.
- *Artwork*: Prints or digital images.

Sample Issue Sample issue available at website.
- "Magic Green Writing," by Claudia Ann Sodaro. A boy finds a creative way to color in green.
- "Colors of Danger," by Carla Mai Jansen. A look at the most poisonous, colorful frogs.

Rights and Payment All rights. Articles and fiction, 3¢ a word. Poetry, $10. Pays within 30 days of publication. PayPal account required for payment; please provide your PayPal email address with your email submission.

Guide

55 West Oak Ridge Drive, Hagerstown, MD 21740. www.guidemagazine.org

Editor: Randy Fishell

Geared to middle school-aged children, *Guide* is a Christian magazine of true stories that apply biblical principles to daily challenges, such as friendship, school, entertainment, and family issues. Each true story should include a clear spiritual element. *Guide* does not accept fiction or poetry.
■ **Circulation** 26,000 ■ **Audience** 10–14 years ■ **Frequency** Weekly

Freelance Potential Publishes 250 freelance submissions yearly: 97% written by nonstaff writers; 20% by authors new to the magazine; 10% by previously unpublished writers. Receives 70 unsolicited manuscripts monthly.

Submissions Guidelines available at website. Send complete manuscript. Prefers email to guide@rhpa.org (attached file); will accept hard copy. Accepts simultaneous submissions if identified. SASE. Responds in 4–6 weeks.
- *Articles*: 450–1,200 words. Personal experience, Christian humor, profiles. Topics: adventure, angels, Bible doctrine, compassion, integrity, faith, family, health, media choices, personal growth, social issues.
- *Depts/columns*: Puzzles, activities, games. Submit seasonal material about Thanksgiving, Christmas, Mother's Day, and Father's Day 8 months in advance.

Sample Issue 32 pages. Sample copy available at website.
- "Fishing in the Dark," by Christina Hoskin. A boy receives forgiveness for a prank.
- "Stopped at the Edge," by Wam Akakfulu. A boy believes his guardian angel stopped him from being seriously hurt on his bike.

Rights and Payment First serial and reprint rights. Articles, 7¢–10¢ a word. Games and puzzles, $30–$40. Pays on acceptance. Provides 3 contributor's copies.

Higher Things

Good Shepherd Lutheran Church, 5009 Cassia Street, Boise, ID 83705. www.higherthings.org

Managing Editor: Adriane Dorr

The mission of *Higher Things* is to show teens how the Gospel messages can be applied to their lives. Its articles contain messages of the importance of service, prayer, and living with God in one's life, as well as information on religion and faith. Articles should tackle serious topics, but should also be written in a style that will appeal to teen readers. ■ **Circulation** Unavailable ■ **Audience** 13–19 years ■ **Frequency** Quarterly

Freelance Potential Publishes 36 freelance submissions yearly: 60% written by nonstaff writers; 30% by authors who are new to the magazine; 40% by previously unpublished writers. Receives 1 query, 2 unsolicited manuscripts monthly.

Submissions Guidelines and theme list available at website. Query or send complete manuscript. Accepts hard copy and email to submissions@higherthings.org. SASE. Response time varies.
- *Articles:* 500–800 words. Informational, how-to, profiles, interviews, personal experience. Topics: religion, current events, recreation, social issues, travel.
- *Depts/columns:* Staff-written.

Sample Issue 32 pages. Advertising. Sample copy available.
- "What's a Body To Do?" by Rev. Mark Beutow. Why it's as important to take care of the body as the soul.
- "Cloning: Understanding the Basics," by Rev. Dr. John I. Lamb. An overview of a controversial topic.

Rights and Payment Rights vary. No payment. Provides several contributor's copies.

Highlights for Children

803 Church Street, Honesdale, PA 18431. www.highlights.com

Manuscript Coordinator

This magazine has been entertaining children for 66 years with its informative articles, engaging stories, and plenty of crafts and activities—all with a mission of getting kids to use their innate creativity, thinking ability, and imagination. It also accepts rebus stories and poetry. ■ **Circulation** 2 million ■ **Audience** 6–12 years ■ **Frequency** Monthly

Freelance Potential Publishes 200 freelance submissions yearly: 99% written by nonstaff writers; 60% by authors new to the magazine; 40% by previously unpublished writers. Receives 800 unsolicited manuscripts monthly.

Submissions Guidelines available at website. Send complete manuscript for fiction. Prefers complete manuscript but will accept query for nonfiction. Accepts hard copy. SASE. Responds to queries in 2–4 weeks, to manuscripts in 6–8 weeks.
- *Articles:* To 800 words. Informational, interviews, profiles, personal experience, how-to. Topics: nature, animals, science, crafts, games, activities, world cultures, history, arts, sports, careers.
- *Fiction:* To 500 words for 6–7 years; to 800 words for 8–12 years. Rebus stories, to 100 words. Genres: contemporary, urban, historical, humor, mystery, sports, adventure, multicultural.
- *Depts/columns:* Word lengths vary. Science experiments, crafts.
- *Other:* Science experiments, crafts, puzzles, games. Poetry, to 16 lines.

Sample Issue 42 pages. No advertising. Sample copy available at website.
- "Who Will Care for Spot?" by Marilyn Kratz. A quick-thinking boy solves a family's pet dilemma.
- "Swing a Dragonfly," by Edna Harrington. A craft project uses sticks to make a dragon fly.

Rights and Payment All rights. Articles and fiction, $150+. Rebus stories, $100+. Poetry, $25+. Other material, $25+. Pays on acceptance. Provides 2 copies.

Highlights High Five

807 Church Street, Honesdale, PA 18431-1895. www.highlights.com

Editor: Kathleen Hayes

Designed with preschoolers in mind, *Highlights High Five* shares the philosophy of the Highlights Foundation that "children are the world's most important people." Its simple stories and activities promote reasoning, problem solving, and creative self-expression; foster a love of language; and encourage a sense of wonder about the world. Most of the magazine's regular features are written in-house, and other content has already been commissioned. Its "no freelance" policy remains in effect for another year. ■ **Circulation** 750,000 ■ **Audience** 2–6 years ■ **Frequency** Monthly

Freelance Potential Publishes few freelance submissions yearly.

Submissions Not accepting freelance submissions at this time.
- *Fiction:* Word lengths vary. Genres vary.
- *Other:* Craft projects, kid-friendly recipes, counting activities, picture puzzles. Poetry.

Sample Issue 40 pages. Sample copy available at website.
- "Ducketty-Duck," by Joy Crowley. Rhyming story about a chicken that helps animals stuck in mud.
- "Perfectly Perfect," by Lissa Rovetch. Story about a family's trip to the mountains.

Rights and Payment Rights and payment rates vary. Payment policy varies.

Hopscotch

P.O. Box 164, Bluffton, OH 45817-0164. www.hopscotchmagazine.com

Editor: Marilyn Edwards

Wholesome information and entertainment for elementary and middle-school aged girls is the focus of this magazine. Free of teen material and articles about boyfriends, fashion, and anything else that makes girls grow up too fast, each themed issue helps young girls enjoy their childhood. It accepts short stories, articles, poetry, and crafts. ■ **Circulation** 16,000 ■ **Audience** Girls, 6–13 years ■ **Frequency** 6 times a year

Freelance Potential Publishes 80–100 freelance submissions yearly: 80% written by nonstaff writers; 40% by authors new to the magazine; 30% by previously unpublished writers. Receives 200 manuscripts monthly.

Submissions Guidelines and theme list available at website. Send complete manuscript. Accepts hard copy. Accepts simultaneous submissions if identified. Availability of artwork improves chance of acceptance. SASE. Responds in 2–3 months.
- *Articles:* 500 words. Informational, how-to, profiles, humor, personal experience. Topics: nature, pets, hobbies, sports, cooking, careers.
- *Fiction:* To 1,000 words. Genres: adventure, mystery, historical, multicultural.
- *Depts/columns:* 500 words. Crafts, cooking.
- *Artwork:* B/W and color prints. Line art.
- *Other:* Poetry. Puzzles and games.

Sample Issue 52 pages. No advertising. Sample copy available at website.
- "A Koala Isn't a Bear," by Shirley Anne Ramaley. All about koalas.
- "How the Kangaroo Got Its Name," by Michael Williams. Rhyme that explains what *kangaroo* means.

Rights and Payment First North American serial rights. Articles and fiction, 5¢ a word. Poetry and puzzles, $10+. Pays on publication. Provides 1 contributor's copy.

Horsepower

P.O. Box 670, Aurora, Ontario L4G 4J9 Canada. www.horse-canada.com/horsepower

Managing Editor: Susan Stafford

Children children who love horses are the targeted readers of this publication. Provided as a pull-out in *Horse Canada*, it features breed profiles and information on horseback riding, equine care, and training. Preference is given to Canadian authors. ■ **Circulation** 10,000 ■ **Audience** 8–15 years ■ **Frequency** 6 times a year

Freelance Potential Publishes 6 freelance submissions yearly: 75% written by nonstaff writers. Receives 4 queries, 2 unsolicited manuscripts monthly.

Submissions Guidelines and editorial calendar available. Query or send complete manuscript with résumé. Accepts hard copy and email submissions to fearless.editor@gmail.com. SAE/IRC. Responds to queries in 1–2 weeks, to manuscripts in 2–3 months.

- *Articles:* 500–1,000 words. Informational, how-to, profiles, no fiction please. Topics: riding and stable skills, equine health, horse breeds, training issues, equine celebrities, equestrian careers.
- *Depts/columns:* Staff-written.
- *Artwork:* Color prints.
- *Other:* Activities, games, puzzles.

Sample Issue 16 pages. Advertising.
- "Horse Hives," by Amy Harris. An explanation of horse allergies.
- "Horse Camp," by Nicole Kitchener. How to narrow down one's choices of horse camps.

Rights and Payment First North American serial rights. Written material, 15¢ a word Canadian. Photos, $25 Canadian. Pays on publication. Provides 1 contributor's copy.

Humpty Dumpty

U.S. Kids Magazines, 1100 Waterway Boulevard, Indianapolis, IN 46206.
www.uskidsmags.com/magazines/humptydumpty

Editor: Terry Harshman

Keeping young minds active is the mission of *Humpty Dumpty*, which publishes a mix of simple stories, puzzles, cartoons, and activities for young readers. Healthy living and protecting the environment are frequent messages. ■ **Circulation** 236,000 ■ **Audience** 5–7 years ■ **Frequency** 6 times a year

Freelance Potential Publishes 45 freelance submissions yearly: 50% written by nonstaff writers; 12% by authors new to the magazine; 5% by previously unpublished writers.

Submissions Guidelines available at website. Send complete manuscript. Accepts hard copy. SASE. Responds in 3 months.
- *Articles:* To 350 words. Informational, how-to. Topics: health, fitness, sports, science, nature, animals, crafts, hobbies.
- *Fiction:* To 350 words. Genres: early reader contemporary, multicultural fiction, fantasy, folktales, humor, mystery.
- *Depts/columns:* Word lengths vary. Recipes, health advice, book excerpts.
- *Other:* Puzzles, activities, games. Poetry, 4–12 lines. Submit seasonal material 8 months in advance.

Sample Issue 36 pages. Little advertising. Sample copy available at website.
- "The Wiggle, Wobble Mystery," by Lois G. Grambling. Story about a boy with a loose tooth.
- "Bully and Peep," by Jodie Mangor. Story about a friendship between a frog and a bird.

Rights and Payment All rights. Written material, to 35¢ a word. Pays on publication. Provides 10 contributor's copies.

Imagination-Café

P.O. Box 1536, Valparaiso, IN 46384. www.imagination-cafe.com

Submissions: Sandie Lee

Through its engaging presentation of career information, *Imagination-Café* encourages kids to dream about their futures. Appearing in ezine format, it also offers regular updates on sports, science, history, and health. Its mission is to offer children tools to discover their passions by providing them with reliable information, resources, and safe opportunities for self-expression. ■ **Hits per month** 1,027 ■ **Audience** 7–12 years ■ **Frequency** Updated daily

Freelance Potential Publishes 12–120 freelance submissions yearly: 75–100% written by nonstaff writers; 10–25% by authors new to the magazine; 1–10% by previously unpublished writers. Receives 25–50 queries, 25–50 unsolicited manuscripts monthly.

Submissions Guidelines available at website. Prefers complete manuscript; will accept query. Accepts email to submissions@imagination-café.com (no attachments). Also accepts requests for assignments. Responds in 1 week.

- *Articles:* Word lengths vary. Informational, how-to, profiles, interviews, reviews. Topics: animals, careers, crafts, hobbies, history, science, technology, sports, celebrities.
- *Fiction:* To 1,000 words. Contemporary stories with young protagonists.
- *Depts/columns:* Word lengths vary. Cool Careers, Before They Were Famous, Celebrity Screw-Ups, School Strategies.
- *Other:* Puzzles, mazes, word games, quizzes, recipes.

Sample Issue Sample copy available at website.
- "Robin's Reality Check," by Latanya West. A girl learns to balance school work with fun.
- "The Whispering," by Caroline Waszek. A scary sound turns out not to be scary at all.

Rights and Payment Non-exclusive print and electronic rights. Written material, $20–$100. Pays on acceptance.

Insight

55 West Oak Ridge Drive, Hagerstown, MD 21740. www.insightmagazine.org

Editor: Dwain Neilson Esmond

Insight's mission is to reach Seventh-day Adventist teens with articles that help them grow in friendship with God. It addresses topics such as friendship, social issues, faith, and serving one's community. Articles should address topics of interest to today's teens from a Christian perspective, and should have a biblical reference. ■ **Circulation** 12,000 ■ **Audience** 13–19 years ■ **Frequency** Weekly

Freelance Potential Publishes 200–300 freelance submissions yearly: 50% written by nonstaff writers; 70% by authors who are new to the magazine; 50% by previously unpublished writers. Receives 60 unsolicited manuscripts monthly.

Submissions Guidelines available at website. Send complete manuscript. Accepts hard copy and email to insight@rhpa.org (Word attachments). SASE. Responds in 1–3 months.
- *Articles:* 500–1,500 words. Informational, profiles, biography, personal experience, humor. Topics: faith, social issues, careers, Christian celebrities, outstanding Seventh-day Adventist youths.
- *Depts/columns:* Word lengths vary. Bible lessons, relationship advice, true stories, personal experience.
- *Other:* Submit seasonal material 6 months in advance.

Sample Issue 16 pages. Little advertising. Sample copy available.
- "Faith that Holds On," by Kimberly Pearson. True story about faith and a girl's sick father.
- "Always There." How a teen was calmed by God's presence.

Rights and Payment First rights. Written material, $50–$125. Reprints, $50. Pays on publication. Provides 5 contributor's copies.

InTeen

1551 Regency Court, Calumet City, IL 60409. www.urbanministries.com

Editor: LaTonya Taylor

Each issue of this Christian teen magazine features thought-provoking Bible studies, inspiring articles, and Scripture passages that link Bible verses to problems facing today's urban teens. It specifically targets African American teens, with a goal to help them develop and nurture their relationships with Jesus Christ and others. All material is assigned. ■ **Circulation** 75,000 ■ **Audience** 15–17 years ■ **Frequency** Quarterly

Freelance Potential Publishes 52 freelance submissions yearly: 90% written by nonstaff writers.

Submissions Guidelines available. All material is written on assignment. Send résumé with writing samples. SASE. Responds in 3–6 months.
- *Articles:* Word lengths vary. Bible study, how-to, profiles, interviews, biography, reviews. Topics: religion, college and careers, black history, music, social issues, multicultural and ethnic issues.
- *Fiction:* Word lengths vary. Stories in Bible lessons. Genres: inspirational, multicultural, ethnic.
- *Other:* Puzzles, activities. Poetry. Submit seasonal material 1 year in advance.

Sample Issue 48 pages. No advertising.
- "Missed Opportunities in Mississippi," by Wil LaVeist. An exploration of modern race issues.
- "The Politics of Hunger," by Christine A. Scheller. An interview with the president of Bread for the World.

Rights and Payment All rights. All material, payment rates vary. Pays 2 months after acceptance. Provides 2 contributor's copies.

International Gymnast

3214 Bart Conner Drive, Norman, OK 73072. www.intlgymnast.com

Editor: Dwight Normile

Preteen and teen gymnasts—and others involved in the sport—are the focus of this magazine. Competition reports, athlete profiles, and training techniques are some of its regular features. Writers should be well-versed in gymnastics and be able to provide interesting facts that readers wouldn't already know. Interviews and profiles are always of interest. ■ **Circulation** 14,000 ■ **Audience** Gymnasts, 10–16 years ■ **Frequency** 10 times a year

Freelance Potential Publishes 5 freelance submissions yearly: 10% written by nonstaff writers; 50% by authors new to the magazine. Receives 1 unsolicited manuscript monthly.

Submissions Guidelines available. Send complete manuscript. Accepts hard copy. Accepts simultaneous submissions if identified. SASE. Responds in 1 month.
- *Articles:* 1,000–2,250 words. Informational, profiles, interviews. Topics: gymnastics competitions, coaching, personalities involved in the sport.
- *Fiction:* To 1,500 words. Gymnastics stories.
- *Artwork:* B/W prints, 35mm color slides for cover art.

Sample Issue 46 pages. Advertising. Sample copy available at website.
- "Flip-Flop Fortunes," by John Crumish. How U.S. gymnast Bridget Sloan went from team alternate to winning the all-around gold.
- "Untouchable," by Dwight Normile. Kohei Uchimura's performance at the world championships.

Rights and Payment All rights. Written material, $15–$25. Artwork, $5–$50. Pays on publication. Provides 1 contributor's copy.

Irish's Story Playhouse

1500 West Lovers Lane, Apartment 107, Arlington, TX 76013. www.irishstoryplayhouse.com

Editor: Irish Monahan

This print magazine and its companion website celebrates the art of storytelling for children, and features fiction, poetry, and the occasional informational article, each grouped in age-appropriate sections. It has been redesigned and now includes podcasts. It is currently closed to submissions.
■ **Circulation** Unavailable ■ **Audience** 3–14 years ■ **Frequency** Monthly

Freelance Potential Of the content published yearly, 25% is written by nonstaff writers.

Submissions Closed to submissions. Check website for changes to this policy.
- *Articles:* 300–1,000 words. Informational. Topics: nature, health, writing.
- *Fiction:* 300–7,500 words. Genres: Contemporary, folktales, adventure.
- *Other:* Poetry, 12-line minimum.

Sample Issue Sample copy available at website.
- "The Old Apple Tree," by Irish Monahan. A young girl remembers her favorite apple tree and the storm that changed it forever.
- "All about Apples." An explanation of the types of apples, their growing habitats, and their uses.

Rights and Payment 6-month exclusive print and electronic rights. Articles, $2. Fiction, $3. Poetry, $1. Pays on publication.

Jack and Jill

U.S. Kids Magazines, 1100 Waterway Boulevard, Indianapolis, IN 46206. www.jackandjillmag.org

Editor: Terry Harshman

A mix of articles, stories, puzzles, and poetry—all designed to encourage children to be happy, healthy, and fit—are found in each issue of this magazine. Editors are particularly interested in profiles of regular kids who are engaged in unusual, challenging, or interesting activities. ■ **Circulation** 200,000
■ **Audience** 6–12 years ■ **Frequency** 6 times a year

Freelance Potential Publishes 24 freelance submissions yearly: 50% written by nonstaff writers; 70% by authors who are new to the magazine. Receives 100 unsolicited manuscripts monthly.

Submissions Guidelines available at website. Send complete manuscript for fiction. Query for nonfiction. Accepts hard copy. Accepts simultaneous submissions if identified. SASE. Responds in 3 months.
- *Articles:* To 700 words. Informational, how-to, humor, profiles, biography. Topics: sports, health, exercise, safety, nutrition, hygiene.
- *Fiction:* To 700 words. Genres: mystery, fantasy, folktales, humor, science fiction, stories about sports and animals.
- *Artwork:* Digital images.
- *Other:* Poetry. Games, puzzles, crafts, activities.

Sample Issue 36 pages. Little advertising. Sample copy available at website.
- "Animal Behavior," by Ed Page. Story about a boy learning correct behavior.
- "My Sister the Dog," by Frances O'Donnell. A girl turns the tables on her mischievous little sister.

Rights and Payment All rights. Articles and fiction, to 25¢ a word. Poetry, $25–$50. Artwork, $15. Pays on publication.

JAKES Country

P.O. Box 530, Edgefield, SC 29824. www.nwtf.org/jakes

Managing Editor: P. J. Perea, Publishing Assistant: Michelle Jones

This publication has replaced *JAKES* (Juniors Acquiring Knowledge, Ethics, and Sportsmanship) and *Xtreme JAKES.* A publication of the National Wild Turkey Federation, *JAKES Country* teaches youth and teens about the importance of conservation and the role that hunting plays in the North American Model. It also features articles on shooting sports, fishing, camping and other traditional outdoor activities. All material must be tailored to the teen outdoorsman. ■ **Circulation** 150,000
■ **Audience** To 17 years ■ **Frequency** Quarterly

Freelance Potential Publishes 30 freelance submissions yearly: 50% written by nonstaff writers; 30% by authors new to the magazine; 10% by previously unpublished writers. Receives 10–16 queries and unsolicited manuscripts monthly.

Submissions Guidelines available on request. Prefers query; accepts complete manuscript. Accepts email to mlindler@nwtf.net. Accepts simultaneous submissions if identified. Responds in 8 weeks.
- *Articles:* 500–1,000 words. Informational, how-tos, member profiles, personal experience written from a teen perspective. Topics: hunting hunting ethics, conservation projects, do-it-yourself outdoor projects, fishing, outdoor sports.
- *Depts/columns:* Word lengths vary. Association news, event coverage, new products and gear.
- *Artwork:* High-resolution digital images. Illustrations.

Sample Issue Sample copy available.
- "Survival Savvy." An explanation of what should be in one's survival pack.
- "Fly Fishing School." What's needed to go fly fishing.

Rights and Payment First North American serial and Web rights. All material, payment rates vary. Kill fee, 20%. Pays on publication. Provides 2 contributor's copies.

Junior Baseball

14 Woodway Lane, Wilton, CT 06897. www.juniorbaseball.com

Editor/Publisher: Jim Beecher

Launched in 1996, this independent magazine focuses on all aspects of youth baseball and aims to connect families to America's favorite pastime. Its articles instruct, inform, and entertain readers with topics ranging from coaching techniques to the secret behind a good knuckleball. ■ **Circulation** 50,000 ■ **Audience** 7–17 years; parents; coaches ■ **Frequency** 6 times a year

Freelance Potential Publishes 20 freelance submissions yearly: 50% written by nonstaff writers; 20% by authors who are new to the magazine; 10% by previously unpublished writers. Receives 4 queries and unsolicited manuscripts monthly.

Submissions Guidelines available. Query with writing samples; or send complete manuscript with artwork. Accepts email submissions to publisher@juniorbaseball.com (Word or text file attachments). Availability of artwork improves chance of acceptance. SASE. Responds in 1–2 weeks.
- *Articles:* 750–1,500 words. Informational, how-to, profiles, interviews. Topics: playing tips, teams and leagues, player safety.
- *Depts/columns:* Player's Story, 500 words. In the Spotlight, news, reviews, 50–100 words. Hot Prospects, 500–1,000 words. Coaches Clinic, 100–1,000 words.
- *Artwork:* Color prints; digital images at 300 dpi.

Sample Issue 40 pages. Advertising. Sample copy available.
- "The Importance of a Great Relationship with Your Catcher." MLB player Cliff Lee provides tips for pitchers and catchers.
- "Seven Steps to Quicker Steps Around the Bases." Base running advice.

Rights and Payment All rights. Articles, 20¢ a word. Depts/columns, $25–$100. Artwork, $50–$100. Pays on publication. Provides 1 contributor's copy.

Junior Shooters

7154 West State Street, Boise, ID 83714. www.juniorshooters.net

Editor in Chief: Andrew Fink

With a mission to get youngsters (and their parents) interested and involved in all types of shooting sports, this magazine covers the shooting disciplines, organizations, events, techniques, and safety issues. About half of the articles are written by juniors about their experiences with shooting. Safety-themed articles are always welcome here. ■ **Circulation** 30,000 ■ **Audience** 8–adult ■ **Frequency** 3 times a year, and weekly website articles

Freelance Potential Publishes several freelance submissions yearly: 80% written by nonstaff writers; 40% by authors new to the magazine; 60% by previously unpublished writers. Receives 15 unsolicited manuscripts monthly.

Submissions Send complete manuscript. Accepts email to articles@juniorshooters.net and CD submissions (PC format) in Word. Materials not returned. Response time varies.
- *Articles:* Word lengths vary. Informational, profiles, personal experience. Topics: all disciplines of shooting sports, techniques, training, coaching, products, gear.
- *Depts/columns:* Word lengths vary. Shooting tips, gun safety, new products, gear.
- *Artwork:* High-resolution digital images.

Sample Issue 68 pages. Advertising. Sample copy available at website.
- "Becoming the Best Shooter You Can Be," by Bob Benbough. Training tips are provided by a coach.
- "Firearms Safety and You!" by Larry Haley. How to safely create your own shooting area in the country.

Rights and Payment Nonexclusive rights. No payment.

JuniorWay

P.O. Box 436987, Chicago, IL 60643. www.urbanministries.com

Editor: Katherine Steward

A publication of Urban Ministries, Inc., *JuniorWay* is a Sunday School magazine with accompanying teacher's guide and activity booklet for fourth to sixth graders. It presents stories, Bible lessons, and activities designed to help children live their lives with Christ in mind. Lessons based on Bible stories must be relevant to the everyday lives of its urban, African American readers and feature a Christ-centered perspective. ■ **Circulation** 75,000 ■ **Audience** 9–11 years ■ **Frequency** Quarterly

Freelance Potential Publishes 10–100 freelance submissions yearly: 95% written by nonstaff writers. Receives 10–25 queries, 10–25 unsolicited manuscripts monthly.

Submissions Guidelines and theme list available. Most material is written on assignment. Query with résumé and writing samples. Query for fiction. Accepts email to ksteward@urbanministries.com. Response time varies.
- *Articles:* Word lengths vary. Bible lessons, personal experience, humor. Topics: religion, relationships, social issues, hobbies, crafts, sports, recreation, multicultural subjects.
- *Fiction:* Word lengths vary. Inspirational stories with multicultural subjects.
- *Artwork:* B/W or color prints or transparencies.
- *Other:* Puzzles, activities, games, jokes. Poetry. Seasonal material about Vacation Bible School.

Sample Issue 32 pages. No advertising. Sample copy available.

Rights and Payment All rights. All material, payment rates vary. Pays on publication.

Just 4 Kids ⭐

P.O. Box 18962, Austin, TX 78760. www.just4kidsmagazine.com

Editor: Mauri Gandy

This Christian print magazine and website gives readers the resources to teach children about Jesus Christ. Written and produced for children, it is designed to "help kids pray and be in a right relationship with God." Each themed issue includes articles, Scripture stories, articles, fiction, poetry, and prayers, as well as games, crafts, and activities. Articles should help children understand how they can become more like Jesus Christ. True stories of children who have experienced miracles, or have shown extra-special virtues, are especially sought. Material written by children is also featured. ■ **Circulation** Unavailable ■ **Audience** 2 years–YA, target reading age of 7–12 years ■ **Frequency** Monthly

Freelance Potential The print magazine is a paying market; donations of material also welcome for the website.

Submissions Guidelines and theme list available at website at http://just4kidsmagazine.com/writer_guidelines.html. Material for print magazine should be sent by regular mail. Donated submissions for use on website should be emailed to mauri@just4kidsmagazine.com. Materials not returned. No previously published material. Response time varies.
■ *Articles:* 300–1,000 words. Informational, profiles, personal experience, seasonal material. Topics: spirituality, living a life honoring Jesus Christ, holidays, virtue, morality, people whose lives reflect Christian values, true stories of miracles.
■ *Fiction:* 400–1,400 words. Scripture-based stories that show children in real-life situations.
■ *Artwork:* Drawings.
■ *Other:* Poetry. Bible quizzes, games, crafts, activities, recipes.

Sample Issue No advertising. A sample of materal is available at website.
■ "Learn to Walk in God's Awesome Power." A child's guide for living a Christian life.
■ "What the Bible Is All About." An introduction of the Old Testament's major prophets.

Rights and Payment Newspaper, periodical, and electronic rights. Rights stay with author for donated material. No payment for material used on website. Pays for content used in print magazine only. Articles and fiction, to 5¢ a word. Family devotions, $5+. Poetry, $2+. Activities and games, $2+. Artwork, $1+. Pays on publication.

Justine

6263 Poplar Avenue, Suite 1154, Memphis, TN 38119. www.justinemagazine.com

Publisher/Editorial Director: Jana Petty

Targeting teenage girls, *Justine* provides articles on topics that interest today's young people without relying on celebrities and gossip. It covers fashion, beauty, and style trends with a focus on reality, affordability, and a healthy lifestyle. Material should be written in a "young" voice without patronizing readers. ■ **Circulation** 250,000 ■ **Audience** YA ■ **Frequency** 6 times a year

Freelance Potential Publishes 25 freelance submissions yearly: 20% written by nonstaff writers; 90% by authors new to the magazine; 25% by previously unpublished writers. Receives 8 queries monthly.

Submissions Query with résumé and clips. Accepts hard copy. SASE. Response time varies.
■ *Articles:* Word lengths vary. Informational, how-to, interviews, profiles. Topics: role models, college, sports, health and fitness, beauty, social issues, school.
■ *Depts/columns:* Word lengths vary. Fashion, fitness, advice, Q&As.

Sample Issue Advertising. Sample copy available.
■ "The 411 on Friendships," by Rachel Smith. Article on making new friends and keeping the old.
■ "10 Ways to Make Life Easier with Your Parents," by Vanessa Van Patten. Advice on strengthening relationships with parents from one of the nations youngest experts on parenting and adolescents.

Rights and Payment Rights vary. Written material, payment rates vary. Pays 30 days after publication.

Kayak ★ ▮

Bryce Hall, Main Floor, 515 Portage Avenue, Winnipeg, Manitoba R3B 0G9, Canada.
www.canadashistory.ca/kids

Editor: Nancy Payne

Published by Canada's National History Society, *Kayak* introduces Canadian children to their country's history with relevant, fun articles and activities. Each themed issue contains an informative article, a story based on a historical event or era, and activities to allow readers to explore and understand their history. Though not accepting unsolicited pieces, writers with experience writing on historical subjects for this age demographic are invited to submit resumes and samples of their work for future assignments. ■ **Circulation** Unavailable ■ **Audience** 7–11 years ■ **Frequency** Quarterly

Freelance Potential Not accepting unsolicited submissions. Send résumé for assignments.

Submissions Guidelines and theme list available at website. Not currently accepting queries or unsolicited submissions. Experienced writers can send résumé and clips for consideration for assignments. Accepts hard copy and email to editor@kayakmag.ca. SASE.
■ *Articles:* Features, 1,200 words. Articles, 350–450 words. Informational. Topics: Canada's history, culture, geography, natural history.
■ *Fiction:* 1,200 words. Genres: historical.
■ *Other:* Games, activities, puzzles, jokes.

Sample Issue 34 pages. No advertising. Sample copy available at website.
■ "Rockin' Discoveries." How archaeologists, paleontologists, and other scientists have discovered important pieces of Canada's history among its rocks.
■ "National Historic Sites to See." A countdown of 16 must-see national historic sites.

Rights and Payment Rights vary. Articles, 35¢ a word. Other material, payment rates vary. Pays on publication.

Key Club

Key Club International, 3636 Woodview Trace, Indianapolis, IN 46268. www.keyclub.org/magazine

Executive Editor: Amberly Peterson

Key Club International is the largest high school service organization in the world. Its magazine is read by service-minded students who want to make a difference in their communities. It features academic, self-help, service, and leadership articles that can help readers become better students and better Key Club members. ■ **Circulation** 260,000 ■ **Audience** 14–18 years ■ **Frequency** Twice a year

Freelance Potential Publishes 4 freelance submissions yearly: 20% written by nonstaff writers; 15% by authors new to the magazine; 5% by previously unpublished writers. Receives 8 queries monthly.

Submissions Guidelines available at website. Prefers query; will accept complete manuscript. Accepts hard copy and email queries to keyclubnews@kiwanis.org. Accepts simultaneous submissions if identified. SASE. Responds in 1 month.
■ *Articles:* 250–1,500 words. Informational, self-help. Topics: education, teen concerns, community service, leadership, school activities, social issues, careers.
■ *Depts/columns:* Staff-written.
■ *Artwork:* Color prints and illustrations.
■ *Other:* Submit seasonal material about back to school, college, and summer activities 3–7 months in advance.

Sample Issue 24 pages. Little advertising. Sample copy available at website.
■ "Rekindle Your Public Relationship," by Shanna Mooney. Boosting public awareness of a club.

■ "Greenbreak," by Shanna Mooney. How to organize an Earth-friendly spring break trip.

Rights and Payment First North American serial rights. Articles, $100–$800. Pays on acceptance. Provides 3 contributor's copies.

Keys for Kids

P.O. Box 1001, Grand Rapids, MI 49501-1001. www.keysforkids.org

Editor: Hazel Marett

CBH Ministries publishes *Keys for Kids* to provide young readers with daily devotionals and Gospel-based stories that will help them develop a closeness with Jesus Christ. Each devotional also includes a "key thought" that readers can bring with them throughout their day. Every submission should include a Scripture passage, a story, a practical application, a key verse, and a key thought.
■ **Circulation** 70,000 ■ **Audience** 6–14 years ■ **Frequency** 6 times a year

Freelance Potential Publishes 30 freelance submissions yearly: 100% written by nonstaff writers; 90% by authors who are new to the magazine; 50% by previously unpublished writers. Receives 10 unsolicited manuscripts monthly.

Submissions Guidelines available at website. Send complete manuscript. Accepts hard copy and email submissions to hazel@cbhministries.org. SASE. Responds in 2 months.
■ *Articles: 375–400 words; key thought, 85 words.* Devotionals with related Scripture passages and a key thought. Topics: contemporary social issues, family life, trust, friendship, salvation, witnessing, prayer, marriage, faith.

Sample Issue 80 pages. Sample copy available at website.

■ "Fences." A lesson that parental rules are for children's protection, not to spoil fun.
■ "A Great Sacrifice." The loving sacrifice of a brother for his sibling.

Rights and Payment First, second, and reprint rights. Articles, $25. Pays on acceptance. Provides 1 contributor's copy.

The Kids' Ark

P.O. Box 3160, Victoria, TX 77903. www.thekidsark.com

Editor: Joy Mygrants

The Kids' Ark is a nondenominational Christian magazine. It appears in themed issues that teach biblical principles through enlightening and entertaining articles and stories. It also publishes activities and games. Stories featuring ethnic and multicultural characters are always welcome. While a biblical lesson should be the underlying foundation of the story, the editors are not interested in heavy-handed preaching. ■ **Circulation** 8,000+ ■ **Audience** 6–12 years ■ **Frequency** Quarterly

Freelance Potential Publishes 12 freelance submissions yearly: 60% written by nonstaff writers; 80–100% by authors new to the magazine. Receives 2 unsolicited manuscripts monthly.

Submissions Guidelines, theme list, and submission due dates available at website. Send complete manuscript with word count noted on the first page. Accepts email to thekidsarksubmissions@yahoo.com (Microsoft Word attachments; indicate theme to which you are submitting in subject line). Responds in 2 months.
■ *Articles:* To 650 words. Informational, inspirational, personal experience. Topics: religion, faith, God's love.
■ *Fiction:* To 650 words. Genres: inspirational, contemporary, historical, science fiction.
■ *Other:* Puzzles, games, comics.

Sample Issue 32 pages. No advertising. Sample copy available at website.

- "A Stubborn Heart," by Michelle Fredrickson. Story about a boy who learns to accept help.
- "Learning to Listen," by Sally Clark. A young baseball player learns to take advice.

Rights and Payment First North American serial, second, worldwide, and electronic rights. Articles and fiction, $100. Reprints, $25. Pays on publication.

Kiki

118 West Pike Street, Covington, KY 41011. www.kikimag.com

Editor in Chief: Jamie G. Bryant

This magazine targets girls who appreciate creativity and style. It rejects the usual subjects of boys and social issues to focus instead on topics relating to fashion, design, personal creativity, and travel. It is for the girl who simply loves to express herself as well as the girl who wants to have a career in design. ■ **Circulation** Unavailable ■ **Audience** Girls, 8–14 years ■ **Frequency** Bimonthly

Freelance Potential Publishes 40 freelance submissions yearly: 50% written by nonstaff writers; 15% by authors new to the magazine. Receives 20 queries monthly.

Submissions Guidelines available at website. Query. Accepts hard copy and email to submissions@ kikimag.com. SASE. Responds in 3 months.
- *Articles:* Word lengths vary. Informational, profiles, interviews. Topics: fashion, design, travel, careers.
- *Depts/columns:* Word lengths vary. Fashion trends, advice, careers.
- *Artwork:* High-resolution digital images.

Sample Issue Sample copy available.
- "History in Fashion," by Sara Rowe. An interview with the director of an historic costume collection.
- "Emi-Jay: A World of Hair Ties and Headbands," by Sara Rowe. Profile of two eighth-graders who started their own hair accessories business.

Rights and Payment All rights. Written material, 50¢–$1 a word. Pays on publication. Provides 2 contributor's copies.

Know

501-3960 Quadra Street, Victoria, British Columbia V8X 4A3 Canada. www.knowmag.ca

Managing Editor: Adrienne Mason

Subtitled *The Science Magazine for Curious Kids, Know* engages children in the study of science through fun, interactive articles, and activities that answer the who, what, why, and how questions that kids ask. Short fiction and poetry submissions must relate to the theme. It is not currently accepting queries or unsolicited submissions for nonfiction articles. However, since a large portion of the content is assigned, writers who have experience writing about science for young children are invited to submit samples of their published work to be considered for assignments. ■ **Circulation** 12,500 ■ **Audience** 6–9 years ■ **Frequency** 6 times a year

Freelance Potential Publishes 12–120 freelance submissions yearly: 75–90% written by nonstaff writers; 75–100% assigned; 1–10% by authors who are new to the magazine; 1–10% by previously unpublished writers. Receives 25–50 queries, 10–25 unsolicited manuscripts monthly.

Submissions Guidelines and theme list available at website. Send résumé and clips to be considered for nonfiction; no unsolicited submissions. Send complete manuscript for fiction and poetry. Accepts email to adrienne@knowmag.ca (Word attachments). Responds to queries in 2 weeks, to manuscripts in 3 months.
- *Articles:* Not accepting submissions.
- *Fiction:* To 500 words. Theme-related. Genres: contemporary, folklore, mythology.

- *Depts/columns:* 200–250 words. Science news and discoveries, scientist profiles, astronomy, paleontology, random facts.
- *Other:* Poetry. Puzzles, games, activities.

Sample Issue 32 pages. No advertising. Sample copy available.
- "The Science of Shells." Article examines the makeup and purpose of animal shells.
- "Home Lab." Explanation of how to turn a shell to dust using a common kitchen ingredient.

Rights and Payment First North American serial and non-exclusive electronic rights. Written material, 50¢ (Canadian) a word. Pays on publication. Provides 2 contributor's copies.

Lad

4200 North Point Parkway, Alpharetta, GA 30022. www.nambstore.com

Content Coordinator: David Nelms

This magazine targets young boys of the Southern Baptist faith. It is filled with inspirational articles, short stories, and fun activities that are designed to foster personal growth and highlight the importance of mission work. It is published by the North American Mission Board. It does not accept unsolicited submissions, but will review résumés from Southern Baptist writers for assignments.
- **Circulation** 13,000 ▪ **Audience** Boys, 6–9 years ▪ **Frequency** Monthly

Freelance Potential Publishes 12 freelance submissions yearly: 90% written by nonstaff writers; 15% by authors new to the magazine; 5% by previously unpublished writers.

Submissions Contract writers only. Send résumé. Accepts hard copy. Response time varies.
- *Articles:* Word lengths vary. Informational, personal experience. Topics: biography, crafts, current events, religion, humor.
- *Fiction:* Word lengths vary. Genres: adventure, mystery, nature, sports, science fiction.
- *Other:* Puzzles, games, jokes.

Sample Issue 22 pages. Advertising. Sample copy available.

Rights and Payment All rights. Written material, payment rates vary. Pays on acceptance. Provides 1 author's copy.

Ladybug

Cricket Magazine Group, 70 East Lake Street, Suite 300, Chicago, IL 60601. www.ladybugmagkids.com, www.cricketmag.com

Submissions Editor

Filled with lively stories that offer a sense of joy and wonder, this magazine is designed to be read aloud to preschoolers. Poems, activities, nonfiction, and rebus stories round out the editorial mix.
- **Circulation** 56,000 ▪ **Audience** 3–6 years ▪ **Frequency** 9 times a year

Freelance Potential Publishes 70 freelance submissions yearly: 90% written by nonstaff writers. Receives 150–200 unsolicited manuscripts monthly.

Submissions Guidelines available at www.cricketmag.com/6-Submission-Guidelines-for-kids-magazines-for-children-from-toddlers-to-teens. Send complete manuscript with word count. Accepts hard copy. Accepts simultaneous submissions if identified. SASE. Responds in 6 months.
- *Articles:* To 400 words. Informational, how-to, humor. Topics: nature, animals, family, the environment, other age-appropriate topics.
- *Fiction:* To 800 words. Rebus stories, 200 words. Read-aloud, early reader, picture, and rebus stories. Genres: adventure, humor, fantasy, folktales, contemporary, multicultural.
- *Other:* Puzzles, learning activities, games, crafts, finger plays, action rhymes, cartoons, songs. Poetry, to 20 lines.

Sample Issue 40 pages. No advertising. Sample copy available at website.

■ ""Manny's Animals," by Julia Durango. In this long poem, Manny pretends to be a monkey, elephant, bullfrog, dolphin, songbird, and bear, with encouragement from his grandmother.

■ "Come Play! Children's Games Around the World," by Tori Telfer. Introduces games children play in Chile, South Africa, Spain, and South Korea.

Rights and Payment Rights vary. Articles and fiction, 25¢ a word ($25 minimum). Poems, $3 a line ($25 minimum). Other material, payment rates vary. Pays after publication. Provides 2 copies.

The Magazine

643 Queen Street East, Toronto, Ontario M4M 1G4 Canada. www.themagazine.ca

Editor: Karen Wong

The Magazine is strictly for older children and young teens. The digest-sized publication is filled with reviews of movies, music, and television; comics; games; celebrity information; articles on healthy lifestyles and the environment; and some short stories and poems. Most of the material comes from writers under age 25. ■ **Circulation** 15,000 ■ **Audience** 8–14 years ■ **Frequency** Monthly

Freelance Potential Publishes 20 freelance submissions yearly: 60% written by nonstaff writers; 30% by authors who are new to the magazine; 60% by previously unpublished writers. Receives 240 queries and unsolicited manuscripts yearly.

Submissions Query or send complete manuscript. Accepts submissions via the website. Response time varies.

■ *Articles:* To 1,000 words. Informational, profiles, interviews, humor. Topics: popular culture, movies, music, video games, books, lifestyle subjects.

■ *Fiction:* Word lengths vary. Short stories. Genres vary.

■ *Depts/columns:* Word lengths vary. Media reviews, news and entertainment briefs, health.

■ *Other:* Contests, quizzes, surveys, posters, horoscopes. Poetry.

Sample Issue 112 pages. Advertising. Sample copy available.

Rights and Payment All rights. Written material, $10–$60 Canadian. Payment policy varies.

M.L.T.S.

1404 East Bristol Street, Philadelphia, PA 19124. www.mltsmag.com

Editor in Chief: Rosella Eleanor LaFevre

Created in the spring of 2011, *M.L.T.S.* (which stands for Most Likely To Succeed) is an online magazine and blog for young college women who want to start their careers while still in school. It targets ambitious, driven older teen and young adult girls with articles on fashion, beauty and fitness, entertainment, careers, education, and relationships. Originally available via a print-on-demand option, it has plans to start full print runs soon. All issues are currently available for free as a digital version. *M.L.T.S.* is looking for pitches for all sections, and is most interested in solid reportage pieces. As a new publication, there are several opportunities for writers here. ■ **Hits per month** 1,500 ■ **Audience** YA girls ■ **Frequency** Quarterly

Freelance Potential Publishes 20 freelance submissions yearly: 25% by nonstaff writers; most by writers new to the magazine.

Submissions Guidelines and editorial calendar available at website. Send complete manuscript for first-person essay; query for all other material. Accepts email to mlts.magazine@gmail.com. Response time varies. Other editorial opportunities are available for interested writers. Contact editor via email for more information.

■ *Articles:* Word lengths vary. Informational, interviews, personal experience. Topics: fashion, beauty,

college, career, relationships.
- *Depts/columns:* Love Lesson (personal essay about something learned about love, 300 words). Send complete essay to editorial@mltsmag.com.

Sample Issue 58 pages. Sample available at website.
- "50 Ways To Rock College." Supplies strategies for getting the most out of one's college experience.
- "You Gotta Be Madd To Start Your Own Business," by Allison Hardin. Interview with a young woman who started her own beauty business, Madd Style Cosmetix.

Rights and Payment Rights vary. No payment yet; anticipates paying writers in the future.

Motivos Bilingual Magazine

P.O. Box 34391, Philadelphia, PA 19101. www.motivosmag.com

Publisher: Jenee Chizick

This bilingual (Spanish and English) magazine features socially and culturally relevant articles about Latino culture, Latino issues, college plans, and career opportunities. High school and college students, as well as adults, are invited to submit material. It seeks work that inspires and empowers Latino youth to explore their full potential and make informed choices about life, college, and career.
- **Circulation** 75,000 - **Audience** YA - **Frequency** Quarterly

Freelance Potential Publishes 30 freelance submissions yearly: 50% written by nonstaff writers; 50% by authors new to the magazine; 40% by previously unpublished writers.

Submissions Guidelines available at website. Send complete manuscript. Accepts hard copy and email to editor@motivosmag.com. SASE. Response time varies.
- *Articles:* 400–1,2000 words. Informational, interviews, creative nonfiction, personal experience. Topics: College prep, career explorations, financial issues, cultural issues, travel.
- *Depts/columns:* Word lengths vary. Health and fitness, relationships, style tips, technology updates.

Sample Issue Advertising. Sample copy available.
- "Two Worlds, Two Languages, One Me," by Gabriela Plumley. Growing up in a bicultural home.
- "College & Baby & Work—Oh My!" by Luz Martinez. From teenage mother to college student.

Rights and Payment First North American serial rights. Written material, payment rates vary. Payment policy varies. Provides 2 contributor's copies.

Muse

Cricket Magazine Group, 70 East Lake Street, Suite 300, Chicago, IL 60601. www.musemagkids.com

Submissions Editor: Elizabeth Preston

This magazine aims to get kids and teens interested in a wide range of topics—including science and technology, history, culture, and the arts—through lively articles and interviews. Never dull, always enlightening, *Muse* gets to the brain via the funny bone. It looks for writers with expertise in their subject, who can convey that knowledge in language that speaks to the target age group and generates excitement. - **Circulation** 38,000 - **Audience** 10+ years - **Frequency** 9 times a year

Freelance Potential 100% written by nonstaff writers; 20% by authors new to the magazine. Receives 1–10 queries monthly.

Submissions Guidelines available at website. All work is assigned. Send résumé and clips. Accepts hard copy and email to muse@caruspub.com. Response time varies.
- *Articles:* To 2,500 words. Informational, interviews. Topics: science, nature, the environment, history, culture, anthropology, sociology, technology, the arts.
- *Depts/columns:* Word lengths vary. Science news, Q&As, math problems, personal experience.
- *Other:* Cartoons, contests, activities.

Sample Issue 40 pages. No advertising. Sample copy available at website.
- "Their Ticket Is Valid," by Anne L. Russon. Up close and personal with the orangutans of a research center in Indonesia.
- "Garden of Surprises," by Paul Baker. An exploration of some of the gardens of English castles.

Rights and Payment Rights vary. Written material, payment rates vary. Payment policy varies.

My Light

www.mylightmagazine.com

Editor in Chief: Jennifer Gladen

This ezine was developed to show children how wonderful a real relationship with God can be. Written for elementary school children who practice the Catholic faith, it includes stories, articles, crafts, poems, profiles of saints, and Bible stories. ■ **Hits per month** 500 ■ **Audience** 4–12 years ■ **Frequency** Bimonthly

Freelance Potential Publishes 180 freelance submissions yearly: 75–90% written by nonstaff writers; 10–25% by assignment; 25–50% by authors who are new to the magazine; 10–25% by previously unpublished writers. Receives 10–25 unsolicited manuscripts monthly.

Submissions Guidelines and theme list available at website. Send complete manuscript with cover letter, author biography, and bibliography for nonfiction. Accepts email to mylightmagazine@msn.com (Microsoft Word attachments). Accepts simultaneous submissions if identified. Also accepts résumés for consideration of contract work. Response time varies.
- *Articles:* Ages 4–6, 300–400 words; ages 7–9, 400–600 words; ages 10–12, 600–900 words. Informational. Topics: prayer, Jesus's teachings and parables, the rosary, Mary, the saints, Holy Mass, creation, spiritual experiences, respect for parents and teachers, Catholic values, the Beatitudes.
- *Fiction:* 300–900 words. Stories that represent Christian lifestyles and morals. Genres: contemporary, inspirational.
- *Depts/columns:* Crafts, 350–500 words. Bible stories, 500–700 words.
- *Artwork:* Digital images at 300 dpi. Illustrations.
- *Other:* Poetry, to 15 lines.

Sample Issue 38 pages. Little advertising. Sample copy available at website.
- "Garden of Dreams," by Jocelyn Ferrer. Working hard to make your dreams come true.
- "Brothers Are Better," by Samantha Bell. A boy learns to appreciate his little sister.

Rights and Payment One-time electronic rights. No payment. PDF version of magazine to contributors upon request.

National Geographic Kids

National Geographic Society, 1145 17th Street NW, Washington, DC 20036-4688. http://kids.nationalgeographic.com

Executive Editor: Julie Agnone

This magazine proves that learning is fun. It offers factually accurate, informative articles in an entertaining and lively format that makes readers want to learn more. Experienced writers who can convey the excitement and wonder of a new discovery, little-known scientific fact, or surprising bit of history are welcome to submit their ideas with examples of their previously published work. ■ **Circulation** 1.3 million ■ **Audience** 6–14 years ■ **Frequency** 10 times a year

Freelance Potential Publishes 20–25 freelance submissions yearly: 85% written by nonstaff writers; 30% by authors new to the magazine; 1% by previously unpublished writers. Receives 30 queries monthly.

Submissions Guidelines available. Query with clips. Accepts hard copy. SASE. Responds if interested.
- *Articles:* Word lengths vary. Informational articles. Topics: geography, archaeology, paleontology, history, entertainment, nature, the environment.
- *Depts/columns:* Word lengths vary. News and trends, amazing animals, fun facts.
- *Other:* Puzzles, games, jokes.

Sample Issue 32 pages. Advertising. Sample copy available.
- "Tiny Frogs Ring in Spring," by Lyssa White. An introduction to spring peepers.
- "Discovered: Oldest Writing in the New World," by Catherine Clarke Fox. Stone blocks discovered in Mexico contain writing from 3,000 years ago.

Rights and Payment All rights. Written material, payment rates vary. Artwork, $100–$600. Pays on acceptance. Provides 3–5 contributor's copies.

National Geographic Little Kids

National Geographic Society, 1145 17th Street NW, Washington, DC 20036-4688
http://littlekids.nationalgeographic.com

Executive Editor: Julie Agnone

Parents and children are meant to enjoy *National Geographic Little Kids* together. Each issue offers stories, articles, and activities that entertain and inform children about the world in which they live. It is interested in material that will capture the imagination of budding scientists and explorers. Most of the material is assigned. ■ **Circulation** Unavailable ■ **Audience** 3–6 years ■ **Frequency** 6 times a year

Freelance Potential Publishes 5 freelance submissions yearly: 10% written by nonstaff writers.

Submissions Most articles are assigned. Query with résumé. Accepts hard copy. SASE. Responds if interested.
- *Articles:* Word lengths vary. Informational. Topics: nature, animals, the environment, science, history, world cultures.
- *Fiction:* Word lengths vary. Rebus stories about animals and other cultures.
- *Depts/columns:* Basic science experiments, craft projects, kid-friendly recipes.
- *Other:* Activities, games, jokes.

Sample Issue 24 pages. No advertising. Sample copy available.
- "Blue Goo." An easy science experiment to make fun blue goo.
- "A Giant Panda Grows Up." Photos and easy text tell about a baby panda's day.

Rights and Payment All rights. Written material, payment rates vary. Pays on acceptance. Provides 3–5 contributor's copies.

Nature Friend

4253 Woodcock Lane, Dayton, VA 22821. www.naturefriendmagazine.com

Editor: Kevin Shank

Nature-themed articles, stories, and activities that foster children's awareness of God are published in this magazine, produced by a conservative Christian publisher. Its mission is to provide a place for children to simply enjoy what God has made without being directed toward a spiritual application. ■ **Circulation** 15,000 ■ **Audience** 8–16 years ■ **Frequency** Monthly

Freelance Potential Publishes 50 freelance submissions yearly: 20% written by nonstaff writers; 10% by authors who are new to the magazine; 5% by previously unpublished writers. Receives 40–60 unsolicited manuscripts monthly.

Submissions Guidelines available at website. Send complete manuscript with word count and bibliography. Accepts hard copy and email to editor@naturefriendmagazine.com (Word attachments). SASE. Response time varies.
- *Articles:* 500–800 words. Informational, how-to, profiles, personal experience. Topics: science, nature, wildlife, astronomy.
- *Fiction:* 300–900 words. Genres: adventure, nature.
- *Depts/columns:* 100–450 words. Seasonal, activities, science experiments.
- *Artwork:* High-resolution digital images with accompanying contact prints.
- *Other:* Nature-related puzzles, games.

Sample Issue 24 pages. No advertising. Sample copy available at website.
- "Green Digging Machine," by Cletus Burkholder. All about the Carolina sphinx moth larva.
- "Cold Hands and Warm Heart," by Caroline Coon. Camping in the La Plata Mountains in Colorado.

Rights and Payment First rights. Written material, 5¢ a word. Artwork, $25–$75 per photo. Pays on publication. Provides 1 contributor's copy.

The New Era

50 East North Temple Street, Room 2420, Salt Lake City, UT 84150-3220. www.newera.lds.org

Managing Editor: Brittany Beattie

Full of inspirational articles and profiles, this magazine is written for young adult members of the Church of Jesus Christ of Latter-day Saints. It seeks submissions that depict the way God works in the lives of teens, and articles that deal with how youth are adapting in wholesome ways to the use of new technology. ■ **Circulation** 230,000 ■ **Audience** YA ■ **Frequency** Monthly

Freelance Potential Publishes 50 freelance submissions yearly: 40% written by nonstaff writers; 5% by authors new to the magazine; 5% by previously unpublished writers. Receives 112 unsolicited manuscripts monthly.

Submissions Guidelines available at website. Send complete manuscript. Accepts hard copy and email to newera@ldschurch.org. SASE. Responds in 2 months.
- *Articles:* Word lengths vary. Informational, self-help, profiles, personal experience, interviews. Topics: Gospel messages, religion, social issues, missionary work, family relationships, testimonies, humor, Scripture.
- *Depts/columns:* Word lengths vary. News items, events, and church activities for youth.
- *Artwork:* Digital images at 300 dpi; color transparencies.
- *Other:* Poetry, to 30 lines. Submit seasonal material 1 year in advance.

Sample Issue 50 pages. No advertising. Sample copy available at website.
- "Like Sweet Milk," by Yolanda Morales Posadas. A young woman finds happiness through God and the church.
- "Breaking New Ground," by Breanna Bennet Olaveson. The building of a new temple helped the author strengthen her faith.

Rights and Payment All rights. Written material, 3¢–12¢ a word. Pays on acceptance. Provides 2 contributor's copies.

New Moon Girls

P.O. Box 161287, Duluth, MN 55816. www.newmoon.com

Executive Editor: Helen Cordes

Created by girls for girls, *New Moon Girls* is dedicated to helping readers discover and honor their true selves. It presents reader-created material created by girls along with occasional adult-written articles and fiction, all designed to speak to the thinking girl. Articles that relate to a planned theme have the best chance of acceptance. ■ **Circulation** 15,000 ■ **Audience** 8+ years ■ **Frequency** 6 times a year

Freelance Potential Publishes 200 freelance submissions yearly: 95% written by nonstaff writers; 95% by authors new to the magazine; 90% by previously unpublished writers. Receives 60 unsolicited manuscripts monthly.

Submissions Guidelines and theme list available at website. Send complete manuscript. Accepts email to submissions@newmoon.com (no attachments). Accepts simultaneous submissions if identified. Responds in 6 months only if interested.
■ *Articles:* 300–1,200 words. Informational, profiles, interviews. Topics: activism, school, fitness, recreation, science, technology, social and multicultural issues.
■ *Fiction:* 900–1,600 words. Empowering stories about girls.
■ *Depts/columns:* 600 words. Herstory, Women's Work, Last Words.

Sample Issue 32 pages. No advertising. Sample copy available at website.
■ "Positive about Pimples," by Claire McCartney. How to prevent and treat acne.
■ "Can We Talk?" by Virginia Harness. Advice on how to speak up when it's difficult.

Rights and Payment All rights. No payment. Provides 3 conributor's copies.

New York Times Upfront

Scholastic Inc., 557 Broadway, New York, NY 10012-3999. www.upfrontmagazine.com

Editor: Elliot Rebhun

High school students learn about current events and the world around them through *New York Times Upfront*, which takes articles about national and international events from the *New York Times* and combines them with profiles of newsworthy young adults and essays by teens. It also includes a teachers' edition to guide classroom discussions. Because most of the material comes from the *New York Times*, it doesn't accept much freelance work. ■ **Circulation** 300,000 ■ **Audience** 14–18 years ■ **Frequency** 14 times a year

Freelance Potential Publishes 2 freelance submissions yearly: 10% written by nonstaff writers; 10% by authors new to the magazine. Receives 12 queries monthly.

Submissions Guidelines available. Editorial calendar available at website. Query with résumé and clips. Accepts hard copy. Availability of artwork improves chance of acceptance. SASE. Responds in 2–4 weeks if interested.
■ *Articles:* 500–1,200 words. Informational, profiles, interviews. Topics: current events, politics, history, media, technology, social issues, careers, the arts, the environment, multicultural and ethnic issues.
■ *Depts/columns:* Word lengths vary. Essays by teens, opinion, news briefs, trends.
■ *Artwork:* Color prints or transparencies.
■ *Other:* Cartoons.

Sample Issue Sample copy available at website.
■ "The New Face of America," by Susan Saulny. An look at the country's changing racial identity.
■ "Egypt: What Now?" by Patricia Smith. What current events in Egypt may mean to the U.S.

Rights and Payment All rights. All material, payment rates vary. Pays on publication.

Odyssey

Cobblestone Publishing, 30 Grove Street, Suite C, Peterborough, NH 03458. www.odysseymagazine.com

Senior Editor: Elizabeth E. Lindstrom

Budding scientists are the audience for this magazine that combines fascinating articles, challenging activities, poetry, and short stories on science, math, and technology themes. A specific need is science-related or science fiction short stories that correspond to an upcoming theme. ■ **Circulation** 25,000 ■ **Audience** 9–14 years ■ **Frequency** 9 times a year

Freelance Potential Publishes 60 freelance submissions yearly: 70% written by nonstaff writers; 25% by authors new to the magazine; 2% by previously unpublished writers. Receives 25 queries monthly.

Submissions Guidelines and theme list available at website. Query with cover letter stating subject and word length, 1-page outline, bibliography, interview source list, and writing sample. Prefers hard copy; will accept email to blindstrom@caruspub.com. SASE. Responds if interested.
■ *Articles:* 750–900 words. Sidebars, 200–500 words. Informational, biographies, interviews. Topics: math, science, technology.
■ *Fiction:* 1,000 words. Genres: science fiction, retold legends, science-themed stories.
■ *Depts/columns:* 400–600 words. Place, Media, People to Discover.
■ *Artwork:* B/W and color prints.
■ *Other:* Activities, to 700 words. Critical-thinking activities, experiments, projects.

Sample Issue 50 pages. No advertising. Sample copy available at website.
■ "Electronic Textiles," by Kathiann M. Kowalski. Scientists are fashioning fabric into electronics.
■ "Emily's Smart New Clothes," by Zareb MacPherson. Young peoples' futuristic clothes.

Rights and Payment All rights. Written material, 20¢–25¢ a word. Artwork, payment rates vary. Pays on publication. Provides 2 contributor's copies.

ONCOURSE

General Council of the Assemblies of God, 1445 North Boonville Avenue, Springfield, MO 65802-1894. www.oncourse.ag.org

Editor: Amber Weigand-Buckley

On Course is published by the National Youth Ministry of the Assemblies of God. Its mission is to empower teens to grow in a real-life relationship with Christ. It looks for fresh voices that can convey the Word of God in language that teen readers can relate to. All articles are assigned, and *On Course* does not accept unsolicited manuscripts. Writers are invited to submit an audition manuscript for evaluation. ■ **Circulation** 155,000 ■ **Audience** 12–18 years ■ **Frequency** Quarterly

Freelance Potential Publishes 32 freelance submissions yearly: 95% written by nonstaff writers; 40% by authors new to the magazine; 30% by previously unpublished writers.

Submissions Guidelines available at website. All work is assigned. To be considered, send sample article that would fit magazine target audience and style—600-800 words with author bio including church involvement. Prefers email submissions to oncourse@ag.org. SASE. Response time varies.
■ *Articles:* To 800 words. Informational, how-to, profiles, humor, personal experience. Topics: social issues, music, health, religion, sports, careers, college, multicultural issues.
■ *Fiction:* To 800 words. Genres: contemporary, humorous, multicultural, sports.
■ *Depts/columns:* Word lengths vary. Profiles, brief news items.

Sample Issue 16 pages. Advertising.
■ "Bucking Illegitimate Shame," by Ann Vande Zande. Embracing God's love over negative social and media influences.
■ "Beckah Shae: Destiny," by Sarah Childs. Review of artist's latest album.

Rights and Payment First and electronic rights. Payment rates vary. Payment policy varies. Provides 5 contributor's copies.

Our Little Friend

Pacific Press Publishing, P.O. Box 5353, Nampa, ID 83653-5353. www.ourlittlefriend.com

Editor: Aileen Andres Sox

Stories and Bible lessons for children in Seventh-day Adventist Sabbath school are published in this magazine. Devotionals are also featured. An ongoing need is for read-aloud stories with messages of Christian love. All material must be consistent with the teachings of the Seventh-day Adventist church. ■ **Circulation** 35,000 ■ **Audience** 1–5 years ■ **Frequency** Weekly

Freelance Potential Publishes 52 freelance submissions yearly: 20% written by nonstaff writers; 10% by authors new to the magazine; 10% by previously unpublished writers. Receives 20 unsolicited manuscripts monthly.

Submissions Guidelines available at website. Send complete manuscript. Prefers email submissions to ailsox@pacificpress.com (Word or RTF attachments); accepts hard copy. SASE. Responds in 4 months.
- *Articles:* 500–650 words. Devotionals, Bible lessons, true stories that teach Christian values. Topics: school, family, faith, love.
- *Fiction:* 500–650 words. Genres: contemporary, inspirational, stories about faith and God's love.
- *Other:* Submit seasonal material 7 months in advance.

Sample Issue 8 pages. No advertising. Sample copy available at website.
- "Mac's Painful Lesson," by Linda Porter Carlyle. Story about kids' injuries and Jesus' suffering.
- "Money Troubles," by Linda Porter Carlyle. A girl learns what money means to people without it

Rights and Payment One-time rights. Written material, $25–$50. Pays on acceptance. Provides 3 contributor's copies.

Owl

Bayard Press Canada, 10 Lower Spadina Avenue, Suite 400, Toronto, Ontario M5V 2Z2 Canada. www.owlkids.com

Submissions Editor

Owl serves Canadian children with timely, reliable, and relevant information on the topics and issues that concern them. The magazine presents informational articles, quirky facts, and fun puzzles and activities regarding everything from sports and the environment to pop culture and peer relationships. ■ **Circulation** 104,000 ■ **Audience** 9–13 years ■ **Frequency** 9 times a year

Freelance Potential Publishes 1–3 freelance submissions yearly: 60% written by nonstaff writers; 10% by authors who are new to the magazine; 5% by previously unpublished writers.

Submissions Guidelines available. Send résumé only. No queries or unsolicited manuscripts. Accepts hard copy. Responds if interested.
- *Articles:* 500–1,000 words. Informational. Topics: adventure, sports, entertainment, pop culture, social issues, relationships.

Sample Issue Advertising. Sample copy available.
- "How Solar Power Works." Solar energy facts.
- "Should You Buy Green School Supplies?" Choosing and making your own eco-friendly products.

Rights and Payment All rights. Articles, $200–$500. Pays on acceptance. Provides 1 contributor's copy.

Partners

Christian Light Publications, P.O. Box 1212, Harrisonburg, VA 22803-1212. www.clp.org

Editor: Etta G. Martin

Partners is filled with short stories, articles, poems, and puzzles that reflect the Mennonite faith. Used

as a Sunday school take-home piece, it is printed in four weekly sections. Submissions should have an age-appropriate spiritual lesson, and they should correlate with an upcoming issue theme.
■ **Circulation** 6,923 ■ **Audience** 9–14 years ■ **Frequency** Monthly

Freelance Potential Publishes 200–500 freelance submissions yearly: 98% written by nonstaff writers; 5% by authors new to the magazine; 5% by previously unpublished writers. Receives 17–25 unsolicited manuscripts monthly.

Submissions Guidelines and theme list available. Send complete manuscript. Prefers email submissions to partners@clp.org; will accept hard copy. Accepts simultaneous submissions if identified. SASE. Responds in 6 weeks.
■ *Articles:* 200–800 words. Informational. Topics: Bible customs, nature, church history and teachings.
■ *Fiction:* 400–1,600 words. Stories that emphasize Mennonite beliefs and biblical standards.
■ *Depts/columns:* Word puzzles, activities. Poetry; no free verse. Submit seasonal material 6 months in advance.

Sample Issue 16 pages. No advertising. Sample copy available.
■ "Love in Action," by Mrs. Silas Bowman. Story of a girl who learns that loving gestures are the best ways to maintain friendships.

Rights and Payment First, reprint, or multiple-use rights. Articles and fiction, 4¢–6¢ a word. Poetry, 50¢–75¢ a line. Activities, payment rates vary. Pays on acceptance. Provides 1 contributor's copy.

Passport

WordAction Publishing, 2923 Troost Avenue, Kansas City, MO 64109. www.wordaction.com

Assistant Editor: Laura Lohberger

Passport is a weekly Sunday school take-home paper for Church of the Nazarene religion students. It offers fun features, devotionals, and Bible lessons for middle elementary and preteen students. It is not currently accepting submissions from freelancers. Check the website for any changes to this policy.
■ **Circulation** 55,000 ■ **Audience** 8–12 years ■ **Frequency** Weekly

Freelance Potential Publishes 30 freelance submissions yearly: 90% written by nonstaff writers; 20% by authors who are new to the magazine; 20% by previously unpublished writers. Receives 20 queries and manuscripts monthly.

Submissions Guidelines and theme list available. Not accepting submissions at this time.
■ *Articles:* "Survival Guide," 400–500 words. "Curiosity Island," 200–300 words.

Sample Issue Sample copy available.

Rights and Payment Multi-use rights. Articles, $15–$25. Pays on publication. Provides 1 contributor's copy.

Plays

P.O. Box 600160, Newton, MA 02460. www.playsmag.com

Editor: Elizabeth Preston

Subtitled *The Drama Magazine for Young People*, the sole focus of this magazine is plays for elementary, middle, and high school students. If features original material as well as adaptations of well-known plays. It is looking for plays that are easy to produce, secular, and wholesome, and that address issues relevant to the actors' age groups. Plays must be simple to produce, with minimal requirements for costumes, sets, and lighting. ■ **Circulation** 3,000 ■ **Audience** 6–17 years
■ **Frequency** 7 times a year

Freelance Potential Publishes 75 freelance submissions yearly: 100% written by nonstaff writers; 50% by authors new to the magazine; 25% by previously unpublished writers. Receives 20 unsolicited manuscripts monthly.

Submissions Guidelines available at website. Send complete manuscript with production notes, number of characters, playing time, costumes, properties, settings, and stage needs. Accepts hard copy. SASE. Responds in 1 month.
- *Fiction:* Skits, 8–10 pages; lower grades, 6–10 pages; middle grades, 12–15 pages; junior and senior high school, 15–20 pages. Genres: patriotic, historical, biographical drama; mystery; melodrama; fairy tales; folktales; comedy; farce.
- *Other:* Submit seasonal material 4 months in advance.

Sample Issue 64 pages. Little advertising. Sample copy available.
- "Stirring Up Trouble," by Tracy Wells. *Much Ado About Nothing* retold in a modern high school.
- "Bee at Your Best," by Dorothy Brandt Marra. Friends work together to pollinate plants.

Rights and Payment All rights. Payment rates vary. Pays on acceptance. Provides 1 contributor's copy.

Pockets

The Upper Room, 1908 Grand Avenue, P.O. Box 340004, Nashville, TN 37203-0004. www.upperroom.org/pockets, http://pockets.upperroom.org

Editor: Lynn W. Gilliam

Through articles, stories, poetry, scripture readings, and activities, this magazine emphasizes that God loves us and calls us into community in order to experience that love. As a devotional magazine for children, it caters to readers from a variety of denominations, cultures, and family backgrounds. Submissions don't need to be overtly religious, but they do need to help young children grow in their faith. ■ **Circulation** 58,000 ■ **Audience** 8–12 years ■ **Frequency** 11 times a year

Freelance Potential Publishes 165–200 freelance submissions yearly: 70% written by nonstaff writers. Receives 50–100 unsolicited manuscripts monthly.

Submissions Guidelines and theme list available at website. Send complete manuscript. Accepts hard copy. SASE. Responds in 2 months.
- *Articles:* 400–1,000 words. Informational, profiles, personal experience. Topics: multicultural and community issues, individuals whose lives reflect their Christian commitment.
- *Fiction:* 600–1,000 words. Genres: inspirational, real-life, stories that demonstrate Christian values.
- *Depts/columns:* Word lengths vary. Scripture readings and lessons, recipes.
- *Artwork:* Color prints; digital images to 300 dpi.
- *Other:* Poetry, to 20 lines. Puzzles, activities, games.

Sample Issue 48 pages. No advertising. Sample copy available.
- "Have a Go." Lily wants to be class president, but needs a friend's encouragement.
- "My Not So Needy Family." A family struggling financially finds a simpler lifestyle.

Rights and Payment First and second rights. Articles and fiction, 14¢ a word. Poetry, activities, games, $25+. Pays on acceptance. Provides 3–5 contributor's copies.

Preschool Playhouse

Urban Ministries,1551 Regency Court, Calumet City, IL 60409. www.urbanministries.com

Editor of Children's Resources: Janet Grier

This is a colorful take-home paper designed to complement Sunday school curricula. It features Bible stories, short fiction, and fun articles that promote family and church values—each written specifically for an African American audience. ■ **Circulation** 50,000–100,000 ■ **Audience** 2–5 years

- **Frequency** Quarterly, with weekly editions

Freelance Potential Assigns 12–120 freelance pieces yearly: 25% written by nonstaff writers; 25% by authors who are new to the magazine; 10% by previously unpublished writers. Receives 1–10 queries monthly.

Submissions Guidelines available. All work is assigned. Send résumé with clips or writing samples. Accepts email to jgrier@urbanministries.com (Word attachments). Response time varies.
- *Articles:* Word lengths vary. Informational, inspirational, Bible lessons. Topics: faith, relationships, God.
- *Fiction:* Word lengths vary. Genres: inspirational.

Sample Issue 52 pages. Little advertising. Sample copy available.

Rights and Payment All rights. Written material, $125. Pays on publication. Provides contributor's copies.

Primary Street

Urban Ministries, P.O. Box 436987, Chicago, IL 60643-6987. www.urbanministries.com

Editor of Children's Resources: Janet Grier

Primary Street, a take-home paper supplementing Sunday school or religious education programs, combines Bible stories and lessons with religious-themed puzzles and other activities. The main article in each weekly issue focuses on instilling specific knowledge about God, with the hope that this will lead to changes in behavior and attitude among the children it serves. All material is assigned. ■ **Circulation** 50,000–100,000 ■ **Audience** 6–8 years ■ **Frequency** Quarterly, with weekly issues

Freelance Potential Publishes 12–120 freelance pieces yearly: 80–90% written by nonstaff writers; 25% by authors who are new to the magazine; 25% by previously unpublished writers. Receives 1–10 queries monthly.

Submissions Guidelines available. All material is assigned. Query with résumé and writing samples. Accepts email to jgrier@urbanministries.com (Word attachments). Response time varies.
- *Articles:* Word lengths vary. Informational, how-to, personal experience, Bible lessons. Topics: religion, Christian values, nature, the environment, animals, pets, crafts, hobbies, African history, multicultural and ethnic subjects, social issues.
- *Fiction:* Word lengths vary. Genres: inspirational, religious.
- *Other:* Bible verses. Puzzles, games, activities.

Sample Issue 4 pages. Little advertising. Sample copy available.

Rights and Payment All rights. Articles, $125. Other material, payment rates vary. Pays on publication. Provides contributor's copies.

Primary Treasure

Pacific Press Publishing, P.O. Box 5353, Nampa, ID 83653-5353. www.primarytreasure.com

Editor: Aileen Andres Sox

Primary Treasure publishes positive, inspiring stories for young children from a Seventh-day Adventist perspective. It also features Bible stories, and stories about children in contemporary Christian settings that help kids learn about faith, God, and making the right decisions. All material submitted must be consistent with Seventh-day Adventist beliefs and practices, but the tone must not be preachy. ■ **Circulation** 250,000 ■ **Audience** 7–9 years ■ **Frequency** Weekly

Freelance Potential Publishes 52 freelance submissions yearly: 10% written by nonstaff writers; 30% by authors new to the magazine; 10% by previously unpublished writers. Receives 20 unsolicited manuscripts monthly.

Submissions Guidelines available at website. Send complete manuscript. Prefers email submissions to ailsox@pacificpress.com (Word or RTF attachments); will accept hard copy. Accepts simultaneous submissions if identified. SASE. Responds in 4 months.
- *Fiction:* 600–1,000 words (4–5 pages). Genres: contemporary, religious, inspirational.
- *Other:* Submit seasonal material 7 months in advance.

Sample Issue 16 pages. No advertising. Sample copy available.
- "Jonahs by Jet," by Melinda Skau. A boy comes to terms with his family's opportunity to become missionaries in Africa.
- "Jungle Missionaries," by Patsy Current. Family members anticipate new adventures as missionaries.

Rights and Payment One-time rights. Written material, $25–$50. Pays on acceptance. Provides 3 contributor's copies.

Rainbow Rumpus

P.O. Box 6881, Minneapolis, MN 55406. www.rainbowrumpus.org

Editor in Chief: Beth Wallace

This online literary magazine is geared to children being raised in lesbian, gay, bisexual, or transgendered (LGBT) families. It looks for stories for early readers through teens that celebrate diversity and the LGBT community. The editors are primarily interested in stories that are written from the point of view of children with LGBT parents or other family members who are connected to the LGBT community. ■ **Hits per month** 9,000 ■ **Audience** 4–18 years ■ **Frequency** Monthly

Freelance Potential Publishes 40 freelance submissions yearly: 40% written by nonstaff writers; 10% by authors who are new to the magazine. Receives 12 queries monthly.

Submissions Guidelines available at website. Query via contact form at website. Responds in 2 weeks.
- *Articles:* Staff-written.
- *Fiction:* For ages 4–12, 800–2,500 words. Teen stories, to 5,000 words. Genres vary.
- *Depts/columns:* Staff-written
- *Other:* Poetry, no line limits.

Sample Issue Sample copy available at website.
- "What Weddings Need," by Amy E. Brandt. Children play dress-up at day care and learn that weddings can take many forms.
- "Knitting the Family," by Rene Ohana. A teen girl and her step-grandmother bond.

Rights and Payment First North American electronic and anthology rights. Fiction, $75. Poetry, payment rates vary. Pays on publication.

Ranger Rick

National Wildlife Federation, 1100 Wildlife Center Drive, Reston, VA 20190-5362. www.nwf.org/rangerrick

Editor: Mary Dalheim

Since 1967 this magazine has been featuring educational yet engaging articles and activities that teach readers about animals and nature, and instill respect for the natural world. It works mostly with staff writers; however, prospective writers can submit their résumé and clips to be considered for assignments. ■ **Circulation** 560,000 ■ **Audience** 7–12 years ■ **Frequency** 10 times a year

Freelance Potential Publishes few freelance submissions yearly.

Submissions All material is assigned. Send résumé and clips only. No queries or unsolicited manuscripts. Accepts hard copy. SASE. Response time varies.
- *Articles:* 900 words. Informational. Topics: animals, nature, preservation, the environment.
- *Depts/columns:* Word lengths vary. Nature news, animal facts.
- *Other:* Games.

Sample Issue 40 pages. No advertising. Sample copy available at website.
- "Frogs," by Kathy Kranking. All about frogs.
- "Horses of a Different Stripe," by Elizabeth Schlechert. The endangered Grevy's zebras.

Rights and Payment Rights vary. Written material, payment rates vary. Pays on acceptance. Provides 2 contributor's copies.

Rangers Now

General Council of the Assemblies of God, 1445 North Boonville Avenue, Springfield, MO 65802-1894. www.royalrangers.ag.org

Editor: John Hicks

The official publication of the National Royal Rangers program of the Assemblies of God, this magazine offers boys of all ages articles designed to foster a closer relationship with Jesus Christ. It focuses on leadership skills, fitness and health, nature, the environment, and outdoor activities as ways to grow in that relationship. It also publishes personal testimonies. *Rangers Now* appears in six different editions, one for each age group in the program and one for leaders. It is not currently accepting submissions from outside sources. ■ **Circulation** 87,000 ■ **Audience** Boys ■ **Frequency** Once a year

Freelance Potential Receives 60 queries yearly.

Submissions Not currently open to submissions.
- *Articles:* 1,000 words. Informational, how-to, personal experience. Topics: faith, Christianity, the outdoors, leadership skills, health and fitness, nature, the environment.
- *Depts/columns:* Word lengths vary. Projects.

Sample Issue Sample copy available.

Rights and Payment First or all rights. Written material, payment rates vary. Pays on publication. Provides 2 contributor's copies.

Recreational Cheerleading Magazine

Recreational Sports Media, 2319 FM 1794 W, Beckville, TX 75631. www.reccheermagazine.com

Editor: Valerie Ninemire

Launched in late 2011, this the only magazine dedicated solely to recreational cheerleaders, their coaches, and their parents. It reports on Pop Warner, scholastic, and all-star cheerleading throughout the country, and shares information on stunts, training, safety, coaching, and fundraising. ■ **Circulation** Unavailable ■ **Audience** Young cheerleaders, coaches, parents ■ **Frequency** Quarterly

Freelance Potential Unavailable.

Submissions Contact valerie@recsportsmedia or info@reccheermag.com for information.
- *Articles:* Word lengths vary. Informational, how-to, profiles. Topics: school and extracurricular cheerleading, coaching, training, techniques, stunting, fundraising, safety.
- *Depts/columns:* Word lengths vary. Program profiles, health, fitness.

Sample Issue Unavailable.

Rights and Payment Unavailable.

RobinAge

504, Shah and Nahar Industrial Estate, Dr. E Moses Road, Worli, Mumbai, 400018, India.
www.robinage.com

Managing Editor: Cherry Divesha-Shethia

This English-language newspaper for children is published in India and provides a way for children all over the world, particularly those of Indian descent, to understand current events and share the love of learning. Readers will also find articles on entertainment, sports, science, history, and cultures. Two areas of India are profiled each week. Twenty-five percent of each issue is written by children, allowing them to express their creativity and opinions. *RobinAge* won a U.S. Parents' Choice Award for quality. ■ **Circulation** Unavailable ■ **Audience** 6–15 years ■ **Frequency** Weekly

Freelance Potential The company is looking for more creative talent.

Submissions Contact for more information at editor@robinage.com
■ *Articles:* Word lengths vary. Informational, profiles. Topics: current events, history, science, pop culture, the environment, multicultural issues.
■ *Depts/columns:* World News, Young Minds, Newsmaker, Experiment.

Sample Issue 16 pages. Sample copy available at website.
■ "Chanting Aloud," by Shweta Ganesh Kumar. A profile of Yogyakarta, a land of many faiths.
■ "Let's Get Brainy." 10 things you may not know about the workings of the brain.

Rights and Payment Unavailable.

The Rock

Cook Communications Ministries, 4050 Lee Vance View, Colorado Springs, CO 80918.
www.davidccook.com

Editor: Doug Mauss

This weekly take-home paper for middle school-age students in religious education classes includes Bible stories, scripture lessons, inspirational stories, and articles that encourage readers to make the right choices. *The Rock* is mostly staff-written, but its editors occasionally assign work to freelancers. Currently it is not accepting any new résumés. ■ **Circulation** 35,000 ■ **Audience** Middle-grade students ■ **Frequency** Quarterly

Freelance Potential Publishes 2–3 freelance submissions yearly: 10% written by nonstaff writers; 20% by previously unpublished writers.

Submissions Guidelines available at website. Not currently accepting résumés for assignments.
■ *Articles:* Word lengths vary. Informational, how-to, personal experience, Bible lessons. Topics vary.
■ *Fiction:* Word lengths vary. Genres: inspirational.

Sample Issue Sample copy available.

Rights and Payment Rights negotiable. Written material, word lengths and payment rates vary. Pays on acceptance. Provides 1 contributor's copy.

Sesame Street Magazine

One Lincoln Plaza, New York, NY 10023. www.sesameworkshop.org

Editor in Chief: Rebecca Herman

Designed for very young children, this magazine features a colorful array of stories, games, and activities. Each issue uses preschoolers' favorite *Sesame Street* characters to teach numbers, letters, and other basic concepts. *Sesame Street Magazine* does not accept queries or unsolicited manuscripts; most material is written in-house. Writers interested in working for the magazine may send a résumé with published clips. ■ **Circulation** 650,000 ■ **Audience** 2–5 years ■ **Frequency** 11 times a year

Freelance Potential 100% staff-written or by assignment.

Submissions All material is written in-house or by assignment. No queries or unsolicited manuscripts. Send résumé and published clips only. Accepts hard copy. SASE.
- *Articles:* Word lengths vary. Informational, factual. Topics: letters, numbers, learning concepts, animals.
- *Other:* Games, activities, coloring projects.

Sample Issue Sample copy available at website.
- "Animals at Play." An introduction to baby animals.
- "Do's and Don'ts." A rhyming activity that teaches the letter D.

Rights and Payment Rights vary. Written material, payment policy varies. Payment policy varies.

Seventeen

300 West 57th Street, 17th Floor, New York, NY 10019. www.seventeen.com

Editor

From fashion to friendship, and popularity to pop culture, this magazine speaks to girls who are looking for answers to the questions of the day. Fiction is offered as well. Writers should be tuned in to the trends, news, and interests of teen girls, as well as to the best way to get readers to tune in. Offer sound advice, but avoid any hint of preachiness. ■ **Circulation** 2 million ■ **Audience** Girls, 13–21 years ■ **Frequency** Monthly

Freelance Potential Publishes 20 freelance submissions yearly: 20% written by nonstaff writers; 40% by authors who are new to the magazine; 5% by previously unpublished writers. Receives 4 queries, 17 unsolicited manuscripts monthly.

Submissions Guidelines available. Query with outline and clips or writing samples for nonfiction. Send complete manuscript for fiction. Accepts hard copy (addressed to appropriate editor; consult masthead). Accepts simultaneous submissions if identified. SASE. Response time varies.
- *Articles:* 650–3,000 words. Informational, how-to, self-help, profiles, interviews, personal experience. Topics: relationships, dating, family issues, current events, social concerns, friendship, pop culture.
- *Fiction:* 1,000–3,000 words. Stories that feature female teenage experiences.
- *Depts/columns:* 500–1,000 words. Fashion, beauty, health, and fitness.
- *Other:* Submit seasonal material 6 months in advance.

Sample Issue 166 pages. Advertising. Sample copy available at newsstands.
- "Look Leaner and Taller." Style tricks that transform.
- "*Pretty Little Liars* Exclusive." A behind-the-scenes look at a popular television show.

Rights and Payment First rights. Written material, $1–$1.50 a word. Pays on acceptance.

Shameless

360A Bloor Street West, P.O. Box 68548, Toronto, Ontario M5S 1X1 Canada. www.shamelessmag.com

Editorial Director: Sheila Sampath

Teen girls and transgender youth in Canada have an alternative to the typical teen-zine. Instead of focusing on cute shoes and boys, *Shameless* offers inspiring articles on social justice and female empowerment. Topics covered include new media and the arts, technology, women's issues, and gender identity. This independent, grassroots publication is committed to empowering young writers, especially those from communities that are underrepresented in the mainstream media. ■ **Circulation** 3,000 ■ **Audience** Girls, YA ■ **Frequency** 3 times a year

Freelance Potential Publishes 25 freelance submissions each year: 30% written by nonstaff writers.

Submissions Guidelines available at website. Query with cover letter and clips. Prefers email queries to sheila@shamelessmag.com; will accept hard copy. SAE/IRC. Response time varies.
- *Articles:* 2,000 words. Informational, profiles, interviews. Topics: women's issues, feminism, activism, socio-political issues, arts and culture, technology.
- *Depts/columns:* News Flash, 200 words. Profiles of organizations, activists, and shameless individuals, 300–700 words. Essays, 800 words. Get-Up, alternative style guide, 300–500 words. Geek Chic, DIY, Sporting Goods, 800 words. Reviews, 100 words.
- *Fiction:* Word lengths vary. Short pieces of fiction or other creative writing.
- *Other:* Poetry.

Sample Issue Sample copy available at website.
- "The Sisterhood," by Allison Martell. Modern-day Canadian sororities and stereotypes.
- "Pant Strap," by Marta Balcewicz. How to make a fashionable, useful cycling pant strap.

Rights and Payment First and electronic rights. No payment.

Shine Brightly

P.O. Box 7259, Grand Rapids, MI 49510. www.gemsgc.org

Managing Editor: Kelli Ponstein

Published by GEMS Girls Clubs (Girls Everywhere Meeting the Savior), this magazine focuses on motivating, inspiring, and equipping girls to use their voices to "shine brightly" and change the world. It is looking for stories, articles, interviews, and activities that are fresh, that present the Christian life realistically, and that cause young readers to see how Christian beliefs apply to daily life. ■ **Circulation** 17,000 ■ **Audience** Girls, 9–14 years ■ **Frequency** 9 times a year

Freelance Potential Publishes 20 freelance submissions yearly: 25% written by nonstaff writers; 90% by authors new to the magazine; 15% by previously unpublished writers. Receives 10–25 unsolicited manuscripts monthly.

Submissions Guidelines and theme list available at website. Send complete manuscript. Accepts email to shinebrightly@gemsgc.org (no attachments). Accepts simultaneous submissions if identified. Responds in 2 months.
- *Articles:* 100–800 words. Informational, how-to, profiles, humor, personal experience. Topics: community service, contemporary social issues, family and friend relationships, peer pressure, animals, the arts, health and fitness, fashion.
- *Fiction:* 700–900 words. Genres: religious, contemporary, science fiction, romance, mystery, adventure.
- *Depts/columns:* Staff-written.
- *Artwork:* 5x7 or larger B/W or color prints.
- *Other:* Poetry. Puzzles, activities, cartoons.

Sample Issue 24 pages. No advertising. Sample copy available.
- "Diana Onyonyi Gets Inspired." A profile of a woman who raises money to create educational opportunities for girls in Nairobi.
- "Micah Road Mysteries." Story of a group of kids who help a woman find her missing jewelry.

Rights and Payment First, second, and simultaneous rights. Articles and fiction, 3¢–5¢ a word, to $35. Poetry, games, and puzzles, $5–$15. Other material, payment rates vary. Pays on publication. Provides 2 contributor's copies.

Simply You Magazine

P.O. Box 284, Phillips, WI 54555-0284. www.simplyyoumagazine.com

Submissions Editor

Teens are the primary focus for this online magazine, but it has began publishing material of interest to readers in their 20s and 30s, with the intent of "growing with the individual." The content of *Simply You* is centered around relationships and coming-of-age issues, as well as real-life teen and young adult stories. It also includes entertainment reviews. ■ **Hits per month** 10,000 ■ **Audience** YA ■ **Frequency** Updated regularly

Freelance Potential Publishes 20–40 freelance submissions yearly: 25% written by nonstaff writers; 50% by authors new to the magazine; 25% by previously unpublished writers. Receives 1–3 unsolicited manuscripts monthly.

Submissions Guidelines available at website. Send complete manuscript. Accepts hard copy and electronic submissions via website. Responds in 1–2 months.
■ *Articles:* Word lengths vary. Informational, inspirational, how-to, opinion, personal experience. Topics: social issues, relationships, coming of age, health.
■ *Fiction:* Word lengths vary. Genres: contemporary, realistic, coming-of-age.
■ *Other:* Poetry.

Sample Issue Sample copy available at website.
■ "The Desperate Optimism of a Fallback Girl," by Elisa G. A young woman's misadventures with guys.
■ "Facial Care Tips & Store." Skin care advice and suggested acne treatments.

Rights and Payment All rights. Written material, word lengths vary. No payment.

Sisterhood Agenda

16213 Spring Garden Street, St. John, VI 00830. www.sisterhoodagenda.com

Editor: Angela D. Coleman

This magazine is designed to empower and uplift women and girls of African descent through sisterhood, self-knowledge, self-development, and self-esteem. It is part of a global, nonprofit organization whose mission is to reach a historically at-risk and traditionally under-served population. It publishes mostly nonfiction articles, but works of fiction are also considered. ■ **Circulation** 500,000 ■ **Audience** 13+ years ■ **Frequency** Quarterly

Freelance Potential Publishes 100 freelance submissions yearly: 90% written by nonstaff writers; 90% by authors new to the magazine; 75% by previously unpublished writers. Receives 8+ unsolicited manuscripts monthly.

Submissions Guidelines and editorial calendar available at website. Send complete manuscript. Accepts email to acoleman@sisterhoodagenda.com (Word attachments). Availability of artwork improves chance of acceptance. Response time varies.
■ *Articles:* To 500 words. Informational, profiles, photo-essays. Topics: Africa, ancestry, heritage, history, current events, nutrition, music, fashion, beauty, self-esteem, fitness, technology, life skills, celebrities, community service.
■ *Fiction:* Word lengths vary. Genres: multicultural, ethnic, inspirational.
■ *Depts/columns:* First-person essays; to 300 words. News briefs, book reviews, hair tips, affirmations; word lengths vary.
■ *Artwork:* Digital images at 300 dpi.
■ *Other:* Poetry, to 15 lines.

Sample Issue 50 pages. Sample copy available.
■ "Haitian Women: The Backbone of Society," by Monica Montufar. The plight and strengths of Haitian women rebuilding after the earthquake.

■ "5 Ways To Be a Great Parent." A parenting primer that is heavy on love and support.

Rights and Payment One-time rights. No payment.

Skipping Stones

P.O. Box 3939, Eugene, OR 97403-0939. www.skippingstones.org

Editor: Arun N. Toké

Skipping Stones is a nonprofit literary and multicultural magazine that serves as a communications forum for children from different lands and backgrounds. Each issue features a mix of multicultural articles, stories, poems, and art, as well as a mix of material written by children and adults. Current needs include articles on nature and cultural awareness. ■ **Circulation** 2,500 ■ **Audience** 7–17 years ■ **Frequency** 5 times a year

Freelance Potential Publishes 175–200 freelance submissions yearly: 50–75% written by nonstaff writers; 75% by authors new to the magazine; 75–100% by previously unpublished writers. Receives 150–200 unsolicited manuscripts monthly.

Submissions Guidelines and editorial calendar available at website. Send complete manuscript with author information. Accepts hard copy and email to editor@skippingstones.org (Word attachments). Accepts simultaneous submissions if identified. Availability of artwork improves chance of acceptance. SASE. Responds in 3–4 months.
■ *Articles:* To 1,000 words. Informational, profiles, biography, photo-essays, interviews, humor, personal experience. Topics: cultural and religious celebrations, history, architecture, living abroad, family, careers, disabilities, sustainable living, social issues, social skills, nature, technology, parenting, activism, current events.
■ *Fiction:* To 1,000 words. Genres: contemporary, multicultural, coming-of-age, adventure, folktales.
■ *Depts/columns:* 100–200 words. Health issues, book reviews, school topics, Q&As.
■ *Artwork:* Color prints or transparencies; JPEG or TIFF images.
■ *Other:* Poetry by children, to 30 lines. Puzzles and games. Submit seasonal material 3–4 months in advance.

Sample Issue 36 pages. No advertising. Sample copy available.
■ "Viewing Problems as Opportunites," by Monique Rider. Advice for accepting life's adversites and how to make them into positive learning experiences.
■ "Joshua's Tree," by Virginia Kroll. Story of a girl who plants a tree she planted for the Jewish festival Tu Bishevat in honor of a newborn.

Rights and Payment First North American serial and non-exclusive reprint rights. No payment. Provides contributor's copies and discounts.

SLAP

High Speed Productions, 1303 Underwood Avenue, San Francisco, CA 94124. www.slapmagazine.com

Editor: Mark Whiteley

An online magazine dedicated to the sport, lifestyle, and attitude of skateboarding, *SLAP* provides users with a forum to exchange tricks, information, and techniques. It also profiles skaters and offers reviews of music and the latest gear. It is only interested in contributors who are in the skateboarding world themselves. ■ **Circulation** 200,000 ■ **Audience** YA ■ **Frequency** Updated daily

Freelance Potential Publishes 24 freelance submissions yearly: 40% written by nonstaff writers: 20% by previously unpublished writers.

Submissions Send complete manuscript. Accepts email to info@slapmagazine.com. Availability of artwork/video improves chance of acceptance. Responds in 2 months.

- *Articles:* Word lengths vary. Informational, how-to, profiles, interviews, personal experience. Topics: skateboarding techniques, equipment, competitions; music; art; pop culture.
- *Depts/columns:* Word lengths vary. Media reviews, interviews, gear, gossip, and skateboard tricks.
- *Artwork:* 35mm B/W negatives; color prints and transparencies.
- *Other:* Photo-essays, cartoons, contests.

Sample Issue Sample copy available at website.
- "S'mores: The Morning Benders," by Cameron Cuchulainn. An interview with a musical group.
- "Turf and Destroy Berkeley," by Stephen Morrison. Report on a skate shop's event.

Rights and Payment First rights. All material, payment rates vary. Pays on publication.

Sparkle!

P.O. Box 7259, Grand Rapids, MI 49510. www.gemsgc.org

Managing Editor: Kelli Ponstein

Published by GEMS (Girls Everywhere Meeting the Savior) Girls' Clubs, *Sparkle!* features articles, fiction, and activities that present Christian life realistically, and show its young readers how God's Word applies to their daily lives. Material should encourage readers to live as Christ would live, and to serve the needs of others. ■ **Circulation** 12,000 ■ **Audience** Girls, 6–9 years ■ **Frequency** 6 times a year

Freelance Potential Publishes 10–20 freelance submissions yearly: 20% written by nonstaff writers; 90% by authors new to the magazine; 90% by previously unpublished writers. Receives 10–25 unsolicited manuscripts monthly.

Submissions Guidelines and theme list available at website. Send complete manuscript. Accepts email submissions to sparkle@gemsgc.org (no attachments). Accepts simultaneous submissions if identified. Responds in 4–6 weeks.
- *Articles:* 100–400 words. Informational. Topics: animals, sports, music, musicians, famous people, interaction with family and friends, service projects, school work.
- *Fiction:* 100–400 words. Genres: Contemporary, adventure, mystery.
- *Other:* Poetry, 5–15 lines. Puzzles, games, recipes, party ideas, humor, cartoons, craft projects.

Sample Issue 16 pages. No advertising. Sample copy available.
- "Sensing God," by Lauri Modrzejewski. Encouragement to sense God's presence in nature.
- "Sharing Our Differences," by Hannah Joy. Two girls come to terms with their different abilities.

Rights and Payment Rights vary. Articles, $20. Other material, payment rates vary. Pays on publication. Provides 2 contributor's copies.

Spider

Cricket Magazine Group, 70 East Lake Street, Suite 300, Chicago, IL 60601. www.cricketmag.com, www.spidermagkids.com

Submissions Editor

This literary magazine for kids is committed to providing readers with high-quality literature, poetry, nonfiction, and activities to encourage a lifelong love of reading. Part of the Cricket Magazine Group, it is interested in humor, adventure, well-told stories, and engaging activities that will appeal to both boys and girls. ■ **Circulation** 45,000 ■ **Audience** 6–9 years ■ **Frequency** 9 times a year

Freelance Potential Publishes 12–120 freelance submissions yearly: 90% written by nonstaff writers; 35% by authors new to the magazine; 35% by previously unpublished writers. Receives 100–150 unsolicited manuscripts monthly.

Submissions Guidelines available at website. Send complete manuscript with word count and author résumé; include bibliography for nonfiction or retold folktales. Accepts hard copy. Accepts simultaneous submissions if identified. SASE. Responds in 6 months.
- *Articles:* 300–800 words. Informational, how-to, profiles, interviews. Topics: nature, animals, science, technology, history, multicultural issues, foreign cultures, the environment.
- *Fiction:* 300–1,000 words. Easy-to-read stories. Genres: realistic, historical, science fiction, humor, fantasy, fairy tales, folktales.
- *Other:* Poetry, to 20 lines. Recipes, crafts, puzzles, games, math and word activities.

Sample Issue 34 pages. No advertising. Sample copy available at website.
- "The Theater Cat," by Marilyn Helmer. Adventures of a very theatrical cat and his friends.
- "Are You a Pack Rat?" by Joan Unterberg. A description of the real pack rats—the desert rodents.

Rights and Payment Rights vary. Articles and fiction, to 25¢ a word. Poetry, to $3 a line. Pays on publication. Provides 2 contributor's copies.

Spirit

Sisters of St. Joseph of Carondelet, 1884 Randolph Avenue, St. Paul, MN 55105-1700. www.goodgroundpress.com

Editor: Joan Mitchell

Designed for a high school, Roman Catholic audience, *Spirit* seeks to help young people connect their life experiences with the Sunday Gospels. It publishes stories and articles about family and social issues, and about finding the holy in everyday life. The editors are particularly interested in stories about youth service projects, and those reflecting the cultural diversity of American Catholic children.
- **Circulation** 25,000 ■ **Audience** YA ■ **Frequency** 28 times a year

Freelance Potential Publishes 1–2 freelance submissions yearly: 25% written by nonstaff writers.

Submissions Theme list available at website. Query or send complete manuscript. Accepts hard copy and email to JMCSJ9@aol.com or julie@goodgroundpress.com. Response time varies.
- *Articles:* 1,100 words. Informational, personal experience. Topics: youth service projects, current events, global issues, social issues.
- *Fiction:* 1,100 words. Genres: contemporary, religious, inspirational, multicultural.

Sample Issue Sample copy available at website.
- "Only the Gold," by Pat Marzolf. The price of expecting perfection.
- "Wind from an Eagle's Wings," by Joan Mitchell. Report on a conference about combining Native and Catholic traditions.

Rights and Payment All rights. Articles and fiction, $300. Pays on publication.

Sporting Youth

P.O. Box 1137, Watkinsville, GA 30677. www.sportingyouthga.com

Editor: Rebecca Mobley

The goal of this magazine is to inspire children to get active. Geared to families living in northeast Georgia, its coverage includes local and professional sporting events, tips from coaches, and profiles of local athletes. It is distributed to area recreation departments, doctor's offices, and schools.
- **Circulation** 5,000 ■ **Audience** 10–18 years ■ **Frequency** 6 times a year

Freelance Potential Publishes 25 freelance submissions yearly: 50% written by nonstaff writers.

Submissions Query or complete manuscript. Accepts email submissions to mail@sporting-youthga.com. Responds in 1 month.

- *Articles:* Word lengths vary. Informational, profiles, interviews. Topics: sports, local athletes.
- *Depts/columns:* Word lengths vary. Opinion, training tips, local events.

Sample Issue 32 pages. Advertising. Sample copy available at website.
- "Second Chance," by Roger Clarkson. Profile of a paralyzed University of Georgia athlete.
- "Where Are They Now?" Interview with athlete and local councilman Brian Brodrick.

Rights and Payment One-time rights. No payment. Provides contributor's copies.

Sports Illustrated Kids

1271 Avenue of the Americas, 32nd Floor, New York, NY 10020. www.sikids.com

Managing Editor: Bob Der

This version of the popular sports magazine targets younger sports fans with articles on professional teams as well as amateur and student athletes. It covers all sports, including the ones that appeal to the younger set, such as skateboarding and BMX racing. It does not use freelancers often. The best chance to break in here is with a short, interesting item. ■ **Circulation** 1.1 million ■ **Audience** 8–14 years ■ **Frequency** Monthly

Freelance Potential Publishes 1–2 freelance submissions yearly: 3–5% written by nonstaff writers. Receives 3–4 queries and unsolicited manuscripts monthly.

Submissions Guidelines and editorial calendar available. Query or send complete manuscript. Accepts hard copy. SASE. Responds in 2 months.
- *Articles:* Lead articles and profiles, 500–700 words. Short features, 500–600 words. Informational, profiles, interviews. Topics: professional and aspiring athletes, sports, fitness, health, safety, hobbies, technology.
- *Depts/columns:* Word lengths vary. Event coverage, team and player profiles, news, pro tips, humor, video game reviews.
- *Other:* Poetry and artwork by children. Puzzles, games, trivia, comics, sports cards.

Sample Issue 56 pages. Advertising. Sample copy available.
- "Ultimate Fantasy Baseball Guide," by Michael Northrop and Rick Zuckerman. Players, rankings, and creating a winning fantasy team.
- "Feel-Good Sports Stories," by David Fischer. Inspirational stories from around the sports world.

Rights and Payment All rights. Articles, $100–$1,500. Depts/columns, payment rates vary. Pays on acceptance. Provides contributor's copies.

Stories for Children Magazine

54 East 490 South, Ivins, UT 84738. www.storiesforchildrenmagazine.org

Assistant Fiction Editor: Roxanne Werner, Assistant Nonfiction Editor: Irene Roth, Assistant Poetry Editor: Jamie DeMumbrum

This ezine publishes enlightening articles, short stories, poetry, and activities designed to strengthen children's interest in reading and academics. In addition to material by adults, it also publishes some work by children. It recently began publishing again after a short hiatus. Current needs include read-aloud stories and fiction for early readers and middle readers. ■ **Hits per issue** 6,000–10,000 ■ **Audience** 3–12 years ■ **Frequency** 9 times a year

Freelance Potential Publishes 225–450 freelance submissions yearly: 60–85% written by nonstaff writers; 75–100% by authors new to the magazine; 10–20% by previously unpublished writers. Receives 100–150 unsolicited manuscripts monthly.

Submissions Guidelines and editorial calendar available at website. Send complete manuscript with cover letter, résumé, and biography; include bibliography for nonfiction material. Accepts email to

FictionAsst@storiesforchildrenmagazine.org for fiction, PoetryAsst@storiesforchildrenmagazine.org for poetry and rebuses, NonfictionAsst@storiesforchildrenmagazine.org for nonfiction, or CAYEditor@ storiesforchildrenmagazine.org for crafts, puzzles, recipes, and activities (Word attachments or put material in body of email). Include title of submission, category, intended age group, and intended issue in subject line. Response time varies.

- *Articles:* Discovery (ages 3–6), 150–400 words. How and Why (ages 7–9), 400–800 words. Tell Me More (ages 10–12), 500–1,200 words. Informational. Topics: nature, animals, science, technology, the environment
- *Fiction:* Read aloud stories, 150–400 words. Rebus stories, to 250 words. Early readers, 400–800 words. Middle readers, 500–1,200 words. Genres: realistic fiction, humor, fantasy, fairy tales, fables, myths, mystery, science fiction.
- *Other:* Poetry, to 16 lines.

Sample Issue No advertising. Sample copy available.

- "Do You See the Moon?" by Ann Stallard. Lesson on the moon's phases and an activity using balls and a flashlight for demonstration.
- "A Thief in the Night," by Kara Hartz. A girl's elaborate plan to photograph the tooth fairy's visit.

Rights and Payment Rights vary. Payment rates vary. Payment policy varies.

Story Mates

Christian Light Publications, Inc., P.O. Box 1212, Harrisonburg, VA 22803-1212. www.clp.org

Editor: Crystal Shank

This publication is used in Sunday schools and as a take-home paper for after-church reflection. Containing stories that correspond to lessons and conform to the conservative Mennonite doctrine, *Story Mates* is geared toward preschool and primary school children. All fiction should show children learning to live in ways that please God. ■ **Circulation** 6,540 ■ **Audience** 4–8 years ■ **Frequency** Monthly (in weekly parts)

Freelance Potential Publishes 200 freelance submissions yearly: 90% written by nonstaff writers. Receives 50 unsolicited manuscripts monthly.

Submissions Guidelines and theme list available. Send complete manuscript. Accepts hard copy and email to storymates@clp.org. SASE. Responds in 6 weeks.

- *Fiction:* Stories related to Sunday school lessons, and true-to-life stories of faith, to 800 words. Picture stories, 120–150 words.
- *Other:* Poetry, word lengths vary. Bible puzzles, activities. Submit seasonal material 6 months in advance.

Sample Issue 16 pages. No advertising. Sample copy available.

Rights and Payment First, reprint, or multiple-use rights. Fiction, 4¢–6¢ a word. Poetry, 50¢–75¢ a line. Puzzles, $10. Other material, payment rates vary. Pays on acceptance. Provides 1 contributor's copy.

Susie

3741 Bloomington Street, #4, Colorado Springs, CO 80922. www.susiemag.com

Editor: Susie Shellenberger

Designed for Christian teen girls, *Susie* publishes fiction and nonfiction, and covers topics such as friendship, family life, fashion, and fitness, all with a "Christian twist." The editors are currently seeking more quizzes, crafts, and general-interest pieces. ■ **Circulation** 60,000 ■ **Audience** Girls, 13–19 years ■ **Frequency** Monthly

Freelance Potential Publishes 75–100 freelance submissions yearly: 90% written by nonstaff writers; 25% by authors who are new to the magazine; 10% by previously unpublished writers. Receives 25 queries monthly.

Submissions Guidelines available. Query. Accepts email submissions to susie@susiemag.com (include "Freelance" in the subject line). Response time varies.
- *Articles:* Word lengths vary. Informational, profiles, interviews. Topics: relationships, social issues, health and fitness, style, the arts, Christ.
- *Fiction:* Word lengths vary. Girl-centered stories that promote a Christ-based view.
- *Depts/columns:* Word lengths vary. Advice, fashion, fitness, health, faith.
- *Other:* Crafts, activities, recipes.

Sample Issue 48 pages. Advertising. Sample copy available at website.
- "Music Mania," by Tracy Darlington. Information on the latest releases of Christian music and artists.
- "This Dollar," by Rachelle Dawson. Six ways to think beyond the impulse to buy.

Rights and Payment First rights. Written material, word lengths vary. No payment. Provides 2 contributor's copies.

Take Five Plus

General Council of the Assemblies of God, 1445 North Boonville Avenue, Springfield, MO 65802-1894. www.gospelpublishing.com

Director of Editorial Services: Paul Smith

This magazine offers daily devotionals for teens to help them consider how God's Word can be applied in their day-to-day lives. Devotionals describe the challenges faced by teens, and then offer Scripture-based advice to handle those challenges. The best devotionals keep language and situations believable, address issues relevant to the age group, and avoid excessive religious jargon and preachiness. Devotionals are meant to be illustrational and applicable, and should help readers mature in their faith. ■ **Circulation** 20,000 ■ **Audience** 12–19 years ■ **Frequency** Quarterly

Freelance Potential Of the content published yearly, 98% is written by nonstaff writers; 10% by authors new to the magazine.

Submissions Guidelines available. All material is assigned. Send letter of introduction with résumé, church background, and clips or writing samples. Accepts hard copy. SASE. Responds in 3 months.
- *Articles:* 200–235 words. Daily devotionals based on Scripture readings.
- *Artwork:* Accepts material from teens only. B/W prints or 35mm color slides. Line art.
- *Other:* Poetry written by teens, to 20 lines.

Sample Issue 104 pages. No advertising. Sample copy available.

Rights and Payment Rights vary. Devotions, payment rates vary. Payment policy varies.

Teen Tribute

71 Barber Greene Road, Toronto, Ontario M3C 2A2 Canada. www.tribute.ca

Editor: Toni-Marie Ippolito

This lifestyle magazine covers the entertainment world and pop culture for its teen readers. It delivers the latest buzz on movies, TV shows, music, video games, and celebrities; and offers advice and fashion inspiration. Movie promos are a great way to break in here. ■ **Circulation** 300,000 ■ **Audience** 14–18 years ■ **Frequency** Quarterly

Freelance Potential Publishes 5–10 freelance submissions yearly: 10% written by nonstaff writers; 1% by authors who are new to the magazine. Receives 2 queries monthly.

Submissions Query with clips or writing samples. Accepts hard copy and email to tippolito@ tribute.ca. Availability of artwork improves chance of acceptance. SAE/IRC. Responds in 1–2 months.
- *Articles:* 400–500 words. Informational, profiles, interviews, personal experience. Topics: movies, the film industry, music, the arts, entertainment, popular culture, social issues.
- *Depts/columns:* Word lengths vary. Media reviews, fashion and beauty tips, new product reviews, relationship advice, gear and gadgets, horoscopes.
- *Artwork:* Color prints or transparencies.

Sample Issue 38 pages. Advertising. Sample copy available at website.
- "Sucker Punch," by Toni-Marie Ippolito. A report on actress Vanessa Hudgens and her latest film.
- "Hollywood It Girl!" by Katharine Watts. An interview with actress Emma Stone.

Rights and Payment First serial rights. Written material, $100–$400 Canadian. Artwork, payment rates vary. Pays on publication. Provides 1 contributor's copy.

Thrasher

1303 Underwood Avenue, San Francisco, CA 94121. www.thrashermagazine.com

Managing Editor: Ryan Henry

Thrasher is all skateboards and snowboards, tricks and tattoos, fearlessness and gnarly injuries. This magazine shares the boarding lifestyle, attitude, and experiences with its readers through articles on the sport, profiles of skaters, skatepark reviews, and music news. To be accepted here, writers must be able to write about skateboarding authoritatively and speak to readers in their own language.
- **Circulation** 200,000 ■ **Audience** Boys, 12–20 years ■ **Frequency** 13 times a year

Freelance Potential Publishes 20 freelance submissions yearly: 20% written by nonstaff writers; 100% by previously unpublished writers. Receives 6–10 unsolicited manuscripts monthly.

Submissions Guidelines available at website. Send complete manuscript. Accepts email to stanislaus@thrashermagazine.com (Microsoft Word or RTF attachments). Accepts simultaneous submissions if identified. Responds in 1 month.
- *Articles:* To 1,500 words. Informational, profiles, interviews. Topics: skateboarding, snowboarding, music.
- *Depts/columns:* 750–1,000 words. News, tips, art, 'zines, and profiles.
- *Artwork:* High-resolution digital images.

Sample Issue 220 pages. Advertising. Sample articles available at website.
- "Fritz Mead Interview," by Kristian Svitak. Interview with the skateboarder and painter.
- "Chico Brenes Interview," by Jake Phelps. Making skateboarding videos.

Rights and Payment First North American serial rights. Written material, 15¢ a word. Artwork, payment rates vary. Pays on publication. Provides 2 contributor's copies.

Time for Kids

1271 6th Avenue, 32nd Floor, New York, NY 10020. www.timeforkids.com

Editor: Martha Pickerill

Distributed through schools to students in kindergarten through seventh grade, *Time for Kids* presents today's top headlines in an age-appropriate format. It is designed as a teaching tool, focusing on the news from around the world, as well as the social and political issues that shape modern life. It has three editions: Big Picture for kindergarten and grade one; News Scoop for grades two and three; and World Report for grades four through seven. All material is assigned, so send a résumé. ■ **Circulation** 4.1 million ■ **Audience** 5–12 years ■ **Frequency** Weekly

Freelance Potential Publishes 4 freelance submissions yearly: 4% written by nonstaff writers.

Submissions Editorial calendar available at website. All work is assigned. Send résumé only. Accepts hard copy. Responds if interested.

- *Articles:* Word lengths vary. Informational, biography. Topics: world news, current events, animals, education, health, fitness, science, technology, math, social studies, geography, multicultural and ethnic issues, music, popular culture, recreation, regional news, sports, travel, social issues.
- *Depts/columns:* Word lengths vary. Profiles, short news items.
- *Artwork:* Color prints and transparencies.
- *Other:* Theme-related activities.

Sample Issue 8 pages. No advertising. Sample copy available.

- "Earthquake Shakes Japan," by Jonathan Rosenbloom. A report on the earthquake and tsunami that struck Japan.
- "Goodbye, Space," by Suzanne Zimbler. A report on the space shuttle *Discovery*'s final mission, and a look ahead at what will become of the retired shuttle.

Rights and Payment All rights. Written material, payment rates vary. Pays on publication.

Turtle

U.S. Kids, 1100 Waterway Boulevard, P.O. Box 567, Indianapolis, IN 46206-0567. www.turtlemag.org

Editor: Terry Harshman

Turtle is filled with entertaining stories, poems, rebuses, experiments, and recipes that teach preschool children about health, nutrition, safety, and exercise. It looks for fun, lively material that promotes healthy living in an age-appropriate way. All work should stimulate and respect young minds without "talking down" to them. ■ **Circulation** 382,000 ■ **Audience** 3–5 years ■ **Frequency** 6 times a year

Freelance Potential Publishes 45 freelance submissions yearly: 50% written by nonstaff writers.

Submissions Guidelines available at website. Send complete manuscript. Accepts hard copy. Accepts simultaneous submissions if identified. SASE. Responds in 3 months.

- *Articles:* To 200 words. Informational. Topics: health, fitness, nutrition, learning concepts, simple science.
- *Fiction:* To 350 words. Rebus stories, to 100 words. Genres: adventure, fantasy, humor, problem-solving mysteries, contemporary, ethnic, and multicultural fiction.
- *Depts/columns:* Word lengths vary. Crafts, health tips, recipes.
- *Other:* Puzzles, activities, games. Poetry, 4–12 lines. Submit seasonal material 8 months in advance.

Sample Issue 36 pages. Little advertising. Sample copy available at website.

- "Three Little Kittens," by Carol Olund. Story about kittens that keep losing their mittens.
- "The Perfect Valentine," by Teresa A. DiNicola. A little mouse wants to show his mother how much he loves her.

Rights and Payment All rights. Articles and fiction, to 35¢ a word. Poetry, $25–$50. Puzzles and games, $25 minimum. Other material, payment rates vary. Pays on publication. Provides up to 10 contributor's copies.

Turtle Trails & Tales

P.O. Box 19623, Reno, NV 89511. www.turtletrailsandtales.com

Editor: Virginia Castleman

Turtle Trails & Tales is an ezine dedicated to celebrating the similarities and differences of the world's children. Multicultural themes run throughout the articles, short stories, and personal experience pieces. New writers are always welcome. ■ **Circulation** Unavailable ■ **Audience** 6–11 years ■ **Frequency** Quarterly

Freelance Potential 80% written by nonstaff writers: 50% by authors new to the magazine; 40% by previously unpublished writers. Receives 5 unsolicited manuscripts monthly.

Submissions Guidelines and theme list available at website. Send complete manuscript. Accepts hard copy and electronic submissions through the website. Responds in 3 months.
- *Articles:* 750 words. Informational, how-to, personal experience. Topics: science, history, ecology, finance, sports, geography.
- *Fiction:* To 800 words. Genres: humor, mystery, adventure, retold folktales, sports, holidays.
- *Artwork:* Illustrations in JPEG or PDF format.
- *Other:* Recipes, activities, games, puzzles.

Sample Issue Sample copy available at website.
- "A Tail That Lost Its Smack," by Karen R. Clarke. Two beavers in danger of being caught by humans.
- "Bubble Trouble: How Humpback Whales Fish." How humpback whales communicate.

Rights and Payment Electronic rights. No payment.

Twist

270 Sylvan Avenue, Englewood Cliffs, NJ 07632. www.twistmagazine.com

Editor in Chief: Tina Donvito

Celebrity news and profiles are the focus of this magazine, which is part of the Bauer Teen Network. In addition to celebrity news, *Twist* offers articles on relationships, fashion, music, and entertainment.
- **Circulation** 230,000 ■ **Audience** Teens ■ **Frequency** 10 times a year

Freelance Potential Publishes 10 freelance submissions yearly: 5% written by nonstaff writers; 5% by authors new to the magazine; 5% by previously unpublished writers. Receives 20 queries monthly.

Submissions Guidelines available. Query. Accepts email to twistmail@twistmagazine.com. Response time varies.
- *Articles:* Word lengths vary. Information, interviews, how-to. Topics: celebrities, popular culture, relationships.
- *Depts/columns:* Word lengths vary. Style trends, fashion tips, music and entertainment briefs.

Sample Issue Sample copy available.

Rights and Payment Rights vary. Written material, payment rates vary. Payment policy varies.

VerveGirl

401 Richmond Street West, Suite 245, Toronto, Ontario M5V 1X3 Canada. www.vervegirl.com

Editor in Chief: Xania Khan

VerveGirl is a lifestyle publication that covers both the fun and serious sides of being a Canadian teen girl. Its French and English editions include articles on fashion, beauty, entertainment, social issues, current events, cultural issues, the environment, and relationships. It is not currently accepting freelance queries. Check the website for updates. ■ **Circulation** 150,000 English; 30,000 French ■ **Audience** Girls, 13–24 years ■ **Frequency** 8 times a year

Freelance Potential Publishes 10–20 freelance submissions yearly: 60% written by nonstaff writers. Receives 17 queries monthly.

Submissions Not accepting queries or submissions from freelancers. Check website for updates.
- *Articles:* Word lengths vary. Informational, self-help, profiles, interviews, personal experience. Topics: health, nutrition, fitness, fashion, beauty, social issues, current events, the environment, education, careers, music.

■ *Depts/columns:* Word lengths vary. Entertainment, fashion and beauty, health and wellness.
■ *Other:* Quizzes.

Sample Issue 50 pages. Sample copy available.
■ "Be a Prom Fairy-Godmother," by Rachel Wildman. How to donate your prom dress.
■ "Be a Different Kind of Model," by Jackie Middletown. The niche opportunities in modeling.

Rights and Payment Rights vary. Written material, payment rates vary. Pays on publication.

YARN

www.yareview.net

Editor: Kerri Major

YARN (Young Adult Review Network) is an award-winning online literary journal for young adult writing that promotes teen literacy and celebrates young adult literature; it is the first such journal to publish teen writers alongside adult and established writers of YA. Each issue offers fiction, essays, poetry, interviews, and an editor's blog. Its editors are open to all genres, topics, and poetic forms, and are especially interested in work that features strong narrative voices and emotional honesty; creative nonfiction particularly welcome; writers can be of any age. ■ **Hits per month** 1,200 ■ **Audience** 14–18 years ■ **Frequency** Weekly

Freelance Potential Publishes 12–120 freelance submissions yearly, 5–10% of the total unsolicited manuscripts received. Likes writers willing to revise pieces for publication. Receives 50–75 unsolicited manuscripts monthly.

Submissions Submission guidelines available at website. Send complete manuscript with author biography and writing history. Accepts email submissions (see guidelines for list of email addresses; no attachments). Accepts simultaneous submissions if identified. Response time varies.
■ *Articles:* To 3,000 words. Essays and other creative nonfiction. Interviews and blogs, staff-written.
■ *Fiction:* To 6,000 words. Genres vary.
■ *Other:* Poetry, 3–7 poems per submission.

Sample Issue Sample copy available at website.
■ "The Lover," by Chris Campbell. Funny story about a young man trying to buy condoms.
■ "Stubb," by Arthur Slade. A boy begins to take on dog characteristics after a severe bite.

Rights and Payment Exclusive first-time Internet rights. No payment.

Yes Mag

501-3960 Quadra Street, Victoria, British Columbia V8X 4A3 Canada. www.yesmag.ca

Managing Editor: Jude Isabella

Yes Mag is a science magazine designed to make science, technology, engineering, and mathematics exciting and fun. Each issue contains entertaining stories, do-at-home projects, brain teasers, and environmental and science news. While open to all science topics, it prefers articles that focus on Canadian science and scientists. At this time, *Yes Mag* is only accepting queries from Canadian writers. ■ **Circulation** 20,000 ■ **Audience** 10–15 years ■ **Frequency** 6 times a year

Freelance Potential Publishes 30 freelance submissions yearly: 70% written by nonstaff writers; 15% by authors new to the magazine; 5% by previously unpublished writers. Receives 25 queries monthly.

Submissions Guidelines and theme list available at website. Canadian writers only. Query with detailed outline. Accepts email to editor@yesmag.ca. Response time varies.
■ *Articles:* Features, 600–1,000 words. Short, theme-related articles, 100–350 words. Informational, profiles. Topics: scientists, astronomy, biology, chemistry, ecology, engineering, math, science, technology, nature, the environment.

■ *Depts/columns:* Science and Technology Watch, 250 words. Hands-on projects, word lengths vary.

Sample Issue 32 pages. No advertising. Sample copy available.
■ "Brain Science, Then and Now," by Kathiann M. Kowalski. The history of brain exploration.
■ "Feeling Touchy: The Parietal Lobes," by Claire Eamer. A report on brain mapping.

Rights and Payment First North American print and one-time electronic rights. Science and Technology Watch, $100. Articles, $145 a page. Pays on publication. Provides 1 contributor's copy.

Young Bucks Outdoors

10350 Highway 80 East, P.O. Box 244022, Montgomery, AL 36117. www.buckmasters.com

Contact: Linda O'Connor

This website for kids interested in hunting, fishing, and other outdoor recreational pursuits offers articles on topics such as animal behavior, weather and astronomy, insects, and forest safety. It also features profiles of young hunters. ■ **Circulation** 200,000 ■ **Audience** 4–18 years ■ **Frequency** Updated regularly

Freelance Potential Publishes 10–20 freelance submissions yearly: 30% written by nonstaff writers. Receives 2 queries monthly.

Submissions Guidelines available. Query with detailed photo information. Availability of artwork improves chance of acceptance. Accepts hard copy and email queries to ybo@buckmasters.com. SASE. Responds in 2 weeks.
■ *Articles:* To 600 words. Informational, how-to, personal experience. Topics: hunting, nature, animals.
■ *Artwork:* Digital images preferred; prints and transparencies.

Sample Issue Website only.
■ "Coyotes Are Here to Stay," by Stewart Abrams. The debate on large-scale coyote control.
■ "Swift Fox Is the Smallest of Its Kind," by Lesley B. Carson. A fox no larger than a house cat.

Rights and Payment First rights. All material, payment rates vary. Pays on publication.

Young Rider

P.O. Box 8237, Lexington, KY 40533. www.youngrider.com

Editor: Lesley Ward

This magazine provides profiles, riding techniques, horse care tips, and articles on other topics of interest to young horseback riders and enthusiasts. It also publishes horse-related short stories.
■ **Circulation** 92,000 ■ **Audience** 6–14 years ■ **Frequency** 6 times a year

Freelance Potential Publishes 12 freelance submissions yearly: 15% written by nonstaff writers; 5% by authors new to the magazine; 5% by previously unpublished writers. Receives 5 queries monthly.

Submissions Guidelines available at website. Query. Accepts hard copy and email to yreditor@bowtieinc.com (Word attachments). Responds in 2 weeks.
■ *Articles:* 800–1,000. Informational, how-to, profiles. Topics: riding, training, careers, riding techniques, general horse care, breeds.
■ *Fiction:* 800–1,000 words. Horse-themed short stories. Genres: realistic, humor, contemporary.
■ *Artwork:* High-resolution digital images.

Sample Issue 48 pages. Advertising. Sample copy available.
■ "English Lesson: Riding Your Off-the-Track Thoroughbred." A how-to about riding a thoroughbred.
■ "Horse Care: Senior Horse Issues." Advice on caring for an aging horse.

Rights and Payment First serial rights. Written material, 10¢ a word. Artwork, payment rates vary. Pays on publication. Provides 2 contributor's copies.

Young Salvationist

The Salvation Army, 615 Slaters Lane, Alexandria, VA 22314. www.thewarcry.com

Editor: Captain Amy Reardon

This magazine deals with the life experiences and social issues that impact teen and young adult Christians. To write for *Young Salvationist,* know about the beliefs and perspectives of the Salvation Army. ■ **Circulation** 48,000 ■ **Audience** Young adults ■ **Frequency** 10 times a year

Freelance Potential Publishes 10 freelance submissions yearly: 5% written by nonstaff writers; 30% by authors new to the magazone; 20% by previously unpublished writers. Receives 4-5 unsolicited manuscripts monthly.

Submissions Guidelines available at website. Prefers complete manuscript; will accept query. Accepts hard copy and email submissions to ys@usn.salvationarmy.org. Accepts imultaneous submissions if identified. SASE. Responds in 4–6 weeks.
■ *Articles:* 1,000-1,500 words. How-to, personal experience, interviews. Topics: inspirational, religious, real-life problems, music, humor, social issues, photo features.
■ *Depts/columns:* Word lengths vary. Q&A.

Sample Issue Sample copy available. Website includes sample article.
■ "The Salvation Army Goes Green." Eco-friendly measures undertaken by the Salvation Army.
■ "Owl City." An interview with musician Adam Young about his relationship with God.

Rights and Payment First and second rights. Written material, 15¢ a word for first rights; 10¢ a word for reprints. Pays on acceptance. Provides 4 contributor's copies

Your Big Backyard

National Wildlife Federation, 11100 Wildlife Center Drive, Reston, VA 20190
www.nwf.org/yourbigbackyard

Editorial Department

Your Big Backyard is the National Wildlife Federation's nature magazine for young children. Its mission is to introduce wildlife and nature, and the concept of protecting it all, in entertaining and education-ally sound ways. It publishes informative articles, stories, games, puzzles, and activities. All work is assigned. Writers should send a résumé for consideration. ■ **Circulation** 400,000 ■ **Audience** 3–7 years ■ **Frequency** 10 times a year

Freelance Potential Publishes 3 freelance submissions yearly: 10% written by nonstaff writers. Receives 100 queries monthly.

Submissions Guidelines available. All work is assigned. Send résumé and clips only. Accepts hard copy. SASE. Response time varies.
■ *Articles:* Word lengths vary. Informational. Topics: nature, animals, outdoor recreation, wildlife, conservation, learning concepts.
■ *Fiction:* Word lengths vary. Short stories about nature.
■ *Other:* Games, puzzles, activities.

Sample Issue Sample copy available at website.
■ "The Travelers," by Kathy Kranking. A story about young animal friends in search of a missing plant.
■ "Seahorse Roundup." Photographs and fun facts about seahorses.

Rights and Payment Rights vary. Written material, payment rates vary. Pays on acceptance. Provides 2 contributor's copies.

Zamoof!

644 Spruceview Place South, Kelowna, British Columbia V1V 2P7 Canada. www.zamoofmag.com

Editor/Publisher: TeLeni Koochin

Zamoof! is vibrant, full of fun, and eaches kids to make healthy choices. Packed with comics, puzzles, crafts, jokes, sports, stories, recipes, interviews, true stories, and more. It encourages reading and creativity. The majority of the work is done in-house or by its readers, but it does accept outside submissions for just-for-fun pet horoscopes and essays by and for parents. *Zamoof!* accepts submissions from Canadian writers only. ■ **Circulation** 9,000 ■ **Audience** 7–14 years ■ **Frequency** 6 times a year

Freelance Potential Publishes 13 freelance submissions yearly: 40% written by nonstaff writers; 100% by authors who are new to the magazine; 50% by previously unpublished writers. Receives about 1 unsolicited manuscript monthly.

Submissions Canadian authors only. Guidelines available at website. Send complete manuscript. Fiction is currently booked for a year ahead; guidelines will be posted when accepting fiction again. Accepts email submissions to mail@zamoofmag.com. Response time varies.
■ *Articles:* Staff-written.
■ *Fiction:* Word lengths vary. Genres: adventure, science fiction, fantasy, humor.
■ *Depts/columns:* Feet Up Chronicles (essays for parents about parenting, 340–350 words). Pet Horoscopes, 25 words per sign.

Sample Issue 76 pages. Sample copy available.
■ "School Store." Lessons learned by a young author who stole while working a cash register.
■ "Pregnant at 17." A teen mom's account of her pregnancy and raising an infant.

Rights and Payment Writer retains rights. Written material, 20¢ a word. Pays on publication. Provides 2 contributor's copies.

Classroom Magazines

Magazines used by students are a second core market for children's writers, and one that can provide regular work if you get an "in" with a publication and become part of a stable of regular writers.

Teachers may use these magazines as an integral part of their classroom lessons, or distribute them to students as a resource.

You'll find that the requirements for writers and submissions may be different for these publications than in the general children's magazine category. Some are very specialized—on chemistry, health, leadership—and others are general interest, but almost all are directly tied to curriculum topics. These magazines represent many opportunities for children's writers.

Become aware of what subjects are taught at different grade levels, become familiar with recent issues of the magazines, and start exploring topics that young readers will be thrilled to read more about in the classroom.

ChemMatters

American Chemical Society, 1155 16th Street NW, Washington, DC 20036. www.acs.org/chemmatters

Editor: Patrice Pages

ChemMatters seeks to demystify everyday chemistry by helping students find connections between the chemistry they learn in school and the world around them. Most articles take a subject that students are familiar with and explain the chemistry behind it. *ChemMatters* is most open to articles on health, materials, and the environment. It also offers assignments on a work-for-hire basis. ■ **Circulation** 35,000 ■ **Audience** Grades 9–12 ■ **Frequency** Quarterly

Freelance Potential Publishes 21 freelance submissions yearly; 90% written by nonstaff writers; 25–50% by authors new to the magazine; 25–50% by previously unpublished writers. Receives 1–10 queries monthly.

Submissions Query with outline and résumé. Accepts email to chemmatters@acs.org (Word or PDF attachments). Responds in 2 weeks.
■ *Articles:* 1,300–2,000 words. Informational. Topics: the chemical aspects of science, sports, technology.
■ *Artwork:* JPEG, EPS, TIFF digital images.

Sample Issue 20 pages. No advertising. Sample copy available.
■ "Tanking Up with Cooking Oil," by Beth Nolte. How cooking oil can be used to fuel a vehicle.
■ "Nuclear Energy: When Will the Lights Go Out?" by Barbara Sitzman & Regis Goode. A discussion of renewable energy.

Rights and Payment First North American serial rights. Articles, $500–$1,000. Pays on acceptance. Provides 5 contributor's copies.

Current Health Kids

Weekly Reader Publishing, 44 South Broadway 18th Floor, White Plains, NY 10601-4425.
www.weeklyreader.com/chkids

Editor: Alicia Zadrozny

General health issues of interest to middle-grade students are tackled in this classroom magazine. Distributed through schools, it contains timely, smart, and straightforward articles on health, fitness, choices, relationships, and emotional well-being. A teacher's guide is included. ■ **Circulation** 100,000 ■ **Audience** Grades 4–7 ■ **Frequency** 8 times a year

Freelance Potential Publishes 30 freelance submissions yearly: 80% written by nonstaff writers; 10% by authors new to the magazine. Receives 1–2 queries monthly.

Submissions Editorial calendar available. Query with letter of introduction outlining areas of expertise, list of publishing credits, and clips. Accepts email to currenthealth@weeklyreader.com. Responds in 1–4 months.
■ *Articles:* 600–850 words. Informational, news-driven articles with emphasis on quality journalism. Topics: personal and public health, fitness, nutrition, disease, psychology, first aid, safety, drug education, risky behavior, relationships.
■ *Depts/columns:* Word lengths vary. Health news, Q&As, fitness.

Sample Issue 24 pages. No advertising. 5 articles; 5 depts/columns. Sample copy available.
■ "Drugs: What You Need to Know NOW." Drugs' effect on mind and body, and making smart choices.
■ "All about Autism," by Melissa Abramovitz. An introduction to autism.

Rights and Payment All rights. Payment rates vary. Kill fee, 20%. Pays on publication. Print and digital copies available.

Current Health Teens

Weekly Reader Publishing, 44 South Broadway 18th Floor, White Plains, NY 10601-4425.
www.weeklyreader.com/chteens

Senior Editor: Erin King

General health issues of interest to tweens and teens are covered in this classroom supplement. Distributed through schools, the magazine contains timely, smart, and straightforward articles on health, fitness, choices, relationships, and emotional well-being. A teacher's guide is included.
■ **Circulation** 120,000 ■ **Audience** Grades 7–12 ■ **Frequency** 8 times a year

Freelance Potential Publishes 36 freelance submissions yearly: 80% written by nonstaff writers; 10% by authors who are new to the magazine. Receives 1–2 queries monthly.

Submissions Editorial calendar available. Query with letter of introduction outlining areas of expertise, list of publishing credits, and clips. Accepts email to currenthealth@weeklyreader.com. Responds in 1–4 months.
■ *Articles:* 700–1,000 words. Informational news-driven articles with emphasis on quality journalism. Topics: personal and public health, fitness, nutrition, disease, psychology, first aid, safety, drug education, risky behavior, relationships. Sexual health issues covered in separate 4-page monthly supplement.
■ *Depts/columns:* Word lengths vary. Health news, safety issues, Q&As, fitness.

Sample Issue 24 pages. No advertising. 5 articles; 4 depts/columns. Sample copy available.
■ "How Slow Can You Go?" by Kirsten Weir. Why slow food is cooler, and healthier, than fast food.
■ "Personal Space," by Cheryl Alkon. Tips on handling privacy issues with parents.

Rights and Payment All rights. Payment rates vary. Kill fee, 20%. Pays on publication. Print and digital copies available.

Dimensions

DECA, Inc., 1908 Association Drive, Reston, VA 20191-1594. www.deca.org

Editor: Christopher Young

Targeting an international group of marketing students, *Dimensions* is a classroom tool used to prepare readers for the business world. It provides information and advice on entrepreneurship, leadership, college admissions, job skills, and volunteerism. ■ **Circulation** 176,000 ■ **Audience** 14–18 years ■ **Frequency** Quarterly

Freelance Potential Publishes 6–8 freelance submissions yearly: 25% written by nonstaff writers; 50–75% by authors new to the magazine.

Submissions Guidelines and editorial calendar available. Query or send complete manuscript with author biography. Accepts hard copy, email to deca_dimensions@deca.org, and Macintosh disk submissions (RTF files). Accepts simultaneous submissions if identified. SASE. Response time varies.
■ *Articles:* 800–1,200 words. Informational, how-to, profiles, interviews, personal experience. Topics: general business, management, marketing, sales, leadership development, entrepreneurship, franchising, personal finance, advertising, e-commerce, business technology, career opportunities.
■ *Depts/columns:* 400–600 words. DECA chapter news briefs, opinions.

Sample Issue 24 pages. Advertising. Sample copy available.
■ "Making a MUSCLE." The first-ever "DECA Dash" raised more than $9,000 for the Muscular Dystrophy Association and matched the amount for a scholarship.
■ "Welcome the Obstacles." By facing obstacles you can aspire to higher things.

Rights and Payment First serial rights. Written material, payment rates vary. Pays on publication. Provides 2 contributor's copies.

KIND News

Humane Society Youth, 67 Norwich Essex Turnpike, East Haddam, CT 06423. www.humanesociety.org/parents_educators/classroom, www.kindnews.org

Manager: Catherine Vincent

KIND News is a classroom newspaper published at three reading levels for children in kindergarten through grade six. Its articles, games, stories, interviews, and profiles all relate to the humane treatment of animals. All material must support the concepts of good character, respect for all living things, and environmental conservation. All articles are assigned. ■ **Circulation** 1 million ■ **Audience** Grades K–6 ■ **Frequency** 5 times a year

Freelance Potential Publishes few freelance submissions yearly: 5% written by nonstaff writers.

Submissions All material is assigned. Send résumé and clips only. Accepts hard copy. SASE. Responds if interested.
■ *Articles:* Word lengths vary. Informational. Topics: animals, cruelty, the environment, conservation and protection.
■ *Other:* Games, activities.

Sample Issue Sample copy available at website.
■ "Orcas: Killers or Victims?" Describes what it's like for an orca to be held in captivity.
■ "The Right Path for Pets." Uses a word search activity to teach about spaying and neutering.

Rights and Payment Exclusive rights. Written material, payment rates vary. Pays on acceptance.

Leadership For Student Activities

1904 Association Drive, Reston, VA 20191-1537. www.nasc.us

Editor: James Paterson

Read by student council members in middle school and high school and their advisors, this magazine is filled with articles about program ideas, motivational techniques, and nurturing leadership skills. It welcomes material from students as well as adult freelancers. ■ **Circulation** 30,000 ■ **Audience** Grades 6–12 ■ **Frequency** 9 times a year

Freelance Potential Publishes 18–25 freelance submissions yearly: 70% written by nonstaff writers; 50% by authors new to the magazine; 75% by previously unpublished writers. Receives 1–2 queries, 4 unsolicited manuscripts monthly.

Submissions Guidelines and theme list available at website. Query with clips, or send complete manuscript. Accepts hard copy and email submissions to leadershipmag@nassp.org. SASE. Responds to queries in 2 weeks, to manuscripts in 1 month.
■ *Articles:* 1,200–1,700 words. Informational, how-to, profiles, interviews. Topics: student activities, leadership development, careers.
■ *Depts/columns:* Reports on special events, 100–350 words. Advice for and by activity advisors, 1,000–1,500 words. National and regional news, leadership plans, opinion pieces, word lengths vary.
■ *Artwork:* B/W or color prints or slides.
■ *Other:* Submit seasonal material 4 months in advance.

Sample Issue 44 pages. Advertising. Sample copy available.

Rights and Payment All rights. Written material, payment rates vary. Payment policy varies. Provides 5 contributor's copies.

Listen Magazine

35 West Oak Ridge Drive, Hagerstown, MD 21740. www.listenmagazine.org

Editor: Céleste Perrino-Walker

Listen Magazine promotes the development of good habits and high ideals of physical, social, and mental health. Written primarily for teens, it focuses on drug-abuse prevention and advocates for total abstinence from tobacco, alcohol, and other drugs. Because the magazine is used extensively in public schools, it does not accept articles that have an overt emphasis on religion. ■ **Circulation** 40,000 ■ **Audience** Grades 7–12 ■ **Frequency** 9 times a year

Freelance Potential Publishes 90+ freelance submissions yearly: 100% written by nonstaff writers; 20% by authors new to the magazine; 15% by previously unpublished writers. Receives 42–50 queries, 2–4 unsolicited manuscripts monthly.

Submissions Guidelines and editorial calendar available at website. Query or send complete manuscript. Accepts hard copy and email to editor@listenmagazine.org. Accepts simultaneous submissions if identified. SASE. Response time varies.
■ *Articles:* 350–750 words. Informational, profiles, self-help. Topics: peer pressure, decision making, drugs, self-esteem, self-discipline, family conflict, sports, hobbies, friendship, healthy choices.
■ *Depts/columns:* Word lengths vary. Opinion pieces, social issues, trends. Alerts (news of emerging drug or behavior trends, or problem-solving tips or resources, 400 words).

Sample Issue 16 pages. No advertising. Sample copy available at website.
■ "Alcohol and Your Body." The effects of alcohol on the body are outlined.
■ "A Dangerous Study Buddy," by Megan Strothman. Information and warnings about Adderall use.

Rights and Payment All rights. Written material, $100–$250. Alerts, $80–$100. Pays on acceptance. Provides 3 contributor's copies.

Minnesota Conservation Volunteer

500 Lafayette Road, St. Paul, MN 55155-4046. www.dnr.state.mn.us/volunteer

Editor: Kathleen Weflen

Published by the Minnesota Department of Natural Resources through donor support, this magazine seeks to entice young naturalists to conserve natural resources. Its articles celebrate the state's natural beauty and environmental activities. ■ **Circulation** 150,000 ■ **Audience** Middle-grade students, teachers ■ **Frequency** 6 times a year

Freelance Potential Publishes 25 freelance submissions yearly: 60% written by nonstaff writers. Receives dozens of queries, 4 unsolicited manuscripts monthly.

Submissions Query with synopsis for feature articles and Field Notes. Send complete manuscript for essays. Accepts hard copy and email queries to kathleen.weflen@dnr.state.mn.us. SASE. Response time varies.
■ *Articles:* 1,200–1,800 words. Informational. Topics: Minnesota's natural resources, wildlife, state parks, lakes, grasslands, groundwater, biofuels, fishing, outdoor recreation.
■ *Depts/columns:* Field Notes (200–500 words). A Sense of Place and Close Encounters (essays, 800–1,200 words).
■ *Other:* Student activities and teacher guides.

Sample Issue 82 pages. Sample copy available at website.
■ "The Place of the Long Rapids," by David Mather. Description of spring life along the Rainy River.
■ "Walleye Stocking Today," by Chris Naskanen. An explanation of the walleye stocking process.

Rights and Payment First North American serial rights with option to purchase electronic rights. Articles and essays, 50¢ a word plus $100 for electronic rights. Payment policy varies.

National Geographic Explorer

1145 17th Street NW, Washington, DC 20036. http://magma.nationalgeographic.com/ngexplorer

Editor in Chief: Jaclyn Mahler

Teachers of grades two through six use this magazine in their classrooms to augment their science and social studies curricula. The same fascinating subjects that have enthralled adult *National Geographic* readers can be found here, but with a kid-friendly presentation. Each issue comes with a teacher's guide. ■ **Circulation** Unavailable ■ **Audience** Grades 2–6 ■ **Frequency** 7 times a year

Freelance Potential Publishes few freelance submissions yearly: 5% written by nonstaff writers.

Submissions All material written on assignment. Send résumé only. Accepts hard copy. Responds if interested.
■ *Articles:* Word lengths vary. Informational. Topics: curriculum-related science, social studies.

Sample Issue 24 pages.
■ "Twister!" What storm chasers do and how tornadoes form.
■ "Flat Sharks." A description of various types of rays.

Rights and Payment All rights. Articles, payment rates vary. Pays on acceptance.

Read

Weekly Reader Publishing, 3001 Cindel Drive, Delran, NJ 08075. www.weeklyreader.com

Senior Editor: Bryon Cahill

Each themed issue of this magazine offers a mix of classic and contemporary fiction and nonfiction. Divided into sections—literature and writing—it features excerpts from well-known works and original literature as well as grammar exercises and author interviews. ■ **Circulation** 160,000 ■ **Audience** Grades 6–10 ■ **Frequency** 10 times a year

Freelance Potential 60% written by nonstaff writers.

Submissions All work is assigned. No queries or unsolicited manuscripts. Send résumé only. Accepts hard copy. Responds if interested.
■ *Articles:* 1,000–2,000 words. Informational, interviews, biography, essays. Topics: writing, literature.
■ *Fiction:* Word lengths vary. Genres: contemporary, mystery, folktales, readers' theater plays.

Sample Issue
■ "A Heavenly Place for a Boy." Mark Twain reflects on his childhood growing up in rural Missouri.
■ "This Is Literary Idol!" This lesson plan lets students face off with reading and performing their favorite literary pieces in front of the class.

Rights and Payment First North American serial and electronic one-time use rights. Written material, payment rates vary. Pays on acceptance. Provides 5 contributor's copies.

Scholastic Choices

Scholastic Inc., 557 Broadway, New York, NY 10012-3999. www.scholastic.com/choices

Editor: Bob Hugel

In *Scholastic Choices*, teens read about other teens who are facing familiar challenges. Sound and helpful advice to meet those challenges is provided. Articles should offer solutions, as well as sidebars that offer additional resources, such as helpline or hotline numbers or websites. ■ **Circulation** 200,000 ■ **Audience** 12–18 years ■ **Frequency** 6 times a year

Freelance Potential Publishes 30–40 freelance submissions yearly: 90% written by nonstaff writers; 10% by previously unpublished writers. Receives 5 queries, 5 unsolicited manuscripts monthly.

Submissions Guidelines and editorial calendar available. Query or send complete manuscript. Accepts hard copy and email submissions to choicesmag@scholastic.com. SASE. Responds to queries in 2 months, to manuscripts in 3 months.
■ *Articles:* 500–1,000 words. Informational, self-help, profiles, personal experience. Topics: health, nutrition, fitness, sports, personal development, personal responsibility, family issues, relationships, safety, social issues, conservation, the environment, popular culture, careers, substance abuse prevention.
■ *Depts/columns:* Staff-written.
■ *Other:* Quizzes, word games, recipes.

Sample Issue 24 pages. Advertising. 5 articles; 4 depts/columns. Sample copy available at website.
■ "Father's Day—Every Day," by Wendy Grossman. Profile of a teenage father and his struggles.
■ "Life with Autism," by Denise Rinaldo. Profile of an autistic teen that explains the autism spectrum.

Rights and Payment All rights. Written material, payment rates vary. Pays on publication. Provides 10 contributor's copies.

Scholastic DynaMath

Scholastic Inc., 557 Broadway, Room 474, New York, NY 10012-3999. www.scholastic.com/dynamath

Associate Editor: Carli Entin

This magazine strives to make math fun. Geared toward kids in grades three to six, it is filled with entertaining articles and interactive activities and puzzles that connect math concepts to the real world. ■ **Circulation** 200,000 ■ **Audience** 8–12 years ■ **Frequency** 8 times a year

Freelance Potential Publishes 16 freelance submissions yearly: 30% written by nonstaff writers; 5% by authors new to the magazine. Receives 2 queries, 2 unsolicited manuscripts monthly.

Submissions Query with outline, or send complete manuscript. Accepts hard copy. Accepts simultaneous submissions if identified. SASE. Responds in 2–4 months.
■ *Articles:* To 600 words. Informational. Topics: critical thinking, chart and graph reading, measurement, fractions, decimals, problem solving, interdisciplinary issues.
■ *Other:* Filler, puzzles, games, jokes. Submit holiday material 4–6 months in advance.

Sample Issue 16 pages. No advertising. 5 articles; 2 activities. Sample copy available at website.
■ "Doc's Bills," by Sarah Kolinovsky. A teen TV star talks about keeping track of his money and bills.
■ "One Cool Chart," by Linda Buchwald. Understanding the wind-chill chart.

Rights and Payment All rights. Articles, $250–$400. Puzzles, $25–$50. Pays on acceptance. Provides 3 contributor's copies.

Scholastic Math Magazine

Scholastic Inc., 557 Broadway, New York, NY 10012-3999. www.scholastic.com/math

Editor: Jack Silbert

This magazine makes learning math fun for students in middle school and high school. It features entertaining and easy-to-follow articles that demonstrate how math concepts are part of daily life, such as with sports, movies, music, and video games. A typical issue includes sections on geometry, pre-algebra, statistics, and theme-related activities. ■ **Circulation** 200,000 ■ **Audience** Grades 6–9 ■ **Frequency** Monthly

Freelance Potential Publishes 10 freelance submissions yearly: 30% written by nonstaff writers; 10% by previously unpublished writers. Receives 2 queries monthly.

Submissions Editorial calendar available at website. Query. Accepts hard copy. SASE. Responds in 2–3 months.
■ *Articles:* 600 words. Informational. Topics: real-world math, math-related news, teen issues, sports, celebrities, TV, music, movies, current events.
■ *Depts/columns:* 140 words. Skill-building exercises, quizzes, practice tests, Q&As.
■ *Other:* Puzzles, games, activities, comic strips, mystery photos.

Sample Issue 16 pages. No advertising. 4 articles; 1 dept/column. Sample copy available at website.
■ "Sad Song for Album Sales," by Linda Buchwald. Uses math to graph CD vs. digital album sales.
■ "NBA Sharp Shooters," by Bill Wise. How to calculate effective field goal percentage.

Rights and Payment All rights. Articles, $300+. Depts/columns, $35. Pays on publication.

Scholastic News

557 Broadway, New York, NY 10012-3999. www.scholasticnews.com

Associate Editor: Elena Cabral

Scholastic News is a newsletter filled with kid-focused, curriculum-connected articles and activities. Every issue presents high-interest, late-breaking news in a variety of engaging formats, all designed to help kids understand and interpret the world around them. Published in six editions, with age-appropriate material for students in grades one through six, the newsletter is complemented by a teacher's edition and interactive website that contains additional instruction material. It is not open to submissions of any kind at this time. ■ **Circulation** 1 million+ ■ **Audience** Grades 1–6 (separate editions) ■ **Frequency** Weekly

Freelance Potential Not open to freelancers at this time.

Submissions Not accepting submissions at this time.
■ *Articles:* Word lengths vary. Informational. Topics: curriculum-based topics, including history, social studies, geography, science, technology, health an dfitness, multicultural, language arts; social skills, learning concepts, current events.
■ *Other:* Games, activities.

Sample Issue Page number varies. No advertising. Sample copy available at website.
■ "Wolf Wars." The controversy over whether to allow hunting of gray wolves.
■ "Are You a Bully?" How to know when joking stops and bullying begins.

Rights and Payment Rights vary. Payment policy varies.

Scholastic Scope

Scholastic Inc., 557 Broadway, New York, NY 10012-3999. www.scholastic.com/scope

Executive Editor: Lucy Lehrer

Scope is designed to entertain teens with high-interest material that grabs their attention while also building vocabulary, writing, and reading comprehension skills. Each issue features fiction, nonfiction, plays, and puzzles. Stories, articles, and activities should be geared to a sixth- to eighth-grade reading level. ■ **Circulation** 550,000 ■ **Audience** 12–18 years ■ **Frequency** 17 times a year

Freelance Potential Of the content published yearly, 10% is written by nonstaff writers: 10% by authors new to the magazine; 2% by previously unpublished writers. Receives 16–25 queries monthly.

Submissions Query with résumé, outline/synopsis, and clips. Accepts hard copy. SASE. Response time varies.
■ *Articles:* 1,000 words. Informational, profiles. Topics: topics that appeal to teens; young adults who have overcome obstacles, performed heroic acts, or had noteworthy experiences; current events; creative nonfiction; classic literature; science; nature and the environment, social studies; multicultural; popular culture.
■ *Fiction:* 1,500 words. Contemporary, realistic, science fiction, plays, myths, fables.
■ *Depts/columns:* Staff-written.
■ *Other:* Puzzles, activities. Submit seasonal material 4 months in advance.

Sample Issue 22 pages. Little advertising. Sample copy available.
■ "I Survived the California Wildfires." The true story of a teen's courage in a dangerous situation.
■ "Readers Theater Play: Greek Myth, King Midas." The classic story for a modern audience.

Rights and Payment Rights vary. Written material, $100+. Pays on acceptance. Provides 2 contributor's copies.

The School Magazine

Private Bag 3, Ryde, New South Wales 2112, Australia
www.curriculumsupport.education.nsw.gov.au/services/schoolmagazine

Editor: Alan Edwards

With four editions that target different age groups (ages 8–9, 9–10, 10–11, and 11–12), this literary magazine for young Australian readers offers a mix of short stories, nonfiction articles, poems, plays, and activities. Teaching units are available for use in the classroom. Nonfiction submissions should include information on sources and/or research material consulted. Authors from around the globe are welcome to submit material. ■ **Circulation** 150,000 ■ **Audience** 8–12 years ■ **Frequency** 10 times a year

Freelance Potential Publishes 100 freelance submissions yearly: 70% written by nonstaff writers; 10% by authors new to the magazine; 10% by previously unpublished writers. Receives 8 queries, 50 unsolicited manuscripts monthly.

Submissions Guidelines available at website. For nonfiction, query with proposed title and topic, why readers would be interested, synopsis, word count, source list, author qualifications, and available artwork to School.Magazine@det.nsw.edu.au. Send complete manuscript for fiction, plays, and poetry. Accepts hard copy only. Material is not returned. Responds via email in 8–12 weeks.
■ *Articles:* 800–2,000 words. Informational. Topics: nature, the environment, history, biography, science, technology, multicultural and ethnic issues.
■ *Fiction:* To 2,000 words. Genres: contemporary, multicultural, historical, humor, fantasy, science fiction.
■ *Depts/columns:* Staff-written.
■ *Other:* Poetry, to 30 lines. Plays, to 2,000 words. Games, activities, puzzles.

Sample Issue 34 pages. No advertising. Sample articles available at website.
■ "Yakka, Yip, and the Yahoos," by Geoffrey McSkimming. Forest creatures build a treehouse.
■ "The Story of Pompeii," by Jonathan Shaw. Description of the fate of the ancient city of Pompeii.

Rights and Payment One-time serial rights. Written material, $270 Australian per 1,000 words. Poetry, payment rates vary. Pays on acceptance. Provides 2 contributor's copies.

Science Weekly

P.O. Box 70638, Chevy Chase, MD 20813. www.scienceweekly.com

Publisher: Claude Mayberry

Science Weekly develops and reinforces reading, writing, mathematics, and critical thinking skills through interactive science content. Its six differentiated editions (based on reading levels) help students "put a little science in their week." It is designed as a complementary supplement to classroom science and math lessons. *Science Weekly* comes in six grade-based editions that center on the same theme. For example, the kindergarten edition on coral reefs introduces new words and compares a reef to a little city; the fifth/sixth-grade edition explains how and where they grow and survive, and includes an experiment. ■ **Circulation** 200,000 ■ **Audience** Grades K–6 ■ **Frequency** 15 times a year

Freelance Potential Publishes 15 freelance submissions yearly: 100% written by nonstaff writers; 5% by authors new to the magazine; 70% by previously unpublished writers.

Submissions Guidelines and theme list available at website. All work is assigned to writers living in the District of Columbia, Maryland, or Virginia. Send résumé. Accepts hard copy. Response time varies.
■ *Articles:* Word lengths vary. Informational. Topics: space exploration, ecology, the environment, nature, biology, meteorology, oceanography, navigation, nutrition, physical science, technology.
■ *Other:* Theme-related puzzles, games, activities.

Sample Issue 4 pages. No advertising. Sample copy available at website.

- "Science in Art." Theme of one of the 2012 issues.
- "Meet the Scientist." Brief profile of marine biologist Niels Lindquist.

Rights and Payment All rights. All material, payment rates vary. Pays on publication.

Science World

Scholastic Inc., 557 Broadway, New York, NY 10012-3999. www.scholastic.com/scienceworld

Editor: Patricia Janes

Science World brings science from around the globe to life with feature articles, hands-on activities, and reproducibles for teachers. All articles are assigned. Writers may submit their qualifications in order to be considered for writing projects. ■ **Circulation** 40,000 ■ **Audience** Grades 6–10 ■ **Frequency** 14 issues a year

Freelance Potential 50% written by nonstaff writers. Receives 10 queries monthly.

Submissions Editorial calendar available. All articles are assigned. Query with list of publishing credits and clips or writing samples. Accepts hard copy. SASE. Responds in 2 months if interested.
- *Articles:* To 750 words. Informational. Topics: science, nature, animals, health.
- *Depts/columns:* 200 words. Hands On Science, Gross Out, Cool Jobs.
- *Other:* Puzzles, activities.

Sample Issue 24 pages. No advertising. 3 articles, 3 depts/columns, 1 activity. Sample copy available at website.
- "Bionic Body Parts," by Jennifer Marino Walters. Scientific machines that replace injured body parts.
- "Who You Callin' Ugly?" by Sara Goudarzi. Odd features of some animals help them survive.

Rights and Payment All rights. Articles, $250–$650. Depts/columns, $100–$125. Kill fee, 50%. Pays on publication. Provides 2 contributor's copies.

Spigot Science Magazine

P.O. Box 103, Blawenburg, NJ 08504. www.spigotsciencemag.com

Editor in Chief: Valeria Girandola

This ezine is intended for use in upper-elementary and middle-school science classes as well as other classes across the curriculum. Its articles reflect skill-based classroom practices and familiarity with national science standards. All articles are written at a fifth- to sixth-grade reading level. Themed issues are built upon one concept, such as oceans, plants, or cells. Writers with a background in the education field are encouraged to submit. ■ **Circulation** Unavailable ■ **Audience** Grades 5–8 ■ **Frequency** Quarterly

Freelance Potential Publishes 10 freelance submissions yearly: 10% written by nonstaff writers.

Submissions Guidelines and editorial calendar available at website. Query or send complete manuscript. Accepts email to vgirandola@spigotsciencemag.com. Response time varies.
- *Articles:* 300–400 words. Informational. Topics: science, nature, animals.
- *Artwork:* Digital images.

Sample Issue
- "Cells." An entire issue devoted to cells.
- "Weather." A theme issue dedicated to weather subjects.

Rights and Payment Limited-time electronic rights. No payment.

SuperScience

Scholastic Inc., 557 Broadway, New York, NY 10012-3999. www.scholastic.com/superscience

Editor: Elizabeth Carney

SuperScience is filled with interesting articles on all aspects of science and how they figure into our daily lives. It also provides teacher guides with classroom experiments and reproducible lesson resources. Authors with experience writing fact-based articles for this age demographic are sought. Each article must have several sidebars and entrance points. ■ **Circulation** 200,000 ■ **Audience** Grades 3–6 ■ **Frequency** 8 times a year

Freelance Potential Publishes 50 freelance submissions yearly: 80% written by nonstaff writers; 15% by authors new to the magazine. Receives 5–10 queries monthly.

Submissions Editorial calendar available at website. All articles are assigned. Query with résumé and clips. Accepts hard copy. SASE. Response time varies.
■ *Articles:* 100–600 words. Informational, how-to. Topics: earth, physical, and life sciences; health; technology; chemistry; nature; the environment.
■ *Depts/columns:* Word lengths vary. Science news, mysteries, experiments.
■ *Artwork:* 8x10 B/W and color prints. Line art.
■ *Other:* Puzzles, activities.

Sample Issue 16 pages. No advertising. 4 articles; 3 depts/columns. Sample copy available at website.
■ "Cheers for Chocolate," by Britt Norlander. How science turns a bitter bean into a delicious delight.
■ "Snow Slide!" by Carli Entin. A scientist studies snow crystals to understand and predict avalanches.

Rights and Payment First rights. Articles, $75–$650. Other material, payment rates vary. Pays on acceptance. Provides 2 contributor's copies.

Tar Heel Junior Historian

North Carolina Museum of History, 5 East Edenton Street, Raleigh, NC 27601-1011. http://ncmuseumofhistory.org

Editor: Lisa Coston Hall

This publication of the North Carolina Museum of History presents a well-balanced selection of scholarly articles about the state's history that appeal to preteens and young adults. Its content is designed to supplement middle school and high school curricula. Because most of the articles are written by history scholars or experts, your best bet is to query with your qualifications and the editors will determine if your background fits their needs. ■ **Circulation** 9,000 ■ **Audience** 9–18 years ■ **Frequency** Twice a year

Freelance Potential Publishes 12 freelance submissions yearly: 50% written by nonstaff writers; 50% by authors new to the magazine; 20% by previously unpublished writers.

Submissions Guidelines and theme list available. Query. Accepts hard copy and email queries to lisa.hall@ncdcr.gov. SASE. Response time varies.
■ *Articles:* 700–1,000 words. Informational, profiles, interviews, personal experience. Topics: regional history; geography; government; social, multicultural, and ethnic issues pertaining to North Carolina history.
■ *Artwork:* B/W and spot color prints or transparencies. Line art.
■ *Other:* Puzzles, activities, word games.

Sample Issue 38 pages. No advertising. Sample copy available.

Rights and Payment All rights. No payment. Provides 10 contributor's copies.

Magazines for Educators, Coaches, and Caregivers

Children's writers who wish to expand their scope of work and diversify their portfolio—while gaining valuable experience, clips, and contacts—can consider this market, which reaches those responsible for the education or direct care of children and teens.

These publications target teachers, administrators, and support professionals who work with or in the service of children. Their readers include administrators, child care administrators, homeschooling parents, coaches, children's librarians, media center professionals, and school administrators; and their goals are to arm their readers with practical ideas, industry news and information, and strategies for working with children.

It is a great market for teachers and education professionals who write, but also for writers with personal knowledge of the subject matter—for example, homeschooling parents, coaches, or parents of special needs students. Writing for this market not only expands a writer's professional repertoire, but creates relationships with publishers that can result in steady work. It also allows an author to illustrate his or her understanding of the needs of children and teens—something children's publishers will value.

Administr@tor

Scholastic, Inc., 557 Broadway, New York, NY 10012-3999. www.scholastic.com/administrator

Editorial Director: Dana Truby

Administrator seeks to provide "smart strategies and proven solutions" to education issues for kindergarten through grade 12. Leadership, staff development, curriculum and instruction, funding, and technology are some of the topics covered. Submissions from school administrators and educators, as well as from freelance writers and journalists, are welcome. ■ **Circulation** 240,000 ■ **Audience** School administrators, grades K–12 ■ **Frequency** 8 times a year

Freelance Potential Publishes 25 freelance submissions yearly: 80% written by nonstaff writers; 10% by previously unpublished writers.

Submissions Guidelines available. Query with résumé. Accepts hard copy and email queries to dtruby@scholastic.com. SASE. Responds in 3–4 months.
■ *Articles:* 1,200 words. Informational, how-to, profiles, interviews. Topics: teacher recruitment and retention, salaries, grants, spending, intervention programs, school boards, gifted education, crisis management, social issues, education trends, legislation, technology.
■ *Depts/columns:* Word lengths vary. News, opinions, technology, book reviews.

Sample Issue 64 pages. Sample copy available at website.
■ "Teach Technique, Not Strategy," by Doug Lemov. Giving teachers practical means instead of theory to manage their classes.
■ "Latest Tech Tools," by Brian Nadel. The leading and best devices for classroom use.

Rights and Payment All rights. All material, payment rates vary. Pays on publication.

The ALAN Review

Louisiana State University, 11M Peabody Hall, Baton Rouge, LA 70803. www.alan-ya.org

Editor: Dr. Steven T. Bickmore

Published three times each year for an audience of English teachers, authors, librarians, publishers, and others, this peer-reviewed journal concentrates solely on literature for adolescents. ■ **Circulation** 2,500 ■ **Audience** Teachers, authors, librarians ■ **Frequency** 3 times a year

Freelance Potential Publishes 38 freelance submissions yearly: 95% written by nonstaff writers; 5% by previously unpublished writers. Receives 8 unsolicited manuscripts monthly.

Submissions Guidelines available in each issue and at website. Send complete manuscript with separate title page containing author contact information and short biography, and a brief statement that the article is original and not previously published. Accepts email submissions to alanreview@lsu.edu (Microsoft Word attachments; include "Manuscript Submission" in subject line). Responds in 2 months.
■ *Articles:* To 3,000 words. Informational, interviews, book reviews. Topics: young adult literature, publishing trends, current research.
■ *Depts/columns:* To 300 words. Short vignettes, membership news.

Sample Issue Sample copy available.
■ "Finding Space and Place for Young Adult Literature: Lessons from Four First-Year Teachers Engaging in Out-of-School Professional Induction," by Wendy J. Glenn and Danielle King. Discussion of innovative practices and strategies to bring young adult books into the classroom.
■ "Social Upheaval and Psychological Scarring: Exploring the Future in Meg Rosoff's *How I Live Now*," by Judith K. Franzak. Review of *How I Live Now*, by Meg Rosoff, which explores the impacts of war on the future.

Rights and Payment Rights vary. No payment. Provides 2 contributor's copies.

American Educator

555 New Jersey Avenue NW, Washington, DC 20001-2079. www.aft.org/pubs-reports/american-educator/index.htm

Editor: Lisa Hansel

Published by the American Federation of Teachers, this professional magazine offers educators news of the field. It also publishes articles on policy, international affairs, trends, and labor issues of interest to AFT members. While its readership is composed of professional educators, articles are not laden with education and research jargon, nor does it publish research papers or doctoral theses as articles. Personal narratives are rarely published, but submissions based on informed opinion are always welcome. ■ **Circulation** 900,000 ■ **Audience** Teachers, professors, policymakers ■ **Frequency** Quarterly

Freelance Potential Publishes 0–1 freelance submissions yearly: 25% written by nonstaff writers; 20% by authors new to the magazine; 10% by previously unpublished writers. Receives 42 queries monthly.

Submissions Guidelines available at website. Prefers query with contact information; will accept complete manuscript. Accepts hard copy and email to amered@aft.org. SASE. Responds in 2 months.
■ *Articles:* Word lengths vary. Informational, profiles, opinion. Topics: trends and problems in education, politics, education law, professional ethics, social and labor issues, international affairs.

Sample Issue 54 pages. Advertising.
■ "Advancing Our Students' Language and Literacy: The Challenge of Complex Texts," by Marilyn Jager Adams. Explores why English texts are much simpler than textbooks written 40 years earlier.
■ "Testing What Has Been Taught: Helpful, High-Quality Assessments Start with A Strong Curriculum," by Laura S. Hamilton. Explains the need for a strong curriculum to build an assessment system.

Rights and Payment All rights. Written material, payment rates vary. Pays on publication. Provides 10 contributor's copies.

American Libraries

American Library Association, 50 East Huron Street, Chicago, IL 60611. www.ala.org/alonline

Acquisitions Editor: Pamela Goodes

This professional journal of the American Library Association features articles that reflect the professional concerns of librarians everywhere. It also covers the news, regulations, and trends of the library industry. It accepts material from professionals in the library sciences only; articles must be well researched and culled from personal experience in a library. ■ **Circulation** 65,000 ■ **Audience** Librarians ■ **Frequency** 10 times a year

Freelance Potential Publishes 10 freelance submissions yearly: 60% written by nonstaff writers; 50% by authors new to the magazine. Receives 41 unsolicited manuscripts monthly.

Submissions Professional librarians only. Guidelines available at website. Send complete manuscript. Accepts hard copy and email submissions to americanlibraries@ala.org. No simultaneous submissions. SASE. Responds in 1–2 months.
■ *Articles:* 600–1,500 words. Informational, profiles, interviews, personal experience. Topics: modern libraries, library and ALA history, technology, leadership, advocacy, funding, privacy.
■ *Depts/columns:* Word lengths vary. News, opinions, profiles, media reviews, information technology, ALA events, career leads, professional development.
■ *Artwork:* Digital images (JPEG) at 300 dpi.

Sample Issue 25 pages. Advertising. 4 articles; 2 depts/columns. Sample copy available.
■ "Booking Passage to a New Home," by Rick Haverinen. Explains how a library collection was relocated after the closing of a U.S. Army library.
■ "One Book for Every Young Child," by Michelle McIntyre. Details on a collaborative library program in Pennsylvania that reinforces early literacy.

Rights and Payment First North American serial rights. Written material, $100–$250. Pays on acceptance. Provides 1+ contributor's copies.

American School & University

9800 Metcalf Avenue, Overland Park, KS 66212-2215. www.asumag.com

Executive Editor: Susan Lustig

This magazine is read by education facilities and business professionals, as well as architects. It offers how-to articles and reports on industry news and trends. Articles should not promote a company or specific product; rather, they should offer the reader new insights into the general trends and market, provide tips about what to look for, and explain processes. Be sure all technical information is correct. ■ **Circulation** 65,000 ■ **Audience** School facilities managers ■ **Frequency** Monthly

Freelance Potential Publishes 40 freelance submissions yearly: 35% written by nonstaff writers; 30% by authors new to the magazine. Receives 180 queries yearly.

Submissions Guidelines and editorial calendar available. Query with outline. Prefers email queries to slustig@asumag.com; will accept hard copy. SASE. Artwork improves chance of acceptance. Responds in 2 weeks.
■ *Articles:* 1,200 words. Informational, how-to. Topics: educational facilities management, maintenance, security, planning, design, construction, operations, furnishings.
■ *Depts/columns:* 250–350 words. Opinions, environmental practices, technology, planning issues, and new products.
■ *Artwork:* Digital images (EPS, TIFF, or JPEG) at 300 dpi.

Sample Issue 58 pages. Advertising. 5 articles; 7 depts/columns. Sample copy available.

- "Going Solar in Green Schools," by Mark Domine. Highlights solar power-generating solutions schools are undertaking to cut operational costs.
- "Managing A Crisis for School Security," by William F. Badzmierowski. Steps to creating an effective crisis communications plan.

Rights and Payment All rights. Written material, payment rates vary. Payment policy varies. Provides 2 contributor's copies.

American Secondary Education

Ashland University, Dwight Schar COE, Room 231, 401 College Avenue, Ashland, OH 44805
www.ashland.edu.ase

Editorial Assistant

With a mix of practical and scholarly articles, this refereed journal examines current issues, theories, and practices of secondary education. It includes articles written by practitioners and researchers that reflect what educators in both the public and private sectors are discussing and thinking.
■ **Circulation** 450 ■ **Audience** Secondary school educators ■ **Frequency** 3 times a year

Freelance Potential Publishes 20 freelance submissions yearly: 99% written by nonstaff writers; 75% by authors new to the magazine. Receives 3–5 unsolicited manuscripts monthly.

Submissions Guidelines available in each issue and at website. Send complete manuscript with 100-word abstract and credentials. Accepts email submissions only to asejournal@ashland.edu. No simultaneous submissions. SASE. Responds in 4–6 months.

- *Articles:* 10–25 double-spaced manuscript pages. Informational. Topics: secondary and middle school education research and practice.
- *Depts/columns:* Word lengths vary. Book reviews.

Sample Issue 96 pages. No advertising. 7 articles; 1 book review. Sample copy available.

- "Overcoming Obstacles in Using Authentic Instruction: A Comparative Case Study of High School Math & Science Teachers," by Jennifer Dennis and Mary John O'Hair. Examination of authentic instruction in three school settings to determine similarities and differences.
- "Expanding Secondary School Chinese Language Programs: A Study of Potential Challenges," by Beverly J. Dretzke and Kelly Jordan. Benefits and challenges of expanding Chinese language instruction.

Rights and Payment All rights. No payment. Provides 3 contributor copies.

American String Teacher

4153 Chain Bridge Road, Fairfax, VA 22030. www.astaweb.com

Editor: Mary Jane Dye

The official publication of the American String Teachers Association and available exclusively to members, this magazine features articles related to the teaching of stringed instruments and/or the performance of music for strings. Topics should not be too broad, nor too narrow. All articles should provide information that will help readers become better string teachers. All articles go through a peer review before acceptance. ■ **Circulation** 11,500 ■ **Audience** String instrument teachers ■ **Frequency** Quarterly

Freelance Potential Publishes 30 freelance submissions yearly: 100% written by nonstaff writers; 50% by authors new to the magazine; 5% by previously unpublished writers. Receives up to 4 queries and unsolicited manuscripts monthly.

Submissions Guidelines available at website. Query or send complete manuscript with brief author biography. Prefers email submissions to ASTarticles@astaweb.com (Microsoft Word attachments); will accept 5 hard copies. SASE. Responds in 3 months.

- *Articles:* 1,500–3,000 words. Informational, profiles. Topics: teaching, methodology, techniques, competitions, auditions, association news.
- *Depts/columns:* Word lengths vary. Teaching tips, opinion pieces, industry news.

Sample Issue 80 pages. Advertising. 4 articles; 9 depts/columns. Sample copy available.
- "Paul Rolland and His Influence," by Mimi Zweig. Profile of this musician and his contributions to the industry.
- "Developing Critical Thinking and Assessment in Music Classrooms," by Maria Stefanova. Discussion of the increased expectations of music educators due to standardized testing.

Rights and Payment All rights. No payment. Provides 5 contributor's copies.

Art Education

Department of Art Education, 128 North Oval Mall, Columbus, OH 43210
www.arteducators.org/publications.html

Editor: Christine Ballengee-Morris

This journal of the National Art Education Association covers a diverse range of topics of interest to professional art educators, including lesson plans and successful model programs. Articles that provide examples of art educators' experiences and practices are welcome; dissertations, research reports, and scholarly papers are not. Each manuscript is peer-reviewed before a final decision is made on whether to accept or reject it. ■ **Circulation** 20,000 ■ **Audience** Art educators ■ **Frequency** 6 times a year

Freelance Potential Publishes 42 freelance submissions yearly: 90% written by nonstaff writers; 40% by authors new to the magazine; 40% by previously unpublished writers. Receives 12–17 unsolicited manuscripts monthly.

Submissions Guidelines available at website. Send complete manuscript with cover letter. Accepts hard copy. SASE. Responds in 3 months.
- *Articles:* To 3,000 words. Experience-based informational, profiles, interviews, personal experience. Topics: visual arts, curriculum planning, art history, art criticism.
- *Depts/columns:* To 2,750 words. "Instructional Resources," lesson plan ideas.
- *Artwork:* 8x10 or 5x7 B/W prints or slides; digital images.

Sample Issue 54 pages. Little advertising. 6 articles; 1 dept/column. Sample copy available.
- "Art Education and Special Education: A Promising Partnership," by Beverly Levett Gerber. Discussion of the benefits of combining art education and special education.
- "An Inevitable Question: Exploring the Defining Features of Social Justice Art Education," by Marit Dewhurst. An exploration of the meaning behind social justice art education.

Rights and Payment All rights. No payment. Provides 2 contributor's copies.

Arts & Activities

12345 World Trade Drive, San Diego, CA 92128. www.artsandactivities.com

Editor-in-Chief: Maryellen Bridge

This art education magazine provides art teachers with the inspiration and information that can help them do their jobs better. It views its articles as conduits for the exchange of professional experiences, advice, lesson plans, and fresh ideas. Readers want practical information about things they can do in their art classes. ■ **Circulation** 20,000 ■ **Audience** Art educators, grades K–12 ■ **Frequency** 10 times a year

Freelance Potential Publishes 100 freelance submissions yearly: 95% written by nonstaff writers; 50% by authors new to the magazine; 50% by previously unpublished writers. Receives 20 unsolicited manuscripts monthly.

Submissions Guidelines and theme list available. Send complete manuscript with cover letter indicating your name, teaching position, and personal and professional contact information; and signed release form of students' art. Accepts disk submissions with hard copy. Availability of artwork improves chance of acceptance. No simultaneous submissions. SASE. Responds in 4–8 months.
- *Articles:* Word lengths vary. Informational, how-to, personal experience. Topics: art education, program development, collage, printmaking, art appreciation, composition.
- *Depts/columns:* Word lengths vary. New product information, news items, media reviews.
- *Artwork:* High-resolution digital images or original art.
- *Other:* Lesson plans for classroom projects.

Sample Issue 66 pages. Advertising. 11 articles; 5 depts/columns. Sample copy available.
- "Here Comes the Sun... and I Say It's An Assemblage," by Karen Skophammer. A lesson plan combining a science lesson about the sun with the creation of an assemblage.
- "Inspired by Nevelson," by Barbara Egenes. Teaching preschoolers about artist Louise Nevelson and her circular assemblage.

Rights and Payment First North American serial rights. All material, payment rates vary. Pays on publication. Provides 2 contributor's copies.

Book Links

American Library Association, 50 East Huron Street, Chicago, IL 60611. www.ala.org/booklinks

Editor: Laura Tillotson

This publication of the American Library Association aims to be a source of ideas and strategies for encouraging a love of reading in children. Articles feature techniques for integrating books in the classroom, bibliographies, and author and illustrator profiles. Each issue focuses on a core curriculum area, such as social studies, science, or history. While not every piece published is theme-related, the bulk of the articles have relevance to one of the subjects. ■ **Circulation** 20,577 ■ **Audience** Teachers and librarians ■ **Frequency** Quarterly

Freelance Potential Publishes 60 freelance submissions yearly: 90% written by nonstaff writers; 30% by authors new to the magazine; 20% by previously unpublished writers. Receives 8 queries and unsolicited manuscripts monthly.

Submissions Guidelines and editorial calendar available at website. Query or send complete manuscript. Accepts email to ltillotson@ala.org. Responds in 2 months.
- *Articles:* Word lengths vary. Informational, how-to, profiles, interviews, annotated bibliographies. Topics: multicultural literature, literacy, language arts, core curriculum subjects, education, the arts, authors, illustrators, teaching techniques.
- *Depts/columns:* Word lengths vary. Curriculum ideas, personal essays, themed book lists.

Sample Issue 64 pages. Advertising. 12 articles; 10 depts/columns. Sample copy available.
- "A Poetry Book of Their Own," by Denise B. Geier. Details how to create a simple bookmaking center in the classroom.
- "Thinking Outside the Book: Responding to Literature with VoiceThread," by Jessica Mangelson & Jill Castek. Explains how to use this free interactive online tool that allows students to create products and share them widely.

Rights and Payment All rights. Articles, $100. Pays on publication. Provides 2 contributor's copies.

Canadian Guider

Girl Guides of Canada, 50 Merton Street, Toronto, Ontario M4S 1A3, Canada. www.girlguides.ca

Submissions: Veveen Gregory

Canadian Guider is the magazine for busy Girl Guide leaders and Rangers who are looking for ideas and inspiring stories that will help them offer dynamic programs to girls. It wants to hear from Guiders throughout the country who have spearheaded a successful project or have some inspiration to share.
■ **Circulation** 40,000 ■ **Audience** Girl Guide leaders ■ **Frequency** 3 times a year

Freelance Potential 75% written by nonstaff writers. Receives 1 query or unsolicited manuscript monthly.

Submissions Girl Guide leaders only. Guidelines available. Query with résumé for articles; send complete manuscript for depts/columns. Accepts hard copy. Availability of artwork improves chance of acceptance. SASE. Responds in 1 month.
■ *Articles:* To 200 words. Informational, how-to, profiles, interviews, personal experience pieces. Topics: leadership, life skills, crafts, activities, community service, camping, outdoor adventure, nature, the arts, social issues, international travel.
■ *Depts/columns:* 50–100 words. Leadership profiles, program ideas, personal experience, contests, organizational business.
■ *Artwork:* B/W and color prints. Digital images at 300 dpi.

Sample Issue 46 pages. Advertising. Sample copy available.
■ "Girl Guides Go 'Over the Top' to Eradicate Hunger and Poverty." Details on a program which organized food, diaper, and clothing drives.
■ "From Canoes to Outer Space: This Is No Ordinary Camp." Description of upcoming camp offered for Girl Guides from all over the world.

Rights and Payment All rights. No payment. Provides 2 contributor's copies.

Catalyst Chicago

332 South Michigan Avenue, Suite 500, Chicago, IL 60604. www.catalyst-chicago.org

Editor in Chief: Lorraine Forte

Published by the Community Renewal Society, this magazine provides a forum for parents, educators, and policy makers to discuss topics related to education reform and policy, particularly as they relate to Chicago's urban schools. Experienced educational journalists are always sought. ■ **Circulation** 9,000 ■ **Audience** Parents and educators ■ **Frequency** 5 times a year

Freelance Potential Publishes 6 freelance submissions yearly: 15% written by nonstaff writers; 25% by authors new to the magazine. Receives 4 queries monthly.

Submissions Guidelines available. Query or send letter of introduction. Accepts hard copy and email queries to editorial@catalyst-chicago.org. SASE. Response time varies. All rights.
■ *Articles:* To 2,300 words. Informational. Topics: education reform, education policy, the state of education in the Chicago area.

Sample Issue 16 pages. No advertising. 5 articles. Sample copy available.
■ "Getting Up to Speed," by Sarah Karp. Report on the academic results at a South Side elementary school after it banned social promotion.
■ "The Good and Bad of Retention," by Sarah Karp. Discusses the downside of student retention, even if fewer students are failing.

Rights and Payment All rights. Articles, $1,700. Pays on acceptance. Provides 1 contributor's copy.

Catholic Library World

Catholic Library Association, 100 North Street, Suite 224, Pittsfield, MA 01201-5178. www.cathla.org

Submissions: Sigrid Kelsey

Library professionals turn to this journal for in-depth reviews of religious and secular books and media, as well as informative articles on professional development. It is the official publication of the Catholic Library Association and welcomes submissions from new writers. Feature articles should be relevant to librarians, library science students, and others interested in the field. ■ **Circulation** 1,100 ■ **Audience** Library professionals ■ **Frequency** Quarterly

Freelance Potential Publishes 12–16 freelance submissions yearly: 90% written by nonstaff writers. Receives 3 queries and unsolicited manuscripts monthly.

Submissions Query or send complete manuscript. Accepts hard copy and email submissions to skelsey@lsu.edu (Word attachments). SASE. Response time varies.
■ *Articles:* Word lengths vary. Informational, reviews. Topics: books, reading, library science, Catholic Library Association news.
■ *Depts/columns:* 150–300 words. Media and book reviews. Topics: biography, fiction, multicultural issues, picture books, reference materials, science, social studies, Catholic values.
■ *Artwork:* B/W or color prints or transparencies. Line art.

Sample Issue 80 pages. Little advertising. Sample copy available.
■ "Information Literacy and the Transition from High School to College," by Donna Dix & Marianne Hageman. Details the most successful ways to prepare high school students to retrieve, analyze and use information effectively.
■ "Check It Out! Books Too Good to Miss for Children," by Charlotte Ecker. Reviews a list of recently published children's books.

Rights and Payment All rights. No payment. Provides 1 contributor's copy.

Childhood Education

Association for Childhood Education International, 17904 Georgia Avenue, Suite 215, Olney, MA 20832. www.acei.org

Editor: Anne W. Bauer

Childhood Education is a magazine for professionals involved in the care and education of children from birth through the early teen years. It presents emerging ideas in the field and serves as a forum for opinions backed by research. The mission of the organization is to promote children's education and development, and to influence educators' professional growth. All manuscripts are judged according to how well they reflect that mission. Unsolicited submissions that focus on topics outlined in the editorial calendar are especially encouraged. ■ **Circulation** 10,000 ■ **Audience** Educators, child-care professionals ■ **Frequency** 6 times a year

Freelance Potential Publishes 40 freelance submissions yearly: 98% written by nonstaff writers; 75% by authors new to the magazine. Receives 10 unsolicited manuscripts monthly.

Submissions Guidelines and editorial calendar available. Send 4 copies of complete manuscript (with information identifying author on only one copy). Accepts hard copy and email submissions to abauer@acei.org. SASE. Responds in 3 months.
■ *Articles:* 1,400–3,500 words. Informational. Topics: innovative teaching strategies, the teaching profession, research findings, parenting and family issues, communities, drug education, safe environments for children.
■ *Depts/columns:* 1,000 words. Research news, education issues, parenting, book and media reviews.
■ *Artwork:* Color or B/W photographs

Sample Issue 62 pages. Sample copy available.

- "The Care and Education of Orphan Children with Disabilities in China," by Ying Hu & Judit Szente. Report on child abandonment in China and the developmental consequences of inadequate care and education.
- "A Novice Teacher Fosters Social Competence with Cooperative Learning," by Stacey Magnesio & Barbara H. Davis. Discusses the benefits of cooperative learning among students, and includes practical solutions for introducing it effectively.

Rights and Payment All rights. No payment. Provides 5 contributor's copies.

Children and Families

1651 Prince Street, Alexandria, VA 22314. www.nhsa.org

Managing Editor: Nicole Klaas

Best practices and the latest developments in the field of early childhood education are discussed in this magazine from the National Head Start Association. Primarily targeting early childhood directors, administrators, educators, and support staff, it provides creative ideas, practical solutions, and expert advice. Writers should be concise and tell readers how they can apply what they learn from the article in the classroom. ■ **Circulation** 50,000 ■ **Audience** Early childhood professionals ■ **Frequency** 3 times a year

Freelance Potential Publishes 25 freelance submissions yearly: 90% written by nonstaff writers; 70% by authors new to the magazine; 30% by previously unpublished writers. Receives 2 queries monthly.

Submissions Guidelines available at website. Query with proposed title, outline, author contact information and short biography, intended audience, objective, brief description of why article is important and how audience will benefit, and possible sidebar information. Accepts email queries to julie@nhsa.org. Responds in 1–3 months.
- *Articles:* 1,800–3,800 words. Informational, how-to. Topics: teaching skills, advocacy strategies, problem-solving, administrative issues, school readiness, professional development, special needs and inclusion, parental involvement and partnerships, child development research.
- *Depts/columns:* Word lengths vary. News, tips for home visits, teaching tactics, leadership advice, lesson plans, literacy projects, baby care issues.

Sample Issue 60 pages. Advertising.
- "The Benefits of Learning with Nature." Ideas for connecting young children with the outdoors.
- "Tactics for Teaching." Suggestions for making families of all economic classes and ethnic backgrounds feel welcome in an early childhood program.

Rights and Payment First rights. No payment. Provides 2+ contributor's copies.

Children's Advocate

Action Alliance for Children, 2150 Allston Way, Suite 400, Berkeley, CA 94704. www.4children.org

Editor: Jessine Foss

Parents, teachers, child-care providers, librarians, and others who advocate for children read this tabloid. It covers legislation that affects children and families and related advocacy efforts. It is distributed free throughout California by the nonprofit Action Alliance for Children. Each issue includes articles written in English and Spanish. ■ **Circulation** 23,000 ■ **Audience** Educators and parents ■ **Frequency** Quarterly

Freelance Potential Publishes 24 freelance submissions yearly: 60% written by nonstaff writers.

Submissions All work is assigned. Guidelines available. Send résumé and writing samples. Accepts hard copy. SASE. Response time varies.

- *Articles:* 1,000 words. Informational, how-to. Topics: parenting, childcare, public policy issues and trends, health, child development, poverty.
- *Depts/columns:* 500 words. News, public policy updates, parent/child activities.

Sample Issue 12 pages. No advertising. Sample copy available at website.
- "Leadership by Immigrant Parents Strengthens Schools," by Annia Castillo. Profile of an elementary school that empowered its parents to get involved.
- "Everyday Math and Science," by Aimee Lewis-Strain. Suggests ways to incorporate learning in everyday life.

Rights and Payment First North American serial rights. Written material, 25¢ a word. Pays on acceptance. Provides 3 contributor's copies.

Children's Voice

Child Welfare League of America, 2345 Crystal Drive, Suite 250, Arlington, VA 22202. www.cwla.org/voice

Editor in Chief: Emily Shenk

A publication of the Child Welfare League of America, *Children's Voice* covers the issues that affect children and families, as well as the organizational and bureaucratic challenges that face advocates and other professionals working within the child welfare system. It seeks articles that highlight new, innovative programs and positive results or present success stories of children or families who have been served by the welfare system. ■ **Circulation** 15,000 ■ **Audience** Child welfare advocates ■ **Frequency** 6 times a year

Freelance Potential Publishes 12 freelance submissions yearly: 20% written by nonstaff writers; 50% by authors new to the magazine; 50% by unpublished writers. Receives 5 queries monthly.

Submissions Guidelines available at website. Query. Accepts email queries to voice@cwla.org (text only). Responds in 1 month.
- *Articles:* 2,000–2,500 words. Informational, how-to, profiles, interviews, personal experience. Topics: child welfare issues, nonprofit management and leadership, legal issues, agency problems and practices.
- *Depts/columns:* 500–700 words. Agency news, public policy alerts, state-level child welfare news, Q&As, reports on special education.

Sample Issue 38 pages. Advertising. Sample copy available.
- "Reading, Writing, and Arugula," by Amber Healy. Examines the expanding role of schools in child nutrition.
- "Trafficked Teens Have New Hope," by Jessica Weiss. Profiles Washington-based Courtney's House, which offers help to commercially sexually exploited teens.

Rights and Payment All rights. No payment. Provides contributor's copies and 1-year subscription.

Community Education Journal

3929 Old Lee Highway, Suite 91A, Fairfax, VA 22030. www.ncea.com

Executive Director: Beth Robertson

This journal is published by the National Community Education Association, a group that advocates the creation of lifelong learning opportunities for all community members. It publishes research reports and articles that explore ways in which schools and communities can better provide educational resources for young children, professionals, and at-risk students. Writers should be professional educators and/or administrators with direct experience in community education. ■ **Circulation** Unavailable ■ **Audience** Community educators ■ **Frequency** Quarterly

Freelance Potential Publishes 24 freelance submissions yearly: 85% written by nonstaff writers; 45% by authors new to the magazine; 20% by previously unpublished writers. Receives 1–2 unsolicited manuscripts monthly.

Submissions Guidelines and theme available. Send complete manuscript. Accepts email submissions to ncea@ncea.com (Word or PDF attachments). Responds in 2 months.
■ *Articles:* 1,500–2,000 words. Informational, opinion. Topics: community education programs, research projects, trends.

Sample Issue 36 pages. No advertising. Sample copy available.
■ "21st Century Community Learning Centers: Do They Affect Student Achievement?" by Everett E. Nance & Debra H. Moore. Discusses research about whether after-school programs have a positive effect on student achievement.
■ "Across the Country: Community Schools' Involvement with Service Learning," by Kathy Gibson Carter. Explains how service learning can be integrated into the curriculum to allow students "real life" applications of the content they are being taught.

Rights and Payment All rights. No payment. Provides up to 5 contributor's copies.

Complex Child E-Magazine

www.complexchild.com

Editor: Susan Agrawal

Parents and guardians of children with special needs, medical conditions, and disabilities read this online magazine. It is intended to provide medical information, along with personal experiences, in simple language that other parents can understand. The articles are authored by writers who are themselves caring for children with these same issues. ■ **Hits per month** Unavailable ■ **Audience** Parents ■ **Frequency** Monthly

Freelance Potential Publishes 50 freelance submissions yearly: 25% written by nonstaff writers. Receives 8 queries monthly.

Submissions Guidelines and upcoming themes available at website. Query. Accepts email queries to submit@complexchild.com (Word or text file attachments). Responds in 1–2 months.
■ *Articles:* 500–2,000 words. Informational, personal experience. Topics: special needs, caring for special needs children, education, advocacy.

Sample Issue No advertising. Sample copy available at website.
■ "One BIG Miracle in Such a Small Girl," by Tiffany Cox. Personal experience piece about a young girl who has defied the odds and is surviving a rare blood disorder.
■ "To the Parents of Kids with Special Needs Who Have Grown Up," by Paxton Moynihan. Essay written by a 25-year-old man about growing up with disabilities.

Rights and Payment Limited time electronic rights. No payment.

Curriculum Review

Paperclip Communications, 125 Paterson Avenue, Suite 4, Little Falls, NJ 07424.
www.curriculumreview.com

Editor: Frank Sennett

Curriculum Review offers teachers and administrators the latest news and research in the field, highlighting "what works in our schools." It features articles on education, lesson plans, reviews of classroom resources, and technology updates. Its goal is to help teachers hone their craft through mutual support and the sharing of ideas. ■ **Circulation** 5,000 ■ **Audience** Teachers, administrators ■ **Frequency** 9 times a year

Freelance Potential Publishes 10 freelance submissions yearly: 2% written by nonstaff writers. Receives 2 queries monthly.

Submissions Query. Accepts hard copy. SASE. Responds in 1 month.
- *Articles:* To 4,000 words. Informational, interviews. Topics: education policy, teaching strategies, social issues.
- *Depts/columns:* Word lengths vary. Personal experience, lesson plans.

Sample Issue Sample copy available.
- "Talking with Children about Violence in Schools." Strategies for informing students about potential dangers without causing fear.
- "Attacking Apartheid Education." An interview with Jonathan Kozol, who wrote a book about urban districts hyper-segregating black children.

Rights and Payment One-time rights. Written material, payment rates vary. Payment policy varies. Provides contributor's copies.

Dance Teacher

110 William Street, 23rd Floor, New York, NY 10038. www.dance-teacher.com

Editor: Karen Hildebrand

This magazine is written exclusively for dance educators in a studio, conservatory, or school setting. Its articles address the challenges of teaching dance, provide practical advice from leading educators, and present age-appropriate program and costume ideas for recitals and the classroom.
- **Circulation** 25,000 ■ **Audience** Dance instructors ■ **Frequency** Monthly

Freelance Potential Publishes 100–120 freelance submissions yearly: 67% written by nonstaff writers; 10–15% by authors new to the magazine; 10% by previously unpublished writers. Receives 8 queries monthly.

Submissions Editorial calendar available at website. Query. Accepts hard copy and email to khildebrand@dancemedia.com. SASE. Responds in 2 months.
- *Articles:* 1,000–2,000 words. Informational, how-to, profiles, interviews. Topics: dance instruction, careers in dance, health and wellness.
- *Depts/columns:* 700–1,200 words. Dance techniques, costumes, news.

Sample Issue Sample copy available at website.
- "How I Teach Tap," by Jenny Dalzell. Explains the improvisational tap techniques one teacher uses.
- "Performance Planner: Heroes and Legends," by Lauren Green. Profiles a "Heroes and Legends" themed recital at a Buffalo, New York, studio.

Rights and Payment All rights. Articles; $200–$300. Depts/columns; $150–$250. Pays on publication. Provides 1 contributor's copy.

Dimensions of Early Childhood

Southern Early Childhood Association, P.O. Box 55930, Little Rock, AR 72215-5930. www.southernearlychildhood.org

Editor: Janet B. Stivers

This publication supports high-quality experiences for young children, their families, and educators by advancing the best practices in, and knowledge base of, early childhood education. Its readership includes teachers of young children, family and group child care providers, administrators, and researchers. ■ **Circulation** 19,000 ■ **Audience** Early childhood professionals ■ **Frequency** 3 times a year

Freelance Potential Publishes 40 freelance submissions yearly: 99% written by nonstaff writers; 80%

by authors new to the magazine; 10% by previously unpublished writers. Receives 4 unsolicited manuscripts monthly.

Submissions Guidelines available. Send complete manuscript. Accepts email submissions to editor@southernearlychildhood.org. No simultaneous submissions. Responds in 3 months.
- ■ *Articles:* Word lengths vary. Informational. Topics: emergent curricula for children, effective classroom practices, theory, research, program administration, family relationships, resource systems.
- ■ *Depts/columns:* Word lengths vary. Reviews.
- ■ *Artwork:* High-resolution digital images.

Sample Issue 40 pages. Little advertising. Sample copy available.
- ■ "Blue Eyes, Brown Eyes, Cornrows, and Curls: Building on Books to Explore Physical Diversity with Preschool Children." Discusses early experiences that can help children develop positive attitudes about diversity.
- ■ "Addressing the 'Epidemic' of Overweight Children By Using the Internet." Online resources that can assist teachers with educational activities about fitness.

Rights and Payment All rights. No payment. Provides 2 contributor's copies.

Dyslexia Online Magazine

P.O. Box 1111, Guilford GU1 9EH, United Kingdom. www.dyslexia-magazine.com

Submissions: John Bradford

Parents, teachers, and caregivers of children with dyslexia turn to this online magazine for information as well as inspiration. Personal experience pieces from parents raising dyslexic children are especially sought. ■ **Hits per month** 150,000 ■ **Audience** Parents and teachers ■ **Frequency** Updated regularly

Freelance Potential Publishes 10 freelance submissions yearly: 25% written by nonstaff writers; 50% by authors new to the magazine; 50% by previously unpublished writers. Receives 1 unsolicited manuscript monthly.

Submissions Send complete manuscript. Accepts email submissions to dyslextest@aol.com (no attachments). Responds in 2 weeks.
- ■ *Articles:* Word lengths vary. Informational, how-to, personal experience. Topics: parenting, education, nutrition, and careers—all as it relates to dyslexia.

Sample Issue Sample copy available at website.
- ■ "Teaching Music Notation to Dyslexic Learners," by Richard Nielsen. Addresses difficulties in learning music among dyslexic students, and explains ways to help them succeed.
- ■ "Test of Early Identification of Dyslexia," by Victoria Zakopoulou. Results of a study among infants to identify early dyslexia.

Rights and Payment Rights vary. No payment.

Earlychildhood News

2 Lower Ragsdale, Suite 200, Monterey, CA 93940. www.earlychildhoodnews.com

Assistant Editor: Susan Swanson

This ezine is written for teachers, childcare workers, and homeschooling parents. Designed as a source of information regarding the education and development of children up to age eight, it features articles on children's behavior and guidance, appropriate practices, health and fitness, assessment, teaching strategies, and classroom ideas. The majority of its writers are education or child development professionals. All articles should have a practical application in the classroom or at home.
■ **Hits per month** 50,000 ■ **Audience** Teachers and parents ■ **Frequency** Updated every 2 weeks.

Freelance Potential Publishes 10+ freelance submissions yearly. Receives 8 queries monthly.

Submissions Guidelines and editorial calendar available. Query with author biography. Accepts email to sswanson@excelligence.com. No simultaneous submissions. Responds in 2 months.
- *Articles:* 800–1,200 words. Informational, how-to, research-based, personal experience. Topics: child development, curricula, family relationships, health and safety, nutrition, behavior management, professional development.

Sample Issue Sample copy available at website.
- "Childhood Overweight: What Teachers and Parents Should Know," by Judy K. Martin. How early childhood educators can help prevent childhood obesity.
- "Calming the Anxious Child," by Ronnie Ginsberg. Explores ways to help anxious children in the classroom.

Rights and Payment All rights. Written material, $75–$300. Pays on acceptance.

Educational Horizons

Pi Lambda Theta, P.O. Box 6626, 4101 East Third Street, Bloomington, IN 47407-6626. www.pilambda.org

Managing Editor

Educational Horizons has been revamped to focus on serving the needs of teacher candidates, graduate students, and new teachers who are members of Pi Lambda Theta It seeks submissions for the Why I Teach column and practical and inspirational tips for I Wish I Had Known…. ■ **Circulation** 14,000 ■ **Audience** Pi Lambda Theta members ■ **Frequency** Quarterly

Freelance Potential Publishes 10–15 freelance submissions yearly: 100% written by nonstaff writers; 65–75% by authors new to the magazine; few by previously unpublished writers. Receives 4–5 queries, 2–3 unsolicited manuscripts monthly.

Submissions Guidelines available at website. Send complete manuscript with author's job title, employer, and city/state. Accepts email submissions to edhorizons@pdkintl.org (Word attachments). Response time varies.
- *Articles:* 300 words. Why I Teach essay.
- *Depts/columns:* Word lengths vary. I Wish I Had Known . . . (personal experience pieces).

Sample Issue 64 pages. Little advertising. Sample copy available at website.
- "Why I Teach," by Chris Graves. Personal experience piece about helping at-risk students capitalize on their strengths.
- "Class Dismissed," by Roxanna Elden. Explores ways to channel personal strengths into classroom success.

Rights and Payment First rights. No payment. Provides 5 contributor's copies.

Educational Leadership

ASCD, 1703 North Beauregard Street, Alexandria, VA 22311-1714. www.ascd.org/el

Editor in Chief: Marge Scherer

This publication of the Association for Supervision and Curriculum Development is read by teachers, school administrators, and other education professionals for timely articles and opinion pieces. Submissions that describe classroom-tested methods and real-life experiences are always needed. Writers are encouraged to review the theme list at the website. ■ **Circulation** 170,000 ■ **Audience** Educators, K–12 ■ **Frequency** 8 times a year

Freelance Potential Publishes 130 freelance submissions yearly: 95% written by nonstaff writers; 75% developed from unsolicited submissions; 50% by authors new to the magazine; 50% by previously unpublished writers. Receives 75 unsolicited manuscripts monthly.

Submissions Guidelines and theme list available at website. Send 2 copies of complete manuscript. Prefers email to elsubmissions@ascd.org (Word document; include "Educational Leadership manuscript submission" in subject line); will accept hard copy. SASE. Responds in 2 months.
- *Articles:* 1,500–2,500 words. Informational, how-to, research-based, program descriptions, personal experience, opinion. Topics: reading, assessment, instructional strategies, student achievement, gifted and special education, science, technology, multicultural issues.
- *Depts/columns:* Word lengths vary. Opinions, accountability issues, research findings, leadership challenges, principals' perspectives, ASCD news, policy reviews.
- *Artwork:* B/W or color prints or slides; digital images at 300 dpi. Line art.

Sample Issue 96 pages. Advertising. Sample copy available.
- "Learning to Love Reading in 30 Minutes," by Kathy King-Dickman. Strategies that boost comprehension skills in struggling adolescent readers.
- "Involvement or Engagement?" by Larry Ferlazzo. Discusses the kinds of school-family connections that will raise student achievement.

Rights and Payment All or first rights. No payment. Provides 5 contributor's copies.

Education Forum

60 Mobile Drive, Toronto, Ontario M4A 2P3, Canada. www.osstf.on.ca

Managing Editor: Rhonda Allan

Education issues, trends, and strategies are covered in this bilingual journal for Ontario-based teachers and administrators. It also features the success stories of professionals in public education. New writers are welcome here. ■ **Circulation** 50,000 ■ **Audience** Educators ■ **Frequency** 3 times a year

Freelance Potential Publishes 35 freelance submissions yearly; 90% written by nonstaff writers; 80% by authors new to the magazine; 20% by previously unpublished writers. Receives 4 queries and unsolicited manuscripts monthly.

Submissions Guidelines available. Query with clips or writing samples; or send complete manuscript. Accepts hard copy. No simultaneous submissions. SAE/IRC. Responds in 1–2 months.
- *Articles:* To 2,500 words. How-to, practical application, essays, opinion. Topics: education trends, teaching techniques, controversial issues relating to education.
- *Depts/columns:* Openers (to 300 words, news and opinion), Forum Picks (word lengths vary, media and software reviews).
- *Artwork:* B/W or color prints or color transparencies. Line art.
- *Other:* Classroom activities, puzzles, games. Submit seasonal material 8 months in advance.

Sample Issue 46 pages. Advertising. Sample copy available.
- "Many Faces, One Community," by Robert Savage & Paul Schaffer. Describes an open gym program at an urban school that keeps students active, in school, and out of trouble.
- "Strong Public Education," by Wendy Anes Hirschegger. Discusses the importance of weaving Canadian values into the social fabric of the education system.

Rights and Payment First North American serial rights. No payment. Provides 5 contributor's copies.

The Education Revolution

417 Roslyn Road, Roslyn Heights, NY 11577. www.educationrevolution.org

Executive Editor: Jerry Mintz

Read by educators, administrators, and parents alike, *The Education Revolution* offers timely information on alternative education. Each issue features profiles of successful alternative schools, both public and private, and informative articles on homeschooling trends. News, conference and event details, and information about job opportunities are also included. It is published by the Alternative Education Resource Organization. ■ **Circulation** 5,000. ■ **Audience** Educators and parents ■ **Frequency** Quarterly

Freelance Potential Publishes 10 freelance submissions yearly: 20% written by nonstaff writers; 40% by authors new to the magazine. Receives 15 queries monthly.

Submissions Query. Accepts hard copy. SASE. Responds in 1 month.
■ *Articles:* Word lengths vary. Informational, profiles. Topics: education, alternative schools, home-schooling,
■ *Depts/columns:* Word lengths vary. Education news, association events

Sample Issue Sample issue available at website.
■ "Being There," by Jerry Mintz. First-person piece about visiting alternative schools in Puerto Rico.
■ "The World Becomes What You Teach," by Zoe Weil. Essay urges educators to create models for humane education.

Rights and Payment Rights vary. No payment.

Education Week

6935 Arlington Road, Suite 100, Bethesda, MD 20814-5233. www.edweek.org

Executive Editor: Greg Chronister

As "American Education's Newspaper of Record," this publication of the nonprofit Editorial Projects in Education reports on critical issues facing American schools. Its articles cover education news, politics, government programs, and trends in education. The majority of articles are written by staff journalists, but educators, administrators, economists, and other professionals knowledgeable about the education field are welcome to submit opinions essays. ■ **Circulation** 50,000 ■ **Audience** Educators ■ **Frequency** 45 times a year

Freelance Potential Publishes 135 freelance submissions yearly: 20% written by nonstaff writers; 75% by authors new to the magazine; 80% by previously unpublished writers. Receives 42 unsolicited manuscripts monthly.

Submissions Guidelines available. Send complete manuscript. Accepts disk submissions. SASE. Responds in 6–8 weeks.
■ *Articles:* Staff-written.
■ *Depts/columns:* To 1,200 words. Commentary (essays about child development and education related to grades K–12).

Sample Issue 40 pages. Advertising. Sample copy available.
■ "Let Us Not Abandon Listening in the Classroom," by Diana Senechal. Essay about the importance of really listening—to cadences, inflection, and tone—to teachers and students.
■ "Collaboration Is Essential in Public Education," by Irving Hamer. Essay takes issue with recent comments made by the former New York City schools chancellor.

Rights and Payment First rights. Commentary essays, $200. Pays on publication. Provides 2 contributor's copies.

EduGuide

Partnership for Learning, 321 North Pine, Lansing, MI 48933. www.eduguide.org

Editor: Mary Kat Parks-Workinger

Published by Partnership for Learning, *EduGuide* offers a "roadmap for student success." As such, it is packed with advice, resources, and strategies for educating children from kindergarten through college. Four editions are offered to serve the needs of students in the elementary, middle school, high

school, and college years. ■ **Circulation** 600,000 ■ **Audience** Parents, students, and teachers
■ **Frequency** Annually

Freelance Potential Publishes 25–30 freelance submissions yearly: 40% written by nonstaff writers;
40% by authors new to the magazine; 10% by previously unpublished writers.

Submissions Guidelines and editorial calendar available. Query. Accepts hard copy. SASE. Responds
in 4–6 weeks.
■ *Articles:* 500–1,000 words. Informational, how-to, profiles, interviews, personal experience. Topics:
the arts, college, careers, computers, gifted education, health, fitness, history, humor, mathematics, music, science, technology, special education, issues related to elementary and secondary
education.
■ *Depts/columns:* Staff-written.
■ *Artwork:* Color prints and transparencies. Line art.
■ *Other:* Submit seasonal material 3 months in advance.

Sample Issue 12 pages: 4 articles; 3 depts/columns. Sample copy available.
■ "Parent Involvement Essential to Successful Middle School Transition to High School," by
Elizabeth Johnson. Explains topics parents should discuss with their children before they begin
high school.
■ "School Stress in Children: What To Expect." Social strategies to help students deal with a variety of
school fears.

Rights and Payment First or second rights. All material, payment rates vary. Pays on acceptance.
Provides 5 contributor's copies.

Edutopia

The George Lucas Educational Foundation, P.O. Box 3494, San Rafael, CA 94912. www.edutopia.org

Executive Editor: Jennifer Sweeney

This magazine, published by the George Lucas Educational Foundation, has a mission to share ideas
about interactive educational environments. It is filled with articles that address the issues of the
current education system and provide innovative ideas on integrated studies, learning, teacher development, and using technology in education. ■ **Circulation** 100,000 ■ **Audience** Teachers, parents,
policy makers ■ **Frequency** 8 times a year

Freelance Potential Publishes 20 freelance submissions yearly: 70% written by nonstaff writers; 30%
by authors new to the magazine. Receives 3–5 queries monthly.

Submissions Query with résumé and clips. Accepts email to edit@edutopia.org. Response time
varies.
■ *Articles:* 300–2,500 words. Informational, how-to, personal experience. Topics: education, computers, science, technology, social issues, current events, health and fitness, nature and the environment, popular culture, recreation, travel.
■ *Depts/columns:* 700 words. Health, education, ethnic and multicultural issues.

Sample Issue 56 pages. Advertising.10 articles; 10 depts/columns. Sample copy available.
■ "Programming Is the New Literacy," by Marc Prensky. Shares reasons why fluency in multimedia
and game-derived devices will be increasingly significant tools for communication.
■ "A Teacher's Guide to Generation X Parents," by Susan Gregory Thomas. Essay describes why
Generation X parents do the obnoxious and self-righteous things that they do.

Rights and Payment First and anthology rights. Written material, 5¢–8¢ a word. Pays on acceptance.
Provides 3 contributor's copies.

The Elementary School Journal

University of Michigan, School of Education, 610 East University Avenue, Suite 3210, Ann Arbor, MI 48109-1255. www.journals.uchicago.edu/ESJ

Editor: Joanne Carlisle

This academic journal offers articles on education theory and research. It is read and written by educators and researchers, and addresses the practical implications of the work presented. All content is peer-reviewed. ■ **Circulation** 2,200 ■ **Audience** Educators ■ **Frequency** 5 times a year

Freelance Potential Publishes several freelance submissions yearly: 100% written by nonstaff writers.

Submissions Guidelines available at website. Send complete manuscript with abstract of 100–150 words. Accepts submissions via Editorial Manager only at http://esj.edmgr.com No simultaneous submissions. Response time varies.
■ *Articles:* To 45 pages. Research. Topics: teaching and learning processes, school leadership and policy, instructional methods and programs, assessment practices, advances in learning technologies.

Sample Issue 8 articles. Sample copy available.
■ "Response to Intervention in Literacy: Problems and Possibilities," by Peter H. Johnston. Study of the structures and belief systems that emphasize the need to identify individuals with disabilities.
■ "Small Group, Computer-Assisted Tutoring to Improve Reading Outcomes for Struggling First and Second Graders," by Bette Chambers & Robert E. Slavin. Study evaluates the relative effects of Tier II computer-assisted tutoring in small groups and one-on-one tutoring provided to struggling readers in high-poverty schools.

Rights and Payment Rights vary. No payment.

Encyclopedia of Youth Studies

130 Essex Street, South Hamilton, MA 01982. www.centerforyouth.org

Editor: Dean Borgman

This website serves as an innovative educational and ministerial resource to those adults who mentor, minister to, study, or otherwise support the world's youth. Its articles summarize topics related to the education of or service to youth, and provide advice support. ■ **Hits per month** Unavailable ■ **Audience** Youth ministry professionals ■ **Frequency** Updated regularly

Freelance Potential Publishes 5–10 freelance submissions yearly: 20% written by nonstaff writers; 85% by authors new to the magazine; 85% by previously unpublished writers. Receives 3 queries, 1 unsolicited manuscripts monthly.

Submissions Guidelines available at website. Query or send complete manuscript with signed copyright release form. Accepts hard copy and email submissions to cys@centerforyouth.org. Responds to queries in 1 week, to manuscripts in 1 month.
■ *Articles:* 600 words. Informational, how-to, book reviews, case studies. Topics: understanding, helping, and counseling youth.

Sample Issue Sample copy available at website.
■ "Sexuality of Middle School Students," by Steve Maturo. Discusses the impact of pop culture and sexuality on preteens.
■ "Race-blind or Racially-open Adoption Policy?" by Dean Borgman. Explores the effects of interracial adoptions on the children.

Rights and Payment All rights. No payment.

eSchoolNews

7920 Norfolk Avenue, Suite 900, Bethesda, MD 20814. www.eschoolnews.com

Editor: Gregg Downey

eSchoolNews appears in print as well as online for teachers and school administrators at all grade levels. It covers education technology in all its aspects—including legislation and litigation, case studies, purchasing practices, and new products. Submissions from educators are preferred, but ed-tech executives are welcome to contribute provided they do not advocate a particular company or product.
■ **Circulation** 100,000 ■ **Audience** Teachers and school administrators ■ **Frequency** Updated monthly

Freelance Potential Publishes 6–8 freelance submissions yearly: 20% written by nonstaff writers. Receives 8 unsolicited manuscripts monthly.

Submissions Prefers query; will accept complete manuscript. Include 1- to 2- sentence biography and headshot. Accepts email submissions to gdowney@eschoolnews.com. No simultaneous submissions. Response time varies.
■ *Articles:* 800–1,200 words. Informational, how-to, opinion pieces, case studies. Topics: software, systems, websites, professional development, school technology challenges and solutions.
■ *Depts/columns:* Word lengths vary. Product reviews, technology news and trends

Sample Issue Sample copy available at website.
■ "Pennsylvania District Settles Webcam Spying Lawsuits for $610K." Report on a lawsuit of illegal webcam photographs.
■ "Summit: U.S. Needs More Computer Science Teachers," by Jenna Zwang. Discusses the lack of properly trained computer science educators and the lack of computer science courses in schools.

Rights and Payment Rights vary. Written material, payment rates vary. Pays on acceptance.

Exchange Magazine

17725 NE 65th Street, Unit B275, Redmond, WA 98052. www.childcareexchange.com

Associate Editor: Donna Rafanello

Formerly listed as *Child Care Exchange*, this magazine is read by early childhood professionals for informative articles about trends in the field and for strategies that work in real-life settings. Though it works primarily with writers found via referral, it accepts submissions. ■ **Circulation** 30,000
■ **Audience** Child-care professionals ■ **Frequency** 6 times a year

Freelance Potential Publishes 120 freelance submissions yearly: 85% written by nonstaff writers; 20–33% by authors new to the magazine; 50% by previously unpublished writers. Receives 6 unsolicited manuscripts monthly.

Submissions Guidelines and theme list available at website. Send complete manuscript with brief author biography, list of article references, updated author photograph, article length, artwork (by mail only) and contact information. Accepts email to submissions@childcareexchange.com (Word attachments). Availability of artwork improves chance of acceptance. SASE. Response time varies.
■ *Articles:* 1,800 words. Informational, how-to, self-help. Topics: child development; education; social, multicultural, and ethnic issues.
■ *Depts/columns:* Word lengths vary. Staff development and training, parent perspectives, child nutrition, program profiles, product reviews.
■ *Artwork:* Color prints. Line art.

Sample Issue 104 pages. Sample copy available.
■ "Children Need Attentive Support During Wartime," by Karen Stephens. Provides tips for giving children affected by war the support they need.

- "Emotional Attachments Motivate Children's Language Mastery," by Karen Stephens. Discusses the importance of realizing a child's full literacy potential.

Rights and Payment All rights. Articles, $300. Depts/columns, payment rates vary. Pays on publication. Provides 2 contributor's copies.

The Forensic Teacher

P.O. Box 5263, Wilmington, DE 19808. www.theforensicteacher.com

Editor: Mark Feil

Information and ideas on teaching forensic topics, such as decomposition, fibers, and toxicology, are the focus of this magazine written by and for teachers. Lab units should be kept simple, and offer practical tips for success. It prefers to work with teachers, but will accept work from others as long classroom applications are included. ■ **Circulation** 30,000 ■ **Audience** Middle school and college teachers ■ **Frequency** Quarterly

Freelance Potential Publishes 18 freelance submissions yearly: 50% written by nonstaff writers. Receives 2–5 queries, 2–3 unsolicited manuscripts monthly.

Submissions Guidelines available at website. Query with clips or writing samples; or send complete manuscript. Accepts email submissions to admin@theforensicteacher.com (Word attachments; attach photos separately). Availability of artwork improves chance of acceptance. Responds to queries in 2 weeks, to manuscripts in 2 months.
- *Articles:* 400–2,000 words. Informational, how-to, lesson plans, photo-essays, personal experience. Topics: forensics, industry news, science, technology, forensic law.
- *Depts/columns:* Word lengths vary. Classroom mystery projects, forensic history and trivia, book reviews.
- *Artwork:* Color prints.
- *Other:* Submit seasonal information 6 months in advance.

Sample Issue 32 pages. Sample copy available.
- "Explosions: Science & Scenarios," by Perry Michael Koussiafes. Lesson plan on the technical aspects of an explosion and its comparison to fire.
- "The Cornflour Bomb," by Brian Bellone. Lesson plan for a combustion experiment.

Rights and Payment First, second, and electronic rights. Articles and depts/columns, 2¢ a word. News items, $10 each. Pays 60 days after publication.

Foster Focus

Hard Times Media, 608 Main Street, Watsontown, PA 17777. www.fosterfocusmag.com

Owner/Editor: Chris Chmielewski

Foster Focus offers an in-depth look at the foster care industry. Its articles cover industry news, legislation, foster family relationships, family getaways, and careers within the industry. Each issue also offers a look at some of the children in the system who are eligible for adoption. Many of its writers work within the foster care system or have grown up in the system. It is actively seeking submissions from people within the system, either as a care professional, advocate, or client. ■ **Circulation** Unavailable ■ **Audience** Foster care professionals, clients ■ **Frequency** Monthly

Freelance Potential Actively looking for submissions.

Submissions Query. Accepts email queries to writers@FosterFocusMag.com. Response time varies.
- *Articles:* Word lengths vary. Informational, profiles, personal experience. Topics: the foster care system, living within foster care, careers in foster care.

- *Depts/columns:* Word lengths vary. Guest Speaker (opinion from foster care professionals), Job Market (helping readers plan a career path in the foster care industry).

Sample Issue Sample copy available at website.
- "The Day I Left Care," by Chris Chmielewski. Personal experience about leaving foster care.
- "Guest Speaker," by Ashley Rhodes Courier. Essay from a best-selling author about the future of foster care.

Rights and Payment Unavailable.

Gifted Education Press Quarterly

10201 Yuma Court, P.O. Box 1586, Manassas, VA 20109. www.giftededpress.com

Editor/Publisher: Maurice D. Fisher

This newsletter, available online as well as in print, addresses issues related to educating gifted students. Written by leaders in the field, the articles and research studies target administrators, program coordinators, academics, and parents. It uses a scholarly tone and demands extensive research and references. ■ **Circulation** 15,000. ■ **Audience** Educators and parents ■ **Frequency** Quarterly

Freelance Potential Publishes 14 freelance submissions yearly: 75% written by nonstaff writers; 67% by authors new to the magazine. Receives 30 queries yearly.

Submissions Query with writing sample. Accepts email queries to mfisher345@comcast.net. Responds in 1 week.
- *Articles:* 2,500–4,000 words. Informational, how-to, research, personal experience, profiles, interviews, scholarly essays. Topics: gifted education; multicultural, ethnic, and social issues; homeschooling; multiple intelligence; parent advocates; academic subjects; the environment; popular culture.

Sample Issue 14 pages. No advertising. Sample copy available at website.
- "Excuses for Not Developing Mathematical Talent," by Susan G. Assouline. Examines issues with the programs and curricula for mathematically talented students.
- "Decoding William Faulkner and the Gifted," by Michael E. Waters. Discusses methods to decoding Faulkner's literary works.

Rights and Payment All rights. No payment. Provides a 1-year subscription

Green Teacher

95 Robert Street, Toronto, Ontario M5S 2K5, Canada. www.greenteacher.com

Editor: Tim Grant

Promoting environmental and global awareness in students in kindergarten through high school is the purpose of *Green Teacher*. It includes classroom-ready activities and general informational articles. Most of its articles are written by teachers in the fields of environmental or global education, but freelance writers are welcome to submit. ■ **Circulation** 7,500 ■ **Audience** Teachers, grades K–12 ■ **Frequency** Quarterly

Freelance Potential Publishes 120 freelance submissions yearly: 100% written by nonstaff writers; 80% by previously unpublished writers. Receives 41+ queries monthly.

Submissions Guidelines available at website. Send query with outline. Prefers email submissions to tim@greenteacher.com (Word, RTF, or text attachments); will accept disk submissions with hard copy. If possible, include 8–10 photographs. Availability of artwork improves chance of acceptance. SAE/IRC. Responds in 1 month.
- *Articles:* 1,500–3,500 words. Informational, how-to, opinion, lesson plans. Topics: environmental and global education.
- *Depts/columns:* Word lengths vary. Reviews, resources, announcements.

■ *Artwork:* JPEG and TIFF images at 300 dpi; B/W and color prints or slides. Line art.
■ *Other:* Submit Earth Day material 6 months in advance.

Sample Issue 48 pages. Advertising. 12 articles; 2 depts/columns. Sample copy available at website.
■ "Social Justice and Language Arts," by Christopher Greenslate. Discusses how teachers and students can connect language arts with current social and global issues.
■ "Last Child in the Woods, First Book in the Field," by Mike Weilbacher. Examines the effects Richard Louv's best-selling book has had on environmental education.

Rights and Payment Rights negotiable. No payment. Provides 5 contributor's copies and a 1-year subscription.

The High School Journal

School of Education, University of North Carolina at Chapel Hill, CB3500 Peabody Hall, Chapel Hill, NC 28599-3500. www.soe.unc.edu/hsj

Managing Editor: Jennifer Job

The High School Journal publishes articles discussing the multiple dimensions of secondary education, including well-researched articles on adolescent growth, development, interests, beliefs, values, and learning. Founded in 1918, it is one of the oldest journals in education and the only nationally circulated, peer-reviewed journal of its kind. *HSJ* is housed in the University of North Carolina at Chapel Hill School of Education and is managed and edited by doctoral students in the Ph.D. in Education; Culture, Curriculum, and Change program. ■ **Circulation** 900 ■ **Audience** High school educators ■ **Frequency** Quarterly

Freelance Potential Publishes 20–30 freelance submissions yearly: 100% written by nonstaff writers; 85% by authors new to the magazine; 25% by previously unpublished writers. Receives 27 unsolicited manuscripts monthly.

Submissions Guidelines available at website. Send complete manuscript. Accepts email submissions via website. Responds in 3–4 months.
■ *Articles:* 20–25 pages. Research. Topics: adolescent growth, development, interests, beliefs, values, and learning—all as they affect school practice; teacher, administrator, and student interaction within secondary school setting.

Sample Issue 3 articles. Sample copy available.
■ "Teacher Perspectives on Career-Relevant Curriculum in Middle School," by Charles P. Akos. Discusses the benefits of a career-relevant curriculum that keep students challenged.
■ "Assessing and Promoting Spiritual Wellness as a Protective Factor in Secondary Schools," by M. Briggs. Reviews literature that links spiritual wellness to thriving in the adolescent population.

Rights and Payment All rights. No payment. Provides 2 contributor's copies.

Home Education Magazine

P.O. Box 1083, Tonasket, WA 98855. www.homeedmag.com

Articles Editor: Jeanne Faulconer

Since 1984, this magazine has brought homeschooling parents timely articles and columns about the issues they deal with, and how homeschooling can enhance the joy of family life. It seeks articles that offer practical lesson ideas, support, and inspiration for homeschoolers, or information on getting started for those considering homeschooling. ■ **Circulation** 110,000 ■ **Audience** Parents ■ **Frequency** 6 times a year

Freelance Potential Publishes 35–40 freelance submissions yearly: 90% written by nonstaff writers;

40% by authors new to the magazine; 25% by previously unpublished writers. Receives 20 queries and manuscripts monthly.

Submissions Guidelines available. Prefers complete manuscript; will accept query. Include 40- to 60-word author biography. Prefers email to articles@homeedmag.com (Word attachments; include author's last name, first name or initial, and title of article in subject line); will accept hard copy. SASE. Responds in 1–2 months.
- *Articles:* 900–1,700 words. Informational, how-to, profiles, interviews, personal experience. Topics: homeschooling, activism, lessons, parenting issues.
- *Depts/columns:* Staff-written.
- *Artwork:* B/W and color prints; digital images at 200 dpi, 300 dpi for cover images.

Sample Issue 42 pages. Advertising. Sample copy available.
- "Beware the Ambition Monster," by Sue Zelle. An essay about stepping back from children's lives so they can learn to depend on themselves.
- "CreekSchooling," by Pamela Jorrick. Personal experience piece about teaching children to enjoy and appreciate nature.

Rights and Payment First North American serial and electronic rights. Articles, $50–$100. Artwork, $12.50; $100 for cover art. Kill fee, 25%. Pays on acceptance. Provides 1+ contributor's copies.

Home Educator's Family Times

P.O. Box 107, Abingdon, MD 21009. www.homeeducator.com/familytimes

Editor: Jane R. Boswell

Now appearing exclusively in digital or PDF format, *Home Educator's Family Times* covers relevant trends and issues in homeschooling. It also offers curriculum ideas and teaching strategies. It does not pay its writers, but will include a short byline to promote a product or service. ■ **Hits per month** 25,000 ■ **Audience** Parents ■ **Frequency** 6 times a year

Freelance Potential Publishes 50 freelance submissions yearly: 90% written by nonstaff writers; 25% by authors new to the magazine.

Submissions Guidelines available at website. Send complete manuscript with author biography and permission statement from website. Accepts disk submissions and email to famtimes@blazenetme.net (Word or text attachments). SASE. Response time varies.
- *Articles:* 1,000–1,500 words. Informational, how-to, opinion, personal experience. Topics: homeschooling methods and lessons, family life, parenting, pets, reading, art, science, creative writing.
- *Depts/columns:* Staff-written.

Sample Issue 24 pages. Advertising. Sample copy available at website.
- "Preparing Our Kids for a Challenging Future," by Barbara Frank. Opinion piece on how to homeschool so the children are better prepared for the real world.
- "If You Give a Boy a Lapbook," by Jodi Whisler. Lesson plan of activities centered around a picture book.

Rights and Payment One-time and electronic reprint rights. No payment.

Homeschooling Today

P.O. Box 244, Abingdon, VA 24212. www.homeschooltoday.com.

Editor

Presenting a mix of practical ideas and inspirational articles, this magazine is read by parents who seek information and support for their homeschooling activities. It reflects a Christian perspective and aims to bring the homeschool community useful information and resources. All material should be supported by a biblical conviction that God uses families to change the world. ■ **Circulation** 25,000 ■ **Audience** Parents ■ **Frequency** 6 times a year

Freelance Potential Publishes 60–70 freelance submissions yearly: 90% written by nonstaff writers; 14% by authors new to the magazine; 6% by previously unpublished writers. Receives 5–10 unsolicited manuscripts monthly.

Submissions Guidelines and theme list available at website. Send complete manuscript. Prefers email to management@homeschooltoday.com (Word attachments; include "Article Submission" in subject line); will accept CD submissions. Responds in 3–6 months.
■ *Articles:* 1,400–2,000 words. Informational, self-help, and how-to, profiles, personal experience. Topics: education, religion, music, technology, special education, the arts, history, mathematics, science.
■ *Depts/columns:* 500–875 words. Time management, history, music, religion, the arts, homeschooling tips. Reviews, 150–475 words.

Sample Issue 68 pages: Sample copy available.
■ "Interview with Authors Mark Thogmartin and Mary Gallagher," by Marilyn Rockett. Discussion about the current research on how the brain works and how children learn to read.
■ "Based on 'The Boy Who Built the Boat,'" by Kara Murphy. Lesson plan for reading Ross Mueller's book with children ages 5–8.

Rights and Payment First North American serial rights. Written material, 10¢ a word. $50 for reprints. Pays on publication. Provides 1 contributor's copy.

Instructor

Scholastic Inc., 557 Broadway, New York, NY 10012-39999. www.scholastic.com/instructor

Editorial Assistant: Megan Kaesshaefer

This magazine is dedicated to helping teachers in kindergarten though eighth grade be as effective as they possibly can. Published by Scholastic, *Instructor* includes articles on facing the everyday challenges of teaching, as well as lesson plans and reviews of teacher resources. Classroom-tested ideas that have been developed by creative elementary and middle school teachers are especially sought. ■ **Circulation** 200,000+ ■ **Audience** Teachers, grades K–8 ■ **Frequency** 6 times a year

Freelance Potential Publishes 55 freelance submissions yearly: 90% written by nonstaff writers; 10% by previously unpublished writers. Receives 8 queries monthly.

Submissions Guidelines available. Query. Accepts email queries to instructor@scholastic.com. Availability of artwork improves chance of acceptance. Responds in 3–4 months.
■ *Articles:* 1,200 words. Informational, how-to, interviews, personal experience. Topics: lesson planning, classroom management, career development, workplace issues, learning and literacy issues, technology.
■ *Depts/columns:* News, Q&A's, technology briefs, book reviews, Teachers' Picks, word lengths vary. Classroom activities, to 250 words. Humorous or poignant personal essays, to 400 words.
■ *Artwork:* Color prints or transparencies.

Sample Issue 64 pages. Advertising. Sample copy available.
■ "Teach Like a Champ," by Caralee Adams. Interview with author Doug Lemov on his book of practical ideas for running a more efficient, inspired, and joyful class.
■ "Tales from a One-Room Schoolhouse," by Megan Kaesshaefer. Interview with a teacher of a 15-student, one-classroom school in rural Nevada.

Rights and Payment All rights. Written material, 80¢ a word. Pays on publication. Provides 2 author's copies.

Journal of Adolescent & Adult Literacy

International Reading Association, 800 Barksdale Road, P.O. Box 8139, Newark, DE 19714-8139. www.reading.org

Managing Editor: James Henderson

This peer-reviewed journal targets those who work with new, struggling, and skilled readers alike. Read by literacy teachers and administrators, it highlights research-based practices aimed at improving literacy achievement in students age 12 and older. It seeks articles that make a significant contribution to advancing and integrating theory and practice. Submissions will be judged on originality, significance, scholarship, audience appropriateness, and writing style. ■ **Circulation** 16,000 ■ **Audience** Reading education professionals ■ **Frequency** 8 times a year

Freelance Potential Publishes 50 freelance submissions yearly: 95% written by nonstaff writers; 50% by authors new to the magazine; 30% by previously unpublished writers. Receives 25 unsolicited manuscripts monthly, of which 15–20% are accepted.

Submissions Send complete manuscript with cover letter, abstract of 150 words written in the third person, one blind copy of the manuscript (author names removed), tables and figures in separate files. Accepts electronic submissions only via http://mc.manuscriptcentral.com/jaal (Word attachments). Responds in 2–3 months.
■ *Articles:* 5,000–6,000 words. Informational. Topics: reading theory, research, and practice; trends in teaching literacy; impact of technology on literacy development; increasing diversity among literacy learners.
■ *Artwork:* Images in TIFF or JPEG format.

Sample Issue Sample copy available.
■ "Did They Get It?" by Jana Echevarria et al. The role of fidelity in implementing proven methods when teaching English learners.
■ "The Shakespeare in All of Us," by Jennifer Ann Savino. Approaching vocabulary instruction with a premeditated, multitudinous approach.

Rights and Payment All rights. No payment. Provides 5 contributor's copies.

Journal of School Health

American School Health Association, 7263 State Road 43, P.O. Box 708, Kent, OH 44240-0708. www.ashaweb.org

Editor: James H. Price

Health educators, school nurses, and school administrators subscribe to this professional journal from the American School Health Association. It covers everything from fetal alcohol syndrome to teen pregnancy and depression. It is interested in all health-related topics affecting preschoolers through high school students. All submissions must be factually accurate and based on rigorous research. ■ **Circulation** 5,000 ■ **Audience** School health professionals ■ **Frequency** 10 times a year

Freelance Potential Publishes 60 freelance submissions yearly: 95% written by nonstaff writers; 90% by authors new to the magazine. Receives 10 unsolicited manuscripts monthly.

Submissions Guidelines available at website. Send complete manuscript with 250-word abstract (include background, methods, results, and conclusion) and title page with author name, academic degree, current position, professional affiliations, and contact information. Accepts email submissions via http://mc.manuscriptcentral.com/josh. No simultaneous submissions. Responds in 3–4 months.
■ *Articles:* 2,500 words. Informational, research, commentaries, practical application. Topics: teaching techniques, health services in the school system, nursing, medicine, substance abuse, nutrition, counseling, ADD/AHD.

Sample Issue 58 pages. No advertising. Sample copy available .
- ■ "Developments in Clinical Neuropsychology: Implications for School Psychological Services," by Michael J. Cleary. Examines the growing specialty of clinical neuropsychology and provides suggestions for integrating the field into school-based psychological services.
- ■ "Prevalence of Food Insecurity and Utilization of Food Assistance Program: An Exploratory Survey of a Vermont Middle School," by Shamina Khan & Richard G. Pinckney. Reports on a study of school children and the relationship between food insecurity, participation in school lunches, exercise, and body mass index.

Rights and Payment All rights. No payment. Provides 2 contributor's copies.

Language Arts Journal

Ohio State University, 333 Arps Hall, 1945 North High Street, Columbus, OH 43210. www.ncte.org

Language Arts Editorial Team

All facets of language arts learning and teaching—focusing on preschool through middle school—are covered in this magazine. Articles discuss both theory and classroom practice, highlight current research, and review children's literature and professional development books. ■ **Circulation** 12,000 ■ **Audience** Language arts teachers ■ **Frequency** 6 times a year

Freelance Potential Publishes 60 freelance submissions yearly: 90% written by nonstaff writers; 30% by authors new to the magazine; 15% by previously unpublished writers. Receives 16 unsolicited manuscripts monthly.

Submissions Guidelines and theme list available via email request to langarts@osu.edu. Send complete manuscript via www.editorialmanager.com/langarts/. Responds in 3–12 months.
- ■ *Articles:* 2,500–6,500 words. Informational, how-to, profiles, photo essays, opinion. Topics: learning and teaching English studies, literacy, language arts.
- ■ *Depts/columns:* Word lengths vary. Professional and children's book reviews.
- ■ *Artwork:* B/W JPEG or TIFF images.

Sample Issue Sample copy available.
- ■ "Writing That Matters: Collaborative Inquiry and Authoring Practices in First-Grade Class," by Maria Paula Ghiso. Lesson plan focusing on student authors investigating their classroom and neighborhood communities.
- ■ "Focus on Policy: Listening to Echoes: Teaching Young Black Men Literacy and the Problem of ELA Standards," by David E. Kirkland. The detrimental effects ELA standards have on the black male school experiences are explored.

Rights and Payment All rights. No payment. Provides 2 contributor's copies.

Learning & Leading with Technology

180 West Eighth Avenue, Suite 300, Eugene, OR 97401-2916. www.iste.org/LL

Editor: Kate Conley

Featuring practical ideas for using today's technology tools to improve teaching and learning, this magazine is targeted to primary and secondary educators. The membership magazine of the International Society of Technology in Education, it offers articles, reviews, and case studies. Writers are typically education professionals. ■ **Circulation** 25,000 ■ **Audience** Educators, grades K–12 ■ **Frequency** 8 times a year

Freelance Potential Publishes 100 freelance submissions yearly: 90% written by nonstaff writers; 75% by authors new to the magazine; 60% by previously unpublished writers. Receives 16 queries monthly.

Submissions Guidelines and theme list available at website. Query with brief description of article idea, why the information is important to magazine's audience, the technology that will be discussed, and the primary outcome or effect on learning or teaching. Accepts email to kconley@iste.org. Responds in 1 week.
- *Articles:* 200–2,000 words. Informational, how-to, personal experience. Topics; computers, computer science, software, technology, media applications, teaching methods, telecommunications.
- *Depts/columns:* Word lengths vary. Research, software reviews, curriculum ideas.
- *Artwork:* Color prints. Line art.

Sample Issue 48 pages. Advertising. Sample copy available.
- "Will the iPad Revoluntionize Education?" by David Wees & Dan Maas. Two technology experts provide their opinions.
- "Harness the Power of Technology," by Arne Duncan. Discusses how best to use technology so students can become effective learners and stay engaged.

Rights and Payment All rights; returns limited rights to author upon request. No payment. Provides 3 contributor's copies.

Library Media Connection

130 Cremona Drive, Suite C, Santa Barbara, CA 93117. www.librarymediaconnection.com

Editor: Marlene Maxwell

Written for and by practicing school librarians, *Library Media Connection* features personal essays and articles on library management, as well as reviews of books and other library materials. Articles must be the author's actual experiences or personal observations. ■ **Circulation** 14,000 ■ **Audience** School librarians, grades K–12 ■ **Frequency** 7 times a year.

Freelance Potential Publishes 215 freelance submissions yearly: 90% written by nonstaff writers; 50% by authors new to the magazine; 50% by previously unpublished writers. Receives 12 queries and unsolicited manuscripts monthly.

Submissions Guidelines and editorial calendar available at website. Query or send complete manuscript with byline (name, title, school, city, and state). Accepts email submissions to wmedvetz@librarymediaconnection.com (Word attachments). Responds in 2 weeks.
- *Articles:* 1,200–3,000 words. Informational, how-to articles, personal experience. Topics: library management and operation, technology, staffing, professional development, literacy.
- *Depts/columns:* Word lengths vary. Book reviews, author profiles, news, tips.
- *Artwork:* High-resolution digital images.

Sample Issue Sample copy available.
- "Internet Safety and High School Students: What Do They Know and What Do They Need to Know?" by Lori Donovan & Kathy Lehman. How libraries can be a critical element in the teaching of twenty-century media skills.
- "Educate the Masses, Educate Yourselves: The School Librarian and Educational Technology," by Cathy Nelson. Provides suggestions for increasing a librarian's resources in the technology department.

Rights and Payment All rights. Written material, payment rates vary. Pays on publication. Provides 4 contributor's copies.

LibrarySparks

401 South Wright Road, P.O. Box 5207, Janesville, WI 53547. www.librarysparks.com

Submissions

Filled with exciting, hands-on program ideas and activities, *LibrarySparks* serves as a resource for children's and elementary school librarians. It also features articles on building reading skills, making curriculum connections, and promoting the library. It is open to ideas that can bring library programs to life. ■ **Circulation** Unavailable ■ **Audience** Librarians and teachers, grades K–6 ■ **Frequency** 9 times a year

Freelance Potential Publishes 15 freelance submissions yearly: 100% written by nonstaff writers; 10% by authors new to the magazine. Receives 2 queries monthly.

Submissions Guidelines and editorial calendar available. Query or send complete manuscript with contact information and school/library name. Accepts hard copy and email to librarysparks@ sfsdayton.com. SASE. Response time varies.
- *Articles:* Word lengths vary. Informational, profiles. Topics: connecting literature to curricula, lesson plans for librarians, teaching library skills, children's authors and illustrators, motivating children to read.
- *Depts/columns:* Word lengths vary. New resources, author profiles, storytelling activities, lesson plans, helpful hints.
- *Other:* Reproducible activities and crafts.

Sample Issue 56 pages. No advertising. Sample copy available.
- "Sports and Good Sports." Explores how themes of fair-mindedness, respect, and effort to learn can permeate library programs across the curriculum.
- "Storytime." Ideas for hosting a storytime with an "I'm Mad" theme.

Rights and Payment Rights vary. Written material, payment rates vary. Pays on publication. Provides 1 contributor's copy.

The Mailbox

The Education Center, P.O. 9753, Greensboro, NC 27429-0753. www.themailbox.com

Editor: Diane Badden

The Mailbox is billed as "America's number one teaching resource. Each issue is filled with creative ideas that can be adapted to fit any lesson plan, and information for teachers on such topics as classroom organization and time management. The magazine was founded by teachers who were frustrated by a lack of practical, ready-to-use material for the classroom. Over the years, other teachers joined in, sharing grade-specific ideas that keep students engaged. The magazine is published in five grade-level editions, from preschool through intermediate. ■ **Circulation** Unavailable ■ **Audience** Teachers ■ **Frequency** 6 times a year

Freelance Potential Open to ideas and contributions; book division also open to submissions.

Submissions Guidelines available. Send complete idea or manuscript to editors@ themailbox.com. Accepts hard copy or electronic submissions via website only. Responds in 6 months.
- *Articles:* Word lengths vary. Informational, how-to. Topics: lesson ideas, creative activities for use in classrooms—all curriculum subjects; classroom management, organization.
- *Other:* Reproducibles for in-class use.

Sample Issue 64 pages. No advertising. Sample pages available at website.
- "Rolling into a New Year." Get your classroom, and your new class, ready for the school year.
- "A Penny for Your Thoughts." An idea to help teach number sense.

Rights and Payment All rights. Contributors receive a $20 gift certificate toward any book or magazine published by The Mailbox.

Momentum

National Catholic Educational Association, 1005 North Glebe Road, Suite 525, Arlington, VA 22201. www.ncea.org

Editor: Brian Gray

Momentum focuses on the ideas, trends, and successes of Catholic school and parish education. It is read by Catholic educators and administrators. In addition to articles that support its monthly themes, it is interested in success stories and ways to encourage vocations. ■ **Circulation** 19,000 ■ **Audience** Teachers, school administrators, and parish catechists ■ **Frequency** Quarterly

Freelance Potential Publishes up to 20 freelance submissions yearly: 50–75% written by nonstaff writers; 25–50% by authors new to the publication; 25–50% by previously unpublished authors. Receives up to 6 queries and unsolicited manuscripts monthly.

Submissions Guidelines and editorial calendar available at website. Query or send complete manuscript. Prefers email submissions to momentum@ncea.org (Word attachments); will accept hard copy with CD. No simultaneous submissions. Responds in 1 month.
■ *Articles:* 1,500–2,000 words. Informational. Topics: teacher and in-service education, education trends, technology, research, management, public relations, finance and development—all as they relate to Catholic schools and parish religious education.
■ *Depts/columns:* Book reviews, 500–750 words. From the Field and opinion pieces, 700 words.

Sample Issue 80 pages. Advertising. Sample copy available.
■ "Battling Bullying," by Scott Alessi. Addresses actions to prevent bullying before it happens, and includes 10 tips for bullying prevention.
■ "Do You Have a Plan?" by Stephen Brown. The importance of planning for leadership succession, because there might not always a volunteer waiting in the wings.

Rights and Payment First North American serial rights. Articles, $75. Depts/columns, $50. Pays on publication. Provides 2 contributor's copies.

Montessori Life

281 Park Avenue South, New York, NY 10010. www.amshq.org

Co-Editors: Kathy Carey & Carey Jones

Written for teachers, administrators, and other professionals working in Montessori education, this peer-reviewed publication covers professional development, provides curriculum ideas, and is a forum for new ideas. ■ **Circulation** 10,500 ■ **Audience** Montessori educators ■ **Frequency** Quarterly

Freelance Potential Publishes 40 freelance submissions yearly: 90% written by nonstaff writers; 30% by authors new to the magazine; 30% by previously unpublished writers. Receives 10–20 unsolicited manuscripts monthly.

Submissions Guidelines and editorial calendar available at website. Send complete manuscript. Accepts email to edmontessorilife@aol.com. Responds in 3 months.
■ *Articles:* 1,000–4,000 words. Informational, how-to. Topics: education, professional development, school support, research, public policy.
■ *Depts/columns:* 500–1,000 words. Reviews, Montessori news, anecdotes.
■ *Artwork:* High-resolution photos.

Sample Issue Sample copy available.
■ "Crossing the Aisle: Conversations about Collaboration." Interviews leaders of American Montessori Society about strengthening the Montessori movement in the future.
■ "The Gift of Silence."The benefits of silence and stillness exercises in the classroom.

Rights and Payment All rights. Written material, payment rates vary. Pays on publication. Provides 1–5 contributor's copies.

MultiCultural Review

194 Lenox Avenue, Albany, NY 12208. www.mcreview.com

Editor: Todd Goldman

Educators and librarians who are interested in multicultural literature and non-print media subscribe to this magazine. It presents discussions of multiculturalism in America and practical pieces on multicultural pedagogy and librarianship. Articles must be timely and geared specifically to the issues relative to or impacted by multiculturalism. Perspectives and opinions should demonstrate knowledge of diversity. ■ **Circulation** 3,500+ ■ **Audience** Teachers and librarians ■ **Frequency** Quarterly

Freelance Potential Publishes 600 freelance submissions yearly: 80% written by nonstaff writers; 20% by authors new to the magazine; 10% by previously unpublished writers. Receives 10 queries monthly.

Submissions Guidelines and editorial calendar available. Query with proposal, outline and writing samples. Accepts hard copy. SASE. Responds in 2–3 months.
■ *Articles:* 2,000–6,000 words. Informational, how-to, bibliographic essays, interviews, opinion. Topics: multiculturalism in the U.S., ethnography of specific groups, books, authors, media, education, libraries.
■ *Depts/columns:* Book and media reviews, 200–500 words. News, 1,500–2,000 words.
■ *Artwork:* Line art. Prints, charts, or graphs.

Sample Issue 98 pages. Advertising. Sample copy available.
■ "The Unbearable Whiteness of Literacy Instruction: Realizing the Implications of the Proficient Reader Research," by Jane M. Gangi. Reports on how a study has changed the way reading comprehension is taught in schools.
■ "Writing about a Forgotten Dictator—An Interview with Cuban-American Historian Frank Argote-Freyre," by Danilo H. Figueredo. Interview with the author about his biography on the life of dictator Fulgencio Batista.

Rights and Payment First serial rights. Articles, $50–$100. Reviews, no payment. Pays on publication. Provides 2 contributor's copies.

MultiMedia & Internet@Schools

14508 NE 20th Avenue, Suite 102, Vancouver, WA 98686. www.mmischools.com

Editor: David Hoffman

This magazine bills itself as "the guide to electronic tools and resources" for school library and media specialists for kindergarten through grade 12. Each issue provides information on the technology products that can be used to further teaching and learning. ■ **Circulation** 12,000 ■ **Audience** School media/technology specialists and teachers ■ **Frequency** 6 times a year

Freelance Potential Publishes 20–24 freelance submissions yearly: 90% written by nonstaff writers; 20% by authors new to the magazine; 20% by previoiusly unpublished writers. Receives 5 queries and unsolicited manuscripts monthly.

Submissions Guidelines available. Query or send complete manuscript. Accepts email submissions to hoffmand@infotoday.com. Availability of artwork improves chance of acceptance. Responds in 6–8 weeks.
■ *Articles:* 1,500 words. Informational, how-to. Topics: K–12 education, the Internet, technology, multimedia and electronic resources, curriculum integration.
■ *Depts/columns:* Word lengths vary. Product news, reviews, ideas from educators.
■ *Artwork:* TIFF images at 300 dpi.

Sample Issue 48 pages. Advertising. Sample copy available.
■ "From Social Networking to Academic Networking... A Paradigm Shift," by Tim Childers. Explores

the different social networking options and how they can be used positively for education.
- ■ "Tools for Learning: Thirty-three Excellent Professional Development Resources for Teachers," by Victor Rivero. A review of professional development resources found online.

Rights and Payment First rights. Written material, $300–$500. Artwork, payment rates vary. Pays on publication. Provides 2 contributor's copies.

Music Educators Journal

MENC, 1806 Robert Fulton Drive, Reston, VA 20191. www.menc.org

Submissions Editor

As the official publication of the National Association for Music Education (abbreviated MENC from an earlier association name), this magazine covers all phases of music education in schools and communities. It accepts material from MENC members only. ■ **Circulation** 80,000 ■ **Audience** MENC members, music teachers ■ **Frequency** Quarterly

Freelance Potential Publishes 30 freelance submissions yearly: 90% written by nonstaff writers; 15% by authors new to the magazine; 10% by previously unpublished writers. Receives 10 unsolicited manuscripts monthly.

Submissions MENC members only. Guidelines available at website. Send complete manuscript with credentials and affiliations. Accepts submissions via http://mc.manuscriptcentral.com/mej. Response time varies.
- ■ *Articles:* 1,800–3,500 words. Informational, instructional, historical studies of music education. Topics: teaching methods and philosophy, current trends in music education and learning.
- ■ *Depts/columns:* 500–700 words. Media reviews, teaching tips, technology updates, association news.
- ■ *Artwork:* TIFF, EPS, JPEG, or PDF files.
- ■ *Other:* Submit seasonal material 8–12 months in advance.

Sample Issue 60 pages. Advertising. Sample copy available.
- ■ "Reflections on Fifty Years of Publishing with MENC," by Bennett Reimer. Author looks back over the 50 years he has been writing to see how music education has changed.
- ■ "Strings Got Rhythm." Offers guidelines for developing rhythmic skills.

Rights and Payment All rights. Written material, no payment. Artwork, $10. Provides 2 contributor's copies.

NASSP Bulletin

2455 Teller Road, Thousand Oaks, CA 91320. http://bulletin.sagepub.com

Submissions: Sage Publications

This is the official journal of the National Association of Secondary School Principals. It accepts scholarly and research-based articles that will advance the vision and performance of middle-level and high school principals. All material is peer reviewed. ■ **Circulation** 2,000 ■ **Audience** Principals ■ **Frequency** Quarterly

Freelance Potential Publishes 20–25 freelance submissions yearly: 100% written by nonstaff writers; 30% by authors new to the magazine; 15% by previously unpublished writers. Receives 12 unsolicited manuscripts monthly.

Submissions Guidelines available at website. Send complete manuscript with title, cover letter stating your commitment to publishing manuscript in the journal, 60- to 80-word abstract, 3–5 keywords, contact information, and 40- to 50-word biographical statement. Accepts submissions via http://mc.manuscriptcentral.com/bul only. Responds in 3–4 months.
- ■ *Articles:* To 30 pages. Scholarly, informational. Topics: school administration, classroom

accountability, disadvantaged students, family and community partnerships, funding, legal issues, literacy, professional development, school reform.

Sample Issue Sample copy available.

■ "Using State Unemployment Insurance Data to Track Student Postsecondary Outcomes," by Ruth Curran Neild. Profile of a community that used state unemployment insurance data, merged with student record data, to investigate early labor market outcomes.

■ "Embedding Due Process Measures Throughout the Evaluation of Teachers," by Joseph J. Matula. Explains preventative measures of fairness that would avoid potential teacher objections due to No Child Left Behind regulations.

Rights and Payment All rights. No payment. Provides 2 contributor's copies.

NextStepU Magazine

2 West Main Street, Suite 200, Victor, NY 14564. www.nextstepu.com

Editor in Chief: Laura Jeanne Hammond

With articles designed to help college and college-bound high school students find the right path in life, *NextStepU Magazine* focuses on "real life" issues such as money management, career decisions, choosing a college, and preparing for the SATs. Queries from professionals within the business or education fields who can share advice and insider tips are sought. ■ **Circulation** 800,000
■ **Audience** 14–21 years ■ **Frequency** 5 times a year

Freelance Potential Publishes 40 freelance submissions yearly: 90% written by nonstaff writers.

Submissions Guidelines available. Query. Accepts email queries to laura@nextstepu.com. Response time varies.

■ *Articles:* 700–1,000 words. Informational, self-help, how-to, profiles, interviews, personal experience, opinion, humor, essays. Topics: college planning, financial aid, campus tours, choosing a career, life skills, résumé writing, public speaking, personal finances, computers, multicultural and ethnic issues, sports, special education.

■ *Depts/columns:* Word lengths vary. Personal experience pieces from college students.

Sample Issue 38 pages. Sample copy available at website.

■ "How to Register for College Classes," by Meghan Carey. Tips to help college freshman narrow their focus when choosing courses.

■ "10 Things to Do Now to Make Senior Year Easier," by Kate Oczypok. Suggests proactive measures that will decrease stress during senior year.

Rights and Payment All rights. Written material, payment rates vary. Pays within 1 month of acceptance.

The Old Schoolhouse

P.O. Box 8426, Gray, TN 37615. www.thehomeschoolmagazine.com

Editors: Paul & Gena Suarez

This magazine publishes articles on homeschooling and family life from a Christian perspective. It also publishes technical and research-based articles on homeschooling. Articles that explore the history, current status, and character of the homeschool movement will always get editors' attention.
■ **Circulation** 50,000. ■ **Audience** Homeschool families ■ **Frequency** Quarterly

Freelance Potential Publishes 160 freelance submissions yearly: 80% written by nonstaff writers; 50% by authors new to the magazine; 30% by previously unpublished writers. Receives 16 queries monthly.

Submissions Guidelines available at website. Query with summary, approximate length, sidebar ideas, and links to published articles. Accepts queries through www.homeschoolblogger.com only;

users should note their user name on query. No simultaneous submissions. Responds in 4–6 weeks.
- *Articles:* 1,000–2,000 words. Informational, how-to, personal experience. Topics: homeschooling, family life, art, music, spirituality, literature, child development, teen issues, science, history, mathematics.
- *Depts/columns:* Word lengths vary. Short news items, styles of teaching, opinion, teaching children with special needs, humor.

Sample Issue 220 pages. Advertising. Sample copy available at website.
- "Welcome to Lumps of Clay Christian Academy," by Deb Turner. Personal experience piece about a woman's fond memories of homeschooling.
- "Hobbies, High School, & Holidays," by Deborah Wuehler. How to use the holidays as a theme for teaching children something new.

Rights and Payment First rights. Written material, payment rates vary. Pays on publication. Provides 2 contributor's copies.

Principal

1615 Duke Street, Alexandria, VA 22314. www.naesp.org

Managing Editor: Vanessa St. Gerard

As the membership publication of the National Association of Elementary School Principals, *Principal* is a source of practical information on topics related to education and elementary school administration issues. Instead of scholarly articles on theories of education, readers turn to the publication for practical information and ideas they can use. ■ **Circulation** 28,000 ■ **Audience** School administrators, K–grade 8 ■ **Frequency** 5 times a year

Freelance Potential Publishes 20 freelance submissions yearly: 90% written by nonstaff writers; 80% by authors new to the magazine. Receives 12 unsolicited manuscripts monthly.

Submissions Guidelines and editorial calendar available at website. Send complete manuscript. Accepts email submissions to publications@naesp.org (Word attachments). No simultaneous submissions. SASE. Responds in 6–8 weeks.
- *Articles:* 1,500–2,000 words. Informational, instructional, profiles, interviews, opinion, personal experience. Topics: elementary education, gifted and special education, parenting, mentoring, technology.
- *Depts/columns:* 800–1,500 words. Parents & Schools, Raise the Bar, Practitioner's Corner, Principal's Bookshelf, Ten to Teen, The Reflective Principal, Speaking Out.

Sample Issue 72 pages. Advertising. Sample copy available.
- "Social Media as a Professional Tool." An interview with two principals who have advanced professionally through social networking.
- "Why Pre-K Is Critical to Closing the Achievement Gap," by Ellen Frede & W. Steven Barnett. Argues the need for higher quality pre-k as a way to improve reading, math, and science scores.

Rights and Payment All North American serial rights. No payment. Provides 3 contributor's copies.

The Reading Teacher

International Reading Association, 800 Barksdale Road, P.O. Box 8139, Newark, DE 19714-8139. www.reading.org

Managing Editor: James Henderson

This peer-reviewed journal shares current theories, research, issues, and practices among literacy educators to help improve literacy instruction for children up to age 12. It is published by the International Reading Association. Submissions focusing on children's literature or the relationship between literacy and other subject areas are welcome. ■ **Circulation** 57,500 ■ **Audience** Literacy educators ■ **Frequency** 8 times a year

Freelance Potential Publishes 50 freelance submissions yearly: 95% written by nonstaff writers; 30% by authors new to the magazine; 20% by previously unpublished writers. Receives 25 unsolicited manuscripts monthly.

Submissions Guidelines available. Send complete manuscript. Accepts online submissions via http://mc.manuscriptcentral.com/rt. Responds in 1–2 months.
- *Articles:* To 6,000 words. Informational, how-to, profiles, personal experience. Topics: literacy, reading education, instructional techniques, classroom strategies, reading research, educational technology.
- *Depts/columns:* 1,500–2,500 words. Reviews of children's books, teaching tips, cultural diversity.

Sample Issue 84 pages. Advertising. Sample copy available.
- "Integrating Literacy and Inquiry for English Learners," by Lindsey M. Guccione. Lesson plan in which students integrate new literacy practices within an inquiry-based classroom learning community.
- "Talking about Talk: Reclaiming the Value and Power of Literature Circles," by Heidi Mills. Reports on research that found a discourse of inquiry to be central to substantive growth and change.

Rights and Payment All rights. No payment. Provides 5 contributor's copies for articles, 2 copies for depts/columns.

Reading Today

International Reading Association, 800 Barksdale Road, P.O. Box 8139, Newark, DE 19714-8139. www.reading.org

Editor in Chief: John Micklos, Jr.

Reading Today is a newspaper for professionals in the field of literacy education. It covers the critical issues facing literacy, and highlights current trends. Other features include classroom strategies and ideas for administrators and parents. Articles about unusual and successful classroom or library reading programs are always of interest. Freelance space is limited, limits nonstaff opportunities.
- **Circulation** 68,000 ■ **Audience** IRA members ■ **Frequency** 6 times a year

Freelance Potential Publishes 30 freelance submissions yearly: 30% written by nonstaff writers; 40% by authors new to the magazine; 10% by previously unpublished writers. Receives 25 queries, 20 unsolicited manuscripts monthly.

Submissions Guidelines available. Prefers query; will accept complete manuscript. Prefers email to readingtoday@reading.org; will accept hard copy and simultaneous submissions if identified. SASE. Responds in 6 weeks.
- *Articles:* 500–1,000 words. Informational, interviews. Topics: reading, reading education, community programs, staffing, assessment, funding, children's books, censorship.
- *Depts/columns:* To 750 words. News; education policy updates; ideas for administrators, teachers, and parents.

Sample Issue 44 pages. Advertising. Sample copy available.
- "Back to School: A First Grader at Heart," by Lauren Grasso. Profile of a Missouri man who is attending first grade at the age of 73.
- "IRA and PAIUnet Partner in e-learning Venture." Report on a new partnership that combines a fast intranet with expert researchers made available to hundreds of teachers across an entire state.

Rights and Payment All rights. Written material, 20¢–30¢ a word. Pays on acceptance. Provides 3 contributor's copies.

Research in Middle Level Education Online

Mercer University, 3001 Mercer University Drive, Atlanta, GA 30341. www.amle.org

Editor: Karen Weller Swanson

This peer-reviewed journal, available online only, features quantitative and qualitative case studies, research studies, and reviews on middle-grade education. It is published by the National Middle School Association. Prospective writers should have a thorough knowledge of the field. ■ **Circulation** 30,000 ■ **Audience** Educators and administrators ■ **Frequency** 10 times a year

Freelance Potential Publishes 10 freelance submissions yearly: 100% written by nonstaff writers: 50% by authors new to the magazine; 20% by previously unpublished writers. Receives 3 unsolicited manuscripts monthly.

Submissions Guidelines available at website. Send complete manuscript with 150- to 200-word abstract. Accepts submissions through www.editorialmanager.com/rmle. Responds in 1 week.
■ *Articles:* 25–40 double-spaced pages. Informational. Topics: quantitative and qualitative studies, case studies, action research studies, research syntheses, integrative reviews, interpretations of research literature—all pertaining to middle-grade education.

Sample Issue 10 articles. No advertising. Sample copy available at website.
■ "Scaffolding Middle School Students' Comprehension and Response to Short Stories," by Lauren Aimonette Liang. Reports on research that focused on the two most popular approaches to teaching literature.
■ "Confirming a Middle Grade's Leadership Model and Instrument," by Dana L. Bickmore. Discusses whether a new study can be used as a research tool to examine which factors will affect student achievement.

Rights and Payment All rights. No payment.

SchoolArts

Davis Publications, 50 Portland Street, Worcester, MA 01608. www.schoolartsonline.com

Editor: Nancy Walkup

Each themed issue of *SchoolArts* shares the successful lessons, ideas, and concepts of art teachers of kindergarten through grade 12. In publication since 1901, its material is divided by grade level. Articles must demonstrate the author's passion, not to mention knowledge, of the topic. ■ **Circulation** 20,000 ■ **Audience** Art teachers, grades K–12 ■ **Frequency** 9 times a year

Freelance Potential Publishes 200 freelance submissions yearly: 75% written by nonstaff writers; 60% by authors new to the magazine; 20% by previously unpublished writers. Receives 25 unsolicited manuscripts monthly.

Submissions Guidelines and editorial calendar available at website. Send complete manuscript with artwork and signed permission forms. Accepts disk submissions, with artwork (if applicable). SASE. Responds in 1–2 months.
■ *Articles:* 300–800 words. Informational, how-to, self-help. Topics: teaching art, artistic techniques, art history, classroom projects and activities, curriculum development, art programs for gifted and disabled students.
■ *Depts/columns:* 500–1,200 words. Crafts, new product reviews, opinions.
■ *Artwork:* Color prints and slides; high-resolution digital images. Line art.

Sample Issue 68 pages. Advertising. Sample copy available.
■ "Presenting Pecha Kucha," by Debi West. Offers a lesson plan in which students learn art critiquing with the Pecha Kucha approach.
■ "The Art of Transformation," by Pam Stephens. Profiles well-known ceramic artist Paula Rice.

Rights and Payment First serial rights. Written material, $25–$150. Artwork, payment rates vary. Pays on publication. Provides 6 contributor's copies.

School Librarian's Workshop

95 Photine Drive, Lowell, MA 01854. www.slworkshop.net

Editor: Hilda Weisburg

Now exclusively online, *The School Librarian's Workshop* provides the latest information that will keep its librarian readers informed, inspired, and indispensable to students, teachers, and administrators. It seeks practical articles that deal with all aspects of library media programs. ■ **Hits per month** 7,000 ■ **Audience** School librarians ■ **Frequency** 6 times a year

Freelance Potential Publishes 20 freelance submissions yearly: 28% written by nonstaff writers; 10% by authors new to the magazine; 10% by previously unpublished writers. Receives 2 unsolicited manuscripts monthly.

Submissions Send 2 copies of complete manuscript. Prefers disk submissions (Word); will accept hard copy. SASE. Responds in 3 weeks.
■ *Articles:* To 1,000 words. Informational, how-to, practical application, profiles, interviews. Topics: librarianship, literature, special education, ethnic studies, computers, technology, social and multicultural issues, the environment.
■ *Artwork:* Line art.
■ *Other:* Submit seasonal material 8 months in advance.

Sample Issue 24 pages. No advertising. Sample copy available.
■ "Who Was Abraham Lincoln?" Lesson plans a teacher can use as mini-units.
■ "High School Life." Reviews three poetry collections that portray high school life.

Rights and Payment First rights. No payment.

School Library Journal

360 Park Avenue South, New York, NY 10010. www.slj.com

Executive Editor: Rick Margolis

School Library Journal offers librarians the timely information needed to integrate libraries into the school curriculum; become leaders in technology, reading, and information; and create high-quality book collections for children and young adults. ■ **Circulation** 34,500 ■ **Audience** School librarians ■ **Frequency** Monthly

Freelance Potential Publishes 25 freelance submissions yearly: 80% written by nonstaff writers; 60% by previously unpublished writers. Receives up to 6 queries and unsolicited manuscripts monthly.

Submissions Guidelines available at website. Query or send complete manuscript. Accepts disk submissions (Word) and email submissions to rmargolis@reedbusiness.com. SASE. Responds to queries in 1 month, to manuscripts in 3 months.
■ *Articles:* 1,500–2,500 words. Informational, interviews. Topics: children's and YA literature, school library management, library careers.
■ *Depts/columns:* 1,500–2,500 words. Book and media reviews, descriptions of successful library programs, opinion.
■ *Artwork:* Color prints. Color tables and charts. Cartoons.

Sample Issue 116 pages. Advertising. Sample copy available.
■ "Insects: Bugged Out," by Kathy Piehl. Discusses how a series of books about bugs can help hone children's observation and investigation skills.

- "The App Squad: *SLJ*'s Advisors Weigh in on Kids' Book Apps," by Kathy Ishizuka. Interview with magazine staff about the best book applications available for children and teens.

Rights and Payment First rights. Articles, $400. Depts/columns, $100–$200. Pays on publication. Provides 4 contributor's copies

---

School Library Media Activities Monthly

3520 South 35th Street, Lincoln, NE 68506. www.schoollibrarymedia.com

Managing Editor: Deborah Levitov

This magazine supports kindergarten through grade 12 school librarians as they work collaboratively with teachers. It reports on ways to teach literacy skills, inquiry, and the research process. It promotes the integration of technology, reports on current issues and trends, and provides links to an array of literature. The articles in each issue are written by school library professionals.
■ **Circulation** 10,000 ■ **Audience** School library and media specialists, grades K–12 ■ **Frequency** 8 times a year

Freelance Potential Publishes 30 freelance submissions yearly: 90% written by nonstaff writers; 30% by authors new to the magazine; 20% by previously unpublished writers. Receives 3 queries, 3 unsolicited manuscripts monthly.

Submissions Guidelines available at website. Query or send complete manuscript with bibliographic citations and brief author biography. Accepts email submissions to dlevitov@abc-clio.com (Word attachments). Responds in 2 months.
■ *Articles:* 1,000–1,800 words. Informational. Topics: media education and promotion, information technology, integration of curriculum materials, library management.
■ *Depts/columns:* Word lengths vary. Activities, lesson plans, tips for professional growth.

Sample Issue 58 pages. Sample copy available at website.
■ "Digital Storytelling: Meeting Standards Across the Curriculum in a WWII/Holocaust Unit," by Dea Borneman & Kathy Gibson. Provides details on using digital storytelling to enhance nontraditional approaches of reading, writing, speaking, and art appreciation.
■ "The Changing Role of the School Library's Physical Space," by Tom Corbett. Profile of a private high school that is enacting a new program that will have students rely almost exclusively on electronic resources for research and reading.

Rights and Payment All rights. Written material, payment rates vary. Pays on publication. Provides 3+ contributor's copies.

Science Activities

Taylor & Francis, 325 Chestnut Street, Suite 800, Philadelphia, PA 19106. www.tandfonline.com/toc/vsca20/current

Executive Editor: Rosanne W. Fortner

This award–winning journal brings K-12 teachers creative, inexpensive, and engaging activities to help make science relevant. The teacher–written and tested activities are hands-on and encourage inquiry to develop thinking scientists in the classroom. Content should be original, grounded in real science, and follow the National Science Education Standards, state standards, or a recognizable teaching philosophy. Activities typically contain a materials list, step-by-step procedure, related background information, cross-curricular applications, and appropriate assessment suggestions or developed rubrics.
■ **Circulation** 1,286 ■ **Audience** Teachers, grades K–12 ■ **Frequency** 4 times a year

Freelance Potential Publishes 25 freelance submissions yearly: 95% written by nonstaff writers; 50% by authors new to the publication; 25% by unpublished writers. Receives 3–4 unsolicited manuscripts monthly.

Submissions Sample copy and guidelines available at website. Send complete manuscript with cover letter that includes title, why your submission is unique, suggested reviewers, and the number of words, tables, and figures. Accepts electronic submissions only through http://mc.manuscriptcentral.com/sa. Responds in 3 months.
- *Articles:* Word lengths vary. Informational, how-to, profiles, personal experience. Topics: hands-on projects in biological, physical, environmental, chemical, earth, and behavioral sciences.
- *Depts/columns:* Staff-written.
- *Artwork:* B/W illustrations. 300 dpi or higher; EPS, TIFF, or PSD format only. Line art.

Sample Issue 40 pages.
- "Oil Spill Cleanup," by Christena Ann Kauble. Classroom activities using a model of a seashore and an oil spill to demonstrate oil spills in oceans.
- "The 'Science' Behind a Successful Field Trip to the Zoo," by Catherine Marie Scott and Catherine E. Matthews. Activities for before, during, and after a zoo trip to maximize learning opportunities.

Rights and Payment All rights. No payment. Provides contributors with free access to articles online.

The Science Teacher

National Science Teachers Association, 1840 Wilson Boulevard, Arlington, VA 22201-3000. www.nsta.org/highschool

Managing Editor: Megan Sullivan

This peer-reviewed journal provides education professionals a forum for sharing ideas and practical experiences with their peers. It is interested in the complete experience of successful programs, including the goals, setup details, and student reactions. All submissions should reflect current issues in science education. ■ **Circulation** 29,000. ■ **Audience** Science teachers, grades 7–12 ■ **Frequency** 9 times a year

Freelance Potential 100% of content written by nonstaff writers: 50% by authors new to the magazine; 70% by previously unpublished writers. Receives 30 unsolicited manuscripts monthly.

Submissions Guidelines available in each issue and at website. Send complete manuscript with abstract of up to 200 words. Accepts submissions through https://mc.manuscriptcentral.com/nsta. Responds in 1 month.
- *Articles:* 2,000 words. Informational, classroom projects, experiments. Topics: science education, biology, earth science, computers, social issues, space technology, sports medicine.
- *Depts/columns:* 500 words. Science.
- *Artwork:* B/W prints. Line art, tables, diagrams.

Sample Issue 84 pages. Advertising. 6 articles; 6 depts/columns. Sample copy available.
- "A Scientific World in a Grain of Sand," by Renee Cleary & James Wandersee. A classroom experiment in Earth history that integrates history, culture, and art.
- "From Misconceptions to Conceptual Change," by Julia Gooding & Bill Metz. Examines how misconceptions occur, and strategies teachers can employ to help students move toward conceptual change.

Rights and Payment First rights. No payment. Provides contributor's copies.

Scouting

Boy Scouts of America, 1325 West Walnut Hill Lane, P.O. Box 152079, Irving, TX 75015-2079. www.scoutingmagazine.org.

Managing Editor: Scott Daniels

Scouting's articles inform, instruct, and inspire its readers, the majority of whom are leaders and

volunteers with the Boy Scouts of America. Its goal is to strengthen volunteers' abilities so they may better perform their leadership roles. It is always interested in successful programs and trips.
■ **Circulation** 1 million ■ **Audience** Scout leaders and volunteers ■ **Frequency** 6 times a year

Freelance Potential Publishes 8 freelance submissions yearly: 50% written by nonstaff writers; 5–10% by authors new to the magazine. Receives 3 queries monthly.

Submissions Guidelines available at website. Query with outline. Accepts hard copy. SASE. Responds in 3 weeks.
■ *Articles:* 500–1,200 words. Informational, how-to, profiles, humor, personal experience. Topics: Boy Scout programs, leadership, volunteering, nature, social issues, history.
■ *Depts/columns:* 500–700 words. Family activities, outdoor activities, short profiles, Scout news.
■ *Other:* Quizzes, puzzles, games.

Sample Issue 48 pages. Advertising. Sample copy available.
■ "Going Rogue," by Bryan Wendall. Describes a trip in which a CEO and Scoutmaster reorganized his priorities on a river rafting trip that required him to be phone- and email-free.
■ "What I've Learned." An interview with a scout who is on the national Aquatics Task Force.

Rights and Payment First North American serial rights. Written material, $300–$800. Pays on acceptance. Provides 2 contributor's copies.

Scuola Calcio Coaching Magazine

P.O. Box 15669, Wilmington, NC 28408. www.soccercoachingmagazine.com

Submissions: Antonio Saviano

This magazine is written for youth soccer coaches in the United States and Canada. It shares coaching tactics, drill instructions, and leadership techniques for improving the skills of young soccer players.
■ **Circulation** 350+ ■ **Audience** Youth soccer coaches ■ **Frequency** 6 times a year

Freelance Potential Publishes 120 freelance submissions yearly: 20% written by nonstaff writers; 10% by authors new to the magazine; 5% by previously unpublished writers. Receives up to 100 queries and unsolicited manuscripts monthly.

Submissions Guidelines available at website. Query or send complete manuscript. Accepts hard copy faxed to 910-795-1674 and email submissions to info@soccercoachingmagazine.com (Word attachments). Responds only if interested.
■ *Articles:* Word lengths vary. Informational, how-to. Topics: soccer methods and drills, practice planning, coaching.
■ *Depts/columns:* Word lengths vary. Q&As, soccer techniques.

Sample Issue Sample copy available.
■ "How Important Is Winning in Youth Soccer?" Coaching techniques that focus more on fun than winning.
■ "Defensive Aspects of a Soccer Player." Explains how to teach young players to identify the defender on the field.

Rights and Payment Worldwide rights. Written material, word lengths and payment rates vary. Payment policy varies.

Spark Action

Forum for Youth Investment, The Cady-Lee House, 7064 Eastern Avenue NW, Washington, DC 20012. http://sparkaction.org

Editor: Caitlin Johnson

This ezine offers advocacy tools for those seeking to make a difference in the lives of children. It covers state and federal policy affecting children, and provides action alerts to help readers make changes in their communities and across the nation. Original and reprinted feature articles that offer a firsthand take on issues affecting children and families are welcome. ■ **Circulation** 50,000+ ■ **Audience** Parents & child welfare professionals ■ **Frequency** 26 times a year

Freelance Potential Publishes 24 freelance submissions yearly: 40% written by nonstaff writers; 25% by authors new to the magazine. Receives 13 queries monthly.

Submissions Query via http://sparkaction.org. Response time varies.
■ *Articles:* 900–1,500 words. Informational, profiles, reviews, photo-essays. Topics: state and federal policy affecting children and youth, contacting elected officials, organizing campaigns, volunteering, research on children's advocacy issues, child care and development, juvenile justice, child abuse and neglect, crime and violence prevention, parental involvement in education, out-of-school time, diversity and awareness, mentoring programs.

Sample Issue 21 articles. Sample copy available at website.
■ "Can Obama Keep the Youth Vote Amid A Bleak Job Market?" by Amanda M. Fairbanks. Examines the mid-term views among recent college graduates on President Barack Obama.
■ "Vilsack: Economic Health of Rural America Dependent on Education," by Lynda Waddington. Discusses recent remarks by the U.S. Secretary of Agriculture that stresses the importance of education in rural America.

Rights and Payment First North American serial rights. No payment.

Sporting Kid

2050 Vista Parkway, West Palm Beach, FL 33411. www.nays.org/sportingkid

Managing Editor: Greg Bach

As the member publication of the National Alliance for Youth Sports (NAYS), *Sporting Kid* is an advocate for positive and safe sports for children. Each issue includes valuable tips to help parents and volunteer coaches in their roles, as well as profiles of outstanding players. It is interested in clever ways coaches can run quality practices that teach kids skills in a safe and productive manner. ■ **Circulation** 300,000 ■ **Audience** Parents, coaches, and officials ■ **Frequency** Quarterly

Freelance Potential Publishes 10 freelance submissions yearly: 15% written by nonstaff writers; 15% by authors new to the magazine; 5% by previously unpublished writers. Receives 1 query, 1 unsolicited manuscript monthly.

Submissions Query or send complete manuscript. Accepts email to sportingkid@nays.org. Responds in 1 month.
■ *Articles:* To 1,000 words. Informational, how-to, profiles. Topics: youth sports, coaching, parenting, officiating, health, safety
■ *Depts/columns:* 750 words. New product information, the culture of youth sports, coaching and parenting tips.

Sample Issue 32 pages.
■ "Reducing Arm Injuries, Soreness—and Errors!" by Heather Holte. Explains throwing progression drills to prevent arm aches and pains.
■ "Impacting Young Lives Through Sports," by Greg Bach. Profiles a coach, parent, and youth leagues that were chosen for the Excellence in Youth Sports Awards.

Rights and Payment First and electronic rights. Written material, payment rates vary. Pays on publication.

Storytelling Magazine

National Storytelling Network, P.O. Box 795, Jonesborough, TN 37659. www.storynet.org

Submissions: Kit Rogers

Storytelling Magazine brings National Storytelling Network members news of important events, trends, people, and publications in the national storytelling community. Geared toward professional story-tellers, librarians, and educators, each issue explores a timely topic through carefully selected articles from leaders in the field. It also includes a story or two for readers to use. ■ **Circulation** 2,000+
■ **Audience** Storytellers, librarians, educators ■ **Frequency** 5 times a year

Freelance Potential Publishes 100 freelance submissions yearly: 100% written by nonstaff writers. Receives about 4 unsolicited manuscripts monthly.

Submissions Query. Accepts email queries to kit@storynet.org. SASE. Response time varies.
■ *Articles:* 1,000–2,000 words. Informational, how–to, profiles, personal experience. Topics: storytelling techniques, news, and trends; people in the field.
■ *Fiction:* Word lengths vary.
■ *Depts/columns:* 500 words. News, reviews.

Sample Issue Sample copy available.
■ "The Art of Storytelling for Filmmaking," by B.Z. Smith. Bringing stories to life on the big screen.
■ "Finn McCool and the Great Fish," by Eve Bunting. A retold Celtic tale of wisdom.

Rights and Payment First North American serial rights. No payment. Provides 2 contributor's copies.

SupportingStudents.com

1270 Rankin Drive, Suite F, Troy, MI 48083. www.supportingstudents.com

Submissions

Previously listed as *Student Assistance Journal*, SupportingStudents.com is an online publication that serves those working with students, particularly students at risk. Its editorial focus includes safety, health and emotional wellness, educational success, professional and organizational development, family, relationships. ■ **Hits per month** 5,000 ■ **Audience** Youth counselors ■ **Frequency** Unavailable

Freelance Potential Publishes 12 freelance submissions yearly: 90% written by nonstaff writers; 50% by previously unpublished writers. Receives 3 queries monthly.

Submissions Query via website only.
■ *Articles:* 1,500 words. Informational, how-to, personal experience. Topics: safety, health, substance abuse and prevention, bullying, violence, self-care.
■ *Depts/columns:* 750–800 words. News updates.

Sample Issue Sample copy available.
■ "Mind Mapping: A New Path to Learning." Describes how mind mapping can make learning easier than taking notes.
■ "Appeals Court Agrees That Cigarette Companies Committed Fraud." Discusses the outcome of an appeal that charges tobacco firms with intentionally misleading the public.

Rights and Payment Rights vary. No payment.

Swimming World and Junior Swimmer

90 Bell Rock Plaza, Suite 200, Sedona, AZ 86351. www.swimmingworldmagazine.com

Editor: Jason Marsteller

Swimming World covers the world of competitive swimming for athletes and coaches. It features instructional tips, competition news, and athlete profiles. *Junior Swimmer*, a section within the main magazine, focuses on young swimmers and includes some content written by the youngsters themselves. It welcomes news and profiles from the junior competition level. ■ **Circulation** 50,000 ■ **Audience** Coaches, youth swimmers ■ **Frequency** Monthly

Freelance Potential Publishes 100 freelance submissions yearly: 60% written by nonstaff writers; 5% by previously unpublished writers. Receives 16 queries monthly.

Submissions Guidelines available. Query. Accepts hard copy and email queries to jasonm@ swimmingworldmagazine.com. SASE. Responds in 1 month.
- *Articles:* 500–3,500 words. Informational, how-to, profiles, personal experience. Topics: swimming, training, competition, medical advice, swim drills, nutrition, dry land exercise, exercise physiology, fitness.
- *Depts/columns:* 500–750 words. Swimming news, new product reviews, nutrition advice.
- *Artwork:* Color prints and transparencies. Line art.
- *Other:* Activities, games, jokes. Submit seasonal material 1–2 months in advance.

Sample Issue 62 pages. Advertising. Sample copy available.
- "The David Nolan Show," by John Lohn. A profile of a high school swimmer who many fans believe may be the greatest scholastic swimmer in history.
- "Pied Piper of the Pool," by John Lohn. A report on Coach Dave Salo's collection of talent at the Trojan Swim Club.

Rights and Payment All rights. Written material, 12¢ a word. Artwork, payment rates vary. Pays on publication. Provides 2–5 contributor's copies.

Teacher Librarian

4501 Forbes Boulevard, Suite 200, Lanham, MD 20706. www.teacherlibrarian.com

Managing Editor: Corinne O. Burton

Targeting librarians who work with children and young adults, this magazine features thought-provoking articles on all aspects of library services. Its articles cover strategies for effective advocacy, techniques for student learning, technology, and management issues. All articles are blind reviewed by at least two members of the advisory board, all of whom are either scholars or recognized professionals. ■ **Circulation** 10,000 ■ **Audience** Library professionals ■ **Frequency** 5 times a year

Freelance Potential Publishes 10 freelance submissions yearly: 60% written by nonstaff writers; 5% by authors new to the magazine; 25% by previously unpublished writers. Receives about 1 query and unsolicited manuscript monthly.

Submissions Guidelines and editorial calendar available. Query or send complete manuscript with biography. Accepts email submissions to admin@teacherlibrarian.com (Word attachments). Responds in 2 months.
- *Articles:* 2,000+ words. Informational, analytical, profiles. Topics: library funding, technology, leadership, library management, audio/visual material, cooperative teaching, young adult library services.
- *Depts/columns:* Staff-written.
- *Artwork:* B/W or color prints. Cartoons, line art.

Sample Issue 86 pages. Advertising.
- "Project ELITE—Technology Training That Works," by Lisa Perez. Explains how a technology training

program in Chicago public school libraries is teaching librarians to use technology tools and other educational resources to engage students.

- "Linking Up L4L: Web Sites to Support the New AASL Standards in Your Library," by Melissa Ahart & Kirstie Miller. Describes the new Standards for the 21st-Century Learner and Learning 4 Life.

Rights and Payment All rights. Written material, $100. Pays on publication. Provides 2 contributor's copies.

Teachers & Writers

520 Eighth Avenue, Suite 2020, New York, NY 10018. www.twc.org

Editor: Susan Karwoska

Innovative techniques and practical methods for teaching the art of writing are explored in this publication. Geared to teachers of kindergarten to grade 12, it is filled with valuable ideas and theories for effective teaching. ■ **Circulation** 3,000 ■ **Audience** Teachers ■ **Frequency** Quarterly

Freelance Potential Publishes 8 freelance submissions yearly: 60% written by nonstaff writers; 50% by authors new to the magazine; 5% by previously unpublished writers. Receives 4 unsolicited manuscripts monthly.

Submissions Guidelines available at website. Send complete manuscript. Prefers email to editors@twc.org; will accept hard copy. SASE. Response time varies.
- *Articles:* 500–2,500 words. Informational, how-to, interview. Topics: all writing genres, oral history, translation, teaching writing in combination with other arts, artists.
- *Depts/columns:* Word lengths vary. Teaching techniques

Sample Issue Sample copy available.
- "Teaching Artist Snapshot," by David McLoghlin. An interview with playwright and poet Melanie Maria Goodreaux of New Orleans.
- "Poetry Inside Out: Teaching Translation to Enhance Literacy," by Marty Rutherford. A curriculum program that heightens participants' awareness of the function of language and their creative self-expression.

Rights and Payment First serial rights. Written material, payment rates vary. Pays on publication. Provides 10 contributor's copies.

Teachers of Vision

227 North Magnolia Avenue, Suite 2, Anaheim, CA 92801. www.ceai.org

Contributing Editor: Judy Turpen

This magazine from the Christian Educators Association International is written for Christian teachers in public and private school systems, with a goal to empower them to be better educators. The vast majority of readers are public school teachers, although some work in Christian or private schools. General education articles are also accepted. All articles need a distinctively Christian viewpoint, but without a preaching tone or religious jargon. ■ **Circulation** 8,000 ■ **Audience** Educators ■ **Frequency** Quarterly

Freelance Potential Publishes 70–75 freelance submissions yearly: 50–75% written by nonstaff writers; 25–50% by authors new to the magazine;10–25% by previously unpublished writers. Receives 10–25 queries, 1–10 complete manuscripts monthly.

Submissions Guidelines available at website. Prefers query with synopsis and brief biography; will accept complete manuscript with brief biography. Prefers email submissions to tov@ceai.org; will accept hard copy. Accepts simultaneous submissions if identified. SASE. Responds in 1–2 months.
- *Articles:* How-to, personal experience pieces, documented reports; 800–2,500 words. Topics: educa-

tion issues, educational philosophy, methodology. Interviews with noted Christian educators; 500–800 words. Teaching techniques, news, special event reports; 400–750 words. Reviews of books, videos, curricula, games, and other resources for K–12 teachers; word lengths vary
- *Other:* Submit seasonal material 4 months in advance.

Sample Issue 32 pages. Little advertising. Sample copy available.
- "Storytelling: A Life-Saving Experience," by Jim Woodward. Personal experience piece about a story-telling class that helped a depressed teenage boy.
- "Introducing Teens to Christian Values in the Classroom Through Popular YA Lit," by SaraBeth Carter. Suggests several YA literature sources that explore Christian principles.

Rights and Payment First and electronic rights. Articles $20–$50. Pays on publication. Provides 3 contributor's copies.

Teaching Theatre

2343 Auburn Avenue, Cincinnati, OH 45219. www.edta.org

Editor: James Palmarini

This is the Educational Theatre Association's journal for theater educators. It features articles on acting, directing, playwriting, and technical theater; program profiles; curriculum design; teaching methodology; and current trends in theater education. If an article can be of use to a theater teacher—either by presenting a model, an innovative idea, or a specific teaching methodology—send along a query. General interest essays on the value of educational theater are likely to be rejected.
- **Circulation** 5,000 ■ **Audience** Theater teachers ■ **Frequency** Quarterly

Freelance Potential Publishes 12–15 freelance submissions yearly: 65% written by nonstaff writers; 50% by authors new to the magazine; 30% by previously unpublished writers. Receives 13 queries monthly.

Submissions Guidelines available. Prefers complete manuscript; will accept query. Prefers email submissions to jpalmarini@edta.org; will accept hard copy. SASE. Responds in six weeks.
- *Articles:* 1,000–4,000 words. Informational, personal experience. Topics: theater education, the arts, curricula.
- *Depts/columns:* Word lengths vary. Classroom exercises, ideas, technical advice, textbook or play suggestions.
- *Artwork:* B/W prints. Line art.

Sample Issue 36 pages. Advertising. Sample copy available.
- "It's Technical: The Movement Towards Standards in Technical Theatre Education," by Dana Taylor. Discusses programs that incorporate technical needs that serve both the show and the student.
- "Deedle Deedle Everyone," by Katie Lebhar Black & John W. White. Profiles a theater program that created a school-wide curriculum based on *Fiddler on the Roof.*

Rights and Payment First rights. Written material, $100–$450. Pays on acceptance. Provides 5 contributor's copies.

Tech & Learning

1111 Bayhill Drive, Suite 125, San Bruno, CA 94066. www.techlearning.com

Managing Editor: Christine Weiser

This magazine, which serves the K–12 school community, champions the integration of technology—particularly digital technology—in the classroom. It can be used as a professional development tool for educators trying to broaden their reach and prepare their students for a global, digital workforce. Its articles are designed to give educators and district-level technology coordinators the information they need to get the most out of the available technology. It accepts pitches from free-lancers, and is most interested in hearing from in-the-field technology directors about what is working in their schools. ■ **Circulation** 90,000 ■ **Audience** Educators, technology coordinators ■ **Frequency** Monthly

Freelance Potential Accepts pitches from freelancers.

Submissions Editorial calendar available at website. Query. Accepts email queries to cweiser@ nbmedia. com. Send pitches only, not complete articles. Response time varies.
■ *Articles:* Word lengths vary. Informational, how-to, personal experience. Topics: using technology in the classroom, school, or district; training teachers; grant writing; information literacy; technology as an instructional tool.
■ *Depts/columns:* Word lengths vary. Product reviews, news and trends, grants and funding. How-To, They Said It (opinion).

Sample Issue Sample issue available at website.
■ "What It Means, How They Do It." How three districts automated assessment for substantive results.
■ "Pick Up the Tabs." Classrooms that have replaced textbooks with digital tablets.

Rights and Payment Unavailable.

Tech Directions

Prakken Publications, 832 Phoenix Drive, P.O. Box 8623, Ann Arbor, MI 48107. www.techdirections.com

Managing Editor: Susanne Peckham

A resource for technical and vocational educators, *Tech Directions* covers the latest teaching methods and projects. Technology-related, hands-on projects must include step-by-step instructions. All material should inform students about technology and careers. ■ **Circulation** 43,000 ■ **Audience** Teachers and administrators ■ **Frequency** 10 times a year

Freelance Potential Publishes 50 freelance submissions yearly: 80% written by nonstaff writers; 50% by authors new to the magazine; 50% by previously unpublished writers. Receives 13 queries, 6 unsolicited manuscripts monthly.

Submissions Guidelines available at website. Query or send complete manuscript. Accepts email submissions to susanne@techdirections.com and disk submissions. Availability of artwork improves chance of acceptance. SASE. Responds in 1–2 months.
■ *Articles:* To 2,000 words. Informational, how-to. Topics: teaching techniques; unusual projects in automotive, building trades, graphics, hydraulics, industrial arts, lasers, manufacturing, radio and television, robotics, software, welding, woodworking, and other vocational education.
■ *Depts/columns:* Word lengths vary. Legislation updates, technology news and history, media reviews, essays,new product information.
■ *Artwork:* High-quality digital images (EPS, TIFF, or JPEG); prints, slides, or transparencies; CAD renderings.
■ *Other:* Puzzles, games, quizzes.

Sample Issue 30 pages. Advertising. Sample copy available at website.
■ "Program Evolves from Basic CAD to Total Manufacturing Experience," by Joel Cassola. Describes one school's transition from a traditional classroom-based, pre-engineering program to one that helps students understand the entire manufacturing process.
■ "Winners of the 'Gimme Shelter' Competition.'" Details on the winners of a challenge to propose designs for inexpensive, portable shelters for people made homeless from natural disasters.

Rights and Payment All rights. Articles, $50+. Depts/columns, to $25. Pays on publication. Provides 3 contributor's copies.

Techniques

ACTE, 1410 King Street, Alexandria, VA 22314. www.acteonline.org

Managing Editor: Susan Emeagwali

Published by the Association for Career and Technical Education, this magazine offers articles that show the connection between education and the workplace. Content is primarily journalistic, and writers are expected to know their material thoroughly. Profiles of individuals making an impact in the field are of particular interest. ■ **Circulation** 30,000 ■ **Audience** Educators ■ **Frequency** 8 times a year

Freelance Potential Publishes 10–20 freelance submissions yearly: 60% written by nonstaff writers; 30% by authors new to the magazine; 15% by previously unpublished writers. Receives up to 8 queries monthly.

Submissions Guidelines and editorial calendar available at website. Query. Accepts email to semeagwali@acteonline.org (Word attachments). Availability of artwork improves chance of acceptance. Responds in 4 months.
■ *Articles:* 1,000–2,500 words. Informational, how-to, case studies, profiles. Topics: career and technical education programming, practices, and policy; integrating career education and academics; technology; environmental issues.
■ *Depts/columns:* To 2,500 words. Research Report.
■ *Artwork:* Digital images at 300 dpi. Charts and graphs.

Sample Issue 62 pages. Advertising.Sample copy available at website.
■ "The End of the School Year—A Time For Reflection," by Susan Reese. Discusses different ways to incorporate reflective writing in the end-of-the-year curriculum.
■ "Making Assessing CTE Programs Meaningful," by Patti Beltram. Describes the changes a school district made to its annual assessment program .

Rights and Payment All rights. No payment.

Texas Child Care Quarterly

P.O. Box 162881, Austin, TX 78716-2881. www.childcarequarterly.com

Editor: Louise Parks

This is a training journal for child-care providers and early childhood education teachers and administrators. Published by the Texas Workforce Commission, it provides information about child growth and development theory, and gives caregivers suggestions for activities to do with children. If submitting an informational article, include all source material at the end. If submitting an activity, include all steps and materials needed. ■ **Circulation** 32,000 ■ **Audience** Teachers and child-care workers ■ **Frequency** Quarterly

Freelance Potential Publishes 12–15 freelance submissions yearly: 50% written by nonstaff writers; 50% by authors new to the magazine; 10% by previously unpublished writers. Receives 2–3 unsolicited manuscripts monthly.

Submissions Guidelines available at website. Send complete manuscript with brief biography. Accepts disk submissions with hard copy and email submissions to editor@childcarequarterly.com. No simultaneous submissions. SASE. Responds in 3 weeks.
■ *Articles:* 2,500 words. Informational, theoretical, how-to. Topics: child growth and development, school-family communication, health and safety, program administration, professional development, hands-on activities.
■ *Depts/columns:* Staff-written.

Sample Issue 44 pages. No advertising. Sample copy available at website.
■ "How To Get More Out of the Outdoors," by Heather Olsen & Kevin Finn. Provides suggestions on how to use fun outdoor activities to keep children active.

- "Talking with Children about Monsters." Discusses activities that can help children conquer their fear about monsters.

Rights and Payment All rights. No payment. Provides 3 contributor's copies and a 1-year subscription.

Today's Catholic Teacher

2621 Dryden Road, Suite 300, Dayton, OH 45439. www.catholicteacher.com

Managing Editor: Betsy Shepard

Focusing on issues and trends affecting elementary and junior high Catholic school education, this magazine targets teachers, principals, superintendents, and parents. Its articles offer practical tips and information in a concise and direct manner. Material directed to teachers in grades four through eight is given preference. ■ **Circulation** 50,000 ■ **Audience** Teachers, grades K–12 ■ **Frequency** 6 times a year

Freelance Potential Publishes 20 freelance submissions yearly: 95% written by nonstaff writers; 50% by authors new to the magazine. Receives up to 16 queries and unsolicited manuscripts monthly.

Submissions Guidelines and editorial calendar available. Prefers query; will accept complete manuscript. Accepts email with hard copy to bshepard@peterli.com. Accepts simultaneous submissions if identified. SASE. Responds to queries in 1 month, to manuscripts in 3 months.
- *Articles:* 600–1,500 words. Informational, self-help, how-to. Topics: technology, fundraising, classroom management, curriculum development, administration, education issues and trends.
- *Depts/columns:* Word lengths vary. Opinion, news, software, character development, curricula, teaching tools, school profiles.
- *Artwork:* Color prints, slides, or transparencies.
- *Other:* Reproducible activity pages.

Sample Issue 76 pages. Advertising. Sample copy available.
- "Not Too Controversial for High School! Bioethics for Science and Religion Students," by Terry Maksymowych. Explores bioethical issues linking science and religion that will engage students.
- "Transforming American Education: The New National Education Technology Plan," by Susan Brooks-Young. Examines the National Education Technology Plan and how teachers can benefit from it.

Rights and Payment All rights. Written material, $100–$250. Pays on publication. Provides contributor's copies.

The Universe in the Classroom

Astronomical Society of the Pacific, 390 Ashton Avenue, San Francisco, CA 94112. www.astrosociety.org/uitc

Editor: Brian Kruse

This electronic, educational newsletter is for teachers and other educators who want to help their students learn more about the universe. Its articles explain astronomical topics and provide hands-on classroom activities that can make the subject come alive for students. The Astronomical Society of the Pacific was formed by a group of Northern California professional and amateur astronomers, and is now one of the largest general astronomy societies in the world. Authors need not be professional astronomers, but they must know of what they write, and gear writing to non-astronomers. ■ **Circulation** 10,000 ■ **Audience** Teachers ■ **Frequency** Quarterly

Freelance Potential Publishes 8 freelance submissions yearly: 75% written by nonstaff writers; 75% by authors new to the magazine; 10% by previously unpublished writers. Receives 1 query monthly.

Submissions Query. Accepts email queries to astroed@astrosociety.org. Availability of artwork

improves chance of acceptance. Responds in 1 month. Guidelines furnished upon acceptance of article query.
- *Articles:* 3,000 words. Informational, classroom activities. Topics: astronomy, astrobiology.
- *Artwork:* Color prints and transparencies.
- *Other:* Hands-on activities.

Sample Issue 5 pages. No advertising. Sample copy available at website.
- "The Drake Equation: 50 Years of Giving Direction to the Scientific Search for Life Beyond Earth," by Sara Scoles & Sue Ann Heatherly. Describes the world's largest and most advanced radio telescopes on Earth.
- "Probing Extrasolar Planets with the Spitzer Space Telescope," by Michelle Thaller. Explains how the Spitzer telescope has revolutionized the study of exoplanets.

Rights and Payment One-time rights. No payment.

Voices from the Middle

National Council of Teachers of English, 1111 West Kenyon Road, Urbana, IL 61801. www.ncte.org/journals/vm

Editor: Doug Fisher

Voices from the Middle appears in themed issues, each devoted to a single concept related to literacy and learning at the middle school level. It publishes informative articles, personal experience pieces, and literature reviews. Writers should note that each issue has a specific deadline for manuscripts.
- **Circulation** 9,000 ■ **Audience** Middle school language arts teachers ■ **Frequency** Quarterly

Freelance Potential Publishes 12 freelance submissions yearly: 70% written by nonstaff writers; 85% by authors new to the magazine; 60% by previously unpublished writers. Receives 13 unsolicited manuscripts monthly.

Submissions Guidelines and editorial calendar/theme list available at website. Send complete manuscript with signed consent form, the proposed issue, 100-word abstract, and bulleted list of key points. Accepts submissions through website only. Responds in 3–5 months.
- *Articles:* 2,000 words. Informational, personal experience, case studies, reviews. Topics: language and visual arts learning, teaching, research focusing on young adolescents.
- *Depts/columns:* Staff-written.
- *Artwork:* High-resolution color images.

Sample Issue Sample copy available at website.
- "Grading Written Work: An Integral Part of Writing Workshop Practice," by Kristen Robbins. Discusses strategies for grading creative writing.
- "Future Directions: A Call for Actions," by Richard Meyer. Introduces steps to changing the reading and writing agenda to go beyond legislation and politics.

Rights and Payment First and second rights. No payment. Provides 2 contributor's copies.

Volta Voices

Alexander Graham Bell Association for the Deaf and Hard of Hearing, 3417 Volta Place NW, Washington, DC 20007-2778. www.agbell.org

Editor: Melody Felzin

Volta Voices is read by the deaf and hearing impaired, their families, and by educators, researchers, and other professionals in the field of hearing loss. Its timely articles cover spoken-language education, new technologies, social aspects of hearing impairment, advocacy and legislation, and health issues. ■ **Circulation** 5,500 ■ **Audience** People affected by or working with hearing loss ■ **Frequency** 6 times a year

Freelance Potential Publishes 6–8 freelance submissions yearly; 90% written by nonstaff writers, 50% by unpublished writers. Receives 24 unsolicited manuscripts yearly.

Submissions Guidelines available at website. Send complete manuscript. Accepts email submissions to editor@agbell.org (Word attachments). Responds in 1–3 months.
- *Articles:* 1,0000–2,000 words. Informational, how-to, personal experience. Topics: technology, education, advocacy, health—all as they relate to hearing loss.
- *Depts/columns:* 50–150 words. Events, association and member news.
- *Artwork:* High-quality digital photos (JPEG, TIFF, or EPS format).

Sample Issue Sample copy available at website.
- "Is Auditory-Verbal Therapy Effective for Children with Hearing Loss?" by Dimity Dornan & Louise Hickson. Reports on a study to determine speech and language outcomes in an auditory-verbal therapy program.
- "Preparing a Global Network of LSL Professionals," by Estelle Roberts. Examines how listening and spoken language communication professionals are trained around the world .

Rights and Payment All rights. No payment. Provides 3 contributor's copies.

VOYA Magazine

4501 Forbes Boulevard, Suite 200, Lanham, MD 20706. www.voya.com

Editor in Chief: RoseMary Honnold

Devoted exclusively to the informational needs of young people and the people who provide it, *VOYA* (Voice of Youth Advocates) is read by librarians and other professionals who work with teens. It reports on teens' reading, writing, and developmental needs. It is interested in libraries' successful teen programs, as well as librarians' philosophies, literary analysis, and experiences in working with teens. ■ **Circulation** 7,000 ■ **Audience** YA librarians ■ **Frequency** 6 times a year

Freelance Potential Publishes 100 freelance submissions yearly: 95% written by nonstaff writers; 60% by authors new to the magazine; 5% by previously unpublished writers. Receives 5 queries monthly.

Submissions Guidelines available at website. Query with synopsis, author biography, target audience, word count, and list of suggested images. Accepts email to rhonnold@voya.com. Availability of artwork improves chance of acceptance. Responds in 2–4 months.
- *Articles:* 750–3,500 words. Informational, how-to, book reviews, interviews, book lists. Topics: young adult literature, contemporary authors, library programs, literary analysis, project ideas.
- *Depts/columns:* Staff-written.
- *Artwork:* B/W and color prints.
- *Other:* Submit seasonal material 1 year in advance.

Sample Issue 174 pages. Advertising. Sample copy available.
- "No Wrong Way to Write," by Joyce Doyle. Provides steps for starting a teen writers group.
- "Our Own Expressions," by Meredith Hale & Jami Schwarzwalder. Describes a popular written and visual arts contest for young adults in Washington State.

Rights and Payment All rights. Written material, $50–$125. Pays on publication. Provides 3 contributor's copies.

Youth Runner Magazine

P.O. Box 1156, Lake Oswego, OR 97035. www.youthrunner.com

Editor: Dan Kesterson

Middle school and high school students, their parents, and their coaches turn to this magazine for reporting on cross-country and track and field running. It includes training tips, and team and athlete

profiles. Submissions students and coaches, as well as professional writers, are encouraged.
■ **Circulation** Unavailable ■ **Audience** Youth runners and their coaches ■ **Frequency** 10 times a year

Freelance Potential Publishes 100 freelance submissions yearly: 30% written by nonstaff writers; 30% by authors new to the magazine; 50% by previously unpublished writers. Receives 5 unsolicited manuscripts monthly.

Submissions Send complete manuscript. Accepts email submissions to editor@youthrunner.com. Response time varies.
■ *Articles:* Informational, how-to, interviews, profiles. Topics: track and field, cross country running, training tips, top athletes and coaches, health and fitness.
■ *Depts/columns:* Product and media reviews, news.

Sample Issue Sample copy available.
■ "Gustafson Back on Track at Palisades," by Steve Galluzzo. Profiles one of the nation's top track and field performers.
■ "P.A.C.E. Trek 2009 Countdown," by Paul Stasos. Describes a youth running event which takes participants on a 500-mile journey through the heart of Alaska.

Rights and Payment First rights. Written material, word lengths and payment rates vary. Payment policy varies.

Youth Today

1331 H Street NW, Washington, DC 20005. www.youthtoday.org

Editor: Nancy Lewis

This industry newspaper is read by professional youth workers and administrators of youth services, youth advocacy, and youth policy programs. It keeps them abreast of news, trends, issues, and programs. Freelancers must have experience writing for daily newspapers, or have extensive experience researching and writing pieces for newspapers and magazines. ■ **Circulation** 12,000 ■ **Audience** Youth workers ■ **Frequency** 10 times a year

Freelance Potential Publishes 25 freelance submissions yearly: 30% written by nonstaff writers. Receives 1 query monthly.

Submissions Query with résumé and clips. Accepts disk submissions (Word attachments) and email queries to nlewis@youthtoday.org. SASE. Responds in 3 months. Guidelines available.
■ *Articles:* 600–2,500 words. Informational, news and research projects, profiles of youth workers and youth programs, interviews, business features. Topics: foster care, child abuse, program management, violence, adolescent health, juvenile justice, job training, school-to-work programs, after-school programs, mentoring, other social issues related to youth development.
■ *Depts/columns:* Viewpoints, 750 words. Book and video reviews, news briefs, people in the news, word lengths vary.

Sample Issue 32 pages. Advertising. Sample copy available.
■ "Q&A: Bryan Samuels, Obama's Top Child Welfare Appointee," by John Kelly. Interview with the Commissioner for the Administration on Children, Youth, and Families.
■ "Education in Juvie," by John Kelly. Discusses how No Child Left Behind offers advocates a chance to improve the lives of incarcerated youth.

Rights and Payment First and reprint rights. Written material, $150–$2,000. Kill fee, $200. Pays on publication. Provides 2 contributor's copies.

Youth Worker Journal

402 BNA Drive, Suite 400, Nashville, TN 37217-2509. www.youthworker.com

Submissions: Amy Lee

This journal for Christian youth workers provides youth ministry resources, games, ideas, fundraiser tools, profiles, and inspirational articles. It works with well-established writers as well as those who have never been published before. Submissions are also accepted for its non-paying digital version.
■ **Circulation** 10,000 ■ **Audience** Youth ministry workers ■ **Frequency** 6 times a year

Freelance Potential Publishes 50+ freelance submissions yearly: 100% written by nonstaff writers; 25% by authors new to the magazine; 15% by previously unpublished writers. Receives 60 queries monthly.

Submissions Guidelines and theme list available at website. Published writers, query with short biography. Unpublished writers, query with outline, introduction, and details on why the article is important to readers and why you should write it. Prefers email to alee@salempublishing.com (include "Query" in subject line); will accept hard copy and faxes to 615-385-4412. SASE. Responds in 6–8 weeks.
■ *Articles:* 200–3,000 words. Informational, practical application, personal experience, reviews. Topics: youth ministry, theology, spreading Christ's word, student worship, family ministry, education, family issues, popular culture, the media, volunteering.
■ *Depts/columns:* Word lengths vary. National and regional trends; youth workers' quotes.

Sample Issue 64 pages. Advertising. Sample copy available .
■ "School's Out? Now What?" by Paul Asay. Discusses the impact of the slow economy on teenagers looking for summer jobs.
■ "We Don't Do Fundraisers," by Luke Trouten. Author's view on why his church doesn't and shouldn't hold fundraisers.

Rights and Payment All rights. Written material, $15–$300. Pays on publication. Provides 1 contributor's copy.

Parenting Magazines

Publications directed toward parents and families present writers with a tremendous number of national, regional, and local publishing opportunities. This is a growing market, and can be a good fit for writers who want to focus their writing on children in some form.

The magazines listed in this section run the gamut from general parenting issues and child deveopment to those that serve families with special challenges such as a child on the autism spectrum; and from national magazines such as *American Baby* to local publications that give parents in their region localized information and resources in their towns.

The parenting market also presents a unique opportunity for writers to increase their publication numbers—and pay days—by writing on a general parenting theme and localizing it for a number of regional magazines, or by taking a child-directed piece written for a children's magazine and refocusing it with a parenting angle.

Some of the local publications may not be paying markets, while those with larger circulations can be quite well-paying. Regardless, the opportunities they each present for getting published and building a résumé can be invaluable to a beginning writer.

ADDitude

39 West 37th Street, 15th Floor, New York, NY 10018. www.additudemag.com

Editorial Assistant: Caitlin Ford

ADDitude covers the news and issues surrounding Attention Deficit Disorder and related syndromes. It is written for families dealing with ADD. Informational articles are written by journalists and mental health professionals. Parents and family members, however, are invited to write first person-stories about their experiences. ■ **Circulation** 40,000 ■ **Audience** Adults ■ **Frequency** 5 times a year

Freelance Potential Publishes 15–20 freelance submissions yearly: 80% written by nonstaff writers; 30% by authors new to the magazine; 30% by previously unpublished writers. Receives 8 queries monthly.

Submissions Guidelines available at website. Query with brief description or outline, why it belongs in the magazine, why you should be the one to write it, and recent clips. Prefers email to submissions@additudemag.com (file attached); will accept hard copy. SASE. Also hires bloggers. Send writing sample, 300-word sample blog post covering the topic you want to blog about, and how often you can post to webmaster@additudemag.com (file attached). Responds in 6–8 weeks.
■ *Articles:* To 2,000 words. Informational, personal experience. Topics: ADD and ADHD, education, medication, recreation, organization, parenting, child development.
■ *Depts/columns:* Word lengths vary. Profiles of students, teachers, and schools, first-person essays, healthy living, organization, product reviews, ADD/ADHD news.

Sample Issue 62 pages. Advertising. Sample copy available.
■ "Reduce Anxiety Naturally," by Sandy Maynard. Tips for treating anxiety without medication.
■ "Shut Up about Your Perfect Kid," by Gina Gallagher and Patricia Konjoian. How parents of ADHD children can deal with negative feelings when other parents brag about their children's successes.

Rights and Payment First rights. Written material, payment rates vary. Kill fee, $75. Pays on publication. Provides a 1-year subscription.

Adoptalk

North American Council on Adoptable Children, 970 Raymond Street, Suite 106, St. Paul, MN 55114-1149. www.nacac.org

Communication Specialist: Diane Riggs

This newsletter, read by foster/adoptive parents, child welfare professionals, and child advocates, covers issues related to adoption and foster care, with a focus on special-needs adoptions. Its goal is to inform membership about current child care policies and legislation, give parenting tips, and present news related to children in and adopted from foster care in North America. It is not interested in submissions about healthy children adopted as infants or in material geared toward children. *Adoptalk* also contains child welfare-related news and resources. Each issue features a personal story from a youth who is currently in, an alumni of, or has been adopted from foster care. ■ **Circulation** 2,500 ■ **Audience** Adults ■ **Frequency** Quarterly

Freelance Potential Publishes 24 freelance submissions yearly: 25–50% written by nonstaff writers; 1–10% by authors new to the magazine; 1–10% by previously unpublished writers. Receives 1–5 queries and 1–5 unsolicited manuscripts monthly.

Submissions Query with cover letter, outline, and description of article. Accepts email submissions (Word, Adobe, PDF, JPEG, TIFF attachments) to dianeriggs@nacac.org. Responds in 1–3 weeks.
■ *Articles:* 500–2,000 words. Informational, profiles, personal experience, essays, interviews. Topics: adoptive and foster care, parenting, child welfare, preparing children for adoption, parenting children exposed to neglect or substance abuse, recruitment, adoption news, conference updates, NACAC membership news and updates.
■ *Depts/columns:* Word lengths vary. Book reviews, first-person essays.

Sample Issue 16 pages. No advertising. Sample copy available.
■ "The Importance of Family," by Wendy Piccus. Young woman's story of being separated from her sisters in foster care and how they were reunited.
■ "Child Welfare's Next Challenge: Parenting Meth's Young Victims," by Diane Riggs. How child welfare is affected by the use of methamphetamine and tips for parents raising these children.

Rights and Payment Rights vary. No payment. Provides 5 contributor's copies.

Adoptive Families

39 West 37th Street, 15th Floor, New York, NY 10018. www.adoptivefamilies.com

Editor: Susan Caughman

This magazine addresses the issues, emotions, and decisions faced by families in all steps of the adoption process. *Adoptive Families* is interested in personal experience stories from people who are part of or work with an adoptive family. It strives to be the leading information resource for families before, during, and after adoption. It is currently looking for articles on: middle–school and teen years, adoptive parent support groups, foster adoption, transracial adoption, adoptive parents of color.
■ **Circulation** 40,000 ■ **Audience** Adoptive parents ■ **Frequency** 6 times a year

Freelance Potential Publishes 100 freelance submissions yearly: 75% written by nonstaff writers; 50% by authors new to the magazine; 20% by previously unpublished writers. Receives 40–50 queries and unsolicited manuscripts monthly.

Submissions Guidelines available at website. Query with a brief description of idea or outline, why you think it belongs in the magazine, why you should write it, where in the magazine you think it belongs (feature or a department; see list below), and recent clips. Send complete manuscript for personal essays. Prefers email to submissions@adoptivefamilies.com (Word attachments); will accept hard copy. SASE. Responds in 6–8 weeks.

- *Articles:* 500–1,800 words. Informational, self-help, how-to, personal experience. Topics: preparing for adoption, health, school and education, birth families, parenting tips, family, friends, and community, talking about adoption, transracial adoption, adoptive parent support groups, foster adoption.
- *Depts/columns:* To 1,200 words. The Waiting Game (pre-adoption issues), Parenting the Child Who Waited (adopting older children), About Birthparents, Been There (adults speak about growing up adopted), Our Story, Adoption and School, In My Opinion, At Home (personal essay), Single Parent, And So It Begins (stories about the first year of parenthood), Living with Diversity.

Sample Issue 66 pages. Advertising. Sample copy available.
- "Showered with Love," by Lisa Milbrand. Planning a baby shower for an adopted baby.
- "A Mother Like Any Other," by Lily Prellezo. How an adoptive mom relates to her daughter's pregnancy.

Rights and Payment All rights. Written material, payment rates vary; personal essays receive a 1-year subscription to the magazine. Payment policy varies. Provides 2 contributor's copies.

AKA Mom

H2O Print Media, 16526 West 78th Street, #359, Eden Prairie, MN 55346-4302. www.akamommagazine.com

Publisher: Sara Conners

Created by moms for moms, this magazine appears in print, online, and even as an iPad app. It made its debut in the summer of 2011, and targets modern and fashion savvy mothers. Each issue offers articles on parenting and children's health that speak to the other roles of its readers: wife, lover, stylish woman, and career woman. ■ **Circulation** 200,000 ■ **Audience** Moms ■ **Frequency** Quarterly

Freelance Potential Unavailable.

Submissions Contact for more information at editorial@akamommagazine.com.
- *Articles:* Word lengths vary. Informational, profiles, personal experience, how-to. Topics: parenting issues, balancing work and home life, relationships, style and fashion, family travel, fitness, pregnancy, careers.

Sample Issue .
- "Taking the Kids." 6 suggestions for traveling smarter during summer vacation.
- "Living the Sweet Life," by Lindsay Walker. An interview with actress and author Jodi Sweetin.

Rights and Payment Unavailable.

Akron Family

TNT Publications, 11630 Chillicothe Road, Chesterfield, OH 44026. www.neohiofamily.com

Editor: Terri Nighswonger

Distributed free through schools, child-care centers, libraries, and grocery stores, *Akron Family* offers features on parenting children of all ages, as well as regional activity calendars and resource guides. ■ **Circulation** 75,000 ■ **Audience** Parents ■ **Frequency** Monthly

Freelance Potential Publishes 40–50 freelance submissions yearly: 50% written by nonstaff writers; 33% by authors new to the magazine. Receives about 40 queries monthly.

Submissions Theme list available at website. Query with clips. Accepts email queries to editor@tntpublications.com. Responds if interested.

- *Articles:* 500+ words. Informational, how–to. Topics: parenting, activities, education, local recreation.
- *Depts/columns:* Word lengths vary. Celebrations (recipes, kitchen crafts and tips), Classroom Corner (homework help, teacher tips), Family Calendar, Special–Needs, Kids (current local news), Mommy Matters/Daddy Dialogue.
- *Artwork:* High resolution JPEG and TIFF images.

Sample Issue Sample issue available at website.
- "Raising More Than Just Hands," by Matthew Rusnak. Explains charter schools and how they work.
- "Cooking Up Giggles for April Fool's or Any Day." Creating "counterfeit food" with kids as a fun prank.

Rights and Payment Exclusive rights. All material, payment rates vary. Pays on publication. Provides 1 contributor's copy.

American Baby

375 Lexington Avenue, 10th Floor, New York, NY 10017. www.americanbaby.com

Editorial Assistant: Jessica Wohlgemuth

This consumer magazine addresses the needs and fears of new parents with articles designed to inform as well as support and encourage. It prefers quick-to-read, hands-on information that readers can put to use immediately rather than theoretical parenting pieces. ■ **Circulation** 2.1 million ■ **Audience** Parents ■ **Frequency** Monthly

Freelance Potential Publishes 24 freelance submissions yearly: 55% written by nonstaff writers; 1% by authors new to the magazine; 1% by previously unpublished writers. Receives about 85 queries and unsolicited manuscripts monthly.

Submissions Guidelines available. Query with clips and writing samples; or send complete manuscript. Accepts hard copy and simultaneous submissions if identified. SASE. Responds in 2 months.
- *Articles:* 1,000–2,000 words. Informational, how-to, profiles, interviews, humor, personal experience. Topics: pregnancy, childbirth, breastfeeding, infancy, parenting, child care and development, health, fitness, nutrition, family travel.
- *Depts/columns:* 1,000 words. Health briefs, fitness tips, new products, fashion.
- *Other:* Submit seasonal material 3 months in advance.

Sample Issue 72 pages. Advertising. Sample copy available.
- "Sleep Like a Baby," by Cynthia Hanson. Explains infant sleep patterns from birth to 18 months.
- "Pregnancy Superstitions." Superstitions and traditions during pregnancy.

Rights and Payment First serial rights. Articles, to $2,000. Depts/columns, to $1,000. Kill fee, 25%. Pays on acceptance. Provides 5 contributor's copies.

Arlington Magazine

1319 North Greenbrier Street, Arlington, VA 22205. www.arlingtonmagazine.com

Editor: Jenny Sullivan

This newly launched regional lifestyle magazine focuses on the needs and interests of residents in the Arlington, McLean, and Falls Church areas of Virginia. Created in late 2011, the magazine covers the region's people, community, history, and arts and entertainment. Articles on parenting and education are also featured. It seeks material that is smart and sophisticated, yet doesn't take itself too seriously. ■ **Circulation** 25,000 ■ **Audience** Parents ■ **Frequency** 6 times a year

Freelance Potential As a new publication, story ideas and specific pitches are welcome.

Submissions For more information as the magazine moves into regular publication, contact editorial@ arlingtonmagazine.com.

■ *Articles:* Informational, interviews. Topics: family, education, parenting, heath and fitness, beauty and fashion, history, the arts.

Sample Issue

■ "Making the Grade." Which schools have the best teachers in Arlington.

Rights and Payment Unavailable.

Athens Parent

P.O. Box 465, Watkinsville, GA 30677. www.athensparent.com

Editor in Chief: Shannon Howell Baker

This regional publication features original articles on issues that interest parents, grandparents, educators, and others living in the Athens area who are involved in the well-being of children and families. It seeks to promote parent/child interaction and community involvement, and to provide a resource for parents and families. It is always in need of articles on health, teens, single parenting, dad's perspective, discipline, and family life. ■ **Circulation** Unavailable ■ **Audience** Parents ■ **Frequency** 6 times a year

Freelance Potential Publishes 40 freelance submissions yearly: 85% written by nonstaff writers. Receives about 42 queries monthly.

Submissions Guidelines and theme list available at website. Query. Accepts hard copy and email queries to editor@athensparent.com. SASE. Response time varies.

■ *Articles:* Word lengths vary. Informational, how–to, personal experience. Topics: parenting, health, family life, community involvement, education, recreational activities, holidays, discipline, single parenting.

■ *Depts/columns:* Word lengths vary. Health, finances, fathering, child development, lifestyle, teen issues.

Sample Issue

■ "How Busy Parents Can Lose Weight," by Rebecca Van Damm. Lifestyle suggestions for parents that will help them achieve and maintain healthy weights.

■ "How Facebook Is Changing the College Admissions Process," by Katherine L. Cohen, Ph.D. Advice for the parents of college-bound teens regarding Facebook and how colleges view it.

Rights and Payment First rights. Written material, payment rates vary. Payment policy varies.

Atlanta Parent

2346 Perimeter Park Drive, Atlanta, GA 30341. www.atlantaparent.com

Managing Editor: Kate Parrott

Parenting advice, educational topics, local recreational opportunities, and children's social and emotional development are all covered in this award–winning magazine for parents living in the greater Atlanta region. Its articles are down-to-earth in tone and are mostly written in the third person, with the exception of humor essays. ■ **Circulation** 120,000 ■ **Audience** Parents ■ **Frequency** Monthly

Freelance Potential 40% written by nonstaff writers.

Submissions Guidelines available at website. Send complete manuscript. Prefers email submissions to editor@atlantaparent.com (Word attachments); will accept hard copy and disk submissions. SASE. Response time varies.

■ *Articles:* 800–1,200 words. Informational, how-to, humor. Topics: education, child care, child development, health, parenting, recreation.

■ *Depts/columns:* Word lengths vary. Health, trends, medical advice, parenting tips, humor.

■ *Other:* Submit seasonal material 6 months in advance.

Sample Issue 82 pages. Advertising. Sample copy available.
- "Best Bets (and Better Nots) for Baby," by Laura Powell and Melanie Wagner. Moms share the best gifts they received for baby and those that were not so useful.
- "Tiger Mom or Pussycat?" by Mary Helen Ramming. A review of the controversial book, *Battle Hymn of the Tiger Mom.*

Rights and Payment One-time and Internet rights. Written material, $35–$50. Pays on publication. Provides 1 contributor's copy.

Austin Family

P.O. Box 7559, Round Rock, TX 78683-7559. www.austinfamily.com

Editor: Melanie Dunham

This free magazine has been providing information about good parenting and raising healthy children since 1992. It serves families who live in the greater Austin area. ■ **Circulation** 35,000 ■ **Audience** Parents ■ **Frequency** Monthly

Freelance Potential Publishes 18 freelance submissions yearly: 85% written by nonstaff writers; 50% by authors new to the magazine; 10% by previously unpublished writers. Receives 100 queries and unsolicited manuscripts monthly.

Submissions Query or send complete manuscript. Accepts email submissions to editor2003@ austinfamily.com. Accepts simultaneous submissions if identified. Availability of artwork improves chance of acceptance. Responds in 3–6 months.
- *Articles:* 800–1,200 words. Informational, how–to, personal experience. Topic: parenting, family life, regional activities, health, education, recreation.
- *Depts/columns:* 800 words. Life Lines (health), Family Matters, The Learning Curve.
- *Artwork:* B/W prints.

Sample Issue Sample copy available.
- "The Spirit of Inclusion," by Jennifer Vanburen. Mainstreaming children with special needs in regular education classrooms.
- "Going Beyond Please and Thank You," by Dr. Betty Richardson. Teaching kids social graces.

Rights and Payment First and second serial rights. All material, payment rates vary. Pays on publication.

Autism Asperger's Digest

P.O. Box 2257, Burlington, NC 27216. www.autismdigest.com

Managing Editor: Kim Fields

This magazine on autism spectrum disorders presents real-life information for readers trying to meet the real-life challenges of ASD. Its articles feature practical, tested strategies and ideas addressing traditional, alternative, and emerging thoughts on ASD. It prefers articles that have a strong hands-on approach to their subject matter, rather than those that simply provide a general overview of a topic. Personal accounts are acceptable as long as they are motivational and have a real-life application. ■ **Circulation** 12,000 ■ **Audience** Parents and ASD professionals ■ **Frequency** 6 times a year

Freelance Potential Publishes 50–60 freelance submissions yearly: 75% written by nonstaff writers; 60% by authors new to the magazine; 60% by previously unpublished writers. Receives 8–10 queries, 20–25 unsolicited manuscripts monthly.

Submissions Guidelines available at website. Query or send complete manuscript. Accepts hard copy and email submissions to editor@autismdigest.com (Word attachments or pasted into body of the email). All submissions must include contact name, address, phone number, and email address in both the email/cover letter and the attachment. SASE. Responds in 2–4 weeks.

- *Articles:* Personal experience, 1,000–1,200 words. Informational, how-to, 1,200–2,000 words. Topics: living with autism, strategies for parents and educators, current research.
- *Depts/columns:* Newsbites, 100–300 words.
- *Artwork:* Color prints; JPEGs at 300 dpi.

Sample Issue 58 pages.
- "A Chip Off the Old Block," by Eric R. Williams. A dad talks about what he's learned from his adopted autistic son.
- "Breaking the Language Barrier," by Karen Emigh. Simple ways to improve language skills for children on the autism spectrum.

Rights and Payment First rights. No payment. Provides contributor's copies and a 1-year subscription.

BabyTalk

2 Park Avenue, 10th Floor, New York, NY 10016. www.babytalk.com

Editor in Chief: Ana Connery

This magazine provides straight talk for new moms and moms-to-be. It features informational and supportive articles on issues faced by parents of babies. Articles should avoid being preachy in tone.
■ **Circulation** 2 million ■ **Audience** Parents ■ **Frequency** 10 times a year

Freelance Potential Publishes 40 freelance submissions yearly: 50% written by nonstaff writers; 20% by authors new to the magazine. Receives about 40 queries monthly.

Submissions Guidelines available. Editorial calendar available at website. Query with clips or writing samples. Accepts hard copy. No simultaneous submissions. SASE. Responds in 2 months.
- *Articles:* 1,500–2,500 words. Informational, how-to, self-help, personal experience. Topics: fertility, pregnancy, childbirth, new motherhood, breastfeeding, infant health and development, baby care, juvenile equipment and toys, day care, nutrition, marital issues.
- *Depts/columns:* 100–500 words. Baby health, milestones, product information, postpartum issues, Q&As, home economics, humor.

Sample Issue 64 pages. Advertising. Sample copy available.
- "36 Tips for Breastfeeding Success," by Megan Aquilina. A round-up of successful breastfeeding strategies.
- "Help! Foods to Avoid During Pregnancy," by Stephanie Wood. Risky foods to avoid while pregnant, and satisfying substitutions.

Rights and Payment First rights. Payment policy varies. Pays on acceptance. Provides 2–4 contributor's copies.

Baltimore's Child

11 Dutton Court, Baltimore, MD 21228. www.baltimoreschild.com

Editor: Dianne R. McCann

In addition to covering local activities, resources, and services for families in the Baltimore region, this magazine emphasizes positive, constructive, and practical advice regarding parenting issues. It prefers articles about living and raising children in the Baltimore region. It will accept general parenting topics, but the article must have local sources. ■ **Circulation** 50,000 ■ **Audience** Parents ■ **Frequency** Monthly

Freelance Potential Publishes 250 freelance submissions yearly: 90% written by nonstaff writers; 10% by authors new to the magazine; 5% by previously unpublished writers.

Submissions Guidelines available at website. Prefers query with proposed subject, description of information article will cover, an indication of style, and clips; will accept complete manuscript. Accepts email submissions to dianne@BaltimoresChild.com. Response time varies.
- ■ *Articles:* 1,200 words. Informational. Topics: parenting, education, health, fitness, child care, social issues, regional news, recreational activities in the region.
- ■ *Depts/columns:* 750 words. Music, family cooking, pet care, baby and toddler issues, parenting teens and children with special needs, family finances.

Sample Issue 92 pages. Advertising. Sample copy available at website.
- ■ "Always in Reach," by Amy Landsman. How families use technology to keep in touch.
- ■ "Globe Trotting at the Library," by Janice Hands. Explains an exciting summer reading program available at the Maryland library system.

Rights and Payment One-time rights. Written material, payment rates vary. Pays within 30 days of publication.

Bamboo Magazine

9012 Haskelll Avenue, North Hills, CA 91343. www.bamboofamilymag.com

Editors: Anni Daulter and Ashley Ess

This digital magazine is designed for parents concerned about the environment and who wish to raise their families in an eco-friendly manner. Articles and columns cover natural living, pregnancy, peaceful parenting, and alternative education. The editors want to hear from writers who are interested in guest-writing the website's blog, in addition to articles. ■ **Hits per month** Unavailable ■ **Audience** Parents ■ **Frequency** Quarterly

Freelance Potential Unavailable.

Submissions Guidelines and edtorial calendar available at website. Query with writing samples or links to samples. Accepts email to submissions@bamboofamilymag.com. Response time varies.
- ■ *Articles:* Word lengths vary. Informational, how-to, interviews, personal experience. Topics: natural living, parenting, education, pregnancy, gardening, the environment.
- ■ *Depts/columns:* Word lengths vary. Health, eco-friendly products, cooking.
- ■ *Artwork:* JPEG or PDF images.

Sample Issue Advertising. Sample copy available at website.
- ■ "The Importance of Play: Making the Case for Creativity in a Media-Driven Society," by Ashley Ess. Explores the social and developmental advantages of creative play.
- ■ "Why Choose Cloth Diapers?" by Kelly Wells. Four reasons for rejecting disposable diapers.

Rights and Payment Rights vary. No payment. Writers receive a short biography at the end of their piece, with a link to a blog, if applicable.

Baton Rouge Parents

11831 Wentling Avenue, Baton Rouge, LA 70816-6055. www.brparents.com

Editor: Amy Foreman-Plaisance

This regional magazine offers articles on parenting issues, children's health topics, education, and family recreation. ■ **Circulation** 55,000 ■ **Audience** Parents ■ **Frequency** Monthly

Freelance Potential Publishes 50+ freelance submissions yearly: 95% written by nonstaff writers; 30% by authors new to the magazine; 15% by previously unpublished writers.

Submissions Guidelines available via email request to brpm@brparents.com. Query with outline, source list, brief author biography, and 2 writing samples. Accepts hard copy and email queries to brpm@brparents.com (include "Article Query" in subject line). SASE. Response time varies.

- *Articles:* Word lengths vary. Informational, how-to. Topics: Parenting, education, child development, regional activities and travel, health.
- *Depts/columns:* Word lengths vary. Stages (child development).

Sample Issue Advertising.
- "Modern Manners in the Tech Age," by Julie Landry Laviolette. New rules to deal with today's high-tech communication methods.
- "The Do's and Don'ts of Homesickness." Strategies for parents to help minimize homesickness for their children.

Rights and Payment First North American serial rights. Written material, $25–$70. Kill fee, $10. Pays on publication. Provides 2 contributor's copies.

Bay Area Parent

1660 South Amphlett Boulevard, Suite 335, San Mateo, CA 94402. www.bayareaparent.com

Editor: Peggy Spear

Catering to families living in the San Francisco Bay area, this publication includes features of national scope with local relevance. Regional family resources and event information are also offered. It is published in three editions: one for the East Bay, one for San Francisco and the Peninsula, and one for Silicon Valley. ■ **Circulation** 80,000 ■ **Audience** Parents ■ **Frequency** Monthly

Freelance Potential Publishes 15–20 freelance submissions yearly: 50% written by nonstaff writers. Receives 10 queries monthly.

Submissions Guidelines available at website. Prefers submissions from local authors. Query. Accepts hard copy. SASE. Responds in 2 months.
- *Articles:* 1,200–1,400 words. Informational, how-to. Topics: parenting, education, health, social skills, regional travel and activities.
- *Depts/columns:* Word lengths vary. Mom's Minute, Green Family, Things We Like, Ask the Doctor, Home Cooking, Health & Safety, Pop Rocks.

Sample Issue Advertising. Sample copy available at website.
- "Virtual Ties," by Jennifer Fogliani. "Visiting" with family using online technology.
- "Waste Not!" by Katherine Ellison. A local mom shares her secrets for a minimalist lifestyle.

Rights and Payment One-time rights. Written material, 6¢ a word. Pays on publication. Provides 1 contributor's copy.

Bay State Parent

117 Elm Street, Millbury, MA 01527. www.baystateparent.com

Editor: Carrie Wattu

Bay State Parent provides up-to-date parenting information and activity guides to families living in eastern and central Massachusetts. Preference is given to queries that come from local writers or cite local sources. ■ **Circulation** 84,000 ■ **Audience** Parents ■ **Frequency** Monthly

Freelance Potential Publishes 72–144 freelance submissions yearly: 95% written by nonstaff writers; 30% by authors new to the magazine; 5% by previously unpublished writers. Receives 10 queries monthly.

Submissions Query. Accepts email queries to editor@baystateparent.com (Word attachments). Availability of artwork improves chance of acceptance. Responds in 1 month.
- *Articles:* To 2,000 words. Informational, how-to, humor. Topics: parenting and family issues, regional

and local events, health, travel, books, arts and crafts, family finance, computers, education, entertainment.
- *Depts/columns:* To 1,500 words. Family health, profiles of fathers, travel pieces.
- *Artwork:* B/W or color prints; JPEG images at 200 dpi.
- *Other:* Submit seasonal material 4 months in advance.

Sample Issue 60 pages. Advertising. Sample copy available.
- "Haiti to Home," by Bonnie J. Toomey. New England families who adopted Haitian children.
- "I Was A Teen Mom," by Heather Kempskie. Women look back on their lives as young moms.

Rights and Payment First Massachusetts exclusive and electronic rights. Articles, $50–$85. Depts/columns, no payment. Kill fee varies. Pays on publication.

BC Parent News Magazine

Sasamat RPO 72086, Vancouver, British Columbia V6R 4P2 Canada. www.bcparent.ca

Editor: Elizabeth Shaffer

This magazine gives parents in British Columbia information on issues that impact children and family life. It also serves as a resource for local events, organizations, and services. ■ **Circulation** 45,000 ■ **Audience** Parents ■ **Frequency** 8 times a year

Freelance Potential Publishes 25 freelance submissions yearly: 80% written by nonstaff writers; 10–30% by authors new to the magazine.

Submissions Guidelines and editorial calendar available. Query or send complete manuscript. Submissions must include a cover page with writer's name, mailing address, phone number, fax number, and email address. Prefers email submissions to eshaffer@telus.net (RTF attachments); will accept disk submissions. No simultaneous submissions. SAE/IRC. Responds in 2 months.
- *Articles:* 500–1,000 words. Informational. Topics: pregnancy, childbirth, adoption, baby and child care, teen issues, family issues, health care, education, computers, sports, money matters, the arts, community events.
- *Depts/columns:* Word lengths vary. Parent health, family news, media reviews.

Sample Issue 24 pages. Advertising. Sample copy available at website.
- "Proactive Preteen Parenting," by Joan Schultz. Practical strategies for parenting preteen children and laying a firm foundation of discipline and communication.
- "Is Spanking Discipline?" by Kathy Lynn. Explores the concept of discipline and getting children to change their behaviors.

Rights and Payment First rights. Articles, $85. Reprints, $50. Depts/columns, payment rates vary. Pays on acceptance.

Birmingham Parent

700-C Southgate Drive, Pelham, AL 35124. www.birminghamparent.com

Publisher/Editor: Carol Muse Evans

This magazine is geared specifically to parents in the Birmingham area of Alabama. Its articles cover parenting with a local slant, and are mostly written by local authors with the goal of helping every parent raise happy, healthy, productive children. ■ **Circulation** 35,000 ■ **Audience** Parents ■ **Frequency** Monthly

Freelance Potential Publishes more than 50 freelance submissions yearly: 50% written by nonstaff writers; 5% by authors new to the magazine.

Submissions Guidelines available at website. Query with résumé, clips, and artwork availability; or send complete manuscript. Accepts email to editor@birminghamparent.com. Responds in 1 month.

- *Articles:* 700–1,500 words. Informational, how-to. Topics: parenting news and advice, health and safety, pregnancy and childbirth, child development, social skills, travel.
- *Depts/columns:* Word lengths vary. News.
- *Artwork:* JPEG files at 300 dpi.

Sample Issue Advertising. Sample copy available at website.
- "Coping with an 'At–Risk' Pregnancy," by Lyn Groom. Support and tips for the mom going through a high–risk pregnancy.
- "Childbirth: Choosing the Right Hospital for You and Your Baby," by Christine del Amo Johnson. Review of Birmingham area hospitals and the birthing options they offer.

Rights and Payment First North American serial and electronic rights. Written material, payment rates vary. Artwork, no payment. Pays within 30 days of publication. Provides 2 conributor's copies.

bNetS@vvy

1201 16th Street NW, Suite 216, Washington, DC 20036. www.bnetsavvy.org

Editor: Mary Esselman

This e-newsletter promotes Internet safety for children and tweens. Read by parents, teachers, and others who work with youth, it offers cyber-safety tools and puts a particular focus on social networking sites. It is published by the National Education Association Health Information Network. *bNetS@vvy* welcomes contributions by parents, teachers, school staff, and tweens who want to share their advice, stories, ideas, and lessons regarding the safe use of technology. ■ **Hits per month** Unavailable ■ **Audience** Parents, teachers, and tweens ■ **Frequency** 6 times a year

Freelance Potential Publishes 20 freelance submissions yearly: 90% written by nonstaff writers; 90% by authors new to the magazine; 80% by previously unpublished writers.

Submissions Guidelines available at website. Query. Accepts email with clips (or links to published work) to internetsafety@nea.org. Responds in 2 weeks.
- *Articles:* 600–950 words. Informational, how-to, reviews. Topics: the Internet, Internet safety, social networking sites.
- 600–950 words. Expert advice, ideas from parents and tweens.

Sample Issue Sample copy available at website.
- "Words Do Hurt . . . National No-Name Calling Week." Details of a week-long campaign filled with educational activities to combat online bullying.
- "Which Social Media Site Is Your Child Visiting?" A round-up of social networking sites that are popular with tweens and the guidelines associated with each of them.

Rights and Payment All rights. Written material, payment rates vary. Payment policy varies.

The Boston Parents' Paper

51 Morgan Drive, Suite 11, Norwood, MA 02062. http://boston.parenthood.com

Associate Editor: Susan Flynn

This magazine gives Boston-area families thought-provoking and service-oriented articles pertaining to parenting and child development issues. It offers features with a national scope and local relevance. This publication also provides information on recreational opportunities and resources in the region. ■ **Circulation** 75,000 ■ **Audience** Parents ■ **Frequency** Monthly

Freelance Potential Publishes 60–75 freelance submissions yearly: 10–12% written by nonstaff writers; 50% by authors new to the magazine; 10% by previously unpublished writers. Receives 10+ queries monthly.

Submissions Guidelines and theme list available. Query with clips or writing samples. Accepts email to susan.flynn@parenthood.com. Availability of artwork improves chance of acceptance. Response time varies.
- *Articles:* Word lengths vary. Informational, how–to. Topics: parenting, environmental concerns, regional activities and travel, social issues, education, entertainment.
- *Depts/columns:* Word lengths vary. 5 Questions.
- *Artwork:* B/W prints. Line art.

Sample Issue Advertising.
- "Striking Out with Baseball," by Susan Flynn. Non–traditional sports for children.
- "Barely Green?" by Susan Simple ways families can be more eco-friendly.

Rights and Payment All rights. All material, payment rates vary. Pays on publication. Provides 5 contributor's copies.

Boulder County Kids

P.O. Box 17114, Boulder, CO 80308. www.bouldercountykids.com

Editor: Jennifer Martin

This guide for families living in Boulder County and surrounding areas features articles on parenting issues, education, children's health, and family recreation. An emphasis is placed on local events, services, and programs. Articles must have a local angle and be resource-oriented, although pieces on local businesses are not accepted. Health-related information must be documented with references.
- **Circulation** Unavailable ■ **Audience** Parents ■ **Frequency** Quarterly

Freelance Potential Local writers are heavily favored.

Submissions Guidelines available at website. Send complete manuscript. Writers are encouraged to call 303-939-8767 before submitting to see if article is a fit. Accepts email to info@ bouldercountykids.com (text or Word attachments). Response time varies.
- *Articles:* Word lengths vary. Informational, interviews. Topics: parenting, education, children's health, recreation, community.
- *Depts/columns:* Word lengths vary. News, education, the environment, health recipes, sports, self-esteem, advice.
- *Artwork:* JPEG, TIFF, GIF, PDF, EPS images.

Sample Issue 56 pages. Advertising. Sample copy available at website.
- "Boulder Art Talk: Why Art Education Matters," by Brenda Neimand. The benefits of art education.
- "The Importance of Self-Care," by Jessica Dancingheart. Tips for staying well and happy when busy.

Rights and Payment Rights vary. No payment; author receives short bio at end of article, promoting a business or organization, if applicable.

Brain, Child

P.O. Box 714, Lexington, VA 24450. www.brainchildmag.com

Associate Editors: Jennifer Niesslein & Stephanie Wilkinson

Parents and grandparents read this publication for entertaining and enlightening articles and stories about raising children. It is the only literary magazine dedicated to motherhood. Its perspective is always insightful and features a range of genres from essay and fiction to lively debates and humor.
- **Circulation** 30,000 ■ **Audience** Parents ■ **Frequency** Quarterly

Freelance Potential Publishes 40 freelance submissions yearly: 90% written by nonstaff writers; 60% by authors new to the magazine; 15% by previously unpublished writers. Receives 25 queries, 200 unsolicited manuscripts monthly.

Submissions Guidelines available. Query with clips for features, news items, and debate essays. Send manuscript for essays and fiction. Prefers email to editor@brainchildmag.com (no attachments; include "Submission" and department in subject line); will accept hard copy. Accepts simultaneous submissions if identified. SASE. Responds in 10 weeks.
- *Articles:* 3,000–6,000 words. Personal essays, 800–4,500 words.
- *Fiction:* 1,500–4,500 words. Genres: contemporary, inspirational.
- *Depts/columns:* Reviews (200–3,000 words), Parody (800 words), Nutshell (news, 200–800 words), Debate (900 words).

Sample Issue Advertising. Sample copy available.
- "Backstep," by Robin Schoenthaler. Essay describing how a child's perception of his/her mother changes with age.
- "The Village," by Jennifer Niesslein. How parents influence and are influenced by other parents.

Rights and Payment Electronic rights. Written material, payment rates vary. Pays on publication.

Calgary's Child

#723–105–150 Crowfoot Crescent NW, Calgary, Alberta T3G 3T2 Canada. www.calgaryschild.com

Editor/Publisher: Ellen Percival

Calgary parents of school-age children read this magazine for timely, in-depth articles on the issues most important to them, from their children's health and safety to community-wide issues. It appears in print and as a digital version. All content is local, and most authors are locally based.
- **Circulation** 150,000; 100,000 hits per month ■ **Audience** Parents ■ **Frequency** 6 times a year

Freelance Potential 99% written by nonstaff writers: 20% by authors new to the magazine. Receives about 85 queries monthly.

Submissions Editorial calendar available at website. Query with outline. Accepts email queries to calgaryschild@shaw.ca. No simultaneous submissions. Response time varies.
- *Articles:* 400–500 words. Informational, how-to. Topics: parenting, education, recreational activities, food, travel, health and safety, work, entertaining, family finances.
- *Depts/columns:* Word lengths vary.

Sample Issue Advertising. Sample copy available at website.
- "Springtime Fun on a Budget," by Stephanie Arsenault. Enjoying spring as a family inexpensively.
- "Over the River and Through the Woods," by Justine Ickes. Tips for family hikes.

Rights and Payment Exclusive Calgary rights. Written material, to $50 Canadian. Payment policy varies.

Canadian Family

111 Queen Street East, Suite 320, Toronto, Ontario M5C 1S2, Canada. www.canadianfamily.ca

Editor: Megan McChesney

Canadian Family has been serving moms and dads for 15 years with information on pregnancy, children's health issues, education, parenting guidance, and reviews of baby and kid products. It has a companion website, billed as Canadian's leading parenting destination, that has just gotten bigger and better. The site recently unveiled a new design with better access to content, more interactive tools, and much more original content. ■ **Circulation** Unavailable ■ **Audience** Parents ■ **Frequency** Monthly

Freelance Potential Unavailable.

Submissions Query with article pitch only. No unsolicited manuscripts. Accepts queries to editorial@canadianfamily.ca.

- *Articles:* Word lengths vary. Informational, how-to, profiles, interviews. Topics: parenting, education, children's health and wellness, relationships, family fun.
- *Depts/columns:* Word lengths vary. Stages of child development, cooking with kids, crafts, party planning, product reviews.

Sample Issue Advertising. Sample copy available at website.
- "Better Sleep Now: School-Age Kids," by Elizabeth Pantley. Advice on naps, night terrors, bedwetting, and bedtime battles.
- "How To Revive Your Libido After Baby." Advice for rekindling the romance once baby comes.

Rights and Payment Unavailable.

Capper's

1503 SW 42nd Street, Topeka, KS 66609-1265. http://cappers.grit.com

Editor in Chief: Katherine Compton

Recently redesigned and now published in a full-color, glossy format, *Capper's* celebrates rural life with practical and inspirational features. It focuses on family gardening and farming, while also offering nostalgia pieces and reflections on the joys of country life. It does not publish fiction or poetry.
■ **Circulation** 100,000 ■ **Audience** Parents ■ **Frequency** 6 times a year

Freelance Potential Publishes 40–50 freelance submissions yearly: 90% written by nonstaff writers; 70% by authors new to the magazine; 50% by previously unpublished writers. Receives 40 queries and unsolicited manuscripts monthly.

Submissions Guidelines available at website. Query. Send complete manuscript for Heart of Home column. Accepts email to jteller@ogdenpubs.com. Responds to queries in 1 month.
- *Articles:* 800–1,500 words. Informational, how–to, historical, inspirational, nostalgia. Topics: rural living, farming, gardening, livestock, cooking, do–it–yourself, machinery, tools, community, seasonal.
- *Depts/columns:* 500–1,500 words. Country Tech, Looking Back, In the Shop (farm items), Comfort Foods, Recipe Box, In the Wild (rural wildlife), Sow Hoe, Heart of the Home (humorous, heartwarming reader–written stories).
- *Artwork:* Photos, JPEGs at 300 dpi.

Sample Issue Advertising. Sample copy available.
- "Chicken Manure Fertilizer for the Vegetable Garden," by Sandi White. The rewards of using chicken manure to fertilize.
- "How to Preserve and Rejuvenate Heirloom Vegetable Seeds," by Craig Idlebrook. Explanation of the development of heirloom seeds and the vegetables they can produce.

Rights and Payment Standard rights. Written material, payment rates vary. Pays on publication. Provides 2 contributor's copies.

Carolina Parent

5716 Fayetteville Road, Suite 201, Durham, NC 27713. www.carolinaparent.com

Editor: Cricket Gibbons

Issues and information relating to the care and education of children from birth through the teen years are presented in this magazine for parents and caregivers. Preference is given to articles that use local references and subjects. ■ **Circulation** 51,000 ■ **Audience** Parents ■ **Frequency** Monthly

Freelance Potential Publishes 156 freelance submissions yearly: 60% written by nonstaff writers; 5% by authors new to the magazine; 2% by previously unpublished writers. Receives 50 queries and 40 unsolicited manuscripts monthly.

Submissions Guidelines and editorial calendar available at website. Query with outline and writing samples or clips. Accepts email submissions to cgibbonsl@carolinaparent.com (Word attachments). Response time varies.
- *Articles:* 850–1,600 words. Informational, self-help, how-to, profiles. Topics: college planning, technology, crafts, hobbies, education, health, fitness, humor, music, nature, the environment, parenting, children's issues, recreation, regional news, sports, travel.
- *Depts/columns:* 650–1,200 words. Family finances, family issues, home and garden, child development, pregnancy, health, news, events, Ages and Stages, Nesting, Family Fun.

Sample Issue 96 pages. Advertising. Sample copy available at website.
- "Unhappy with Your Child's Friends?" by Tammy Holoman. Do's and don'ts for parents of tweens and teens as they venture out and form their own friendships.
- "Technology Tips Help You 'Talk' with Your Teen," by Karen Taylor. How today's technological devices can aid family communication.

Rights and Payment First and electronic rights. Written material, payment rates vary. Pays on publication.

Central Penn Parent

1500 Paxton Street, Harrisburg, PA 17104. www.centralpennparent.com

Editor: Andrea Ciccocioppo

Informative articles about regional parenting topics appears in *Central Penn Parent*. Targeting families in Pennsylvania's Dauphin, Lancaster, Lebanon, Cumberland/Perry, and York counties, it includes regional updates, travel tips, and event calendars. This publication prefers to work with local writers.
■ **Circulation** 40,000 ■ **Audience** Parents ■ **Frequency** Monthly

Freelance Potential Publishes 120 freelance submissions yearly: 50–75% written by nonstaff writers; 10–25% by authors new to the magazine; 1–10% by previously unpublished writers. Receives 10–25 queries and 1–10 unsolicited manuscripts monthly.

Submissions Guidelines available at website. Query with contact information. Prefers email queries to editor@centralpennparent.com. Accepts simultaneous submissions and reprints. Send cover letter and clips for work-for-hire assignments. Responds in 2 weeks.
- *Articles:* 1,200–1,500 words. Informational, reviews. Topics: local family events and activities, health, nutrition, discipline, education, home life, technology, literature, parenting, travel.
- *Depts/columns:* 700 words. Family finances, health, infant issues, news, education.
- *Artwork:* Color prints and transparencies; JPEGs. Line art.
- *Other:* Submit seasonal material at least 3 months in advance.

Sample Issue 54 pages. Advertising. Sample copy available.
- "More Than a Headache," by Angelique Caffrey. Understanding and treating migraines in children.
- "Getting Away Without Breaking the Bank," by Robyn Passante. Budget-friendly vacation ideas for families.

Rights and Payment First rights. Written material, $50–$125. Reprints, $35. Pays on publication. Provides contributor's copies upon request.

Charlotte Parent

2125 Southend Drive, Suite 253, Charlotte, NC 28203. www.charlotteparent.com

Associate Publisher/Editor: Eve C. White

This magazine for families living in the Charlotte area of North Carolina offers articles on parenting and local events. It is most interested in articles with a regional slant and encourages submissions from writers who live in the region. ■ **Circulation** 52,000 ■ **Audience** Parents ■ **Frequency** Monthly

Freelance Potential Publishes 45 freelance submissions yearly: 50% written by nonstaff writers; 25% by authors new to the magazine; 15% by previously unpublished writers. Receives 85 queries and 65 unsolicited manuscripts monthly.

Submissions Guidelines and editorial calendar available at website. Query or send complete manuscript with résumé, bibliography, and word count. Prefers email to editorial@ charlotteparent.com; will accept hard copy or Macintosh disk submissions. Accepts simultaneous submissions. SASE. Responds if interested.
- *Articles:* 500–1,200 words. Informational, how-to, profiles, personal experience. Topics: parenting, family life, finances, education, health, fitness, vacations, entertainment, regional activities, the environment.
- *Depts/columns:* Word lengths vary. Child development, restaurant and media reviews, children's health.
- *Artwork:* High-density Macintosh images, 300+ dpi.
- *Other:* Activities. Submit seasonal material 2–3 months in advance.

Sample Issue 72 pages. Advertising. Sample copy available.
- "Making Friends Without Facebook," by Marilyn Randall. Tips for helping children maintain a social balance in a digital world.
- "Better Sleep for the Whole Family," by Michelle Huggins. How busy families can ensure everyone gets the sleep they need.

Rights and Payment First and Internet rights. Written material, $45–$125. Reprints, $15–$35. Pays on publication. Provides 1 contributor's copy

---

Chesapeake Family

929 West Street, Suite 210, Annapolis, MD 21401. www.chesapeakefamily.com

Editor: Mary McCarthy

Family activities and resources are the focus of this magazine for parents living in Maryland's Chesapeake Bay region. It prefers articles that are written in an easy-to-read, accessible tone and pack plenty of information into a few words. ■ **Circulation** 40,000 ■ **Audience** Parents ■ **Frequency** Monthly

Freelance Potential Publishes 40 freelance submissions yearly: 80% written by nonstaff writers; 40% by authors new to the magazine; 10% by previously unpublished writers. Receives 100 queries and 40 unsolicited manuscripts monthly.

Submissions Guidelines and editorial calendar available at website. Prefers query with list of previously published work and one clip; will accept complete manuscript. Accepts email to editor@ chesapeakefamily.com. Response time varies.
- *Articles:* 1,000 words. Informational, how-to. Topics: parenting, child development, education, the environment, entertainment, regional news and events, family health, family travel.
- *Depts/columns:* 750 words. Money management, relationships, media reviews.
- *Other:* Submit seasonal material 6 months in advance.

Sample Issue 60 pages. Advertising. Sample copy available at website.
- "Catching Up with First Lady Katie O'Malley," by Mary McCarthy. Interview with the wife of the governor of Maryland.
- "Time with Dad: How to Connect Amidst Busy Schedules," by Mindy Ragan Wood. Ways for busy fathers to spend meaningful time with their children.

Rights and Payment One-time print and electronic rights. Articles, $75–$200. Depts/columns, $50. Reprints, $35. Kill fee, $25. Pays on publication.

Chicago Parent

141 South Oak Park Avenue, Oak Park, IL 60302. www.chicagoparent.com

Editor: Tamara O'Shaughnessy

This magazine is filled with articles on a range of topics of interest to parents in the Chicago area. It also offers a family events calendar. All content has a local angle and most articles and columns are written by Chicago-area writers and/or parents. ■ **Circulation** 138,000 ■ **Audience** Parents ■ **Frequency** Monthly

Freelance Potential Publishes 50+ freelance submissions yearly: 85% written by nonstaff writers; 45% by authors new to the magazine; 30% by previously unpublished writers. Receives 130 queries monthly.

Submissions Query with résumé and clips. Accepts email queries to tamara@chicagoparent.com. Responds in 6 weeks.
■ *Articles:* 1,500–2,500 words. Informational, profiles, personal experience, humor. Topics: pregnancy, childbirth, parenting, grandparenting, foster care, adoption, day care, child development, health, education, recreation, family issues.
■ *Depts/columns:* 850 words. Crafts, activities, media reviews, health, nutrition, travel, finance, events.
■ *Other:* Cartoons for parents. Submit seasonal material 2 months in advance.

Sample Issue 100 pages. Advertising. Sample copy available.
■ "Siblings Sharing a Room Is Making a Comeback," by Laura Amann. The benefits and logistics of this once-common family living arrangement.
■ "This Spring Break, Try a Staycation Right Here in Chicago," by Cindy Richards. Tips for a fun stay-at-home vacation in the Chicago area.

Rights and Payment One-time northwest Indiana and Illinois exclusive rights. Articles, $125–$350. Depts/columns, $25–$100. Kill fee, 10%. Pays on publication. Provides contributor's copies on request.

The Christian Science Monitor

210 Massachusetts Avenue, Boston, MA 02115. www.csmonitor.com

Home Forum Editors: Susan Leach & Marjorie Kehe

This popular news and opinion magazine also features a regular section of articles dedicated to family issues and parenting in its "Home Forum" section. It accepts essays on a variety of topics. Humor, if present, should be gentle. Poetry for this section should be uplifting; nothing about death, aging, or illness. ■ **Circulation** 80,000 ■ **Audience** Adults ■ **Frequency** Weekly

Freelance Potential Publishes 150 freelance submissions yearly: 95% written by nonstaff writers; 40% by authors new to the magazine; 10% by previously unpublished writers. Receives 500 unsolicited manuscripts monthly.

Submissions Guidelines available at website. Send complete manuscript with contact information and word count. Accepts email submissions to homeforum@csmonitor.com. Responds in 3 weeks if interested.
■ *Articles:* 400–800 words. Personal experience, humor. Topics: home life, family, parenting, travel, gardening.
■ *Other:* Short informational bits, 150–400 words. Poetry, to 20 lines. Submit seasonal material 6 weeks in advance.

Sample Issue 48 pages. Advertising. Sample copy available.
■ "God's Family: There's Always Room for One More," by Kathy Chicoine. Loving ways to relate.
■ "How Large Should Your Emergency Fund Be?" by Trent Hamm. Keeping family money available.

Rights and Payment Exclusive rights. Essays, $75–$160. Poetry, $20–$40. Pays on publication.

Cincinnati Family Magazine

10945 Reed Hartman Highway, Suite 221, Cincinnati, OH 45242. www.cincinnatifamilymagazine.com

Editor: Sherry Hang

In addition to activity calendars and camp directories, this regional publication offers news and feature articles of interest to parents living in the greater Cincinnati area. ■ **Circulation** 55,000 ■ **Audience** Parents ■ **Frequency** Monthly

Freelance Potential Publishes 20–24 freelance submissions yearly: 25% written by nonstaff writers; 5% by authors new to the magazine; 5% by previously unpublished writers. Receives 10–15 queries, 4–8 unsolicited manuscripts monthly.

Submissions Guidelines and editorial calendar available. Query or send complete manuscript. Accepts hard copy and email submissions to sherryh@daycommail.com. SASE. Response time varies.
■ *Articles:* Word lengths vary. Informational, how-to. Topics: parenting, education, family health, social issues, social skills, regional activities.
■ *Depts/columns:* Word lengths vary.

Sample Issue
■ "Eating Good Matters," by Deborah Bohn. How to introduce one's family to healthier eating habits.
■ "It's Called Sexting," by Sherry Hang. An exposé of this disturbing new teen trend and what parents can do about it.

Rights and Payment First rights. Written material, $75–$125. Pays 1 month after publication.

Cincinnati Parent

9435 Waterstone Boulevard, Suite 140, Cincinnati, OH 45249. www.cincinnatiparent.com

Managing Editor: Megan Kirschner

Articles on healthy families and positive parenting along with regional service directories of interest to parents in the greater Cincinnati and northern Kentucky regions are the focus of this publication. The editors also like well-researched articles on surviving all stages of childhood. Preference is given to local writers. ■ **Circulation** 110,000 ■ **Audience** Parents ■ **Frequency** Monthly

Freelance Potential Publishes 30 freelance submissions yearly: 25–40% written by nonstaff writers. Receives 100+ queries and manuscripts monthly.

Submissions Guidelines available at website. Query with central theme, intended sources, and outline; or send complete manuscript with author byline and biography, photos (if applicable), photo of author, and contact information. Accepts email to editor@cincinnatiparent.com (include Manuscript: "Topic of Article" in subject line). Responds if interested.
■ *Articles:* 300–1,000 words. Informational, how-to, humor. Topics: education, health, child development, local current events, working parents, dad's perspective. organizing, holidays.
■ *Depts/columns:* 300–1,000 words. Rave Reviews, Publisher's Note, Women's/Pediatric Health, Museum Note, Local Profiles, News You Can Use, Community Spotlight.
■ *Artwork:* JPEG, TIFF, EPS, or PDF images at 200 dpi.

Sample Issue: Advertising. Sample copy available.
■ "A Holistic Approach to Healthy Kids," by Carrie Bishop. Exploring holistic healthcare options for children.
■ "Arts & Enrichment," by Krista Bocko. A round-up of summer arts education and performance programs for families.

Rights and Payment First rights. Written material, 10¢ a word. Reprints, $35–$50. Pays on publication.

Cleveland Family

11630 Chillicothe Road, Chesterland, OH 44026. www.neohiofamily.com

Editor: Terri Nighswonger

Parents of tots through teens pick up this publication to learn about local events and to get up-to-date information about Cleveland-area family resources. It is distributed through schools, child care centers, libraries, retail outlets, and grocery stores. The editors prefer factual pieces to first-person essays. Local writers are preferred here. ■ **Circulation** 7,500 ■ **Audience** Parents ■ **Frequency** Monthly

Freelance Potential Publishes 40–50 freelance submissions yearly: 50% written by nonstaff writers; 33% by authors new to the magazine. Receives 750 queries monthly.

Submissions Editorial calendar available. Query. Accepts email to editor@tntpublications.com. Responds if interested.
- *Articles:* 500+ words. Informational, self-help, how-to, profiles, reviews. Topics: the arts, animals, computers, crafts, health, fitness, education, popular culture, sports, the environment, religion, family travel, regional issues.
- *Depts/columns:* Word lengths vary. News, advice, education, teen issues, humor, stepfamilies.
- *Artwork:* High-resolution JPEG and TIFF images.

Sample Issue 42 pages. Advertising.
- "Seven Tools to Help You Decide if a Video Game is Right for Your Child." Tips for determining if a game is appropriate for a child.
- "Childhood Obesity," by Donna L. Robinson. Steps to help children maintain a healthy weight.

Rights and Payment Exclusive rights. Written material, payment rates vary. Pays on publication. Provides 1 contributor's copy.

Columbus Parent

34 South Third Street, Columbus, OH 43215. www.columbusparent.com

Editor: Jane Hawes

Practical and locally relevant information fills the pages of this magazine that is distributed throughout the greater Columbus area of Ohio. Its focus is on raising happy, healthy children and on the needs and concerns of parents. It rarely accepts material that does not have a local slant or uses local sources. While the magazine does not accept unsolicited manuscripts, local writers may submit résumés and writing samples to be considered for assignments. ■ **Circulation** 58,500 ■ **Audience** Parents ■ **Frequency** Monthly

Freelance Potential Publishes 50 freelance submissions yearly: 75% written by nonstaff writers; 25% by authors new to the magazine. Receives 75–100 queries monthly.

Submissions Currently not accepting unsolicited submissions. Writers based in Central Ohio interested in being considered for assignments may submit résumé and 3 writing samples that reflect the magazine's style and content. Accepts hard copy. Response time varies.
- *Articles:* 700 words. Informational, self-help, how-to, profiles, interviews, reviews. Topics: current events, family health, child development, education, humor, music, recreation, travel.
- *Depts/columns:* 300 words. Recipes, travel, health, nutrition, education, news, events, sports, family humor, behavioral development, media and product reviews.
- *Other:* Submit seasonal material at least 2 months in advance.

Sample Issue 56 pages. Advertising. Sample copy available.
- "To Pierce or Not to Pierce," by Heather Weekley. The issue of ear piercings in children.
- "Why Do You Dress like That?" by Anietra Hamper. Clothes as cultural identifiers in children.

Rights and Payment Rights vary. Written material, 10¢–20¢ a word. Pays on publication.

Complete Woman

875 North Michigan Avenue, Suite 3434, Chicago, IL 60611-1901.
www.thecompletewomanmagazine.com

Executive Editor: Lora Wintz

This women's magazine covers a range of topics from a woman's perspective, including parenting and family life. ■ **Circulation** 875,000 ■ **Audience** Women ■ **Frequency** Quarterly

Freelance Potential Publishes 75 freelance submissions yearly: 90% written by nonstaff writers; 30% by authors new to the magazine; 20% by previously unpublished writers. Receives 60 queries monthly.

Submissions Query with clips; or send complete manuscript. Accepts hard copy. Accepts simultaneous submissions if identified. SASE. Responds in 3 months.
■ *Articles:* 800–1,200 words. Informational, self-help, profiles, humor, confession, personal experience, interviews. Topics: health, fitness, beauty, skin care, fashion, dining, relationships, romance, business, self-improvement, celebrities, careers, money, entertainment, pop culture.
■ *Depts/columns:* Word lengths vary. Careers, new products, beauty tips, news briefs.

Sample Issue 106 pages. Advertising. Sample copy available.
■ "11 Free or Cheap Ways to Start and Run Your Online Business," by Natalie Williams. Getting started in an online business without investing a lot of money.
■ "The Stress of Being a Woman." Tips for de-stressing.

Rights and Payment Rights vary. Written material, payment rates vary. Pays on publication. Provides 1 contributor's copy.

Connecticut Parent Magazine

420 East Main Street, Suite 18, Branford, CT 06405. www.ctparent.com

Editor/Publisher: Joel MacClaren

This magazine offers Connecticut families a complete guide to regional attractions, events, and news. In addition, it features articles with practical information and tips on topics of general interest to parents and families. Its readers are primarily parents of children up to age 12. ■ **Circulation** 60,000 ■ **Audience** Parents ■ **Frequency** Monthly

Freelance Potential Publishes about 50 freelance submissions yearly: 20% written by nonstaff writers; 10% by authors new to the magazine. Receives 25–50 queries, 25–50 unsolicited manuscripts monthly.

Submissions Query with outline; or send complete manuscript. Prefers email to editorial@ctparent.com (Word attachments); will accept hard copy. SASE. Availability of artwork improves chance of acceptance. Response time varies.
■ *Articles:* 1,000–1,500 words. Informational, self-help, how-to, profiles, interviews. Topics: maternity and childbirth issues, parenting, regional news, family relationships, social issues, education, special education, health, fitness, nutrition, safety, entertainment, travel.
■ *Depts/columns:* 600 words. Family news, new product information, book reviews.

Sample Issue 100 pages. Advertising. 6 articles; 1 guide; 3 depts/columns. Sample copy available.
■ "A Mother's Altruistic Gift," by Jillian Orlando. Describes how to donate cord blood to be used by families in need.
■ "Help Them Hear the Music," by Bill Corbett. Ways for parents to help children tap into their creative talents.

Rights and Payment One-time rights. Written material, payment rates vary. Pays on publication. Provides 1 contributor's tearsheet.

County Parents Magazine

P.O. Box 1666, Bel Air, MD 21014. www.countyparents.com

Publisher: Joan Fernandez

Serving parents in Maryland's Harford County, *County Parents Magazine* provides localized parenting and educational resources, as well as articles on family-friendly topics and regional recreational opportunities. Because of its emphasis on local information, writers from the region are preferred.
■ **Circulation** 22,000 ■ **Audience** Parents ■ **Frequency** Monthly

Freelance Potential Publishes 20 freelance submissions yearly: 75% written by nonstaff writers.

Submissions Guidelines available at website. Query. Accepts hard copy and email queries to countyparents@aboutdelta.com. SASE. Response time varies.
■ *Articles:* Word lengths vary. Informational, how-to. Topics: child care topics, health matters, child development, regional recreational activities, education.
■ *Depts/columns:* Word lengths vary.

Sample Issue
■ "Growing Up Online: Making Smart Decisions about Smart Phones," by Carolyn Jabs. The risks associated with the use of smart phones by children and teens.
■ "10 Tips to Finding the Right Day Camp," by Denise Morrison Yearian. Considerations for parents trying to choose the camp that will be the best fit for their child.

Rights and Payment First print and electronic rights. Written material, payment rates vary. Pays on publication. Provides 1 contributor's copy.

Curious Parents

2345 Bethel Avenue, Merchantville, NJ 08109–2715. www.curiousparents.com

Submissions: Jackie Piccone

Parenting issues as well as general topics that are of interest to parents are covered in this family-oriented magazine. It is published in four local editions serving the Pennsylvania, New Jersey, and Delaware triangle. Parents also look to this publication for information about educational and recreational opportunities in their area. ■ **Circulation** 375,000 ■ **Audience** Parents ■ **Frequency** Monthly

Freelance Potential Publishes 45 freelance submissions yearly: 80% written by nonstaff writers; 40% by authors new to the magazine; 60% by previously unpublished writers. Receives 10 unsolicited manuscripts monthly.

Submissions Guidelines available at website. Send complete manuscript with brief description and brief author biography. Accepts email submissions to editor@curiousparents.com. Response time varies.
■ *Articles:* Word lengths vary. Informational, how-to, self-help. Topics: crafts, hobbies, current events, recreation, education, college prep, safety, health, family entertainment, networking, parenting, travel, camps, going green, seasonal fun, family gardening, family finances.
■ *Depts/columns:* Word lengths vary. Health, automobile safety, book reviews.

Sample Issue 30 pages. Advertising. Sample copy available.
■ "Multilingual Families," by Janine Boldrin. How and why three families tackle teaching their children multiple languages.
■ "Tender Parenting Through Good Times and Bad," by Julia M. Rahn, Ph.D. Strategies to create a home that runs smoothly and helps family members live peacefully and in harmony.

Rights and Payment All rights. No payment.

The Dabbling Mum

508 West Main Street, Beresford, SD 57004. www.thedabblingmum.com

Editor: Alyice Edrich

The articles and essays found in this online magazine are geared to busy parents who want information to help them be better parents, small business owners, writers, or with their home-based businesses. Some of the writing is Christian-oriented. It is currently seeking original articles on business ideas and reprints on social networking, customer service, or hosting an event. *The Dabbling Mum* welcomes new writers. ■ **Hits per month** 20,000–40,000 ■ **Audience** Parents ■ **Frequency** Weekly

Freelance Potential Publishes 48–96 freelance submissions yearly: 75–100% developed from unsolicited submissions; 75–100% written by nonstaff writers; 50–75% by authors new to the magazine; 25–50% by previously unpublished writers. Receives 10 queries, 10 manuscripts monthly.

Submissions Editorial calendar and guidelines available at website. Query or send complete manuscript. Accepts email to dm@thedabblingmum.com. Also offers work-for-hire assignments. Check website for current needs and submission information. Responds in 4–8 weeks.
■ *Articles:* 500–1,500 words. Informational, how-to, personal experience. Topics: family life, parenting, women's issues, grief support, marriage, arts and crafts, cooking, home businesses, sales and marketing, ecofriendly living.

Sample Issue
■ "Is It a Sin to Swear?" by Donna J. Shepherd. Opinion piece about why swearing is wrong according to the Bible.
■ "Monitoring Television Time," by Alyice Edrich. Setting limits on children's television viewing.

Rights and Payment One-month exclusive online rights; indefinite archival rights. Written material, $15–$25 per original article; reprints $5–$10. Payment policy varies.

Dallas Child

Lauren Publications, 4275 Kellway Circle, Suite 146, Addison, TX 75001. www.dallaschild.com

Editorial Content: Joylyn Niebes

Dallas Child offers a local perspective on issues affecting families in the Dallas region, with a special focus on children from prenatal through adolescence. It prefers to work with writers living in the region. Articles should inspire, inform, and entertain. ■ **Circulation** 80,000 ■ **Audience** Parents ■ **Frequency** Monthly

Freelance Potential Publishes 25 freelance submissions yearly: 30% written by nonstaff writers; 5–10% by authors new to the magazine. Receives about 35 queries monthly.

Submissions Guidelines available at website. Query with résumé. Accepts hard copy, email to editorial@dfwchildmagazines.com, and fax to 972-447-0633. Accepts simultaneous submissions if identified. SASE. Responds in 2–3 months, if interested.
■ *Articles:* 1,000–2,000 words. Informational, self-help, how-to, profiles, interviews, humor, personal experience. Topics: parenting, education, child development, family travel, regional news, recreation, entertainment, recreation, current events, social issues, multicultural and ethnic subjects, health, fitness, crafts.
■ *Depts/columns:* 800 words. Local events, travel tips, health news.

Sample Issue 74 pages. Advertising. Sample copy available at website.
■ "Stress: The Trickle–Down Effect," by Jeanne Albanese. How the stress parents experience gets passed on to their children, and ways to diminish the negative effects for the entire family.
■ "The Anatomy of a Cool Mom," by Nancy Myers. Secrets of a busy mom for looking chic and stylish.

Rights and Payment First rights. Written material, payment rates vary. Pays on publication. Provides contributor's copies upon request.

Denver Reign

1945 South Humboldt Street, Denver, CO 80210, www.denverreign.com

Publisher and Editor in Chief: Betsy Martin

"Denver's authority on fabulous," this new digital magazine covers everything the mile-high city has to offer young women, from culture to dining and style. It also has an active section on parenting and family fun featuring articles and short, fun items on topics ranging from school readiness to shopping for kids' fashions. Special themed issues will include a focus on back to school, babies, and hearth and home. ■ **Circulation** 9,000 ■ **Audience** Parents ■ **Frequency** Twice a week

Freelance Potential Unavailable.

Submissions Contact for more information at betsy@denverreign.com.
■ *Articles:* Word lengths vary. Informational, how-to, profiles. Topics: children's fashions, shopping, parenting, culture, entertainment, style, beauty.

Sample Issue Sample copy available at website.
■ "You Go, Girlfriend!" A Colorado mother's apparel business aids impoverished women globally.
■ "Too Cool for School." Puts the spotlight on kids' clothes made by Colorado designers.

Rights and Payment Unavailable.

Dirt

Straus News, 20 West Avenue, Chester, NY 10918. www.dirt-mag.com

Editor: Becca Tucker

Subtitled "Healthy Living from the Ground Up," this natural lifestyle magazine presents information on living sustainably, acting responsibly, and thinking locally. Started in May 2011, it includes articles on farming, organic gardening, ecofashion, alternative lifestyles and energies, holistic health, education, parenting, and maintaining a green home. Material that has a local personality or angle is highly preferred. ■ **Circulation** Unavailable ■ **Audience** Families ■ **Frequency** 6 times a year

Freelance Potential Welcomes article ideas and new writers.

Submissions Query. Accepts hard copy or email queries to editor.dirt@strausnews.com. SASE. Materials not returned. Response time varies.
■ *Articles:* Word lengths vary. Informational, profiles, interviews, personal experience. Topics: farming, gardening, parenting, education, homebirths, alternative energies.
■ *Depts/columns:* Word lengths vary. Get Out (travel around New York), Griterati (profiles), Homemade (food), Born Again (creative re-uses), News and Reviews.
■ *Other:* Poetry.

Sample Issue 32 pages.
■ "Home Babies Are Back," by Shawn Dell Joyce and Becca Tucker. The renaissance of home births.
■ "Meet the Unschool Class of 2011," by Becca Tucker. A family that allowed their son to "unschool."

Rights and Payment Unavailable.

Early Years

128 North Royal Avenue, Front Royal, VA 22630. www.rfeonline.com

Editor: Tia Gibbo

Early Years is a reproducible newsletter for parents of preschool and kindergarten-age children. Its brief articles offer practical advice on parenting skills and how to improve children's school readiness.
■ **Circulation** 60,000 ■ **Audience** Parents and teachers ■ **Frequency** 9 times a year

Freelance Potential Publishes 80 freelance submissions yearly: 100% written by nonstaff writers; 28% by previously unpublished writers. Receives 3 queries monthly.

Submissions Query with résumé and clips. Accepts hard copy. SASE. Responds in 1 month.
■ *Articles:* 225–300 words. Informational, how–to, personal experience. Topics: child development, learning skills, discipline, reading and math support, social skills, life skills, moral issues, parenting.
■ *Depts/columns:* 175–200 words. Short information bits, Q&As.

Sample Issue Sample copy available.
■ "Better Behavior." Gives parents tips for loving and effective discipline.
■ "Pattern Practice." Activities that teach children about patterns, for a head start in math.

Rights and Payment All rights. Written material, 60¢ a word. Pays on acceptance. Provides 5 contributor's copies.

Exceptional Parent

416 Main Street, Johnstown, PA 15901. www.eparent.com

Managing Editor: Laura Apel

This magazine examines the social, psychological, legal, financial, and educational issues faced by individuals with disabilities and the people who care for them. It is filled with practical information and valuable advice to make life easier and happier. Its articles are written by laypeople and health care practitioners. It strives to be upbeat in tone for an audience faced with difficult realities.
■ **Circulation** 70,000 ■ **Audience** Parents and professionals ■ **Frequency** Monthly

Freelance Potential Publishes 250 freelance submissions yearly: 90% written by nonstaff writers; 30% by authors new to the magazine; 30% by previously unpublished writers. Receives 70 queries monthly.

Submissions Guidelines and editorial calendar available at website. Query only (no more than 500 words) with contact information, summary, word length, intended audience, and estimated completion date of article. Accepts email queries to lapel@eparent.com (include "Query letter for *EP Magazine* or website" in subject line) and hard copy. Responds in 3–4 weeks if interested.
■ *Articles:* To 2,500 words. Informational articles, profiles, interviews, personal experience. Topics: the social, psychological, legal, political, technological, financial, and educational concerns of individuals with disabilities and their caregivers.
■ *Depts/columns:* Word lengths vary. Opinions, personal essays, news, new products, media reviews.

Sample Issue 98 pages. Advertising. Sample copy available.
■ "Mainstreaming Children with Disabilities."
■ "Comprehenisve Newborn Screening." From an issue highlighting newborn screening awareness.

Rights and Payment All rights. No payment. Provides 6 contributor's copies.

Families on the Go

Life Media, P.O. Box 55445, St. Petersburg, FL 33732. www.familiesonthego.org

Editor: Barbara Doyle

With separate print and online versions, *Families on the Go* offers a mix of parenting-related articles and travel and destination pieces for families looking to enjoy some vacation or adventure time. It has three editions, each focused on a particular region of Florida. All articles should include at least one sidebar and a list of local resources. Once accepted, an article may be used for one or several editions, or the website. ■ **Circulation** 120,000 ■ **Audience** Parents ■ **Frequency** 6 times a year

Freelance Potential Publishes 50 freelance submissions yearly: 80% written by nonstaff writers; 20% by authors new to the magazine; 25% by previously unpublished writers.

Submissions Guidelines available at website. Query or send complete manuscript. Accepts email submissions to editor@familiesonthego.org (Word attachments). Responds if interested.
- *Articles:* 350–750 words. Informational. Topics: health, wellness, fitness, parenting issues, education, family relationships, home and garden, the arts, travel, entertainment.
- *Depts/columns:* Word lengths vary. Community news.

Sample Issue 48 pages. Advertising. Sample copy available at website.
- "Social Networking," by David Geldbart. How to maximize the usefulness of social networks and avoid the pitfalls associated with this form of communication.
- "Cyber–Bullying," by David Geldbart. Tips and resources for preventing and halting online bullying.

Rights and Payment Exclusive regional rights. Written material, payment rates vary. Pays on publication. Provides 2 contributor's copies.

Family Circle

Meredith Corporation, 375 Lexington Avenue, 9th Floor, New York, NY 10017. www.familycircle.com

Executive Editor: Darcy Jacobs

Family Circle offers smart, practical advice on parenting issues, with a particular emphasis on the concerns faced by mothers of tweens and teens. It also provides suggestions for fun family activities, delivers the latest health news, and showcases projects to create a comfortable home. It is always on the lookout for true stories about women making a difference in their communities, and reports on newsworthy social issues that affect American families. It welcomes new writers with national magazine experience. ■ **Circulation** 3.8 million ■ **Audience** Families ■ **Frequency** 15 times a year

Freelance Potential Publishes many freelance submissions yearly: 80% written by nonstaff writers. Receives 20+ queries monthly.

Submissions Guidelines available. Query with clips (including 1 from a national magazine) and author bio. Accepts hard copy and email to fcfeedback@familycircle.com. No simultaneous submissions. SASE. Responds in 6–8 weeks if interested.
- *Articles:* 1,000–2,000 words. Informational, how-to, profiles, personal experience. Topics: parenting, relationships, health, safety, social issues, fitness, home decor, travel, fashion, cooking.
- *Depts/columns:* 750 words. "My Hometown," "My Family Life," "Good Works," recipes, beauty tips, shopping tips, fitness routines, advice.

Sample Issue 210 pages. Advertising. Sample copy available.
- "Garden Variety Giving," by Sondra Forsyth. A mom's garden surplus feeds families in need.
- "Your Brain on Tech," by Christina Tynan–Wood. The downside to being connected 24/7 and how to set appropriate social boundaries.

Rights and Payment All rights. Written material, payment rates vary. Kill fee, 25%. Pays on acceptance. Provides 1 contributor's copy.

FamilyFun

47 Pleasant Street, Northampton, MA 01060. www.familyfun.go.com

Department Editor: Jonathan Adolph

For the past 20 years, *FamilyFun* has been providing parents with ideas for having fun with their children. Original ideas for family projects and family-friendly travel destinations are always welcome. The emphasis is on activities and practical ways to build strong, healthy families. ■ **Circulation** 2 million+ ■ **Audience** Parents ■ **Frequency** 10 times a year

Freelance Potential Publishes 100+ freelance submissions yearly: 80% written by nonstaff writers; 2% by authors new to the magazine; 1% by previously unpublished writers. Receives 100+ queries and unsolicited manuscripts monthly.

Submissions Guidelines available at website. Query for features; include content, structure, and tone of article. Send complete manuscript for depts/columns. Include photographs or sketches, if appropriate. Accepts hard copy and email queries to queries.familyfun@disney.com. SASE. Responds in 6–8 weeks.
- *Articles:* 850–3,000 words. Informational, how-to. Topics: food, crafts, parties, holidays, sports, games, travel.
- *Depts/columns:* 50–1,000 words. Let's Cook, Let's Party, Let's Go, Success Story, My Great Idea, Healthy Fun, Family Home, Our Favorite Things. See guidelines for details. Crafts, nature activities, recipes, family getaways and traditions, household hints, healthy fun, home decorating and gardening tips, product reviews.
- *Other:* Submit seasonal material 6 months in advance.

Sample Issue 116 pages. Advertising. Sample copy available.
- "Mechanical Bird," by Heather Swain. Instructions for making a whimsical bird.
- "Cupcake Cakes," by Joy Howard and Amy Kaldor–Bull. Clever party treats assembled from cupcakes.

Rights and Payment First serial rights. Written material, payment rates vary. Pays on acceptance.

Family Health & Life

Toronto Airport Corporate Centre, 2680 Matheson Boulevard, Suite 102, Mississauga, Ontario L4W 0A5 Canada. www.thefamilymag.com

Publisher/Editor in Chief: Ian Khan

In addition to general articles on health and well-being, this magazine presents information on alternative health modalities, recreational opportunities, and other topics of interest for residents of the greater Toronto area. Writers who are passionate about health issues are welcome to query.
- **Circulation** 5,000 ■ **Audience** Parents ■ **Frequency** Monthly

Freelance Potential Publishes several freelance submissions yearly.

Submissions Guidelines available at website. Query with clips. Accepts email queries to contact@ thefamilymag.com. Writers may also be considered for regular writing or columnist positions. . Response time varies.
- *Articles:* 500–2,000 words. Informational, how–to. Topics: natural healing, yoga, massage therapy, green living, meditation, child psychology, relationships, local family attractions and activities.
- *Depts/columns:* Word lengths vary.

Sample Issue Advertising. Sample copy available at website.
- "Foods that Protect Against Cancer," by Rod Charles. Incorporating cancer–fighting foods.
- "What Are the Top 5 Fruits?" by Iva Young. Fruits with the most health benefits and least sugar.

Rights and Payment Rights vary. Written material, payment rates vary. Payment policy varies.

Family Life Magazine

100 Professional Center Drive, Suite 104, Rohnert Park, CA 94928. www.sonomafamilylife.com

Publisher/Editor: Sharon Gowan

This publication is for families living in California's Sonoma, Mendocino, and Lake counties. Each issues provides information of general interest to parents as well as regional news, recreation, and resources. A local slant and local authors are preferred. ■ **Circulation** 40,000 ■ **Audience** Parents ■ **Frequency** Monthly

Freelance Potential Publishes 24–36 freelance submissions yearly: 40% written by nonstaff writers; 10% by unpublished writers. Receives 10+ unsolicited manuscripts monthly.

Submissions Guidelines and editorial calendar available at website. Send complete manuscript. Accepts email submissions to sharon@family-life.us (Word attachments). Accepts simultaneous submissions with exclusivity in Northern California, and reprints. Responds if interested.

■ *Articles:* 650–1,150 words. Informational, how-to, profiles. Topics: education, health, parenting, travel, regional news and recreation.

■ *Depts/columns:* Word lengths vary.

■ *Artwork:* Color and B/W photos.

Sample Issue 42 pages. Advertising. Sample copy available at website.

■ "Shopping for Nana and Pop-Pop," by Claire Yezbak Fadden. Special, loving gifts for grandparents.

■ "Meet Teacher Ramon Ramirez," by Suzanne Maggio-Hucek.An inspiring high school teacher.

Rights and Payment All rights. Written material, 8¢ a word. Reprints, $35–$50. Pays on publication. Provides 1 contributor's copy.

Family Motor Coaching

8291 Clough Pike, Cincinnati, OH 45244. www.fmcmagazine.com

Editor: Robbin Gould

This magazine is for families who travel by motor home and RV. It covers topics ranging from vehicle maintenance and reviews to destination ideas. It is the official publication of the Family Motor Coach Association. ■ **Circulation** 110,000 ■ **Audience** Parents ■ **Frequency** Monthly

Freelance Potential Publishes 50 freelance submissions yearly: 75% written by nonstaff writers; 10% by authors new to the magazine; 10% by previously unpublished writers. Receives 50 queries, 25 unsolicited manuscripts monthly.

Submissions Prefers query with résumé, outline, and clips; will accept complete manuscript with résumé. Accepts hard copy and email submissions to magazine@fmca.com. SASE. Response time varies.

■ *Articles:* 1,200–2,000 words. Informational, how–to. Topics: motorhome maintenance, reviews, news, destinations.

■ *Depts/columns:* 1,000 words.

Sample Issue Sample copy available.

■ "Lassoing History," by Lazelle Jones. Profile of rodeo star Trevor Brazile, who travels the rodeo circuit in an RV.

■ "Entegra Insignia," by Lazelle Jones. Review of a new model motorhome from Entegra Coach.

Rights and Payment First North American serial and electronic rights. Written material, $50–$500. Pays on acceptance. Provides 1 contributor's copy.

Family Safety & Health

1121 Spring Lake Drive, Itasca, IL 60143–3201. www.nsc.org

Editor: Tim Hodson

Published by the National Safety Council, *Family Safety & Health* is known as "the official magazine for on-the-job safety," although it does also report on safety concerns relevant to families in the areas of home, community, and roads. ■ **Circulation** 225,000 ■ **Audience** Parents ■ **Frequency** Quarterly

Freelance Potential Publishes 5 freelance submissions yearly: 1% written by nonstaff writers; 20% by authors new to the magazine.

Submissions No queries or unsolicited manuscripts; send résumé and clips only. All assignments are made on a work-for-hire basis. Accepts hard copy.
■ *Articles:* 1,200 words. Informational, how–to. Topics: safety in the workplace, home, community, car.
■ *Depts/columns:* Word lengths vary.

Sample Issue
■ "Practice Window Safety to Prevent Falls." Protecting children from falling out of windows.
■ "Holiday Traffic Fatality Estimates." Simple ways to avoid holiday dangers on the road.

Rights and Payment All rights. Payment rate varies. Pays on acceptance. Provides 2 contributor's copies.

Family Time for You and Your Crew

P.O. Box 334, Selbyville, DE 19975. www.familytimemag.biz

Publisher: Caine Boyden

Serving families in Delaware's Sussex County region, this magazine is published in print and online. It features parenting information, recreational opportunities, and articles of general interest to residents of this region. Local articles will trump all others. It does not offer payment for accepted submissions at this time but hopes to do so in the future. ■ **Circulation** Unavailable ■ **Audience** Parents ■ **Frequency** 5 times a year

Freelance Potential Publishes 12–24 freelance submissions yearly. Receives 4–5 queries and unsolicited manuscripts monthly.

Submissions Calendar available at website. Prefers query; will accept complete manuscript. Accepts email to info@familytimemag.biz. Response time varies.
■ *Articles:* 500–700 words. Informational, how–to. Topics: education, home, gardening, travel, regional.
■ *Depts/columns:* Word counts vary.

Sample Issue Advertising. Sample copy available at website.
■ "A Plan for Spending," by Carrie Boyden. Tips for maximizing savings using coupons.
■ "Step Right Up!" by Tanya Ehlers. Teaching children initiative.

Rights and Payment Rights vary. No payment.

Family Tree Magazine

4700 East Galbraith Road, Cincinnati, OH 45236. www.familytreemagazine.com

Editorial Director: Allison Stacy

This is the leading how–to publication for those who want to discover and celebrate their roots. It covers all areas of interest to family history enthusiasts, going beyond genealogy research. *Family Tree* provides engaging, easy–to–understand instructions that make genealogy a hobby anyone can do. It does not publish personal experience pieces, and is not interested in articles directed specifically to children or teens. ■ **Circulation** 75,000 ■ **Audience** Families ■ **Frequency** 7 times a year

Freelance Potential Publishes 12–120 freelance submissions yearly: 75–100% written by nonstaff writers; 10–25% developed from unsolicited submissions; 1–10% by authors new to the magazine; 1–10% by previously unpublished writers. Receives 25–50 queries, 25–50 manuscripts monthly.

Submissions Guidelines available at website. Query only with cover letter; include suggestions for sidebars, tips, and resources ; and clips. Prefers email queries to familytreeeditorial@fwmedia.com (JPEG, TIFF, or PDF); accepts hard copy. No simultaneous submissions. SASE. Responds in 6–8 weeks.
■ *Articles:* 2,000–3,500 words. Informational, how–to, historic. Topics: genealogy, ethnic heritage, family reunions, memoirs, oral history, scrapbooking, historical travel.
■ *Depts/columns:* 300–1,000 words.

Sample Issue 76 pages. Advertising. Sample copy available.
- "Dazzling Destinations," by David A. Fryxell. The 101 best websites for family history.
- "Monumental Makeover," by Cheryl Felix McClellan. Care and repair tips for grave markers.

Rights and Payment All rights. Written material, payment rates vary. Kill fee, 25%. Pays on acceptance. Provides contributor's copies.

FamilyWorks Magazine

4 Joseph Court, San Rafael, CA 94903. www.familyworks.org

Editor: Lew Tremaine

FamilyWorks Magazine's readership resides in Marin and Sonoma counties in California. The publication covers issues of interest to parents and also offers regional event coverage. It strives to help its readers enhance and strengthen personal and family well–being, improve communication skills, build compassion, increase self-awareness, and learn essential life skills. ■ **Circulation** 20,000 ■ **Audience** Parents ■ **Frequency** 6 times a year

Freelance Potential Publishes 75 freelance submissions yearly: 80% written by nonstaff writers; 25% by authors new to the magazine. Receives 10+ unsolicited manuscripts monthly.

Submissions Guidelines available. Send complete manuscript. Accepts hard copy, disk submissions, and email submissions to familynews@familyworks.org. Availability of artwork improves chance of acceptance. SASE. Responds in 1 month.
- *Articles:* 1,000 words. Informational, profiles, interviews. Topics: parenting, family issues, recreation, education, finance, crafts, hobbies, sports, health, fitness, nature, the environment.
- *Depts/columns:* Word lengths vary. Community news, reviews, recipes.
- *Artwork:* B/W and color prints.

Sample Issue 24 pages. Advertising. Sample copy available at website.
- "Don't Focus on Your Child's Happiness," by Gary Direnfeld. Making children responsible and accountable instead of happy.
- "The Year of No Regrets," by Dottie DeHart. How to focus time and energy on what really matters.

Rights and Payment One-time rights. No payment. Provides 3 contributor's copies.

Farm & Ranch Living

5400 South 60th Street, Greendale, WI 53129–1404. www.farmandranchliving.com

Editor

For nearly 30 years farming and ranching families from all over the country have read and contributed to this lifestyle magazine. It is devoted to topics of interest to those who love the land and rural living. It features articles, profiles, first-person stories, photo-essays, and a kids' section. ■ **Circulation** 350,000 ■ **Audience** Parents and children ■ **Frequency** 6 times a year

Freelance Potential Publishes 36 freelance submissions yearly: 90% written by nonstaff writers; 50% by authors new to the magazine; 50% by previously unpublished writers. Receives 10 queries and unsolicited manuscripts monthly.

Submissions Guidelines available at website. Query or send complete manuscript with photos if appropriate. Accepts hard copy and email submissions to editors@farmandranchliving.com. Availability of artwork improves chance of acceptance. SASE. Responds in 6 weeks.
- *Articles:* To 1,500 words. Informational, how–to, personal experience. Topics: farming and crops, farm animals and livestock, profiles of successful farmers, daily life, fairs, food.
- *Depts/columns:* 350 words.
- *Artwork:* Digital images, color prints; at least 300 dpi.

Sample Issue
- "Mending Fences." Profile of a fence mender who works in the high desert of northern Arizona.
- "New! Tractor Restoration Stories & Photos." A sneak preview of the upcoming Old Iron calendar, featuring tractors old and new, tractor trivia, and show dates.

Rights and Payment One-time rights. Written material, $10–$150. Pays on publication. Provides 1 contributor's copy.

FatherMag.com

P.O. Box 231891, Houston, TX 77223. www.fathermag.com

Managing Editor: John Gill

Fatherhood from all angles is explored in this online magazine. *FatherMag.com* is a source of practical advice, inspiration, and support for dads living with or without their children. Separate "strife" and "life" sections address the challenges and joys of being a dad. Submissions are welcome from anyone who has something worthwhile to say about fatherhood. ■ **Circulation** 1 million ■ **Audience** Parents ■ **Hits per month** Unavailable

Freelance Potential Publishes 50 freelance submissions yearly: 95% written by nonstaff writers; 50% by authors new to the magazine.

Submissions Guidelines available at website. Query. Accepts email queries through website only. Response time varies.
- *Articles:* Word lengths vary. Informational, how–to, interviews, reviews, humor. Topics: parenting, everything to do with the joys and challenges of being a dad.
- *Depts/columns:* Word lengths vary.
- *Fiction:* Word lengths vary. Short stories.
- *Other:* Poetry.

Sample Issue Sample copy available at website.
- "House Bill 1208: Teen Sex Offenders–Intimacy and Sex." Legislation on underage sex offenders.
- "Parenting a PPD–NOS Child," by Jos Haring. Understanding a mild but common form of autism.

Rights and Payment One-time rights. No payment.

Fertility Today

P.O. Box 117, Laurel, MD 20725-0177. www.fertilitytoday.org

Editor: Diana Broomfield

Fertility Today serves as a comprehensive and up-to-date resource for all aspects of fertility and infertility. Nearly all articles are written by experts and cover medical and legal issues, as well as the spiritual, emotional, and physical aspects of infertility. Also features some personal experience pieces. It strives to be the nation's leader in educating the public on reproductive health. ■ **Circulation** 225,000 ■ **Audience** Parents ■ **Frequency** 4 times a year

Freelance Potential Publishes 150 freelance submissions yearly: 75% written by nonstaff writers; 15% by authors new to the magazine. Receives 12 queries monthly.

Submissions Writers' guidelines and editorial calendar available at website. Query with author biography; physicians should also include address of practice. Accepts email queries to articles@ fertilitytoday.org. Responds in 2 months.
- *Articles:* 800–1,500 words. Informational, profiles, interviews, opinion, personal experience. Topics: fertility issues and treatments, male and female reproductive health.
- *Depts/columns:* 1,500 words. Exercise and Nutrition, Adoption/Child-Free Living, Mind, Body & Soul, My Story. Reviews of books on fertility topics. "Health Forum," written by physicians.

Sample Issue 96 pages. Advertising. Sample copy available.
- "Fertile Hope for Cancer Survivors," by Lindsay Nohr Beck. Preserving fertility despite cancer.
- "Male Infertility." Describes the factors of male fertility that can affect a couple's ability to conceive.

Rights and Payment All rights. Written material, 50¢ a word. Pays on acceptance. Provides 3 contributor's copies.

FitPregnancy

21100 Erwin Street, Woodland Hills, CA 91367. www.fitpregnancy.com

Executive Editor: Sharon Cohen

This magazine is a pregnant woman's guide to health, nutrition, exercise, and beauty. It also offers content on infant and baby care, as well as postpartum issues. It is interested in articles that have something new and fresh to offer. ■ **Circulation** 500,000 ■ **Audience** Women ■ **Frequency** 6 times a year

Freelance Potential Publishes 50 freelance submissions yearly: 40% written by nonstaff writers; 30% by authors new to the magazine. Receives 30 queries monthly.

Submissions Editorial calendar available at website. Query with clips; specify whether idea is for a feature or column. Accepts email to scohen@fitpregnancy.com. Responds in 1 month.
- *Articles:* 1,000–1,800 words. Informational, profiles, personal experience. Topics: prenatal fitness and nutrition, postpartum issues, breastfeeding, baby care, psychology, health.
- *Depts/columns:* 550–1,000 words. Essays by fathers, family issues, prenatal health, newborn health, psychology, childbirth, prenatal nutrition, news briefs. "Time Out," 550 words.
- *Other:* Recipes and meal plans.

Sample Issue 128 pages. Advertising. Sample copy available.
- "Oh Your Aching Head," by Danielle Braff. Tips for combatting postpartum headaches.
- "Alcohol: Just Say Maybe," by Kim Schworm Acosta. Research on alcohol use during pregnancy.

Rights and Payment Rights vary. Written material, payment rates vary. Pays on publication. Provides 2 contributor's copies.

Fort Lauderdale Family Magazine

7045 SW 69th Avenue, South Miami, FL 33143. www.familymagazine.biz

Publisher: Janet Jupiter

Parents living in Fort Lauderdale and its environs read this magazine's general interest articles, news of local events, reviews, recreation ideas, and product information. All content has a regional focus.
- ■ **Circulation** Unavailable ■ **Audience** Parents ■ **Frequency** Monthly

Freelance Potential Publishes 15–20 freelance submissions yearly: 30% written by nonstaff writers.

Submissions Query. Accepts hard copy and email queries to familymag@bellsouth.net. SASE. Response time varies.
- *Articles:* Word lengths vary. Informational, how-to. Topics: child care, family finances, relationships, education, health, safety, fitness, pets, regional activities and entertainment.
- *Depts/columns:* Word lengths vary.

Sample Issue Advertising. Sample copy available at website.
- "To Change or Not to Change," by Julie Casey. Opinion piece on restaurants and changing tables.
- "Veggin' Out Is So In." Tips for starting your own vegetable garden.

Rights and Payment One-time rights. Payment rates vary. Pays on publication. Provides contributor's copies.

Fort Myers & Southwest Florida

15880 Summerlin Road, Suite 189, Fort Myers, FL 33908. www.ftmyersmagazine.com

Publisher: Andrew Elias

This regional magazine covers the various scenes of southwestern Florida—the arts scene, the cultural scene, and the entertainment scene. It also publishes regional lifestyle pieces about health, sports, recreation, travel, food, gardening, and family. It caters to sophisticated adults who have a strong interest in the arts. All submissions must focus on a local subject, be impeccably researched, and present a high caliber of writing. ■ **Circulation** 20,000 ■ **Audience** Educated adults, 20-70 years ■ **Frequency** 6 times a year

Freelance Potential Publishes 10–20 freelance submissions yearly: 90% written by nonstaff writers; 15% by authors new to the magazine; 25% by previously unpublished writers. Receives 5 unsolicited manuscripts monthly.

Submissions Guidelines and editorial calendar available at website. Query or send complete manuscript with suggested headlines and subheads, author biography, contact information, and photos or artwork that may enhance the article. Prefers email submissions to ftmyers@optonline.net (Word attachments or pasted into body of email). Responds in 6–12 weeks.
- *Articles:* 750–1,500 words. Informational, profiles, interviews, reviews, local news. Topics: the arts, media, entertainment, travel, recreation, health, fitness, nutrition, gardening, local history, popular culture, recreation, environmental issues, reviews.
- *Depts/columns:* 750–1,500 words. Informational, interviews, profiles, news, reviews. Topics: books, music, fine arts, theater, film, video profiles, health and wellness, travel and leisure, sports and recreation, food and drink, home and garden.
- *Artwork:* JPEG, TIFF, or PDF images.

Sample Issue 40 pages. Advertising. Sample copy available.
- "The Art of Botany," by Ann Drew. Review of an art exhibition, "Gardens in Perpetual Bloom."
- "Bein' Green by Design," by Cindy-jo Dietz. Profile of the owners of a local business, Renzos Designs Green Developers.

Rights and Payment One-time rights. Written material, approximately 10¢ a word. Artwork, $10–$50. Pays about 30 days from publication. Provides 1 contributor's copy.

FortWorthChild

Lauren Publications, 4275 Kellway Circle, Suite 146, Addison, TX 75001. www.dwfchild.com

Editor in Chief: Joylyn Niebes

Entertaining information, valuable advice, and helpful resources are packed into this publication for parents living in Texas's Tarrant County. *FortWorthChild* and its sisters, *DallasChild* and *NorthTexasChild,* look for fresh voices, ideas, and perspectives with a focus on children of all ages. All queries must have a local focus; preference is given to authors who live in the region. ■ **Circulation** 133,000 for all the publications ■ **Audience** Parents ■ **Frequency** Monthly

Freelance Potential Publishes 12–15 freelance submissions yearly: 25% written by nonstaff writers; 20% by authors new to the magazine. Receives 20 queries monthly.

Submissions Guidelines available at website. Query with résumé. Prefers email queries to editorial@dfwchildmagazines.com; accepts hard copy and faxes to 972-447-0633. Accepts simultaneous submissions if identified. SASE. Response time varies.
- *Articles:* 1,000–2,500 words. Informational, self-help, how-to, humor, profiles, personal experience. Topics: parenting, education, child development, family travel, regional news, recreation, entertainment, current events, social issues, multicultural and ethnic subjects, health, fitness, crafts.
- *Depts/columns:* 800 words. Family activities, health, safety, news briefs, education, child development, humor, fathers' perspectives, reviews.

Sample Issue 74 pages. Advertising. Sample copy available.
- "So Your Child Wants to Be a Star," by Shelley Hawes Pate. Pros and cons of a child in entertainment.
- "A Whole Lotta Love," by Margie Jacinto. Profile of Fort Worth–based celebrity chef Tim Love.

Rights and Payment First rights. Written material, payment rates vary. Pays on publication. Provides contributor's copies upon request.

Fostering Families Today

541 East Garden Drive, Unit N, Windsor, CO 80550. www.fosteringfamiliestoday.com

Editor: Richard Fischer

Practical information and personal experiences that help foster parents and adoptive parents deal with the challenges and joys of raising children are found in this magazine, which is published in both print and online editions. It also offers articles of interest to professionals working in the field of child welfare. ■ **Circulation** 26,000 ■ **Audience** Adoptive and foster parents ■ **Frequency** 6 times a year

Freelance Potential Publishes 40–45 freelance submissions yearly: 85% written by nonstaff writers; 30% by authors new to the magazine; 30% by previously unpublished writers. Receives 6–10 unsolicited manuscripts monthly.

Submissions Sample copy available at website. Send complete manuscript with permission agreement form (available at website). Accepts hard copy and email submissions to louis@adoptinfo.net (attach file). SASE. Response time varies.
- *Articles:* 500–1,200 words. Informational, how-to, profiles, personal experience. Topics: adoption, foster parenting, child development, relevant research, health, education, legal issues.
- *Depts/columns:* Word lengths vary. News, opinions, advice, profiles, book reviews, child advocacy.

Sample Issue 62 pages. No advertising. Sample copy available at website.
- "Secrecy vs. Privacy in Adoption." A child's preferences about knowing adoption information.
- "Definition of Adoption." Ways for adoptive families to give back during the holiday season.

Rights and Payment Non-exclusive print and electronic rights. No payment. Provides 3 contributor's copies and a 1-year subscription.

Gay Parent Magazine

P.O. Box 750852, Forest Hills, NY 11375-0852. www.gayparentmag.com

Editor: Angeline Acain

This magazine is filled with articles that address parenting issues faced by LGBT parents. It also provides helpful resources for choosing private schools, day and overnight camps, and vacation spots. ■ **Circulation** 10,000 ■ **Audience** Gay and transgender parents ■ **Frequency** 6 times a year

Freelance Potential Publishes 6 freelance submissions yearly: 3% written by nonstaff writers; 1% by authors new to the magazine. Receives about 6 manuscripts monthly.

Submissions Guidelines available at website. Send complete manuscript. Accepts email submissions to gayparentmag@gmail.com. Artwork improves chance of acceptance. Response time varies.
- *Articles:* 700 words. Informational, how–to, personal experience. Topics: LGBT parenting.
- *Depts/columns:* Word counts vary.
- *Artwork:* Color prints or digital images.

Sample Issue Advertising. Sample copy available.
- "A Chat with Reality TV's Guncles." Profile of gay dads on a reality TV show.
- "Local Support Groups and Events." A roundup of resources in the greater New York area.

Rights and Payment One-time rights. Written material, 10¢ a word. Photography, payment rates vary. Pays on publication. Provides contributor's copies.

Genesee Valley Parent

266 Alexander Street, Rochester, NY 14607. www.gvparent.com

Editor: Jillian Melnyk

This regional magazine offers parents in the greater Rochester, New York, area coverage of local events, as well as articles on family and child-rearing issues starting with birth and going right up through college. It also features profiles and personal experience pieces. ■ **Circulation** 30,000 ■ **Audience** Parents ■ **Frequency** Monthly

Freelance Potential Publishes 50 freelance submissions yearly: 75% written by nonstaff writers; 5% by authors new to the magazine. Receives 20 queries monthly.

Submissions Guidelines and editorial calendar available. Query with clips or writing samples. Accepts hard copy. Accepts simultaneous submissions if identified. SASE. Responds in 1–3 months.
■ *Articles:* 700–1,200 words. Informational, how-to, profiles, reviews, humor, personal experience. Topics: regional family events, local goods and services, special and gifted education, social issues, family problems, health and fitness, parenting.
■ *Depts/columns:* 500–600 words. Family health, teen issues, toddler issues, short news items.
■ *Other:* Submit seasonal material 4 months in advance.

Sample Issue 68 pages. Advertising.
■ "Home Alone," by Myrna Beth Haskell. Tips for parents on leaving teenagers home alone safely.
■ "Fostering Happy Campers," by Claire Yezbak Fadden. The value of day camp and how to choose the right one for your child.

Rights and Payment Second rights. Articles, $30–$45. Depts/columns, $25–$30. Pays on publication. Provides 1 tearsheet.

GeoParent

16101 North 82nd Street, Suite A-9, Scottsdale, AZ 85260. wwwgeoparent.com

Editors: Betsy Bailey & Nancy Price

GeoParent is an online information site that is part of SheKnows.com. It covers topics of general interest to parents and families, as well as state-specific regional articles on recreation and travel. This site also offers features related to homeschooling. ■ **Circulation** Unavailable ■ **Audience** Parents ■ **Frequency** Weekly

Freelance Potential Publishes 50 freelance submissions yearly: 90% written by nonstaff writers. Receives about 4–5 queries and unsolicited manuscripts monthly.

Submissions Guidelines available at website. Send complete manuscript with a 50-word summary, author biography, and signed writer's agreement form from the website. Accepts reprints. Accepts email submissions to skwriters@gmail.com. Response time varies.
■ *Articles:* 450–600 words. Informational, how-to. Topics: parenting, child development, family issues, pregnancy and childbirth, infancy, child care, nutrition, health, education, gifted and special education, homeschooling, travel, regional recreation.
■ *Depts/columns:* Word lengths vary. Parenting tips and advice.
■ *Artwork:* JPEG, PNG or GIF images.

Sample Issue Advertising. Sample copy available at website.
■ "Thinking about Homeschooling?" by Suzi Milovanovic. Ohio homeschooling requirements.
■ "The Bites," by Michele Borboa. Common insect bites and how to treat them.

Rights and Payment Rights vary. Written material, $25–$50; $10 for reprints. Pays on publication.

Georgia Family Magazine

523 Sioux Drive, Macon, GA 31210. www.georgiafamily.com

Executive Editor/Publisher: Olya Fessard

This regional parenting magazine delivers information on all topics related to parenting and serves as a resource for families living in the state of Georgia. It looks for well-developed storylines, careful research, and independent reporting, and it prefers articles with regional interest. ■ **Circulation** 17,000 print; 200,000+ hits online ■ **Audience** Parents ■ **Frequency** Monthly

Freelance Potential Publishes 100-125 freelance submissions yearly: 50–75% written by nonstaff writers; 10–25% by authors new to the magazine; 25–50% by previously unpublished writers. Receives 25–50 queries and unsolicited manuscripts monthly.

Submissions Guidelines, editorial calendar, and sample copy available online. Query with cover letter and author biography; or send complete manuscript. Accepts email submissions (Word attachments) to georgiafamilyeditorial@gmail.com. Accepts simultaneous submissions. Responds in 5 days. Availability of artwork improves chance of acceptance. First rights. Written material, word lengths vary. No payment.
■ *Articles:* 400–800 words. Informative, how–to. Topics: child development, family relationships, family recreation, arts, career/education, entertainment, holidays/seasonal, outdoors, parenting children and teens, social skills, social issues, technology, home and garden, party planning, sandwich generation, summer camps.
■ *Depts/columns:* Word lengths vary. Reviews.
■ *Artwork:* PDF or JPEG.

Sample Issue 64 pages. Advertising.
■ "The Craft of Cursive," by Jamie Lober. Georgia schools debate teaching children cursive writing.
■ "Best Public School for Your Kid," by Olya Fessard. Choosing a school that best fits a child's needs.

Rights and Payment Reprint rights and more rarely first time rights. Reprints, $10–$30. Original articles, $20–$60. Pays on publication. Provides 1 tearsheet.

Good Housekeeping

Hearst Corporation, 300 West 57th Street, 28th Floor, New York, NY 10019-5288. www.goodhousekeeping.com

Executive Editor: Judith Coyne

Understanding the challenges women face in balancing family, house duties, and time for themselves, this magazine informs and supports readers with articles on everything from home and gardening tips to parenting issues. ■ **Circulation** 25 million ■ **Audience** Women ■ **Frequency** Monthly

Freelance Potential Publishes 50+ freelance submissions yearly: 80% written by nonstaff writers. Receives 1,500–2,000 queries monthly.

Submissions Query with résumé and clips for nonfiction. Send complete manuscript for fiction; manuscripts not returned. Accepts hard copy. SASE. Responds in 4–6 weeks.
■ *Articles:* 750–2,500 words. Informational, how–to. Topics: parenting young children through tweens and teens, social issues. Essays, to 1,000 words. Personal experience.
■ *Fiction:* To 3,000 words.
■ *Depts/columns:* Word lengths vary.

Sample Issue Advertising. Sample copy available.
■ "Parent–Teacher Talk," by Hilary Quinn. Tips for fostering a good parent/teacher relationship.
■ "Are You A Pushover Parent?" by Charlotte Latvala. How to become an authoritative parent.

Rights and Payment All rights for nonfiction; first North American serial rights for fiction. Articles, to $2,000; essays, to $750; fiction, payment rates vary. Pays on acceptance. Provides 1 contributor's copy.

Grandparents.com

589 8th Avenue, 6th Floor, New York, NY 10018. www.grandparents.com

Editor

Grandparents.com serves as a hub of information for engaged and involved grandparents. Dedicated to fostering family connections, it offers a wide range of activities that grandparents and grandchildren can do together, as well as personal experience pieces that give insight into the unique grandparent/grandchild relationship. The editors are always looking for fresh, new story ideas and freelance writers to add to their editorial team. ■ **Hits per month** Unavailable ■ **Audience** Grandparents ■ **Frequency** Unavailable

Freelance Potential Publishes several freelance submissions yearly.

Submissions Guidelines available at website. Query. Accepts email queries to contribute@grandparents.com. Response time varies.
■ *Articles:* Word lengths vary. Informational, how–to, essays, interviews. Topics: entertaining and educational activities, travel, lifestyle, real–life problems, social issues, social skills, recipes, gifts.
■ *Depts/columns:* Word lengths vary. Reviews. Topics: toys, games, books, gear, movies, and other family-friendly products.

Sample Issue Advertising. Sample copy available at website.
■ "Do Your Speak Up or Hold Your Tongue?" by Sherri Lerner. A survey of grandparents on the question of stepping in when they feel moms and dads are making mistakes with their children.
■ "How Do They Grow Up So Fast?" by Beverly Beckham. A grandmother reflects on watching her grandchildren grow up.

Rights and Payment Electronic rights. No payment.

Grand Rapids Family

549 Ottawa Avenue NW, Suite 201, Grand Rapids, MI 49503-1444. www.grfamily.com

Editor: Carole Valade

Families living in western Michigan look to this award–winning publication for local resources and activities. It addresses myriad issues of both general and regional interest to parents. ■ **Circulation** 20,000 ■ **Audience** Parents ■ **Frequency** Monthly

Freelance Potential Publishes 15 freelance submissions yearly: 20% written by nonstaff writers.

Submissions Guidelines available with #10 SASE. Query or send complete manuscript. Accepts hard copy. SASE. Responds to queries in 2 months, to manuscripts in 6 months.
■ *Articles:* Word lengths vary. Informational, how–to, profiles, interviews. Topics: local events and activities, travel, child care, education, local personalities.
■ *Depts/columns:* Word lengths vary. Frontlines (short news features), Baby Knows (experts speak on infant care), Pop Life (the humorous side of parenting), Family Dates (regional guide to family fun), What They Say (local children's photos/interviews). Also reviews, health, fitness, finances.
■ *Artwork:* B/W and color prints.

Sample Issue Advertising.
■ "Home Is Where the School Is," by Paul R. Kopenkoskey. One family's homeschooling success.
■ "Moving in the Right Direction," by Melissa Black. An active working mom with young children gets a fashion and beauty makeover.

Rights and Payment All rights. Written material, payment rates vary. Kill fee, $25. Photographs, $25. Pays on publication.

Grit

1503 Southwest 42nd Street, Topeka, KS 66609-1265. www.grit.com

Senior Associate Editor: Jean Teller

Grit brings readers articles about living a self-sustaining life and raising a family on a farm, ranch or in other rural setting. It celebrates country lifestyles of all kinds and emphasizes the importance of community and stewardship. Its readers are well–educated and are either already living a rural life or aspire to do so. ■ **Circulation** 150,000 ■ **Audience** Parents ■ **Frequency** 6 times a year

Freelance Potential Publishes 80–90 freelance submissions yearly: 90% written by nonstaff writers; 50% by authors new to the magazine; 50% by previously unpublished writers. Receives 200 queries monthly.

Submissions Guidelines available at website. Query only. Accepts email queries to jteller@grit.com (include "Query" and subject of query in subject line). Response time varies.
■ *Articles:* 800–1,500 words. Informational, how–to, humor, profiles, personal experience. Topics: country living, land management, wildlife, pets, livestock, gardening, cooking, seasonal food, machinery and tools, do–it–yourself, community.
■ *Depts/columns:* 350–1,500 words. *GRIT* Gazette (news and quirky briefs of interest to farmers), Country Tech (farm equipment), Looking Back (nostalgic look at life on the farm), In the Shop (how–to for specialty farm items), Comfort Foods, Recipe Box, Wild *GRIT*, Sow Hoe (gardening).
■ *Artwork:* 35mm color prints and slides, digital images.

Sample Issue Advertising. Sample copy available.
■ "All about Spiders in America," by Jerry Schleicher. A primer on spiders, safe or dangerous.
■ "The Benefits of Raising Ducks," by Heather Head. The proper care and feeding of ducks.

Rights and Payment Shared rights. Written material, 35¢ a word. Photographs, $35–$175. Pays on publication. Provides 3 contributor's copies.

Happiness

P.O. Box 388, Portland, TN 37148. www.happiness.com

Editor: Diane Lynn Wilks Nolan

Happiness is a television guide centered around the family that also features uplifting articles about self-improvement, good health, and family relationships. Poems, activities, and children's stories are also included. Articles should be based on incidents that are true, or true-to-life. They should build character and emphasize a more fulfilling or happier life in health, personality, or behavior. *Happiness* does not publish religious material with a specific doctrinal slant. ■ **Circulation** 150,000 ■ **Audience** Families ■ **Frequency** Weekly

Freelance Potential 75% written by nonstaff writers: 25% by authors new to the magazine; 25% by previously unpublished writers.

Submissions Guidelines available. Send complete manuscript. Accepts hard copy. SASE Responds in 3 months.
■ *Articles:* 450 words. Informational, self-help, how-to, humor, personal experience. Topics: careers, education, health, fitness, hobbies, animals, pets, nature, recreation, travel.
■ *Depts/columns:* 25–75 words. Cooking, health, humor, tips from readers.
■ *Other:* Poetry. Submit seasonal material 4 months in advance.

Sample Issue 16 pages. No advertising.
■ "A Breath of Fresh Air," by Melissa Hoffman. The health and mood–lifting benefits of fresh air.
■ "How to Lose Weight Without Even Trying," by Suzan L. Wiener. Painless ways to cut the fat from your family budget.

Rights and Payment First rights. All material, payment rates vary. Pays on publication.

Hawaii Parent

350 Ward Avenue, Suite 106-304, Honolulu, HI 96814. www.hawaii-parent.com

Publisher: Charles H. Harrington

This is Hawaii's original and longest-running parenting magazine. Its articles are designed to help parents face the challenges of raising happy and healthy children, as well as to provide information on local resources, activities, and events. ■ **Circulation** 45,000 ■ **Audience** Parents ■ **Frequency** 6 times a year

Freelance Potential Actively looking for writers.

Submissions Editorial calendar available at website. Query with story ideas, résumé, and writing samples. Accepts email to to hpks@hawaii.rr.com.
■ *Articles:* Word lengths vary. Informational, personal experience. Topics: positive parenting, family life, pregnancy, child development, education.
■ *Depts/columns:* Word lengths vary. Health issues, family safety.

Sample Issue Advertising. Sample copy available at website.
■ "Appealing Parenting Apps," by Lisa Gmur. Reports on several "apps" for mobile devices that can either provide parenting tips or keep the kids happy with educational games.
■ "Teaching Our Children Appreciation," by Nicole Hempeck. Five ideas for instilling in children empathy for others and an appreciation for what they have.

Rights and Payment Rights vary. Payment information unavailable.

Healthy Mom & Baby Magazine

1208 Weston Pine Circle, Sarasota, FL 34240. www.health4mom.org

Editor: Carolyn Davis Cockey

Designed for expectant and new mothers, this magazine addresses all the issues, topics, and challenges associated with pregnancy and caring for a newborn. It is usually distributed by nurses to women in health care settings. Prospective writers must be experts in the medical or wellness fields. New authors can find the best chance of acceptance through pitching an expert advice column. ■ **Circulation** 300,000 ■ **Audience** Parents ■ **Frequency** 4 times a year

Freelance Potential 50% written by nonstaff writers; 10% by authors new to the magazine.

Submissions Query. Accepts hard copy. SASE. Response time varies.
■ *Articles:* Word lengths vary. Informational, how–to, profiles. Topics: pregnancy, health, fitness, birth, newborn care, baby products, family, parenting, travel.
■ *Depts/columns:* Word lengths vary. Expert advice.

Sample Issue Advertising. Sample copy available.
■ "Putting the Brakes on Pertussis," by Carolyn Davis Cockey. Race car driver Jeff Gordon and his wife spread the word on the importance of getting a pertussis booster if you're caring for a baby.
■ "Stilettos and the Baby Bump," by Brea Samuel. Proper footwear for pregnant women.

Rights and Payment Rights vary. Payment rates vary. Payment policy varies.

High School Years

128 North Royal Avenue, Front Royal, VA 22630. www.rfeonline.com

Publisher: Nan Grambo

Distributed to parents by subscribing high schools, this reproducible newsletter features topics such as improving school success, parenting skills, and challenges facing teens. It is written by educators and journalists who are knowledgeable about the issues facing teens today. ■ **Circulation** 300,000 ■ **Audience** Parents ■ **Frequency** 9 times a year

Freelance Potential Publishes 80 freelance submissions yearly: 100% written by nonstaff writers; 25% by unpublished writers. Receives 3 unsolicited manuscripts monthly.

Submissions Guidelines and editorial calendar available. Query with résumé and clips. Accepts email to rfecustomer@wolterskluwer.com. Responds if interested.
- *Articles:* 225–300 words. Informational, how-to. Topics: education, study skills, parenting, teen issues, social issues.
- *Depts/columns:* 175–200 words.

Sample Issue Sample copy available at website.
- "Let's Get Organized." Tips for helping teens keep track of assignments and budgeting their time.
- "Guidance vs. Independence." The balance between guiding teens and letting them make decisions.

Rights and Payment Rights vary. Payment rates vary. Pays on acceptance. Provides 5 copies.

Hip Mama

P.O. Box 82539, Portland, OR 97202. www.hipmamazine.com

Advising Editor: Kerlin Richter

A reader-written magazine, *Hip Mama* targets parents who are outside of the mainstream. Young parents, gay parents, and homeschooling parents are among its readership. Published on an irregular basis, in print and online, it looks for daring, honest essays about family life. ■ **Circulation** 5,000 ■ **Audience** Parents ■ **Frequency** Irregular

Freelance Potential Publishes 32–48 freelance submissions yearly: 100% written by nonstaff writers. Receives 5–6 unsolicited manuscripts monthly.

Submissions Guidelines and theme list available at website. Send complete manuscript and short author biography. Accepts email submissions to submissions@hipmamazine.com (Word attachments) and hard copy. Responds in 1 month.
- *Articles:* 250–1,500 words. Opinion, personal experience. Topics: parenting, child development, education, social issues, health, nutrition, family, home.
- *Artwork:* B/W prints, digital images in JPEG format, line art.

Sample Issue Sample copy available at website.
- "The Zen of Miscarriage," by Cheryl Dumsinil. A mom who miscarries finds healing through surrender and a sweet tattoo.
- "Rewriting the Questions," by Amy Daniewicz. One mom searches for answers to her son's inquiries about death.

Rights and Payment Rights vary. No payment.

Home & School Connection

128 North Royal Avenue, Front Royal, VA 22630. www.rfeonline.com

Publisher: Nan Grambo

This reproducible newsletter is distributed to parents by subscribing elementary schools. Filled with ideas that families can use to promote school success, it is written by educators and journalists who understand the issues facing young school children. ■ **Circulation** Unavailable ■ **Audience** Parents ■ **Frequency** 9 times a year

Freelance Potential Publishes 80 freelance submissions yearly: 100% written by nonstaff writers; 14% by authors who are new to the publication; 28% by unpublished writers.

Submissions Guidelines and editorial calendar available. Query with résumé and clips. Accepts email to rfecustomer@wolterskluwer.com. Responds if interested.
■ *Articles:* 225–300 words. Informational, how-to. Topics: education, study skills, parenting, social issues, social skills.
■ *Depts/columns:* 175–200 words.

Sample Issue Sample copy available at website.
■ "After School Chats." How to get children to open up about their day at school.
■ "A Recipe for Respect." How to model and teach this character trait.

Rights and Payment Rights vary. Payment rates vary. Pays on acceptance. Provides 5 copies.

The Hood Magazine

Hoodlum Production, www.thehoodmagazine.com

Editor: Taryn Sonnenfeld

"The hood" that this title refers to is childhood, familyhood, parenthood, and grandparenthood. *The Hood* celebrates them all with informative articles designed to promote strong families. It reports on local organizations, events, and programs that advocate community and family togetherness. Parenting articles, health advice, and local resources fill *The Hood*'s pages. ■ **Circulation** 10,000 ■ **Audience** Parents ■ **Frequency** 9 times a year

Freelance Potential Unavailable.

Submissions Query or send complete manuscript. Accepts material via electronic form at website only. Response time varies.
■ *Articles:* Word lengths vary. Informational, profiles, personal experience. Topics: family values, parenting issues, education, social issues, child development.
■ *Depts/columns:* Word lengths vary. Health, advice, events.

Sample Issue 36 pages. Advertising. Sample copy available at website.
■ "Is Your Child Being Bullied?" by Greta Stewart. Discusses the warning signs that a child is being bullied.
■ "Celebrating Our Differences," by Taryn Sonnenfeld. Profiles a day care center in which diversity is celebrated every day.

Rights and Payment All rights. Payment information unavailable.

Houston Family Magazine

5131 Braesvalley, Houston, TX 77096. www.houstonfamilymagazine.com

Editor: Dana Donovan

Houston Family Magazine focuses on practical information that Houston-area parents can use in their everyday life. It offers articles on a wide variety of topics of interest to parents, all written from a regional perspective. ■ **Circulation** 60,000 ■ **Audience** Parents ■ **Frequency** Monthly

Freelance Potential Publishes 20 freelance submissions yearly: 20% written by nonstaff writers; 25% by authors new to the magazine.

Submissions Guidelines available at website. Query or send complete manuscript. Accepts email submissions to editor@houstonfamilymagazine.com. Response time varies.
- *Articles:* Word lengths vary. Informational, how–to, profiles. Topics: child care, education, recreation, travel, health, local news and current events affecting families, entertainment, regional activities, recipes.
- *Depts/columns:* Word lengths vary. Ask Amy (financial advice), Book Bites, Family Finds, Family Table, Parents Ask, Reel Life With Jane (family entertainment news), Talk to the Doc.

Sample Issue Advertising. Sample copy available at website.
- "Basics of Boarding School," by Kristin Bustamante. Deciding if a boarding school education is right for your child and what the options are for Houston parents.
- "A Pirate's Life Is a Wonderful Life," by Krysten Davis. A travel guide to North Carolina's Outer Banks.

Rights and Payment First and limited-time electronic rights. Payment rates vary. Pays on publication. Provides 2 contributor's copies.

Hudson Valley Parent

174 South Street, Newburgh, NY 12550. www.hvparent.com

Editor: Pauline Liu

Targeting families in New York State's mid-Hudson Valley, this magazine focuses on resources for raising happy, healthy children ages newborn to 14, and family-oriented, regional events and activities. It prefers first–person accounts that are carefully researched. ■ **Circulation** 25,000 ■ **Audience** Parents ■ **Frequency** Monthly

Freelance Potential Publishes 52 freelance submissions yearly: 60% written by nonstaff writers; 20% by authors new to the magazine; 5% by previously unpublished writers. Receives 20 queries and 10 unsolicited manuscripts monthly.

Submissions Guidelines and editorial calendar available. Query with writing samples, or send complete manuscript with sidebar and author biography. Also accepts reprints. Accepts email submissions to editor@excitingread.com. Responds in 3–6 weeks.
- *Articles:* 700–1,200 words. Informational, how-to, personal experience. Topics: child care and development, discipline, education, learning disabilities, family health, recreation, travel, entertainment.
- *Depts/columns:* 700 words. Health, education, behavior, kid-friendly recipes.
- *Artwork:* 8x10 B/W and color prints.
- *Other:* Submit seasonal material 6 months in advance.

Sample Issue 58 pages. Advertising. Sample copy available.
- "A Special Family," by Pauline Liu and Sandy Tomcho. The story of a family who adopted a girl with Down's Syndrome.
- "Computing Is Not Playtime," by Dr. Paul Schwartz. The dangers of screen time activities for young children.

Rights and Payment First time rights and online rights; one–time reprint rights. Written material, $80–$120; $25–$35 for reprints. Pays on publication. Provides 1 contributor's copy.

Indy's Child

921 East 86th Street, Suite 130, Indianapolis, IN 46240. www.indyschild.com

Managing Editor: Megan Kirschner

Articles on parenting topics, with a focus on Indianapolis, are the mainstay of this magazine. It serves as a guide to regional resources and expects well-researched articles that will offer readers information they can use in real life. Humor is always welcome. ■ **Circulation** 120,000 ■ **Audience** Parents ■ **Frequency** Monthly

Freelance Potential Publishes 240+ freelance submissions yearly: 95% written by nonstaff writers; 60% by authors new to the magazine; 35% by previously unpublished writers. Receives hundreds of queries and about 50 unsolicited manuscripts monthly.

Submissions Query with writing samples, main idea of article and how you will organize it, list of sources. Accepts email to editor@indyschild.com (Word attachments). Responds if interested.
- *Articles:* 300–1,000 words. Informational, how-to, profiles, humor. Topics: parenting, child development, family-oriented events and activities, sports, travel, health, balancing career and family, fatherhood.
- *Depts/columns:* 800–1,000 words. News, education, pediatric/women's/men's health, special needs, local profiles, and budget related stories.
- *Artwork:* Color digital images at 200 dpi.
- *Other:* Submit seasonal material 2 months in advance.

Sample Issue Advertising. Sample copy available at website.
- "March Against Bullying," by Katie Wynne. Tips for recognizing and preventing bullying in honor of National Stop Bullying Month.
- "Pediatric Asthma," by Raminder Sufi, M.D. Symptoms and treatment of pediatric asthma.

Rights and Payment First rights. Written material, 10¢–15¢ a word for original articles; $40–$75 for reprints. Pays on publication.

Inland Empire Family

1451 Quail Street, Suite 201, Newport Beach, CA 92660. www.inlandempirefamily.com

Editor: Lynn Armitage

This magazine is for families living in Riverside and San Bernadino counties in California. It covers a range of parenting topics specific to the region. All submissions must have a local connection and include online sources and current information for places referenced. ■ **Circulation** 55,000 ■ **Audience** Parents ■ **Frequency** Monthly

Freelance Potential Publishes several freelance submissions yearly: 95% written by nonstaff writers.

Submissions Query. Accepts hard copy. SASE. Response time varies.
- *Articles:* Word lengths vary. Informational, how-to, essays. Topics: parenting, child care and development, education, entertainment, sports, recreation, travel, health, nutrition, summer camp, pets.
- *Depts/columns:* Word lengths vary. Parenting advice by age group, self-help for parents and couples, children's health, fashion, food and dining, education, media reviews.

Sample Issue Advertising.
- "Blow-'Em-Away Birthday Parties," by Jennifer Sbranti. New trends for kids' birthday parties.
- "Why Reading Remains Lesson No. 1," by Amy Bentley. How parents can lay a foundation for strong reading development through everyday activities.

Rights and Payment All rights. Articles, $100–$500. Depts/columns, payment rates vary. Kill fee, $50. Pays within 45 days of publication.

Inspired Mother

The Design Center, 10816 Millington Court, Suite 110, Cincinnati, OH 45242. www.inspiredmother.com

Editor: Jennifer Hogan Redmond

Both the personal and professional sides of mothers (and an occasional father) are explored in this online magazine. Readers find profiles of moms who are successfully raising their children in today's world, as well as inspiration for themselves. Humor is always welcome, as are book and product reviews. ■ **Hits per month** Unavailable ■ **Audience** Mothers ■ **Frequency** Monthly

Freelance Potential Publishes 15–30 freelance submissions yearly: 40% written by nonstaff writers; 75% by authors new to the magazine; 15% by previously unpublished writers.

Submissions Guidelines available at website. Send complete manuscript. Prefers email submissions to editor@inspiredmother.com. Response time varies.
■ *Articles:* To 1,500 words. Informational, profiles. Topics: inspirational mothers who have achieved success in their personal and/or professional lives, overcome difficulties, and made positive contributions to their communities.
■ *Depts/columns:* To 750 words. Short stories, narratives. Creative pieces about motherhood. Media and product reviews.
■ *Other:* Poetry.

Sample Issue Sample copy available at website.
■ "Boomerang Discipline," by Sharon K. Trumpy. Disciplining a preschooler.
■ "A Not–So–Simple Day," by Jennifer Redmond. A mom's attempt to turn off the communication technology in her home and have a "simple" day.

Rights and Payment Limited-time electronic rights. No payment.

Jeunesse

Centre for Research in Young People's Texts and Cultures, University of Winnipeg, 515 Portage Avenue, Winnipeg, Manitoba MB R3B 2E9 Canada. http://jeunessejournal.ca

General Editor: Mavis Reimer

This interdisciplinary academic journal publishes research and opinion on literature and other media for, by, and about children. It focuses on the cultural functions and representations of "the child." Though international in scope, it has a special interest in Canada. It welcomes articles in both English and French. ■ **Circulation** 400 ■ **Audience** Parents, educators, scholars, librarians ■ **Frequency** 2 times a year

Freelance Potential Publishes 25 freelance submissions yearly: 95% written by nonstaff writers; 40% by authors new to the magazine; 10% by previously unpublished writers. Receives 3–4 unsolicited manuscripts monthly.

Submissions Guidelines and theme list available at website. Send complete manuscript. Prefers email submissions to jeunesse@uwinnipeg.ca (Word or RTF attachments); name and contact information should not appear on the submission itself, but on a separate file or piece of paper (along with a 100-word abstract) so it may undergo a blind review by peers. Will accept 3 hard copies. SAE/IRC. Responds in 3 months.
■ *Articles:* 2,000–6,000 words. Informational, reviews, essays, profiles, interviews. Topics: children's literature; film, video, drama, authors, toys, digital culture, material culture.

Sample Issue Sample copy available.
■ "Breaking Faith: Disrupted Expectations and Ownership in Stephenie Meyer's Twilight Saga," by Rachel Hendershot Parkin. Abstract examines the relationship between the author, text, and young adult fans of this popular book series.

■ "The Mirror Staged: Images of Babies in Baby Books," by Perry Nodelman. A look at how baby books with photographs of babies relate to the "mirror stage" in baby development.

Rights and Payment First serial rights. No payment. Provides 1 contributor's copy.

Kaboose.com

Disney Online Mom and Family Portfolio, 5161 Lankershin Boulevard, 4th Floor, North Hollywood, CA 91601. http://kaboose.com

Vice President: Emily Smith

This online parenting resource center provides parents and other caretakers with the information they seek to raise a happy, healthy family. It is updated regularly and covers a wide range of topics of interest to families. ■ **Hits per month** 3.6 million ■ **Audience** Parents ■ **Frequency** Unavailable

Freelance Potential Publishes 30 freelance submissions yearly: 95% written by nonstaff writers; 30% by authors new to the magazine; 10% by previously unpublished writers. Receives about 12 queries monthly.

Submissions Query only with outline; does not accept unsolicited manuscripts. Accepts hard copy. SASE. Response time varies.
■ *Articles:* 2,000 words. Informational, how–to, personal experience. Topics: family health, education, child development, finding "mom time."
■ *Depts/columns:* 500 words. Parties, costumes, crafts.

Sample Issue Sample copy available at website.
■ "No More Whining," by Julie Tilsner. A roundup of ideas for getting young children to stop whining.
■ "Helping Preschoolers Cope with Separation," by Joan E. LeFebvre. Ways for parents to help their children learn how to deal with separation anxiety.

Rights and Payment Rights vary. Written material, 85¢ a word. Pays on acceptance.

Kalamazoo Parent

8248 West Q Avenue, Kalamazoo, MI 49009. www.kalamazooparent.com

Editor: Vicky Girard

Kalamazoo Parent launched in 2011 with the goal of helping readers find family-friendly activities every day of the year. To that end, the magazine covers child- and family-oriented events, destinations, and activities throughout southwest Michigan. It also offers articles on family fun and parenting issues. "Local" is the key word for all material submitted here. ■ **Circulation** 10,000 ■ **Audience** Parents ■ **Frequency** Monthly

Freelance Potential Unavailable.

Submissions Guidelines available. Query or send complete manuscript. Accepts hard copy and email to editor@kalamazooparent.com.
■ *Articles:* Word lengths vary. Informational, how-to, personal experience. Topics: parenting, education, family recreation.
■ *Depts/columns:* Word lengths vary. Health, media reviews, product reviews, family life.

Sample Issue 24 pages. Advertising. Sample copy available at website.
■ "An 'Electronics Police-Mom' Goes Digital," by Eileen Wacker. A mom tries to balance her children's love of electronic gadgetry with a love of reading and learning.
■ "Back To School, Back to You," by Christina Katz. Ideas about how mothers can spend just a few minutes a day focusing on themselves.

Rights and Payment All rights. Payment information unavailable.

Kansas 4-H Journal

116 Umberger Hall, Kansas State University, Manhattan, KS 66506-3417.
www.kansas4hfoundation.org

Editor: Rhonda Atkinson

Members of 4-H in Kansas turn to this journal for news and information about club events and activities. It welcomes submissions from writers who have a solid understanding of Kansas 4-H clubs, including members, leaders, and parents. ■ **Circulation** 9,000 ■ **Audience** Families ■ **Frequency** 6 times a year

Freelance Potential Publishes 100 freelance submissions yearly: 60% written by nonstaff writers; 20% by authors new to the magazine; 10% by previously unpublished writers. Receives 58 queries and unsolicited manuscripts monthly.

Submissions Query or send complete manuscript, using the form at website. Accepts email to ratkinso@ksu.edu and hard copy. SASE. Response time varies.
■ *Articles:* 500 words. How–to, informational, personal experience. Topics: careers, education, camping, communication, community service, 4H projects and programs.
■ *Artwork:* Photographs.
■ *Other:* Photo-essays.

Sample Issue Advertising. Sample copy available.

Rights and Payment Rights vary. Payment rates vary. Payment policy varies.

Keeping Family First Online

P.O. Box 36594, Detroit, MI 48236. www.keepingfamilyfirst.org

Executive Editor: Anita S. Lane

This publication describes itself as "an online community of moms and dads who are dedicated to building strong families." Each issue offers practical advice on topics such as the challenges of parenting and balancing family life with work, as well as resources for families. It also accepts personal experience and inspirational pieces. ■ **Hits per month** 40,000 ■ **Audience** Parents ■ **Frequency** Monthly

Freelance Potential Publishes 70 freelance submissions yearly: 100% written by nonstaff writers; 10% by authors new to the magazine; 56% by previously unpublished writers.

Submissions Guidelines available at website. Query. Accepts email queries using form on website only. Response time varies.
■ *Articles:* Word lengths vary. Informational, how–to, personal experience. Topics: parenting, education, family health and wellness, inspirational, home, leisure, entertainment.
■ *Depts/columns:* Word lengths vary. Blended Families, Fashion, Fitness, Food Factor, HomeSpot, Lawn & Garden, Marriage, Mom–to–Mom, Parenting for Dads, Sextime Prayers, Spiritually Speaking, Tazmanian Mom, Teen Time, Wise Words for Women.

Sample Issue Sample copy available at website.
■ "How to Nail That Job Interview," by Joy Gendusa. Expert advice on how to exhibit the qualities most likely to get you hired.
■ "Is It Cold In Here? Learning to Touch Your Dream Each Day," by Racquel R. Robinson. How a family can keep dreams and goals from gradually slipping away.

Rights and Payment Rights vary. No payment.

Kids Life

1426 22nd Avenue, Tuscaloosa, AL 35401. www.kidslifemagazine.com

Publisher: Mary Jane Turner

Kids Life is dedicated to providing information that is relevant to families in western Alabama, including event calendars, regional activities, and resources. It welcomes material from writers everywhere, but gives preference to local freelancers. All articles must have a local angle and relate to families living in our region. ■ **Circulation** 30,000 ■ **Audience** Parents ■ **Frequency** 6 times a year

Freelance Potential Publishes 12 freelance submissions yearly: 75% written by nonstaff writers; 10% by authors new to the magazine; 50% by previously unpublished writers. Receives 20 queries, 20 unsolicited manuscripts monthly.

Submissions Editorial calendar available at website. Query or send complete manuscript. Accepts email submissions to kidslife@comcast.net. Availability of artwork improves chance of acceptance. Responds in 2 weeks.
■ *Articles:* 1,000 words. Informational, personal experience. Topics: parenting, education, sports, child care, religion, cooking, crafts, health, travel, current events.
■ *Depts/columns:* Staff-written.
■ *Artwork:* Color prints, JPEG files. Line art.
■ *Other:* Filler.

Sample Issue About 50 pages. Advertising. Sample copy available.
■ "Summer Camps." A round-up of area summer camps and what they offer.
■ "Back to School Tips." Suggestions for making a smooth transition back to the classroom.

Rights and Payment Rights vary. Written material, to $30. Pays on publication. Provides 1 contributor's copy.

Kids Off the Couch

www.kidsoffthecouch.com

Founders: Sarah Bowman, Diane Phillips Shakin

Kids Off the Couch is a free email newsletter and website based on the belief that the best way to get kids off the couch is to first get on the couch with them. Each article pairs a child-friendly film with a complementary local event, exhibit, or idea for a family adventure. The result is kids getting excited about film, culture, and family time. There are multiple editions for cities throughout the country. It welcomes adventure ideas from parents. ■ **Hits per month** Unavailable ■ **Audience** Parents ■ **Frequency** Weekly

Freelance Potential Publishes many freelance submissions yearly.

Submissions Query. Accepts email queries to info@kidsoffthecouch.com or via submission form at website. Response time varies.
■ *Articles:* Word lengths vary. All are formatted as follows: The Film (a suggested film with synopsis that gives the good points, "red flags," and further viewing suggestions); The Adventure (a regional activity or site that complements the film; also includes insider tips, logistical details, and further suggestions of related activities).

Sample Issue Sample copy available at website.
■ "Get Caught Shreking." A review of Shrek and a visit to a local exhibit about monsters and miracles in Jewish picture books.
■ "Get Caught Reading." *Diary of a Wimpy Kid* is the featured film in this article, paired with suggestions for getting a child hooked on using the local library in a variety of ways.

Rights and Payment Rights vary. No payment.

Kids VT

P.O. Box 1184, Burlington, VT 05402. www.kidsvt.com

Editor: Cathy Resmer

Vermont's young families find regional information on parenting and events in this free tabloid. It is always interested in upbeat material that makes parenting easier and life more fun for families living in the state of Vermont. Most pieces have a distinct regional angle, so submissions from authors living in Vermont are preferred. Readers rely on this publication for support and as a connection to the communities where they live and work. The tone is positive and practical. ■ **Circulation** 25,000 ■ **Audience** Parents ■ **Frequency** 11 times a year

Freelance Potential Publishes 40–50 freelance submissions yearly: 80% written by nonstaff writers; 20% by authors new to the magazine. Receives dozens of unsolicited manuscripts monthly.

Submissions Editorial calendar available at website. Send complete manuscript. Accepts email submissions to cathy@kidsvt.com (no attachments). Accepts simultaneous submissions if identified. Responds if interested.
■ *Articles:* 500–1,500 words. Informational, profiles, interviews, humor. Topics: local events and activities, the arts, education, recreation, nature, the environment, music, camps, health, pregnancy, infancy, parenting.
■ *Depts/columns:* Word lengths vary. The Kids Beat (news), Eat. Learn. Play! (food, facts, and fun), Hands–On (crafts and activities). News and media reviews.
■ *Other:* Activities and games. Submit seasonal material 2 months in advance.

Sample Issue Advertising.
■ "Tiny Dancers," by Kate Laddison. Zumba classes for children.
■ "Endless Summer...Camp," by Paula Routly. Interviews about their camp experiences , paired with offerings of regional camps today.

Rights and Payment One-time and reprint rights. Written material, payment rates vary. Pays 30 days after publication. Provides 1–2 contributor's copies.

Ladies' Home Journal

Meredith Corporation, 375 Lexington Avenue, 9th Floor, New York, NY 10017. www.lhj.com

Deputy Editor: Margot Gilman

This popular consumer magazine is dedicated to American women who want to look good, be healthy, and do well in life. Its goal is to empower women to lead the kind of lives they *want* to have, and so this magazine looks for articles that inspire as well as inform. *Ladies' Home Journal* is a high-profile magazine and accepts only the highest quality writing. ■ **Circulation** 4.1 million ■ **Audience** Women ■ **Frequency** Monthly

Freelance Potential Publishes 25 freelance submissions yearly: 85% written by nonstaff writers; 5% by authors new to the magazine; 1% by previously unpublished writers. Receives 200 queries monthly.

Submissions Query with résumé, outline, and clips or writing samples for nonfiction. Accepts fiction through literary agents only. Accepts hard copy. SASE. Responds in 1–3 months.
■ *Articles:* 1,500–2,000 words. Informational, how-to, profiles, interviews, personal experience. Topics: family issues, parenting, social concerns, fashion, beauty, women's health, marriage, relationships, healthy lifestyles, fitness, home decor.
■ *Depts/columns:* Word lengths vary. Motherhood, marriage, self-help, beauty, home, health, food, news, lifestyle features.
■ *Fiction:* Word lengths vary. Genres vary.

Sample Issue Advertising. Sample copy available.
■ "Ree Drumond: The Pioneer Woman Tells All," by Ree Drummond. A modern "pioneer woman" describes how she went from city girl to country wife.

- "Cheap Summer Fun for the Whole Family," by Lambeth Hochwald. Twenty-four mom–tested ways to have fun and save money too.

Rights and Payment All rights. All material, payment rates vary. Pays on publication. Provides 2 contributor's copies.

Lake/Geauga Family

TNT Publications, 11630 Chillicothe Road, Chesterland, OH 44026. www.neohiofamily.com

Editor: Terri Nighswonger

Helping parents of tots to teens, this publication provides valuable parenting and child development information alongside regional guides for recreational activities. ■ **Circulation** 75,000 ■ **Audience** Parents ■ **Frequency** Monthly

Freelance Potential Publishes 40–50 freelance submissions yearly: 50% written by nonstaff writers; 33% by authors new to the magazine. Receives 500 queries monthly.

Submissions Guidelines available. Theme list available at website. Query with clips. Accepts email queries to editor@tntpublications.com. Responds if interested.
- *Articles:* 500+ words. Informational, how–to. Topics: parenting, child development, health and fitness, regional activities, travel, birthday parties, summer camps.
- *Depts/columns:* Word lengths vary.
- *Artwork:* High-resolution JPEG and TIFF images.

Sample Issue Advertising. Sample copy available at website.
- "Get in the Get–Fit Games," by Matthew Rusnak. Reviews video games that get kids moving.
- "Behind the Shot," by Dr. Arthur Lavin. A look at the pros and cons of vaccines and the controversy surrounding them.

Rights and Payment Exclusive rights. All material, payment rates vary. Provides 1 contributor's copy. Pays on publication.

L.A. Parent

443 East Irving Drive, Burbank, CA 91504. www.losangeles.parenthood.com

Editor: Carolyn Graham

This regional parenting magazine is dedicated to all aspects of raising children in the Los Angeles area. While it will work with authors who do not live in the area, all material must have a local angle or perspective and include information that readers can use in their own communities. Regional resources should be highlighted whenever possible. ■ **Circulation** 120,000 ■ **Audience** Parents ■ **Frequency** Monthly

Freelance Potential Publishes 20 freelance submissions yearly: 50% written by nonstaff writers; 10% by authors new to the magazine; 5% by previously unpublished writers. Receives 10 queries monthly.

Submissions Query with clips. Prefers email queries to carolyn.graham@parenthood.com; will accept hard copy. SASE. Responds in 6 months.
- *Articles:* 400–1,500 words. Informational, practical application, how-to, profiles, interviews. Topics: parenting, health, fitness, social issues, regional activities, travel, gifted and special education.
- *Depts/columns:* 1,000 words. Family life, technology, travel destinations, crafts.
- *Artwork:* B/W or color prints or transparencies.

Sample Issue Advertising. Sample copy available.
- "Should Your Kids Play the Ocarina," by Christina Elston. How to get children interested in learning to play an instrument.

- "Why Girls Need Sports," by Hannah Storm. The benefits of playing sports for girls and how to get them involved.

Rights and Payment First serial rights. Written material, payment rates vary. Pays on publication. Provides contributor's copies.

Lexington Family

138 East Reynolds Road, Suite 201, Lexington, KY 40517. www.lexingtonfamily.com

Editor: John Lynch

Useful information, sound advice, and a parent perspective are the trademarks of this publication. The focus must be local. ■ **Circulation** 30,000 ■ **Audience** Parents ■ **Frequency** Monthly

Freelance Potential Publishes 36 freelance submissions yearly: 50% written by nonstaff writers; 40% by authors new to the magazine. Receives 20 unsolicited manuscripts monthly.

Submissions Guidelines and theme list available. Query or send complete manuscript. Accepts hard copy and email to info@lexingtonfamily.com. SASE. Response time varies.
- *Articles:* 500–1,500 words. Informational, how-to. Topics: parenting, the arts, hobbies, current events, education, health, fitness, recreation, regional history, multicultural issues, popular culture, science, technology, family travel, women's issues.
- *Depts/columns:* 800 words. News briefs, family health tips.
- *Artwork:* B/W and color prints. Line art.
- *Other:* Poetry, puzzles, activities.

Sample Issue 32 pages. Advertising. Sample copy available.
- "The Truth about Food Allergies," by Zac Betts. How to recognize and treat food allergies.
- "Serving the Disadvantaged at DeLima Stables," by Laurie Evans. A local stable offers a free horseback riding camp to children of low income families in Mercer County, Kentucky.

Rights and Payment All rights. Written material, payment rates vary. Pays on publication. Provides 2 contributor's copies.

Literary Mama

1416 11th Avenue, San Francisco, CA 94122. www.literarymama.com

Editor in Chief: Caroline Grant

Fiction, poetry, and creative nonfiction written by moms and reflecting the many facets of motherhood appear in this ezine. It seeks submissions from self–identified mothers of all ages and types including biological, non–biological, step, transgendered, foster, grand, or adoptive. Book reviews are also published. ■ **Hits per month** 55,000 ■ **Audience** Mothers ■ **Frequency** Monthly

Freelance Potential Publishes 150 freelance submissions yearly: 80% written by nonstaff writers; 50% by authors new to the magazine; 15% by previously unpublished writers. Receives about 10 queries, 200 unsolicited manuscripts monthly.

Submissions Guidelines available at website. Query for profiles, reviews, op-ed, and columns. Send complete manuscript for all other work. Accepts email submissions only; see website for appropriate editor, email address, and specific requirements. Also considers reprints. Responds in 1–4 months.
- *Articles:* To 6,000 words. Creative nonfiction, literary reflections, profiles, interviews. Topics: various aspects of mothering or motherhood.
- *Fiction:* To 6,000 words.
- *Depts/columns:* 1,000–6,000 words. Book reviews, columns, op–ed. Mothering and motherhood.
- *Other:* Poetry. No line limit. Any form.

Sample Issue Sample copy available at website.

- "The Garden Party," by Marcelle Soviero. A mom's memory of the first birthday her daughter celebrated after her dad moved out.
- "No Thank You," by Jennifer Itell. Fiction about the desire to be more than ordinary.

Rights and Payment Non-exclusive rights. No payment.

Little Bit

Dooby Design Group, 124 Pearl Street, Suite 503, Ypsilanti, MI 48197. www.littlebitmag.com

Founder: Aisha Holly

Little Bit is a digital magazine that covers design trends and ideas for children's spaces, children's parties, and related activities. It was founded in 2011, and seeks "real moms with an eye for all things beautiful." The emphasis here is on chic, savvy, and stylish design or products for children up to age 16. It accepts trend pieces, details of completed projects, and do-it-yourself ideas that mothers can replicate at home. ■ **Hits per month** Unavailable ■ **Audience** Parents ■ **Frequency** 6 times a year

Freelance Potential Seeks "real moms with an eye for all things beautiful" to submit design concepts and products.

Submissions Guidelines available at website. Query with description of project, artwork, and all vendors and clients involved. Accept email to contribute@littlebitmag.com (attach low-resolution images). Response time varies.

- *Articles:* Word lengths vary. Informational, how-to. Topics: children's room designs, cake designs, baby shower/birthday parties, children's fashions, table design.
- *Artwork:* Digital images.

Sample Issue Sample copy available at website.

- "Karen and Dejuan." Spotlights a high-end, "Baby Wears Prada" themed baby shower.
- "Sugar + Spice." Chronicles how a design team and event planner created a child's first birthday party that delighted the stylish adults as well as the kids.

Rights and Payment Unavailable.

Little Rock Family

122 East Second Street, Little Rock, AR 72201. www.littlerockfamily.com

Submissions Editor: Jennifer Pyron

Little Rock Family is written for busy parents in need of timely local information for their families. Distributed throughout Arkansas's capital region, it not only features a comprehensive calendar of events but also articles that cover important parenting issues. Writers should have a strong knowledge of the region and articles should have a Little Rock focus. ■ **Circulation** 20,000 ■ **Audience** Parents ■ **Frequency** Monthly

Freelance Potential Publishes few freelance submissions yearly: 1% written by nonstaff writers.

Submissions Query. Accepts hard copy. SASE. Response time varies.

- *Articles:* Word lengths vary. Informational, how–to. Topics: health, religion, education, special needs, recreational activities, the arts, sports, outdoors, dining, seasonal.
- *Depts/columns:* Word lengths vary.

Sample Issue Advertising.

- "The Truth about Tattling," by Abby Hartz. Sifting through tattlers' tales and how to teach children better ways of communicating.

- "Over the River and Through the Woods," by Kelcie Huffstickler. Surefire ways to make family road trips go smoothly.

Rights and Payment First rights. Payment rates vary. Payment policy varies.

Living with Teenagers

One LifeWay Plaza, Nashville, TN 37234-0174. www.lifeway.com/magazines

Editor: Bob Bunn

This parenting magazine is designed to give Christian parents of teenagers the information and inspiration they need to raise children who are close to God and who proudly proclaim their faith
■ **Circulation** 35,000 ■ **Audience** Parents ■ **Frequency** Monthly

Freelance Potential Publishes several freelance submissions yearly: 90% written by nonstaff writers.

Submissions All material written on assignment. Send résumé and writing samples to be considered. Accepts hard copy. SASE. Responds if interested.
■ *Articles:* 600–1,200 words. Informational, how–to. Topics: the Bible, family, parenting, youth culture.
■ *Depts/columns:* Word lengths vary.

Sample Issue Sample copy available at website.
■ "Reel Life Concerns," by Drew Dyck. Discerning appropriate movies for teens.
■ "Snapshots," by Robert Smith. A round-up of media news that relates to teenagers.

Rights and Payment All rights with nonexclusive license to the writer. Articles, $100–$300. Pays on acceptance. Provides 3 contributor's copies.

Long Island Parent

152 West 19th Street, Huntington Station, NY 11746. www.liparentonline.com

Editor: Liza Burby

Published for, by, and about Long Island moms and dads, this publication provides valuable information and expert advice for raising children from birth through age 16. Regional issues as well as topics of general interest to parents are covered. ■ **Circulation** 55,000 ■ **Audience** Parents ■ **Frequency** 6 times a year

Freelance Potential Publishes 20 freelance submissions yearly: 25–30% written by nonstaff writers; 30% by authors new to the magazine.

Submissions Guidelines available. Query or send complete manuscript. Accepts hard copy and email submissions to editor@liparentonline.com. SASE. Responds in 2–4 months.
■ *Articles:* Word lengths vary. Informational, how–to. Topics: education, travel, health and fitness, family recreation, regional news and activities.
■ *Depts/columns:* Word lengths vary.

Sample Issue Advertising. Sample copy available.
■ "A Plan for Bringing Baby Home," by Joan Swirsky. Planning ahead practically and emotionally for a new baby to enter your home and your life.
■ "Tempering Those Tantrums," by Dianne Galante. Tips for dealing with toddler temper tantrums.

Rights and Payment First rights. Written material, payment rates vary. Pays on publication. Provides 2 contributor's copies.

Long Island Woman

P.O. Box 176, Malverne, NY 11565. www.liwomanonline.com

Managing Editor: Arie Nadboy

With a readership consisting of upscale, educated women, this regional magazine features general interest articles on topics of interest to its audience. It also spotlights local entertainment venues, and provides a comprehensive list of area support groups. It seeks submissions on any topic that would be of interest to women age 35 and over, with a local focus. ■ **Circulation** 40,000 ■ **Audience** Women ■ **Frequency** Monthly

Freelance Potential Publishes 25 freelance submissions yearly: 50% written by nonstaff writers. Receives about 40 queries, 30 unsolicited manuscripts monthly.

Submissions Query or send complete manuscript with suggested headlines and subheads. Accepts email submissions only to editor@liwomanonline.com. Availability of artwork improves chance of acceptance. Responds in 8–10 weeks.
■ *Articles:* 350–2,000 words. Informational, how-to, profiles, interviews. Topics: regional news, family, health, lifestyles, sports, fitness, nutrition, fashion, beauty, business, finance, decorating, gardening, entertainment, media, travel, celebrities.
■ *Depts/columns:* 500–1,000 words. Book reviews, health advice, personal essays, profiles.
■ *Artwork:* Electronic B/W and color prints. Line art.
■ *Other:* Submit seasonal material 3 months in advance.

Sample Issue Advertising. Sample copy available.
■ "Jodi Picoult: Family Values," by Debbi Honorof. Interview with author Jodi Picoult, a Long Island native.
■ "Midlife, No Crisis for Today's Women," by Judith Reichman. How today's women get more out of life in middle-age years.

Rights and Payment One-time and electronic rights. Written material, $70–$200. Kill fee, 20%. Pays on publication. Provides 1 tearsheet.

Lowcountry Parent

134 Columbus Street, Charleston, SC 29403. www.lowcountryparent.com

Submissions Editor: Shannon Brigham

Families living in Charleston, South Carolina, and the surrounding area read this magazine. Each issue features articles of regional interest, and also covers topics of general interest to parents. Profiles of local personalities are also published. It is only interested in receiving submissions from local writers. ■ **Circulation** 42,000 ■ **Audience** Parents ■ **Frequency** Monthly

Freelance Potential Publishes few freelance submissions yearly: 10% by authors new to the magazine. Receives 8–10 queries monthly.

Submissions Send résumé. Accepts email to editor@lowcountryparent.com. Responds if interested.
■ *Articles:* Word lengths vary. Informational, how-to, profiles. Topics: parenting, family travel and recreation, education, health and safety, personal finance.
■ *Depts/columns:* Word lengths vary.

Sample Issue Advertising. Sample copy available at website.
■ "If You Don't Smile, I'm Gonna..." by Angie Mizzell. A humorous look at supposedly "picture perfect" moments of family life.
■ "Men Who Cook," by Ryan Nelson. Profiles of area restaurant chefs who are also dads.

Rights and Payment One-time rights. Written material, $15–$100. Pays on publication. Provides 3 contributor's copies.

Mahoning Valley Parent

100 DeBartolo Place, Suite 210, Youngstown, OH 44512. www.forparentsonline.com

Editor & Publisher: Amy Leigh Wilson

Parents in Ohio's Mahoning Valley turn to this magazine for the latest information on where to go and what to do in the area, as well as topics of general interest to families. Articles should feature local sources, local information, and local resources. ■ **Circulation** 50,000 ■ **Audience** Parents ■ **Frequency** Monthly

Freelance Potential Publishes 100 freelance submissions yearly: 99% written by nonstaff writers; 20% by authors new to the magazine; 5% by previously unpublished writers. Receives about 40 unsolicited manuscripts monthly.

Submissions Send complete manuscript. Accepts hard copy and email to editor@mvparent-magazine.com. Retains all material for possible use; does not respond until publication. Include SASE if retaining manuscript is not acceptable.
- ■ *Articles:* 1,000–1,800 words. Informational, how-to, profiles, reviews. Topics: parenting, child development, education, family relationships, regional news, current events, the environment, nature, health, crafts, travel, recreation, hobbies, ethnic and multicultural subjects.
- ■ *Depts/columns:* Word lengths vary. Parenting issues, book reviews, events for kids.
- ■ *Artwork:* B/W or color prints.
- ■ *Other:* Submit seasonal material 3 months in advance.

Sample Issue Advertising. Sample copy available.
- ■ "The New Parent Trap," by Heidi Smith Luedtke. Dealing with the ambiguous feelings and needs of being a new parent.
- ■ "Often Overlooked Safety Traps Put Children at Risk," by Melissa Kay. Surprising home safety dangers for children.

Rights and Payment One-time rights. Articles, $20–$50. Pays on publication. Provides tearsheets.

Maryland Family

Baltimore Sun Company, 501 North Calvert Street, Third Floor, Baltimore, MD 21202. www.marylandfamilymagazine.com

Editor: Betsy Stein

Updates on regional family events, news of interest to parents, and substantive articles on child health, behavior, and learning appear in this free publication. It targets families living in and around Baltimore and looks for useful information for busy parents. Articles that have a local angle and are written by freelancers from the Baltimore area have a better chance of being accepted. ■ **Circulation** 50,000 ■ **Audience** Parents ■ **Frequency** Monthly

Freelance Potential Publishes 50 freelance submissions yearly: 75% written by nonstaff writers; 10% by authors new to the magazine; 10% by previously unpublished writers. Receives 30–50 queries monthly.

Submissions Query stating areas of expertise. Accepts hard copy. SASE. Responds in 1 month.
- ■ *Articles:* 800–1,000 words. Informational, how-to, profiles, personal experience. Topics: family issues, parenting, education, recreation, travel, summer camp, sports, health.
- ■ *Depts/columns:* Word lengths vary. News briefs, local events, health tips. Family Matters, 100–400 words.
- ■ *Artwork:* Color prints and transparencies.
- ■ *Other:* Submit seasonal material 2–3 months in advance.

Sample Issue Advertising. Sample copy available.
- ■ "Recess and Results." Fitness initiatives that are fun and yield results for kids.

- "Revolve Tour to Inspire Young Girls." Christian bands and inspirational speakers are offered as part of an inspirational weekend for young women.

Rights and Payment First and electronic rights. Written material, payment rates vary. Pays on publication. Provides 1 contributor's copy.

MASK

8937 East Bell Road, Suite 202, Scottsdale, AZ 85260. www.maskmatters.org

Editor in Chief: Michelle Jacoby

MASK is the publication of the nonprofit organization Mothers Awareness on School-age Kids, founded by mothers concerned with the exposure of school-aged children to social, sexual, and substance abuse issues. Articles, many written by experts in the field, provide awareness of issues, prevention tactics, and conversation starters for families. ■ **Circulation** 20,000 ■ **Audience** Parents ■ **Frequency** Quarterly

Freelance Potential 35% of content written by nonstaff writers.

Submissions Send complete manuscript. Accepts email to info@maskmatters.org.
- *Articles:* Word lengths vary. Informational, personal experience, how-to. Topics: substance abuse, parenting, education, self-esteem, bullying, health and fitness, family relationships.

Sample Issue Sample copy available at website.
- "Synthetic Evolution 'Designer Drugs' Quickly Becoming the New Norm for High School Students," by Preslie Hirsch & Sarah Dinnel. An explanation of the newest drugs making the scene at schools.
- "Cyberbullying: A Victim Tells His Story," by Alex Clearwater. A student's experience with cyberbullying, and the effects it had on him.

Rights and Payment First rights. No payment; writers get a short biography at end.

MetroFamily

725 Northwest 11th Street, Suite 204, Oklahoma City, OK 73103. www.metrofamilymagazine.com

Editor: Mari Farthing

A parenting magazine for residents of central Oklahoma, *MetroFamily* features articles that inform and empower families. Its goal is to educate, inspire, and uplift its readers. This publication prefers to work with writers from the region, and all articles must have a local perspective. It does not shy away from humor, so writers should feel free to brighten their submissions with levity.■ **Circulation** 35,000 ■ **Audience** Parents ■ **Frequency** Monthly

Freelance Potential Publishes 45 freelance submissions yearly: 60% written by nonstaff writers; 10% by authors new to the magazine; 10% by previously unpublished writers. Receives over 80 queries and unsolicited manuscripts monthly.

Submissions Guidelines available at website. Query or send complete manuscript. Considers reprints. Accepts email to editor@metrofamilymagazine.com (no attachments). May not respond if not interested. Queries sent via standard mail are not considered.
- *Articles:* 300–600 words. Informational, how-to, profiles, personal experience. Topics: parenting, education, health and fitness, child development, family relationships, travel, recreational activities.
- *Depts/columns:* Staff-written.

Sample Issue Advertising. Sample copy available at website.
- "Food Fight in the Public Schools," by Julie Dill. Describes changes the local school districts are making to their cafeteria food and lunch offerings.
- "Exploring Oklahoma: The Chicksaw Cultural Center," by Kevin Mitchell. What visitors will find at this area attraction.

Rights and Payment First North American serial rights. Articles, $25–$50. Pays on publication. Provides 1 contributor's copy.

MetroKids

412-1414 Pine Street, Philadelphia, PA 19102. www.metrokids.com

Executive Editor: Tom Livingston

The articles in *MetroKids* offer readers a fresh approach to common parenting issues. It provides parenting resources, tips, and ideas tailored to parents in the greater Philadelphia region. It prefers articles with a local angle. General topics will be considered, however, especially if they can be localized with sidebars. ■ **Circulation** 115,000 ■ **Audience** Parents ■ **Frequency** Monthly

Freelance Potential Publishes 12–100 freelance submissions yearly: 25–50% developed from unsolicited submissions; 25–50% written by nonstaff writers; 10–25% by authors new to the magazine; 1–10% by previously unpublished writers. Receives 50–75 queries, 50–75 unsolicited manuscripts monthly.

Submissions Guidelines available. Query or send complete manuscript with cover letter. Accepts email submissions only to editor@metrokids.com (Word or plain text attachments). Accepts simultaneous submissions. Also considers reprints and résumés for work-for-hire. Availability of artwork improves chance of acceptance. Responds if interested.
■ *Articles:* 450–900 words. Informational, how-to, self-help, personal experience. Topics: pregnancy, childbirth, parenting, pets, computers, education, health, fitness, beauty, careers, finances, birthday parties, summer camps, special needs, nature, the environment, travel, recreation, social issues.
■ *Depts/columns:* 550–700 words. School news, product recalls, health notes, opinions, book reviews, nature activities, special education information, local events.
■ *Artwork:* Color prints or transparencies; 300 dpi or greater.

Sample Issue 52 pages. Advertising. Sample copy available.
■ "For Divorced and Separated Parents, A Plan Can Foster Cooperation," by Suzanne Koup–Larsen. Tips for divorced parents on creating a parenting plan that works for their children.
■ "Diet and Sleep: They're Connected," by Lori Samlin Miller. The effects of food on sleep quality.

Rights and Payment One-time and electronic rights. Written material, $35 for reprints; $50 for original articles. Artwork, payment rates vary. Pays on publication. Provides 1 contributor's copy.

Metro Parent (MI)

22041 Woodward Avenue, Ferndale, MI 48220–2520. www.metroparent.com

Executive Editor: Julia Elliott

Metro Parent Magazine and *MetroParent.com* mix ideas for family fun with more serious, substantive pieces on child development, health, education, and family management. Parents can pick up the print edition free of charge at various sites throughout Detroit and southeast Michigan. It looks for writing that reflects the communities it covers; southeast Michigan topics and sources are preferred. ■ **Circulation** 80,000 ■ **Audience** Parents ■ **Frequency** Monthly

Freelance Potential Publishes 250 freelance submissions yearly: 75% written by nonstaff writers; 35% by authors new to the magazine; 5% by previously unpublished writers. Receives 80+ queries and unsolicited manuscripts monthly.

Submissions Guidelines available at website. Query, or send complete manuscript or previously published articles for reprint. Accepts email submissions to jelliott@metroparent.com. Accepts simultaneous submissions. Responds in 1 month, if interested.
■ *Articles:* 1,500–2,500 words. Informational, self-help, how-to, interviews, personal experience. Topics: pregnancy, childbirth, parenting, family life, education, child development, social issues,

travel, finance, fitness, health, recreation, entertainment, nature.
- *Depts/columns:* 600–700 words. Along the Way (personal essays), Family Health, Little Ones, Big Kids, Tweens & Teens, Family Finance, Little Lessons (how–to column for teaching kids simple skills), Shop Around the Corner (local business profiles), Let's Go! (travel), Family Fun, new product information, women's health, media reviews, computers, crafts.

Sample Issue 68 pages. Advertising. Sample copy available at website.
- "10 Reasons to Send Your Child to Camp," by Diana Christensen. The many benefits of a camp experience and a round-up of some of the many Michigan camp choices.
- "Equal Parenting," by Kristen J. Gough. Finding ways to balance parenting tasks and responsibilities.

Rights and Payment First rights and electronic rights. Articles, $100–$250. Depts/columns, $35–$75. Reprints, $35. Pays on publication. Provides 1 contributor's copy.

Metro Parent (OR)

P.O. Box 13660, Portland, OR 97213-0660. www.metro-parent.com

Editor: Marie Sherlock

Parents living in Oregon's Portland area find practical information on parenting in each issue of *Metro Parent*. It also features a local event calendar and regional news. Preference is given to writers living in the region. ■ **Circulation** 45,000 ■ **Audience** Parents ■ **Frequency** Monthly

Freelance Potential Publishes 50 freelance submissions yearly: 75% written by nonstaff writers; 20% by previously unpublished writers. Receives 20 queries monthly.

Submissions Query with outline. Accepts hard copy and email to editor@metro-parent.com. Accepts simultaneous submissions if identified. SASE. Responds in 1 month.
- *Articles:* Word lengths vary. Informational, how–to. Topics: education, travel, recreation, health, child development.
- *Depts/columns:* Word lengths vary.

Sample Issue Advertising. Sample copy available.
- "Mother Nature's Child," by Sue Campbell. Green options for pregnancy and birth.
- "What's Normal for New Moms?" by Teresa Carson. Helpful information and common physical issues associated with birth recovery.

Rights and Payment Rights vary. Written material, payment rates vary. Pays on publication.

Metro Spirit

700 Broad Street, Augusta, GA 30901. www.metrospirit.com

Editor: Stacey Eidson

Subtitled "Augusta's Independent Voice," *Metro Spirit* targets parents living in and around this Georgia city. Each issue features comprehensive coverage of local recreational activities and educational programs, along with parenting advice. ■ **Circulation** Unavailable ■ **Audience** Parents ■ **Frequency** Monthly

Freelance Potential Publishes 50 freelance submissions yearly: 80% written by nonstaff writers; 5% by authors new to the magazine; 5% by previously unpublished writers. Receives 20 queries monthly.

Submissions Guidelines available. Query. Accepts hard copy and email queries to spirit@metrospirit.com. SASE. Response time varies.
- *Articles:* Word lengths vary. Informational, how–to, profiles. Topics: parenting, child development, social issues, the arts, local news, current events, entertainment, people, places, events.
- *Depts/columns:* Word lengths vary.

Sample Issue Advertising. Sample copy available.
- "Breaking the Cycle," by Judy S. Freedman, L.C.S.W. Changing attitudes about bullying and violence.
- "About Attitudes and Actions," by James A. Perkins. Preparing parents for the tween and teen years.

Rights and Payment First rights. Written material, payment rates vary. Payment policy varies. Provides 1 contributor's copy.

Miami Family Magazine

7045 SW 69 Avenue, South Miami, FL 33143. http://familymagazine.biz

Publisher: Janet Jupiter

This magazine provides parents with the information they need to happily raise children in Florida's Miami, Fort Lauderdale, and Boca Raton regions. Local angles and personalities are always preferred.
■ **Circulation** Unavailable ■ **Audience** Parents ■ **Frequency** Monthly

Freelance Potential Publishes 15–20 freelance submissions yearly: 30% written by nonstaff writers.

Submissions Editorial calendar available at website. Query. Accepts hard copy and email queries to familymag@bellsouth.net. SASE. Response time varies.
- *Articles:* Word lengths vary. Informational, how–to. Topics: education, health, nutrition, home improvement, travel, camps, party planning, cooking, outdoor activities, regional activities.
- *Depts/columns:* Word lengths vary. Local events calendar, book and movie reviews.

Sample Issue Advertising. Sample copy available at website.
- "Going Green on Your Next Remodel? Sustainable home remodeling products.
- "To Change or Not to Change," by Julie Casey. Opinion piece on restaurants and changing tables.

Rights and Payment One-time rights. Written material, payment rates vary. Pays on publication. Provides contributor's copies.

Minnesota Parent

Minnesota Premier Publications, 1115 Hennepin Avenue South, Minneapolis, MN 55403. www.mnparent.com

Editor: Kathleen Stoehr

The articles in *Minnesota Parent* highlight the rewarding, exciting, hectic, and fun times parents have while raising their children. It only considers submissions with local angles. ■ **Circulation** 52,500
■ **Audience** Parents ■ **Frequency** Monthly

Freelance Potential Publishes 24 freelance submissions yearly.

Submissions Query. Accepts email queries to kstoehr@mnpubs.com. Response time varies.
- *Articles:* Word lengths vary. Informational, how–to, interviews, profiles. Topics: education, social issues, parenting, child development, family finances, regional activities.
- *Depts/columns:* Word lengths vary. Book, toy, and movie reviews.

Sample Issue Advertising.
- "The Sporting Life," by Kelly Jo McDonnell. The cost and commitment of childhoods sports.
- "Grows on Trees," by Kara McGuire. An online tool to help kids track and budget their allowances.

Rights and Payment First serial and electronic rights. Written material, $50–$350. Pays on publication. Provides 2 contributor's copies.

Mirror Moms

301 Cayuga Avenue, Altoona, PA 16602. www.mirrormoms.com

Editor: Barbara Cowan

Appearing as print publication with an online presence, *Mirror Moms* is published by the *Altoona Mirror* daily newspaper. It is filled with news, features, and advice relevant to parents in central Pennsylvania, including family issues, education, and children's health and safety. Local authors, and local sources, are preferred. *Mirror Moms* was launched in 2010. ■ **Circulation** *Altoona Mirror,* 30,000 ■ **Audience** Parents ■ **Frequency** Quarterly

Freelance Potential Website provides additional writing opportunities and is host to blogs about the parenting experience

Submissions Contact bcowan@altoonamirror.com for more information.
■ *Articles:* Word lengths vary. Informational, opinion, personal experience, profiles. Topics: parenting, family life, safety, health, education, news relevant to local young people.

Sample Issue
■ "Home School," by Kristy MacKaben. Profile of a mother who decided to homeschool her children, and how parents can incorporate unconventional learning methods into their kids' day.
■ "Hold All Calls," by Kristy MacKaben. The pros and cons to working from home, juggling child care.

Rights and Payment Unavailable.

Mobile Bay Parents

Watson Media, 555 Farmington Road, Montgomery, AL 36109. www.mobilebayparents.com

Publisher & Editor in Chief: Lynn Knighton

This magazine for parents along Alabama's Gulf Coast launched in 2011. It features parenting information, local resources for family entertainment, and guides for camps, after-school activities, and summer fun. The editorial is a mix of child development advice from local experts and practical tips for busy families. ■ **Circulation** 25,000 ■ **Audience** Mothers ■ **Frequency** Monthly

Freelance Potential Unavailable.

Submissions For information on freelancing opportunities, or to pitch a story idea, email info@ mobilebayparents.com.
■ *Articles:* Word lengths vary. Informational, profiles, personal experience, how-to. Topics: parenting issues, education, child development.
■ *Depts/columns:* Word lengths vary. Children's Health, Living With Children, Krafts for Kids, Parent of the Month.

Sample Issue Sample articles are available to view at website.
■ "Tips To Raising an Independent Child," by Julia Garstecki. Teaching a child to rely on Mom less.
■ "Transitioning to Middle School," by Susan McConnell. The physical, social, and intellectual changes of middle school.

Rights and Payment Unavailable.

MOM Magazine

2532 Santiam Highway SE, #102, Albany, OR 97322. www.mommag.com

Editor: Krista Klinkhammer

This magazine is written for mothers with children under the age of 12. It welcomes articles on parenting issues and family recreation, as well as personal experience pieces that share the joy, challenges, and sometimes sadness of motherhood. ■ **Circulation** 60,000 ■ **Audience** Mothers ■ **Frequency** 6 times a year

Freelance Potential Publishes 50 freelance submissions yearly: 5% written by nonstaff writers; 50% by authors new to the magazine; 50% by previously unpublished writers. Receives about 42 queries, 12 manuscripts monthly.

Submissions Query or send complete manuscript. Accepts email to editor@mommag.com (Word attachments). Also accepts reprints. Availability of artwork improves chance of acceptance. Response time varies.
■ *Articles:* To 500 words. Informational, how–to, personal experience. Topics: parenting, child development, recreation, education, health, fitness.
■ *Depts/columns:* Word lengths vary.
■ *Artwork:* 5x7 JPEG or TIFF images at 300 dpi.

Sample Issue Advertising.
■ "Making Music Together." Tips for cultivating a love of music in young children.
■ "The HPV Vaccine: Can It Protect Your Children?" by Kay Yanit, RN, BSH, CLNC. What is currently known about the HPV vaccine and why it's important to protect women from this virus.

Rights and Payment One–time or reprint rights. No payment.

MOMSense

2370 South Trenton Way, Denver, CO 80231-3822. www.mops.org

Editor: Mary Darr

Filled with equal parts information, inspiration, and support for mothers of preschool children, *MOMSense* is a parenting magazine with a Christian perspective. It is published by Mothers of Preschoolers, and is always interested in articles that suggest ways in which mothers can help other mothers. While the articles are Christian based, they should not preachy in style or tone.
■ **Circulation** 120,000 ■ **Audience** Mothers ■ **Frequency** 6 times a year

Freelance Potential Publishes 45–50 freelance submissions yearly: 70% written by nonstaff writers; 20% by authors new to the magazine; 20% by previously unpublished writers. Receives 30–40 unsolicited manuscripts monthly.

Submissions Guidelines and editorial theme list available at website. Send complete manuscript with word count and author biography. Prefers email submissions to MOMSense@mops.org (Word attachments); will accept hard copy. Availability of artwork improves chance of acceptance. SASE. Responds in 3 months.
■ *Articles:* 450 words. Informational, how–to, profiles, personal experience. Topics: parenting, religion, humor.
■ *Depts/columns:* Word lengths vary. Parenting and family life.
■ *Artwork:* B/W or color prints or transparencies.
■ *Other:* Submit seasonal material 6–12 months in advance.

Sample Issue 32 pages. Advertising. Sample copy available at website.
■ "Mom, You're the Expert," by Alexandra Kuykendall. Where to find answers to mothering questions.
■ "Quiz: Mom Artist or Mom Scientist?" by Shelly Radic. Analytical and creative parenting approaches.

Rights and Payment First and electronic rights. Written material, 15¢–25¢ a word. Payment policy varies. Provides contributor's copies.

Nashville Parent

2270 Rosa L. Parks Boulevard, Nashville, TN 37228. www.nashvilleparent.com

Editor in Chief: Susan Day

This regional magazine covers topics of interest to parents of infants through teens, living in Nashville and its environs. *Nashville Parent*'s focus is always on the region. It welcomes submissions from local writers or writers who know Nashville well. Articles should be lively as well as informative.
■ **Circulation** 85,000 ■ **Audience** Parents ■ **Frequency** Monthly

Freelance Potential Publishes 400 freelance submissions yearly: 15–20% written by nonstaff writers; 40% by authors new to the magazine. Receives 100 unsolicited manuscripts monthly.

Submissions Guidelines available at website. Send complete manuscript. Accepts hard copy and Macintosh disk submissions with hard copy. Availability of artwork improves chance of acceptance. SASE. Response time varies.
■ *Articles:* 800–1,000 words. Informational, how-to, profiles, interviews, photo-essays, personal experience. Topics: parenting, family life, current events, social issues, health and fitness, music, travel, recreation, religion, the arts, crafts, computers, multicultural and ethnic issues.
■ *Depts/columns:* Staff-written.
■ *Artwork:* B/W and color prints.
■ *Other:* Submit Christmas, Easter, and Halloween material 2 months in advance.

Sample Issue Advertising. Sample copy available at website.
■ "Back to School Jitters," by Maila Jacobson. Smooth transitions from summer to school days.
■ "On Solid Ground," by Susan Day. Getting infants started on solid foods in a healthful way.

Rights and Payment One-time rights. Written material, $35. Pays on publication. Provides 3 contributor's copies.

Native Magazine

1150 Hungryneck Boulevard, Suite C-351, Mt. Pleasant, SC 29464. www.thenativelife.com

Publisher & Editor in Chief: Deona Smith

This regional lifestyle, culture, and arts magazine made its debut in 2011. Written for residents of and people interested in the Lowcountry of South Carolina, *Native Magazine* also includes some coverage of parenting issues and family relationships. ■ **Circulation** 30,000 ■ **Audience** Parents, adults ■ **Frequency** 6 times a year

Freelance Potential Unavailable.

Submissions For more information, email contact@thenativelife.com.
■ *Articles:* Word lengths vary. Informational, profiles, interviews, personal experience. Topics: culture, travel, cuisine, business, careers, the arts, health, parenting, education, style.

Sample Issue 34 pages. Advertising. Sample copy available at website.
■ "Kid in Development Services," by Kristen Gehrman. Profile of a program that helps families with children with disabilities.
■ "Toddlers Have a Way with Words," by Kristen Wright-Matthews. Personal experience about teaching a child language that increases the potential for learning.

Rights and Payment Unavailable.

Natural Child Magazine

Life Media, B2-125 The Queensway, Suite 52, Toronto, Ontario M8Y 1H6, Canada.
www.naturalchildmagazine.com

Editor: Wendy Priesnitz

This subscription-based digital magazine is a spinoff from *Natural Life* magazine's popular The Natural Child column, which began in 1992. With a focus on green family living, its articles cover subjects such as natural lifestyles, healthy pregnancy, homebirth, co-sleeping, organic eating, natural childhood remedies, and the environment. It enjoys a readership from around the globe. The tone is positive, but not preachy. ■ **Hits per month** Unavailable ■ **Audience** Parents ■ **Frequency** 6 times a year

Freelance Potential Unavailable.

Submissions Guidelines available at website. Query with outline, author biography, and experience with the topic and writing. Accepts email to nceditor@lifemedia.ca. Accepts simultaneous submissions if identified.
■ *Articles:* Word lengths vary. Informational, how-to, personal experience. Topics: eco-friendly living, natural childbirth, health pregnancy, parenting, organic gardening, peaceful parenting, alternative education, homeopathic medicine, breastfeeding.

Sample Issue Sample copy available at website.
■ "Choosing Toys for Babies," by Elizabeth Panthley. Examines which home-grown and store-bought toys are best for babies.
■ "For the Sake of Our Children," by Léandre Bergeron. Excerpts from a father's journal explaining how he's raising his children with respect and openness—and what he's receiving in return.

Rights and Payment Rights returned to author after publication. No payment; authors are given a link to their blog or website, if applicable.

Natural Life

Life Media, B2-125 The Queensway, Suite 52, Toronto, Ontario M8Y 1H6 Canada.
www.naturallifemagazine.com

Editor: Wendy Priesnitz

This magazine is written for an international audience of families who want progressive information about natural family living. It describes environmentally friendly, sustainable practices and principles while focusing on natural parenting, gardening, and housing. It looks for contributors who can write simply and clearly, in concise, non-academic prose, rather than as professional "experts." The aim is for a style that's friendly, but not folksy. ■ **Circulation** 35,000 ■ **Audience** Parents ■ **Frequency** 6 times a year

Freelance Potential Publishes 40 freelance submissions yearly: 50% written by nonstaff writers; 20–30% by authors new to the magazine; 20% by previously unpublished writers. Receives several queries monthly.

Submissions Guidelines available at website. Query with detailed outline and 50- to 200-word synopsis that highlights the main points of the article, how it will benefit the reader, why it's timely, intended sources, and your qualifications to write it. Accepts hard copy and email to editor@natural-lifemagazine.com. Accepts simultaneous submissions if identified. Responds in 3–5 days to email queries; 2 months for regular mail.
■ *Articles:* 2,500–3,500 words. Informational, how-to, profiles, interviews, personal experience. Topics: green living, eco-travel, natural parenting, unschooling, lifelong learning, self-directed learning, social issues, gardening, education, food and recipes, sustainable housing.
■ *Depts/columns:* Staff-written.
■ *Artwork:* Color prints. High-resolution TIFF images at 300 dpi.

Sample Issue 62 pages. Advertising. Sample copy available.
- "Crafting for a Greener World," by Robyn Coburn. One family's love of crafts and creating with a green theme.
- "Can We Save Money by Going Solar?" Q&A regarding the feasibility of using solar power instead of conventional electricity.

Rights and Payment One-time print and non-exclusive electronic rights. No payment. Provides author's copies.

Natural Solutions

2995 Wilderness Place, Suite 205, Boulder, CO 80301-5408. www.naturalsolutionsmag.com

Editor: Lauren Piscopo

Since 1994, this magazine has presented information to readers who are committed to healthy, natural living. Articles must use authoritative resources and offer readers practical advice. ■ **Circulation** 225,000 ■ **Audience** Parents ■ **Frequency** 10 times a year

Freelance Potential Publishes 40–50 freelance submissions yearly: 95% written by nonstaff writers; 25% by authors new to the magazine. Receives 2–3 queries monthly.

Submissions Guidelines available at website. Query with brief explanation of why your story is a good fit for *Natural Solutions* and 3 published clips. Accepts email queries to editor@ natural-solutionsmag.com. Responds only if interested.
- *Articles:* 1,200–2,000 words. Informational, how–to. Topics: natural beauty, health, herbs, healing foods, natural household products, family, pets, home, natural lifestyle.
- *Depts/columns:* 50–1,200 words. Health Matters & Simple Solutions (news and innovative ideas), Healing Foods (includes recipes), Natural Radiance, Healthy Tonics (alternative therapies), Inner Balance (mind, body, and spirit).

Sample Issue Advertising. Sample copy available.
- "Overcoming Loneliness," by O'rya Hyde–Keller. How loneliness can negatively impact health and some ways to combat it.
- "Hugs, Not Depression Drugs," by Melaina Juntti. For mild to moderate depression, natural remedies like feel–good nutrients and talking with friends are proven more effective than drugs.

Rights and Payment All rights. Written material, payment rates vary. Pays within 45 days of acceptance. Provides 2 contributor's copies.

Neapolitan Family

P.O. Box 110656, Naples, FL 34108. www.neafamily.com

Publisher: Andrea Breznay

With a focus on local events, recreation, and resources, this magazine offers articles on topics of interest to parents in Collier County, Florida. *Neapolitan Family* strives to give its readers information and resources that will enhance all aspects of parenting and family life. ■ **Circulation** 12,000 ■ **Audience** Parents ■ **Frequency** Monthly

Freelance Potential Publishes 40 freelance submissions yearly: 90% written by nonstaff writers; 20% by authors new to the magazine. Receives about 40 unsolicited manuscripts monthly.

Submissions Guidelines and editorial calendar available at website. Send complete manuscript. Prefers email submissions to andrea@neafamily.com/ Accepts hard copy. SASE. Responds in 1 month.
- *Articles:* Word lengths vary. Informational, how–to. Topics: parenting, education, family life, local issues, family-friendly local events, social issues, real-life problems.
- *Depts/columns:* Word lengths vary.

Sample Issue Advertising. Sample copy available.
- "When Is the Best Time to Move Your School Age Child?" by Mara Muller. Surprising information about the best time to make a move to ensure your child makes a smooth transition.
- "Teen Angst," by Christine Holmes. Signs that indicate when teenagers are veering off in the wrong direction and strategies for getting them back on track.

Rights and Payment Rights vary. Written material, payment rates vary. Pays on publication.

New Jersey Family

480 Morris Avenure, Summit, NJ 07091. www.njfamily.com

Editor: Farn Dupre
Managing Editor: Lucy Banta

New Jersey Family is distributed in northern and central New Jersey. Its content has a strong regional focus and preference is given to local writers. This publication strives to help New Jersey parents be the best they can be and to offer a good mix of fun and substantive articles. ■ **Circulation** 130,000 ■ **Audience** Parents ■ **Frequency** Monthly

Freelance Potential Publishes about 120 freelance submissions yearly: 25–50% developed from unsolicited submissions; 75% written by nonstaff writers; 10–25% by authors new to the magazine; 1–10% by previously unpublished writers. Receives 25–50 queries, 25–50 manuscripts monthly.

Submissions Guidelines available at website. Query or send complete manuscript with cover letter and writing samples. Prefers email queries to editor@njfamily.com (no attachments). Accepts simultaneous submissions. Response time varies.
- *Articles:* 600–1,000 words. Informational, how–to. Topics: health and fitness, education trends, culture and the arts, recreation, social skills, social issues, child care, crafts and hobbies, entertainment, parenting, food and recipes, activities.
- *Depts/columns:* Word lengths vary.
- *Other:* Seasonal material must be submitted 4 months in advance.

Sample Issue Advertising.
- "What's Good about Video Games," by Carolyn Jabs, MA. Latest research reveals that there are some educational, social, and emotional benefits from playing video games.
- "NJ Gets Tough On Bullies," by Dr. Kenneth Shore. Describes New Jersey's Anti–Bullying Bill of Rights, which is the strongest anti–bullying legislation in the nation.

Rights and Payment First rights. Written material, payment rates vary. Pays on publication.

New Jersey Suburban Parent

Middlesex Publications, 850 Route 1 North, North Brunswick, NJ 08902. www.njparentweb.com

Editor: Melodie Dhondt

In addition to its guide to fun and educational family activities in the tri–state area, *New Jersey Suburban Parent* provides valuable information on parenting and general topics of interest to families. It is distributed throughout New Jersey. ■ **Circulation** 70,000 ■ **Audience** Parents ■ **Frequency** Monthly

Freelance Potential Publishes 12 freelance submissions yearly: 80% written by nonstaff writers; 40% by authors new to the magazine; 20% by previously unpublished writers. Receives 1 query a month.

Submissions Guidelines and editorial calendar available. Query with writing samples. Accepts hard copy. Accepts simultaneous submissions if identified. SASE. Responds in 1–2 months.
- *Articles:* 700–1,000 words. Informational, how–to. Topics: family health, child care, education, summer camps, the sandwich generation, after–school activities, local news and recreational activities,

home improvement, food and recipes, beauty.
- *Depts/columns:* Word lengths vary.
- *Artwork:* B/W or color prints.

Sample Issue Advertising. Sample copy available.
- "Age–Related Macular Degeneration Takes a Devastating Toll," by Prevent Blindness Tri–State. The financial and emotional impacts of macular degeneration and tips for prevention.
- "Turkey . . . More Than A Holiday Treat," by Susie Napsa. The economic and nutritional benefits of adding turkey to a family's meal plans regularly.

Rights and Payment Rights vary. Written material, $30. Pays on acceptance. Provides 1+ contributor's copies.

New York Family

79 Madison Avenue, 16th Floor, New York, NY 10016. www.newyorkfamily.com

Editor: Eric Messinger

This regional parenting magazine tackles topics of general interest to parents—including articles on child development and educational issues—but prefers articles to be filled with local information and resources. Its readership consists of affluent, sophisticated, active parents. The ideal author for this publication knows and understands the issues related to raising children in the city. ■ **Circulation** 30,000 ■ **Audience** Parents ■ **Frequency** Monthly

Freelance Potential Publishes 40 freelance submissions yearly: 50% written by nonstaff writers; 40% by authors new to the magazine. Receives about 15 queries monthly.

Submissions Guidelines available. Query with clips. Accepts hard copy and email to newyorkfamily@ manhattanmedia.com. SASE. Response time varies.
- *Articles:* 800–1,200 words. Informational, profiles, interviews, photo-essays, personal experience. Topics: education, music, recreation, regional news, social issues, travel, parenting advice and techniques, health, fashion.
- *Depts/columns:* 400–800 words. News and media reviews.

Sample Issue 82 pages. Advertising. Sample copy available.
- "Camera Ready," by Alessandra Hickson. Profile of a unique New York city photo studio for family portraits.
- "Born & Bred." Round-up of entries from the magazine's blog for expectant and new parents.

Rights and Payment First rights. Written material, $25–$300. Pays on publication. Provides 3 contributor's copies.

North State Parent

P.O. Box 1602, Mount Shasta, CA 96067. www.northstateparent.com

Editor: Lisa Shara

North State Parent is a resource for parents, grandparents, and caregivers living in the northern counties of California. It features articles on topics of interest to parents of infants through teens, and includes things to do and see in the region. All material must have a local angle. ■ **Circulation** 17,000 ■ **Audience** Parents and childcare providers ■ **Frequency** Monthly

Freelance Potential Publishes 20 freelance submissions yearly: 90% written by nonstaff writers.

Submissions Guidelines available at website. Query with potential title, premise of article, approach and potential sources; or send manuscript or published article for reprint. Prefers email submissions to editorial@northstateparent.com. with "Reprint," "Query," or "Article" and topic in subject line. Response time varies.

- *Articles:* 700–1,000 words. Informational, how-to. Topics: child development, childhood heath and fitness, family relationships, education, multicultural, regional activities, parenting, community, teens and youth, camps, art instruction, seasonal and holiday festivities.
- *Depts/columns:* 400–600 words.
- *Artwork:* JPEG images, 300 dpi.
- *Other:* Send seasonal material 4–6 months in advance.

Sample Issue Advertising.
- "Bay Area Students Provide Hands–On Help in Haiti," by Libby Strichartz. High school students raise funds and travel to Haiti to help earthquake victims.
- "Don't Sell the Sequel Short," by Jeff Bogle. A dad talks about the differences between parenting his first daughter and his second.

Rights and Payment First rights. Written material, $35–$75. Pays on publication. Provides 2 contributor's copies.

North Texas Kids

Scissortail Publishing, 2220 Coit Road, Suite 480-214, Plano, TX, www.northtexaskids.com

Publisher: Minette Riordan

After eight years as a print publication, *North Texas Kids* has gone exclusively digital. Still free, it gives parents in the region timely and thoughtful information on parenting, education, and social issues. It also serves as a guide to all parenting resources in the area, from entertain to education. ■ **Hits per month** Unavailable ■ **Audience** Parents ■ **Frequency** Monthly

Freelance Potential Unavailable.

Submissions Guidelines available on request. Send complete manuscript. Accepts hard copy and email to info@northtexaskids.com. Materials not returned. Response time varies.
- *Articles:* 500–800 words. Informational, how-to, personal experience. Topics: parenting, education, child development, entertainment, local recreation.
- *Depts/columns:* Word lengths vary. Local events, recreation, and resources.

Sample Issue 58 pages. Advertising. Sample copy available at website.
- "Backpack Safety—Is Your Child's Backpack Too Heavy," by Mitchell Brooks. A doctor discusses the weight guidelines for backpacks, and the dangers of children too heavy a load.
- "How To Create a Better Morning Routine with Kids," by Minette Riordan. Strategies for getting the kids up, dressed, fed, and out to school without stress.

Rights and Payment Unavailable.

Northumberland Kids

39 Queen Street, Suite 203, Coburg, Ontario K9A 1M8 Canada. www.northumberlandkids.com

Editor: Susan Stanton

Topics that are of interest to parents in Northumberland County can be found in this magazine, along with information on local recreational and educational resources. All material must contain information that Northumberland parents will find helpful and include local resources. ■ **Circulation** Unavailable ■ **Audience** Parents ■ **Frequency** Monthly

Freelance Potential Publishes 25 freelance submissions yearly: 40–50% written by nonstaff writers. Receives 20–30 queries monthly.

Submissions Guidelines available at website. Prefers query; accepts complete manuscripts. Prefers email queries to sstanton@northumberlandkids.com (Word or text file attachments). Response time varies.

- *Articles:* 1,200–1,400 words. Informational articles, profiles, interviews. Topics: parenting, health and fitness, current events, nature, the environment, family recreation, social issues,education.
- *Depts/columns:* 750 words. Safety, health and nutrition, recreation, organization, media reviews, alternative medicine, the environment.
- *Artwork:* High-resolution digital images at 300 dpi; drawings.

Sample Issue 32 pages. Advertising. Sample copy available at website.
- "Talking Sex: Puberty & Beyond," by Ruth Walker, RN, BScN. How to have a frank and informative dialogue with your teen about his or her changing body and sexuality.
- "Snowshoeing: A Winter World at Your Feet," by Donald Fraser. Tips on how families can enjoy this popular winter sport.

Rights and Payment First rights. Written material, payment rates vary. Pays on publication.

NYMetro Parents

1440 Broadway, Suite 501, New York, NY 10018. www.nymetroparents.com

Managing Editor: Dawn Roode

The largest publisher of parenting magazines in New York, NYMetroParents publishes *Big Apple Parent,* as well as editions for Brooklyn, Queens, Westchester, Long Island, and Connecticut. The focus is on raising happy and healthy children, and providing regional news. It likes articles that pack a punch—submissions that offer a lot of practical advice and information to parents in a few words. Writers are not required to have previous publishing credits, but must have thorough knowledge of the topic. ■ **Circulation** 500,000 ■ **Audience** Parents ■ **Frequency** Monthly

Freelance Potential Publishes 300 freelance submissions yearly: 50% written by nonstaff writers; 10% by authors new to the magazine; 20% by previously unpublished writers. Receives 1–2 queries, 6 unsolicited manuscripts monthly.

Submissions Query or send complete manuscript with two clips (if available), sidebar, a pull quote, and sources. Accepts email submissions to DRoode@davlermedia.com. Responds if interested.
- *Articles:* 800–900 words. Informational, profiles, interviews, personal experience. Topics: family issues, education, camp, health, nutrition, fitness, current events, regional news.
- *Depts/columns:* 600 words. Cultural offerings; family vacations; financial planning; book, video, movie, and software reviews.
- *Other:* Submit seasonal material 4 months in advance.

Sample Issue 66 pages. Advertising. Sample copy available.
- "Stuttering in Children: Diagnosis, Treatment, and Finding Support," by Lois Barrett. Expert advice on what this disorder is and how to manage it.
- "How to Avoid Being an Overprotective Parent." Tips for parents who "bubble–wrap" their children.

Rights and Payment First New York area rights. No payment.

OC Family

1451 Quail Street, Suite 201, Newport Beach, CA 92660. www.ocfamily.com

Editor: Kim Porrazzo

Distributed throughout Orange County, California, this magazine covers general parenting topics. It also includes information on child-related events, goods, and services in the county. ■ **Circulation** 55,000 ■ **Audience** Parents ■ **Frequency** Monthly

Freelance Potential Publishes 50 freelance submissions yearly: 82% written by nonstaff writers; 1% by authors new to the magazine; 1% by previously unpublished writers. Receives 12 queries monthly.

Submissions Editorial calendar available. Query. Accepts hard copy. SASE. Responds in 1 month.

- *Articles:* 800–2,500 words. Informational, profiles. Topics: education, health, nutrition, family travel, regional food and dining, youth sports and recreation, child care and development.
- *Depts/columns:* Word lengths vary. Parenting advice, children's book reviews, family movie reviews, fashion, beauty.
- *Artwork:* B/W or color prints.

Sample Issue 204 pages. Advertising. Sample copy available at website.
- "National Children's Study Is Underway," by Sandy Bennett. The most comprehensive long–term research project ever conducted in the U.S., on child development and health.
- "Stress and Oral Health," by Robin Barr. Stress in children can cause canker or cold sores.

Rights and Payment One-time rights. Written material, $100–$500. Artwork, $90. Kill fee, $50. Pays 45 days after publication. Provides 3 contributor's copies.

Ottawa Family Life

Coyle Publishing, 362 Terry Fox Drive, Suite 220, Kanata, Ontario K2K 2P5, Canada.
www.ottawafamilylife.com

Editor: Pan den Boer

Targeting local families and parents with young children, *Ottawa Family Life* launched a year ago to help readers make the most of their kids' childhood years. In addition to parenting and education information, each seasonal issue offers family-friendly activities and local resources. Local sources for articles are preferred. ■ **Circulation** 50,000 ■ **Audience** Parents ■ **Frequency** Quarterly

Freelance Potential Unavailable.

Submissions For more information, contact editor@coylepublishing.com.
- *Articles:* Word lengths vary. Informational, how-to. Topics: parenting issues, education, child health and safety, behavior, development.
- *Depts/columns:* Word lengths vary. Busy Families, Development, Education, Food and Nutrition, Healthwise, Homework, Parents@Work (profiles of businesses that cater to families), Time Out (spotlights an upcoming family-friendly event).

Sample Issue 84 pages. Sample copy available at website.
- "No Place Like Home," by Heather Cameron. How to handle the ups and downs of a move.
- "Success Comes from Strong Roots" by Stephen Johnson. How to build strong family values.

Rights and Payment Unavailable.

Our Children

National PTA Headquarters, 1250 North Pitt Street, Alexandria, VA 22314. www.pta.org

Editor: Marilyn Ferdinand

With both a print and an online version, this National PTA publication is interested in articles on how parents can become more involved with their children's education. It also covers issues that affect children's productivity and those that impact their education and welfare. ■ **Circulation** 31,000 ■ **Audience** Parents and teachers ■ **Frequency** 5 times a year

Freelance Potential Publishes 20–25 freelance submissions yearly: 50% written by nonstaff writers; 75% by authors new to the magazine. Receives 15–20 queries monthly.

Submissions Guidelines and editorial calendar available at website. Query with description of article, credentials, and clips. Prefers email to mferdinand@pta.org. No simultaneous submissions. Responds in 2 months.
- *Articles:* 600–1,000 words. Informational, how–to. Topics: education, parenting, child welfare, school/parent connection.

- *Depts/columns:* Word lengths vary.

Sample Issue Sample issue available.
- "Avoid the 'Senior Scramble,'" by Karen Daluga. Using the summer between junior and senior year to get a jump-start on the college application process.
- "Parents Can Prevent Cyberbullying," by Meline Kevorkian, EdD. Tips for Internet safety aimed at preventing cyberbullying.

Rights and Payment First North American serial, electronic, and reproduction rights. Written material, no payment. Provides 3 contributor's copies.

Parentguide News

419 Park Avenue South, New York, NY 10016. www.parentguidenews.com

Editor: Jenna Hammond

Catering to the needs of parents in the New York metropolitan area, this tabloid-sized publication (the oldest and largest local parenting publication covering New York City, Queens, Long Island, Westchester County, Rockland County, and New Jersey) and its online edition offer guidance and insight to parents with children under the age of 12. It covers everything from family matters and pregnancy to health and education. The best bet for new writers is to query on a personal experience piece with important, engaging, or seldom-discussed family concerns. ■ **Circulation** 285,000 **Audience** Parents ■ **Frequency** Monthly

Freelance Potential Publishes 120–300 freelance submissions yearly: 25–50% developed from unsolicited submissions; 75% written by nonstaff writers; 75–100% by authors new to the magazine. Receives 100–150 queries, 10–25 unsolicited manuscripts monthly.

Submissions Guidelines available online. Query with cover letter. Prefers email queries to jenna@ parentguidenews.com. Responds in 6 months.
- *Articles:* 700–950 words. Informational, how-to, profiles, interviews, personal experience. Topics: parenting, pregnancy, child development, health and fitness, special and regular education, technology, recreation, activities, the arts, entertainment, girls, boys, travel, crafts, nutrition.
- *Depts/columns:* 200–1,000 words. Crafts, health tips, recipes, products, travel destinations, regional news and events.
- *Other:* Submit seasonal material 5 months in advance.

Sample Issue 86 pages. Advertising.
- "What a Pretty Plate," by Laura Gibofsky, RD. How to use color to boost your family's nutrition and up your children's interest in healthy eating.
- "Infantile Spasms," by W. Donald Shields, M.D. Recognizing how this seizure disorder affects young children.

Rights and Payment Regional rights for 1 year. No payment. Provides 2 contributor's copies.

Parenting

2 Park Avenue, New York, NY 10016. www.parenting.com

Submissions Editor

Parenting covers the psychological as well as the practical aspects of raising a child from birth to age 12. Its articles also deal with the emotional issues that mothers face—issues such as maintaining their friendships and juggling their various roles. Best opportunities for writers new to parents are the departments. ■ **Circulation** 2 million+ ■ **Audience** Parents ■ **Frequency** 11 times a year

Freelance Potential Publishes 10–15 freelance submissions yearly: 80% written by nonstaff writers; 10% by authors new to the magazine; 5% by previously unpublished writers. Receives 80+ queries monthly.

Submissions Guidelines available at website. Query with clips. Accepts hard copy. SASE. Responds in 2 months.
- *Articles:* 1,000–2,500 words. Informational, how-to, self-help, profiles, personal experience. Topics: child development, behavior, health, pregnancy, family activities, women's issues.
- *Depts/columns:* 100–500 words. Parenting tips, child development by age range, work and family, health, fitness, beauty.

Sample Issue 184 pages. Advertising. Sample copy available.
- "How to Boost Your School's Literacy Development Program," by Barbara Rowley. Research shows that parent volunteers make a difference in closing the early childhood literacy gap.
- "Is It Quitting Time?" by Kristen J. Gough. How to tell when your child is ready to quit an activity.

Rights and Payment First world rights with 2 months exclusivity. Written material, payment rates vary. Pays on acceptance. Provides 1 contributor's copy.

Parenting Children with Special Needs

30905 East Stony Point School Road, Grain Valley, MO 64029. www.pcwsn.com

Editor: Kara Cowie

Distributed in the Kansas City area through schools, hospitals, medical clinics, and businesses, this magazine is filled with practical articles for parents of special needs children. Each issue spotlights local resources, presents timely information from healthcare and other professionals, and offers poetry and personal experience pieces written by parents. Its mission is to offer support, understanding, encouragement, and guidance through the struggles and emotional turmoil parents face raising a special needs child. ■ **Circulation** 50,000 ■ **Audience** Parents ■ **Frequency** 6 times a year

Freelance Potential Publishes several freelance submissions yearly.

Submissions Send complete manuscript. Accepts email submissions to kara@pcwsn.com. Response time varies.
- *Articles:* Word lengths vary. Informational, how-to, profiles, personal experience. Topics: special education, health, medical care, nutrition, social issues, social skills.
- *Depts/columns:* Word lengths vary. Self-care for parents, educational programs, local resources, advice from healthcare and education professionals.
- *Other:* Poetry by parents, line lengths vary.

Sample Issue Sample copy available at website.
- "The Cleek Family's Fight Against Autism," by Han Cheung. A family's treatment plans and lifestyle choices to help their autistic son.
- "Summer Savings," by Jason Armstrong. Planning ahead for an affordable vacation.

Rights and Payment Rights vary. Written material, payment rates vary. Payment policy varies.

Parenting for High Potential

National Association for Gifted Children, 1331 H Street NW, Washington, DC 20005. www.nagc.org

Editor: Dr. Jennifer Jolly

This quarterly helps parents and teachers of gifted children assist students in developing their talents and reaching their highest potential. Expertly written articles and columns ,reviews, and a children's section make up the editorial mix. Writers should have experience working with gifted children. ■ **Circulation** 4,000 ■ **Audience** Parents and teachers ■ **Frequency** 4 times a year

Freelance Potential Publishes 10–12 freelance submissions yearly: 100% written by nonstaff writers; 50% by authors new to the magazine. Receives 2–3 unsolicited manuscripts monthly.

Submissions Guidelines available. Send complete manuscript with cover letter, brief biographical statement, and a 3-sentence description of the article. Does not accept simultaneous submissions. Prefers email submissions to jjolly@lsu.edu (Word, WordPerfect, Adobe PageMaker, or InDesign attachments). Responds in 6–8 weeks.

■ *Articles:* 2,500–4,500 words. Informational, how–to, personal experience. Topics: recognizing and nurturing gifted children, collaborating with educators, suggestions for challenging programming in home, school, and community, issues related to gifted and talented programming.

■ *Depts/columns:* Word lengths vary.

Sample Issue Sample copy available.

■ "Susan and Goliath: A Seventh-Grade Girl's Skipping Odyssey," by Mary Reed. A mom describes what her daughter went through to skip from seventh grade to high school.

■ "Laureates," by Dr. Bill Phillips. Parental influence on Nobel Laureate winners.

Rights and Payment First rights. No payment.

Parenting New Hampshire

150 Dow Street, Manchester, NH 03101. www.parentingnh.com

Editor: Melanie Hitchcock

All aspects of parenting—from childbirth through managing adolescents—are covered in this magazine for New Hampshire families. It also provides updates on family-friendly events and resources in the area. Preference is given to New Hampshire writers. ■ **Circulation** 27,500 ■ **Audience** Parents ■ **Frequency** Monthly

Freelance Potential Publishes 25–35 freelance submissions yearly: 85% written by nonstaff writers; 50% by authors new to the magazine; 20% by previously unpublished writers. Receives 100 queries, 20–30 unsolicited manuscripts monthly.

Submissions Guidelines available at website. Query or send complete manuscript with writing samples. Accepts hard copy, disk submissions, and email submissions to editor@parentingnh.com. SASE. Responds if interested.

■ *Articles:* Word lengths vary. Informational, how-to, profiles, interviews. Topics: parenting, education, maternity, childbirth, special needs, gifted education, fathering, child development, summer fun, regional activities, family–related businesses, product round–ups, birthday parties, holidays, back-to-school issues, health.

■ *Depts/columns:* 500–800 words. Chit Chat (nonfiction essays, poetry, or vignettes). Child development, parenting issues, health and wellness.

■ *Other:* Submit seasonal material 3 months in advance.

Sample Issue 54 pages. Advertising. Sample copy available.

■ "How Summer Camp Teaches Life Lessons," by Morgen Thiboult. Summer camp experiences help develop valuable skills for children in the areas of friendship, leadership, and citizenship.

■ "Snowboarding in NH," by Jacqueline Tourville. A guide to snowboarding in the state.

Rights and Payment All rights. Articles, $30. Other material, payment rates vary. Pays on acceptance. Provides 3 contributor's copies.

Parenting Special Needs

310 21st Court SW, Vero Beach, FL 32962. www.parentingspecialneeds.org

Editorial Director: Chantai Snellgrove

Parenting Special Needs is a free online publication serving the special needs community. It covers all ages and stages of guiding children with special needs, and empowers their parents, caregivers, teachers, and friends by providing information, and inspiration. The mission is to provide practical tips, share life lessons, help tackle challenges, and celebrate the joys related to raising children with special needs. ■ **Hits per month** 70,000+ ■ **Audience** Parents ■ **Frequency** 6 times a year

Freelance Potential Publishes several freelance submissions yearly.

Submissions Guidelines available at website. Query or send complete manuscript with cover letter and brief author biography. Accepts hard copy and email submissions to submit@parentingspecial-needs.org (Word attachments). Accepts simultaneous submissions, résumés for work-for-hire, and published articles for reprints. Availability of artwork improves chance of acceptance. May hold submissions for possible future use. SASE. Response time varies.
■ *Articles:* 400–1,000 words. Informational, how–to, personal experience. Topics: health, discipline, alternative treatments, fitness, nutrition, family travel, developmental stages—all as they relate to children with special needs.
■ *Depts/columns:* Word lengths vary. New product information, book reviews, essays.
■ *Artwork:* B/W or color prints; JPEG, TIFF, or PDF images at 150 dpi (minimum).

Sample Issue Sample copy available at website.
■ "What Every Parent Should Know about Brain Injury," by the May Institute. Prevention, symptoms, and treatment for this leading cause of death and disability for children and adolescents.
■ "Eating Green?" by Christina Bartlett. Small steps to healthier eating and living.

Rights and Payment Rights vary. No payment.

Parent Life

One LifeWay Plaza, Nashville, TN 37234-0172. www.lifeway.com/parentlifeblog

Content Editor

Parent Life has a distinctly Christian perspective. Its articles offer help, information, and advice in all the areas in which parents seek godly guidance for their children, including health, education, safety, and spiritual development. Its focus is on parents of younger children rather than teens. All articles should be informative above all else, as well as upbeat and encouraging. ■ **Circulation** 50,000
■ **Audience** Parents ■ **Frequency** Monthly

Freelance Potential Publishes 8–12 freelance submissions yearly: 10% developed from unsolicited submissions; 90% written by nonstaff writers; 10–15% by previously unpublished writers. Receives 25–50 queries, 10–25 unsolicited manuscripts monthly.

Submissions Guidelines available online. Editorial calendar available via email request to parentlife@lifeway.com. Query with cover letter and outline or send complete manuscript. Accepts email submissions to parentlife@lifeway.com. Accepts simultaneous submissions. Also accepts applications for work-for-hire through form on website. Response time varies.
■ *Articles:* 300–1,200 words. Informational, how-to, personal experience, profiles. Topics: family issues, religion, regular and special education, health, hobbies, games, social issues, travel, child care, entertainment.
■ *Depts/columns:* 500 words. Parenting Matters, Growth Spurts (age-appropriate advice), A Life of Worship, Real Life Solutions, Mom's Life, Dad's Life, Funny Life. Expectant parents, single parenting, medical advice.
■ *Artwork:* Color prints and transparencies.
■ *Other:* Accepts seasonal material for Christmas and Thanksgiving.

Sample Issue 50 pages. Sample copy available at website.
■ "The Coolest Grandparents," by Christi McGuire. Grandparents active part in their grandkids' lives.
■ "The Table Game," by Pat Baker. Bringing conversation back to the family dinner table.

Rights and Payment Nonexclusive rights. Written material, $125–$350. Pays on publication. Provides 1 contributor's copy.

Parents

375 Lexington Avenue, New York, NY 10017. www.parents.com

Editor

This magazine is read by parents and parents-to-be for its informative articles and personal experience pieces. It also features new product reviews, profiles, and interviews. Articles on discipline and baby-related articles are particularly sought at this time. ■ **Circulation** 2.2 million ■ **Audience** Parents ■ **Frequency** Monthly

Freelance Potential Publishes 300 freelance submissions yearly; 80% written by nonstaff writers; 15% by authors new to the magazine. Receives 40–50 queries monthly.

Submissions Query. Accepts email queries to mailbag@parents.com. Responds in 6 weeks.
■ *Articles:* Word lengths vary. Informational, how–to, profiles, interviews, personal experience. Topics: all aspects of parenting, newborn care, child development, safety, nutrition, education, behavioral issues, health, fitness, relationships, food, travel, home, fashion, beauty, finance, technology, culture.
■ *Depts/columns:* Word lengths vary. New product reviews, news.

Sample Issue Advertising. Sample copy available.
■ "9 Ways Life Is Better with Baby," by Bari Nan Cohen. Benefits to being a new parent.
■ "Raise a Child Who Loves Life," by Robin Westin. Latest research about teaching optimism.

Rights and Payment Rights vary. Payment rates vary. Pays on acceptance.

Parents & Kids

785 North President Street, Suite B, Jackson, MS 39202. www.parents-kids.com

Editor: Gretchen W. Cook

Parenting, education, health and safety, and local recreation are among the topics covered in this regional magazine, published in print and digital editions. It strives to offer parents helpful information from conception through the teen years, with resources specific to the Jackson, Mississippi, community. ■ **Circulation** 35,000 ■ **Audience** Parents ■ **Frequency** Monthly

Freelance Potential Publishes 80 freelance submissions yearly; 80% written by nonstaff writers; 50% by previously unpublished writers. Receives about 35 manuscripts monthly.

Submissions Guidelines and editorial calendar available at website. Send complete manuscript for reprints; query for original features. Accepts email submissions to gretchen@parents-kids.com (text in body of email and as Word attachment). Responds in 6 weeks.
■ *Articles:* 700 words. Informational, self-help, how-to. Topics: parenting, education, the arts, computers, crafts and hobbies, health and fitness, multicultural and ethnic issues, recreation, regional news, social issues, regular and special education, sports, family travel.
■ *Depts/columns:* 500 words. Travel, cooking, computers.
■ *Artwork:* Prefers digital images; will accept B/W prints or transparencies. Line art.
■ *Other:* Submit seasonal material 3–6 months in advance.

Sample Issue 48 pages. Advertising. Sample copy available at website.
■ "Giving Back, Getting More," by Leah Kackley. The benefits of working on volunteer projects with children.
■ "Summer Camp Listings." A round-up of the various camps in the region.

Rights and Payment One-time rights. Written material, $25. Pays on publication. Provides 1 tearsheet.

Parents' Choice

Parents' Choice Foundation, 201 West Padonia Road, Suite 303, Timonium, MD 21093. www.parents-choice.org

Editor: Claire Green

This online publication of the Parents' Choice Foundation strives to provide parents with reliable and unbiased information about tools to help their children learn and grow imaginatively, physically, morally, and mentally. It offers themed articles, written by experts, on books, toys, software, music, websites, magazines, and television. ■ **Hits per month** 1 million ■ **Audience** Parents ■ **Frequency** Unavailable

Freelance Potential Publishes numerous freelance submissions yearly: 80% written by nonstaff writers.

Submissions Query or send complete manuscript. Accepts hard copy and email submissions to info@parents-choice.org. Accepts simultaneous submissions if identified. SASE. Response time varies.
■ *Articles:* To 1,500 words. Informational, how–to. Topics: reviews of toys, books, software, games, websites, music, magazines, television, movies; arts and crafts; learning; regular and special education; child development; social skills; social issues.
■ *Depts/columns:* Word lengths vary.

Sample Issue Sample copy available at website.
■ "Shopping for Children with Special Needs," by Elisa Mintz Delia and Claire S. Green. Expert tips on how to pick out a toy that is appropriate and fun for a child with special needs.
■ "Tips for Teaching Kids to Enjoy Reading," by Kristi Jemtegaard. Encouraging reading.

Rights and Payment All rights. Written material, payment rates vary. Pays on acceptance.

Parents Express

290 Commerce Drive, Fort Washington, PA 19034. http://montgomerynews.com

Editor: Mike Morsch

Parents Express is a magazine for families living in the Philadelphia region and southern New Jersey. It covers parenting issues as well as regional events, news, and resources. ■ **Circulation** 49,000 ■ **Audience** Parents ■ **Frequency** Monthly

Freelance Potential Publishes 25–30 freelance submissions yearly: 30% written by nonstaff writers; 75% by authors new to the magazine; 25% by previously unpublished writers. Receives several queries monthly.

Submissions Query with clips or writing samples. Accepts hard copy. SASE. Responds in 1 month.
■ *Articles:* 300–1,000 words. Informational, how–to, interviews, profiles. Topics: regional news and activities, parenting, health, sports, education, camps, recreation, social issues.
■ *Depts/columns:* 600–800 words.

Sample Issue Advertising. Sample copy available.
■ "An Unexpected Single Father," by Lisa B. Samalonis. An interview with a dad whose wife died unexpectedly while giving birth to their daughter.
■ "Local Families Spread the Word about Rare Genetic Disease," by Mindy Toran. A rare genetic disease leads a family to host a "Path to the Cure" event.

Rights and Payment One-time rights. Written material, payment rates vary. Pays on publication. Provides contributor's copies.

Parents' Press

1416 Park Avenue, Alameda, CA 94501. www.parentspress.com

Editor: Judith M. Gallman

Published for families that live in the San Francisco area, *Parents' Press* specializes in practical information about the care and development of children. It looks for factual, researched-based articles on topics such as health, education, and relationships that include information about local resources. Parents' Press does not publish personal experience and opinion pieces. ■ **Circulation** 40,000 ■ **Audience** Parents ■ **Frequency** Monthly

Freelance Potential Publishes 25–50 freelance submissions yearly: 15–20% written by nonstaff writers; 15% by authors new to the magazine. Receives 10+ unsolicited manuscripts monthly.

Submissions Send complete manuscript. Accepts hard copy, email submissions to editor@parents-press.com, and reprints. SASE. Responds in 2 months.
■ *Articles:* To 1,500 words. Informational, how-to. Topics: child development, education, health, safety, party planning, local family events and activities.
■ *Depts/columns:* Staff-written.
■ *Artwork:* B/W prints and transparencies. Line art.
■ *Other:* Submit seasonal material 2 months in advance.

Sample Issue 32 pages. Advertising. Sample copy available.
■ "A Good Night's Sleep," by Sarah Handelsman, M.D. Helping infants and toddlers get to sleep.
■ "About Breastfeeding," by Meg Zweiback, R.N., M.P.H. Q&A on breastfeeding.

Rights and Payment All or second rights. Articles, $50–$500. Pays 45 days after publication.

Parent:Wise Austin

5501–A Balcones Drive, Suite 102, Austin, TX 78731. www.parentwiseaustin.com

Editor in Chief: Kim Pleticha

In addition to fact-filled, interview-based articles about parenting, this magazine features humor, essays, and poetry that reflect the day-to-day concerns of families. It was created specifically for families living in central Texas. Articles must be well-researched, tightly written, and directed at an audience of parents who want to be educated. ■ **Circulation** 32,000 ■ **Audience** Parents ■ **Frequency** Monthly

Freelance Potential Publishes 15+ freelance submissions yearly: 10–25% developed from unsolicited submissions; 25–50% written by nonstaff writers; 50% by authors new to the magazine; 15% by previously unpublished writers. Receives 150–200 queries, 25–50 unsolicited manuscripts monthly.

Submissions Guidelines available at website. Send complete manuscript. (Cover stories are by assignment only.) Accepts email submissions only to editor@parentwiseaustin.com. Accepts simultaneous submissions. Also accepts queries for contract writing from journalists in Texas. Responds in 1–6 months.
■ *Articles:* 550–1,000 words. Informational, essays, personal experience, humor. Topics: parenting, family life, regular and special education, regional news, and people in the Austin community who work to make life better for other families.
■ *Depts/columns:* To 650 words. Humor about parenting and family life; medical advice, reviews of books, music, and products.
■ *Other:* Poetry for Mother's Day and Father's Day about parenting, children, or families; to 24 lines.

Sample Issue 32 Pages. Advertising. Sample copy available at website.
■ "Strength That Few Have," by Tina Callison. A mom writes of the joy and heartbreak of having a child who lived for only 20 months.

- "We Can't Cut Our Way Out of This," by Jenny LaCoste–Caputo. Budget woes in Texas schools and possible solutions.

Rights and Payment First North American serial and Internet rights. Essay and humor articles, $50. Pays on publication. Provides contributor's copies.

Pathways to Family Wellness

327 North Middletown Road, Media, PA 19063. www.pathwaystofamilywellness.org

Editor

The purpose of this publication is to provide parents with the information they need to make good health care choices for their children and themselves. Guided by a natural wellness philosophy, it explores new approaches to health and wellness. ■ **Circulation** 12,000 ■ **Audience** Parents ■ **Frequency** 4 times a year

Freelance Potential Publishes 40–50 freelance submissions yearly: 80% written by nonstaff writers. Receives 2 unsolicited manuscripts monthly.

Submissions Guidelines available at website. Send complete manuscript with word count and 50-word author biography. Accepts email submissions to editor@icpa4kids.com. Accepts simultaneous submissions if identified. Responds in 3 weeks.
- *Articles:* 900–2,000 words. Informational, how–to, personal experience. Topics: parenting, education, pregnancy, childbirth, infant and child care, the mind-body connection, nutrition.
- *Depts/columns:* Word lengths vary.
- *Artwork:* 5x7 b/w or color prints; digital photos, JPEG or TIFF format, 300 dpi.

Sample Issue
- "What Can Be Done to Prevent Autism Now?" by Maureen H. McDonnell, R.N. Prevention and treatment of this growing disorder.
- "The Lancet Retraction Changes Nothing," by David Kirby. The debate over the link between autism and vaccines.

Rights and Payment First or reprint rights. All material, no payment. Provides 2 contributor's copies.

Pediatrics for Parents

P.O. Box 219, Gloucester, MA 01931. www.pedsforparents.com

Editor: Richard J. Sagall, M.D.

Known as "The Children's Medical Journal for Parents," this publication offers carefully researched information in language accessible to the lay reader. It will publish only material that is medically accurate, contains resource citations where applicable, and is useful to parents of children from pre-natal to early teens. Submissions of previously published articles from medical and dental journals will be considered only if rewritten for a lay audience. The emphasis of this publication is on prevention. ■ **Circulation** 250,000 ■ **Audience** Parents ■ **Frequency** 6 times a year

Freelance Potential Publishes 30 freelance submissions yearly: 50% written by nonstaff writers; 50% by authors new to the magazine; 50% by previously unpublished writers. Receives 4–5 queries and unsolicited manuscripts monthly.

Submissions Guidelines available at website. Query or send complete manuscript with cover page. Prefers email submissions to submissions@pedsforparents.com (Word attachments). Response time varies.
- *Articles:* 750–1,500 words. Informational. Topics: prevention, fitness, medical advances, new treatment options, wellness, pregnancy.
- *Depts/columns:* Word lengths vary. Article reprints, new product information.

Sample Issue 32 pages. Advertising. Sample copy available at website.
- "Protect Children from Acetaminophen Overdoses," by the Institute for Safe Medical Practices. How to avoid accidental overdoses of this common over–the–counter medication.
- "Parental Monitoring Is Crucial During Adolescence," by Barbara Stanton, M.D. Proof that teens who have adult supervision are at lower risk for danger, and how to monitor them successfully.

Rights and Payment First rights or reprint rights. Written material, to $25. Pays on publication. Provides 3 contributor's copies and a 1-year subscription.

Piedmont Parent

P.O. Box 530, King, NC 27021. www.piedmontparent.com

Editor: Myra Wright

Essays and articles that have a local spin are found in *Piedmont Parent*, a tabloid targeting families in the Winston-Salem, Greensboro, and High Point regions of North Carolina. Child care, education, and family entertainment are among the topics it covers. Features require thorough research (citing a minimum of three reliable sources) and concise writing skills. ■ **Circulation** 36,000 ■ **Audience** Parents ■ **Frequency** Monthly

Freelance Potential Publishes 36–40 freelance submissions yearly: 50% written by nonstaff writers; 50% by authors new to the magazine; 25% by previously unpublished writers. Receives about 85 queries and unsolicited manuscripts monthly.

Submissions Guidelines and theme list available at website. Query with story outline and clips or send complete manuscript with word count. Accepts email to editor@piedmontparent.com (Word attachments). Accepts simultaneous submissions if identified. Responds in 1–2 months, if interested.
- *Articles:* 500–1,200 words. Informational, how-to, interviews, personal experience. Topics: child development, day care, child care, summer camps, birthday parties, food, frugal living, gifted and special education, local and regional news, social issues, sports, popular culture, health, pregnancy, travel.
- *Depts/columns:* 600–900 words. Family health, parenting news.
- *Art:* Digital photos, 300 dpi minimum.
- *Other:* Family games and activities.

Sample Issue 40 pages. Advertising. Sample copy available at website.
- "What to Do When You Dislike Your Child's Friends," by Tammy Holoman. How to share your values and give your teen the necessary freedom to choose peers wisely.
- "Too Much Homework in Kindergarten," by Peggy Gisler and Marge Eberts. What a parent can do if it appears a child is getting too much homework.

Rights and Payment One-time rights. Written material, payment rates vary. Pays on publication. Provides 1 tearsheet.

Pikes Peak Parent

30 South Prospect Street, Colorado Springs, CO 80903. www.pikespeakparent.com

Editor: George Lewis

The latest parenting news for families in the greater Colorado Springs area appears in *Pikes Peak Parent*, a section of the *Colorado Springs Gazette*. All articles focus on raising, educating, and entertaining children. Distributed free, it is more interested in practical articles with local sources than opinions and essays about parenting. Articles about local businesses are okay, as long as they offer insights and information parents can use. ■ **Circulation** 30,000 ■ **Audience** Parents ■ **Frequency** Monthly

Freelance Potential Publishes 4 freelance submissions yearly: 5% written by nonstaff writers; 2% by authors new to the magazine. Receives 5 queries monthly.

Submissions Query with writing samples. Accepts reprints. Accepts hard copy and email queries to parent@gazette.com. SASE. Response time varies.
- *Articles:* 800–1,500 words. Informational, how-to, profiles. Topics: regional news and resources, parenting issues, family life, travel, health, safety, sports, social issues, recreation.
- *Depts/columns:* Word lengths vary. News, opinions, grandparenting, health, family issues, profiles, local events.

Sample Issue 20 pages. Advertising.
- "Dissolvable Tobacco New to Colorado, But Old Questions Arise," by Barbara Cotter. Local concerns that this new and easily ingestible form of tobacco is appealing to children.
- "Depressed Friend Led Senior to Her Passion," by Anslee Wolfe. A high school senior plans to become a psychologist because of her best friend's illness.

Rights and Payment All rights on assigned pieces; second rights on reprints and unsolicited pieces. Written material, payment rates vary. Pays on publication. Provides 1 contributor's copy.

The Pink Chameleon

www.thepinkchameleon.com

Editor: Dorothy Paula Freda

This ezine provides wholesome reading material for the whole family. It features fiction of all genres, creative nonfiction, and poetry. Among its current needs are works about "rare moments in time," inspirational stories, words of wisdom, helpful advice, and nostalgia pieces. It will not accept violence, cursing, or any other material unsuitable for families. ■ **Hits per month** 100 ■ **Audience** Families ■ **Frequency** Unavailable

Freelance Potential Publishes 50–100 freelance submissions yearly: 95% written by nonstaff writers; 60% by authors new to the magazine; 40% by previously unpublished writers. Receives 25 unsolicited manuscripts monthly.

Submissions Guidelines available at website. Send complete manuscript with brief author biography. Accepts email submissions to dpfreda@juno.com (no attachments). No simultaneous submissions. Responds in 1 month.
- *Articles:* To 2,000 words. Personal experience, short anecdotes, words of wisdom. Topics: family-oriented, children.
- *Fiction:* To 2,000 words. Short stories. Genres: family-oriented, fantasy, historical, mystery, romance, science fiction, Western.
- *Other:* Poetry. Maximum 24 lines.

Sample Issue Sample copy available at website.
- "Caregivers, Guardians of Human Dignity," by Paula Freda. Reflection on the qualities needed when a loved one needs care.
- "The Willie Button Series," by Albert J. Manachino. Short stories about a man who has to unload an evil book to gain access to heaven.

Rights and Payment Electronic rights for 1 year. No payment.

Pittsburgh Parent

P.O. Box 374, Bakerstown, PA 15007. www.pittsburghparent.com

Editor: Patricia Poshard

Loads of parenting advice from local resources and experts can be found in each issue of this magazine along with up-to-date information on local activities and events. It covers a variety of family topics of interest to parents of newborns to teens. Well-written and fresh articles with a local angle are always in demand. ■ **Circulation** 50,000 ■ **Audience** Parents ■ **Frequency** Monthly

Freelance Potential Publishes 120–250 freelance submissions yearly: 10–25% developed from unsolicited submissions; 50–75% written by nonstaff writers; 1–10% by authors new to the magazine. Receives 25–50 queries, 50–75 unsolicited manuscripts monthly.

Submissions Sampley copy, guidelines, and editorial calendar available at website. Query for nonfiction; send complete manuscript for fiction. Prefers email to editor@pittsburghparent.com (Word attachments). Accepts simultaneous submissions if identified and résumés for work-for-hire. Availability of artwork improves chance of acceptance. Response time varies.
- *Articles:* To 950 words. Informational, profiles, interviews. Topics: family issues, parenting, preschool, child care, maternity, party ideas, discipline, drug abuse, education, science, fitness, health and safety, nature, college, computers, multicultural subjects.
- *Depts/columns:* Word lengths vary. Education, teen issues, book reviews, humor.
- *Other:* Submit seasonal material 3 months in advance.

Sample Issue 40 pages. Advertising. Sample copy available at website.
- "How Can I Talk with My Teen about Weight Issues?" by Kathy Sena. How to tackle this sensitive subject successfully.
- "Online Privacy for Kids," by Carolyn Jabs. Protecting your child's personal information online.

Rights and Payment First serial rights. Written material, $50. Pays on publication. Provides 1 tearsheet.

Positive Parenting

P.O. Box 1312, Ventura, CA 93002. www.positiveparenting.com

Owner: Deborah Godfrey

This ezine provides information to make parenting more rewarding, effective, and fun. Articles support the belief that children should be raised lovingly, nonviolently, and with discipline that motivates through love. A professional background in child development is not needed to contribute to this site. It is about parents (and professionals) helping parents understand how to raise their children in a loving, self esteem-building manner. Articles on discipline issues and success stories are most open to new writers. ■ **Hits per month** Unavailable ■ **Audience** Parents ■ **Frequency** Updated regularly

Freelance Potential Publishes 2–3 freelance submissions yearly: 30% written by nonstaff writers; 80% by authors new to the magazine; 10–20% by previously unpublished writers. Receives 4–6 unsolicited manuscripts monthly.

Submissions Send complete manuscript. Accepts email submissions to info@positiveparenting.com. Response time varies.
- *Articles:* 500–1,000 words. Informational, how-to, personal experience. Topics: parenting, discipline, family relationship issues.
- *Depts/columns:* Word lengths vary. Success stories, reviews.
- *Other:* Seasonal and holiday-related parenting tips.

Sample Issue Sample copy available at website.
- "Contribution Makes a Difference," by Deborah Godfrey. The positive benefits of having children learn the value of working and contributing.
- "Teach Your Kids to Think!" by Maria Chesley Fisk, Ph.D. Excerpt from a book on how to get children to think for themselves and be resourceful.

Rights and Payment Rights vary. No payment.

Premier Baby and Child

4818 Six Forks Road, Suite 204, Raleigh, NC 27609. www.premierbaby.com

Editor/Publisher: Robyn Mangrum

This upscale parenting magazine is packed with tips for raising children up to age 6. Fresh, fun articles are meant to inspire readers while providing information on local products and resources. It is distributed to hospitals and pediatricians' offices throughout North Carolina's Triangle region.
■ **Circulation** 32,000 ■ **Audience** Parents ■ **Frequency** Annually

Freelance Potential Publishes several freelance submissions yearly: 100% written by nonstaff writers; 50% by previously unpublished writers.

Submissions Guidelines available. Query with résumé and clips. Accepts hard copy and email queries to publisher@premierbaby.com. SASE. Response time varies.
■ *Articles:* 250–500 words. Informational, how–to, personal experience. Topics: baby and child care, health, fashion, decorating, parties, healthcare services.
■ *Depts/columns:* Word lengths vary.

Sample Issue Advertising. Sample copy available.
■ "Common Infant Conditions." Ailments that may appear early but will be resolved easily.
■ "How to Choose a Preschool." Factors to consider when choosing a preschool in the Triangle area.

Rights and Payment All rights. Written material, $50–$100. Pays on publication. Provides 2 contributor's copies.

PTO Today

100 Stonewall Boulevard, Suite 3, Wrentham, MA 02093. www.ptotoday.com

Queries Editor

This magazine's mission is to serve as a resource to the leaders of parent groups in elementary and middle schools across the United States. The content specifically focuses on helping parent-teacher organizations be more effective and have a greater impact at their schools. ■ **Circulation** 80,000 ■ **Audience** Parents ■ **Frequency** 7 times a year

Freelance Potential Publishes 15–20 freelance submissions yearly: 70% written by nonstaff writers; 15% by authors new to the magazine; 5% by previously unpublished writers. Receives 8–10 queries monthly.

Submissions Guidelines available. Prefers queries with clips and cover letter that includes: subject, angle, possible interview sources, why the article will interest readers, and author's group leadership experience. Art suggestions to accompany article are appreciated. Accepts hard copy and email queries to queries@ptotoday.com. Responds in 2 months.
■ *Articles:* 1,200–2,200 words. Informational, how–to, profiles. Topics: parent involvement, leadership, fundraising, group management and organization, working with school staff, playgrounds, the role of parent groups in education.
■ *Depts/columns:* 600–1,200 words.

Sample Issue Sample copy available at website.
■ "Putting Meetings in Perspective," by Tim Sullivan. Why groups should stop focusing on increasing meeting attendance and use more relevant ways of measuring the success of the organization.
■ "What I Learned in School," by Sharon Kahn Luttrell. 10 hard–earned lessons from a decade of volunteering.

Rights and Payment All rights. Written material, $150–$700. Pays on acceptance. Provides 1 contributor's copy.

Purple Circle

14200 FM 1062, Canyon, TX 79015. www.purplecircle.com

Editor: Melita Cramblet

This magazine is read by parents of Junior Livestock Show exhibitors, and by show producers and suppliers. Its articles promote the Junior Livestock Show industry, and cover all topics, news, and trends relevant to the show circuit. ■ **Circulation** 3,300 ■ **Audience** Parents ■ **Frequency** 10 times a year

Freelance Potential Publishes 40 freelance submissions yearly: 50% written by nonstaff writers; 99% by previously unpublished writers.

Submissions Query or send complete manuscript. Accepts hard copy. SASE. Response time varies.
■ *Articles:* Word lengths vary. Informational, how-to, profiles. Topics: breeding, selection, care, and showing of champion cattle, goats, hogs, and sheep; youths active in the show circuit.
■ *Depts/columns:* Word lengths vary.

Sample Issue Advertising. Sample copy available.
■ "Junior Spotlights: Southern Belle," by Kristi McCurdy. Profile of an 18-year-old girl who shows Hereford heifers.

Rights and Payment Exclusive rights. No payment. Provides 2 contributor's copies.

Rainbow Kids

P.O. Box 202, Harvey, LA 70059. www.rainbowkids.com

Editor: Martha Osborne

Rainbow Kids is an adoption advocacy website dedicated to helping people adopt from other countries. In addition to its listings of children, agencies, and adoption resources, it features articles on the intricacies of the adoption process and personal essays from those involved. All writers must have experience—either personal or professional—with adoption. ■ **Hits per month** 1.5 million
■ **Audience** Adoptive families ■ **Frequency** Monthly

Freelance Potential Publishes 10–20 freelance submissions yearly: 10% written by nonstaff writers; 50% by authors new to the magazine.

Submissions Send complete manuscript. Prefers email submissions to martha@rainbowkids.com (Word attachments). Responds in 2–3 days.
■ *Articles:* Word lengths vary. Informational, personal experience. Topics: all matters related to adoption and adoptive families, both domestic and foreign including finances, special needs, support groups, transracial adoptions. Also publishes adoption guidelines, adoption events, photo listings.

Sample Issue Sample copy available at website.
■ "Not Wonderful, Not Lucky, Just Parents," by Barbara Kerr. Adopting a preteen daughter.
■ "Lilah's Turn," by Anne and Mike. Adopting a child with limb differences.

Rights and Payment Limited electronic rights. No payment.

Raising Arizona Kids

7000 East Shea Boulevard, Suite 1470, Scottsdale, AZ 85254-5275. www.raisingarizonakids.com

Assistant Editor: Mary L. Holden

The idea behind *Raising Arizona Kids* is that sharing ideas and local resources furthers the raising children in Arizona. This guide to local family-friendly events and services is geared to parents of babies through teens. All articles should quote local experts and parents, and be written by Arizona-based writers only. ■ **Circulation** Unavailable ■ **Audience** Parents ■ **Frequency** Monthly

Freelance Potential Publishes 12 freelance submissions yearly: 65% written by nonstaff writers; 1% by authors new to the magazine; 1% by previously unpublished writers. Receives 4–5 queries monthly.

Submissions Guidelines available at website. Arizona-based writers only. Query with clips. Accepts hard copy and email queries to editorial@raisingarizonakids.com. SASE. Responds in 3 months if interested.
- *Articles:* 1,000–3,000 words. Informational, how-to, profiles, interviews, personal experience, photo-essays. Topics: parenting issues, children, health and fitness, college and careers, current events, education, social issues, travel, recreation.
- *Depts/columns:* 250–750 words. News, parenting issues, family matters, profiles.
- *Other:* Journal articles, 500 words.

Sample Issue 46 pages. Advertising. Sample copy available.
- "The Good Divorce," by Brook Mortensen. How to divorce with maturity, grace, and the kids' best interests in mind.
- "Overnight Camps," by Mala Blomquist. A round-up of overnight camps in the Southwest.

Rights and Payment Rights vary. Articles, $150+. Journal articles, payment rates vary. Depts/columns, $25+. Pays 30 days after publication.

Redbook

Hearst Corporation, 300 West 57th Street, 22nd Floor, New York, NY 10019. www.redbookmag.com

Submissions: Alison Brower

This popular consumer magazine targets women and strives to present information on all aspects of their lives, including parenting. It accepts informative articles as well as personal experience pieces. ■ **Circulation** 2.3 million ■ **Audience** Women ■ **Frequency** Monthly

Freelance Potential Publishes 10 freelance submissions yearly: 5% written by nonstaff writers; 2% by previously unpublished writers. Receives 850+ queries monthly.

Submissions Query with clips and source list. Accepts hard copy and email to redbook@hearst.com. SASE. Responds in 3–4 months.
- *Articles:* 1,000–3,000 words. Informational, how-to, personal experience. Topics: relationships, beauty, fashion, careers, sex, home and garden, health, parenting, the trials of being a mother, childhood development issues.
- *Depts/columns:* 1,000–5,000 words.

Sample Issue Advertising. Sample copy available.
- "Women Cheat, Too: The Other Side of Ashley Madison," by Justin Rocket Silverman. A reporter uncovers why married women go online to find sex partners.
- "Should Parents Put Their Kids on a Diet?" by Carmen Stacier and Liz Nord. The pros and cons of this controversial question.

Rights and Payment All rights. Articles, 75¢–$1 per word. Depts/columns, payment rates vary. Pays on acceptance.

Red River Family Magazine

P.O. Box 7654, Lawton, OK 73506. www.redriverfamily.com

Executive Editor: Laura Clevenger

Written specifically for parents living in southwest Oklahoma and north Texas, this publication focuses on children's health, development, and education, while also offering features on regional family fun and recreation. Many of its readers are military families. ■ **Circulation** 20,000 ■ **Audience** Parents ■ **Frequency** Monthly

Freelance Potential Publishes 100 freelance submissions yearly: 34% written by nonstaff writers; 80% by authors new to the magazine; 10% by previously unpublished writers.

Submissions Guidelines available via email request. Query with clips or writing samples. Accepts email queries to publisher@redriverfamily.com. Response time varies.
■ *Articles:* Word lengths vary. Informational, how-to, profiles, interviews, personal experience. Topics: parenting and family life, social issues, regular and special education, health and fitness, college and careers, technology, nature, the environment, recreation.
■ *Depts/columns:* Word lengths vary. Military life, education, green living, media reviews, fitness, safety, regional news.

Sample Issue 34 pages. Advertising. Sample copy available at website.
■ "National Poison Prevention Week." The many ways children are unintentionally poisoned each year.
■ "Meet Alex," by Jamie Lober. A profile of the National PTA Reflections contest.

Rights and Payment One-time print and 2-year electronic rights. Articles, $20–$50. Payment policy varies.

Richmond Family

P.O. Box 28597, Richmond, VA 23228. http://richmondfamilymagazine.com

Submissions

This magazine inspires, informs, and entertains parents and children of all ages in the greater Richmond area. It features articles of general interest to parents as well as those that highlight regional activities and resources. Using local information and sources is a requirement for writers.
■ **Circulation** Unavailable ■ **Audience** Parents ■ **Frequency** Monthly

Freelance Potential Publishes several freelance submissions yearly.

Submissions Guidelines available at website. Send complete manuscript. Accepts email submissions to editor@richmondfamilymagazine.com. Response time varies.
■ *Articles:* 800–1,000 words. Informational, how-to, profiles, essays, opinion, personal experience. Topics: health, family relationships, travel, local recreation, education, local celebrities, working parents, seasonal.
■ *Depts/columns:* Word lengths vary. The DAD Zone, Reaching Out, Expert Advice, Family Health, Legal Ease, Pages for All Ages, Kids Can–Do, What's Cooking?

Sample Issue Advertising. Sample copy available at website.
■ "Naturally Dramatic," by Diane York. Introducing children to the performing arts.
■ "Kindergarten Time!" by Jenny Adlakha. How to decide if a child is ready for kindergarten.

Rights and Payment Exclusive print and electronic rights. Written material, payment rates vary. Pays on acceptance.

Richmond Parents Monthly

1506 Staples Mill Road, Suite 102, Richmond, VA 23230. www.richmondparents.com

Editor: Ann Marie Griffith

For more than 20 years, *Richmond Parents Monthly* has provided information and resources that help parents raise children and build a better family life. It is distributed free through more than 400 community sites in central Virginia. Prefers local writers. ■ **Circulation** 30,000 ■ **Audience** Parents ■ **Frequency** Monthly

Freelance Potential Publishes 50–60 freelance submissions yearly: 75% written by nonstaff writers; 5% by authors new to the magazine. Receives 50 queries and manuscripts monthly.

Submissions Guidelines and editorial calendar available at website. Query with 3–5 clips and résumé (optional), or send complete manuscript. Accepts email submissions to mail@richmondpublishing.com. No simultaneous submissions. Availability of artwork improves chance of acceptance. Responds in 1–3 weeks.
■ *Articles:* 400–2,200 words. Informational, self-help, essays. Topics: the arts, camps, pets, home and garden, parties, education, health, holidays.
■ *Depts/columns:* "Your Turn" essays, 400–900 words. Family-related news, media reviews, technology.
■ *Artwork:* Color prints or transparencies.

Sample Issue 30 pages. Advertising. Sample copy available.
■ "Page Turners," by Becky Robinette Wright. A local author is living her dream, writing biographies for young readers.
■ "Family and Determination Make This Student Shine," by Ann Harmon. Profile of a top student at a local school.

Rights and Payment One-time rights. Written material, $52–$295. Pays on publication.

Roanoke Valley Woman

916 Roanoke Avenue, P.O. Box 520, Roanoke Rapids, NC 27870. www.roanokevalleywoman.com

Editor: Kris Smith

Launched in 2011, this regional magazine is published by the *Daily Herald* and targets women in North Carolina's Halifax, Northampton, and Lake Gaston areas who want to "get more out of life." Parenting and family issues are covered here, as are career development, money management, and current events. All stories are local. Profiles of local women complete the mix. ■ **Circulation** Unavailable ■ **Audience** Women ■ **Frequency** Quarterly

Freelance Potential Unavailable.

Submissions For more information, contact rvwoman@rrdailyherald.com.
■ *Articles:* Word lengths vary. Informational, personal experience, profiles. Topics: balancing work and family, parenting issues, marriage.
■ *Depts/columns:* Word lengths vary. Health and Wellness, Good Eats, Entertainment & Social.

Sample Issue 28 pages. Advertising. Sample copy available at website.

■ "In the Line of Duty: Roanoke Valley Wives Cope," by Roger Bell. A profile of several women who work in law enforcement or emergency services, or are married to someone who does.
■ "Direct Sales: Area Women Bring Home the Bacon," by Jacqueline Hough. Profiles of women who are balancing their motherhood duties with direct sales jobs, such as Pampered Chef and Mary Kay Cosmetics.

Rights and Payment Unavailable.

Sacramento Parent

457 Grass Valley Highway, Suite 5, Auburn, CA 95603. www.sacramentoparent.com

Editor: Amy Crelly

Offering timely information on news that affects parents in the Sacramento region, this magazine also features articles of general interest on parenting issues, education challenges, and the realities of raising children in a modern world, with an emphasis on sound, practical advice. It is edited and published by moms who have educational backgrounds in child development. ■ **Circulation** 50,000 ■ **Audience** Parents ■ **Frequency** Monthly

Freelance Potential Publishes 50 freelance submissions yearly: 75% written by nonstaff writers; 25% by authors new to the magazine; 10% by previously unpublished writers. Receives 65 queries monthly.

Submissions Guidelines and theme list available at website. Send complete manuscript with writing samples. Accepts email queries to amy@sacramentoparent.com. Availability of artwork improves chance of acceptance. Also accepts reprints. Response time varies.
■ *Articles:* 600–1,000 words. Informational, how-to, personal experience, humor. Topics: parenting, health, fitness, finance, family travel, education, grandparenting, adoption, sports, recreation, learning disabilities, regional news.
■ *Depts/columns:* 300–500 words. Child development, opinions, hometown highlights.
■ *Other:* Submit seasonal or themed material 3 months in advance.

Sample Issue 50 pages. Advertising. Sample copy available.
■ "How to Get Hubby More Involved," by Helen Worster, MFT. How to keep dad involved as a family adjusts to the changing roles and dynamics that a new baby brings.
■ "The Importance of Preschool," by Linda Morgan. How to identify a quality preschool that's a good fit for your child.

Rights and Payment Exclusive regional rights (6 months–1 year) for original articles; second rights for reprints. Original articles, $50–$200. Depts/columns, $25–$40. Reprints, $25–$45. Pays on publication. Provides contributor's copies.

San Diego Family

P.O. Box 23960, San Diego, CA 92193-3960. www.sandiegofamily.com

Editor: Kirsten Flournoy

This magazine provides informative, locally focused articles for families living in the San Diego area. Its goal is to provide parenting information and resources that enhance the quality and emphasize the pleasures of family life. ■ **Circulation** 120,000 ■ **Audience** Parents ■ **Frequency** Monthly

Freelance Potential Publishes 120–200 freelance submissions yearly: 90% written by nonstaff writers; 10% by authors new to the magazine; 5% by previously unpublished writers. Receives 10 queries, 10 unsolicited manuscripts monthly.

Submissions Guidelines and editorial calendar available at website. Query or send complete manuscript. Prefers email to kirsten@sandiegofamily.com; include "article submission" or "query" in subject line. Responds in 1 month.
■ *Articles:* 500–1,200 words. Informational, self-help, how-to. Topics: parenting, pregnancy, childbirth, child care, education, summer camp, health, safety, nutrition, gardening, dining out, recreation, arts and crafts, travel, sports, family finance, local events, multicultural issues, parties, finances, home and garden, green living.
■ *Depts/columns:* Word lengths vary. News briefs, tips, trends, restaurant reviews, book reviews, cooking, gardening.

Sample Issue 134 pages. Advertising. Sample copy available.

- "Does Your Child Have Allergies or Asthma?" by Paul Ehrlich et al. Questions for parents to help them distinguish between cold symptoms, allergies, and asthma.
- "Taking Charge of Your Memories," by Geeta Shreedar. Digital solutions for organizing family photos.

Rights and Payment First or second, and all regional rights. Written material, $1.25 per column inch. Pays on publication. Provides 1 contributor's copy.

Santa Barbara Family Life

P.O. Box 4867, Santa Barbara, CA 93140. www.sbfamilylife.com

Editor: Nansie Chapman

This community-oriented magazine covers events and resources of interest to families living in the Santa Barbara area of California. It focuses on regional arts and entertainment, local destinations, and health and relationship issues. ■ **Circulation** 60,000 ■ **Audience** Parents ■ **Frequency** Monthly

Freelance Potential Publishes 10 freelance submissions yearly: 5% written by nonstaff writers; 10% by authors new to the magazine; 5% by previously unpublished writers. Receives about 42 queries monthly.

Submissions Query or send complete manuscript. Accepts email to nansie@sbfamilylife.com. Responds if interested.
- *Articles:* 500–1,200 words. Informational, profiles, photo-essays, personal experience. Topics: regional events and activities, parenting, family life, education, recreation, crafts, hobbies, current events.
- *Depts/columns:* Word lengths vary. Love and relationships, arts and entertainment, health issues.
- *Other:* Puzzles and activities.

Sample Issue 36 pages. Advertising. Sample copy available at website.
- "Bored with the Same ol' Beautiful Orchids Every Day?" by Mike Bush. A primer on growing orchids outside.
- "Events." Highlights 3 upcoming events in the Santa Barbara area.

Rights and Payment Rights vary. Written material, $25–$35. Payment policy varies.

Scholastic Parent & Child

Scholastic Inc., 557 Broadway, New York, NY 10012-3999. www.parentandchildonline.com

Senior Editor: Samantha Brody

Targeting parents of children from birth to age 12, this magazine helps readers celebrate the joys of family living and learning. It covers topics important to parents everywhere, including child development, health and fitness, juggling work and home, and child-related products.
■ **Circulation** 7.8 million ■ **Audience** Parents ■ **Frequency** 8 times a year

Freelance Potential Publishes 20 freelance submissions yearly: 60% written by nonstaff writers; 15% by authors new to the magazine. Receives 100 queries, 50 unsolicited manuscripts monthly.

Submissions Guidelines available. Query or send complete manuscript. Accepts hard copy. SASE. Responds to queries in 3 months, to manuscripts in 2 months.
- *Articles:* 500–1,000 words. Informational, how–to, interviews. Topics: child development, education, parenting.
- *Depts/columns:* Word lengths vary. Literacy, health, parent/teacher relationships, arts and crafts, child development, product reviews, travel, cooking, family issues.

Sample Issue 88 pages. Advertising. Sample copy available.
- "A Different Kind of Strength," by Jennifer Fox. How to recognize and optimize a child's strengths.
- "9 Marvelous Months," by Lambeth Hochwald. Expert advice and fascinating facts for each trimester of pregnancy.

Rights and Payment All rights. Written material, payment rates vary. Pays on publication. Provides contributor's copies.

Scooter

New York Observer, 321 West 44th Street, 6th Floor, New York, NY 10036. www.observer.com/scooter

Editor in Chief: Peter Feld

Scooter is a new magazine, published by the *New York Observer*, about raising children in New York City. The free magazine specifically targets parents in Manhattan and Brooklyn, and features articles on trends, education, parenting issues, and recreation. The magazine will cover subjects such as playgrounds, outings, family-friendly brunches, and the city's hidden gems, and report on issues such as family moves and preschool admission. ■ **Circulation** 40,000 ■ **Audience** Parents ■ **Frequency** Twice a year

Freelance Potential Unavailable.

Submissions For more information, contact scooter@observer.com.
■ *Articles:* Informational. Topics: parenting, education, recreation, home and family.
■ *Depts/columns:* Word lengths vary. Children's book, film, and music reviews.

Sample Issue 80 pages.
■ "Back to School." Spotlighting the latest school fashion trends and the best city schools.
■ "Best Books." A review of recent books for children and parents.

Rights and Payment Unavailable.

Seattle's Child

1463 East Republican Street, #193, Seattle, WA 98112. www.seattleschild.com

Managing Editor: Ruth Schubert

With an emphasis on local resources and services, this magazine provides Seattle-area families with a wealth of relevant parenting information. Each issue also features health, travel, and education information. Local issues that relate to national trends are always of interest, as long as sources from the area can be incorporated. ■ **Circulation** 80,000 ■ **Audience** Parents ■ **Frequency** Monthly

Freelance Potential Publishes 30 freelance submissions yearly: 80% written by nonstaff writers; 25% by authors new to the magazine; 10% by previously unpublished writers. Receives 10+ queries monthly.

Submissions Guidelines and theme list available. Query with outline. Accepts hard copy and email queries to rschubert@seattleschild.com. Accepts simultaneous submissions if identified. SASE. Responds in 1 month.
■ *Articles:* Word lengths vary. Informational, how-to, personal experience. Topics: family, parenting, social issues, health, fitness, nutrition, regional news, family travel, recreation.
■ *Depts/columns:* Word lengths vary. Profiles, cooking, media reviews.

Sample Issue 46 pages. Advertising. Sample copy available.
■ "Writers in the Schools Program," by Taryn Zier. Local writers share their expertise to help students discover the power and joy of writing.
■ "Seattle School Board Ousts Superintendent Goodloe–Johnson," by Cheryl Murfin. What's behind the firing of this prominent school administrator.

Rights and Payment Rights vary. Written material, $100–$450. Pays 30 days after publication. Provides 2 contributor's copies.

See Jane Fly

1212 Mariner Way, #1, Tiburon, CA 94920. www.seejanefly.com

Submissions: Erica Rogers

Air travel, whether for business or recreation, can be a hassle. This website was created in 2007 to give travelers informational travel guides, how-to's, and scores of helpful tips and advice from people who have learned to travel well. Updated regularly, a portion of its content is geared toward traveling with children. It accepts articles and blogs from travel experts who have seen it all and done it all—with kids. ■ **Hits per month** 30,000+ ■ **Audience** Women ■ **Frequency** Unavailable

Freelance Potential Publishes several freelance submissions yearly.

Submissions Query with author interests, credentials, and writing samples. Accepts email queries to partner@seejanefly.com. Response time varies.
■ *Articles:* Word lengths vary. Informational, how–to, personal experience, interviews. Topics: air travel, destinations and activities, themed trips, packing, traveling with children, fashion and beauty.
■ *Depts/columns:* Word lengths vary.

Sample Issue Sample copy available at website.
■ "10 Tips for Packing Light," by Erica Dublin. Tips for packing efficiently and avoiding overpacking when traveling with a family.
■ "Stay–Trim Tricks of the Trade: What Diet & Fitness Experts Eat," by Alexa Joy Sherman. What nutrition and fitness experts do when traveling to keep themselves fit and avoid weight gain.

Rights and Payment Rights vary. Written material, payment rates vary. Payment policy varies.

Singlemom.com

www.singlemom.com

Editor

SingleMom.com presents free information, support, resources, and tools for single mothers who are single by circumstance or by choice. This website focuses on the issues that affect single moms and their children and strives to provide them with guidance, emotional support, and ultimately the means for them to become self–sufficient and reliant. A popular feature of the site is its "Amazing Mom Stories" department, which features inspiring accounts of sacrifice, determination, will, and the desire to overcome adversity. ■ **Hits per month** Unavailable ■ **Audience** Mothers ■ **Frequency** Unavailable

Freelance Potential Publishes several freelance submissions yearly.

Submissions Send complete manuscript. Accepts email submissions to contact@singlemom.com. Response time varies.
■ *Articles:* Word lengths vary. Informational, how–to, personal experience. Topics: government grants, scholarships, careers, health care, finances, housing, legal issues, child care, social issues, real–life problems, media reviews, cooking and recipes.

Sample Issue Sample copy available at website.
■ "Parenting Insight? Like Everyone, You'll Learn to Trust Me," by Darcey Blain. A single mom shares her experiences and advice.
■ "Is It Harder to Raise Boys or Girls?" by Paula Spencer. The debate has much to do with what aspect of parenting is being considered and the age and developmental stage of the child.

Rights and Payment No payment.

South Florida Parenting

1701 Green Road, Suite B, Deerfield Beach, FL 33064. www.southfloridaparenting.com

Editor: Kyara Lomer Camarena

Serving three counties in southeastern Florida, this publication provides its readers with the most up-to-date regional information on child development, recreational activities, and travel. It prefers to work with local writers. ■ **Circulation** 95,000 ■ **Audience** Parents ■ **Frequency** Monthly

Freelance Potential Publishes 90 freelance submissions yearly: 85% written by nonstaff writers; 10% by authors new to the magazine. Receives 7-10 queries and unsolicited manuscripts monthly.

Submissions Editorial calendar available at website. Guidelines available. Prefers complete manuscript; will accept query. Accepts hard copy and email submissions to krlomer@tribune.com. SASE. Responds in 2–3 months.
■ *Articles:* 800–1,500 words. Informational, how-to, profiles, interviews, personal experience. Topics: family life, travel, parenting, education, leisure, music, health, regional events and activities.
■ *Depts/columns:* To 750 words. Family finances, health, nutrition, infant care, preteen issues.

Sample Issue 118 pages. Advertising. Sample copy available at website.
■ "Young at Art Hosts Tree Houses Exhibit," by Scott Fishman. A look at a new exhibit at a local children's museum.
■ "Migraines: Not Just for Adults," by Sue Hubbard. Recognizing the symptoms of migraines in children.

Rights and Payment One-time regional rights. Written material, $50–$300. Pays on publication. Provides contributor's copies upon request.

South Jersey Mom

P.O. Box 2413, Vineland, NJ 08362-2413. www.southjerseymom.com

Executive Editor: Adrienne Richardson

This regional magazine focuses on providing support and advice for moms with children under the age of 12, including expectant moms. It shares real stories from real moms that highlight the joys, wonders, headaches, and heartaches that go along with parenting. It features debates over hot parenting issues and local opinions about national issues. The stories are about regional children and families and are written by local writers using sources and settings in South Jersey. ■ **Circulation** 38,000 ■ **Audience** Parents ■ **Frequency** Monthly

Freelance Potential Publishes 50–75 freelance submissions yearly: 98% written by nonstaff writers; 10% by authors new to the magazine; 40% by previously unpublished writers. Receives 15 queries monthly.

Submissions Guidelines and editorial calendar available at website. Query with 2 writing samples and author biography. Prefers email queries to adrienne@southjerseymom.com. Response time varies.
■ *Articles:* To 600 words. Informational, profiles, personal experience. Topics: parenting, trends, family issues, pregnancy, technology, education, exercise, safety, sports, recreation.
■ *Depts/columns:* Up to 600 words. Health topics, gear, technology.

Sample Issue 36 pages. Advertising. Sample copy available at website.
■ "Planning Your Family Summer Vacation," by Makema T. Douglas. Vacations in the South Jersey vicinity that provide fun activities without a lot of travel.
■ "Nana's 2 Sense," by Nana Jean. A mom bewails the assault on children's sensibilities and values in the media.

Rights and Payment Rights vary. No payment.

SweetMama

www.sweetspot.ca/SweetMama

Editor

This website, part of the family of online trend-spotting guides at www.sweetspot.ca, caters to mothers who want cool, helpful information quickly. *SweetMama* focuses on parenting advice, tips, and sweet finds to help raise kids well. It has articles with information relevant to mothers across Canada, as well localized guides to entertainment, services, and shopping. ■ **Hits per month** Unavailable ■ **Audience** Canadian mothers ■ **Frequency** Updated regularly

Freelance Potential *SweetMama* is "always looking for talented writers with a knack for finding sweet spots!"

Submissions Guidelines available at website. To query about general freelance opportunities, query with a short blurb about why you'd be great at uncovering sweet finds in Toronto, Montreal, Calgary or Vancouver. To send a specific pitch, query with as many details as possible. Accepts email to contact@sweetspot.ca
■ *Articles:* Word lengths vary. Informational, personal experience. Topics: parenting, child development, education, kid-related gear, style, reviews.

Sample Issue Sample copy available at website.
■ "Great Gear for Back-to-School Cool." More than 50 great finds for school gear and fashions.
■ "Babysitter Must-Haves." Essential things to have on hand for the sitter, besides pizza and an emergency contact list.

Rights and Payment Unavailable.

Syracuse Parent

5910 Firestone Drive, Syracuse, NY 13206. www.syracuseparent.net

Editor: Jennifer Wing

This parenting magazine is distributed at family-friendly locations around central New York. Its purpose is to arm New York parents with the local information they need to raise a family there. It also publishes an array of articles on parenting and family issues. It seeks local information and local sources. ■ **Circulation** 26,500 ■ **Audience** Parents ■ **Frequency** Monthly

Freelance Potential Publishes 15 freelance submissions yearly: 40% written by nonstaff writers; 10% by authors new to the magazine; 25% by previously unpublished writers. Receives about 8 queries monthly.

Submissions Guidelines and editorial calendar available. Query. Accepts hard copy. SASE. Responds in 4–6 weeks.
■ *Articles:* 800–1,000 words. Informational, how-to, profiles, interviews, personal experience, practical application, humor. Topics: parenting, family issues, pets, education, health, current events, regional news, social issues, nature, the environment, technology, music, travel, recreation, sports.
■ *Depts/columns:* Staff-written.
■ *Other:* Submit artwork 3–4 months in advance.

Sample Issue 24 pages. Advertising. Sample copy available.
■ "How to Encourage Your Baby to Self–Soothe." What parents can do to encourage babies to calm themselves and fall asleep.
■ "Snap, Crackle, Fiber? How to Look for a Healthy Cereal," by Mary Ann Russo. A dietician's advice on buying nutritious cereal.

Rights and Payment First North American serial rights. Articles, $25–$30. Pays on publication.

This Week Community Newspapers

7801 North Central Drive, Lewis Center, OH 43035. www.thisweeknews.com

Editor: Sandy Wallace

Readers in central Ohio turn to one of the 22 region-specific *ThisWeek* publications for articles on family life, parenting, and education, as well as local news, events, and sports coverage. *ThisWeek* also has a website that is updated daily. Preference is given to local writers who have a strong connection to the community. ■ **Circulation** 200,000 ■ **Audience** Parents ■ **Frequency** Weekly

Freelance Potential Publishes 100 freelance submissions yearly: 100% written by nonstaff writers.

Submissions Guidelines available at website. Query. Accepts email queries to editorial@thisweek-news.com (no attachments). Responds in 1 month.
■ *Articles:* Word lengths vary. Informational, news. Topics: regional news, sports, community, family.
■ *Depts/columns:* Word lengths vary.

Sample Issue Advertising. Sample copy available at website.
■ "Historical Society Honors Longtime Volunteers," by Margo Bartlett. Historical society pays tribute to those who have worked to preserve area history.
■ "Crime Summit Draws a Crowd," by Eric George. Community concerns about area crime.

Rights and Payment First or reprint rights. Written material, word lengths vary; 10¢–20¢ a word. Pays on publication. Provides 2 contributor's copies.

Thriving Family

Focus on the Family, 8605 Explorer Drive, Colorado Springs, CO 80920, www.thrivingfamily.com

Submissions Editor

Thriving Family is part of the ministry of Focus on the Family, a global Christian organization that supports marriages reflecting God's design and equips parents to raise their kids according to biblical principles. The articles offer reliable solutions, practical advice, and parenting and marriage guidance. It also addresses the needs of single-parent families, blended families, and extended families.
■ **Circulation** Unavailable ■ **Audience** Parents ■ **Frequency** 6 times a year

Freelance Potential Freelance material is accepted for use in print, and addtional material is accepted for the website.

Submissions Guidelines available at website. Query for Family Life columns; send complete manuscript for all material. Accepts hard copy or email to thrivingfamilysubmissions@family.org. SASE. Response time varies.
■ *Articles:* 1,200–1,500 words: well-known personalities in the Christian world.
■ *Depts/columns:* Family Stages (practical ideas, 50–200 words), Family Media (entertainment trends kids ages 2–6, 250 words), Family Life (husband's or wife's insight into marriage, blended families, extended families, adoption/special needs, word lengths vary).

Sample Issue Sample articles are available to view at the website.
■ "Uncomfortable Questions about Your Child's Adoption," by Sue Johnson. Suggestions for answering an adopted child's questions about his or her life.
■ "Remembering 9/11," by Nathan Davidson and Andrea Jewell. Profiles of several families affected by the September 11 terrorist attacks, and how they worked to retain strong familial bonds and faith.

Rights and Payment First non-exclusive rights. Family Stages, $50. Written material, 25¢+ a word. Payment policy varies.

Tidewater Parent

150 West Brambleton Avenue, Norfolk, VA 23510. www.mytidewatermoms.com

Editor in Chief: Jennifer O'Donnell

Tidewater Parent is a comprehensive magazine showcasing articles and news for active parents and families in the coastal regions of Virginia. It sees itself as the primary source for local parenting information, giving readers articles on regional activities and resources as well as parenting issues and child development. Many of its readers are military families. ■ **Circulation** 35,000+ ■ **Audience** Parents ■ **Frequency** Monthly

Freelance Potential Publishes 40 freelance submissions yearly: 90% written by nonstaff writers; 50% by authors new to the magazine; 10% by previously unpublished writers. Receives about 6 unsolicited manuscripts monthly.

Submissions Editorial calendar available at website. Send complete manuscript. Will accept previously published manuscripts that can be reprinted. Accepts hard copy. SASE. Response time varies.
■ *Articles:* 800–1,200 words. Informational, how–to, personal experience. Topics: parenting, child development, regional activities, recreation, health, seasonal, education, military families, green living, social issues, summer camps, finances, pregnancy, balancing work and family.
■ *Depts/columns:* Word lengths vary. Parenting advice, book and movie reviews.

Sample Issue 76 pages. Advertising. Sample copy available at website.
■ "Tiny Carbon Footprints." Simple suggestions for families to help take care of the environment.
■ "What Kids Think about Military Life." Three children who have parents in the military.

Rights and Payment Rights vary. Articles, $25. Kill fee, 50%. Pays on publication. Provides 1 contributor's copy.

Today's Parent

1 Mount Pleasant Road, 8th floor, Toronto, Ontario M4Y 2Y5, Canada. www.todaysparent.com

Managing Editor: Nadine Silverthorne

Today's Parent is Canada's number one parenting magazine, and it hosts a website with content that is distinct from the magazine's. Together they provide information—both philosophical and practical—on a range of parenting issues, from children's health and development to family fun. Material should be grounded in the reality of Canadian family life, and strike a balance between the practical and the reflective. Though open to all writers, Canadian writers are favored. ■ **Circulation** 215,000 ■ **Audience** Parents ■ **Frequency** Monthly

Freelance Potential Freelancers are welcome to submit feature articles as well as several regular departments.

Submissions Guidelines available at website. Send complete manuscript for Your Turn column only. Query with detailed proposal, writings samples, and proposed length for all other material. Accepts hard copy and email to queries@tpg.rogers.com. Responds in 6 weeks.
■ *Articles:* 1,500–2,500 words. Informational, personal experience, profiles. Topics: parenting issues, relationships, child discipline, pregnancy, party ideas, balancing work and family, fathers' roles.
■ *Depts/columns:* 500–700 words. Your Turn (personal experience), Mom Time (fitness, beauty, relationships), Education, Health, Behaviour, Money.

Sample Issue Sample articles are available to view at the website.
■ "How Teens Communication," by Randi Chapnik Myers. How technology has changed the way teens talk to each other, and what parents needs to know about it.
■ "What Is HypnoBirthing," by Jenn Hardy. Examines hypnosis as part of a less stressful birth.

Rights and Payment All rights. Your Turn, $200. Other written material, word lengths vary. Pays 30 days after acceptance.

Toledo Area Parent News

1120 Adams Street, Toledo, OH 43604. www.toledoparent.com

Assignment Editor: Christy Penka

Distributed through more than 1,000 sites in northwestern Ohio and southeastern Michigan, *Toledo Area Parent News* provides important, up-to-date parenting information in an easy-to-read style. Most of its material has a regional angle. It is most interested in articles that provide practical information that parents can use in their day-to-day family lives. ■ **Circulation** 81,000 ■ **Audience** Parents ■ **Frequency** Monthly

Freelance Potential Publishes 12 freelance submissions yearly: 75% written by nonstaff writers; 20% by authors new to the magazine; 10% by previously unpublished writers. Receives about 4 queries and unsolicited manuscripts monthly.

Submissions Guidelines and editorial calendar available. Query with clips; or send complete manuscript. Prefers email to editor@toledoparent.com; will accept hard copy. SASE. Responds in 1 month.
■ *Articles:* 700–2,000 words. Informational, profiles, interviews. Topics: family issues, parenting, teen issues, education, social issues, health, fitness.
■ *Depts/columns:* Word lengths vary. Restaurant reviews, brief news items related to family issues.

Sample Issue 48 pages. Advertising. Sample copy available via email request to kdevol@toledocitypaper.com.
■ "On the Air," by Christy Penka. A local family with a child who has Williams Syndrome is featured on a national news program.
■ "Meet the Mummies," by Karen L. Zickes. Review of an exhibit at the Toledo Museum of Art.

Rights and Payment All North American serial rights. Written material, $30–$200. Pays on publication.

Tots To Teens

P.O. Box 1233, Plainfield, IL 60544. www.totstoteensmagazine.com

Editor in Chief: Phyllis Pometta

This digital magazine is celebrating its second anniversary. It continues to bring readers information on best picks in products, apparel, toys, fashions and gadgets, accompanied by a healthy dose of parenting articles on all stages of child development, motherhood, and healthy eating. ■ **Hits per month** Unavailable ■ **Audience** Parents ■ **Frequency** Quarterly

Freelance Potential Freelancers are invited to pitch article ideas.

Submissions Editorial calendar available at website. Accepts email queries to editor@totstoteens-magazine.com.
■ *Articles:* Word lengths vary. Informational, how-to, profiles, personal experience. Topics; child fashion trends, parenting, social issues, family relationships, family travel
■ *Depts/columns:* Word lengths vary. Baby gear, product reviews, cooking with children, book and media reviews.

Sample Issue 64 pages. Advertising. Sample copy available at website.

■ "How Family Dinners Improve Students' Grades." The benefits of a family sitting together to dine.
■ "Making Motherhood Work for You." Advice for moms of all ages on balancing home and work.

Rights and Payment No payment, but writers receive a link to personal webpage or blog.

Treasure Valley Family

13191 West Scotfield Street, Boise, ID 83713-0899. www.treasurevalleyfamily.com

Publisher/Editor: Liz Buckingham

This regional magazine targets parents with children under the age of 12. It offers informational articles on education, child care, and health issues, as well as ideas for family activities and excursions.
■ **Circulation** 20,000+ ■ **Audience** Parents ■ **Frequency** Monthly

Freelance Potential Publishes 10–15 freelance submissions yearly: 50% written by nonstaff writers; 1–2% by authors new to the magazine. Receives 150 queries and unsolicited manuscripts monthly.

Submissions Guidelines and theme list/editorial calendar available at website. Prefers query with clips; will accept complete manuscript with 1-sentence author biography. Accepts hard copy and email submissions to magazine@treasurevalleyfamily.com (Word attachments). SASE. Responds in 2–3 months.
■ *Articles:* 1,000–1,300 words. Informational, how-to. Topics: health, preschool, child care, education, summer camp, sports, travel, recreation, teen issues, college, party planning, crafts, hobbies, the arts, family fun.
■ *Depts/columns:* 700–900 words. Events, activities, advice, news, product reviews, age-specific issues, book reviews, women's health, profiles of local agencies, interviews with area families.

Sample Issue 48 pages. Advertising. Sample copy available.
■ "Tutors Help Make the Grade," by Pamela Kleibrink Thompson. How tutors can help children become successful academically.
■ "Bits and Pieces." A round-up of brief news items and reviews that pertain to children and families.

Rights and Payment First North American serial rights. All material, payment rates vary; pays an additional 10% for Web rights. Pays on publication. Provides 2 contributor's copies.

Trumbull County Parent

100 DeBartolo Place, Suite 210, Youngstown, OH 44512. www.forparentsonline.com

Editor: Amy Leigh Wilson

This magazine, distributed in the Ohio county of Trumbull, offers families information on local kid-friendly activities as well as parenting articles of general interest. ■ **Circulation** 50,000
■ **Audience** Parents ■ **Frequency** Monthly

Freelance Potential Publishes 100 freelance submissions yearly: 99% written by nonstaff writers; 20% by authors new to the magazine; 5% by previously unpublished writers. Receives about 42 unsolicited manuscripts monthly.

Submissions Query or send complete manuscript. Prefers email to editor@mvparentmagazine.com. Response time varies.
■ *Articles:* Word lengths vary. Informational, how–to. Topics: child development, parenting, education, health, regional activities and resources.
■ *Depts/columns:* Word lengths vary.
■ *Other:* Submit seasonal material 3 months in advance.

Sample Issue Advertising. Sample copy available.
■ "Avoid 'Summer Slide' in Your House." Ways to help children keep their academic skills sharp over the summer.
■ "Moms' Favoritism Tied to Depression." Results of a study that shows middle–aged adults who perceived their mother favored one sibling over another often have symptoms of depression.

Rights and Payment Rights vary. Payment varies. Payment policy unavailable.

Tulsa Kids

1820 South Boulder, Suite 400, Tulsa, OK 74119-4409. www.tulsakids.com

Editor: Betty Casey

Tulsa parents read this magazine in print and online for information on parenting, education, and regional activities. Most articles are focused on the greater Tulsa region. It looks for well-researched articles on current parenting topics, preferably with a local angle or interview. It seeks to inform and support its readers. ■ **Circulation** 20,000 ■ **Audience** Parents ■ **Frequency** Monthly

Freelance Potential Publishes 1–10 freelance submissions monthly: 90% written by nonstaff writers; 10% by authors new to the magazine; 20% by previously unpublished writers. Receives 75–100 queries, 50–75 unsolicited manuscripts monthly.

Submissions Send complete manuscript. Prefers email submissions to editor@tulsakids.com (Word attachments). Accepts simultaneous submissions if identified. Responds in 2–3 months.
■ *Articles:* 500–800 words. Informational, profiles, interviews, humor, personal experience. Topics: family life, education, parenting, recreation, entertainment, college, health, sports, fashion, maternity, decorating, fitness, careers, crafts, social issues.
■ *Depts/columns:* 100–300 words. News; book, CD, and product reviews; social issues; family cooking.

Sample Issue 84 pages. Advertising. Sample copy available at website.
■ "The Change to Daylight Saving Time Can Disrupt Sleep in Some Children," by Bob Haring. How to deal with this twice annual event.
■ "Battling Baby Blues and More," by Holly Wall. How to deal with depressive disorders as a mom.

Rights and Payment One-time rights for print and 6 months online locally. Written material, $25–$100. Payment policy varies. Provides contributor's copy if requested.

Twins

30799 Pinetree Road, #256, Cleveland, OH 44124. www.twinsmagazine.com

Editor in Chief: Christa D. Reed

Since 1984, parents of twins, triplets, and higher-order multiples have been reading this magazine for the valuable information it provides. From health concerns and child development issues to humorous and touching tales of the joys and challenges, *Twins* covers it all. It is interested in new research specific to twins and multiples, as well as personal experience pieces about growing up as a twin.
■ **Circulation** 40,000 ■ **Audience** Parents ■ **Frequency** 6 times a year

Freelance Potential Publishes 10–12 freelance submissions yearly: 50% written by nonstaff writers. Receives 20 queries monthly.

Submissions Guidelines available at website. Query or send complete manuscript with brief author biography and head shot image. Accepts email queries to twinseditor@twinsmagazine.com (Word or pdf attachments). Responds in 3 months.
■ *Articles:* 800–1,000 words. Informational, how-to, profiles, personal experience. Topics: parenting, family life, health, fitness, education, music, the arts, the home, nutrition, diet, sports, social issues, crafts, hobbies.
■ *Depts/columns:* To 800 words. Mom-2-Mom, A Word from Dad, Family Health, LOL, Research Column, Resource Round Up, Tales from Twins, Twin Star Spotlight, news, new product information, opinion pieces, short items on child development

Sample Issue 56 pages. Advertising. Sample copy available.
■ "Pregnant with Twins," by Francoise von Trapp Gibson. Reassuring information for pregnant women explaining that not all twin pregnancies are high risk.
■ "Preschool Twins," by J. Cameron Tew. Getting twins ready for "real" school.

Rights and Payment All rights. Written material, $50–$100. Pays on publication. Provides 2 contributor's copies.

Urbanbaby & Toddler

928 West 20th Avenue, Vancouver, British Columbia V5Z 1Y5, Canada. www.urbanbaby.ca

Editor: Emma Lee

This publication targets British Columbia's parents and expectant parents with information on everything from pregnancy to local family events. Many features are written by local experts in child development, family nutrition, breastfeeding, education, and parenting. It also carries a resource list and calendar of events to aid parents. ■ **Circulation** 40,000 ■ **Audience** Parents ■ **Frequency** Quarterly

Freelance Potential Unavailable.

Submissions For more information, contact info@urbanbaby.ca.
■ *Articles:* Word lengths vary. Informational. Topics: parenting, education, child health and development, family recreation.
■ *Depts/columns:* Word lengths vary. Nutrition, health, education, postpartum pregnancy, new products.

Sample Issue 40 pages. Advertising. Sample copy available at website.
■ "Baby Meets Trails," by Michael Boronowski. The best stroller-friendly hiking trails in Vancouver.
■ "Parenting: Where and How Does Dad Fit?" by Marilee Peters. Advocates for parental leave regulations that allow fathers time to bond with their babies.

Rights and Payment Unavailable.

Vancouver Family

P.O. Box 820264, Vancouver, WA 98682. www.vancouverfamilymagazine.com

Editor: Nikki Klock

Offering the information and resources needed to raise healthy, well-adjusted children, this magazine serves parents in the Clark County area of Washington State. Its emphasis is on family businesses and events located in the region. Local writers are preferred and a local angle is required for consideration. ■ **Circulation** 10,000 ■ **Audience** Parents ■ **Frequency** Monthly

Freelance Potential Publishes 25–30 freelance submissions yearly: 90% written by nonstaff writers; 40% by authors new to the magazine; 30% by previously unpublished writers. Receives about 35 queries monthly.

Submissions Guidelines and editorial calendar available. Query. Accepts hard copy. SASE. Response time varies.
■ *Articles:* Word lengths vary. Informational, how–to. Topics: parenting, family-related issues, health and fitness, relationships, recreation, regional activities and resources, travel.
■ *Depts/columns:* Word lengths vary. Parenting and family issues, local family businesses, local news.

Sample Issue 32 pages. Advertising. Sample copy available at website.
■ "Preparing Siblings for a New Baby," by Jacqueline Bodnar. How to pave the way for a new member of the family and tend to the needs of baby's siblings.
■ "Staycation: Olympic Peninsula," by Nikki Klock. Family fun at this local recreation hotspot.

Rights and Payment Rights vary. Assigned articles, 10¢ a word. Payment policy varies.

Vegetarian Journal

P.O. Box 1463, Baltimore, MD 21203. www.vrg.org

Managing Editor: Debra Wasserman

Launched in 1982, *Vegetarian Journal* targets well-educated readers of various backgrounds who share a common interest in the vegan or vegetarian lifestyle. Its goal is to make vegetarian living easily accessible at any stage of life. ■ **Circulation** 20,000 ■ **Audience** Parents ■ **Frequency** 4 times a year

Freelance Potential Publishes 10 freelance submissions yearly: 50% written by nonstaff writers; 5% by authors new to the magazine.

Submissions Query with brief author biography. Accepts hard copy. SASE. Responds in 1 week.
■ *Articles:* Word lengths vary. Informational. Topics: health, nutrition, animal rights, ecology, recipes, cooking tips, scientific updates.
■ *Depts/columns:* Word lengths vary.
■ *Other:* Submit seasonal material 1 year in advance.

Sample Issue Sample copy available at website.
■ "Do Vegetarians and Vegans Stay Vegetarian?" by Charles Stahler. A survey about vegetarians and a look at its meaning.
■ "Have a Panini Party," by Nanette Blanchard. Suggestions for hosting a party with these sandwiches as the culinary centerpiece; recipes included.

Rights and Payment One-time rights. Articles, $200. Pays on acceptance. Provides 3+ contributor's copies.

VegFamily

4920 Silk Oak Drive, Sarasota, FL 34232. www.vegfamily.com

Editor: Cynthia Mosher

Families who are living, or want to live, a vegan lifestyle turn to this ezine for information and encouragement. While not absolutely imperative, a vegan perspective is expected to be evident in submissions. Well-written articles on other healthy-living topics, including organic, green, and sustainable living, will also be considered. ■ **Hits per month** 10,000 ■ **Audience** Parents ■ **Frequency** Monthly

Freelance Potential Publishes 150+ freelance submissions yearly: 50% written by nonstaff writers; 50% by authors new to the magazine; 90% by previously unpublished writers. Receives 5 queries monthly.

Submissions Query. Accepts email queries to cynthia@vegfamily.com. Responds in 2 weeks.
■ *Articles:* 700+ words. Informational, self-help, how-to, profiles, personal experience. Topics: vegan pregnancy and health, vegan cooking, natural parenting, animal rights, the environment, green living.
■ *Depts/columns:* 700+ words. Opinions, profiles. Nutrition advice, recipes, cooking tips, health issues, vegan news, family profiles, parenting issues by age group.
■ *Artwork:* JPEG and GIF files.
■ *Other:* Activities. Submit seasonal material 2 months in advance.

Sample Issue Sample copy available at website.
■ "Are Vaccines Really Safe and Effective?" by Jock Doubleday. Some current thinking regarding the pros and cons of vaccines.
■ "A Uniquely Positive Hospital Experience," by Linda Muehlbauer. A vegan mom describes her hospital experience and how her vegan preferences were respected.

Rights and Payment First and electronic rights. Articles, $10–$30. Pays on publication.

Vibrant Life

55 West Oak Ridge Drive, Hagerstown, MD 21740. www.vibrantlife.org

Editor: Heather Quintana

This Christian magazine sets itself apart from the competition by taking a holistic approach that incorporates spirituality with overall health. It features articles that offer practical suggestions for living a healthier, happier, and more satisfying life. Its readers expect practical, affordable suggestions that fit into their demanding schedules while helping them prevent and fight disease. ■ **Circulation** 21,711 ■ **Audience** Parents ■ **Frequency** 6 times a year

Freelance Potential Publishes 25 freelance submissions yearly: 95% written by nonstaff writers; 60% by authors new to the magazine; 30% by previously unpublished writers. Receives 25 queries, 12 unsolicited manuscripts monthly.

Submissions Guidelines available at website. Send complete manuscript (with photos if applicable). Accepts hard copy and email to vibrantlife@rhpa.org (Word attachments). No electronic photo submissions. SASE. Also accepts reprints. Responds in 1 month.
■ *Articles:* 450–1,00 words. Informational, how-to, self-help, profiles, interviews. Topics: health, fitness, nutrition, family, spiritual balance, challenges and triumphs, safety, environmental stewardship.
■ *Depts/columns:* Word lengths vary. Health news, medical advice, green living, spiritual guidance, family life, recipes.

Sample Issue 32 pages. Sample copy available at website.
■ "Seven Ways to Boost Your Energy Level." Seven life strategies to feel more invigorated.
■ "Is Road Biking for You?" Questions to answer to help decide if this fitness activity is right for you.

Rights and Payment First world serial rights, *Vibrant Life* reprint and website rights. Written material, $100–$300. Pays on publication. Provides 3 contributor's copies.

The Village Family

501 40th Street S, Suite 201, Fargo, ND 58103. www.thevillagefamily.org

Editor: Laurie Neill

Targeting parents living in North Dakota's Fargo region, *The Village Family Magazine* offers positive stories and valuable information that help improve the quality of life for families. It is published by the Village Family Service Center. ■ **Circulation** 25,000 ■ **Audience** Parents ■ **Frequency** 6 times a year

Freelance Potential Publishes 18 freelance submissions yearly: 90% written by nonstaff writers; 5–10% by authors new to the magazine. Receives 60 queries, 2 unsolicited manuscripts monthly.

Submissions Guidelines available. Query or send complete manuscript with author biography. Accepts email submissions to magazine@thevillagefamily.org. Response time varies.
■ *Articles:* 1,000–2,500 words. Informational, self-help, how-to, profiles, interviews, personal experience. Topics: current events, social issues, relationships, parenting, health and fitness, elder care, wellness.
■ *Depts/columns:* Word lengths vary. Crafts, health tips, recipes, relationships, opinion pieces.

Sample Issue 46 pages. Advertising. Sample issue available.
■ "Good News: Colon Cancer Is Preventable," by Heidi Tetzman. Screening and early intervention are the keys to preventing this disease.
■ "Forgiveness," by Roxane B. Salonen. An in–depth look at the hard work of forgiveness as related through the story of a mother whose daughter committed suicide.

Rights and Payment First and electronic rights. Written material, 10¢ a word. Reprints, $30–$50. Pays on publication.

Washington Family

485 Spring Park Place, Suite 500, Herndon, VA 20170. www.washingtonfamily.com

Managing Editor: Marae Leggs

Parents living in the Washington, D.C. area find advice on topics ranging from health and safety to fun and games. It offers regional activities and resources as well. ■ **Circulation** 100,000 ■ **Audience** Parents ■ **Frequency** Monthly

Freelance Potential Publishes 90 freelance submissions yearly: 75% written by nonstaff writers; 50% by authors new to the magazine; 50% by previously unpublished writers. Receives 100 queries monthly.

Submissions Guidelines and editorial calendar available. Query with outline. Accepts email queries to editor@thefamilymagazine.com (Word attachments). No simultaneous submissions. Response time varies.
- *Articles:* 800–900 words. Informational, self-help, how-to, personal experience. Topics: parenting, family life, relationships, fitness, crafts, hobbies, the arts, education, music, multicultural and ethnic issues, social issues, travel.
- *Depts/columns:* Word lengths vary. Health, cooking, activities, tips and trends.
- *Artwork:* 8x10 B/W prints and transparencies. Line art.
- *Other:* Submit seasonal material at least 3 months in advance.

Sample Issue 126 pages. Advertising. Sample copy available at website.
- "Creativity and Learning," by Heidi Smith Luedtke. Exploring the creative nature and how to nurture it in children.
- "A Rockin' Family Vacation," by Jolie Perara. A review of the all–inclusive resort, the Hard Rock Hotel & Casino Punta Cana.

Rights and Payment Exclusive regional and Web rights. Articles, $50. Depts/columns and artwork, payment rates vary. Pays on publication. Provides 1 tearsheet for contributors.

Washington Parent

4701 Sangamore Road, Suite N270, Bethesda, MD 20186-2528. www.washingtonparent.com

Editor: Margaret Hut

Washington Parent serves as a resource and support for families living in D.C., Maryland, and Northern Virginia. Its themed issues include articles written by local professionals in the fields of child development, the arts, education, and special needs. It covers topics that appeal to parents of newborns through teens. ■ **Circulation** 75,000 ■ **Audience** Parents ■ **Frequency** Monthly

Freelance Potential Publishes 20 freelance submissions yearly: 90% written by nonstaff writers. Receives 80+ queries monthly.

Submissions Guidelines and editorial calendar available. Query. Accepts email queries to contactus@washingtonparent.net (Word attachments). Response time varies.
- *Articles:* 1,000–1,200 words. Informational, how-to. Topics: regional news and events; parenting and family issues; entertainment; gifted, special, and regular education; child development; health; fitness; the environment; multicultural and ethnic issues; camps; parties.
- *Depts/columns:* Word lengths vary. Family travel, book and media reviews, education, topics relating to children with special needs, short news items.

Sample Issue 98 pages. Advertising. Sample copy available.
- "The Perks and Pitfalls of Raising an Only Child," by Robyn Des Roches. Strategies for maximizing the benefits and minimizing the disadvantages of being an only child.
- "Wowed by Women," by Justine Ickes. Fun facts about prominent women in all fields in honor of Women's History Month.

Rights and Payment First rights. Written material, payment rates vary. Provides 3 contributor's copies.

Westchester Family

7 Purdy Street, Suite 201, Harrison, NY 10528. www.westchesterfamily.com

Editor: Jean Sheff

Targeted to parents living in New York's Westchester County and Connecticut's Fairfield County,

Westchester Family provides parenting, health and safety, and education articles. Additionally, the magazine features a comprehensive event and activity calendar. While it is open to a variety of parenting and family topics, all articles must be well-researched, written in an engaging style, and have a local angle that pertains to people and events in the area. ■ **Circulation** 59,000 ■ **Audience** Parents ■ **Frequency** Monthly

Freelance Potential Publishes 20 freelance submissions yearly: 60% written by nonstaff writers; 5% by authors new to the magazine; 5% by previously unpublished writers. Receives 100 queries monthly.

Submissions Guidelines available. Query with clips. Accepts hard copy. SASE. Response time varies.
■ *Articles:* 800-1,200 words. Informational, profiles, interviews, photo-essays, personal experience. Topics: education, music, recreation, regional news, social issues, special, gifted, and regular education, travel, women's issues.
■ *Depts/columns:* 400–800 words. News, media reviews.

Sample Issue 82 pages. Advertising. Sample copy available.
■ "The Camp Director," by Jamie Sirkin. Ten questions parents should ask about summer camps to make the best choice for their child.
■ "Inspire Me!" by Sarah Niss. Book review of *Soar, Elinor*, the story of the youngest licensed female pilot in the United States.

Rights and Payment First rights. Written material, $25-$200. Pays on publication. Provides 1 contributor's copy.

West Coast Families

Unit #140, 2nd Floor, 13988 Maycrest Way, Richmond, British Columbia V6V 3C3 Canada.
www.westcoastfamilies.com

Managing Editor: Anya Levykh

West Coast Families is a local guide to family-related information in the Vancouver region. It puts a focus on the active, green, West Coast lifestyle that more of the families in this area are choosing. It covers parenting, family, and health issues for babies to tweens. It seeks original article ideas that can provide local, useful information for parents. ■ **Circulation** 40,000+ ■ **Audience** Parents ■ **Frequency** 9 times a year

Freelance Potential Publishes 12–40 freelance submissions yearly: 80% written by nonstaff writers; 25% by authors new to the magazine. Receives 35–65 queries monthly.

Submissions Guidelines and editorial calendar available at website. Query with résumé or relevant experience and writing sample. Accepts email queries only to editor@westcoastfamilies.com. Responds in 6–8 weeks, if interested.
■ *Articles:* 600–1,200 words. Informational, self-help, how-to, profiles, interviews, personal experience. Topics: family life, parenting, recreation, travel, religion, current events, health, fitness, finance, education, sports, hobbies, science, technology, nature, pets.
■ *Depts/columns:* Word lengths vary. Health, travel, finances, crafts.
■ *Other:* Puzzles, activities, jokes. Submit seasonal material 3 months in advance.

Sample Issue 32 pages. Advertising. Sample copy available at website.
■ "Tweens and Cell Phones," by Sara Dimerman. A family psychologist explains her reasons for not allowing her 11–year-old to have a cell phone.
■ "You Can Eat to Starve Cancer," by Debbie Bowman. Nutrients that can help prevent and battle cancers and the right foods to eat to get these nutrients.

Rights and Payment One-time and electronic rights. Written material, $50–$100. Kill fee, 50%. Pays on publication. Provides contributor's copies.

Western New York Family

3147 Delaware Avenue, Suite B, Buffalo, NY 14217. www.wnyfamilymagazine.com

Editor: Michele Miller

The articles in this family magazine address current parenting issues, with a western New York tie-in whenever possible. Strong emphasis is placed on local, family-oriented events and services for children. It is interested in articles that present practical information for parents in the region.
■ **Circulation** 25,000 ■ **Audience** Parents ■ **Frequency** Monthly

Freelance Potential Publishes 150 freelance submissions yearly: 90% written by nonstaff writers; 30% by authors new to the magazine; 30% by previously unpublished writers. Receives 100 unsolicited manuscripts monthly.

Submissions Guidelines and editorial calendar available at website. Prefers complete manuscript with 2-sentence biography. Accepts email submissions only to michele@wnyfamilymagazine.com (text in body of email along with Word attachments). Accepts simultaneous submissions if identified, and reprints. Responds if interested.

■ *Articles:* 950–3,000 words. Informational, how-to, self-help, creative nonfiction, humor, personal experience. Topics: parenting, education, children with special needs, family relationships, seasonal and holiday, working parents, newborn care, tweens, teens.
■ *Depts/columns:* Word lengths vary. News briefs, reviews, family travel, recipes, fatherhood, single parenting, Internet, technology.
■ *Other:* Submit seasonal material 3 months in advance

Sample Issue 64–80 pages. Advertising. Sample copy available at website.

■ "Seeking Spring," by Katrina Cassel. Activities that spark the imagination and fill those days of "April showers."
■ "Pops for All Seasons." Sweets on a stick for all occasions and seasons; recipes included.

Rights and Payment First or reprint and electronic rights. Written material, $35–$200 plus an additional 10% for online rights. Pays on publication.

West Virginia Family

P.O. Box 107, Buckhannon, WV 26201. www.wvfamilymagazine.com

Editor: Carla Cosner

This magazine focuses on all areas of interest to busy families living in the state of West Virginia. It seeks articles and tips on topics such as safety, travel, education, family traditions, and pets. Its editorial content is very specific to the season. *West Virginia Family* prefers articles that offer solutions and use local sources. ■ **Circulation** 15,000 ■ **Audience** Parents ■ **Frequency** 4 times a year

Freelance Potential Publishes 10–15 freelance submissions yearly: 75% written by nonstaff writers; 25% by authors new to the magazine; 15% by previously unpublished writers. Receives 100+ unsolicited manuscripts monthly.

Submissions Guidelines and editorial calendar available at website. Accepts email submissions to editor@wvfamilymagazine.com. Response time varies.
■ *Articles:* 250–600 words. Informational, how-to. Topics: summer camps, education, current events, health and fitness, recreation, social issues, safety, home life, travel, holidays and seasonal, pets.
■ *Depts/columns:* Word lengths vary. Child development, safety, parenting issues, finance, regional news, children's book and product reviews.

Sample Issue 28 pages. Advertising. Sample copy available at website.
■ "Sleep Loss and Fat Loss: What is the Connection?" by Kathy Sena. Losing sleep may also inhibit your ability to lose weight.

■ "Volunteer Guide," by Michele Boom. A regional guide on ways to give back during the holidays.

Rights and Payment One-time print and electronic rights; reprint rights. Original articles, $25. Filler, payment rates vary. Pays on publication. Provides 1 contributor's copy.

What's Up

3145 Wolfedale Road, Mississauga, Ontario L5C 3A9 Canada. www.whatsupfamilies.com

Editor in Chief: Erin Ruddy

Billed as "a busy mom's best friend," each issue of this Canadian magazine is filled with ideas for maximizing family time. Its practical strategies for time–strapped families helps parents enjoy their kids—whether at the dinner table, in the garden, or on the playground. It accepts submissions from Canadian authors only. ■ **Circulation** 100,000 ■ **Audience** Families ■ **Frequency** 6 times a year

Freelance Potential Publishes 30 freelance submissions yearly: 80% written by nonstaff writers; 60% by authors new to the magazine. Receives about 30 queries monthly.

Submissions Canadian authors only. Query. Accepts email queries to editor@whatsupfamily.ca. Response time varies.
■ *Articles:* Word lengths vary. Informational, how-to, profiles, interviews. Topics: education, family issues, travel, fitness, nutrition, health, the arts, entertainment.
■ *Depts/columns:* Word lengths vary. Mom Time, Health Matters, Finances, Baby Steps, From the Kitchen, Learning Curves, Family Travel, What's Up with Dad, Kid's Space, Cool Careers, Kid Craft.

Sample Issue 82 pages. Advertising.
■ "Health and Your DNA." What your genes have to do with your health.
■ "How to Host a Ghoulishly Good Gathering." Putting together the ultimate Halloween costume party.

Rights and Payment All rights. Written material, payment rates vary. Payment policy varies. Provides conributors copies.

Women Today Magazine

Power To Change, 20385 64th Avenue, Langley, British Columbia, V2Y 1N5, Canada. http://powertochange.com/women/

Senior Editor: Claire Colvin

This online magazine offers a Christian perspective on contemporary issues of relevance to today's women. It also offers information on how to minister to others. ■ **Hits per month** Unavailable ■ **Audience** Women ■ **Frequency** Unavailable

Freelance Potential Publishes 20–30 freelance submissions yearly: 30–50% written by nonstaff writers; 25% by authors new to the magazine; 5% by previously unpublished writers. Receives about 40 unsolicited manuscripts monthly.

Submissions Guidelines available at website. Send complete manuscript with author biography. Accepts submissions through online submission system only. Responds in 4–6 weeks.
■ *Articles:* 500–1,200 words. Informational, how-to. Topics: relationships, parenting, marriage, careers, personal finances, health, beauty, fitness, home and garden, faith.
■ *Depts/columns:* Word lengths vary.

Sample Issue Advertising. Sample copy available at website.
■ "Understanding Cutting," by Dena Yohe. A mother with a daughter who cuts explains the issue.
■ "Gift-Giving Strategies for Growing Families," by Stacy Wiebe. Gift-giving when families grow and live a distance apart.

Rights and Payment Reprint rights only. No payment.

Religious Magazines

The religious publishing market can be yet another way for children's writers to reach an audience. Writers can find religious magazines for children and those directed for Sunday school use in the "Magazines for Children and Teens" category, beginning on page 29. Listed here are publications that serve religious educators and youth ministry leaders, as well as those that present family, parenting, and social issues for audiences of all ages from a distinctly religious perspective.

When targeting these publications, take care to notice their requirements regarding content and style. Some may be tightly focused and Scripture-based, while others may be much more mainstream in their topics but want a spiritual or inspirational tone.

Birmingham Christian Family

P.O. Box 383203, Birmingham, AL 35238. www.christianfamilypublications.com

Editor: Laurie Stroud

Parents read *Birmingham Christian Family* for its uplifting articles and stories, with all content originating from a Christian perspective. It specifically addresses families living in and around Birmingham. While submissions on a variety of topics are welcome, a local angle is mandatory. ■ **Circulation** 35,000 ■ **Audience** Families ■ **Frequency** Monthly

Freelance Potential Publishes 15 freelance submissions yearly: 75% written by nonstaff writers; less than 5% by authors new to the magazine; 5% by previously unpublished writers. Receives 20 queries monthly.

Submissions Editorial calendar available. Query with artwork, if applicable. Accepts email queries to laurie@christianfamilypublications.com. Availability of artwork improves chance of acceptance. Responds in 1 month.
■ *Articles:* To 500 words. Informational, self-help, how-to, profiles, personal experience. Topics: love, family life, parenting, Christianity, church, philanthropy, education, recreation, the arts, travel, sports.
■ *Fiction:* To 500 words. Genres: inspirational, humorous.
■ *Depts/columns:* To 500 words. Media and restaurant reviews, faith in the workplace, financial, health, home improvement, business tips, recipes, family travel.
■ *Artwork:* B/W and color prints.

Sample Issue 32 pages. Advertising. Sample copy available at website.
■ "Roxanne & Radio," by Laurie Stroud. Profile of a Christian radio personality.
■ "Cool Stuff with A Mighty Message." Information on an Easter Cross Witness project.

Rights and Payment Rights vary. No payment.

Catholic Digest

1 Montauk Avenue, Suite 200, New London, CT 06320. www.catholicdigest.com

Assistant Editor: Kathryn Oates

Since its beginning in 1936, *Catholic Digest* has used stories of real people to demonstrate that a life guided by faith can be exciting, enlivening, and joyous. Informational articles and personal stories of faith—with an emphasis on the family experience—fill its pages, along with meaningful ways to connect faith with everyday life, and tips for strengthening family ties and friendships. Due to the large volume of submissions, *Catholic Digest* no longer accepts unsolicited submissions, except for its Good Egg and Open Door columns. Previously published professional writers may query with clips.
■ **Circulation** 285,000 ■ **Audience** Families ■ **Frequency** 11 times a year

Freelance Potential Publishes 100–200 freelance submissions yearly: 45% written by nonstaff writers; 10–15% by authors new to the magazine. Receives 400 unsolicited manuscripts monthly.

Submissions Guidelines available at website. Accepts submissions for Open Door and Good Egg departments only. For Good Egg, email essay and photo of nominee to goodegg@catholicdigest.com. For Open Door, email article and author headshot to opendoor@catholicdigest.com. Previously published writers may query with 1–2 relevant published writing samples to queries@catholicdigest.com. No hard copy accepted. No simultaneous submissions. Responds in 2–3 weeks.
■ *Articles:* 1,000–1,500 words. Informational, profiles, personal experience pieces. Topics: religion, prayer, spirituality, relationships, family issues, history, nostalgia.
■ *Depts/columns:* 350–500 words. Good Egg (profile of someone who has demonstrated their faith), Open Door (true, personal experience piece about converting to the Catholic faith or recovering faith that has been lost).
■ *Artwork:* JPEG files at 300 dpi.

Sample Issue 128 pages. Advertising. Sample copy available.
■ "The Easiest Way to Pray," by James Martin. An examination of conscience can open up prayer.
■ "A Q&A with Author Frank Cottrell Boyce," by Julie Rattey. Boyce talks about his children's books.

Rights and Payment One-time rights. Articles, $100–$300. Open Door, $100. Good Egg, no payment. Pays on publication. Provides 2 contributor's copies.

Catholic Forester

P.O. Box 3012, Naperville, IL 60566-7012. www.catholicforester.org

Associate Editor: Patricia Baron

The Catholic Order of Foresters, a century-old Catholic fraternal life insurance society, publishes this magazine for its members. It features industry news, general interest articles, articles pertaining to family life, and inspirational articles. Although primarily interested in informational articles, the editors do entertain the occasional light fiction, children's story, or humor piece. ■ **Circulation** 87,000
■ **Audience** Catholic Forester members ■ **Frequency** Quarterly

Freelance Potential Publishes 4–8 freelance submissions yearly: 20% written by nonstaff writers. 20% by authors new to the magazine. Receives 20 unsolicited manuscripts monthly.

Submissions Guidelines available at website. Send complete manuscript. Prefers email to pbaron@catholicforester.org; will accept hard copy. SASE. Responds in 4 months.
■ *Articles:* 1,000 words. Informational, inspirational. Topics: money management, fitness, health, family life, investing, senior issues, parenting, nostalgia.
■ *Fiction:* 500–1,000 words. Genres: inspirational, humorous, children's stories.
■ *Depts/columns:* Staff-written.

Sample Issue 40 pages. No advertising. 6 articles; 5 depts/columns. Sample copy available.

- "Saint of the POW Camp," by Victor M. Parachin. The work of Father Joseph Kapaun, a POW during the Korean War.
- "Sorting Through Vitamin D Claims," by Carolyn Maille-Petersen. The role of vitamin D in heath.

Rights and Payment First North American serial rights. Written material, 50¢ a word. Reprints, $50. Pays on acceptance. Provides 3 contributor's copies.

Children's Ministry

1515 Cascade Avenue, Loveland, CO 80539. www.childrensministry.com

Associate Editor: Carmen Kamrath

Children's Ministry publishes practical ideas for running successful religious education classes for kids and ministering to children. It features articles on Christian education, emerging church and ministry trends, motivating volunteers, and developmental trends and insights. Writers who are new to the magazine have the best chance for publication with an article that describes a teaching technique that has worked for them. ■ **Circulation** 65,000 ■ **Audience** Children's ministry leaders ■ **Frequency** 6 times a year

Freelance Potential Publishes 180 freelance submissions yearly: 90% written by nonstaff writers; 60% by authors new to the magazine; 60% by previously unpublished writers. Receives 8 unsolicited manuscripts monthly.

Submissions Send complete manuscript. Prefers email submissions to ckamrath@cmmag.com; will accept hard copy. SASE. Responds in 2–3 months.
- *Articles:* 500–1,700 words. Informational, how-to, personal experience. Topics: Christian education, children's ministry, family issues, child development, faith.
- *Depts/columns:* 50–300 words. Educational issues, activities, devotionals, family ministry, parenting, crafts, resources.
- *Other:* Activities, games, tips. Submit seasonal material 6–8 months in advance.

Sample Issue 122 pages. Advertising. Sample copy available.
- "Essential Strategies for Classroom Management," by Jody Capehart. Disciplinary tips for teachers.
- "10 Ways to Lose a Volunteer," by Carmen Kamrath. Recruiting missteps and tips for transforming interested people into active volunteers.

Rights and Payment All rights. Articles, $40–$400. Depts/columns, $40–$75. Pays on acceptance. Provides 1 contributor's copy.

Christian Home & School

3350 East Paris Avenue SE, Grand Rapids, MI 48512-3054. www.csionline.org/chs

Managing Editor: Rachael Heyboer

Christian parents read this magazine for articles on education, parenting, health, and matters related to Christian schooling. Articles must have real-world applications to education and offer a mature, biblical perspective. *Christian Home & School* is a publication of Christian Schools International. Refer to the editorial calendar for upcoming needs. ■ **Circulation** 66,000 ■ **Audience** Parents ■ **Frequency** 3 times a year

Freelance Potential Publishes 12–15 freelance submissions yearly: 90% written by nonstaff writers; 10–25% by authors new to the magazine; 50–75% by previously unpublished writers. Receives 25–50 queries, 1–10 unsolicited manuscripts monthly.

Submissions Guidelines and editorial calendar available at website. Query or send complete manuscript. Prefers email to rheyboer@csionline.org (Word attachments); will accept hard copy. No simultaneous submissions. SASE. Responds in 7–10 days.

- *Articles:* 1,000–2,000 words. Informational, how-to, inspirational, personal experience. Topics: education, parenting, life skills, decision-making, discipline, family travel, faith, children's health, tutoring, learning difficulties, standardized testing.
- *Depts/columns:* Parent Stuff (100–250 words). Reviews and parenting tips.

Sample Issue 40 pages. Advertising. Sample copy available.
- "Cultivating Character in Our Children," by Tammy Darling. Parents' role in developing kids' character.
- Education Trend. Description of Spanish immersion program at one Christian school.

Rights and Payment First rights. Written material, $50–$300. Pays on publication. Provides 3 contributor's copies.

Christian Work at Home Moms

P.O. Box 974, Bellevue, NE 68123. www.cwahm.com

Submissions: Pebbles Jacobo

Support, information, and advice for mothers who are establishing work-at-home careers are found in this online resource, which includes a website, electronic newsletter, and blogging center. It also offers inspirational pieces and devotionals. It welcomes contributions to its website and weekly newsletter. Though it doesn't compensate writers, it includes an "About the Author" section at the end of each article with a link to author's website. Practical at-home business information is needed, as well as pieces on Christian parenting, marriage, and topics of interest to women. ■ **Hits per month** 1.5 million ■ **Audience** Mothers ■ **Frequency** Weekly

Freelance Potential Publishes 12–120 freelance submissions yearly: 75–100% written by nonstaff writers; 25–50% by authors new to the magazine; 10–25% by previously unpublished writers. Receives 1–10 queries, 1–10 unsolicited manuscripts monthly.

Submissions Query or send complete manuscript. Accepts email to pebbles@cwahm.com (Word attachments). Responds in 2 weeks.
- *Articles:* 500+ words. Informational, how-to, profiles, personal experience. Topics: telecommuting, home businesses, business technology, website management and design, search engine optimization, copywriting, money management, marriage, parenting, spiritual growth, homeschooling.
- *Depts/columns:* Word lengths vary. Book and media reviews, career information, blogs, devotionals.

Sample Issue Sample copy available at website.
- "Gym & Physical Education Options for Homeschoolers," by Michelle Shaeffer. Physical activities for children that are easy to do at home.
- "Teach Your Children to Be Different," by Carey Scott. Biblical inspirations for helping children build self-esteem and be supportive of others.

Rights and Payment First rights. No payment.

EFCA Today

418 Fourth Street NE, Charlottesville, VA 22902. www.efcatoday.org

Editor: Diane McDougall

Written primarily by and for members of the Evangelical Free Church of America (EFCA), this ezine focuses on spirituality and evangelism and the role they play in today's society. It publishes articles of interest to church pastors, elders, and deacons, while also targeting ministry volunteers and religious educators. Each issue features a series of articles on a particular theme, plus regular departments.
 ■ **Circulation** 40,000 ■ **Audience** EFCA members ■ **Frequency** Quarterly

Freelance Potential Publishes several freelance submissions yearly: 80% written by nonstaff writers.

Submissions Guidelines available at website. Send complete manuscript. Accepts email to editor@

efca.org (Word attachments) and hard copy. SASE. Response time varies.
- *Articles:* 300–800 words. Informational, how-to, inspirational, personal experience. Topics: church business, church planting, ministry, family issues.
- *Depts/columns:* 300–600 words. Engage (church and the community), Leader to Leader (thoughts from church leaders), Catalyst (profiles of young leaders), Face to Face (profiles of global EFCA groups).

Sample Issue Sample copy available at website.
- "Adventures in Church Planting," by Kristen Kimmel. The realities of a calling to plant a church.
- "Listen to the Hum," by Regina Robinson. Personal experience of someone starting a church.

Rights and Payment First rights. Theme articles, 300–800 words. Departments, 300–600 words. Written material, 23¢ a word. Pays on acceptance.

Faith & Family

432 Washington Avenue, North Haven, CT 06473. www.faithandfamilylive.com

Assistant Editor: Robyn Lee

Written for educated, professional, "real-world" Catholic moms, *Faith & Family* focuses on spirituality, raising children, homekeeping, and finances. It is read by women from diverse Catholic traditions who seek information, inspiration, resources, and encouragement as they embrace marriage and motherhood. ■ **Circulation** 35,000 ■ **Audience** Catholic mothers ■ **Frequency** 6 times a year

Freelance Potential Publishes 35 freelance submissions yearly: 75% written by nonstaff writers; 10% by authors new to the magazine; 15% by previously unpublished writers. Receives 25 queries monthly.

Submissions Query. Accepts email queries to editor@faithandfamilylive.com. Responds in 2–3 months.
- *Articles:* 1,800–2,500 words. Informational, inspirational, how-to, self-help, profiles, interviews, personal experience. Topics: home, family, parenting, marriage, relationships, spirituality, personal growth.
- *Depts/columns:* Children's book reviews (1,000 words), What's Cooking (300 words plus 6 recipes and 1–3 sidebars), My Faith & Family (1,000 words).

Sample Issue 96 pages. Advertising.
- "How To Love a Homosexual," by Melinda Selmys. Helping Catholics hate the sin but love the sinner.
- "Love: The Path of Least Resistance," by Tim Drake. Communication helps save a dissolving marriage.

Rights and Payment First North American serial rights. Feature articles, $400. Departments, $400–$450. Children's book reviews, $250. Pays on publication.

For Every Woman

General Council of the Assemblies of God, 1445 North Boonville Avenue, Springfield, MO 65802–1894. http://women.ag.org

Administrative Coordinator: Deborah Hampton

This e-zine is hosted by the National Women's Ministries Department of the Assemblies of God and features inspirational writing on relationships, family, careers, and ministering to others. The aim is to support Christian women in all stages of life, especially with inspirational stories that have basis in Scripture. Topics of interest include blended families, dealing with divorce, forgiveness, character, compassion, and loving our neighbors. ■ **Circulation** Hits per month: 83,000. ■ **Audience** Women ■ **Frequency** Ongoing

Freelance Potential 50% written by nonstaff writers: 10% are by authors new to the magazine; 80% are by unpublished writers. Receives 20–30 unsolicited mmanuscripts monthly.

Submissions Send complete manuscript. Accepts email submissions to dhampton@ag.org (Word attachments). Response time varies.

- *Articles:* 500–800 words. Informational, inspirational, self-help; personal experience. Topics include blended families, marriage, family life, special education, health, crafts, hobbies, multicultural and ethnic issues, music, popular culture, religion, faith, social issues.
- *Other:* Submit seasonal material 4–6 months in advance.

Sample Issue
- "I Want to Start Giving My Children an Allowance," by Deborah McNaughton. Guidelines to follow.
- "Help Her Through" by Darla Knoth. Ministering to women with breast cancer.

Rights and Payment Electronic rights. Payment varies. Payment policy varies.

Group

Group Publishing, P.O. Box 481, Loveland, CO 80539-0481. www.youthministry.com/group

Associate Editor: Scott Firestone

Group provides practical resources and inspiration for leaders of Christian youth groups. It focuses on strategies and ideas for effectively working with teens to encourage their spiritual development. It is an interdenominational publication, and welcomes descriptions of successful youth ministry strategies, as well as articles about understanding kids and youth culture. ■ **Circulation** 40,000 ■ **Audience** Youth ministry leaders ■ **Frequency** 6 times a year

Freelance Potential Publishes 200 freelance submissions yearly: 60% written by nonstaff writers; 80% by authors new to the magazine; 50% by previously unpublished writers. Receives 25 unsolicited manuscripts monthly.

Submissions Guidelines available at website. Send complete manuscript with brief cover letter that includes author information. Accepts email to sfirestone@group.com and hard copy. SASE. Responds in 8–10 weeks.
- *Articles:* 500–2,000 words. Informational, how-to. Topics: youth ministry strategies, recruiting and training adult leaders, understanding youth culture, professionalism, time management, leadership skills, professional and spiritual growth of youth ministers.
- *Depts/columns:* Try This One (to 300 words), Hands-On Help (to 175 words).

Sample Issue 82 pages. Advertising. Sample copy available.
- "Tips on Evaluating a Ministry," by Mike Kupferer. Questions a youth minister should ask himself.
- "Thankful Teens?" by Grant T. Byrd. Teaching teens to live a life of gratitude.

Rights and Payment All rights. Articles, $150–$350. Depts/columns, $50. Pays on acceptance.

Indian Life Newspaper

P.O. Box 3765, Redwood Post Office, Winnipeg, Manitoba R2W 3R6 Canada. www.indianlife.org.

Editor: Jim Uttley

Published by Intertribal Christian Communications (Indian Life Ministries), this newspaper covers the social, cultural, political, and spiritual issues facing Native North Americans in the U.S. and Canada. All material should have a Christ-based perspective. A small amount of fiction and poetry is also published. Native writers, while not used exclusively, are preferred. ■ **Circulation** 20,000 ■ **Audience** Native American families ■ **Frequency** 6 times a year

Freelance Potential Publishes 20 freelance submissions yearly: 80% written by nonstaff writers; 40% by authors new to the magazine; 10% by previously unpublished writers. Receives 25 unsolicited manuscripts monthly.

Submissions Guidelines available at website. Query. Prefers email to ilm.editor@indianlife.org; will accept hard copy. For return of materials, Canadian writers should send SAE; U.S. writers should send $3.50 money order with SAE. Responds in 6 weeks.

- *Articles:* 300–1,200 words. Informational, inspirational, personal experience. Topics: current issues faced by Native people, family issues, spirituality, overcoming problems—all with biblical overtones.
- *Fiction:* Word lengths vary. Genres: contemporary, historical, inspirational.
- *Depts/columns:* 100–800 words. News, legends.
- *Artwork:* B/W or color JPEG or TIFFs at 300 dpi.
- *Other:* Poetry, word lengths vary. Filler. Submit seasonal material 6 months in advance.

Sample Issue Sample copy available at website.
- "A Handful of Coins," by K. Marie Quartz. Inspirational piece about helping others.
- "Strawberries and Forgiveness," by Crying Wind. Narragansett Indian legend.

Rights and Payment First rights. Articles, depts/columns, and fiction, 15¢ a word, to $150. Filler, $30. Poetry, $40. Pays on publication. Provides 3 contributor's copies.

InSite

405 West Rockrimmon Boulevard, P.O. Box 62189, Colorado Springs, CO 80919. www.ccca.org

Editor: Jackie M. Johnson

Both practical and inspirational articles about Christian camp and conference management are found in *InSite*. It is written for members of the Christian Camp and Conference Association. It seeks practical articles that show what God is doing in and through Christian camp and conference ministries, with an emphasis on ways to maximize performance and impact. Profiles and interviews are the best bet for writers new to the magazine. ■ **Circulation** 8,500 ■ **Audience** Christian camp leaders ■ **Frequency** 6 times a year

Freelance Potential Publishes 40 freelance submissions yearly: Articles, 90% written by nonstaff writers; 25% by authors new to the magazine; 15% by previously unpublished writers. Receives 1 query monthly.

Submissions Guidelines and editorial calendar available at website. Query with résumé and writing samples. Accepts email queries to editor@ccca.org. Availability of artwork improves chance of acceptance. Responds in 1 month.
- *Articles:* 1,200–1,500 words. Informational, how-to, profiles, interviews. Topics: Christian camp and conference operations, programs, fundraising, leadership, personnel, recreation, religion, social issues, crafts, hobbies, health, fitness, multicultural and ethnic issues, nature, popular culture, sports.
- *Depts/columns:* Staff-written.
- *Artwork:* Color prints and digital images.
- *Other:* Submit seasonal material 6 months in advance.

Sample Issue 50 pages. Advertising. Sample copy available at website.
- "Opening Doors to Diversity," by Ami Neiberger-Miller. Building ethnic diversity in Christian camping.
- "He Made the Stars," by Ann-Margret Hovsepian. How astronomy is a tool to share the gospel.

Rights and Payment First rights. Articles, 20¢ a word. Pays on publication. Provides 1 contributor's copy.

InTeen Teacher

1551 Regency Court, Calumet City, IL 60409. www.urbanministries.com

Editor: LaTonya Taylor

One of the curriculum publications of Urban Ministries, *InTeen Teacher* features comprehensive teaching plans and Bible study guides that are used in conjunction with the student magazine, *InTeen*. Its content specifically addresses the needs and concerns of urban teens. New writers are welcome to contact Urban Ministries, which looks for stimulating educational materials. ■ **Circulation** 75,000 ■ **Audience** Religious educators ■ **Frequency** Quarterly

Freelance Potential Publishes 52 freelance submissions yearly: 90% written by nonstaff writers.

Submissions All material is written on assignment. Send résumé with writing samples. SASE. Responds in 3–6 months.
- *Articles:* Word lengths vary. Bible study plans, guides for teaching Christian values to African American teens, how-to. Topics: career/college, health, finances, relationships, family, religion.
- *Fiction:* Word lengths vary. Stories may be included as part of study plans. Genres: inspirational, multicultural, and real-life/problem-solving.
- *Other:* Puzzles, activities, poetry. Submit seasonal material 1 year in advance.

Sample Issue No advertising.
- "Precepts for Living." Commentary and in-depth Bible study.

Rights and Payment All rights. Written material, payment rates vary. Pays 2 months after acceptance. Provides 2 contributor's copies.

Journal of Adventist Education

12501 Old Columbia Pike, Silver Spring, MD 20904-6600. http://JAE.adventist.org

Editor: Beverly J. Robinson-Rumble

This professional journal is for teachers in Seventh-day Adventist learning institutions covers Christian education, the integration of faith and learning in the classroom, and educator training. ■ **Circulation** 15,000 ■ **Audience** Seventh-day Adventist educators ■ **Frequency** 5 times a year

Freelance Potential Publishes 30 freelance submissions yearly: 90% written by nonstaff writers; 30% by previously unpublished writers. Receives 2–4 queries monthly.

Submissions Guidelines available. Query. Accepts email to rumbleb@gc.adventist.org (Word attachments). Availability of artwork improves chance of acceptance. Responds in 3–6 weeks.
- *Articles:* To 2,000 words. Informational, how-to, inspirational, personal experience. Topics: classroom management, religion, classroom spirituality, education trends, teacher training, and methodology.
- *Artwork:* Color prints and slides, JPEG or TIFF digital images.

Sample Issue
- "The Day Bruce Threw a Chair," by Harvey R. Burnett Jr. and Faith-Ann McGarrell. Perspectives on classroom management and discipline.
- "Trial or Trail? The Path to Redemptive Discipline," by John Wesley Taylor V. An analysis of classroom discipline in a religious education setting.

Rights and Payment First North American serial rights. Articles, to $100. Artwork, payment rates vary. Pays on publication. Provides 2 contributor's copies.

Kids' Ministry Ideas

55 West Oak Ridge Drive, Hagerstown, MD 21740. www.kidsministryideas.com

Editor: Candy DeVore

This magazine, written for youth ministry leaders within the Seventh-day Adventist faith, aims to be a practical resource of how-to's, inspiring true stories, and project ideas. It prefers articles written in the first person using personal experiences to illustrate the point. Articles should be clear, concise, practical, relevant, and current. ■ **Circulation** 4,500 ■ **Audience** Adventist youth ministry leaders ■ **Frequency** Quarterly

Freelance Potential Publishes 60 freelance submissions yearly: 100% written by nonstaff writers.

Submissions Guidelines available at website. Query or send complete manuscript. Accepts hard copy and email to KidsMin@rhpa.org (Word attachments). SASE. Response time varies.

■ *Articles:* To 800 words. Informational, how-to, essays. Topics: religious education, youth ministry, family issues, working with volunteers, lesson plans and props, faith, prayer.
■ *Depts/columns:* Word lengths vary. Leadership training, teaching tips, crafts.
■ *Other:* Submit seasonal material 6–12 months in advance.

Sample Issue 32 pages. Sample copy available.
■ "Vacation Bible School: Making God Real," by Candy Harvey. Vacation Bible School do's and don'ts.
■ "Experience Outdoor Learning," by Ann E. Slaughter. How to find and teach Jesus in nature.

Rights and Payment First North American serial rights. Written material, $20–$100. Pays 5–6 weeks after acceptance. Provides 1 contributor's copy.

Kyria

465 Gundersen Drive, Carol Stream, IL 60188. www.kyria.com

Acquisitions Editor

The former *Today's Christian Woman* has been revamped as this *digizine*. Published electronically, its articles offer in-depth biblical insight into topics of faith and ministry for mature Christian women. Articles should have a distinct evangelical Christian perspective. It is published by Christianity Today International. ■ **Hits per month** Unavailable ■ **Audience** Christian women ■ **Frequency** Monthly

Freelance Potential Publishes 30 freelance submissions yearly: 70% written by nonstaff writers; 20% by authors new to the magazine; 20% by previously unpublished writers. Receives 30 queries monthly.

Submissions Guidelines and theme list available at website. Send query letter with article summary, purpose, and value to reader; author qualifications on topic; suggested length; and anticipated completion date. Accepts hard copy and electronic queries through the website. No simultaneous submissions. SASE. Responds in 2 months.
■ *Articles:* 600–1,500 words. Informational, how-to, essays, interviews, personal experience. Topics: women's ministry, family, marriage, church leadership, social issues, spiritual formation, Bible study, devotionals.

Sample Issue Sample copy available at website.
■ "The Goodness of God," by Corrie Cutrer. Interview with author Nancy Guthrie about submission.
■ "The Symphony of Submission," by Stephanie Voiland. How yielding to one another can create harmony.

Rights and Payment Exclusive online rights and non-exclusive rights. Articles, 600–1,500 words; $50–$150. Pays on acceptance.

Live

General Council of the Assemblies of God, 1445 North Boonville Avenue, Springfield, MO 65802-1894. www.gospelpublishing.com/store/startcat.cfm?cat=twritguid

Editor: Richard Bennett

This take-home paper for adult religious education classes publishes upbeat informational articles, true stories, and fiction that encourage Christian readers to apply biblical principles to everyday problems, including parenting and family relationships. True stories, nonfiction, how-to's, and fiction are accepted. ■ **Circulation** 32,000 ■ **Audience** Adults ■ **Frequency** Quarterly, in weekly sections

Freelance Potential Publishes 110 freelance submissions yearly: 75–100% written by nonstaff writers; 10–25% by authors new to the magazine; 25–50% by previously unpublished writers. Receives 100–150 unsolicited manuscripts monthly.

Submissions Guidelines available at website. Send complete manuscript. Accepts email submissions to rl-live@gph.org (Word attachments). Accepts simultaneous submissions if identified. SASE. Responds in 1–6 weeks.
- *Articles:* 300–1,100 words. Informational, how-to articles, humor, inspirational, personal experience. Topics: family issues, parenting, general Christian living issues.
- *Fiction:* 300–1,100 words. Genres: inspirational, religious.
- *Other:* Poetry, 12–25 lines. Submit seasonal material 18 months in advance.

Sample Issue 8 pages. No advertising. Sample copy available.
- "My Father's Prayers," by Judi Peers. A woman realizes the impact of her father's faith on family.
- "Puppy Problems," by Barbara Bryden. A mother struggling with her faith is changed.

Rights and Payment First and second rights. Written material, 10¢ a word for first rights; 7¢ a word for second rights. Pays on acceptance. Provides 2 contributor's copies.

The Lutheran Digest

6160 Carmen Avenue East, Inver Grove Heights, MN 55076. www.lutherandigest.com

Editor: Nick Skapyak

Inspiration, hope, and even some humor can be found in this general interest magazine. Its blend of secular and light theological articles include home and family topics. In true "digest" form, the majority of material is reprinted from other publications, with the balance coming from unsolicited material from freelance writers. It seeks articles about how God intervened in a person's life, seasonal material, and articles reflecting God's presence in nature. ■ **Circulation** 70,000 ■ **Audience** Lutheran church members ■ **Frequency** Quarterly

Freelance Potential Publishes 80 freelance submissions yearly: 80% written by nonstaff writers; 30% by authors new to the magazine. Receives 25 unsolicited manuscripts monthly.

Submissions Guidelines available at website. Send complete manuscript with author biography. Prefers articles as email attachments to editor@lutherandigest.com (Word or PDF attachments). SASE. Responds in 2–3 months.
- *Articles:* 3,000–7,000 characters. Informational, inspirational, personal experience. Topics: spirituality, prayer, Bible lessons, God's presence in everyday life.
- *Other:* Poetry, to 3 poems per submission. Recipes, jokes. Submit seasonal material 6 months in advance.

Sample Issue Sample copy available.
- "My Partner in Parenting," by Lynn Klammer. How God and church can help in parenting.
- "The Teachings of a Three-Legged Dog," by A. Trevor Sutton. An amputee support group.

Rights and Payment One-time and second rights. Articles, $35. Poetry and filler; no payment. Pays on publication. Provides 1 contributor's copy.

The Majellan

P.O. Box 43, Brighton, Victoria 3186 Australia. www.majellan.org.au

Editor: Father Michael Gilbert

A magazine of the Australian Redemptorists, *The Majellan* fosters Christian family life and marriage. Its articles contain information and inspiration to help couples build strong relationships based on Catholic values. Most of its readers are Catholics living in Australia and New Zealand. Child development issues and teen topics are of special interest. ■ **Circulation** 17,500 ■ **Audience** Parents ■ **Frequency** Quarterly

Freelance Potential Publishes 20 freelance submissions yearly: 50% written by nonstaff writers; 20%

by authors new to the magazine; 15% by previously unpublished writers. Receives several unsolicited manuscripts monthly.

Submissions Send complete manuscript. Accepts hard copy and email submissions to editor@majellan.org (Word or RTF attachments). SAE/IRC. Response time varies.
- *Articles:* 750–1,500 words. Informational, personal experience. Topics: marriage, parenting, Catholic family life.
- *Depts/columns:* Staff-written.
- *Other:* Filler, photos.

Sample Issue 48 pages. Advertising. Sample copy available at website.
- "Cutting to the Quick," by Michael Leunig. Anti-violence piece.
- "Anger: A Positive Force?" by Margie Ulbrick. Using Christ's lessons to help diffuse anger.

Rights and Payment Rights vary. Articles, $50–$80 Australian. Pays on acceptance.

Prairie Messenger

Box 190, 100 College Drive, Muenster, Saskatchewan S0K 2Y0 Canada. www.prairiemessenger.ca

Associate Editor: Maureen Weber

This Catholic newspaper covers local, national, and international religious news for readers living in Saskatchewan and Manitoba. Work may be submitted by Canadian writers only. Human-interest stories and opinion pieces have the best chance of acceptance. ■ **Circulation** 5,800 ■ **Audience** Canadian Catholics ■ **Frequency** Weekly

Freelance Potential Publishes 10 freelance submissions yearly: 60% written by nonstaff writers. Receives 3 queries, 3 unsolicited manuscripts monthly.

Submissions Canadian authors only. Guidelines available at website. Query for longer features; send complete manuscript for all others. Accepts hard copy and email to pm.canadian@stpeterspress.ca. Responds in 1 month if interested.
- *Articles:* Features, 2,500 words. Articles, to 800 words. Opinion pieces, to 900 words. Informational, inspirational, profiles, opinion, essay.
- *Artwork:* B/W prints.
- *Other:* Poetry.

Sample Issue 20 pages. Sample copy available.
- "Development and Peace." Canadian peace workers' trip to Cambodia.
- "Liturgy and Life," by Leah Perrault. Lessons of human weakness and hope.

Rights and Payment First rights. Features, $55–$75. Articles, $3 per column inch. Photos, $20. Pays at the end of the month. Provides 1 contributor's copy.

PresenTense

214 Sullivan Street, Suite 2A, New York, NY 10012. www.presentensemagazine.org

Editor: Ariel Beery

The PresenTense Group is an international grassroots effort to inspire and enable socially minded pioneering work in the Jewish community. *PresenTense* magazine covers modern Jewish life, Jewish activism, giving back to society, the arts, and current events. Poetry and fiction with Jewish themes are also accepted. ■ **Circulation** 30,000 ■ **Audience** Jewish YA–Adult ■ **Frequency** 3 times a year

Freelance Potential Publishes 40 freelance submissions yearly: 80% written by nonstaff writers; 70% by authors new to the magazine; 40% by previously unpublished writers.

Submissions Guidelines available at website. Query with author biography, statement of author qualifications, and what article is and how it is relevant to audience; or send complete manuscript with submission type, title, and word count in subject line of email. Writers may also query with an assignment request. Accepts email to appropriate editor as listed in the guidelines, or via the website. Responds to queries and assignment requests in 2 weeks, to manuscripts in 2 months.

- *Articles:* 800–1,200 words. Profiles, 600–700 words. Sidebars, 50–250 words. Topics: Judaism, the Diaspora, Zionism, Israel, activism, community, education, relationships, health.
- *Fiction:* 1,000–3,000 words. Genres vary.
- *Depts/columns:* Paradigm Shift (essays, 1,200–2,000 words), Around the World (600–800 words), news and pop culture briefs (400–500 words), reviews (300–800 words).
- *Artwork:* JPEG images at 300 dpi.
- *Other:* Photo-essays, 12 photos, 600 words. Poetry, to 300 words.

Sample Issue 64 pages. Sample copy available at website.
- "Electric in Demand," by Lianna Wolfson. The development and future of electric vehicles.
- "Seeds of Pluralism," by Jakir Manela, et al. Service-based programs at Kayam Farm in Maryland.

Rights and Payment First rights. No payment. Provides 3 contributor's copies and a 1-year subscription.

Seek

Standard Publishing Company, 8805 Governor's Hill Drive, Suite 400, Cincinnati, OH 45249. www.standardpub.com

Editor: Margaret K. Williams

Seek is a take-home paper designed to supplement religious education or Bible study lessons. It is directed at young adults and adults, and contains inspirational stories and Bible lessons. Articles should encourage readers in their walk with Jesus Christ and help them apply biblical truths in their lives. ■ **Circulation** 27,000 ■ **Audience** YA–Adult ■ **Frequency** Weekly (on a quarterly basis)

Freelance Potential Publishes 150 freelance submissions yearly: 80% written by nonstaff writers; 50% by authors new to the magazine. Receives 40–50 unsolicited manuscripts monthly.

Submissions Guidelines and theme list available at www.standardpub.com/view/seek-guidelines.aspx. Send complete manuscript. Prefers email submissions to seek@standardpub.com; will accept hard copy. SASE. Responds in 3–6 months.
- *Articles:* 600–1,200 words. Inspirational, devotionals, personal experience. Topics: religious and contemporary issues, Christian living, coping with moral and ethical dilemmas, controversial subjects.
- *Fiction:* 400–1,200 words. Genres: religious.
- *Other:* Submit seasonal material 1 year in advance.

Sample Issue 8 pages. No advertising. Sample copy available at website.
- "Worshipping God," by Terry L. Brensinger. The values of heartfelt worship.
- "Fresh Ways to Pray Every Day," by Christine Sobania Johnson. Prayer inspirations.

Rights and Payment First and second rights. Written material, 5¢–7¢ a word. Pays on acceptance. Provides 5 contributor's copies.

Sharing the Victory

Fellowship of Christian Athletes, 8701 Leeds Road, Kansas City, MO 64129. www.sharingthevictory.com

Editorial Assistant: Ashley Burns

Sharing the Victory targets athletes and coaches who are members of the Fellowship of Christian Athletes. Its articles, profiles, and first-person pieces are meant to inform and inspire readers. Profiles and interviews are most open to freelance writers. All profile articles must contain an authentic spiritual angle depicting the person's struggles and successes while including a strong tie to the FCA ministry. ■ **Circulation** 75,000 ■ **Audience** Athletes & coaches, grades 7+ ■ **Frequency** 9 times a year

Freelance Potential Publishes 20 freelance submissions yearly: 40% written by nonstaff writers; 10% by authors new to the magazine; 25% by previously unpublished writers. Receives 4 queries and unsolicited manuscripts monthly.

Submissions Guidelines available. Prefers query with outline and writing samples; will accept complete manuscript. Prefers email to stv@fca.org; will accept hard copy. Availability of artwork improves chance of acceptance. SASE. Response time varies.
- *Articles:* 1,000–2,000 words. Informational, profiles, interviews, personal experience. Topics: sports, athletes, coaches, competition, training, focus, faith, missions, Christian education.
- *Depts/columns:* Staff-written.
- *Artwork:* Color prints or digital images at 300 dpi.
- *Other:* Submit seasonal material 3–4 months in advance.

Sample Issue 30 pages. Advertising. Sample copy available.
- "Cheers for Camp!" by Jennifer Borgognoni. Cheerleading camp brought the author closer to God.
- "Sports Liars," by Roger Lipe. The negative impact of success and failure in sports.

Rights and Payment First serial rights. Articles, $150–$400. Pays on publication.

Young Adult Today

1551 Regency Court, Calumet City, IL 60409. www.youngadulttoday.net

Editor: Aja Carr

Urban Ministries publishes this magazine for Christian African-Americans living in urban communities who are about to face college, career, and adulthood. It includes Bible lessons, study guides, daily devotions, and articles on issues of importance to young adults. Articles are assigned; freelancers should become familiar with the specific style of the magazine before inquiring about joining its team of writers. ■ **Circulation** 25,000 ■ **Audience** 18–24 years ■ **Frequency** Quarterly

Freelance Potential Publishes 52 freelance submissions yearly: 90% written by nonstaff writers; 50% by authors new to the magazine; 50% by previously unpublished writers. Receives 20 queries monthly.

Submissions All material is assigned. Query with résumé. No unsolicited manuscripts. Accepts hard copy. SASE. Responds in 2 months.
- *Articles:* To 400 words. Informational, inspirational, Bible studies, devotionals—all in modern life.

Sample Issue 80 pages. Little advertising. Sample copy available.
- "Five Ways to Look Like Jesus." How to live a Christian life.
- "Christ as Healer." The ability of Jesus to cure the sick.

Rights and Payment Rights negotiable. Written material, $150 per lesson. Pays on publication.

Young Adult Today Leader

1551 Regency Court, Calumet City, IL 60409. www.youngadulttoday.net

Editor: Aja Carr

A companion publication to Urban Ministries' *Young Adult Today*, this magazine prepares youth ministry leaders and Bible study teachers to lead Christian education groups with young adults. Each quarterly issue includes 13 weekly lessons. Urban Ministries makes writing assignments to a team of writers; it is open to receiving résumés. ■ **Circulation** 15,000 ■ **Audience** Religious educators ■ **Frequency** Quarterly

Freelance Potential Publishes 52 freelance submissions yearly: 90% written by nonstaff writers; 50% by authors new to the magazine; 50% by previously unpublished writers. Receives 20 queries monthly.

Submissions All work is assigned. Query with résumé. No unsolicited manuscripts. Accepts hard copy. SASE. Responds in 2 months.
■ *Articles:* Word lengths vary. Devotionals, 400 words. Informational, inspirational, devotionals. Topics: current events, social issues in relation to Christianity and the Bible.

Sample Issue 96 pages. No advertising. Sample copy and guidelines available by mail.
■ "Open My Heart." A lesson plan on welcoming people openly to a church community.
■ "Wise Speakers." The biblical basis for speaking the right way to others.

Rights and Payment Rights negotiable. Written material, $150. Pays on publication.

Youth and Discipleship Leadership

1080 Montgomery Avenue, Cleveland, TN 37311. www.pathwaypress.org

Editor: Shelia Stewart

Christian educators and youth ministry workers find useful tips and inspiring stories in each issue of this magazine. Its focus is on discipling readers and instructing them on ways to incorporate acts of Christian living into everyday life. Profiles of individuals or groups who are advancing Christian education with distinctive ministries and practical how-to articles are particularly welcome. ■ **Circulation** 10,000 ■ **Audience** Adults ■ **Frequency** Quarterly

Freelance Potential Publishes 10 freelance submissions yearly: 10% written by nonstaff writers; 10% by authors new to the magazine; 90% by previously unpublished writers. Receives 2–3 queries, 2 unsolicited manuscripts monthly.

Submissions Guidelines available at website. Send complete manuscript. Accepts hard copy and email to Editorial Assistant at tammy_hatfield@pathwaypress.org (Word attachments). SASE. Responds in 3 weeks.
■ *Articles:* 500–1,000 words. Informational, inspirational, how-to, profiles, interviews, humor, personal experience. Topics: Christian ministry, programming ideas, discipleship, Christian education.
■ *Depts/columns:* Staff-written.

Sample Issue 32 pages. Little advertising. Sample copy available at website.
■ "Work with What You've Got," by Dave Cox. Optimize resources for a successful ministry program.
■ "Middle School Calling and Gifts," by Joel Daniels. Defining and developing a tween's faith.

Rights and Payment First rights. Written material, $25–$50. Kill fee, 50%. Pays on publication. Provides 1–10 contributor's copies.

Magazines of Interest to Children and Teens

In order to provide writers with as many opportunities as possible to get published in a children's-related area, we have included this category of listings for authors who may be interested in ancillary markets. While not specifically directed toward children, these publications cover subjects that may be of interest to young adults, especially older teens and college students, and sometimes to younger children as well.

They include magazines that cover scholastic sports or sports popular with kids and teens; hobby magazines; science fiction magazines; magazines for video and computer gamers; career-oriented magazines; magazines about history, pets, youth travel, and outdoor recreation; and even a couple of book publishers who accept children-, or YA-directed short fiction for anthologies. Some are even markets for young writers themselves, accepting fiction and nonfiction from children and teens.

These magazines, ezines, and websites can be fruitful markets for children's writers, and can provide opportunities to reach more publishers and, ultimately, more readers.

The Acorn

138 East Holly Avenue, Pitman, NJ 08071

Editor: Stefanie Collum

The Acorn, published and distributed by Pitman Middle School in New Jersey, offers a place for budding young writers to grow. It features short fiction, poetry, personal experience pieces, and reviews written by students ages 9 to 18 on topics appropriate for, and of interest to, this age group.
■ **Circulation** 100+ ■ **Audience** 9–18 years ■ **Frequency** 3 times a year

Freelance Potential Publishes 100 freelance submissions yearly: 100% written by nonstaff writers; 75–100% by authors new to the magazine; 50–75% by previously unpublished writers. Receives 20 unsolicited manuscript monthly.

Submissions Guidelines available. Send complete manuscript. Accepts hard copy and email to scollum@pitman.k12.nj.us (no attachments). Accepts simultaneous submissions if identified. SASE. Responds in 6 weeks.
■ *Articles:* 250 words. Personal experience, reviews. Topics: sports, animals, nature, social issues.
■ *Fiction:* 500 words. Genres: adventure, animals, coming-of-age, mysteries, nature, humor, fantasy, sports, historical, inspirational fiction.
■ *Other:* Poetry, to 35 lines.

Sample Issue 22 pages. No advertising. Sample copy available.
■ "Paisley and Her Paisins," by Megan Isbitski. Short story about a girl who loved peaches and raisins.
■ "Old Crooked Tree," by Rachel Wilson. An ode to a girl's favorite spot in her yard.

Rights and Payment No rights. No payment. Provides 1 contributor's copy.

Action Pursuit Games

2400 East Katella Avenue, Anaheim, CA 92806. www.actionpursuitgames.com

Editor: Bryan Sullivan

Paintball enthusiasts subscribe to this magazine to find out about the latest techniques and cutting-edge strategies. It also includes league information and product reviews. ■ **Circulation** 80,000 ■ **Audience** YA–Adult ■ **Frequency** Monthly

Freelance Potential Publishes 150+ freelance submissions yearly: 60% written by nonstaff writers; 30% by authors new to the magazine; 20% by previously unpublished writers. Receives 40 unsolicited manuscripts monthly.

Submissions Guidelines available at website. Query with title, short description, artwork, and signed release form. Accepts hard copy and email to bryansullivanapg@gmail.com. Availability of artwork increases chance of acceptance. No simultaneous submissions. SASE. Responds in 1 month.
■ *Articles:* 400–500 words. Informational, how-to, profiles. Topics: paintball techniques, strategies, players and teams, products.
■ *Depts/columns:* 300–500 words. Gear, news, safety, techniques, tournaments and events, reviews, young adults in the sport.
■ *Artwork:* High-resolution JPEGs or TIFFs.

Sample Issue Sample copy available.
■ "Male Dominated," by Wendy Wilson. Why women are slow to take up the sport of paintball.
■ "Going Solo," by Jason Lineberger. How a lone paintballer can compete against larger teams.

Rights and Payment All rights. All material, payment rates vary. Pays on publication. Provides 1 contributor's copy.

Ad Astra

1155 15th Street NW, Suite 500, Washington, DC 20005. www.nss.org

Assignment Editor: Katherine Brick

As the member publication of the National Space Society, *Ad Astra* features the latest news and research in space exploration and aerospace science. Its readership is made up of avid space enthusiasts as well as scientists and technologists. ■ **Circulation** 20,000 ■ **Audience** YA–Adult ■ **Frequency** Quarterly

Freelance Potential Publishes 40–50 freelance submissions yearly: 80% written by nonstaff writers. Receives 5–6 queries and unsolicited manuscripts monthly.

Submissions Guidelines and theme list available at website. Query or send complete manuscript with résumé and writing samples. Accepts disk submissions and email to adastra@nss.org. SASE. Response time varies.
■ *Articles:* Word lengths vary. Informational, factual, profiles, interviews. Topics: science and technology relating to space exploration, issues related to the aerospace industry.
■ *Depts/columns:* 600–750 words. Reviews, opinion.
■ *Artwork:* Color digital images at 300 dpi.

Sample Issue 64 pages. Advertising. Sample copy available.
■ "Solar Power Satellite Design Competition," by Don Flournoy. Reports on a competition to design next-generation satellites that will collect solar energy in space and deliver it to Earth.
■ "The New Face of the Moon," by Marianne J. Dyson. Discoveries about the moon's topography.

Rights and Payment First North American serial rights. Written material, payment rates vary. Artwork, payment rates negotiable. Payment policy varies.

AKC Family Dog

American Kennel Club, 260 Madison Avenue, New York, NY 10016. www.akc.org/pubs/familydog

Features Editor: Mara Bovsun

AKC Family Dog is a lifestyle magazine for families who want to enjoy a mutually happy relationship with their pet. Articles highlight common breeds and offer advice on dog behavior, grooming, and canine health. ▪ **Circulation** 180,000 ▪ **Audience** Dog owners ▪ **Frequency** 6 times a year

Freelance Potential Publishes 24–30 freelance submissions yearly: 70% written by nonstaff writers; 15% by authors new to the magazine. Receives 5–10 queries monthly.

Submissions Guidelines available. Query with outline. Accepts email to mbb@akc.org. Responds immediately.
▪ *Articles:* 1,000–2,000 words. Informational, how-to, profiles. Topics: Owning a dog; breeds; canine health, behavior, grooming.
▪ *Depts/columns:* Staff-written.

Sample Issue Sample issue available.
▪ "A Measure of Difficulty," by Robert Rodi. Reports on an agility novice's first try in the ring.
▪ "She's a Mantrailer," by Dave Schwartz. Profiles a young bloodhound winning her first AKC title.

Rights and Payment First North American serial rights. Written material; $125–$500. Pays on publication. Provides 1 contributor's copy.

Amazing Kids!

20126 Ballinger Way NE, Suite 239, Shoreline, WA 98155. www.amazing-kids.org

Editor: Alyse Rome

This online magazine is a kid-created publication featuring fiction, nonfiction, art, and photography. It also publishes reviews of family-friendly books, new products, events, and travel destinations. Its content is created by, and directed toward, children ages 5 to 18 and their parents. ▪ **Hits per month** 640,000 ▪ **Audience** 5–18 years ▪ **Frequency** Updated regularly

Freelance Potential Publishes 50+ freelance submissions yearly: 30% written by nonstaff writers; 70% by authors new to the magazine; 90% by previously unpublished writers. Receives hundreds of queries monthly.

Submissions Guidelines available at website. Query. Accepts email to editor@amazing-kids.org. Response time varies.
▪ *Articles:* Word lengths vary. Informational, how-to, personal experience. Topics: science, technology, cultural diversity, travel, holiday traditions, cooking, adventures.
▪ *Fiction:* To 2,000 words. All genres.
▪ *Depts/columns:* Word lengths vary. Book and media reviews, science and technology.
▪ *Artwork:* Digital photos.
▪ *Other:* Poetry, no line limites. Recipes, activities.

Sample Issue Sample copy available at website.
▪ "Freedom," by Inikki Mitchell. Short story about a young slave pining for freedom.
▪ "A Writer's World," by Allison Stein. Profile of the author's mother and a late start to a writing career.

Rights and Payment All rights. No payment.

American History

Weider History Magazine Group, 19300 Promenade Drive, Leesburg, VA 20176. www.historynet.com

Submissions: Sarah Richardson

American History contains factually accurate articles about U.S. history, presented in an engaging, entertaining format. It focuses on the significant events and people that contributed to the creation of the nation. Its readership includes historians and the general public. ■ **Circulation** 100,000 ■ **Audience** YA–Adults ■ **Frequency** 6 times a year

Freelance Potential Publishes 30 freelance submissions yearly: 75% written by nonstaff writers; 50% by authors new to the magazine. Receives 25 queries monthly.

Submissions Guidelines available. Query with 1-page proposal and writing experience. Accepts hard copy and email to acw@weiderhistorygroup.com. SASE. Responds in 10 weeks.
■ *Articles:* 2,000–4,000 words. Informational. Topics: people, places, and events that shaped American history.
■ *Depts/columns:* Word lengths vary. Interviews, reviews, news.

Sample Issue Sample copy available.
■ "What We Owe Jehovah's Witnesses," by Sarah Barringer Gordon. How the actions of Jehovah's Witnesses led to more freedoms for all Americans.
■ "Founding Foodie," by Kristen Hinman. Thomas Jefferson's passion for gardening and cuisine.

Rights and Payment All rights. Articles, 20¢ a word. Depts/columns, $75. Pays on acceptance. Provides 5 contributor's copies..

Analog Science Fiction and Fact

Dell Magazine Group, 267 Broadway, New York, NY 10007. www.analogsf.com

Editor: Stanley Schmidt

Fiction exploring future science or technology is the mainstay of this magazine. It also publishes factual articles, mostly on current and future scientific topics. Because it covers such a broad spectrum of science fiction subgenres, all well-crafted submissions are welcome. Stories must be believable, no matter how fantastic the circumstances. ■ **Circulation** 40,000 ■ **Audience** YA–Adult ■ **Frequency** 10 times a year

Freelance Potential Publishes 80–90 freelance submissions yearly: Articles and stories, 100% written by nonstaff writers; 10% by authors new to the magazine; 10% by previously unpublished writers. Receives 500 unsolicited manuscripts monthly.

Submissions Guidelines available at website. Send complete manuscript with word count and publishing history. Query for serials only. Accepts submissions through online submission program, accessible via website. Responds in 5 weeks.
■ *Articles:* To 6,000 words. Informational. Topics: science, technology.
■ *Fiction:* Serials, 40,000–80,000 words. Novellas and novelettes, 10,000–20,000 words. Short stories, 2,000–7,000 words. Genres: Physical, sociological, psychological, and technological science fiction.
■ *Depts/columns:* Staff-written.

Sample Issue 240 pages . Little advertising. Sample copy available.
■ "Phantom Sense," by Richard A. Lovett & Mark Niemann-Ross. A father looking to make up lost time with his adult daughter.
■ "Tower of Worlds," by Rajnar Vajra. A young prisoner shares his thoughts before his execution.

Rights and Payment First North American serial and non-exclusive rights. Serials, 4¢ a word; other written material, 5¢–8¢ a word. Pays on acceptance. Provides 2 contributor's copies

Asimov's Science Fiction

Dell Magazine Group, 267 Broadway, 4th Floor, New York, NY 10007. www.asimovs.com

Editor: Sheila Williams

Serving a readership of young adult and adult science fiction fans, this journal features stories in which the characters, rather than the science, are the main focus. It also publishes poetry and book reviews. It accepts "borderline" fantasy—no sword and sorcery, please. ■ **Circulation** 60,000 ■ **Audience** YA–Adult ■ **Frequency** 10 times a year

Freelance Potential Publishes 85 freelance submissions yearly: 97% written by nonstaff writers; 30% by authors new to the magazine; 10% by previously unpublished writers. Receives 700 unsolicited manuscripts monthly.

Submissions Guidelines available at website. Send complete manuscript with word count and publishing history via website. No simultaneous submissions. Responds in 5 weeks.
■ *Fiction:* To 20,000 words. Genres: science fiction, fantasy.
■ *Depts/columns:* Word lengths vary. Book and website reviews.
■ *Other:* Poetry, to 40 lines.

Sample Issue 112 pages. Advertising. Sample copy available.
■ "The Day the Wires Came Down," by Alexander Jablokov. An ancient city with unusual transport.
■ "Becalmed," by Kristine Kathryn Rusch. Tells of a woman held prisoner on a futuristic ship.

Rights and Payment First worldwide, English-language serial rights. Fiction, 5¢–6¢ a word. Poetry, $1 a line. Depts/columns, payment rates vary. Pays on acceptance. Provides 2 contributor's copies.

Athlon Sports

220 25th Avenue North, Suite 200, Nashville, TN 37203. www.athlonsports.com/monthly-magazine

Editorial Director: Charlie Miller

From the leading publisher of sports annuals comes *Athlon Sports*, which made its debut a year ago, as a monthly insert into major daily newspapers. It provides a full range of sports coverage, athlete profiles, predictions, perspective, and inside analysis. In addition to all the major professional and collegiate sports, it also covers some youth sports, the Olympics, and horse racing. ■ **Circulation** 7 million ■ **Audience** YA-Adult ■ **Frequency** Monthly

Freelance Potential Unavailable.

Submissions For information, contact charlie.miller@athlonsports.com or athlonmedia3@athlonsports.com.
■ *Articles:* Word lengths vary. Informational, profiles, interviews. Topics: all major professional and collegiate sports, athletes, teams, leagues.
■ *Depts/columns:* Word lengths vary. Q&A, opinion.

Sample Issue
■ "Heart of the Saints." Why NFL quarterback Drew Brees has captivated New Orleans.
■ "Another Yankee Dynasty?" An analysis of the New York Yankees, and the legacy of Jeter and crew.

Rights and Payment Unavailable.

The Black Collegian

140 Carondelet Street, New Orleans, LA 70130. www.blackcollegian.com

Chief Executive Officer: Preston J. Edwards, Sr.

This career and self-development magazine targeting African American college students provides information about careers, job opportunities, and employment trends. Profiles of corporations and graduate programs are regular features. ■ **Circulation** 121,000 ■ **Audience** 18–30 years ■ **Frequency** Twice a year

Freelance Potential Publishes 20 freelance submissions yearly: 95% written by nonstaff writers; 33% by authors new to the magazine. Receives 2 queries monthly.

Submissions Guidelines available at website. Query. Prefers email to preston@imdiversity.com; will accept hard copy. SASE. Responds in 3 months.
■ *Articles:* 1,500–2,000 words. Informational, self-help, how-to, profiles, personal experience. Topics: careers, graduate and professional school, internships, study-abroad, personal development, financial aid, history, technology, multicultural and ethnic issues.
■ *Depts/columns:* Word lengths vary. Health issues, media reviews.
■ *Artwork:* B/W and color transparencies. B/W and color line art.

Sample Issue 72 pages: 16 articles. Sample copy available at website
■ "Professions and College Degrees in the Oil Industry," by Reginald Thomas. Oil Careers post-BP spill.
■ "Tyra Banks: It All Began Right here," by Pearl Stewart. Profile of the model and entrepreneur.

Rights and Payment One-time rights. All material, payment rates vary. Pays after publication. Provides 1 contributor's copy.

Bull Spec

P.O. Box 13146, Durham, TX 27709. www.bullspec.com

Editor: Samuel Montgomery-Blinn

Available in print and digital versions, *Bull Spec* is a journal of speculative fiction. It accepts short stories, poetry, interviews with authors, and book reviews. Though it focuses on fantasy and science fiction, it is open to many genres. ■ **Circulation** 500 ■ **Audience** YA–Adults ■ **Frequency** Quarterly

Freelance Potential 90% of content written by nonstaff writers: 50% by authors new to the magazine; 35% by previously unpublished writers. Receives 50 unsolicited manuscripts monthly.

Submissions Guidelines available at website. Send complete manuscript with author's city and state, word count, and whether submission has been published before. Accepts email to submissions@bullspec.com (attach file). Accepts simultaneous submissions, if identified. Responds in 3 months.
■ *Articles:* Word lengths vary. Interviews, book reviews.
■ *Fiction:* 1,000–8,000 words. Genres: fantasy, science fiction.
■ *Other:* Poetry, submit up to 3 poems at once

Sample Issue 64 pages. Sample copy available.
■ "Perchance," by Stuart Jaffe. A woman decides to give up sleeping for the rest of her life.
■ "Less than Absent," by Kenneth Schneyer. A missing persons investigation.

Rights and Payment First worldwide rights. Written material, 5¢ a word. Payment policy varies. Provides 1 contributor's copy.

Camping Magazine

American Camp Association, 5000 State Road 67 North, Martinsville, IN 46151-7902. www.acacamps.org/campmag

Editor in Chief: Harriet Lowe

Read by camp owners and administrators, *Camping* covers the news and trends in educational camps. Articles on innovative programming, safety issues, and management are featured. Many of the articles are written by people in the field who have hands-on experience. ■ **Circulation** 7,500 ■ **Audience** Camp managers and educators ■ **Frequency** 6 times a year

Freelance Potential Publishes 30–35 freelance submissions yearly: 90% written by nonstaff writers; 30% by authors new to the magazine; 50% by previously unpublished writers. Receives 8 unsolicited manuscripts monthly.

Submissions Guidelines and editorial calendar available at website. Send complete manuscript. Accepts disk submissions with hard copy and email submissions to magazine@acacamps.org (Word attachments). SASE. Response time varies.
- *Articles:* 1,500–3,000 words. Informational, how-to. Topics: camp management, special education, social issues, careers, health, recreation, crafts, hobbies.
- *Depts/columns:* 800–1,000 words. News, opinion, risk management, building and construction.
- *Artwork:* Color prints; JPEG or TIFF images at 300 dpi.

Sample Issue 72 pages. Advertising. Sample copy available.
- "Looking Back: Education in a 'Formal Sense,'" by Gwynn Powell & Joy James. The most instrumental educational partners for the camp profession over the years.
- "Working Toward a Healthier Camp: Five Strategies for Camp Administrators to Reconsider Now!" by Linda Ebner. Strategies for improved health and safety guidelines.

Rights and Payment All rights. No payment. Provides 3 contributor's copies.

Camping Today

Family Campes & RVers, 126 Hermitage Road, Butler, PA 16001. www.fcrv.org

Editor: DeWayne Johnston

Camping Today offers articles on family camping and the outdoors. Topics include road safety, wildlife, and destinations. Pieces written from personal experience that include the author's opinions and impressions are welcome. ■ **Circulation** 10,000 ■ **Audience** YA–Adult ■ **Frequency** 6 times a year

Freelance Potential Publishes 10 freelance submissions yearly: 40% written by nonstaff writers; 10% by previously unpublished writers. Receives 2 unsolicited manuscripts monthly.

Submissions Guidelines and theme list available. Send complete manuscript with artwork. Accepts hard copy. SASE. Responds in 2 months.
- *Articles:* 1,000–3,000 words. Informational, how-to, personal experience. Topics: camping, destinations, travel, equipment, road safety.
- *Depts/columns:* Word lengths vary. News, events, wildlife.
- *Artwork:* JPEG images.

Sample Issue 40 pages. Advertising. Sample copy available at website.
- "Myrtle Beach," by Tom Reed. Destination story about Myrtle Beach, South Carolina.
- "DAT to DASAT," by Marilyn Rausch. Changes to the new Disaster and Safety Awareness Training.

Rights and Payment One-time rights. Written material, $35–$150. Pays on publication. Provides 1+ contributor's copies.

Canoe & Kayak

236 Avenida Fabricante, Suite 201, San Clemente, CA 92672. www.canoekayak.com

Managing Editor: Jeff Moag

Each issue of this magazine is packed with canoe and kayak destination pieces, the latest paddling techniques, expert reviews of paddle and camping gear, and family paddling tips. Writers must have experience canoeing, kayaking, and rafting. ■ **Circulation** 50,000 ■ **Audience** YA–Adults ■ **Frequency** 6 times a year

Freelance Potential Publishes 25 freelance submissions yearly: 90% written by nonstaff writers; 25% by authors new to the magazine; 5% bypreviously unpublished writers. Receives 10 queries monthly.

Submissions Guidelines available at website. Query with photos and publishing experience. Accepts email submissions to appropriate editor (see guidelines for full list). Responds in 6–8 weeks.
- *Articles:* 400–2,000 words. Informational, how-to, personal experience, profiles. Topics: destinations; boat news and trends; retailer, outfitter and manufacturer profiles.
- *Depts/columns:* 150–750 words. Personalities, adventures, trends.
- *Artwork:* Digital images.

Sample Issue Sample copy available.
- "Ghosts of the Dubawnt River," by Bill Layman. Personal experience piece about a trip to the Northwest Territories of Canada.
- "Cobra Eliminator–Fast and Fit Boats." Review of a new canoe.

Rights and Payment All rights. Written material, 50¢ a word. Pays on publication. Provides 1 contributor's copy.

Cat Fancy

P.O. Box 6050, Mission Viejo, CA 92690. www.catchannel.com

Query Editor

Informative articles on cats, feline behavior, and breeds are published in this magazine that is dedicated to the love of cats. It is open to receiving queries from new writers. ■ **Circulation** 290,000 ■ **Audience** YA–Adults ■ **Frequency** Monthly

Freelance Potential Publishes 150 freelance submissions yearly: 95% written by nonstaff writers; 70% by authors new to the magazine; 10% by previoiusly unpublished writers. Receives 42+ queries monthly.

Submissions Guidelines available at website. Query with clips between January 1 and May 1 only (news and trend queries accepted year-round). Accepts hard copy and email queries to query@catfancy.com. Availability of artwork improves chance of acceptance. Response time varies.
- *Articles:* 100–1,000 words. Informational, how-to, profiles. Topics: cat breeds; feline health, nutrition, grooming, behavior, and training; cat personalities; human-animal bond.
- *Depts/columns:* 500 words. Champion for Cat, Rescue of the Month.
- *Artwork:* 35mm slides, high-resolution digital images with contact sheets.

Sample Issue Sample copy available.
- "Russian Gift," by Elisa Jordan. Profile of the Siberian cat.
- "A Flea's Life," by Fran Pennock Shaw. Explains the biology of a flea, and offers strategies for getting rid of and preventing their reoccurrence.

Rights and Payment First rights. All material, payment rates vary. Pays on publication. Provides 2 contributor's copies.

Chess Life

P.O. Box 3967, Crossville, TN 38557-3967. www.uschess.org

Editor: Daniel Lucas

For more than 20 years, the U.S. Chess Federation has been publishing this magazine for players of all ages. Each issue includes information on playing strategies for novices through experts, as well as reports on tournaments around the globe. It welcomes articles about chess in everyday life or a profile of a relatively unknown player. ■ **Circulation** 80,000 ■ **Audience** YA–Adult ■ **Frequency** Monthly

Freelance Potential Publishes 30 freelance submissions yearly: 75% written by nonstaff writers; 30% by unpublished writers. Receives 15–35 queries monthly.

Submissions Query with clips or writing samples. Accepts hard copy and email queries to dlucas@uschess.org. SASE. Responds in 1–3 months.

■ *Articles:* 800–3,000 words. Informational, how-to, historical, profiles, humor, personal experience, opinion. Topics: chess games and strategies, tournaments and events, personalities in the game.
■ *Depts/columns:* To 1,000 words. Book and product reviews, short how-to's, player profiles.
■ *Artwork:* B/W or color prints.
■ *Other:* Chess-oriented cartoons, contests, games.

Sample Issue 72 pages. Advertising. Sample copy available.
■ "Looks at Books," by Al Lawrence. A new book about the rise and fall of chess player Bobby Fischer.
■ "Karpov on Fischer." Interview with seven-time World Champion Anatoly Karpov.

Rights and Payment All rights. Written material, $100 a page. Artwork, $15–$100. Kill fee, 30%. Pays on publication. Provides 2 contributor's copies.

Chicken Soup for the Soul

P.O. Box 700, Cos Cob, CT 06807-0700, www.chickensoup.com

Editor

Inspirational, true stories that touch the hearts of readers are the mainstay of the popular Chicken Soup for the Soul anthologies. Contributors of all ages are accepted, and all topics are fair game. The company continues to publish anthologies to a variety of target audiences, including children, young adults, and parents. A typical piece is a true story about ordinary people doing extraordinary things, and touching the lives of others. ■ **Circulation** Not applicable ■ **Audience** Children, YA, adults ■ **Frequency** Anthologies

Freelance Potential Contributions from new as well as established writers are welcome here.

Submissions Guidelines available at website. Submit complete manuscript. Accepts electronic submissions via website only. Mailed material will be returned unopened.
■ *Articles:* 1,2000 words. Creative nonfiction. True, inspirational stories or essays.
■ *Other:* Poetry.

Sample Issue Not applicable.
■ "Chicken Soup for the Soul: Just for Preteens." True stories designed to help tweens navigate life.
■ "Chicken Soup for the Soul: Power Moms." Celebrates stay-at-home and work-from-home moms.

Rights and Payment Rights vary. Written material, $200. Pays on publication. Provides 10 contributor's copies.

Children's Writer

Institute of Children's Literature, 95 Long Ridge Road, West Redding, CT 06896-1124
www.childrenswriter.com

Editor in Chief: Susan Tierney

Children's Writer is a newsletter, now available in an electronic edition, for writers that reports on and analyzes trends in children's book and magazine publishing. It covers all categories, from picture books through YA, and magazines for all ages. The Marketplace section highlights publishers' needs. Its departments offer strategies on business issues, writing techniques, motivation, and research. ■ **Circulation** 14,000 ■ **Audience** Writers ■ **Frequency** Monthly

Freelance Potential Publishes 75 freelance submissions yearly: 90% written by nonstaff writers; 15% by authors new to the magazine; 10% by previously unpublished writers. Receives 5+ queries monthly.

Submissions Guidelines available at website. Query with detailed outline, potential length, potential sources, and proposed submission date. Prefers email query to cwtierney@ChildrensWriter.com, and attachments (Word). Accepts simultaneous submissions if identified. SASE. Responds if interested.
■ *Articles:* 1,700–2,000 words. Informational, analytical, how-to, interviews. Topics: children's book

and magazine publishing trends, new markets, genres, writing techniques and craft, career.

■ *Depts/columns:* To 750 words, plus 125-word sidebar. Writing techniques, business issues, commentary, technology, research strategies, motivation, editor and publisher profiles.

Sample Issue 12 pages. No advertising. Sample copy available.

■ "Memorable Seasons in Children's Writing." Writing fiction and nonfiction about holidays and seasons.

■ "Sound Like Who You Are." Tips on developing a distinct writing voice.

Rights and Payment First-time rights. Features, $300; columns $200. Pays on acceptance.

CKI Magazine

Circle K International, 3636 Woodview Trace, Indianapolis, IN 46268-3196. www.circlek.org

Executive Editor: Amberly Peterson

Targeting members of Circle K International, a collegiate service organization affiliated with the Kiwanis Club, this magazine reports on chapter events and activities and offers advice on college life, job hunting, and service to the community. It is published digitally and delivered to members' inboxes.

■ **Hits per month** 10,000 ■ **Audience** YA–Adult ■ **Frequency** Twice a year

Freelance Potential Publishes 2–4 freelance submissions yearly: 20% written by nonstaff writers; 5% by authors new to the magazine. Receives 2–4 queries monthly.

Submissions Guidelines available at website. Query. Accepts email queries to ckimagazine@kiwanis.org. Responds in 2 weeks.

■ *Articles:* 1,500–2,000 words. Informational, self-help. Topics: social issues, collegiate trends, community service, leadership, fundraising, career planning and development.

■ *Depts/columns:* Word lengths vary. News and information about Circle K activities.

■ *Artwork:* TIFF or JPEG images at 300 dpi or higher.

Sample Issue 16 pages. Sample copy available at website.

■ "One Cause, One Family." A service aimed at eliminating maternal/neonatal tetanus worldwide.

■ "Service on a Large Scale." Reports on the services and goals of the Aids Housing Alliance.

Rights and Payment First North American serial rights. Written material, $150–$400. Artwork, payment rates vary. Pays on acceptance.

Classic Toy Trains

21027 Crossroads Circle, Waukesha, WI 53187. www.classictoytrains.com

Editor: Carl Swanson

This photo-filled magazine is read by model train hobbyists for how-to articles and pieces on collecting and train history. It also publishes profiles of collectors. Of special interest are articles dealing with wiring or scenery techniques and interesting layouts. ■ **Circulation** 55,000 ■ **Audience** YA–Adults ■ **Frequency** 9 times a year

Freelance Potential Publishes 40–50 freelance submissions: 60% written by nonstaff writers yearly; 20% by authors new to the magazine; 20% by previously unpublished writers. Receives 8 queries, 5 unsolicited manuscripts monthly.

Submissions Guidelines available at website. Prefers query; will accept manuscript. Accepts hard copy, disk submissions (Word files), and email submissions to editor@classictoytrains.com. No simultaneous submissions. SASE. Responds in 3 months.

■ *Articles:* 500–5,000 words. Informational, how-to, profiles. Topics: model train collecting, layouts, train history.

■ *Depts/columns:* Word lengths vary. Reviews, techniques, tips.

Sample Issue Sample copy available.

■ "Build a Busy Harbor Scene," by Fred M. Dole. Step-by-step instructions for adding a bay, coal loading dock, and a scratchbuilt barge to a harbor train scene.

■ "Lionel's Forgotten Printing Kit," by Joe Algozzini. A look back at a 1950s kit that helped kids design their dream railroad.

Rights and Payment All rights. Articles, $75 a page. Depts/columns, payment rates vary. Pays on acceptance. Provides 1 contributor's copy.

Coins

4700 East Galbraith Road, Cincinnati, OH 45236. www.coinsmagazine.net

Editor: Robert Van Ryzin

Coins is the go-to publication for timely information on coin market trends, buying and selling tips, and pricing. It also offers articles on the history of coin collecting and how to start a collection. Personal experience pieces, profiles, and show coverage round out each issue. All content is authored by coin experts, and assignments are given on a work-for-hire basis. ■ **Circulation** 60,000 ■ **Audience** Coin collectors ■ **Frequency** Monthly

Freelance Potential Publishes 70 freelance submissions yearly: 40% written by nonstaff writers; 5% by authors new to the magazine. Receives 3–5 queries monthly.

Submissions Guidelines available. Query. Accepts hard copy. SASE. Responds in 1–2 months. Also offers work-for-hire assignments.

■ *Articles:* 1,500–2,500 words. Informational, how-to, profiles, personal experience. Topics: the history, trends, pricing, buying, selling, and collecting of coins.

■ *Depts/columns:* Staff-written.

Sample Issue Sample copy available.

■ "Time Is Right for Morgan and Peace Dollars," by Mark Benevenuto. Examines some high-end Morgan and Peace dollars that have increased in value.

■ "Roosevelt on the Dime," by Tom LaMarre. Discusses how the dime was designed in 1945.

Rights and Payment All rights. Articles, 4¢ a word. Pays on publication. Provides contributor's copies upon request.

College News

39 South LaSalle, Unit 420, Chicago, IL 60603. www.collegenews.com

Editor: Janelle Vreeland

This magazine gives college students information on career opportunities, education trends, money issues, and travel in a contemporary format. It also offers college lifestyle pieces and articles on the latest entertainment, music, sports, and global news. It prefers to work with college-age writers, but considers all queries from other writers. Articles about the serious side of college are especially sought. ■ **Circulation** Unavailable ■ **Audience** 18–25 years ■ **Frequency** Quarterly

Freelance Potential Publishes 20 freelance submissions yearly: 30% written by nonstaff writers; 20% by authors new to the magazine; 70% by previously unpublished writers. Receives 50 queries monthly.

Submissions Guidelines available. Query. Accepts email to editor@collegenews.com. Response time varies.

■ *Articles:* 400 words. Informational, how-to, personal experience, interviews. Topics: college life, careers, education.

■ *Depts/columns:* Word lengths vary. Entertainment, politics, health, college, careers, money.

Sample Issue Sample copy available at website.
- "Graduation Day," by Marisa Amorasak. The eagerness and anxiety of a soon-to-be college graduate.
- "Stop and Stare at One Republic," by Alina Dain. Interview with One Republic's lead guitarist Zach Filkins.

Rights and Payment All rights. No payment. Provides 1 contributor's copy.

Craftbits.com

P.O. Box 3106, Birkdale, Queensland 4159, Australia. www.craftbits.com

Editor: Shellie Wilson

Family-oriented and kid- and senior-friendly, this online magazine has craft projects for all ages and skill levels. Directions for more complicated crafts are presented in a detailed, step-by-step format. Candle- and soap-making, beading, and scrapbooking, as well as holiday-themed and recycled crafts, are among the projects featured. ■ **Hits per month** 60,000 ■ **Audience** YA–Adult ■ **Frequency** Updated regularly

Freelance Potential 5% of content written by nonstaff writers.

Submissions Guidelines available at website. Query with artwork. Accepts email queries to staff@craftbits.com. Responds in 1–2 months.
- *Articles:* Word lengths vary. How-to. Topics: crafts for all ages, including bath and body, beads, candle making, holidays, crochet and knitting patterns, gifts in a jar, jewelry, paper, recycled goods, scrapbooking, sewing, weddings.
- *Artwork:* JPEG files.

Sample Issue Sample copy available at website.
- "Kasbah Beaded Scarf." Make a plain, store-bought scarf into a statement piece.
- "Recycled Bottle Cap Pocket Mirror." Instructions on how to turn bottle caps into pocket mirrors.

Rights and Payment All rights. Written material, word lengths vary. Kill fee, $10. Pays on publication.

Dance International

677 Davie Street, Vancouver, British Columbia V6B 2G6 Canada. www.danceinternational.org

Managing Editor: Maureen Riches

Dance International brings global coverage of both classical and contemporary dance to its readers. It offers reviews, criticism, profiles, and interviews. Writers are often dancers themselves, or they have extensive professional experience within (or covering) the dance world. It covers contemporary dance and ballet companies from around the globe, and it is always in need of reviews of productions on foreign soil. ■ **Circulation** 4,000 ■ **Audience** YA–Adult ■ **Frequency** Quarterly

Freelance Potential Publishes 95 freelance submissions yearly: 85% written by nonstaff writers; 9% by authors new to the magazine.

Submissions Guidelines available at website. Send complete manuscript. Accepts email to danceint@direct.ca (attach file) and disk submissions (RTF files). SASE. Responds in 2 months.
- *Articles:* 1,500 words. Informational, profiles, interviews, opinion, media reviews. Topics: dance, performers, performances.
- *Depts/columns:* 1,000 words. Commentaries, book and performance reviews.
- *Artwork:* Digital images at 300 dpi or higher.

Sample Issue 62 pages. Advertising. Sample copy available.
- "The Truth Behind *Black Swan*," by Jeffrey Taylor. A former dancer on the movie's accuracy.
- "Former National Ballet of Canada Star Frank Augustyn: An Update," by Victor Swoboda. Augustyn's new career path as a professor at Adelphi University.

Rights and Payment First rights. Articles, $100–$150. Depts/columns, $100. Kill fee, 50%. Pays on publication. Provides 2 contributor's copies.

Dance Magazine

110 William Street, 23rd Floor, New York, NY 1003. www.dancemagazine.com

Editor in Chief: Wendy Perron

Dance students, teachers, and professionals read this magazine for articles that keep them abreast of what is going on in all disciplines of dance. It features techniques, training strategies, and profiles of dancers, companies, and productions. Writers should have a history with dance, either in performance, teaching, or critiquing. Though most of its coverage leans toward ballet and contemporary, it is open to pieces about any style. ■ **Circulation** 50,000 ■ **Audience** YA–Adult ■ **Frequency** Monthly

Freelance Potential Publishes 200 freelance submissions yearly: 80% written by nonstaff writers; 25% by authors new to the magazine; 5% by previously unpublished writers.

Submissions Query. Accepts hard copy and email queries to wperron@dancemedia.com. SASE. Response time varies.
■ *Articles:* To 1,500 words. Informational, profiles, interviews. Topics: dance, dance instruction, choreography, the arts, family, health concerns.
■ *Depts/columns:* Word lengths vary. New product information, reviews, dance news, instruction.

Sample Issue 138 pages. Advertising. Sample copy available at website.
■ "A Female Force," by Victoria Looseleaf. The small number of women in artistic director positions.
■ "Wide Open Spaces," by Martha Ullman West. Profiles the Trey McIntyre Project, which is touring in America's heartland.

Rights and Payment Rights vary. Written material, payment rates vary. Pays on publication.

Dog Fancy

BowTie Inc., P.O. Box 6050, Mission Viejo, CA 92690-6050. www.dogfancy.com

Editor: Ernie Slone

Dog Fancy is devoted to all dogs, whether purebred or mixed breed. It seeks articles that cover training, canine health and behavior, and living happily with a dog. It is accepting articles on holistic health for its new supplement, *Natural Dog*. New contributors with fresh ideas are welcome to query.
■ **Circulation** 270,000 ■ **Audience** Dog owners ■ **Frequency** Monthly

Freelance Potential Publishes 20–25 freelance submissions yearly: 95% written by nonstaff writers; 10% by authors new to the magazine. Receives 0 queries monthly.

Submissions Guidelines available at website. Query with résumé, outline, and clips. Accepts email queries to barkback@dogfancy.com. Responds in 1 month.
■ *Articles:* 1,000–1,600 words. Informational, how-to, profiles. Topics: breeds; dog health, behavior, grooming, and training; products.
■ *Depts/columns:* 650 words. News, trends, grooming and training tips, health news.

Sample Issue Sample copy available.
■ "The Big Show," by Eve Adamson. A look behind the scenes of the Westminster Dog Show.
■ "Clean and Green," by Wendy Bedwell-Wilson. All-natural tips for keeping a dog-owning home looking and smelling good.

Rights and Payment First North American serial rights. Written material, payment rates vary. Pays on publication. Provides 2 contributor's copies.

Doll House Miniatures

68132 250th Avenue, Kasson, MN 55944. www.dhminiatures.com

Editor in Chief: Kelly Rud

Dollhouse Miniatures informs, entertains, and inspires dollhouse hobbyists of all levels of experience. It seeks unique projects with clear directions accompanied by step-by-step photos. Contributors must fully understand not only the hobby, but the magazine as well. ■ **Circulation** 25,000 ■ **Audience** YA–Adult ■ **Frequency** Six times a year

Freelance Potential Publishes 8–10 freelance submissions yearly: 30% written by nonstaff writers; 30% by authors new to the magazine; 10% by previously unpublished writers. Receives 5 queries monthly.

Submissions Query with title and brief introduction; include list of tools and materials for how-to projects. Accepts hard copy and email to kelly@dhminiatures.com. SASE. Responds in 2 months.
■ *Articles:* 500–2,500 words. Informational, how-to. Topics: collecting and creating dollhouses, dollhouse accessories.
■ *Artwork:* JPEG images at 300 dpi; color photos. Line art.

Sample Issue Sample copy available.
■ "A Wonderful Day in a Beautiful Setting," by Joyce Dean. Meeting the artists from Rosalind Mercy, a UK company specializing in miniature porcelain.
■ "World Wide Collection Download," by Fiona Martin. Report on the best dollhouse items sold online.

Rights and Payment All rights. Payment rates vary. Pays on publication.

Dolls

P.O. Box 5000, Iola, WI 54945-5000. www.dollsmagazine.com

Editor: Joyce Greenholdt

Doll collectors turn to this magazine for its comprehensive coverage of other doll collectors and collections, as well as articles on doll history and doll making. Product reviews and current prices are also included. ■ **Circulation** 10,000 ■ **Audience** YA–Adult ■ **Frequency** Monthly

Freelance Potential Publishes 50 freelance submissions yearly: 75% written by nonstaff writers; 10% by authors new to the magazine. Receives 4 unsolicited manuscripts monthly.

Submissions Send complete manuscript. Accepts email submissions to editor@dollsmagazine.com. Availability of artwork improves chance of acceptance. Response time varies.
■ *Articles:* 1,000–2,000 words. Informational, profiles. Topics: doll makers, history, collecting.
■ *Depts/columns:* Staff-written.
■ *Artwork:* Color prints, slides, or transparencies; JPEG images at 300 dpi.

Sample Issue Sample copy available.
■ "Peek into the Past," by Kerra Davis. How to differentiate an authentic Lenci doll from a copycat.
■ "Couture Creations," by Stephanie Finnegan. Profiles the creator of the popular OOAK dolls.

Rights and Payment Perpetual and assignable license. Written material, $200. Pays on publication.

Elementary School Writer

Writer Publications, P.O. Box 718, Grand Rapids, MI 55744-0718. www.writerpublications.com

Editor: Emily Benes

For more than 25 years, *Elementary School Writer* has been showcasing the stories, poems, essays, and articles of young authors. It was founded by an English teacher to foster student creativity, and to enable students to learn from the writing of their peers. Submissions from young writers must come from teachers who are subscribers. ■ **Circulation** Unavailable ■ **Audience** Children–YA ■ **Frequency** 6 times a year

Freelance Potential Publishes 300 freelance submissions yearly: 100% written by nonstaff writers; 75% by authors new to the magazine; 95% by previously unpublished writers. Receives 8 unsolicited manuscripts monthly.

Submissions Guidelines available in each issue and at website. Accepts complete manuscripts from subscribing teachers only. Accepts hard copy and email submissions to writer@mx3.com (text file attachments). Accepts simultaneous submissions if identified. SASE. Response time varies.
■ *Articles:* To 1,000 words. Informational, how-to, profiles, humor, opinion, personal experience. Topics: current events, multicultural and ethnic issues, nature, the environment, popular culture, sports, travel.
■ *Fiction:* To 1,000 words. Genres: humor, science fiction, and stories about nature and sports.
■ *Other:* Poetry, no line limits. Seasonal material.

Sample Issue 8 pages. No advertising.
■ "The Dog Who Dug Lake Superior." Story about the creation of Lake Superior.
■ "First Class Luxury." Personal experience piece about a trip from Beirut to Minneapolis, Minnesota.

Rights and Payment One-time rights. No payment.

Enchanted Conversation

www.fairytalemagazine.com

Editor: Kate Wolford

Lovers of fairy tales read this magazine for articles about the genre and for short stories and poems. Each themed issue features fiction in which the storylines and characters from existing fairy tales are expanded; also includes nonfiction that relates to the theme. Though not intended for children, young adult fans of the genre will find this appealing. ■ **Circulation** Unavailable ■ **Audience** YA–Adults ■ **Frequency** Quarterly

Freelance Potential Accepts work from established writers and encourages submissions from new writers.

Submissions Guidelines and theme list available at website. Send complete manuscript with word count. Accepts email submissions only to enchantedconversation@gmail.com (no attachments; include author's name and issue theme in subject line). Take note of specific submission windows and deadlines, as they vary. Response time varies.
■ *Articles:* Word lengths vary. Informational. Topics: the fairy tale genre.
■ *Fiction:* 1,500 words. Short stories that expand upon an existing fairy tale or fairy tale theme. Must relate to issue theme.
■ *Other:* Poetry.

Sample Issue
■ "Finding Beauty," by Breanna Teintze.
■ "Roses on Snow," by Ariel Woodruff.

Rights and Payment Rights vary. Articles and fiction, 10¢ a word. Poetry, $50. Payment policy varies.

Entertainment Magazine

P.O. Box 3355, Tucson, AZ 85722. www.emol.org

Publisher: Robert Zucker

This online magazine provides daily updates on all aspects of the entertainment industry. Included are profiles and interviews, movie and TV updates, and other entertainment news of worldwide interest. The ezine does not publish material promoting products or businesses. ■ **Hits per month** 500,000+ ■ **Audience** YA–Adult ■ **Frequency** Updated regularly

Freelance Potential Publishes dozens of freelance submissions yearly: 60% written by nonstaff writers; 25% by authors new to the magazine; 75% by previously unpublished writers. Receives 10+ queries monthly.

Submissions Query. Accepts email queries to emol@emol.org. Responds in 1–2 days.
■ *Articles:* To 1,000 words. Informational, reviews. Topics: movies, music, TV, celebrities, books, the entertainment industry.
■ *Artwork:* B/W digital images.
■ *Other:* Calendar of events.

Sample Issue Sample copy available at website.
■ "Outlaw Laboratories Sets New Film Plans." A studio plan to develop 10 feature films over 5 years.
■ "2011 Billboard Music Awards." Discusses expectations of the upcoming awards show.

Rights and Payment Author retains rights. No payment.

Equestrian

4047 Iron Works Parkway, Lexington, KY 40511. www.usef.org

Editor: Brian Sosby

The United States Equestrian Federation publishes this magazine for its members, offering comprehensive coverage of events, news, and competitions. It also features articles on equine health, breeding, and training. ■ **Circulation** 90,000 ■ **Audience** YA–Adult ■ **Frequency** 10 times a year

Freelance Potential Publishes 50 freelance submissions yearly: 50% written by nonstaff writers; 10% by authors new to the magazine. Receives 17 queries monthly.

Submissions Guidelines available. Query with résumé and writing samples. Accepts email queries to bsosby@usef.org. Responds in 1 week.
■ *Articles:* 2,000–3,000 words. Informational, how-to. Topics: equine health, breeding, training, competitions.
■ *Depts/columns:* 500–1,000 words. Breed profiles, USEF news and events.

Sample Issue 56 pages. Sample copy available at website.
■ "USET Foundation Supports America's Equestrians," by Rebecca Walton. Describes the goals and services of the United States Equestrian Team Foundation.
■ "Our Town: New Jersey's Somerset Hills," by Nancy Jaffer. A communtiy that is home to many large horse farms, stables, and training facilities.

Rights and Payment First rights. Written material, payment rates vary. Kill fee, 50%. Pays on publication. Provides 1 contributor's copy.

Equine Journal

102 Roxbury Street, Keene, NH 03431. www.equinejournal.com

Editor: Kelly Ballou

Amateur and professional equestrians, as well as horse enthusiasts, read this journal to stay on top of horse-related news and activities. It covers breeds, riding styles, equine health, and competitions. It is open to any horse-related topic that would be of interest to riders, owners, breeders, trainers—or anyone who simply loves horses. ■ **Circulation** 19,000 ■ **Audience** 14 years–Adult ■ **Frequency** Monthly

Freelance Potential Publishes 100 freelance submissions yearly: 90% written by nonstaff writers; 10% by authors new to the magazine. Receives 3–5 queries monthly.

Submissions Guidelines and editorial calendar available at website. Query with résumé and clips. Accepts hard copy and email submissions to editorial@equinejournal.com. Accepts simultaneous submissions if identified. Responds in 2 months.
- *Articles:* 1,500–2,000 words. Informational, how-to. Topics: breeds, riding tips, carriage driving, training, stabling, transportation, equine care, ranch management, equine insurance.
- *Depts/columns:* Word lengths vary. Horse Health, Last Laugh.

Sample Issue 146 pages. Advertising. Sample copy available at website.
- "Just Right," by Kandace York. Barn plans to fit an owner's style and budget.
- "Effective Pasture Management," by Nancy Humphrey Case. Strategies for turning unproductive lots into thriving, nutritious pastures.

Rights and Payment First North American serial rights. Articles, $100–$225. Depts/columns, $25–$125. Pays on publication. Provides 1 contributor's copy.

Fido Friendly

P.O. Box 160, Marsing, ID 83639. www.fidofriendly.com

Submissions: Claudine Randazzo

This magazine is read by dog owners looking for information about pet-friendly travel destinations in the U.S. and Canada. Also published are articles on canine health and wellness, behavior and training, and even canine fashion. ■ **Circulation** 44,000 ■ **Audience** YA–Adult ■ **Frequency** 6 times a year

Freelance Potential Publishes 20 freelance submissions yearly: 75% written by nonstaff writers; 10% by authors new to the magazine; 10% by previously unpublished writers. Receives 8 queries monthly.

Submissions Query with sample paragraph. Accepts email queries to editorial@fidofriendly.com. Responds in 1 month.
- *Articles:* 800–1,200 words. Informational, how-to, profiles. Topics: canine health, behavior, and training; travel; rescue; celebrity dog owners.
- *Depts/columns:* Word lengths vary. Profiles, nutrition, health, training, adoptions, gear.

Sample Issue 98 pages. Advertising. Sample copy available at website.
- "Get in the Doghouse—21st Century Style," by Carol Bryant & Tiffany Keeth. Offers suggestions for creating a comfortable, attractive, and unique doghouse.
- "Chewing Through the Apron Strings," by Tiffany Keeth. Making a kennel stay successful.

Rights and Payment First rights. Articles,10¢ a word. Pays on publication. Provides 1 contributor's copy.

FineScale Modeler

21027 Crossroads Circle, P.O. Box 1612, Waukesha, WI 53187. www.finescale.com

Editor: Matthew Usher

This magazine is read for its detailed and well-illustrated how-to articles on scale modeling. Readers include beginners to the hobby as well as advanced enthusiasts. Writers who are submitting to the magazine for the first time, or who are unpublished, will find a brief article on a popular subject, such as repairing and polishing clear parts, to be their best chance for acceptance. ■ **Circulation** 60,000 ■ **Audience** YA–Adult ■ **Frequency** 10 times a year

Freelance Potential Publishes 40 freelance submissions yearly: 85% written by nonstaff writers; 20% by authors new to the magazine. Receives 17 queries monthly.

Submissions Guidelines available at website. Query with photos; include biography if first-time author. Accepts hard copy and disk submissions with hard copy. No simultaneous submissions. Availability of artwork improves chance of acceptance. SASE. Responds in 1–4 months.
- *Articles:* 750–2,500 words. Informational, how-to. Topics: modeling techniques; making, repairing, and polishing parts; painting; color schemes; displays and dioramas; workshop techniques.
- *Depts/columns:* Staff-written.
- *Artwork:* Digital images; slides, prints. Scale drawings.

Sample Issue Advertising. Sample copy available.
- "Giving a Flat Authentic Flavor," by Aaron Skinner. Techniques for a layered approach to weathering.
- "Mort Künstler: "America's Artist"," by Mark Hembree. Profile of a renowned illustrator.

Rights and Payment All rights. All material, payment rates vary. Pays on acceptance. Provides 1 contributor's copy.

Games

Kappa Publishing Group, Inc., 6198 Butler Pike, Suite 200, Blue Bell, PA 19422-2600.
www.gamesmagazine-online.com

Editor in Chief: R. Wayne Schmittberger

Teens and adults who are fascinated by games and puzzles read this magazine to challenge their minds. Each issue offers engaging games and puzzles, and articles on the history of, and creative processes behind, game and puzzle development. It welcomes ideas for feature articles about games, puzzles, wordplays, and the people who create them .Game reviews are by assignment only.
- **Circulation** 75,000 ■ **Audience** YA–Adult ■ **Frequency** 10 times a year

Freelance Potential Publishes 200+ freelance submissions yearly: 86% written by nonstaff writers; 20% by authors new to the magazine; 10% by previously unpublished writers. Receives 80 queries and unsolicited manuscripts monthly

Submissions Guidelines available. Prefers query; will accept complete manuscript. Accepts hard copy and email to wschmittberger@kappapublishing.com. SASE. Responds in 6–8 weeks.
- *Articles:* 1,500–3,000 words. Informational, profiles, humor. Topics: game-related events and people, wordplay, human ingenuity.
- *Depts/columns:* Gambits, word lengths vary.
- *Other:* Visual and verbal puzzles, quizzes, contests, two-play games, adventures.

Sample Issue 80 pages. Little advertising. Sample copy available.
- "Hail to the Veep," by Gunnar Johnson. Quiz tests reader's knowledge of U.S. vice presidents.
- "Punch Lines," by Walter Klis. Scramblers of humorous cartoon captions.

Rights and Payment All North American serial rights. Articles, $500– $1,000., Depts/columns, $100–$250. Pays on publication. Provides 1 contributor's copy.

Good Dog

Nomad Editions, 245 Fifth Avenue, Room 2345, New York, NY 10016.
www.nomadeditions.com/good-dog

Editor: Sonia Zjawinski

Good Dog celebrates the dogs that are part of our lives, from energetic puppies to the faithful family friend. Its publisher is Nomad Editions, which delivers magazines directly to readers' tablets or mobile devices via a downloaded app. *Good Dog* features essays in honor of great or quirky canines, profiles of dogs and their owners, do-it-yourself pet projects, and information on dog health and care.
- **Circulation** Unavailable ■ **Audience** Families ■ **Frequency** Weekly

Freelance Potential Nomad Editions and its apps for original magazine content represent a new business model for digital media, and is looking for writers to help take on the challenge. It accepts specific article ideas as well as applications for assignments.

Submissions Query or send complete manuscript. Also accepts writers interested in being a regular contributor. Contact the editors via the form at website, or szjawinski@nomadeditions.com.
- *Articles:* Word lengths vary. Informational, personal experience, essay, photo-essay. Topics; dogs, pet nutrition, life with dogs.

Sample Issue Sample issue available.
- "Bliss." A photo-essay about the joys of cruising through the country with a dog.
- "The Dish Behind Dog Food." A report on what your dog is *really* eating.

Rights and Payment Unavailable.

Alfred Hitchcock's Mystery Magazine

267 Broadway, 4th Floor, New York, NY 10007. www.themysteryplace.com

Editor: Linda Landrigan

This mystery magazine publishes well-written, and entertaining stories of crime, either as an outright act or an insinuated one. It accepts nearly every kind of mystery, including stories of detection of the classic kind, police procedurals, private investigator tales, suspense, courtroom dramas, and tales of espionage. ■ **Circulation** 75,000 ■ **Audience** YA–Adults ■ **Frequency** 10 times a year

Freelance Potential Publishes 90–100 freelance submissions yearly: 98% written by nonstaff writers; 25–50% by authors new to the magazine; 5–10% by previously unpublished writers. Receives 50–100 unsolicited manuscripts monthly.

Submissions Guidelines available at website. Send complete manuscript. Accepts hard copy. No simultaneous submissions. SASE. Responds in 3–5 months.
- *Fiction:* To 12,000 words. Genres: classic crime mysteries, detective stories, suspense, private investigator tales, courtroom drama, espionage.
- *Depts/columns:* Word lengths vary. Reviews, puzzles, profiles of bookstores.

Sample Issue 192 pages. Little advertising. Sample copy available.
- "The Case of the Telephoning Ghost," by Joe Helgerson. A small-town detective searches for a ghost who preys on residents when they are using a telephone.
- "Watts Up," by Doc Finch. An energy consultant is pulled into an investigation of a suspicious death.

Rights and Payment First serial, anthology, and foreign rights. Written material, payment rates vary. Pays on acceptance. Provides 2 contributor's copies.

The Horn Book

56 Roland Street, Suite 200, Boston, MA 02129. www.hbook.com

Editorial Assistant: Cynthia Ritter

Individuals interested in children's literature turn to *The Horn Book Magazine* for informative articles on the industry. Book reviews, interviews, and essays are also regularly featured. Articles about fiction and reviews of children's literature are sought. ■ **Circulation** 8,500 ■ **Audience** Parents, teachers, librarians ■ **Frequency** 6 times a year

Freelance Potential Publishes 12–15 freelance submissions yearly: 50–75% written by nonstaff writers; 25–50% by authors new to the magazine; 75–100% by previously unpublished writers. Receives up to 10 queries and unsolicited manuscripts monthly.

Submissions Guidelines available at website. Query or send complete manuscript. Prefers email to info@hbook.com (Word attachments, include "Horn Book Article Submission" in the subject line); will accept hard copy. SASE. Responds in 3–4 months.
- *Articles:* 1,000–2,800 words. Informational, interviews, essays, criticism, book reviews. Topics: children's and young adult literature, authors, illustrators, editors.
- *Depts/columns:* Word lengths vary. Perspectives from illustrators, children's publishing updates, special columns.

Sample Issue 104 pages. Advertising. Sample copy available.
- "New Knowledge," by Marc Aronson. Discusses how current YAbooks differ from those in the past.
- "Sing a Song of Science," by Erica Zappy. New YA books that discuss ongoing scientific research.

Rights and Payment All rights. Written material, payment rates vary. Pays on publication. Provides 3 contributor's copies.

Horse & Rider

2520 South 55th Street, #210, Boulder, CO 80301. www.horseandrider.com

Managing Editor: Jennifer Paulson

This magazine educates, informs, and entertains competitive and recreational Western riders. It seeks tightly focused articles on training, stable management techniques, hands-on health care tips, and safe trail riding practices. ■ **Circulation** 165,000 ■ **Audience** YA–Adult ■ **Frequency** Monthly

Freelance Potential Publishes 20–30 freelance submissions yearly: 15% written by nonstaff writers; 1% by authors new to the magazine; 3% by previously unpublished writers. Receives 10 queries monthly.

Submissions Query with detailed outline. Accepts hard copy. No simultaneous submissions. SASE. Responds in 3 months. Guidelines available at website.
- *Articles:* 600–1,200 words. Informational, how-to. Topics: Western riding and training, stable management, equine health, safe riding, competitions and events.
- *Depts/columns:* To 900 words. Equine news, events.
- *Artwork:* High-resolution digital images.

Sample Issue 4 articles. Sample copy available.
- "Wounds: Nightmare or Nuisance." Tips for differentiating surface wounds from serious injuries.
- "Horse Sports for the 21st Century." Describes six new sports for Western riders.

Rights and Payment All rights. Written material, $25–$400. Payment policy varies. Provides 1 contributor's copy.

Horse Illustrated

P.O. Box 8237, Lexington, KY 40533. www.horseillustrated.com

Editor: Elizabeth Moyer

This glossy magazine targets horse owners as well as riders. Both Western and English disciplines are covered. It promotes responsible ownership by providing tips on better horse care and training, and also provides up-to-date news from within the equine community. ■ **Circulation** 200,000 ■ **Audience** YA–Adult ■ **Frequency** Monthly

Freelance Potential Publishes 10–20 freelance submissions yearly: 80% written by nonstaff writers. Receives 40 queries, 20 unsolicited manuscripts monthly.

Submissions Guidelines available at website. Prefers complete manuscript; will accept query with detailed outline, resources, sample paragraphs, and clips. Accepts hard copy. No simultaneous submissions. Availability of artwork improves chance of acceptance. SASE. Responds in 3–4 months.

- *Articles:* 1,500–2,000 words. Informational, how-to. Topics: equine health, care, training, stable management.
- *Depts/columns:* 1,000–1,400 words. Equine events and news, horse profiles, techniques.
- *Artwork:* Color transparencies or prints.

Sample Issue Sample copy available.
- "Threat Level" by Sharon Biggs. Discusses the health benefits of vaccinations.
- "Bounce Back to Fitness," by Holly Werner Caccamise. Getting a horse back into shape for spring.

Rights and Payment First North American serial rights. Articles, $300–$425. Depts/columns, $50–$100. Artwork, payment rates vary. Pays on publication. Provides 2 contributor's copies.

Horseman's Yankee Pedlar

83 Leicester Street, North Oxford, MA 01537. www.pedlar.com

Editor: Elisabeth Gilbride

This magazine serves as a resource for horse owners, breeders, riders, and trainers in the northeastern region of the U.S., offering show and tournament coverage in addition to informative articles on all things equine. New writers who are familiar with the region's horse show circuit are encouraged to submit their well-written coverage of events, personal experience pieces, or interviews. ■ **Circulation** 50,000 ■ **Audience** YA–Adult ■ **Frequency** Monthly

Freelance Potential Publishes 40 freelance submissions yearly: 85% written by nonstaff writers; 5% by authors new to the magazine. Receives 30 queries, 20 unsolicited manuscripts monthly.

Submissions Guidelines available. Query or send complete manuscript. Accepts hard copy and simultaneous submissions, if identified. SASE. Responds to queries in 1–2 weeks, to manuscripts in 2–3 months.
- *Articles:* 500–800 words. Informational, how-to, interviews, reviews, personal experience. Topics: horse breeds, disciplines, training, health care, equestrian management.
- *Depts/columns:* Word lengths vary. News, book reviews, business and legal issues, equine nutrition.
- *Artwork:* B/W and color prints.

Sample Issue 226 pages. Advertising. Sample copy available.
- "An Introduction to Canine Good Citizenship," by Charlene Arsenault. How to train a dog to become an AKC Canine Good Citizen.
- "Getting Fit for Spring," by Sue Perry. Important conditioning to get a horse in shape for competitions.

Rights and Payment First North American serial rights. Written material, $2 a published column inch. Show coverage, $75 a day. Pays 30 days after publication. Provides 1 tearsheet.

Kronicle

Height of Land Publications, 60 Main Street, Suite 201, P.O. Box 190, Jeffersonville, VT 05464. www.kroniclemag.com

Editor in Chief: Mike Horn

This magazine and its readers are dedicated to backcountry snowboarding. Helping snowboarders get away from packed slopes and lines, *Kronicle* keeps fans in the know with informational articles, profiles, and snowboarders' own experiences. Launched in late 2011, it also features gear and techniques. ■ **Circulation** Unavailable ■ **Audience** YA–Adult ■ **Frequency** Quarterly

Freelance Potential Unavailable.

Submissions For information, email mike@holpublications.com.
- *Articles:* Word lengths vary. Informational, profiles, interviews, essays. Topics: backcountry snowboarding, locations, terrain, techniques, athletes.

■ *Depts/columns:* Word lengths vary. Gear tests, analysis, snow skills, safety.

Sample Issue Sample articles are available to view at the website.
■ "Aaron Robinson's 'Manifest,'" by Mike Horn. Report on the late snowboarder Aaron Robinson.

Rights and Payment Unavailable.

The Illuminata

5486 Fairway Drive, Zachary, LA 70791. www.tyrannosauruspress.com

Editor in Chief: Bret Funk

This electronic journal is written and read by avid fans of fantasy and science fiction. It accepts fiction, essays, critiques, and reviews. It actively seeks regular as well as occasional contributors.
■ **Hits per month** 600 ■ **Audience** YA–Adult ■ **Frequency** Quarterly

Freelance Potential Publishes 5–10 freelance submissions yearly: 25% written by nonstaff writers; 50% by authors new to the magazine; 95% by previously unpublished writers. Receives 1 query monthly.

Submissions Guidelines available at website. Query. Accepts email to info@tyrannosauruspress.com (no attachments). Responds in 1–3 months.
■ *Articles:* 1–2 pages. Informational. Topics: writing science fiction, fantasy, horror.
■ *Fiction:* Word lengths vary. Genres: science fiction, fantasy, horror
■ *Depts/columns:* 500–1,000 words. Reviews.

Sample Issue 26 pages. no advertising. Sample copy available at website.
■ "Digital Evolution," by Bret Funk. How the publishing business has been affected by the digital age.
■ "The Other Side," by David Emmitt. A woman's spirit is watches her last moments before a car crash .

Rights and Payment Rights vary. No payment.

I Love Cats

16 Meadow Hill Lane, Armonk, NY 10504. www.iluvcats.com

Editor: Lisa Allmendinger

I Love Cats celebrates feline companionship by offering profiles of owners and cats, articles on health and behavior, and stories about life with cats. It is more likely to accept articles accompanied by JPEG images. ■ **Circulation** 25,000 ■ **Audience** Cat owners ■ **Frequency** 6 times a year

Freelance Potential Publishes 50 freelance submissions yearly: 50% written by nonstaff writer; 70% by authors new to the magazine; 60% by previously unpublished writers. Receives 500 unsolicited manuscripts monthly.

Submissions Guidelines available at website. Query with sample 1–2 paragraphs; or send complete manuscript. Accepts hard copy and email queries to ilovecatseditor@sbcglobal.net. SASE. Responds in 1–2 months.
■ *Articles:* 500–1,000 words. Informational, how-to. Topics: feline care, health, behavior, training.
■ *Depts/columns:* Word lengths vary. Short fillers.

Sample Issue Sample copy available.
■ "Talking to the Community about Caring for Cats" by Becky Robinson. The need for education on feral cats.
■ "Feline Nutrition." Provides nutrition tips for keeping cats fit and healthy.

Rights and Payment All rights. Written material, $25–$50. JPEG images; payment rates vary. Pays on publication. Provides 1 contributor's copy.

Inside Kung-Fu

Action Pursuit Group, 2400 East Katella Avenue, #300, Anaheim, CA 92806. www.insidekung-fu.com

Editor: Dave Cater

Each issue of *Inside Kung-Fu* offers articles on traditional forms of fighting and weaponry. It also features pieces about the history of this martial art, along with profiles of master martial artists. It is read by beginners and experts. ■ **Circulation** 65,000 ■ **Audience** YA–Adult ■ **Frequency** Monthly

Freelance Potential Publishes 120 freelance submissions yearly: 80% written by nonstaff writers; 50% by authors new to the magazine; 50% by previously unpublished writers. Receives 80 queries monthly.

Submissions Guidelines available at website. Query. Accepts hard copy and email queries to dcater@beckett.com. No simultaneous submissions. SASE. Responds in 4–6 weeks.
■ *Articles:* 1,500 words. Informational, how-to, profiles, personal experience. Topics: martial arts history, weapons, training, techniques, philosophy, well-known martial artists.
■ *Depts/columns:* 750 words. Training tips and techniques, products.

Sample Issue Sample copy available.
■ "50 Kickin' Kung-Fu Classics," by Ric Meyers. Reviews the best all-time kung-fu action DVDs.
■ "Eric the Trainer's Fit to Fit," by Eric Fleishman. Shares training secrets to increase fighting fitness

Rights and Payment First rights. Written material, payment rates vary. Pays on publication.

Kaleidoscope

701 South Main Street, Akron, OH 44311-1019. www.udsakron.org

Editor in Chief: Gail Willmott

Celebrating 30 years, *Kaleidoscope* expresses the experiences of disability from the perspective of individuals, families, health care professionals, and society as a whole. Thought-provoking essays, stories, and poems fill its pages. It is especially interested in reviewing humor pieces from writers with or without disabilities. ■ **Circulation** 1,000 ■ **Audience** YA–Adult ■ **Frequency** Twice a year

Freelance Potential Publishes 40 freelance submissions yearly: 90% written by nonstaff writers; 75% by authors new to the magazine; 10% by previously unpublished writers. Receives 20 queries, 52 unsolicited manuscripts monthly.

Submissions Guidelines available at website. Query or send complete manuscript with author biography. Accepts hard copy and email submissions to kaleidoscope@udsakron.org (Word attachments). Accepts simultaneous submissions if identified. SASE. Responds to queries in 2 weeks, to manuscripts in 6 months.
■ *Articles:* To 5,000 words. Informational, profiles, interviews, reviews, humor, personal experience, book reviews. Topics: art, literature, biography, multicultural and social issues, disabilities.
■ *Fiction:* To 5,000 words. Genres: folktales, humor, multicultural, problem solving.
■ *Artwork:* High-resolution digital images at 300 dpi.
■ *Other:* Poetry.

Sample Issue 64 pages. No advertising. Sample copy available.
■ "It's Not about the Dog," by Deshae E. Lott. How the author eventually bonded with her service dog.
■ "Raffles," by Kathy Nimmer. An essay about dealing with a seriously ill service dog.

Rights and Payment First rights. Written material, $25–$125. Poetry, $10. Pays on publication. Provides 2 contributor's copies.

Keyboard

1111 Bay Hill Drive, Suite 125, San Bruno, CA 94066. www.keyboardmag.com

Managing Editor: Debbie Greenberg

Written for professional and amateur keyboard players, this magazine provides product reviews, recording and playing tips, as well as artist profiles. It covers the keyboard in all genres of music.
■ **Circulation** 61,000 ■ **Audience** YA–Adult ■ **Frequency** Monthly

Freelance Potential Publishes 120 freelance submissions yearly: 25–35% written by nonstaff writers; 55% by authors new to the magazine; 35% by previously unpublished writers. Receives 5–10 unsolicited manuscripts mmonthly.

Submissions Guidelines available. Send complete manuscript with résumé. Accepts hard copy and email submissions to keyboard@musicplayer.com. SASE. Responds in 3 months.
■ *Articles:* 500–3,000 words. Informational, how-to, interviews, profiles, reviews. Topics: keyboard techniques, keyboard artists, equipment.
■ *Depts/columns:* 400–600 words. Techniques, products.

Sample Issue Sample copy available.
■ "The Flaming Lips." Interview with the alternative rock band about their keyboard instruments.
■ "5 Ways to Play Like Chick Corea." Provides 5 techniques that will improve one's sound.

Rights and Payment All rights. Written material, payment rates vary. Pays on publication. Provides 5 contributor's copies.

KidSpirit

77 State Street, Brooklyn, NY 11201. www.kidspiritonline.com

Editor: Elizabeth Dabney Hochman

This online magazine publishes the works of children, ages 11 to 16, who are curious about the meaning of life. Each issue is themed and includes poetry, reviews, feature articles, and art. A small amount of fiction is used, but writers should consult wth the editor before submitting. ■ **Hits per month** 5,000 ■ **Audience** 11–16 years ■ **Frequency** Quarterly

Freelance Potential Publishes 40 freelance submissions yearly: 100% written by nonstaff writers; 100% by unpublished writers. Receives 3 queries, 2 unsolicited manuscripts monthly.

Submissions Guidelines available at website. Accepts submissions from children ages 11–16 only. Query with author biography for features; send complete manuscript for other works. Accepts hard copy and email to submissions@kidspiritonline.com. SASE. Responds in 1 month.
■ *Articles:* Word lengths vary. Informational. Topics: relationships, health, social issues and current events that affect preteens/teens.
■ *Fiction:* Word lengths vary. Stories related to theme. Genres: Inspirational and other genres of interest to preteens/teens.
■ *Other:* Poetry, puzzles, cartoons.

Sample Issue Sample issue available at website.
■ "Teen Depression," by Madison Friedman. The prevalence of teen depression and how to get help.
■ "Success for Kids," by Gautama Mehta.A successful, inner-city school program that focuses on behavioral awareness and self-esteem.

Rights and Payment Rights vary. No payment. Provides 2 contributor's copies.

Kids' Storytelling Club

P.O. Box 205, Masonville, CO 80541-0205. www.storycraft.com/co

Editor: Vivian Dubrovin

This website features a series of downloadable booklets of storytelling activities, crafts, telling tips, and creative story ideas for elementary and junior high students. Also in the works is a new magazine feature. Information on local storytelling clubs, programs, and festivals for young storytellers is always of interest. Writers are advised to check the website for updates. ■ **Hits per month** Unavailable ■ **Audience** 5–12 years ■ **Frequency** Updated six times a year

Freelance Potential 70% of content written by nonstaff writers.

Submissions Guidelines available at website. Query. Accepts email to vivian@storycraft.com. Response time varies.
■ *Articles:* Word lengths vary. How-to. Topics: creating storytelling stories, telling tips, creative story ideas.
■ *Other:* Activities and crafts related to storytelling.

Sample Issue Sample copy available at website.
■ "Create a Storytelling Story," by Vivian Dubrovin. Gives 3 tips to create an interesting story.
■ "If You Want to Be a Storyteller, You Must Tell Stories." How everyday activities can become stories.

Rights and Payment First rights. Written material, payment rates vary. Pays on acceptance.

Kids X-Press

P.O. Box 374, White Plains, NY 10603. www.kidsxpress.net

Publisher: Nivia Viera

Kids X-Press is a nonprofit magazine devoted to promoting literacy and self-expression. It publishes work by children ages 6 to 14 for their peers to enjoy. It accepts articles, interviews, and personal experience pieces on pop culture, sports, animals, and multicultural topics. ■ **Circulation** 140,000 ■ **Audience** 6–14 years ■ **Frequency** Quarterly

Freelance Potential Publishes 90 freelance submissions yearly: 90% written by nonstaff writers; 80% by authors new to the magazine. Receives 5–6 queries monthly..

Submissions Guidelines and theme list/editorial calendar available. Child authors only. Send complete manuscript. Accepts submissions via website (attach documents). Availability of artwork improves chance of acceptance. SASE. Responds in 1 week.
■ *Articles:* To 250 words. Informational, interviews, personal experience, reviews. Topics: pop culture, sports, animals, multicultural issues.
■ *Artwork:* Color prints or transparencies. Line art.
■ *Other:* Poetry, games.

Sample Issue Sample copy available.
■ "Kids Are Teachers, Too!" by Kiara Cruz & Ivan Maldonado. Skit about kids conserving energy and the environment.
■ "I Want To Be A Teacher," by Christina Hood. Essay about why author wants to be a teacher when she grows up.

Rights and Payment Rights vary. No payment.

Lacrosse

113 West University Parkway, Baltimore, MD 21210. www.laxmagazine.com

Editor: Paul Krome

Lacrosse players, coaches, and fans read this magazine for athlete profiles, how-to articles on training and playing strategies, and collegiate team coverage. Product reviews and news from US Lacrosse—the sports' national governing body—appear as well. ■ **Circulation** 275,000 ■ **Audience** YA–Adults ■ **Frequency** Monthly

Freelance Potential Publishes 60 freelance submissions yearly: 30% written by nonstaff writers; 10% by authors new to the magazine; 5% by previously unpublished writers. Receives 5 queries monthly.

Submissions Guidelines available at website. Query with clips or résumé. Accepts email to pkrome@uslacrosse.org (Word attachments). Artwork accepted via email or CD. Responds in 6 weeks.
■ *Articles:* 800–1,000 words. Informational, how-to, profiles. Topics: lacrosse training, playing strategies, athlete profiles, collegiate team coverage.
■ *Depts/columns:* 300 words. Product reviews, US Lacrosse news.
■ *Artwork:* JPEG images. Color prints.

Sample Issue Sample copy available.
■ "Recruiting U." Discusses options for students wishing to play lacrosse in college.
■ "All Roads Lead to Orlando." Profiles the U15 teams preparing for regional championships.

Rights and Payment Exclusive rights. Articles, $100–$300. Depts/columns, $100–$150. Pays on publication. Provides 1+ contributor's copies.

Leading Edge

4087 JKB, Provo, UT 84602. www.leadingedgemagazine.com

Fiction or Poetry Director

Leading Edge is a journal of science fiction and fantasy stories. It also accepts poetry, as long as it has a science fiction or fantasy theme. Each submission receives a written critique, whether it is published or not. ■ **Circulation** 200 ■ **Audience** YA–Adult ■ **Frequency** Twice a year

Freelance Potential Publishes 18 freelance submissions yearly: 95% written by nonstaff writers; most by previously unpublished writers. Receives 25 unsolicited manuscripts monthly.

Submissions Guidelines available in each issue and at website. Send complete manuscript. Accepts hard copy. No simultaneous submissions. SASE. Responds in 2–4 months.
■ *Fiction:* To 15,000 words. Genres: science fiction, fantasy.
■ *Other:* Poetry, no line limit.

Sample Issue Sample copy available.
■ "Cryonic Sushi," by Meagan Hutchins. Fantasy fiction.
■ "A Fair Trade," by Emily Adams. Science fiction tales.

Rights and Payment First North American serial rights. Fiction, 1¢ a word, minimum $10. Poetry, $10 for first 4 pages, $1.50 for additional pages. Pays on publication. Provides 2 contributor's copies.

Lightspeed

www.lightspeedmagazine.com

Editor: John Joseph Adams

Lightspeed is an online science fiction magazine that was nominated for the Hugo Award. It seeks original science fiction of all types, from futuristic to the star-spanning and everything in between. No subject is considered off-limits, and the editors encourage writers to push the envelope of the genre as well as their writing style. Nonfiction articles about the genre are generally staff-written but occasionally assigned to freelancers. ■ **Hits per month** 40,000 ■ **Audience** YA–adults ■ **Frequency** Monthly

Freelance Potential An open market for original fiction.

Submissions Guidelines available at website. Send complete manuscript for fiction. Accepts submissions through online submission system, accessible via website.For consideration for article assignments, send résumé and credentials to Esther Inglis-Arkell, nonfiction editor, via contact form in submission guidelinesNo simultaneous or multiple submissions. Responds in two weeks.
■ *Articles:* Staff-written or assigned.
■ *Fiction:* 1,500–7,500 words. Genres: science fiction, all types.

Sample Issue Some stories and articles available for free at website.
■ "Bubbles," by David Brin.
■ "Universe," by Pamela L. Gay.

Rights and Payment Rights vary. Fiction, 5¢ a word. Payment policy varies.

The Lion

Lions Clubs International, 300 West 22nd Street, Oak Brook, IL 60523-8842. www.lionsclubs.org

Senior Editor: Jay Copp

This publication of the world's largest service organization covers the community-oriented activities—many of them benefitting children and families—of its clubs on the local, national, and international levels. Writers need not be a Lions Clubs member to write about one of its members or projects. High-quality photographs are always needed. ■ **Circulation** 425,000 ■ **Audience** Lions Clubs members ■ **Frequency** 11 times a year

Freelance Potential Publishes 30 freelance submissions yearly: 50% written by nonstaff writers; 20% by authors new to the magazine. Receives 10 queries, 5 unsolicited manuscripts monthly.

Submissions Guidelines available. Prefers query; will accept complete manuscript. Accepts hard copy and email submissions to magazine@lionsclubs.org. SASE. Responds to queries in 10 days, to manuscripts in 2 months.
■ *Articles:* To 2,000 words. Informational, profiles, humor, photo-essays. Topics: Lions Clubs service projects, disabilities, social issues, special education.
■ *Depts/columns:* Staff-written.
■ *Artwork:* Color prints; JPEG or TIFF images at 300 dpi.

Sample Issue 156 pages. Little advertising. Sample copy available.
■ "I Got My Glasses from Lions... and Went On To Be A Success," by Maria Blackburn. Profiles adults who were helped by the Lions when they were children.
■ "Pedal Power," by Cliff Terry. Highlights a go-cart trip through Europe and Africa that raised awareness for vision loss.

Rights and Payment All rights. Written material, $100–$1,000. Pays on acceptance. Provides 4–10 contributor's copies.

Living Safety

Canada Safety Council, 1020 Thomas Spratt Place, Ottawa, Ontario K1G 5L5, Canada
www.safety-council.org

President: Jack Smith

The Canada Safety Council publishes this magazine as a tool for employers to use in their safety programs. Its goal is to raise safety awareness to the point where safety becomes a personal value and a conscious lifestyle choice. It serves as a credible, reliable source of safety information, education, and awareness in all aspects of Canadian life—in traffic, at home, at work, and at leisure. ■ **Circulation** 60,000 ■ **Audience** All ages ■ **Frequency** Quarterly

Freelance Potential Publishes 25 freelance submissions yearly: 75% written by nonstaff writers; 10% by authors new to the magazine; 65% by previously unpublished writers. Receives 2 queries monthly.

Submissions Guidelines available. Query with résumé and clips or writing samples. Accepts hard copy. SAE/IRC. Responds in 2 weeks.
- *Articles:* 1,000–2,500 words. Informational. Topics: recreational, home, and traffic safety; family health and safety; environmental concerns.
- *Depts/columns:* Word lengths vary. Safety news, research findings, opinions, product recalls.
- *Other:* Children's activities.

Sample Issue 30 pages. No advertising. Sample copy available.
- "Children and Airbags." Discusses the safety benefits of airbags for children.
- "Taking the School Bus." Provides steps for preparing children to take the school bus.

Rights and Payment All rights. Articles, to $500. Depts/columns, payment rates vary. Pays on acceptance. Provides 1–5 contributor's copies.

Mad

1700 Broadway, New York, NY 10019. www.madmag.com

Submissions Editor

Each issue of *Mad Magazine* is filled with hard-hitting satire, parodies, and comic strips on such subjects as politics, celebrities, sports scandals, and cultural fads. Writers with a twisted sense of humor and a peculiar way of looking at the world are wanted. ■ **Circulation** 250,000 ■ **Audience** YA–Adult ■ **Frequency** Monthly

Freelance Potential Publishes 25 freelance submissions each year: 90% written by nonstaff writers.

Submissions Guidelines available at website. Query with brief premise of article, 3–4 examples, and art plan. Prefers email to submissions@madmagazine.com; will accept hard copy if submission includes artwork. SASE. Responds if interested.
- *Articles:* Word lengths vary. Humor. Topics: cultural themes and trends, political blunders, celebrity/sports scandals, pop culture, sex and dating, politics, the Internet, media, music, fashion, video games, child/parent and student/teacher relationships.
- *Depts/columns:* Word lengths vary. Topical humor.
- *Artwork:* Rough sketches.
- *Other:* Comic strips.

Sample Issue Sample copy available.
- "100% Superficial," by Desmond Devlin. Humorous look at Justin Bieber's new autobiography.
- "Wild, Unfounded Rumors Surrounding the Xbox Kinect," by John Caldwell. Cartoon about the rumors behind new gaming breakthroughs.

Rights and Payment All rights. Written material, $500 a printed page. Graphic artwork, payment rates vary. Pays on acceptance. Provides 1 contributor's copy.

The Magazine of Fantasy & Science Fiction

P.O. Box 3447, Hoboken, NJ 07030. www.sfsite.com/fsf

Editor: Gordon Van Gelder

Founded in 1949, *The Magazine of Fantasy & Science Fiction* publishes stories in these genres from writers in all stages of their careers. Although fiction is the only avenue open to freelancers, the magazine is also home to profiles, reviews, and critiques. It would like to see more fantasy stories that are character-oriented. ■ **Circulation** 45,000 ■ **Audience** YA–Adult ■ **Frequency** 6 times a year

Freelance Potential Publishes 60–90 freelance submissions yearly: 98% written by nonstaff writers; 20% by authors new to the magazine; 10% by previously unpublished writers. Receives 500–700 unsolicited manuscripts monthly.

Submissions Guidelines available at website. Send complete manuscript. Accepts hard copy. No electronic or simultaneous submissions. SASE. Responds in 2 months.
■ *Articles:* Staff-written.
■ *Fiction:* To 25,000 words. Short stories and novellas. Genres: science fiction, fantasy, humor.
■ *Depts/columns:* Staff-written.

Sample Issue 258 pages. Little advertising. Sample copy available.
■ "You Are Such A One." Story about a woman who discovers a ghost is haunting her house.
■ "Hunchster." Story about a disabled young man who creates a video time machine.

Rights and Payment First world rights with option of anthology rights. Written material, 6¢–9¢ a word. Pays on acceptance. Provides 2 contributor's copies.

Massive Online Gamer

4635 McEwen Drive, Dallas, TX 75244. www.massiveonlinegamer.com

Editor: Douglas Kale

Enthusiasts of massively multiplayer online (MMO) games read this magazine for game reviews and descriptions, strategies, and techniques. It covers all types of games, including fantasy, science fiction, adventure, and war games. It also includes interviews and in-game item giveaways. Writers are encouraged to send leveling guides, reviews, previews, and exclusive interviews with personalities in the world of MMO. ■ **Circulation** 100,000 ■ **Audience** YA–Adult ■ **Frequency** 6 times a year

Freelance Potential Publishes 120+ freelance submissions yearly: 90% written by nonstaff writers; 70% by authors new to the magazine; 20% by previously unpublished writers. Receives 15+ queries monthly.

Submissions Guidelines available. Query with writing sample and list of MMO experience. Prefers email queries to dkale@beckett.com; will accept hard copy. SASE. Response time varies.
■ *Articles:* Word lengths vary. Informational, how-to, personal experience, interviews. Topics: MMO game descriptions, strategies, gaming techniques.
■ *Depts/columns:* Word lengths vary. MMO etiquette, technology, contests, news.

Sample Issue 88 pages. Sample copy available.
■ "PAX East Roundup," by Jason Winter. Recap of the trade show and new game launches.
■ "Rift Officially Launches," by Jason Winter. Reviews the newly released game.

Rights and Payment All rights. Written material, $25–$150. Pays 45 days after publication.

Model Airplane News

Air Age Publishing, 20 Westport Road, Wilton, CT 06897. www.modelairplanenews.com

Executive Editor: Debra Cleghorn

This magazine promotes the model airplane hobby through its coverage of new products, building techniques, after-market customization, competitions and events across the country. ■ **Circulation** 95,000 ■ **Audience** YA–Adults ■ **Frequency** Monthly

Freelance Potential Publishes 100+ freelance submissions yearly: 80% written by nonstaff writers; 33% by authors new to the magazine. Receives 12–24 queries monthly.

Submissions Guidelines available. Query with outline and biography describing model experience. Accepts hard copy. Availability of artwork improves chance of acceptance. SASE. Responds in 6 weeks.
- *Articles:* 1,700–2,000 words. Informational, how-to, personal experience. Topics: model airplanes, building and flying techniques, new products, reviews.
- *Artwork:* 35mm color slides.

Sample Issue Sample copy available.
- "Flight Technique: Harness the Wind," by John Reid. Gives instructions for flying an electric-powered model in slope lift.
- "Sneak Peak: Visiting Hitec RCD," by Holly Hansen. Describes a visit to the Hitec warehouse to see new telemetry sensors.

Rights and Payment First North American serial rights. Articles, $175–$600. Pays on publication. Provides up to 6 contributor's copies.

New York Tennis Magazine

United Sports Publications, 1220 Wantagh Avenue, Wantagh, NY 11793. www.newyorktennismagazine.com

Editor in Chief: Eric C. Peck

This magazine, which launched in 2011, is designed to promote and develop the sport of tennis on every level in the New York state community. As the official publication of the United States Tennis Association (USTA) Eastern-Metro region, it reports on the clubs, the camps, rising players, coaches, trends, and events surrounding tennis in New York. It publishes articles on junior tennis, high school and college tennis, and the professional level. ■ **Circulation** 20,000 ■ **Audience** Tennis players of all ages, coaches ■ **Frequency** 6 times a year

Freelance Potential Unavailable.

Submissions For information, contact info@usptennis.com
- *Articles:* Word lengths vary. Informational, interviews, profiles, personal experience. Topics: tennis, youth tennis, coaching, event coverage.
- *Depts/columns:* Word lengths vary. News items, events, fitness and nutrition.

Sample Issue E-editions of the magazine are archived online.
- "Mythbusters: The Only People Who Are about College Tennis Are Friends and Family," by Ricky Becker. Provides highlights and insights into the NCAA Tennis Championships.
- "Hall of Fame Class of 2011 to Be Honored at the Legends Ball." Offers a preview of a New York event.

Rights and Payment Rights vary. No payment.

NJCAA Review

1755 Telstar Drive, Suite 103, Colorado Springs, CO 80920. www.njcaa.org

Executive Editor: Wayne Baker

This publication of the National Junior College Athletic Association covers the issues facing the organization, as well as its athletes, schools, coaches, programs, and events. It is always looking for people who can report on the myriad sporting activities of the nation's junior colleges. Writers familiar with the schools in question and/or the junior college system are preferred. ■ **Circulation** 3,300 ■ **Audience** YA–Adult ■ **Frequency** 10 times a year

Freelance Potential 30–40% written by nonstaff writers. Publishes 3–5 freelance submissions yearly: 30–40% written by nonstaff writers. Receives 1+ unsolicited manuscripts monthly.

Submissions Editorial calendar available. Send complete manuscript. Accepts hard copy. Availability of artwork improves chance of acceptance. SASE. Responds in 2 months.
- *Articles:* 1,500–2,000 words. Informational, profiles. Topics: sports, college, careers, health, fitness, NJCAA news.
- *Artwork:* B/W prints or transparencies.

Sample Issue 20 pages. Advertising. Sample copy available.
- "Men's Ice Hockey Championships." Provides an overview of the championship game in which Erie Community College won its first-ever championship.
- "College of the Mont." Profiles Western Wyoming Community College.

Rights and Payment One-time rights. No payment. Provides 3 contributor's copies.

The Numismatist

American Numismatic Association, 818 North Cascade Avenue, Colorado Springs, CO 80903-3279. www.money.org

Editor in Chief: Barbara J. Gregory

Members of the American Numismatic Association read this magazine for the latest news on coin, medal, token, and paper money collecting. ■ **Circulation** 30,500 ■ **Audience** YA–Adult ■ **Frequency** Monthly

Freelance Potential Publishes 36 freelance submissions yearly: 60% written by nonstaff writers; 10% by authors new to the magazine; 20% by previously unpublished writers. Receives 4+ unsolicited manuscripts monthly.

Submissions Guidelines available. Send complete manuscript with biography. Prefers email submissions to editor@money.org; will accept hard copy and disk submissions. SASE. Responds in 8–10 weeks.
- *Articles:* To 3,500 words. Informational. Topics: coin, medal, token, and paper money collecting.

Sample Issue Sample copy available.
- "A Novel Approach," by Henry Mitchell. Discusses the coins from the Roman Republic.

Rights and Payment Perpetual non-exclusive rights. Articles, 12¢ a word. Pays on publication. Provides 5 contributor's copies.

Off Track Planet

www.offtrackplanet.com

Editor: Sara White

The concept for *Off Track Planet* was created by a group of young travelers while staying at a youth hostel. They decided to create a magazine, website, and social community where young people could share the wonders of traveling the globe. It works with young, professional travel writers as well as young folks who have experiences and advice on youth travel to share. *Off Track Planet's* prime audience is college students and recent college grads. ■ **Circulation** 600,000 print; 100,000+ online ■ **Audience** YA ■ **Frequency** Quarterly

Freelance Potential Written by young professional travel writers and locals. It occasionally puts a call out for travel writers and contract freelancers.

Submissions Check the website under About and Opportunities. For information, email contact@offtrackplanet.
- *Articles:* Word lengths vary. Informational. Topics: destinations, budget travel, culture, events and festivals around the world.
- *Depts/columns:* Word lengths vary. Hostel reviews, advice, volunteer and study abroad opportunities.

Sample Issue Articles available on the website.
■ "Top 10 Things To Do in Columbia on a Backpacker's Budget." An array of places to see and activities in Columbia that don't cost much.
■ "The 10 Coolest Subways Around the World." The world's subway subcultures.

Rights and Payment All rights.

Pageantry

1855 W. State Road 434, Suite 254, Longwood, FL 32750. www.pageantry-digital.com

Editor: Ashley Burns

Written for teens and adults who participate in beauty pageants, this magazine immerses readers in the glamour of the gowns, jewelry, and hairstyles needed to win competitions. Articles also focus on the more demanding side, such as fitness and talent. It welcomes news articles and photos on events and programs. ■ **Circulation** Unavailable ■ **Audience** YA–Adult ■ **Frequency** Quarterly

Freelance Potential Publishes 5 freelance submissions yearly: 10% written by nonstaff writers.

Submissions Guidelines available at website. Query. Accepts hard copy and email queries to editor@pageantrymag.com. SASE. Response time varies.
■ *Articles:* Word lengths vary. Informational, profiles, interviews, personal experience. Topics: beauty pageants, celebrities, fitness, modeling, makeup tips, interviewing techniques, dance, winning psychology, judges' perspectives, etiquette, coaching, talent competitions, fashion.
■ *Depts/columns:* Word lengths vary. Jewelry, makeup, hairstyles, fitness, body shaping, modeling, personal advice, teen issues, winner profiles, etiquette, news, opinions, show business, celebrities.
■ *Artwork:* JPEG digital images.

Sample Issue 144 pages. Sample copy available.
■ "A Lifetime of Memories." Covers the American Coed National Pageants held in Orlando, Florida.
■ "A Holiday Miracle." Describes the inaugural American Spirit Pageant in Iowa.

Rights and Payment First North American serial rights. Written material, payment rates vary. Payment policy varies. Provides 1 contributor's copy.

Peloton

Move Press, 1000 Freemont Avenue, Suite H, South Pasadena, CA 91030. www.pelotonmagazine.com

Managing Editor: Paige Dunn

Staffed by editors and writers who are self-professed "bike junkies," this magazine aims to share the many joys of cycling with readers, from the thrill of racing to the tranquility of peaceful rides. Articles cover the sport of cycling, the gear, the people, and the cycling lifestyle. It was founded in 2010.
■ **Circulation** Unavailable ■ **Audience** Cycling enthusiasts ■ **Frequency** 9 times a year

Freelance Potential Describes itself as "a collective of writers, photographers, designers."

Submissions For information, email paige@movepress.com.
■ *Articles:* Word lengths vary. Informational, profiles, historical. Topics: bike technology, racers, manufacturers, race courses, cycling history.
■ *Depths/columns:* Word lengths vary. Biking news, technology, products, photo-essays, race coverage.

Sample Issue Some articles and reports available online.
■ "Six Day Racing." A report on racing in the early nineteenth century.
■ "New England Genesis." A look at the heritage of bike manufacturing in New England.

Rights and Payment Unavailable.

PKA's Advocate

1881 Little Westkill Road, Prattsville, NY 12468. http://advocatepka.weebly.com

Publisher: Patricia Keller

Fiction, personal essays, and poetry, appealing particularly to horse-, nature-, and animal-lovers, are featured here. The Gaited Horse Association Newsletter is also included in each issue. Original, previously unpublished pieces from beginning writers are preferred. It is especially interested in horse-related stories, poetry, art, and photos. ■ **Circulation** 10,000 ■ **Audience** YA–Adult ■ **Frequency** 6 times a year

Freelance Potential Publishes 150 freelance submissions yearly: 90% written by nonstaff writers; 35% by authors new to the magazine; 65% by previously unpublished writers. Receives 125 queries and unsolicited manuscripts monthly.

Submissions Guidelines available at website. Send query or complete manuscript. Accepts hard copy. SASE. No simultaneous submissions. Responds in 6–10 weeks.
- *Articles:* To 1,500 words. Informational, personal experience, profiles, essays. Topics: horses, animals, the arts, humor, nature, recreation.
- *Fiction:* To 1,500 words. Genres: contemporary, historical, realistic, and science fiction; adventure; fantasy; romance; mystery; suspense; stories about animals, nature, and the environment.
- *Artwork:* 8x10 B/W or color prints. Line art.
- *Other:* Poetry, no line limit. Puzzles and recipes.

Sample Issue Advertising. Sample copy available.

Rights and Payment First rights. No payment. Provides 2 contributor's copies.

Playground Magazine

360 B Street, Idaho Falls, ID 83402. www.playgroundmag.com

Editor: Lane Lindstrom

Professionals and others involved in the design, planning, installation, and operation of playground systems read this magazine for informative articles. Profiles of companies are also published. While playground structures play a very important part in the editorial mix, it also welcomes articles that prove and promote the value of play itself. ■ **Circulation** 35,000 ■ **Audience** Adults ■ **Frequency** 7 times each year

Freelance Potential Publishes 8 freelance submissions yearly: 25% written by nonstaff writers; 30% by authors new to the magazine. Receives 1–4 queries monthly.

Submissions Guidelines and editorial calendar available. Query or send complete manuscript. Accepts hard copy and email submissions to lindstrom@harrispublishing.com. SASE. Responds in 1–2 months.
- *Articles:* 800–1,200 words. Informational, how-to. Topics: the planning, design, and installation of playgrounds; types of play structures; surfacing; safety; maintenance; skate parks; aquatic features; fundraising.
- *Depts/columns:* Word lengths vary. Legal issues, news, industry updates, manufacturer profiles, landscaping, design, and the developmental value of play.

Sample Issue 32 pages: Sample copy available.
- "Playful City USA Program Inspires Communities," by Ben Duda. Highlights communities that increased play opportunities for children.
- "It's Like the Magic Mulch," by Lane Lindstrom. The benefits of bonded wood fiber for surfacing.

Rights and Payment First serial rights. Articles, $100–$300. Depts/columns, $50–$175. Payment policy varies.

Pointe

110 William Street, 23rd Floor, New York, NY 10038. www.pointemagazine.com

Managing Editor: Carol Rubin

Dedicated exclusively to ballet, *Pointe* magazine is read by students, professional dancers, teachers, and amateur enthusiasts. It covers all topics related to ballet, including profiles of dancers, teachers, and choreographers; auditioning; injury prevention; and training programs. It seeks writers with dance experience and a winning way with words. ■ **Circulation** 40,000 ■ **Audience** All ages ■ **Frequency** 6 times a year

Freelance Potential Publishes 1–2 freelance submissions yearly: 75% written by nonstaff writers; 25% by authors new to the magazine; 10% by previously unpublished writers. Receives 1+ queries monthly.

Submissions Guidelines and editorial calendar available. Query. Accepts hard copy. SASE. Responds in 2 months.
■ *Articles:* 1,200 words. Informational, profiles, interviews, personal experience, photo-essays. Topics: ballet companies, dancers, choreographers, news, trends, festivals and events, premieres, auditions.
■ *Depts/columns:* 800–1,000 words. Topics: Premieres, news, interviews with directors, profiles of dancers and companies, advice, and tips on technique.
■ *Artwork:* B/W and color prints or transparencies; digital photos. Line art.

Sample Issue Advertising. Sample copy available.
■ "Dollars and Sense," by Kristin Schwab. Discusses the critical components of a contract.
■ "Married to Normal Folk," by Nancy Wozny. Interviews four dancers about their relationships with their non-dancer spouses.

Rights and Payment All rights. Written material, payment rates vary. Pays on acceptance. Provides 2 contributor's copies.

Prehistoric Times

145 Bayline Circle, Folsom, CA 95630-8077. www.prehistorictimes.com

Editor: Mike Fredericks

Prehistoric Times unearths facts and offers speculations about dinosaurs and other species. It is read by enthusiasts for its scientific articles, as well as for its how-to modeling instructions, collector news, and media reviews. Interviews with scientists, collectors, and model makers are of particular interest.
■ **Circulation** Unavailable ■ **Audience** YA–Adult ■ **Frequency** Quarterly

Freelance Potential Publishes 20+ freelance submissions yearly: 30% written by nonstaff writers; 75% by authors new to the magazine; 75% by previously unpublished writers. Receives 2+ unsolicited manuscripts monthly.

Submissions Guidelines available via email request to pretimes@comcast.net. Send complete manuscript. Accepts email submissions to pretimes@comcast.net (attach file). Response time varies.
■ *Articles:* 1,500–2,000 words. Informational, profiles, interviews. Topics: dinosaurs, paleontology, prehistoric life, drawing dinosaurs, dinosaur-related collectibles.
■ *Depts/columns:* Word lengths vary. Field news, dinosaur models, media reviews, interviews, detailed descriptions of dinosaurs and other prehistoric species.

Sample Issue Advertising. Sample copy available.
■ "Professor Earl Douglass." Profiles a renowned geologist and paleontologist.
■ "Age of Reptiles." Interview with Ricardo Delgado, comic book artist.

Rights and Payment All rights. Written material, payment rates vary. Payment policy varies.

Ellery Queen's Mystery Magazine

267 Broadway, 4th Floor, New York, NY 10007. www.themysteryplace.com/eqmm

Editor: Janet Hutchings

Since 1941, *Ellery Queen* has been entertaining its audience with every type of mystery short story—from the psychological suspense tale and detective puzzle to the private eye case. It accepts work from both new and established writers. Submissions from unpublished writers are eligible for the magazine's Department of First Stories. Though *Ellery Queen* occasionally features one or two short novels each year, that space is usually reserved for established writers. ■ **Circulation** 120,000 ■ **Audience** YA–Adult ■ **Frequency** 10 times a year

Freelance Potential Publishes 120 freelance submissions yearly: 100% written by nonstaff writers; 25% by authors new to the magazine; 7% by previously unpublished writers. Receives 215 unsolicited manuscripts monthly.

Submissions Guidelines available at website. Send complete manuscript. Accepts manuscripts through online submission system only, accessible at website. Responds in 3 months.
■ *Fiction:* 2,500–8,000 words. Feature stories. Minute Mysteries, 250 words, novellas by established authors, to 20,000 words. Genres: contemporary, historical crime, psychological thriller, mystery, suspense, detective/private eye stories.
■ *Depts/columns:* Book reviews.
■ *Other:* Poetry.

Sample Issue 112 pages. Little advertising. Sample copy available.
■ "The Children," by Lia Matera. A nanny who loses her job after being stricken by the Spanish flu.
■ "Showtime," by Marilyn Todd. A Wild West mystery with showdowns, gunslingers, and magic tricks.

Rights and Payment First and anthology rights. Written material, 5¢–8¢ a word. Pays on acceptance. Provides 3 contributor's copies.

The Red Bulletin

RBNA Headquarters, 1740 Stewart Street, Santa Monica, CA 90404. www.redbullusa.com

Deputy Editor: Ann Donahue

In 2011, the makers of Red Bull energy drink launched this lifestyle magazine for young adults. It covers sports, music, people, travel, arts, and culture. It is inserted into major market newspapers and is being available at newsstands. *Red Bulletin* was also launched in 9 other countries. All content should have a contemporary, pithy style. ■ **Circulation** 1.2 million ■ **Audience** YA–adult, mostly male ■ **Frequency** Monthly

Freelance Potential Unavailable.

Submissions For infromation, email ann.donahue@us.redbull.com or contact@us.redbulletin.com.
■ *Articles:* Word lengths vary. Informational, profiles, interviews. Topics: sports, athletes, pop culture, travel, food, music, film, celebrities.

Sample Issue 100 pages.
■ "Red Hot Mysteries." An interview with the Red Hot Chili Peppers, and a review of their new album.
■ "Carbon Feet, Steel Mind." A report on runner Oscar Pistorius and his prosthetic feet, and the controversy over whether they actually give him an advantage in races.

Rights and Payment Unavailable.

Reptiles

P.O. Box 6050, Mission Viejo, CA 92690. www.reptilechannel.com

Editor: Russ Case

This magazine is used as a guide for owners of reptiles and amphibians. Geared to the beginner or intermediate hobbyist, articles are written by experts on the care and breeding of these pets.
■ **Circulation** 40,000 ■ **Audience** YA–Adult ■ **Frequency** Monthly

Freelance Potential Publishes 55 freelance submissions yearly: 60% written by nonstaff writers; 40% by authors new to the magazine; 50% by previously unpublished writers. Receives 10 queries monthly.

Submissions Guidelines available at website. Query with description of herp background. Accepts email queries to reptiles@ bowtieinc.com (Microsoft Word attachments). No simultaneous submissions. Responds in 2–3 months.
■ *Articles:* Word lengths vary. Informational, how-to, interviews, profiles. Topics: owning and caring for reptiles and amphibians, husbandry, breeding, field herping, travel, tips and techniques, health issues.
■ *Depts/columns:* Word lengths vary. Breed and retailer profiles, health Q&As, trends.
■ *Artwork:* Digital images at 300 dpi or higher; 35mm color slides.

Sample Issue Sample copy available.
■ "Breeding the Angel Island Chuckwalla," by Jerry D. Fife. The popularity of the Sauromalus hispidus.
■ "Alligator Snapping Turtle," by Paul Vander Schouw. Explains the differences between the alligator snapping turtle and the more common snapping turtle.

Rights and Payment First North American serial rights. Written material, payment rates vary. Pays on publication. Provides 2 contributor's copies.

Reunions

P.O. Box 11727, Milwaukee, WI 54311-0727. www.reunionsmag.com

Editor: Edith Wagner

Professionals and others directly involved with family, military, class, and association reunion planning find ideas, inspiration, and resources in this magazine. It considers only submissions directly related to reunions, and particularly about planning them. Stories about successful reunions, accompanied by photographs that capture that success, are always welcome. ■ **Circulation** 20,000 ■ **Audience** Adults ■ **Frequency** Quarterly

Freelance Potential Publishes 100 freelance submissions yearly: 75% written by nonstaff writers; 80% by authors new to the magazine; 60% by previously unpublished writers.

Submissions Guidelines and editorial calendar available. Query. Prefers email queries to editor@reunionsmag.com (Microsoft Word attachments); will accept hard copy. Responds in 12–18 months.
■ *Articles:* Word lengths vary. Informational, factual, how-to, profiles, personal experience. Topics: organizing reunions, choosing locations, entertainment and activities, genealogy.
■ *Depts/columns:* 250–1,000 words. Opinion, personal experience, resource information, reviews.
■ *Artwork:* Digital images at 300 dpi or higher.

Sample Issue Advertising. Sample copy available.
■ "'The Gathering' Draws Descendants," by Grace Elting Castle. Shares reunion story of more than 200 descendants of New Paltz, New York.
■ "Triumph Over Adversity." Discusses how one family overcame obstacles related to the meeting space for their reunion.

Rights and Payment One-time and electronic rights. Written material, payment rates vary. Payment policy varies. Provides contributor's copies.

Reverb Monthly

10008 Western Avenue, Suite 300, Seattle, WA 98104. www.seattleweekly.com/reverbmonthly

Editor: Chris Kornelis

Started in September 2011, this new magazine covers the local music scene in Seattle, from garage bands and young musicians to about-to-make-it-big bands. Each issues offers interviews with and profiles of the people propelling the city's music, as well as reviews of shows and albums. It is inserted into *Seattle Weekly* magazine as well as distributed to locations across the city. ■ **Circulation** 75,000 ■ **Audience** YA–Adults ■ **Frequency** Monthly

Freelance Potential Unavailable.

Submissions Email via website only for information.
■ *Articles:* Word lengths vary. Informational, interviews, profiles, opinion, personal experience. Topics: music, performers, songwriters, producers—all related to Seattle.
■ *Depts/columns:* Word lengths vary. Reviews, critiques, essays.

Sample Issue Sample issue available at website.
■ "Faustine Hudson: She Bangs!," by Todd Hamm. Profiles a female drummer from Seattle.
■ "Dreya Weber: Aerial Pink," by Erika Hobart. An interview with a performance artist and choreographer.

Rights and Payment Unavailable.

Rugby

33 Kings Highway, Orangeburg, NY 10962. www.rugbymag.com

Editor in Chief: Alex Goff

This magazine gives fans of American rugby news about their favorite sport. It provides readers with player and team profiles, training tips, and competition coverage for both the college and club levels. ■ **Circulation** 10,500 ■ **Audience** YA–Adult ■ **Frequency** 6 times a year

Freelance Potential Publishes 400 freelance submissions yearly: 50% written by nonstaff writers; 50% by authors new to the magazine; 50% by previously unpublished writers. Receives up to 50 queries and unsolicited manuscripts monthly.

Submissions Guidelines available. Query or send complete manuscript. Accepts hard copy and disk submissions. SASE. Responds in 2 weeks.
■ *Articles:* Word lengths vary. Informational, how-to, profiles. Topics: rugby players, teams, training, and competitions.
■ *Depts/columns:* Word lengths vary. Coaching and refereeing techniques, skill development, training and nutrition advice, equipment.

Sample Issue Sample copy available.
■ "High School and U19 Top 20s." Predicts the best boys and girls high school and U10 teams.
■ "The Story Behind 'Play On,'" by Pat Clifton. Behind-the-scenes production of a new rugby movie.

Rights and Payment All rights. Written material, payment rates vary. Pays on publication. Provides 3 contributor's copies.

Scott Stamp Monthly

Scott Publishing Company, P.O. Box 828, Sidney, OH 45365. www.amospublishing.com

Editor: Donna Houseman

Philatelists of all ages can find articles in this magazine to help them further their collecting hobby. New stamp releases, collecting news, and profiles of collectors are offered here. ■ **Circulation** 35,000 ■ **Audience** YA–Adult ■ **Frequency** Monthly

Freelance Potential Publishes 100 freelance submissions yearly: 70% written by nonstaff writers; 15% by authors new to the magazine; 15% by previously unpublished writers. Receives up to 15 queries and unsolicited manuscripts monthly.

Submissions Guidelines available. Prefers query; will accept complete manuscript. Accepts hard copy and disk submissions (Microsoft Word). SASE. Responds in 1 month.
■ *Articles:* 1,000–2,000 words. Informational, how-to, profiles. Topics: stamp collecting tips, products, and personalities.
■ *Depts/columns:* Word lengths vary. Postal history, historical subjects on stamps, new products.

Sample Issue Sample copy available.

Rights and Payment First rights. Articles, $75–$150. Depts/columns, payment rates vary. Pays on publication. Provides 1 contributor's copy.

Sierra

85 Second Street, 2nd Floor, San Francisco, CA 94105. www.sierraclub.org/sierra

Managing Editor

With the motto "Explore, enjoy, and protect the planet," *Sierra* features articles about the natural world. It prefers to work with professional writers, ideally those who have covered environmental issues. Submissions should have painstaking reporting and smart writing. ■ **Circulation** 620,000 ■ **Audience** YA–Adult ■ **Frequency** 6 times a year

Freelance Potential Publishes 50 freelance submissions yearly: 45% written by nonstaff writers; 10% by authors new to the magazine. Receives 40–60 queries monthly.

Submissions Guidelines available at website. Query. Accepts email queries to Submissions. Sierra@sierraclub.org. Responds in 6–8 weeks.
■ *Articles:* 500–5,000 words. Informational, essays. Topics: environmental issues, conservation, adventure travel, nature, self-propelled sports, green living, Sierra Club campaigns.
■ *Depts/columns:* To 1,500 words. Enjoy (upbeat look at green living), Explore (destinations), Grapple (environmental issues), Act (personality profiles), Comfort Zone (environmental design), Mixed Media (book and media reviews).

Sample Issue Advertising. Sample copy available.
■ "Life After Wartime," by Karen J. Coates. Discusses the long-term effects of bombings in Laos.
■ "Beyond Oil in 20 Years," by Paul Rauber. Essay on how to end the country's addiction to oil.

Rights and Payment First North American serial, reproduction, and archival rights. Articles, payment rates vary. Depts/columns, $50–$1,000. Pays on acceptance. Provides 2 contributor's copies.

Skating

United States Figure Skating Association, 20 First Street, Colorado Springs, CO 80906. www.usfigureskating.org

Director of Publications: Troy Schwindt

Figure skating and the personalities, programs, trends, and events that affect the sport are the focus of this magazine. It is written for members and fans of the United States Figure Skating Association. It seeks up-and-coming skaters from around the world, as well as coaches with interesting stories.
■ **Circulation** 45,000 ■ **Audience** 5 years–Adult ■ **Frequency** 11 times a year

Freelance Potential Publishes 15 freelance submissions yearly: 70% written by nonstaff writers; 20% by authors new to the magazine; 10% by previously unpublished writers. Receives up to 6 queries and unsolicited manuscripts monthly.

Submissions Guidelines available. Query with résumé, clips or writing samples, and photo ideas; or send complete manuscript. Accepts hard copy, Macintosh zip disk submissions, and email to skating-magazine@usfigureskating.org. SASE. Responds in 1 month.
■ *Articles:* 750–2,000 words. Informational, profiles, interviews. Topics: association news, competitions, techniques, personalities, training.
■ *Depts/columns:* 600–800 words. Competition results, profiles of skaters and coaches, sports medicine, fitness, technique tips.
■ *Artwork:* B/W and color prints, slides, or transparencies; digital images at 300 dpi.

Sample Issue 56 pages. Sample copy available.
■ "Even If the Roof Is Falling Down," by Lorraine Hanlon Comanor. First-person piece by former World Champion skater about the course of events that shaped her skating life.
■ "Unforgettable Experience," by Renee Felton. The annual U.S. Adult Figure Skating Championships.

Rights and Payment First serial rights. Articles, $75–$150. Depts/columns, $75. Artwork, payment rates vary. Pays on publication. Provides 5–10 contributor's copies.

Skiing

5720 Flatiron Parkway, Boulder, CO 80301. www.skiingmag.com

Editor: Jake Bogoch

Targeting people of all skill levels who just can't get enough of the slopes, Skiing features articles on ski destinations, tips on techniques, profiles of skiers, and information on the latest gear.
■ **Circulation** 300,000 ■ **Audience** YA–Adult ■ **Frequency** 6 times a year

Freelance Potential Publishes 50 freelance submissions yearly: 60% written by nonstaff writers; 5% by authors new to the magazine; 2% by previously unpublished writers. Receives 1+ queries monthly.

Submissions Query with clips or writing samples. Prefers email to editor@skiingmag.com; will accept hard copy. No simultaneous submissions. SASE. Responds in 2–4 months.
■ *Articles:* Word lengths vary. Informational, how-to, profiles. Topics: ski destinations and resorts, techniques, gear.
■ *Depts/columns:* Word lengths vary. Gear, fitness and nutrition, safety.

Sample Issue Sample copy available.
■ "Five-Question Interview," by Kevin Luby. Interview with the founder of Toy Soldier Production.
■ "The Secret to Tree Skiing," by Berne Broudy. Describes how to learn to tree ski.

Rights and Payment First universal and all media rights. Written material, $1 a word. Pays on acceptance. Provides 2 contributor's copies.

Smithsonian Zoogoer

Friends of the National Zoo, P.O. Box 37012, MRC 5516, Washington, DC 20013-7012
www.fonz.org/zoogoer.htm

Editor: Cindy Han

Members of Friends of the National Zoo read this magazine for information relating to the animals and staff of the National Zoo. Articles, written by field experts, also discuss wildlife biology and conservation. ■ **Circulation** 40,000 ■ **Audience** YA–Adults ■ **Frequency** 6 times a year

Freelance Potential Publishes 8–10 freelance submissions yearly: 15% written by nonstaff writers; 5% by authors new to the magazine. Receives 5 queries monthly.

Submissions Guidelines available. Query with sources, author biography, and clips. Accepts hard copy and email queries to zoogoer@fonz.org (Microsoft Word or text attachments). SASE. Responds in 1–2 months.
■ *Articles:* 2,000 words. Informational. Topics: zoo updates, wildlife conservation, scientific research.
■ *Depts/columns:* 800–1,500 words. Staff profiles, animal facts, species profiles, zoo news, book reviews.

Sample Issue 3 articles; 5 depts/columns. Sample copy available.
■ "The Zoo's Pride," by Lindsay Renick Mayer. Provides updates on the building of the lion pride.
■ "Two Thousand Eye Exams," by Devin Murphy. Explains how zoo veterinarians conduct eye exams.

Rights and Payment First rights. Written material, 80¢ a word. Pays on acceptance. Provides 5 contributor's copies.

Sportsnet Magazine

Rogers Sportsnet, One Mount Pleasant Road, Toronto, Ontario M4Y 3A1, Canada. www.sportsnet.ca

Publisher & Editor in Chief: Steve Maich

Sportsnet Magazine was launched in late 2011 by by Rogers Media, the same company that owns the Sportsnet sports television channels in Canada. The magazine and its companion website publish expert commentary and analysis of teams in the major professional leagues and premier amateur sporting events. Hockey, baseball, football, soccer, MMA—and the personalities behind them—are all covered. ■ **Circulation** 100,000 ■ **Audience** YA–Adults ■ **Frequency** Biweekly

Freelance Potential Unavailable.

Submissions For information, email rogersdigitalmedia@rci.rogers.com.
■ *Articles:* Word lengths vary. Informational, profiles, interviews, opinion. Topics: major league sports, top amateur sports, athletes, coaches, programs, sports issues, sporting events.

Sample Issue Unavailable.

Rights and Payment Unavailable.

Stone Soup

P.O. Box 83, Santa Cruz, CA 95063. www.stonesoup.com

Editor: Gerry Mandelr

This "magazine by young writers and artists" is made up of stories, poems, book reviews, and art from contributors all over the world. It accepts work from children up to the age of 14 only; no adult submissions. ■ **Circulation** 15,000 ■ **Audience** 8–13 years ■ **Frequency** 6 times a year

Freelance Potential Publishes 72 freelance submissions yearly: 75–100% written by nonstaff writers; 1–10% assigned; 75–100% by authors new to the magazine; 75–100% by previously unpublished writers. Receives 150–200 unsolicited manuscripts monthly.

Submissions Guidelines available at website. Writers under age 14 only. Guidelines available at website. Send complete manuscript. Accepts hard copy. No simultaneous submissions. No SASE. Responds in 6 weeks if interested.
■ *Fiction:* To 2,500 words. Genres: contemporary, multicultural, ethnic, historical, science fiction, adventure, mystery, suspense.
■ *Depts/columns:* Word lengths vary. Book reviews.
■ *Artwork:* Color only.
■ *Other:* Poetry, line lengths vary.

Sample Issue 48 pages. No advertising. Sample copy available at website.
■ "Flynn," by Hugh Cole. Wilderness adventures of a boy who can communicate with animals.
■ "Irah, the Princess," by Lena Greenberg. Story of a young, sensitive girl who finds a soulmate in a new student.

Rights and Payment All rights. Written material, $40. Artwork, $25. Pays on publication. Provides 2 contributor's copies.

The Storyteller

2441 Washington Road, Maynard, AR 72444. www.freewebs.com/fossilcreek/storyteller.html

Editor: Regina Williams

This family magazine offers wholesome reading material only—no erotica, violence, racial or religious bias, or graphic language. Articles, essays, short stories, and poetry are welcome; however, material for children is not accepted. ■ **Circulation** 700 ■ **Audience** YA–Adults ■ **Frequency** Quarterly

Freelance Potential Publishes 300 freelance submissions yearly: 90% written by nonstaff writers; 50–75% by authors new to the magazine; 75–100% by previously unpublished writers. Receives 200 unsolicited manuscripts monthly.

Submissions Guidelines available at website. Send complete manuscript with word count. Accepts hard copy. Accepts simultaneous submissions if identified. SASE. Responds in 1–2 weeks.
■ *Articles:* To 2,500 words. Personal experience, humor. Topics of interest to families.
■ *Fiction:* To 2,500 words. Genres: contemporary and inspirational fiction, fantasy, horror, humor, mysteries, romance, science fiction, westerns.
■ *Other:* Poetry, to 40 lines.

Sample Issue 72 pages. Little advertising. Sample copy available.

Rights and Payment First North American serial rights. No payment.

Surfing

950 Calle Amanecer, Suite C, San Clemente, CA 92673. www.surfingmagazine.com

Editor: Travis Ferre

Experienced surfers read this publication for information on surfing destinations, techniques, surfer profiles, product reviews, and the surfing lifestyle. With content applicable to all surfers, its targeted audience is young surfers. ■ **Circulation** 105,000 ■ **Audience** YA–Adult ■ **Frequency** Monthly

Freelance Potential Publishes 15 freelance submissions yearly: 20% written by nonstaff writers; 50% by previously unpublished writers. Receives 5+ unsolicited manuscripts monthly.

Submissions Query or send complete manuscript. Accepts hard copy and disk submissions (Quark XPress or Microsoft Word). Accepts simultaneous submissions if identified. SASE. Responds in 1 month.
■ *Articles:* 2,000–3,000 words. Informational, profiles. Topics: surfing destinations, personalities, events.
■ *Depts/columns:* 135–500 words. Techniques, product reviews.

Sample Issue Sample copy available.

Rights and Payment One-time rights. Written material, 10¢–25¢ a word. Pays on publication. Provides 2 contributor's copies.

Sweet Designs

www.sweetdesignsmagazine.com

Editor-in-Chief: Stephanie Lynn

Sweet Designs Magazine, an online magazine for (and by) teenage girls and young adult women, covers teen lifestyle issues. Writers passionate about their topics who can submit fresh, interesting material every month are welcome to query. ■ **Hits per month** Unavailable ■ **Audience** YA girls ■ **Frequency** Updated monthly

Freelance Potential Publishes several freelance submissions yearly.

Submissions Guidelines available at website. Query with writing sample. Accepts email queries to sweet2685@gmail.com. Response time varies.
■ *Articles:* Word lengths vary. Informational, how-to, personal experience. Topics: family, school, dating, friendships, self-esteem, substance abuse, politics, college, fashion, beauty, health and fitness, entertainment.
■ *Other:* Poetry.

Sample Issue Sample copy available at website.
■ "Social Blunders," by Shanice. Offers tips on staying safe on social networking sites.
■ "Transferring Colleges." Discusses the pros and cons of transferring colleges.

Rights and Payment Rights vary. Articles, payment rates vary.

Teen Graffiti

P.O. Box 452721, Garland, TX 75045-2721. www.teengraffiti.com

Publisher: Sharon Jones-Scaife

Teen Graffiti aims to become the voice of teenagers across the nation by providing a platform for the expression of their styles, concerns, ideas, talents, achievements, and community involvement. Although it accepts some submissions from adult writers, most of its articles, essays, and opinions are written by teens for teens. ■ **Circulation** 10,000 ■ **Audience** 12–19 years ■ **Frequency** 6 times a year

Freelance Potential Publishes 30–40 freelance submissions yearly: 70% written by nonstaff writers. Receives several queries and unsolicited manuscripts monthly.

Submissions Teen writers preferred. Guidelines available. Query or send complete manuscript. Prefers email submissions to sharon@teengraffiti.com; will accept hard copy. SASE. Response time varies.
■ *Articles:* 250–500 words. Informational, personal experience, opinion, essays. Topics: college, careers, current events, popular culture, sex, health, social issues.
■ *Depts/columns:* 100–200 words. Advice from teachers, teen-to-teen advice, media reviews.
■ *Artwork:* B/W and color prints. Accepts submissions from teens only.
■ *Other:* Poetry.

Sample Issue 30 pages. Little advertising. Sample copy available.
- "Better Health for Teen Girls Starts at Breakfast."
- "Qualities of a Good Friend."

Rights and Payment One-time rights. No payment.

Teen Voices

80 Summer Street, Suite 400, Boston, MA 02110–1210. www.teenvoices.com

Managing Editor: Becca Steinitz

Written by and for teen girls, this magazine empowers its readers with inspiring and thoughtful articles about the real issues that teens face. It accepts original writing, poetry, and artwork from teen girls across the country. ■ **Circulation** 55,000 ■ **Audience** Teen girls ■ **Frequency** Monthly (website); 2 times a year (print)

Freelance Potential Publishes 100 freelance submissions yearly: 95% written by nonstaff writers; 95% by authors new to the magazine; 95% by previously unpublished writers. Receives about 170 unsolicited manuscripts each month.

Submissions Accepts manuscripts written by girls ages 13–19 only. Send complete manuscript. Accepts hard copy, email submissions to teenvoices@teenvoices.com, and submissions through the website. SASE. Response time varies.
- *Articles:* Word lengths vary. Informational, self-help, interviews, profiles. Topics: ethnic and religious traditions, the Internet, multicultural issues, surviving sexual assault, family relationships, teen motherhood, disability, health, nutrition, cooking, the arts, activism.
- *Fiction:* Word lengths vary. Humorous, inspirational, contemporary, ethnic, multicultural.
- *Depts/columns:* Word lengths vary. Media reviews, arts and culture, international issues, food, opinion pieces.
- *Other:* Poetry; comic strips.

Sample Issue 56 pages. Advertising.
- "One Graceful Musician." Profile of 16–year–old jazz saxophonist, Grace Kelly.
- "Become a Working Girl."The inside scoop for teen girls who want to get a job.

Rights and Payment First or one-time rights. No payment. Provides 5 contributor's copies.

Toy Farmer

7496 106th Street SE, LaMoure, ND 58458-9404. www.toyfarmer.com

Editorial Assistant: Cheryl Hegvik

Toy Farmer offers avid collectors and enthusiasts informative articles on farm toy history, collecting, and pricing. It profiles collectors and collections, as well as manufacturers. Show coverage is also included in each issue. ■ **Circulation** 27,000 ■ **Audience** YA–Adult ■ **Frequency** Monthly

Freelance Potential Publishes 50 freelance submissions yearly: 100% written by nonstaff writers; 20% by authors new to the magazine; 20% by previously unpublished writers. Receives several queries monthly.

Submissions Editorial calendar available. Query with writing samples. Accepts hard copy. SASE. Responds in 1 month.
- *Articles:* 1,500 words. Informational, how-to, profiles. Topics: farm toy history, collecting, pricing, collectors, manufacturers.
- *Depts/columns:* 800 words. Events, new products.

Sample Issue Sample copy available.
- "2011 National Farm Toy Show Tractor," by Peter D. Simpson and Don Wadge. Tells the history of

the four wheel-drive tractor.
- "Custom Built and Scratch Built Projects," by Cindy Ladage. Profiles a builder of custom planters.

Rights and Payment First rights. Written material, 10¢ a word. Pays on publication. Provides 2 contributor's copies.

Toy Trucker & Contractor

7496 106th Avenue SE, LaMoure, ND 58458-9404. www.toytrucker.com

Editorial Assistant: Cheryl Hegvik

Toy Trucker & Contractor is read by model truck and equipment collectors. Each issue offers how-to instruction, profiles of collectors, and articles on collecting. Coverage of model truck shows is also provided. ■ **Circulation** 8,000 ■ **Audience** YA–Adult ■ **Frequency** Monthly

Freelance Potential Publishes 60 freelance submissions yearly: 100% written by nonstaff writers; 20% by authors new to the magazine; 10% by previously unpublished writers. Receives 1 query monthly.

Submissions Editorial calendar available. Query with writing samples. Accepts hard copy. SASE. Responds in 1 month.
- *Articles:* 1,000–5,000 words. Informational, how-to, personal experience, profiles. Topics: truck and equipment collecting, history, personalities.
- *Depts/columns:* Word lengths vary. Events, new products.

Sample Issue Sample copy available.
- "Tigercat 630," by Fred Moses. Explains how the toy truck was built.
- "Fire Truck and Firemen Need Homes Too," by Richard Marmo. Describes how the author designed a firehouse from a 1913 plan.

Rights and Payment First North American serial rights. Written material, 10¢ a word. Pays on publication. Provides 2 contributor's copies.

Trains

21027 Crossroads Circle, P.O. Box 1612, Waukesha, WI 53187-1612. www.trainsmag.com

Editor: Jim Wrinn

News stories, feature articles, and personal recollections make up the bulk of this magazine for train buffs of all ages. All types of trains are covered, past and present, in entertaining and edifying articles. Material on trains of the eastern and southern U.S. is of particular interest. ■ **Circulation** 95,000 ■ **Audience** YA–Adult ■ **Frequency** Monthly

Freelance Potential Publishes 300–400 freelance submissions yearly: 65% written by nonstaff writers; 25% by authors new to the magazine; 25% by previously unpublished writers. Receives 25 queries monthly.

Submissions Guidelines available at website. Query. Accepts email to editor@trainsmag.com (Microsoft Word attachments). Responds in 3 months.
- *Articles:* Word lengths vary. Informational, personal experience, profiles. Topics: railroad companies, industry trends, train history, industry personalities.
- *Depts/columns:* Word lengths vary. Railroad news, technology, train preservation, Q&As.
- *Artwork:* Digital images at 300 dpi; color transparencies.

Sample Issue Sample copy available.
- "Presenting the Past at the Mount Washington Cog Railway," by Karl Zimmerman. Explores the history of New Hampshire's cog.
- "Confused about PTC Yet?" by Steve Ditmeyer. Explains positive train control and how it will work.

Rights and Payment All rights. Written material, 10¢–15¢ a word. Pays on acceptance. Provides 2 contributor's copies.

Transworld Snowboarding

2052 Corte del Nogal, Suite B, Carlsbad, CA 92011. www.snowboarding.transworld.net

Managing Editor: Annie Fost

The very best of snowboarding is celebrated in this magazine. It profiles the raddest boarders and the best snowboarding destinations in the world, covers the latest gear, reports on competitions, and provides insight into the sharpest tricks. ■ **Circulation** 1.4 million ■ **Audience** YA–Adult ■ **Frequency** 8 times a year

Freelance Potential Publishes 10 freelance submissions yearly: 10% written by nonstaff writers; 5% by authors new to the magazine. Receives 10 queries monthly.

Submissions Guidelines and theme list available. Query. Accepts email queries to annie.fast@ transworld.net. Responds in 1 month.
■ *Articles:* To 1,600 words. Informational, how-to, profiles, photo-essays. Topics: snowboarding personalities, destinations, events, and news.
■ *Depts/columns:* 300 words. Gear, techniques.

Sample Issue Sample copy available.
■ "Retrospect Week: Caught Up with Harrison Gordon." Interview with snowboarder Harrison Gordon.
■ "The Art of Flight Is Comin," by Scott Serfas. Photo-essay depicting snowboarding adventures in Alaska's Tordrillo Range in anticipation of the upcoming movie.

Rights and Payment Rights vary. Written material, 35¢ a word. Pays on publication. Provides 2 contributor's copies.

Uncle John's Bathroom Readers

Readers Institute, P.O. Box 1117, Ashland, OR 97520. www.bathroomreader.com

Editor: Amy Miller

Since 1987, Bathroom Readers Institute has published books of trivia and fun facts on an array of topics. Their purpose is to give people reading that is entertaining anywhere. The company continues to publish collections, and has started to create targeted publications, including some for children. The possibilities are endless here. Humor is not required, but it is appreciated. The only requirement is that the items be short, and the topic be informative or entertaining. ■ **Circulation** 40,000 readers ■ **Audience** Children, teens, adults ■ **Frequency** New editions published frequently

Freelance Potential Open to freelance contributors.

Submissions To be considered for freelance contributions to upcoming books, send résumé and original, unedited samples of work. Accepts hard copy and email to mail@bathroomreaders.com. SASE. Response time varies.
■ *Articles:* 1,000 words. Topics: Fun facts, trivia, science, pop culture, history, sports, nature humor.
■ *Fiction:* 1,000 words. Short fiction. Genres: contemporary, mystery, Western, science fiction, humor.

Sample Issue Sample copy available at newsstands and bookstores.
■ "Uncle John's Creature Feature Bathroom Reader for Kids Only."
■ "Uncle John's Did You Know . . . ? Bathroom Reader For Kids Only."

Rights and Payment North American serial rights and electronic rights. Payment rates vary. Payment policy varies.

USA Synchro Magazine

132 East Washington, Suite 820, Indianapolis, IN 46204. www.usasynchro.org

Editor: Taylor Payne

The latest information on synchronized swimming can be found in this online member publication of U.S. Synchronized Swimming. It spotlights noteworthy teams, coaches, and judges, and offers competition results, member news, and gear and equipment information. It also features a section dedicated to its younger members. New writers are welcome to send submissions. ■ **Hits per month** 7,000 ■ **Audience** YA–Adult ■ **Frequency** Quarterly

Freelance Potential Publishes 12 freelance submissions yearly: 50% written by nonstaff writers; 50% by authors new to the magazine; 50% by previously unpublished writers.

Submissions Query or send complete manuscript. Accepts hard copy. SASE. Response time varies.
■ *Articles:* Informational, how-to, profiles. Topics: synchronized swimming teams, coaches and judges, competition results, health and safety.
■ *Depts/columns:* Association news, Q&As, gear.

Sample Issue Sample copy available at website.
■ "World's Largest Synchro Meet," by Taylor Payne. A reports on this recent event for ages 11–19.
■ "Concussions in Synchronized Swimming," by Dr. Jim Miller. Risk factors and prevention methods.

Rights and Payment All rights. Written material, word lengths vary. No payment.

The Water Skier

USA Water Ski, 1251 Holy Cow Road, Polk City, FL 33868-8200. www.usawaterski.org

Editor: Scott Atkinson

USA Water Ski publishes this glossy magazine for fans and water skiers alike. Features, athlete profiles, how-to articles, new product reviews, event coverage, and USA Water Ski news updates are offered in each photo-packed issue. The sports of kneeboarding and wakeboarding are also covered. ■ **Circulation** 20,000 ■ **Audience** YA–Adult ■ **Frequency** 7 times a year

Freelance Potential Publishes 10–12 freelance submissions yearly: 20% written by nonstaff writers; 10% by authors new to the magazine. Receives 1–3 queries monthly.

Submissions Query. Accepts hard copy. SASE. Responds in 1 month.
■ *Articles:* 1,000 words. Informational, how-to, profiles. Topics: water skiing athletes, techniques, and events; kneeboarding; wakeboarding.
■ *Depts/columns:* 500–1,000 words. Association news and events.

Sample Issue Sample copy available.
■ "Strong Mind," by Chris Rossi. Provides on and off-water tips for slalom water skiing.
■ "Taking the Handle with You," by Freddy Krueger. The optimal body position to improve jumping.

Rights and Payment All rights. Written material, payment rates vary. Pays on publication. Provides 1 contributor's copy.

Weatherwise

Taylor and Francis Group, LLC, 325 Chestnut Street, Suite 800, Philadelphia, PA 19106
www.weatherwise.org

Managing Editor: Margaret Benner

Weatherwise publishes articles and photos chronicling the world's weather phenomena. It seeks writers that are meteorologists and articles that are anecdotal, analytical, and illuminating. ■ **Circulation** 5,800 ■ **Audience** YA–Adult ■ **Frequency** 6 times a year

Freelance Potential Publishes 25 freelance submissions yearly: 50% written by nonstaff writers; 30% by authors new to the magazine. Receives 5+ queries monthly.

Submissions Guidelines available at website. Certified meteorologists only. Query with outline, résumé, list of potential sources and illustrations, and clips. Accepts queries to margaret.benner@ taylorandfrancis.com. No simultaneous submissions. Availability of artwork improves chance of acceptance. Responds in 2 months.
■ *Articles:* 1,500–2,500 words. Informational. Topics: the history, trends, discoveries, technology, and issues of meteorology and climatology.
■ *Depts/columns:* 800–1,500 words. Book and media reviews; essays; news items on weather-related people, events, trends.
■ *Artwork:* Digital images at 300 dpi, color prints or slides. Line art.

Sample Issue Sample copy available.
■ "The Weather and Climate of West Virginia," by Kevin T. Law and H. Michael Mogil. Explains West Virginia's variable climate due to its dramatic topography.
■ "The Russian Inferno of 2010," by Tim Vasquez. Russia's unusual,severe heat wave and its effects.

Rights and Payment All rights. Payment rates vary. Pays on publication.

Wire Tap

Independent Media Institute, 77 Federal Road, San Francisco, CA 94107. www.wiretapmag.org

Associate Editor

Featuring "ideas and action for a new generation," this independent news and culture ezine is a platform for progressive journalists. It covers education, the environment, politics, racial justice, and arts and lifestyle issues. The goal is to highlight, mentor, and amplify some of the most compelling and urgent young voices in the country today. ■ **Hits per month** 60,000 ■ **Audience** 18–30 years ■ **Frequency** Updated daily

Freelance Potential Publishes 120 freelance submissions yearly: 95% written by nonstaff writers. Receives 25 queries monthly.

Submissions Query. Accepts email queries to submissions@wiretapmag.org (no attachments). Response time varies.
■ *Articles:* Word lengths vary. Informational, profiles, interviews, personal experience. Topics: social issues, politics, culture, current events, the environment, immigration, relationships, peace, education, youth activism.
■ *Depts/columns:* Word lengths vary. Reviews, politics, news.
■ *Other:* Poetry.

Sample Issue 8 articles. Sample copy available at website.
■ "Cedric Michael Cox: Structured Soul," by Geoffrey Dobbins. Profiles this visual artist and an exhibit.
■ "The Greening of Hip Hop," by Eric Arnold. Rap and hip hop artists engaged in social change.

Rights and Payment Electronic rights. Written material, $50–$400 for assigned pieces. No payment for unsolicited submissions. Payment policy varies.

Woodall's Camper Ways

Woodall Publications Group, 2575 Vista Del Mar Drive, Ventura, CA 93001. www.woodalls.com

Managing Editor: Maryanne Sullivan

RV and camping enthusiasts in the Mid-Atlantic U.S. turn to this publication for how-to information on vehicle maintenance and safety, recreational activities, and destination ideas. ■ **Circulation** Unavailable ■ **Audience** YA–Adult ■ **Frequency** Monthly

Freelance Potential Publishes several freelance submissions yearly: 90% written by nonstaff writers; 10% by authors new to the magazine. Receives 25 queries monthly.

Submissions Guidelines available. Query. Accepts email queries to editor@woodallpub.com (Microsoft Word attachments). Artwork required for acceptance. Responds in 2 months.
■ *Articles:* 1,000–1,400 words. Informational, how-to. Topics: RV and tent camping, vehicle maintenance and safety, destinations, recreational activities.
■ *Depts/columns:* By assignment only.
■ *Artwork:* Digital images.

Sample Issue Sample copy available.
■ "Life's a Beach When You Can Find a Beach Campground." Suggestions for great beach campgrounds.
■ "Camping Near Aquariums Can Be Educational and Fun," by Rick Hazeltine. Explores the best aquariums around the country.

Rights and Payment First North American serial rights. Articles, $50–$200. Pays on acceptance. Provides 2 contributor's copies.

Writers' Journal

Val-Tech Media, P.O. Box 394, Perham, MN 56573-0394. www.writersjournal.com

Editor: Leon Ogroske

Writers' Journal wants to be known as the "complete writer's magazine." To that end, it covers such topics as the business side of writing, self-publishing, income venues, and writing skills. It welcomes short, lively, and witty poems, especially if they are about writing. ■ **Circulation** 10,000 ■ **Audience** YA–Adult ■ **Frequency** 6 times a year

Freelance Potential Publishes 40 freelance submissions yearly: 50% written by nonstaff writers; 80% by authors new to the magazine; 20% by previously unpublished writers. Receives up to 17 queries and unsolicited manuscripts monthly.

Submissions Guidelines available at website. Query with clips, or send complete manuscript. Prefers hard copy; will accept email submissions to writersjournal@writersjournal.com (text only). SASE. Responds in 2–6 months.
■ *Articles:* 1,200–2,200 words. Informational, how-to, profiles, interviews. Topics: fiction writing, travel writing, technical writing, business writing, screenwriting, journalism, poetry, writing skills and styles, punctuation, interviewing techniques, research, record-keeping, income venues, finance, self-publishing.
■ *Depts/columns:* Staff-written.
■ *Other:* Poetry, to 15 lines.

Sample Issue 64 pages: Advertising. Sample copy available.
■ "Taking Your Act on the Road and Writing about It," by Dee Dee McNeil. Discusses how one can use a trip as subject matter for a book.
■ "Self Editing versus Pro Editing," by John Robert Marlow. Provides tips for editing one's work so that an agent or publisher will pay attention.

Rights and Payment First North American serial rights. Articles, $30. Poetry, $5 a poem. Pays on publication. Provides 2 contributor's copies upon request and a 1-year subscription.

Contests
& Awards

Selected Contests & Awards

One way to have your work read by editors and other writers is to enter writing contests. Winning or placing in a contest can open the door to publication and recognition. If you don't win, you are still refining your craft, and increasing your submissions. Read winning entries when published, to gain insight into how your work compares with the competition.

Contests generate excitement. For editors, contests are a way to discover new writers. Entries are more focused because of the contest guidelines, and therefore closely target an editor's current needs. For writers, the benefit is that every contest entry is read, often by more than one editor. Submissions are not relegated to an untouched slush pile. And you don't have to be the grand-prize winner to benefit—non-winning manuscripts are often purchased by the publication for future issues.

To be considered for the contests and awards that follow, fulfill all of the requirements carefully. For each listing, we've included the address, a description, the entry requirements, the deadline, and the prize. In some cases, the 2012 deadlines were not available at press time. We recommend that you write to the addresses provided or visit the websites to request an entry form and the contest guidelines, which usually specify the current deadline.

The AAAS Kavli Science Journalism Awards

AAAS Office of Public Programs, 1200 New York Avenue NW, Washington, DC 20005. www.aaas.org/SJAwards

Description Begun in 1945, these awards honor distinguished science reporting. They recognize scientific accuracy, initiative, originality, clarity of interpretation, and fostering a better public understanding of science and its impact. A category for children's science news recognizes excellence in science reporting for children to age 14.

Requirements The children's award is open to U.S. and international reporters. Science reports published in print, broadcast, or online are eligible. Submit 9 copies of the text, each with a completed entry form (available at website). An entry may consist of a single story; no more than 3 segments of a thematic series; or a group of 3 unrelated stories. Each entrant may submit up to 3 entries.

Prizes Category winners receive $3,000.

Deadline August 1.

Abilene Writers Guild Annual Contest

726 Davis Drive, Abiline, TX 79605. www.abilenewritersguild.org

Description The Guild's annual contest is open to all writers; its monthly contests are open to members only. The categories for the yearly competition include children's stories for ages 3 to 8 and a novel category that accepts YA fiction. Other categories include flash fiction, general interest articles, poetry, and adult fiction.

Requirements Entry fees are $10 for novels, $5 for short entries. Guidelines vary for each category.

Children's stories may target one age range—preschool, for example, or age 8—and do not have to appeal to all ages. Submit the entire story, which must be original and unpublished. For YA and other novels, send the first 10 pages and a 1-page synopsis.

Prizes First place, $100; second place, $65; third place, $35.

Deadline Between October 1 and November 30.

Amy Writing Awards

Amy Foundation, P.O. Box 1609, Lansing, MI 48901-6091. www.amyfound.org

Description The Amy Foundation Writing Awards program recognizes nonfiction articles that apply biblical principles in a sensitive, though-provoking manner to current issues, with an emphasis on discipling. Winning entries will employ creative, skillful writing.

Requirements No entry fee. Articles must have been published in a mainstream, non-religious publication and contain at least one passage of scripture. Books, poetry, and fiction are not eligible. Submit tearsheet for print works, or a hard copy of online works with URL clearly visible. Entries not returned. Limit 10 submissions per author.

Prizes First-prize winner receives $10,000; other awards range from $1,000–$5,000.

Deadline Entries must be postmarked by January 31 following the calendar year in which the work was published. Winners notified by May 1.

Arizona Literary Contest

Contest Coordinator, 6145 West Echo Lane, Glendale, AZ 85302. www.azauthors.com

Description This annual contest sponsored by the Arizona Authors Association accepts work from writers anywhere in the world, as long as the work is written in English. It accepts entries of unpublished short stories, poems, articles, essays, and true stories, as well as published books and children's literature.

Requirements Entry fees range from $15 to $30, depending on the category. Check website for fees and word length requirements. Accepts hard copy. Manuscripts are not returned. Visit the website or send an SASE for complete guidelines.

Prizes First-place winners in each category receive $100. Second- and third-place winners receive $50 and $25, respectively. The top 3 winners for all categories are published or featured in *Arizona Literary Magazine*.

Deadline Entries are accepted between January 1 and July 1.

Atlantic Writing Competition

Writers' Federation of Nova Scotia, 1113 Marginal Road, Halifax NS B3H 4P Canada. www.writers.ns.ca

Description Open to writers living in Atlantic Canada, this annual contest includes categories for children's writing and juvenile/YA novels. Entries must be unpublished. Established writers are eligible to enter only in a category that is new to them. The competition has been held since 1975.

Requirements Entry fees range from $20 to $35. The writing for children's category accepts picture books, fiction, nonfiction, poetry, or stage plays for children up to age 12; 20,000 words maximum. The juvenile/YA novel category accepts manuscripts for readers ages 8 to 12; 75,000 words maximum. Only 1 entry per category. Send complete manuscript. Do not include your real name on the manuscript itself; select a pseudonym. Also include a 1-paragraph description of yourself, and a list of writing credits, if any.

Prizes Prizes in each of the categories are $150, $75, and $50.

Deadline November 4.

Baker's Plays High School Playwriting Contest

45 West 25th Street, New York, NY 10010. www.bakersplays.com

Description As an advocate for theater in schools for more than 100 years, Baker's Plays sponsors this high school playwriting competition to foster creativity among teens involved in drama. All subjects are welcome.

Requirements Open to high school students only. No entry fee or length limitations. Plays must be accompanied by the signature of a sponsoring high school English teacher. Manuscripts must be firmly bound and typed. Plays will not be returned. A postcard or email will be sent as notification of receipt of manuscript. Multiple submissions and co-authored scripts are welcome. Visit the website for contest rules and entry form.

Prizes First-place winner receives $500; second- and third-place winners receive $250 and $100, respectively. Each winning play is published in a collection by Baker's Plays, with a royalty-earning contract.

Deadline Entries are accepted between September 1 and January 31.

Waldo M. and Grace C. Bonderman Youth Theatre Playwriting Competition

Indiana Repertory Theatre, 140 W. Washington Street, Indianapolis, IN 46204. www.irtlive.com

Description This biennial competition, which is connected to a playwriting workshop and symposium, was launched to encourage the development of theatrical scripts that attract young audiences. It accepts plays that are intended for audiences in third grade through high school, written by adult writers. Scripts must not be committed to publication at the time of submission.

Requirements No entry fee. Scripts for grades 3–5 should have a running time of 30–40 minutes. Scripts for grades 6 and up should run a minimum of 45 minutes. Send complete manuscript with a brief synopsis and cast list. Author's name should not appear on the manuscript. Accepts email submissions to bonderman@irtlive.com. Visit the website for complete guidelines. Playwrights are expected to be in residence in Indianapolis throughout the workshop and symposium.

Prizes Prizes vary. Winning plays will be performed at the Bonderman Symposium.

Deadline June 30.

Canadian Writer's Journal Short Fiction Contest

Box 1178, New Liskeard, Ontario P0J 1P0 Canada. www.cwj.ca

Description Original, unpublished short stories of any genre are accepted for this contest. Submitting writers must be Canadian citizens or landed immigrants.

Requirements Entry fee, $10 per story. Maximum length, 2,500 words. Multiple entries accepted. Accepts hard copy. Author's name must not appear on manuscript. Include a cover sheet with author's name, address, and short biography. Manuscripts are not returned. Send SASE for contest results only, or watch the website. Visit the website for complete guidelines.

Prizes First-place winner receives a cash prize of $150. Second- and third-place winners receive cash prizes of $100 and $50, respectively. Winning entries are published in *Canadian Writer's Journal*.

Deadline April 30.

CAPA Competition

Connecticut Authors and Publishers Association, c/o Dan Uitti, 223 Buckingham Street, Oakville, CT 06779. www.aboutcapa.com

Description Prizes for poems, short stories, personal essays, and children's stories are awarded annually by the Connecticut Authors and Publishers Association. While the competition was previously open to Connecticut residents only, it is now open to all writers. All entries must be original and previously unpublished.

Requirements Entry fees, $10 for 1 story or essay, or up to 3 poems. Children's stories to 2,000 words (no illustrations). Personal essays, to 1,500 words. Short stories, to 2,000 words. Poetry, to 30 lines. See website for entry form. Multiple entries are accepted. Accepts hard copy. Submit 4 copies of each entry. Manuscripts are not returned. Winning entries are published in a special issue of *The Authority*, CAPA's monthly newsletter.

Prizes First-place winners in each category receive $100. Second-place winners receive $50.

Deadline December 23.

Children's Writer Contests

Children's Writer, 93 Long Ridge Road, West Redding, CT 06896-1124. www.childrenswriter.com

Description *Children's Writer* is a monthly newsletter covering the children's publishing industry. It sponsors two writing contests each year. Subjects include children's poetry, children's fiction, children's nonfiction, or writing that is targeted to specific age groups and/or genres. Check the website for the latest calls for submissions. Top-ranked entries and authors are featured in the newsletter, and winning submissions are published.

Requirements No entry fee for subscribers. For non-subscribers, a $15 entry fee includes an 8-month subscription to the newsletter. Manuscripts accepted online or by mail. Manuscripts are not returned. Visit the website for complete contest rules.

Prizes First place is awarded $500; second place is awarded $250; and $100 goes to third, fourth, and fifth places. Winning entries are published in *Children's Writer*.

Deadline February 28 and October 31. Check website for details.

Delacorte Press Contest for a First YA Novel

Random House, 1745 Broadway, 9th Floor, New York, NY 10019. www.randomhouse.com/kids/writingcontests

Description This annual contest for a first young adult novel is open to previously unpublished U.S. and Canadian writers. It looks for stories that feature contemporary settings, suitable for readers ages 12 to 18. Winners are awarded a book contract.

Requirements No entry fee. Length, 100–224 pages. Send complete manuscript with brief plot summary and cover page with author's name and contact information. Manuscripts will not be returned. SASE for notification only. No simultaneous submissions. Authors may submit up to 2 manuscripts.

Prizes Winner receives a book contract from Delacorte Press Books for Young Readers, a $7,500 advance against royalties, and a cash prize of $1,500.

Deadline Entries are accepted between October 1 and December 31.

Family Circle Fiction Contest

Family Circle Magazine, 375 Lexington Avenue, New York, NY 10017. www.familycircle.com/family-fun/fiction

Description *Family Circle* magazine sponsors this annual contest to celebrate the short story in all its forms, although stories about family are preferred. Stories are judged on topic creativity, originality, and overall excellence. Unpublished writers are encouraged to enter.

Requirements No entry fees. Word length, to 2,500 words. Original work only. Entrants may submit up to two stories. Must be legal resident of the U.S. and at least 21 years old.

Prizes Grand prize winner will receive $750, a gift certificate to one mediabistro.com course, one year membership mediabistro.com and more. Second place winner receives $250 and membership. Third place $250 and membership. The grand prize winner may be published in *Family Circle*. Runners-up may be published at the *Family Circle* website

Deadline September 9; winners announced in October.

Shubert Fendrich Memorial Playwriting Contest

Pioneer Drama Service, P.O. Box 4267, Englewood, CO 80155-4267. www.pioneerdrama.com

Description This annual playwriting contest was established to honor the founder of Pioneer Drama Service. Its purpose is to recognize and encourage the development of quality theatrical material for the educational, community, and children's theater markets. All original, unpublished plays submitted to Pioneer Drama Service for publication will be automatically entered into the contest.

Requirements No entry fee. Plays should run between 20 and 90 minutes. Accepts hard copy or electronic submissions via the website. All entries must include the completed application form (available at website), musical score if applicable, and proof of production. Writers who are currently published by Pioneer Drama Service are not eligible.

Prizes Winning entry is published by Pioneer Drama Service; winner receives a $1,000 advance on royalties.

Deadline Ongoing; winner announced each June 1 from plays submitted during the previous calendar year.

Foster City International Writing Contest

c/o Foster City Parks & Recreation Department, 650 Shell Boulevard, Foster City, CA 94404. http://bwstore.biz/foster

Description The Foster City International Writing Contest is held each year, and accepts entries of children's stories, fiction, humor, personal essays, and poetry. Only submissions of original, unpublished work will be considered.

Requirements Entry fee, $10. Multiple entries are accepted. Children's stories, fiction, humor, and personal experience pieces, to 3,000 words. Poetry, to 500 words. Accepts hard copy and email submissions to fostercity_writers@yahoo.com (Word, RTF, PDF, or TXT attachments; include "Writer's Contest Entry," category, and author name in subject field). Visit the website for complete information and entry form.

Prizes First-place winners are awarded $150; second-place winners, $75.

Deadline March 11.

H. E. Francis Contest

Department of English, Morton Hall, Room 222, University of Alabama at Huntsville, Huntsville, AL 35899. www.uah.edu/hefranciscontest

Description Judged by a panel of nationally recognized authors, creative writing program directors, and literary journal editors, this contest is sponsored by the Ruth Hindman Foundation and the University of Alabama Huntsville English department. It is for short stories only.

Requirements Entry fee, $15 per submission. Word length, to 5,000 words. Send 3 copies of manuscript. No identifying information should appear on the manuscript itself. Enclose a cover sheet with story title, word count, and author name and address. Accepts simultaneous submissions if identified. Manuscripts are not returned; send SASE for announcement of winner. Visit the website for more information.

Prizes First-place winner receives a cash prize of $1,000.

Deadline December 31. Winner is announced in March.

Friends of the Library Contest

Decatur Public Library, 130 North Franklin Street, Decatur, IL 62523. www.decatur.lib.il.us.writingcontest.aspx

Description Sponsored by the public library in Decatur, Illinois, this writing contest is open to writers from all over the world. It awards prizes for essays, fiction, juvenile fiction, and poetry. It is judged by professional, published writers who live in Illinois. The main criterion is salability. Writers should avoid using the present tense in fiction and near rhyme in rhymed poetry.

Requirements Entry fee, $3; limit 5 entries per person. Essays, to 2,000 words. Fiction and juvenile fiction, to 3,000 words (no illustrations). Poetry, to 40 lines. Accepts hard copy. Author's name should not appear on the manuscript. All entries must be accompanied by an entry form. Complete contest rules and entry form available at website.

Prizes First-place winner receives a cash award of $50. Second- and third-place winners receive $30 and $20, respectively.

Deadline September 25. Winners announced in December.

Funds For Writers Contest

Address, www.fundsforwriters.com/annualcontest.htm

Description Funds for Writers has been sponsoring this annual, themed writing contest for 10 years. See website for 2012 theme. It accepts nonfiction essays only, including memoir, creative nonfiction, and journalistic writing. No fiction is accepted. Entrants are given the choice to enter for free, or pay an entry fee and vie for a higher prize purse.

Requirements Zero entry fee category and $5 entry fee category. See website for detailed submission guidelines. Word limit, 750 words. Accepts email entries only to hope@fundsforwriters.com. Include the following in the body of the email (no attachments): title of essay, name and contact information, word count, "fee" or "no fee" category, and essay. Multiple submissions accepted.

Prizes First prize $400. Five additional cash prizes. Winner published in Funds for Writers newsletters.

Deadline October 31.

John Gardner Memorial Prize for Fiction

Harpur Palate, English Department, Binghamton University, Box 6000, Binghamton, NY 13902-6000. http://harpurpalate.binghamton.edu

Description Previously unpublished short fiction is accepted for this contest, sponsored by Binghamton University. All genres are accepted. The annual award is given in memory of John Gardner, a fiction writer, dramatist, and teacher.

Requirements Entry fee, $15; includes a 1-year subscription to *Harpur Palate*. Length, to 8,000 words. Accepts hard copy. Include a cover sheet with author's name, address, phone number, email address, and title of the story. Author's name should not appear on entry. Manuscripts are not returned; enclose SASE for contest results. See website for contest details.

Prizes Winner receives a cash award of $500 and publication in the summer issue of *Harpur Palate*.

Deadline Entries are accepted between February 1 and April 15.

Ghost Story Contest

Friends of the Dr. Eugene Clark Library, P.O. Box 821, Lockhart, TX 78644. www.clarklibraryfriends.com

Description Each year, the Dr. Eugene Clark Library in Lockhart, Texas, sponsors a "Scare The Dickens Out of Us" short story contest in conjunction with its "A Dickens Christmas in Lockhart" festival. The contest accepts unpublished ghost stories of any genre, written on any subject. Published as well as unpublished writers are invited to submit. In addition to the adult category, a junior category accepts stories written by teens ages 12 to 18.

Requirements Entry fee, $20 for adults; $5 for juniors. Limit, 1 entry per writer. Length, to 5,000 words. Accepts hard copy accompanied by an entry form. Manuscripts are not returned. Visit the website for full contest rules and entry form.

Prizes First-place winners receive $1,000; second-place, $500; third-place, $250. Juniors, $25.

Deadline Between July 1 and October 1.

Paul Gillette Awards

c/o Pikes Peak Writers, 427 East Colorado #116, Colorado Springs, CO 80903. www.ppwc.net/html/paul_gillette_awards.html

Description The Pikes Peak Writers organization sponsors this contest for unpublished writers of short stories and novels. Short stories may be any genre. It accepts book-length fiction for children (ages 8–12) and young adults (ages 12–18), as well as historical, mainstream, science fiction, mystery, suspense, intrigue, and romance.

Requirements Entry fee, $30 per entry for Pikes Peak Writers members; $40 for non-members. Up to 2 entries in the same category will be accepted; writers may submit entries in more than one category. Word lengths vary for each category. Accepts email submissions only to pgcontest@gmail.com (RTF attachments). Check website for full contest rules and checklist.

Prizes First-place winners receive $100. Second- and third-place winners receive $50 and $30.

Deadline November 15.

Good Housekeeping Short Story Contest

3 West 57th Street, 28th Floor, New York, NY 10019-5288.
www.goodhousekeeping.com/win/fiction-contest

Description This popular consumer magazine sponsors an annual fiction contest that is open to all writers, published or unpublished. All work must be original. Themes and genres are open. The only requirement is that stories should reflect any aspect of women's lives today.

Requirements Writers must be a legal resident of the U.S. and at least 21 years old. Only one submission per entrant. Word length, to 3,500. Accepts email submissions to fictioncontest@ goodhousekeeping.com (include title of story in subject line), include author name and contact information in email.

Prizes Grand prize winner will receive $3,000. Two runners-up will each receive $750. Winning entries may be published in *Good Housekeeping* magazine.

Deadline September 1; winners notified the following February.

Highlights for Children Fiction Contest

Fiction Contest, 803 Church Street, Honesdale, PA 18431.
www.highlights.com/highlights-fiction-contest

Description This year's *Highlights for Children* Fiction Contest welcomes short, funny stories inspired by a newspaper headline. All stories must be for young readers. Writers must be at least 16 years old to submit their work. Stories cannot include derogatory humor, crime, or violence. Published and unpublished writers are welcome to submit. All submissions must be previously unpublished.

Requirements No entry fee. Length, to 750 words; to 475 words for beginning readers. Accepts hard copy. Include SASE for return of manuscript. All submissions should be clearly marked "Fiction Contest." Visit the website for complete guidelines.

Prizes Three winning entries will receive a cash award of $1,000 or tuition for the Highlights Foundation Writers Workshop at Chautauqua, and will be published in *Highlights*.

Deadline Entries must be postmarked between January 1 and January 31.

Insight Writing Contest

55 West Oak Ridge Drive, Hagerstown, MD 21740-7390. www.insightmagazine.org

Description Adults and students (up to age 22) are invited to enter this contest from *Insight Magazine*. It awards prizes for student short stories and poetry, as well as for short stories written by adults. Submissions must be true, unpublished, and have a strong spiritual message. The use of Bible texts is encouraged. Non-winning entries are considered for purchase at regular *Insight* rates.

Requirements No entry fee. Length, to 7 pages for short fiction; to 1 page for poetry. Accepts hard copy and email to insight@rhpa.org. Multiple entries accepted; each accompanied by the cover sheet available for download at website, and author biography. Visit the website for complete guidelines.

Prizes Winners receive awards ranging from $50 to $220. Winning entries are published in *Insight*.

Deadline June 1.

Magazine Merit Awards

Society of Children's Book Writers & Illustrators, 8271 Beverly Boulevard, Los Angeles, CA 90048. www.scbwi.org

Description This annual award is granted by the SCBWI to recognize outstanding and original published magazine writing for young people in the categories of fiction, nonfiction, illustration, and poetry. Winning entries will reflect the interests and concerns of young readers.

Requirements No entry fee. Entrants must be members of SCBWI. Members submit 4 copies of each entry in publication form with proof of publication date, indicating the magazine name and date of publication. Cover sheet must contain member's name and contact information, category, and name and date of publication. See website for details.

Prizes Winners in each category are given a plaque. Honor certificates are also awarded.

Deadline December 15; winners announced in April.

Memoirs Ink Writing Contest

10866 Washington Boulevard, Suite 518, Culver City, CA 90232. www.memoirsink.com

Description Writers of personal essays, memoirs, and stories based on autobiographical experiences are welcome to submit their work to this contest, which is held twice a year. Writing can be funny, sad, serious, artsy, or fragmented; however, all entries must be written in the first person. It is open to writers of all ages and from all countries, as long as the writing is in English.

Requirements Entry fee, $15; $13 for previous entrants. Length, to 1,500 words for February contest; to 3,000 words for August contest. Multiple submissions are accepted; $10 entry fee for each additional submission. Accepts hard copy and submissions through website. Author's name should appear only on entry form. Manuscripts not returned. Visit the website for details and entry form.

Prizes First-place winner receives $1,000. Second- and third-place winners receive $500 and $250, respectively. Winning entries will be published in *Memoirs Ink*.

Deadline February 15 and August 15 (additional $5 fee for late entries).

Milkweed Prize for Children's Literature

Milkweed Editions, 1011 Washington Avenue South, Suite 300, Minneapolis, MN 55415. www.milkweed.org

Description This prize is awarded to novels written for children ages 8 to 13. The publishers of Milkweed Editions choose a winner from the best manuscripts that have been submitted during the calendar year, by a writer they have not previously published. Books that introduce young readers to memorable characters struggling with difficult decisions are favored. Picture books and collections of stories are not eligible.

Requirements No entry fee. All children's manuscripts submitted to Milkweed for publication are automatically entered. Prefers electronic submissions through the website; will accept hard copy. SASE. Submissions should adhere to Milkweed's children's literature submission guidelines, available on website.

Prizes Winner receives $10,000 in addition to a negotiated publishing contract.

Deadline Ongoing. Submission periods are January–March, and July–September.

National Children's Theatre Competition

Actors' Playhouse/Miracle Theatre, 280 Miracle Mile, Coral Gables, FL 33134.
www.actorsplayhouse.org

Description Judged by panelists from both professional and academic theater, this competition seeks original, unpublished scripts for children's musicals. Musicals should lend themselves to being simplified and be suitable for touring. The target audience is ages 5 to 12, but submissions that also appeal to adults will have an advantage. Contemporary relevance is preferred over topicality. New adaptations of traditional, public-domain titles are also accepted.

Requirements Entry fee, $10. Multiple entries are accepted; each must be accompanied by entry fee and official entry form. Musicals should have a running time of 45–60 minutes and require no more than 8 adult actors to play any number of roles. Accepts hard copy. Visit the website for complete guidelines and entry form.

Prizes Winner receives a cash prize of $500; winning musical will be a featured production of the National Children's Theatre Festival.

Deadline April 1.

New Millennium Writing Awards

Room M2, P.O. Box 2463, Knoxville, TN 37901. www.newmillenniumwritings.com

Description Each year, *New Millennium Writings* sponsors a contest to recognize outstanding fiction, short-short fiction, poetry, and nonfiction. Nonfiction can include humor, memoir, creative nonfiction, travel pieces, opinions, essays, interviews, and investigative reporting. It accepts previously published works if they appeared online or in a publication with a circulation of less than 5,000.

Requirements Entry fee, $17. Fiction and nonfiction, to 6,000 words. Short-short fiction, to 1,000 words. Poetry, up to 3 poems; limit 5 pages total per entry. Accepts hard copy and submissions through the website. Author name and contact information should appear on cover page only. Visit the website for complete guidelines.

Prizes First-place winners in each category receive $1,000.

Deadline See website.

New Voices Award

Lee & Low Books, 95 Madison Avenue, New York, NY 10016. www.leeandlow.com

Description This children's book publisher awards an annual prize to a picture book that addresses the needs of children of color. Children should be able to relate to the story, and it should promote understanding among cultures and ethnicities. Submissions may be fiction, nonfiction, or poetry. The contest is open to writers of color who are U.S. residents and who have not previously published a children's picture book.

Requirements No entry fee. Length, to 1,500 words. Limit 2 submissions per entrant. Include cover letter with author name, contact information, and brief biographical note, including cultural and ethnic background. Accepts hard copy. Visit the website for complete guidelines.

Prizes Winner receives $1,000 and a publishing contract from Lee & Low Books.

Deadline Entries are accepted between May 1 and September 30.

Oregon Writers Colony Short Story Contest

c/o Lill Ahrens, 306 NW 32nd Street, Corvallis, OR 97330.
http://oregonwriterscolony.org/short-story-contest/

Description The Oregon Writers Colony supports writers at all stages of the writing experience. It offers skill-building classes, critique and inspiration from writing teachers and other writers, and hosts a writing retreat. This writing contest honors the short story—both true and imagined. Therefore, both fiction and nonfiction submissions are accepted. Stories are judged on plot, emotion, theme, mechanics, sensory detail, depth of character/character arc, and, of course, originality.

Requirements Entry fee: $10/OWC member, $15/non-member, $10 optional fee for judges' constructive critiques. Original work only. Word length, to 2,500 words. Send 4 hard copies of manuscript (with envelope labeled fiction or nonfiction). Complete submission details available at website. Failure to follow submission requirements will affect judging.

Prizes First prize, $200; second prize, $100; third prize, $50; first Honorable Mention, certificate of achievement. Additional Honorable Mentions credited in *Colonygram* and on OWC website. First place winners are featured on the cover of the *Colonygram*. All winners listed inside *Colonygram* and on website. Winners are invited to read from their winning entry at awards ceremony.

Deadline August 15.

Pacific Northwest Writers Association Literary Contest

PMB 2717, 1420 NW Gillman Boulevard, Suite 2, Issaquah, WA 98027. www.pnwa.org

Description This contest accepts entries in 12 categories, including children's fiction (from picture books through middle-grade fiction), young adult novels, and poetry. It is sponsored annually by the Pacific Northwest Writers Association.

Requirements Entry fee, $35 for members; $50 for non-members. Limit one entry per category. Word lengths vary for each category. Book-length works may require a synopsis. Send 3 hard copies of submission, a complete contest registration form, entry fee, and #10 SASE. Author's name should not appear on manuscript. Visit the website for entry form and complete guidelines.

Prizes Winners of each category receive $700; second-place winners receive $300.

Deadline February 18.

Pockets Annual Fiction Contest

P.O. Box 340004, Nashville, TN 32703-0004. http://pockets.upperroom.org/annual-fiction-contest

Description This annual contest is sponsored by *Pockets*, a magazine published by Upper Room Ministries that is designed to connect children to God. The contest accepts all types of previously unpublished fiction and short stories that target children ages 6 to 12.

Requirements No entry fee. Word length, 750–1,000 words. Manuscripts outside this word length will be disqualified. Accepts hard copy; include accurate word count on cover sheet. Multiple submissions are permitted. SASE for return of materials only. Visit website for detailed guidelines.

Prizes Winner receives $500 and publication in *Pockets*.

Deadline Submissions must be postmarked between March 1 and August 15.

Purple Dragonfly Awards

Five Star Publications, 4696 West Tyson Street, Chandler, AZ 85226-2903. www.fivestarpublications.com

Description Conceived with children in mind, the Purple Dragonfly Awards are designed to recognize published authors in the field of children's literature. The 35 award categories range from short story collections to board books, picture books, chapter books, YA fiction, and nonfiction. The awards are sponsored by Five Star Publications, a book publisher and publishing consulting firm.

Requirements Entry fee, $50 for singular submission, $45 each for multiple submissions. Mail 2 copies of each book for each category entered, along with a completed entry form. Ebooks are not eligible. See website for details, entry forms, and judging criteria.

Prizes Grand prize, $300 and a marketing consultation with Five Star Publications, and $100 worth of the company's books. First-place winners in each category receive a certificate, foil award seals for their books, and are entered into a drawing for a $100 prize.

Deadline May 1.

San Antonio Writers Guild Writing Contests

San Antonio Writers Guild, P.O. Box 100717, San Antonio, TX 78201-8717. www.sawritersguild.com

Description This annual contest recognizes exceptional work in the categories of novel, short story, flash fiction, memoir or personal essay, and poetry. It is open to submissions of unpublished work by members of the San Antonio Writers' Guild and non-members.

Requirements Entry fee, $10 for members; $20 for non-members. Word lengths vary according to category. Multiple entries are accepted in up to 3 different categories; each entry must have its own entry form. Submit 2 hard copies with entry form. Visit the website for complete contest guidelines.

Prizes First-place winners receive a cash prize of $150. Second- and third-place winners receive cash prizes of $75 and $50 respectively.

Deadline Entries must be postmarked by the first Thursday of October each year.

Seven Hills Literary Contest

TWA Seven Hills Contest, P.O. Box 3428, Tallahassee, FL 32315. www.twaonline.org

Description Sponsored annually by the Tallahassee Writers Association (TWA), this contest accepts entries in the categories of short story, creative nonfiction, and flash fiction. It also recognizes children's chapter books and short stories, alternating yearly with children's picture books. The 2012 contest will accept chapter books and children's short stories.

Requirements Entry fee, $12 for members; $17 for non-members. Length, to 2,500 words; to 500 words for flash fiction. Accepts electronic submissions through website; or 3 hard copies with TWA cover sheet. Author's name should not appear on the manuscript itself. Manuscripts are not returned. Visit the website for cover sheet and contest guidelines.

Prizes First-place winners in each category receive $100. Second- and third-place winners receive $75 and $50, respectively. All winning entries appear in *Seven Hills Review*.

Deadline August 31.

Seventeen's Fiction Contest

Hearst Communications, Inc., 300 West 57th Street, 17th Floor, New York, NY 10019. www.seventeen.com/fiction

Description Female fiction writers between the ages of 13 and 21 are encouraged to submit their best stories to this competition. Judging is based on originality, creativity, and the author's writing ability. Entrants must be residents of the U.S. or Canada, and all submissions must be unpublished. The winning story appears in *Seventeen* magazine.

Requirements No entry fee. Length, to 500 words. Multiple entries are accepted. Accepts hard copy and electronic submissions through the website; each submission must be accompanied by the entry form posted at the website.

Prizes Grand-prize winner receives $5,000 and publication in *Seventeen*.

Deadline December 31.

Skipping Stones Youth Honor Award Program

Skipping Stones, P.O. Box 3939, Eugene, OR 97403. www.skippingstones.org

Description Sponsored by the international multicultural magazine *Skipping Stones,* the Youth Honor Awards recognize creative works by young people ages 7 to 17. All works should be intended for readers of the same ages. The judges look for essays, interviews, short stories, poems, plays, and artwork that promote multicultural and nature awareness. Non-English and bilingual writings are welcome.

Requirements Entry fee, $3; low-income entrants and subscribers may enter free. Length, to 1,000 words. Poetry, to 30 lines. Accepts hard copy. Include SASE and certificate of originality from parent or teacher. Visit the website for complete guidelines.

Prizes Ten winners will have their work published in *Skipping Stones* and will receive an Honor Award Certificate, a subscription, and 5 books.

Deadline June 20.

Kay Snow Writing Contest

Willamette Writers, 2108 Buck Street, West Linn, OR 97068. www.willamettewriters.com

Description Sponsored by the largest writers' organization in Oregon, and one of the largest in the United States, this contest confers awards in fiction, nonfiction, juvenile short stories (or YA novel excerpt or article), poetry, screenplays, and student writing (for ages 18 and under). All entries must be original and unpublished.

Requirements Entry fee, $10 per entry for members; $15 per entry for non-members; student entries are free. Juvenile submissions, to 1,500 words. Other word lengths vary with category. Multiple submissions are accepted. For each submission, send 2 hard copies with entry form and 3x5 card with author name, address, phone, title of entry, and category. Author's name should not appear on the manuscript itself. Manuscripts are not returned. Visit the website for complete guidelines and entry forms.

Prizes First-place winners receive a cash prize of $300. Second- and third-place winners receive cash prizes of $150 and $50 respectively. Student category award winners receive cash prizes of $10–$50.

Deadline April 23.

SouthWest Writers Contest

SouthWest Writers, 3721 Morris NE, Suite A, Albuquerque, NM 87111. www.southwestwriters.com

Description The SouthWest Writers organization offers annual prizes in 14 categories, including middle-grade and young adult novel, children's fiction or nonfiction picture book, adult fiction in a variety of genres, and poetry. The goal is to reward and encourage excellence.

Requirements Entry fees, word lengths, and other requirements vary for each category; check website for specific information. Send hard copy of submission with entry form. Author's name and contact information should not appear on the entry itself.

Prizes First-place winners in each category receive $150. Second- and third-place winners in each category receive $100 and $50, respectively. All winners are eligible for a $1,000 Storyteller Award.

Deadline May 1.

Sydney Taylor Manuscript Award

Aileen Grossberg, 204 Park Street, Montclair, NJ 07042-2903. www.jewishlibraries.org

Description First awarded in 1985 and sponsored by the Association of Jewish Libraries, this award recognizes works of fiction for readers ages 8 through 11, written by unpublished writers. Submitted stories should deepen the understanding of Judaism for all children, Jewish and non-Jewish, and present positive aspects of Jewish life.

Requirements No entry fee. Length, 64–200 pages. Accepts hard copy. Manuscripts must be accompanied by a release form, entry form, and cover letter with a short personal statement, synopsis, and curriculum vitae. No multiple submissions. Visit the website or send an SASE for complete guidelines.

Prizes Winner receives $1,000.

Deadline December 15.

Tennessee Williams Fiction Contest

Tennessee Williams/New Orleans Literary Festival, 938 Lafayette Street, Suite 514, New Orleans, LA 70113. www.tennesseewilliams.net

Description The judges of this contest seek the best works of fiction from writers who have not yet published a book of fiction. Stories can be of any theme or genre; those that have won any other writing contest are ineligible.

Requirements Entry fee, $25. Length, to 7,000 words. Multiple entries and simultaneous submissions accepted. Accepts hard copy and submissions through website. Author's name should not appear on the manuscript. Include a separate page with story title, word count, author's name, address, phone, and email. Visit the website for complete guidelines.

Prizes Winner receives $1,500, domestic airfare to attend the literary festival, a public reading of the entry at the festival, and publication in *Bayou*.

Deadline November 15.

Tennessee Williams One-Act Play Contest

Tennessee Williams/New Orleans Literary Festival, 938 Lafayette Street, Suite 514, New Orleans, LA 70113. www.tennesseewilliams.net

Description The Tennessee Williams/New Orleans Literary Festival sponsors a contest each year to recognize and reward writers of one-act plays. Submissions must not have been previously produced, published, or performed. "Workshopped" readings are accepted.

Requirements Entry fee, $25. Plays should be no more than one hour in length. Multiple entries are accepted. Accepts electronic entries through the website or hard copy. Include 2 title pages, one with the play title only and another with play title and author's name, address, phone, and email. Visit the website for complete guidelines.

Prizes Winner receives $1,500, a staged reading at the festival, and publication in *Bayou*.

Deadline November 1.

Utah Original Writing Competition

617 East South Temple, Salt Lake City, UT 84102. http://arts.utah.gov

Description Sponsored by the Utah Division of Arts & Museums, this competition was established to honor the state's finest writers. It is open to Utah residents only, and accepts entries in a number of categories, including novel, general nonfiction, poetry, short story, personal essay, and young adult fiction or nonfiction. Entrants must be unpublished in the category they are entering. Submissions are reviewed in a blind process by judges from outside Utah.

Requirements No entry fee. Word lengths vary for each category; check website for specific information. Young adult book (or compilation of stories for young readers), no word limit. Limit 1 entry per category. Manuscripts accepted via website only. Visit website for submission instructions and contest details.

Prizes Young adult book category first prize is $1,000; second prize, $750.

Deadline June 30.

Paul A. Witty Short Story Award

Steven L. Layne, Chairing, Poetry and Prose Awards Subcommittee, Judson University, 1151 North State Street, Elgin, IL 60123-1404. www.reading.org

Description This annual award is presented to the author of an original short story published for the first time during the past year in a periodical for children under the age of 12. Sponsored by the International Reading Association (IRA), it does not consider retellings of folktales, legends, or myths. Both fiction and nonfiction stories are eligible.

Requirements No entry fee. No word length limitations. Accepts hard copy accompanied by a copy of the periodical in which the article or story appeared. Entries must be mailed separately to each member of the judging committee. Visit website or send an SASE for additional information. Nominations may be made by publishers, IRA members, or authors.

Prizes Winners receive $1,000.

Deadline November 15.

WOW! Women on Writing Flash Fiction Contests

Contest Coordinator.
www.wow-womenonwriting.com

Description The *WOW! Women on Writing* ezine sponsors a quarterly competition for very short stories. Winners of each contest are chosen by a guest judge. While all styles of writing are acceptable, it is suggested that writers consider the sensibilities of the guest judge if they wish to be serious contenders.

Requirements Entry fee, $10; entry with critique, $20. Length, 250–750 words. Multiple entries are accepted. Accepts electronic submissions through the website only. Contest closes when 300 stories have been submitted.

Prizes First-place winners receive $300. Second- and third-place winners receive $200 and $100, respectively. All winning stories are published in the ezine.

Deadline Visit website for current quarterly entry deadlines.

Writer's Digest Competitions

WD Young Adult Competition, 4700 East Galbraith Road, Cincinnati, OH 45236
www.writersdigest.com/competitions/writing-competitions

Description Each year, *Writer's Digest* hosts several writing contests, including young adult fiction, short story, and science fiction writing. Full descriptions of the contests, their requirements, and prizes, are available at the website.

Requirements $20 entry fee. Detailed guidelines available for each contest at website. Word lengths vary by competition. Submit via electronic link at website, or send hard copy with entry form found on website.

Prizes Prizes vary by category. Young adult fiction: First place, $1,000; second place, $500. Also Honorable Mentions. All winners receive promotion in *Writers' Digest*.

Deadline Deadlines vary by contest. Young adult fiction competition deadline, October 1.

Writers-Editors Network Annual Competition

CNW/FFWA, P.O. Box A, North Stratford, NH 03590. www.writers-editors.com

Description This annual writing competition is sponsored by the Cassel Network of Writers (CNW), and accepts entries from both members and non-members. The contest is divided into four categories: nonfiction, fiction, children's literature, and poetry. Within each category there are subcategories. Except for nonfiction, all submissions must be unpublished or self-published only. The children's literature category includes short stories, nonfiction article, book chapter, or poetry.

Requirements Entry fees vary based on membership and length of submission. Word lengths vary depending on type of entry and category; see website for details. No stapled entries. Manuscripts are not returned. Visit the website for official entry form, list of categories, category guidelines, and judging criteria.

Prizes Each first-place winner receives $100; second-place winners, $75; third-place winners, $50. All winners also receive certificates.

Deadline March 15.

Writers' Journal Writing Contests

P.O. Box 394, Perham, MN 56573.
www.writersjournal.com

Description Each year, *Writers' Journal* sponsors an array of contests in a number of categories, including fiction, short story, horror/ghost story, romance, science fiction/fantasy, and poetry. The contests it sponsors are open to all writers.

Requirements Entry fees range from $3 to $15 depending on category. Word lengths and guidelines vary. Writers may enter as many manuscripts in as many categories as they wish; include a separate entry form and fee for each manuscript. Accepts hard copy. Visit the website or send an SASE for complete contest information.

Prizes Winners receive cash prizes ranging from $15 to $500, publication in *Writers' Journal*, and a 1-year subscription.

Deadline Varies for each category.

The Writing Conference, Inc. Writing Contests

P.O. Box 664, Ottawa, KS 66067-0664.
www.writingconference.com

Description Each year, the Writing Conference, Inc. sponsors writing contests for elementary, junior high/middle school, and high school students. Entries must be relevant to each year's contest topic, which is available on the website. The contests recognize outstanding, unpublished student submissions in the areas of poetry, narrative, or essay.

Requirements No entry fee. Visit the website or send an SASE for contest topic, complete guidelines, and entry form. Writers' names should appear on the entry form only.

Prizes Winning entries appear in *The Writers' Slate*, an online magazine for students and teachers.

Deadline Check website for deadline date.

Writing for Children Competition

Writers' Union of Canada, 90 Richmond Street, Suite 200, Toronto, Ontario M5C 1P1 Canada.
www.writersunion.ca

Description The best writing for children is recognized each year by the Writers' Union of Canada. It accepts any writing for children up to 1,500 words written in the English language. Entrants must be unpublished Canadian citizens or landed immigrants.

Requirements Entry fee, $15 per entry. Length, to 1,500 words. Multiple entries are accepted. Accepts hard copy accompanied by separate cover letter with author's name, address, phone number, email address, and number of pages of entry. Manuscripts are not returned. Visit the website or send an SASE for complete guidelines.

Prizes Winner receives $1,500. Winning entries and finalists will be submitted to 3 children's book publishers.

Deadline April 24.

Indexes

2012 Market News

New Listings

AKA Mom
Arlington Magazine
Art Dawg
Athlon Sports
Bamboo Magazine
Bayard Magazines
Boulder County Kids
Canadian Family
Chicken Soup for the Soul
ChopChop
Complex Child E-Magazine
Dancing With Bear Publishing
Denver Reign
Dirt
Disney Magazines
DNA Ya!
Enchanted Conversation
ESPNHS
Exchange Magazine
Family Circle Fiction Contest
Foster Focus
Friends of the Library Contest
Funds for Writers Contest
Good Dog
Good Housekeeping Short Story Contest
Hawaii Parent
The Hood Magazine
JAKES Country
Just 4 Kids
Kalamazoo Parent
Kayak
Kronicle

Lightspeed
Little Bit
The Mailbox
MASK
Mirror Moms
M.L.T.S.
Mobile Bay Parents
Native Magazine
Natural Child Magazine
New York Tennis Magazine
North Texas Kids
Off Track Planet
Oregon Writers Colony Short Story Contest
Ottawa Family Life
Peloton
Recreational Cheerleading Magazine
The Red Bulletin
Reverb Monthly
Roanoke Valley Woman
RobinAge
Scooter
Sportsnet Magazine
SweetMama
Tech & Learning
Thriving Family
Today's Parent
Tots to Teens
Uncle John's Bathroom Readers
Urbanbaby & Toddler
USA Synchro Magazine
Writer's Digest Competitions

2012 Market News

Deletions

The following publications have been removed from this year's directory because they have ceased publishing, are unresponsive to submissions, or have proven to be too small a niche.

American School Board Journal
AMomsLove.com
Apples
The Apprentice Writer
Beckett Plushie Pals
Better Homes & Gardens
Bop
Christian Storyteller
City Parent
The Claremont Review
Coastal Family
Community College Week
Conceive
Cookie
Co-Op Thymes
Creative Kids
Crow Toes Quarterly
Delmarva Youth Magazine
Faith Today
The Family Digest
Gwinnett Parents Magazine
Home Times Family Newspaper
I.D.
Impact Magazine
Inkling Magazine
Junior Storyteller
JVibe

Kahani
Kids Magazine Writers
Kittens USA
Kiwibox.com
Midwifery Today
Mission
Mondo Times
Mothering
Mysteries Magazine
North Start Family Matters
Organic Family
Pack-O-Fun
ParentingHumor.com
Popcorn Magazine for Children
Racquetball
Read America!
Scholastic News English/Español
Six78th
Southwest Florida Parent & Child
Student Assistance Journal
Supertwins
TC Magazine
Unique Magazine
Weekly Reader
What If?
World Around You

Name Changes

Child Care Information Exchange: Replaced by Exchange Magazine
JAKES: Replaced by JAKES Country
Synchro Swimming USA: Renamed USA Synchro
Xtreme JAKES: Replaced by JAKES Country
Youth & Christian Education & Leadership: Replaced with Youth & Discipleship Leadership

Fifty+ Freelance

You can improve your chances of selling by submitting to magazines that fill their pages with freelance material. We have listed below markets that buy at least 50 percent of their freelance material from writers who are new to the magazine. Of course, there are no guarantees. But if you approach these magazines with well-written manuscripts targeted to their subject, age range, and word-limit requirements, you can increase your publication odds.

The Acorn
Adoptive Families
Akron Family
Alateen Talk
Amazing Kids
American History
American Libraries
American Secondary Education
American String Teacher
Arts & Activities
Austin Family
Autism Asperger's Digest
Babybug
bNetS@vvy
The Boston Parents' Paper
Brain, Child
Broomstix
Bull Spec
Capper's
Cat Fancy
Childhood Education
Children and Families
Children's Voice
Cicada
ColumbiaKids
Cricket
The Dabbling Mum
Davey and Goliath's Devotions
Devozine
Dig
Dimensions
Dimensions of Early Childhood
Discovery Girls
Dramatics
Dyslexia Online Magazine
Eco-Kids Magazine
Educational Horizons
Educational Leadership
Education Forum
Education Week
Elementary School Writer
Encyclopedia of Youth Studies
Farm & Ranch Living
FatherMag.com

Gifted Education Press Quarterly
Girlworks
Grit
Group
Guardian Angel Kids
Highlights for Children
The High School Journal
The Illuminata
I Love Cats
Indy's Child
Inside Kung-Fu
Insight
Inspired Mother
International Gymnast
Jack and Jill
Journal of Adolescent & Adult Literacy
Journal of School Health
Justine
Kaleidoscope
Keyboard
Keys for Kids
The Kids' Ark
Kids X-Press
Leadership for Student Activities
Learning & Leading with Technology
Library Media Connection
Literary Mama
Massive Online Gamer
Mom Magazine
Motivos Bilingual Magazine
New Moon Girls
The Old Schoolhouse
Our Children
Parentguide News
Parenting for High Potential
Parenting New Hampshire
Parents Express
Parent:Wise Austin
Pediatrics for Parents
Piedmont Parent
The Pink Chameleon
Plays

Positive Parenting
Prehistoric Times
PresenTense
Principal
Rainbow Kids
Red River Family Magazine
Research in Middle Level Education Online
Reunions
Rugby
SchoolArts
Science Activities
The Science Teacher
Seek
Shine Brightly
Simply You
Sisterhood Agenda
Skipping Stones
Sparkle!
Stone Soup
Stories for Children Magazine
The Storyteller
Tar Heel Junior Historian
Teachers & Writers
Teaching Theatre
Tech Directions
Teen Voices
Texas Child Care Quarterly
Tidewater Parent
Today's Catholic Teacher
Turtle Trails & Tales
The Universe in the Classroom
USA Synchro Magazine
VegFamily
Vibrant Life
Voices from the Middle
VOYA Magazine
Washington Family
What's Up
Writers' Journal
Young Adult Today
Young Adult Today Leader
Zamoof!

Category Index

To help you find the appropriate market for your manuscript or query letter, we have compiled a category and subject index listing magazines according to their primary editorial interests. Pay close attention to the markets that overlap. For example, when searching for a market for your rock-climbing adventure story for 8- to 12-year-old readers, you might look under the categories "Adventure Stories" and "Middle-grade (Fiction)." If you have an idea for an article about blue herons for early readers, look under the categories "Animals/Pets" and "Early Reader (Nonfiction)" to find possible markets. Always check the magazine's listing for explanations of specific needs.

For your convenience, we have listed below all of the categories that are included in this index. If you don't find a category that exactly fits your material, try to find a broader term that covers your topic.

Adventure Stories
Animals (Fiction)
Animals (Nonfiction)
Audio/Video
Bilingual (Nonfiction)
Biography
Boys' Magazines
Canadian Magazines
Career/College
Child Care
Computers
Contemporary Fiction
Crafts/Hobbies
Current Events
Drama
Early Reader (Fiction)
Early Reader (Nonfiction)
Education/Classroom
Factual/Informational
Fairy Tales
Family/Parenting
Fantasy
Folktales/Folklore
Games/Puzzles/Activities
Geography
Girls' Magazines
Health/Fitness

Historical Fiction
History
Horror
How-to
Humor (Fiction)
Humor (Nonfiction)
Inspirational Fiction
Language Arts
Mathematics
Middle-grade (Fiction)
Middle-grade (Nonfiction)
Multicultural/Ethnic
 (Fiction)
Multicultural/Ethnic
 (Nonfiction)
Music
Mystery/Suspense
Nature/Environment
 (Fiction)
Nature/Environment
 (Nonfiction)
Personal Experience
Photo-Essays
Poetry
Popular Culture
Preschool (Fiction)
Preschool (Nonfiction)

Profile/Interview
Read-aloud Stories
Real life/Problem-solving
Rebus
Recreation/Entertainment
Regional (Fiction)
Regional (Nonfiction)
Religious (Fiction)
Religious (Nonfiction)
Reviews
Romance
Science Fiction
Science/Technology
Self-help
Services/Clubs
Social Issues
Special Education
Sports (Fiction)
Sports (Nonfiction)
Travel
Western
Writing
Young Adult (Fiction)
Young Adult (Nonfiction)
Young Author (Fiction)
Young Author (Nonfiction)

Humor

Preschool

Profiles/Biography

Index

If you do not find a particular magazine, turn to Market News on page 348.

★ Indicates a newly listed publisher, agent, or contest